W9-AEH-260

# Human Resource Management

# Human Resource Management

## A GENERAL MANAGER'S PERSPECTIVE

*Text and Cases*

*Michael Beer*

*Bert Spector*

*Paul R. Lawrence*

*D. Quinn Mills*

*Richard E. Walton*

THE FREE PRESS
*A Division of Macmillan, Inc.*
New York

Collier Macmillan Publishers
London

The Free Press
A Division of Macmillan, Inc.
866 Third Avenue, New York, N.Y. 10022

Collier Macmillan Canada, Inc.

Printed in the United States of America

printing number

3 4 5 6 7 8 9 10

Case material of the Harvard Graduate School of Business Administration is made possible by the cooperation of business firms and other organizations which may wish to remain anonymous by having names, quantities and other identifying details disguised while maintaining basic relationships. Cases are prepared as the basis for class discussion rather than to illustrate either effective or ineffective handling of administrative situations.

*Library of Congress Cataloging in Publication Data*

Main entry under title:

Human resource management.

Includes index.
1. Personnel management. 2. Personnel management—
Case studies. I. Beer, Michael.
HF5549.H873 1985 658.3 84-21080
ISBN 0-02-902360-2

# Contents

# Preface

This is not a traditional personnel textbook. We do not review theory, research, and practice in personnel administration, labor relations, and organization behavior and development, the three major research and practice traditions represented in many personnel functions and courses. It is a book for *any* manager or prospective manager, particularly general managers, who want to learn about the critical issues and the strategic questions they will have to consider in managing large aggregates of employees in the 1980s and beyond.

In response to a developing consensus among our alumni and faculty that there is a need in many corporations for better management of human resources, the Harvard Business School (HBS) launched a new required course in Human Resource Management (HRM) in 1981. This book and a supplementary readings book present the cases, text, and readings that comprise that course.

The last new required course, managerial economics, was introduced into the curriculum nearly 20 years ago. The introduction of a new course, therefore, communicates important changes in the knowledge and skills the school judges general managers will require in the future, just as it communicates important developments in the underlying building blocks of practice, research, and theory upon which a new course such as HRM must be built.

The development of the new HRM course was stimulated by practicing managers, graduates of HBS and other institutions, who were telling us that human resource problems increasingly dominated their calendars and significantly influenced the effectiveness of their corporations. Competitive pressures, changing values in the work force and society, government legislation, slower growth or decline in mature industries, and rapid growth in high-technology firms are making human resources an increasingly important competitive factor. Despite HBS's leadership and strong tradition in the field of organizational behavior, with its emphasis on managing people, process, structures, and change in organizations, we felt that something more was needed in the knowledge and skills of our graduates. Graduates themselves also expressed a desire to learn more about the management of human resources in our executive programs.

We also learned, through our research, case development, and consulting, that changes were taking place in the practice of HRM. Old problems of productivity, employee commitment, employee development, fair employment practice, union-management relations, and compensation were taking on new urgency and importance in the wake of changes in the competitive environment and society. Furthermore, new developments in the field of organizational behavior and development, personnel administration, and labor relations cried out for representation in our curriculum. Moreover, developments in these three fields are increasingly becoming intertwined in their application by both general managers and personnel specialists. Line managers trying to improve organizational effectiveness perceive conflicting perspectives, directions, and values emanating from various specialists in the personnel function. Personnel specialists in one discipline are finding that their assumptions are being challenged by initiatives and developments in other personnel specialties. General managers, faced with an array of external and internal pressures, are beginning to demand that managing human resources be approached in an integrated, proactive, and strategic way, one relevant to their business and management problems.

The new HRM course is a response to these discontinuities. It is not surprising, therefore, that this book is significantly different from traditional textbooks in personnel. There are many excellent personnel textbooks that review theory, research, and practice in personnel administration, labor relations, and organizational behavior and development needed by the student who aspires to a career in personnel. But while these books, and the courses in which they are used, do an excellent job of presenting research findings and current practices in all three disciplines, they fall short, in our view, of presenting HRM in a way that will be experienced as relevant by practicing managers who are not personnel specialists, or by MBAs who do not aspire to become such specialists. At HBS, where the vast majority of MBAs and executives in residence fall into this category, we have had to search for an approach to teaching about important human resource issues that *all* managers need to understand without teaching about personnel practices, techniques and theory. In short, we have had to develop an HRM course and a book that provides a general management perspective.

The general management perspective places HRM in the context of business strategy and society. It attempts to stimulate students to ask important questions about managing human resources in a changing environment, while at the same time giving them sufficient information about existing institutional arrangements and known personnel practices to facilitate a realistic discussion. It asks them to grapple with the many dilemmas and problems managers encounter in fashioning short- and long-term solutions and taking action. There are several ways in which we have tried to operationalize the general management perspective in this book.

We have chosen the title human resource management because this newer term is being adopted by firms who are trying to do the same thing we are trying to do: integrate practice traditions and make the personnel function responsive to the needs of business, employees, and society. In doing this, we are mindful that the term human resource management communicates excessively instrumental values about people and insufficient human values. We do not wish to communicate this. We do, however, like the fact that HRM communicates the notion that people, no less than physical plant and financial resources, may be viewed and managed as assets and not merely as costs. The most important implication of this approach is that the development of trust between employees, management, and unions, for example, may be seen as a long-term investment, one that must, of course, be justified by the long-term benefits it produces. We chose several cases (Bethoney, Webster, Nippon Steel, and Hewlett-Packard, to name a few) that allow students to evaluate what pattern of HRM develops employees and employer–employee relationships.

We have chosen to write the text for this book in essay form, avoiding extensive review and citations of research, theory, and practice. There are two introductory chapters, one chapter for each of four major human resource policy areas, and a concluding chapter. Each chapter presents conceptual background as well as some knowledge about institutional arrangements and personnel practice which students must possess to tackle the cases. While we do not review research, theory, and practice in exhaustive detail, the text material is based on our knowledge of both research and practice. We have tried to synthesize that knowledge in the interest of articulating more general issues and questions of concern to general managers. We realize full well that in doing this we are leaving unstated many important qualifications that a detailed review of research and theory would allow. We have tried to deal with this potential problem by only making assertions about general directions, considerations, and questions rather than about specific solutions. The issues and questions we raise can, of course, only provide a general framework for analysis and action. HRM problems and practices found in each situation require a situation specific analysis such as the one we require in a case discussion.

There are several reasons why we have taken this approach to the text material. First, it is our experience that general managers do not always want or need the expertise of a functional specialist to grapple with important human resource problems facing them. Indeed, getting into the details of personnel practice can sometimes preclude getting at the fundamental management problem or at the underlying implication of a human resource management policy or practice.

Second, by including knowledge relevant for the functional specialist (techniques, methods, procedures, and accepted practice), we would send the message that managing human resources wisely depends largely on that knowledge and/or the help of the personnel function that has it. We wish to communicate something different. The specialist's methods and approaches can be helpful, but they represent no permanent truths. They can be judged only by their capacity to solve relevant management problems within the realistic constraints of the situation. Thus, an approach that confronts students with human resource problems for which they must design relevant solutions and actions seem to us to be better suited for prospective line managers.

Third, consistent with the pedagogy of HBS, we teach HRM by the case method. The case method puts students in a real situation and forces them to diagnose that situation and take action. If the case presents a given company's approach to HRM, it offers students the opportunity to evaluate the effectiveness of that approach. The text which precedes each section is aimed at giving students the general background and perspective required to analyze and discuss the cases in that section. By asking students to diagnose, evaluate, and take action with classroom challenges from peers and faculty, we are helping students develop their own research findings, ones they are likely to remember because they come from their own experience. So long as the discussion is guided by someone who knows the research and understands the constraints of reality, this approach is, we believe, preferable to providing them with our own analysis of the cases or with comprehensive reviews of research studies which deal with the problem.

Naturally, instructors are an important part of this type of learning process. They guide the discussion by asking relevant questions, providing expertise and experience where needed and encouraging students to grapple with important questions. The teacher's manual which accompanies this book provides our analysis of the cases and recommendations on how to teach them. It also suggests a number of audiovisual materials which we have found invaluable in stimulating excitement and interest when used with specific cases.

Though limited by the number of classes we can teach and the number of pages we can include in this book, we have included a range of cases that will acquaint students with the human resource management issues they need to understand in order to manage in the 1980s and beyond. In many instances these cases were developed explicitly for the HRM course and include up-to-date issues, practices, and problems. Naturally, we have made some judgments about the scope and content of human resource management by the choice of cases, but we believe these judgments are validated by our experience as researchers and practitioners.

Finally, we have limited our text to a more general treatment of human resource management, because we are supplying a companion book of supplementary readings. In several instances these readings were developed by us to provide the minimum knowledge of theory, institutional arrangements, or current law or practice needed by students as background for an informed discussion. The notes on Labor Relations in the United States, Why Employees Unionize, Japanese Management and Employment Systems, and Performance Appraisal are examples. In other instances we have included articles. In still other instances the cases themselves provide information about relevant methods or laws; for example, the Dana case explains the Scanlon plan and the Highland Products case provides information about equal employment legislation and litigation.

In most instances, however, the supplementary readings book is intended as a backdrop to the more fundamental questions the instructor raises about the cases. The questions that should dominate the discussion are "what is the problem here, and what short- and long-term action do you recommend?" Or if the case is descriptive of human resource policies and practices in a given company, the key questions are "how do you evaluate the company's approach and under what circumstances can it be applied elsewhere?" Given the varied experience and values of students, the class can arrive at a much more complete understanding of the situation and a more complete plan of action than any single individual. Of course, this complete understanding requires that the instructor bring out the different viewpoints in the class rather than lecture about the case or use it as an illustration. An alternative approach is to subdivide the class into small groups which are asked to present their analysis and recommendations for action.

In addition to their successful use in the MBA program at HBS, some of the cases and text in the book have been used successfully in various executive programs in and out of the school. Finally, one of the authors has used virtually the whole HRM course as presented in this book in an MBA program at another school. Students were surprised not to get a standard personnel course, but they were delighted with the range and depth of the issues raised by the cases and notes.

The development of a new course and case textbook requires the help and cooperation of many people. We wish to acknowledge some of them here. The course required the approval of the whole HBS faculty which took risks in doing so. We thank them for their confidence in us. John McArthur, Dean of HBS, supported the idea of a new required HRM course and was instrumental in bringing two separate groups, production and operations management as well as organizational behavior, together to undertake the development of the new course. Wick Skinner was a member of the original teaching group which planned and taught this course for the first time. We appreciate his support and contributions. Richard von Werssowetz contributed significantly by writing several cases which appear in this book. His dedication to this task contributed to the success of the new course. Our thanks also go to Rita McSweeney, who typed some of the chapters. And special thanks should go to the dedicated people of the Word Processing Center at HBS, who typed the final version of all chapters. Finally, we wish to acknowledge the financial support of the Division of Research and its director, Raymond E. Corey. The division made it possible for Michael Beer and Bert Spector to dedicate a year to course development.

*Chapter 1*

# Introduction

IN ORDER FOR A CORPORATION to meet effectively its obligations to shareholders, employees, and society, its top managers must develop a relationship between the organization and employees that will fulfill the continually changing needs of both parties. At a minimum, the organization expects employees to perform reliably the tasks assigned to them and at the standards set for them, and to follow the rules that have been established to govern the workplace. Management often expects much more: that employees take initiative, supervise themselves, continue to learn new skills, and be responsive to business needs. At a minimum, employees expect the organization to provide fair pay, safe working conditions, and fair treatment. Like management, employees often expect more, depending on the strength of their needs for security, status, involvement, challenge, power, and responsibility. Just how ambitious the expectations of each party are will vary from organization to organization.

Human resource management (HRM) involves all management decisions and actions that affect the nature of the relationship between the organization and employees—its human resources. General managers make important decisions daily that affect this relationship, but that are not immediately thought of as HRM decisions: introducing new technology into the office place in a particular way, or approving a new plant with a certain arrangement of production operations, each involves important HRM decisions. In the long run, both the decisions themselves and the manner in which those decisions are implemented have a profound impact on employees: how involved they will be in their work, how much they trust management, and how much they will grow and develop new competencies on the job. Deciding how fast a company should grow in response to market demand is another significant HRM decision made by general managers. A decision on growth affects the stress employees will experience as circumstances change, as well as the probabilities that employees will be able to avoid obsolescence and that the organization will have employees with the required talents and skills for the future. Deciding on whether investments are to be financed through internally generated funds or through debt or equity is yet another general management HRM decision. Such financing decisions can make the firm more or less dependent on external stockholders, bankers, and the investment community, thereby influencing a number of HRM policies, most notably, decisions of employment security and investments in employee development. Similarly, general management decisions concerning geographic location of facilities, diversification through acquisition, and business strategy all have, in our view, important implications for the human resources of the firm. Finally, the manner in which supervisors deal with their subordinates, particularly in the expectations they create, the feedback they provide, the trust they generate, and the responsibility they delegate, can do more than any personnel policy or system to shape and reshape the employee-organization relationship. Their actions can reinforce the effective utilization of human resources by the organization; they can also undermine that effectiveness.

None of the above decisions and actions reside in the personnel or labor relations function. Indeed, functional specialists are often not even involved in these or other decisions which affect in a profound way the relationship between the organization and its employees. Just as important, personnel and labor relations departments are sometimes engaged in the administration of policies and systems that have little relationship to the needs of line managers or to the central strategic thrust of the corporation or division. Furthermore, many of these personnel and labor relations activities and systems seem to have a life of their own, isolated from and independent of other personnel and labor relations activities and systems.

The general isolation of personnel decisions has taken place because general managers have counted upon the personnel department and its specialists to play a key role in the management of human resources. Our approach emphasizes two features which are appropriate to HRM. First, the general manager accepts more responsibility for ensuring the alignment of competitive strategy, personnel policies, and other policies impacting on people. Second, the personnel staff has the mission of setting policies which govern how personnel activities are developed and implemented in ways that make them more mutually reinforcing. This is what we mean by a general manager's perspective. The reasons for this are best understood by reviewing the past development of personnel activities.

Ask managers what their personnel departments do or what their own personnel responsibilities are and they will list a series of seemingly disjointed activities such as labor relations, compensation, staffing (recruitment, placement, and promotion), performance appraisal, training, organization development, equal employment opportunity, and health and safety. Indeed, personnel or labor relations functions are generally composed of many separate departments each performing one or more of these activities. Historically, at least, each of these departments has developed a set of policies and systems which provide guidelines for personnel decisions by line managers. These personnel departments also provide a diverse set of services to line management that often bear little relationship to each other and sometimes conflict with each other. The policies, systems, and services developed by each personnel activity or department are generally determined by the tradition of that practice field. For example, compensation departments develop bonus pay plans, organization development departments engage in team building, and labor relations departments deal with grievances and union negotiations.

The disunity of the personnel and labor relations approaches is not surprising, given that personnel activities in corporations have been added in reaction to specific problems and needs rather than as a response to a stated purpose. Personnel departments originally emerged because as corporations grew in size and complexity, there was a need for a central administrative department to hire and pay people. Labor relations departments were added later to negotiate and administer increasingly complex contracts in those corporations organized by unions. Organization development departments were added to solve problems of conflict, motivation, communication, and coordination which emerged as corporations grew even larger, more diverse, and more complex. And equal employment opportunity departments were added to ensure corporate compliance with government legislation and policy in this area. As a result, HRM often emerged as a set of staff activities lacking a coherent structure or central purpose imprinted by general managers. It is also not surprising that, lacking a coherent structure for policy decisions, HRM tends to be reactive rather than proactive in shaping a relationship between the organization and its employees that is suitable to its long-term needs.

Such coherent structure and central purpose will be added only when HRM is seen as more than just the responsibility of a specific functional department. This will occur only when general managers develop a viewpoint of how they wish to see employees involved in and developed by the enterprise, and of what HRM policies and practices might achieve these goals. Without either a central philosophy or a strategic view—whch can be provided *only* by general managers—HRM is likely to remain a set of independent activities, each guided by its own practice tradition.

In our opinion, the ability to develop a coherent HRM policy that contributes to corporate performance, employee needs, and societal well-being does not require general managers to be experts in personnel and labor relations. Therefore, much of the theory and methodology of those two fields has not been included in this book. Developing an HRM strategy does require that general managers be able to ask the right quesitons when confronted with HRM problems, questions that will allow them to link alternative HRM approaches to business strategy, to assumptions about employee needs and values, to societal expectations and government regulations, and to their own management style and values. With the help of HRM specialists, general managers must then create the HRM policies and systems that will make it possible for managers at all levels of the organization to attract, select, promote, reward, motivate, utilize, develop, and keep and/or terminate employees consistent with business requirements, employee needs, and standards of fairness. In short, *HRM is the development of all aspects of an organizational context* so that they will encourage and even direct managerial behavior with regard to people.

## THE EMERGENCE OF HUMAN RESOURCE MANAGEMENT AS A CONCERN OF GENERAL MANAGEMENT

In the past, general managers were content to delegate rather narrowly defined personnel responsibilities to functional specialists. Today, however, a great many pressures are demanding a broader, more comprehensive and more strategic perspective with regard to the organizations' human resources. A list of such pressures would include the following:

1. *Increasing international competition* is creating the need for dramatic improvements in human productivity. The competitive crises in the automobile and steel industries are two such examples. American executives look overseas, especially to Japan, and see employment and management practices that appear to

increase employee commitment while ensuring companies a long-term supply of people with necessary competencies and skills.

2. *Increasing complexity and size* of organizations has resulted in multiple layers of bureaucracy. Some companies are concerned with the high costs of such layers. Others see over-bureaucratization as serving to isolate employees from both the organization and the competitive environment in which that organization must operate. By reducing levels, these organizations hope to put employees in closer touch with their environment, thereby increasing their commitment to the organization as well as their ability and competence to work more effectively. Geographical spread, particularly the emergence of multinational firms, presents new challenges in managing human resources in diverse societies where laws and prevailing social values may be quite different.
3. *Slower growth* and in some cases declining markets have dramatically affected an organization's ability to offer advancement opportunities to high potential employees and employment security to long-service employees.
4. *Greater government involvement* in human resource practices such as employment security (particularly in Europe) and fair employment practices (in the United States) are causing corporations to reexamine their HRM policies and practices and to develop new ones. In the United States, individual employee suits and class action suits for large employee groups have raised the possibility of costly settlements, thereby increasing the importance of HRM in the eyes of general managers.
5. *Increasing education of the work force* is causing corporations to reexamine their assumptions about the capacity of employees to contribute and therefore the amount of responsibility they can be given.
6. *Changing values of the work force*, particularly relative to authority, are causing corporations to reexamine how much involvement and influence employees should be given and what mechanisms for employee voice and due process need to be provided.
7. *More concern with career and life satisfaction* is causing corporations to reexamine traditional assumptions about career paths, to provide more alternative career paths and to take into account employee lifestyle needs in transferring employees and scheduling work.
8. *Changes in work force demography*, particularly the infusion of women and minorities into organizations, are causing corporations to reexamine all policies, practices, and managerial values

that affect the responsibilities, treatment, and advancement of these employee groups.

It is not surprising that such pressures have created the need for more institutional attention to people, a longer time perspective in managing people, and consideration of people as a potential asset rather than merely a variable cost. But why has the potential for greater effectiveness inherent in better management of human resources eluded many managers until now? In part there has been a tendency in the education, development, and training of managers to emphasize the analytical and technical aspects of work, leaving some companies with managers who have wide variance in terms of their skills in managing people fairly and effectively. So why are companies now turning more to the human side of the enterprise in order to solve business problems? In part that answer lies in societal pressures. Just as concern over the condition of blue-collar workers found its way into labor legislation during the 1930s, concern over equitable and fair treatment found its way into civil rights and equal opportunity legislation in the 1960s and 1970s. Such legislation called attention to and helped shape companies' HRM practices, as did social values concerning individual satisfaction and well-being. In part, the reason lies in the failure of other approaches to live up to their expectations of improving organizational effectiveness. Administrative systems, marketing, technology, operations management, industrial engineering, diversification, portfolio management, and more recently computerization have all solved some problems. But they have created new ones; often human problems.

Many managers who eagerly adopted new technology or new approaches to portfolio management, for instance, face redesign of HRM with far greater reluctance. Technology or portfolio management seem easier to implement because such approaches do not *seem* to require managers to confront basic values and assumptions about human nature. They do not *seem* to raise questions about personal style and individual power. Of course, such perceptions are not entirely correct. The introduction of new technology, for instance, *does* affect people and power relationships. Indeed, it is often the failure to recognize the intricate relationships between "impersonal" systems and people that causes such approaches either to fail or to fall short of their promise. HRM issues, on the other hand, require that fundamental and sometimes threatening questions about our personal values and assumptions be addressed. Nevertheless, competitive pressures and changes in employees have highlighted fundamental HRM questions about how to unleash people's energies and creativity. In fact, a number of major American corporations have begun to address these HRM issues and are leading a trend that will fundamentally alter the practice of human resource management.

Experience has shown that severe external pressures may be required for a firm to reexamine and dramatically change HRM policies. Indeed both research and experience suggest that fundamental changes are rarely addressed until dissatisfaction with the status quo is high and models for new behavior exist. The factors listed earlier have led to such dissatisfaction, while new HRM models, such as Japanese employment and management systems and union-management quality of work life projects, to name only two of the more prominent ones, are also emerging. Unfortunately, companies that undertake fundamental changes in the relationship between management and employees while they are under competitive pressure have little slack in time, money, and good will of employees to engineer such changes. To avoid the difficulties of trying to change longstanding approaches to HRM virtually "overnight" in response to competitive pressures, it can be suggested that companies continually reexamine HRM policies. That way they might evolve a relationship with employees that will stand the rigorous test of constantly shifting competitive pressures.

Unfortunately, companies with a good deal of growth and profitability seldom see a reason to innovate in HRM practices in order to build a relationship between the organization and its employees that will pass the tests of greater competition and the shrinking economic pie. There are exceptions, however. Companies like Hewlett-Packard, Lincoln Electric, and IBM, whose founders had a strong set of values concerning what the relationship between employees and their employing organization ought to be, have devoted a good deal of attention to developing and maintaining consistent and effective HRM policies, even in the absence of strong competitive pressures. Other companies not yet under competitive pressures can, if they so choose, make a conscious decision to examine systematically and continuously the effectiveness of their HRM policies and practices. New rapid-growth companies can develop HRM policies with long-term perspective because it is generally more difficult to change a culture than to develop one from the beginning. The cases and text in this book can help managers and prospective managers grapple with some of the major human resource issues that corporations should examine.

## FOUR MAJOR HRM POLICY AREAS

We propose that many diverse personnel and labor relations activities may be subsumed under four human resource policy areas. Each of the following policy areas defines a major HRM task that general managers must attend to whether or not the firm is unionized, whether blue-collar or managerial employees are involved, and whether the firm is growing or declining.

### *Employee Influence*

A corporation has a variety of stakeholders, among them shareholders, unions, various groups of employees, government, and the community. This policy area has to do with a key question that all managers must ask: How much responsibility, authority, and power should the organization voluntarily delegate and to whom? If required by government legislation to bargain with unions or consult with worker councils, how should management enter into these institutional relationships? Will they seek to minimize the power and influence of these legislated mechanisms? Or will they share influence and work to create greater congruence of interests between management and the employee groups represented through these mechanisms? The managerial task here is to develop the organization's policy regarding the amount of influence employee stakeholders have with respect to such diverse matters as business goals, pay, working conditions, career progression, employment security, or the task itself; and to attempt to implement these policies. Inevitably, decisions about employee influence affect traditional management prerogatives and can reshape the very purpose of the firm. Employee influence decisions are therefore critical general management decisions whether they are made explicitly, or as is often the case, implicitly.

In many situations managers are the only ones who can initiate a decision-making process about how much participation and due process employees are to have and what mechanisms to develop for their voice to be heard and their influence to be felt. Unless challenged by employees through unions, turnover, government legislation, or lawsuits, managers possess much of the decision-making power in the organization, so a lack of action in regard to employee influence amounts to a decision not to share and delegate much of that power and influence. Self-management groups in Japan, task forces or group decision making at the management level, membership on quality of work life committees at the working level, open-door policies, and ombudsmen are examples of mechanisms managers can select. It is our assumption that choices about employee influence, in the long run, are inevitable. Democratic societies have tended to legislate influence mechanisms whenever employees have felt aggrieved or underrepresented in decisions governing their welfare.

*Human Resource Flow*

This policy area has to do with the responsibility shared by all managers in an organization for managing the flow of people (at all levels) into, through, and out the organization. Traditional personnel practice areas such as recruitment, internal staffing, performance appraisal, and outplacement are all subsumed in this area. But the task goes further. Personnel specialists and general managers must work in concert to ensure that personnel flow meets the corporation's long-term strategic requirement for the "right" number of people and mix of competencies. Selection, promotion, and termination decisions must also meet the needs of employees for job security, career development, advancement, and fair treatment, and they must meet legislated standards of society. General managers must ask themselves how much employment security employees should be granted and how much the corporation should invest in employee development. Inevitably, decisions in this area will affect and be affected by fundamental business decisions about profit goals, growth rates, and dividend policy, to name only a few. When characterized as a whole the pattern of practices in this area constitutes the organization's flow policies. Such policies affect the very capacity of the organization to achieve its strategic objectives and obligations to employees and society. Human resource flow policy decisions must be made and reviewed by general managers.

*Reward Systems*

Rewards, both financial and otherwise, send a powerful message to employees of an organization as to what kind of organization management seeks to create and maintain, and what kind of behavior and attitudes management seeks from its employeees. It is up to all managers of an organization, and not just pay specialists, to attend to certain questions under this HRM managerial task: Do we want an organization that rewards individual or group behavior? How shall we use money: as an incentive to stimulate desired behavior, or as equitable recognition of effective performance? Do we wish to share economic gains (profits or improvements in costs, for example) with various employees or employee groups? The answers to these questions lead to the task of designing and administering equitable and fair reward systems to attract, motivate, and retain (satisfy) employees at all levels. Management may have complete control over the design and administering of the organization's reward system, or they may have to negotiate these policies and systems with a union. There are choices to be made by managers concerning rewards for nonunion workers, as managers consider the extent to which they want to involve those workers in design and administration. Decisions about participation and the mix of rewards offered need to be consistent with business strategy, management philosophy, employee needs, and other HRM policies. The extent to which compensation should be used as an incentive, the mix between extrinsic and intrinsic rewards, and the extent to which rewards should be tied to individual versus organizational performance are some of the questions that only general managers can decide. Such decisions have a fundamental and pervasive effect on the nature of the organization-employee relationship, and the extent to which that relationship is based on an individual calculation of personal gains or on identification with the firm's tasks and goals.

*Work Systems*

At all levels of an organization, managers must face the task of arranging people, information, activities, and technology. In other words, they must define and design work. Management choices about these arrangements affect the quality of the decisions people make, coordination between functions and tasks, the extent to which people's competencies are utilized, the extent to which people are committed to organizational goals, and the extent to which people's needs for development and quality of work life are met. Decisions by managers about manufacturing processes at the plant level (extent of divisions of labor and application of technology, for example), about new information technology in the office (such as computerized information systems), about organization design, and about planning and goal-setting systems at the management level are examples of policy decisions in the work systems area. General managers, not personnel or labor relations specialists, make conscious or unconscious choices about the quality of decisions and commitment of employees when they make decisions in the work system area or when they allow such decisions to be made by others.

The four-policy framework can stimulate managers to plan how to accomplish the four major HRM tasks in a unified, coherent manner rather than in a disjointed approach based on some combination of past practice, accident, and ad hoc response to outside pressures. An HRM policy involves a choice by managers about how employees will be managed; a choice that ultimately influences the nature of the relationship between the organization and its employees. For such a choice to be effective it must be put into operation through the development of HRM policies and practices. Conscious choices about policies then can lead to the development of HRM systems and practices consistent with them.

## THE HRM PERSPECTIVES GUIDING THIS BOOK

The preceding discussion of the HRM policy areas reflects a number of the choices we made about how to view the HRM task. These choices can be made more explicit.

The first central theme cuts across all four policy areas and is the conceptual framework we will propose in Chapter 2: *stakeholder interests*. We view the role of top management as balancing and, where possible, integrating the interests of the many stakeholders of the enterprise: shareholders, employees, customers, suppliers, host communities, labor unions, trade associations, governments, and so on. This view of employees as important stakeholders in the enterprise underscores the need of top managers to consider how the interests of various stakeholders differ, how much weight those distinct interests should be given, and the mechanisms by which those various stakeholders can exercise influence over the enterprise. Because this book is about human resource management, the tensions between the interests of employees or institutions that represent them (unions and government) and the interests of management and shareholders receive most of our attention.

If employees are major stakeholders in the enterprise, then it is critical that managers design and administer various mechanisms for *employee influence*, a second major theme of this book. This policy area will be discussed in depth in Chapter 3. For now, we wish to make the point that employee influence in its broadest sense is a central perspective in the formulation of all human resource management policies (see Figure 1-1). All policies, the design and implementation of technology and work systems, the design and administration of compensation, and the design and administration of systems for hiring, promoting, placing, and terminating employees should be examined from the perspective of how much influence employees are given over decisions in these areas. Thus, the employee influence policy area goes well beyond the traditional activities of union-management relations or employee relations or even participative management initiatives that some companies have undertaken. The policy area poses a question much broader than that typically associated with these personnel practices: how to develop a process of mutual influence between two sets of stakeholders—management and employees. Stating the task this way allows the inclusion of worker councils, grievance systems, sensing groups, open-door policies, attitude surveys, ombudsmen, and other due process mechanisms as alternatives or additions to the mix of practices that may be applied in the interest of achieving a mutual influence process appropriate to the strategy of the firm, the values of top management, and the expectations of employees and society. The task of designing and managing a process of mutual influence is primary; the means or the activity is secondary, and is to be judged on the basis of its contribution to this basic HRM task.

After the stakeholder and employee influence perspectives, a third perspective of the book involves an emphasis on the need for a reasonable amount of consistency, or *fit*, between each of the four policy areas. For example, efforts to increase commitment to the goals of the enterprise through increasing the responsibility of workers and their participation in work decisions will probably have to be supported eventually by flow policies that provide some job security, and by compensation systems that encourage the acquisition of skills and provide some form of sharing with employees of cost or profit improvement. Internal consistency between policies is needed to provide clear signals to people about the behavior that is expected and that will be rewarded.

Fourth, we view human resources as *social capital*. The implication is that the development of work-force capabilities, attitudes, and internal relations must be thought of within an investment paradigm. People can seldom be thought of mainly as budgeted expenses. Rather they constitute the firm's social capital, which results from front-end investments and which yields a stream of benefits over time. Broad employee competencies, for example, can lead to flexible assignment practices, while a relationship of trust between management and workers can increase employee commitment to reassignments that respond to shifting business conditions. This capital can also be degraded by neglect or poor maintenance and can become obsolete unless retrained in line with changing requirements. As with other investments, there are risks

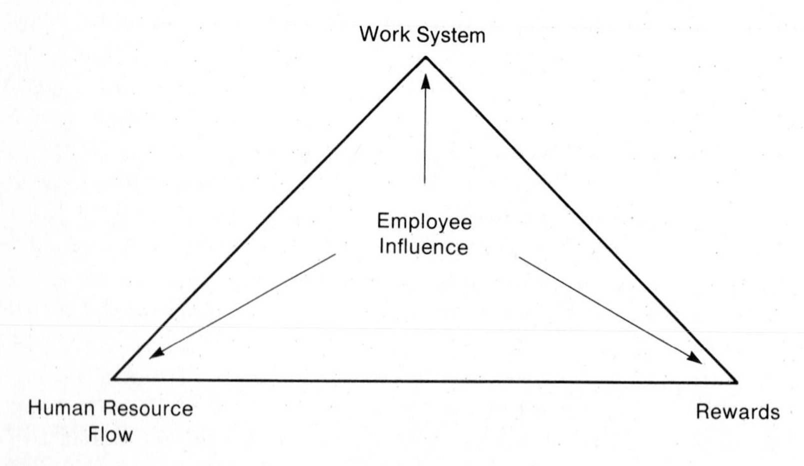


**FIGURE 1–1 Human Resource System**

associated with the estimates of future stream of benefits—for example, whether an investment in developing employee attitudes and skills will, in fact, lead to enhanced product quality or some other key success factor. As with other investment decisions, a long-term perspective, sometimes well beyond the current accounting period, is required.

Fifth, we view the management of human resources from a *strategic* perspective. An enterprise has an external strategy—a chosen way of competing in the marketplace. It also needs an internal strategy to determine how its human resources are to be developed, deployed, motivated, and controlled. There are several implications of this perspective. One implication is that the internal and external strategies must be *linked*. Each provides goals and constraints for the other. A competitive strategy based on becoming the low-cost producer may indicate different approaches to compensation and employment security than a competitive strategy that depends on product innovation. The very idea of an internal strategy implies there is consistency among all of the specific tactics or activities which affect human resources. Hence, the need for practices to be guided by conscious policies—to increase the likelihood that practices will reinforce each other and will be consistent over time.

The analytical framework we advance in Chapter 2 requires the analysis of fit: fit between competitive strategy and internal HRM strategy and fit among the elements of the HRM strategy.

Sixth, we emphasize the need for *multiple levels of social evaluation* in assessing the outcomes of HRM policies and practices. It is not enough to ask how well the management of human resources serves the interests of the *enterprise*. One should ask how well the enterprise's HRM policies serve the well-being of the *individual employee*. At a higher level of analysis, one should ask how well the company's HRM policies and practices serve the interests of *society*. Of course, other stakeholders may be relevant in particular cases. Moreover, the relative weighting that management will give to these three evaluative considerations will vary from management to management and from case to case. Our view is that the weighting should be more explicit in the future than it has been in the past. This perspective serves to raise the following question: Are there HRM policies that increase the likelihood that they will *simultaneously* serve the interests of the enterprise, the individual, and society?

Our seventh perspective derives from all of the above. It is that *HRM is a part of the general management function*. If the HRM strategy must fit the competitive strategy, if human resource development involves investment decisions with long-term implications, and if employees are viewed as one of the groups of major stakeholders of the enterprise whose interests must be balanced by top management, then surely HRM policy decisions cannot be delegated to a functional specialty.

## THE ORGANIZATION OF THE BOOK

Before proceeding, a few words about the organization of *Human Resource Management* might be useful. Now that we have staked out in general terms the territory we wish to cover in our HRM approach, we will move in Chapter 2 to a conceptual overview of the subject. It is our intent in that chapter to present readers with a set of analytical levers which can be brought to bear generally on HRM issues and specifically on the cases included in the text. We will suggest seven groups of factors—laws and societal values, task technology, unions, work force characteristics, labor market conditions, business strategy, and management philosophy—that need to be considered when making HRM policy choices. We will suggest the four Cs—competence, commitment, congruence, and cost effectiveness—as a way for managers to consider the impact of HRM policy choices. Finally, we will propose that the ultimate consequences of HRM policies be viewed on three levels: organizational effectiveness, employee well-being, and societal well-being.

From there we will move sequentially through each of the four HRM policy areas—employee influence, human resource flow, reward systems, and work systems—and close with an integrative chapter. These chapters are not meant to be exhaustive examinations of the many practice fields such as labor relations or wage and salary administration subsumed under our policy areas. Consistent with the general manager's perspective, we have tried to sketch an overview of each policy area based on our knowledge of relevant personnel and labor relations issues and practices and our experience with the policy issues they raise for general managers.

Since each of these chapters will be followed by cases, it might also be useful here to state our feelings on what purpose these cases can serve. We include these cases not as examples of revealed truths or as illustrations of the proper, or for that matter, improper ways of handling a particular HRM problem. Readers would seriously err, we believe, to seek *the* answer or answers within the cases. The cases present HRM problems and approaches in a variety of real-world settings. Readings in a companion book provide background information about the content of relevant personnel practices that helps readers to diagnose problems and consider action alternatives. We urge that cases be used to trigger ways of thinking about HRM issues; that they be read and discussed to illuminate the dilemmas, the issues, the problems, and the possibilities for action inherent in the task of managing human resources. Ultimately the effectiveness of human resource management in corporations can only be enhanced by general managers who have mastered a way of thinking our text and cases are designed to stimulate.

*Chapter* 2

# A Conceptual Overview of HRM

IF GENERAL MANAGERS are to determine what human resource policies and practices their firm should employ, they need some way to assess the appropriateness or effectiveness of those policies. In this chapter, we will offer some ways of diagnosing not only the impact of management decisions on the human resources of the firm, but also whether the policies that guide those decisions continue to make sense and what changes might be considered in them.

The analytical approach depicted in Figure 2-1 is a broad causal mapping of the determinants and consequences of HRM policies. The HRM map shows that HRM policies are influenced by two major considerations: situational factors and stakeholder interests. By situational factors we mean those forces—laws and societal values, labor market conditions, unions, work-force characteristics, business strategies, management philosophy, and task technology—that exist in the environment or inside the firm. These factors can act as constraints on the formation of HRM policies and can also be influenced by HRM policies. HRM policies are and indeed should be influenced by the interests of various stakeholders: shareholders, management employees, unions, community, and government. Unless these policies are influenced by all stakeholders, the enterprise will fail to meet the needs of these stakeholders in the long run and it will fail as an institution.

HRM policies affect certain immediate organizational outcomes and have certain long-term consequences. Policy choices made by managers affect the overall *competence* of employees, the *commitment* of

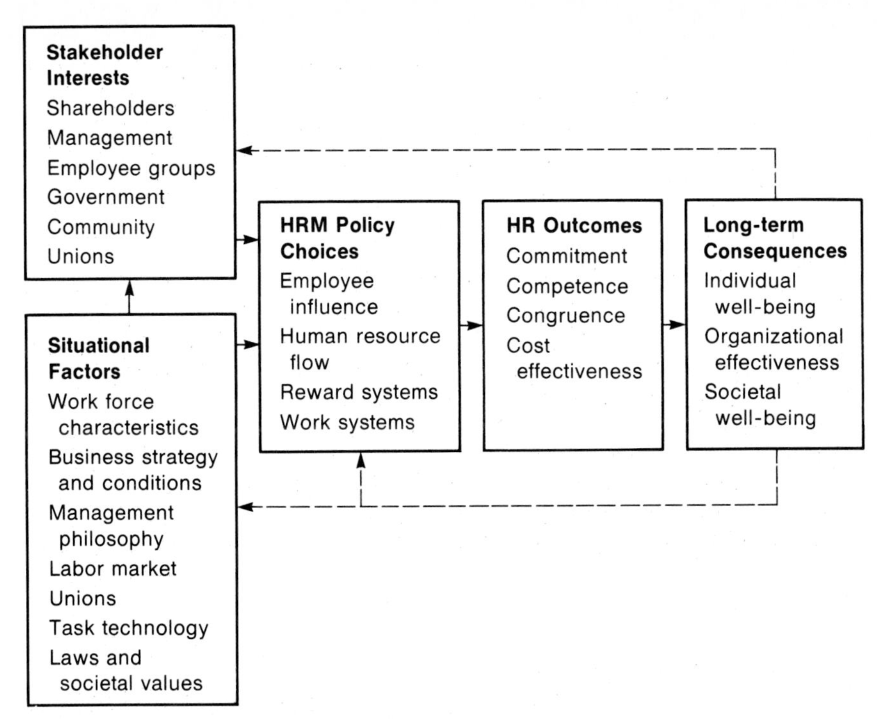


**FIGURE 2–1 Map of the HRM Territory**

employees, the degree of *congruence* between the goals of employees and those of the organization, and the overall *cost effectiveness* of HRM practices. These four Cs are not exhaustive of the criteria that HRM policy makers may find useful in evaluating the effectiveness of human resource management, but they are reasonably comprehensive. The reader may find it useful to add to the four Cs other criteria suggested by a particular case or problem.

In the long run, striving to enhance all four Cs will lead to favorable consequences for individual well-being, societal well-being, and organizational effectiveness (i.e., long-term consequences, the last box in Figure 2-1). By organizational effectiveness we mean the capacity of the organization to be responsive and adaptive to its environment. We are suggesting, then, that human resource management has much broader consequences than simply last quarter's profits or last year's return on equity. Indeed, such short-term measures are relatively unaffected by HRM policies. Thus HRM policy formulation must incorporate this long-term perspective.

The HRM map in Figure 2–1 also illustrates the circularity of HRM policy choices. HRM policy choices affect the four Cs and have long-term consequences for individual well-being, organizational effectiveness, and societal well-being. But long-term consequences also affect situational factors and stakeholder interests. For example, protests by mistreated, insecure employees in the society can lead to government legislation regarding fair employment practice or can result in the industrial democracy legislation seen in Europe. Strikes that affect society negatively can influence changes in labor legislation. Poor profitability over an extended period will affect shareholder interest and must inevitably result in changes of HRM policies regarding wages, training, and perhaps employee influence. There are other feedback effects. The central point is that the long-term consequences of HRM policies for individual well-being, organizational effectiveness, and societal well-being will affect those policies and the context within which they are formulated.

How can the analytical framework just presented be used by the readers of this book, including practicing managers?

We find that it is necessary, as a central matter, to clarify who has a stake in the issue at hand, to identify these stakes, and to determine how much power they may be able to apply. These questions are analytically important whether the decision-maker ultimately wants to accommodate or deny the interests of another stakeholder.

One can use other aspects of the analytical framework in various ways. If managers want to understand why their company is currently pursuing a particular approach to an HRM issue, such as an adversarial stance toward labor relations or a policy of lifetime employment, they must analyze the situational factors, both their current force and their historical influence.

On the other hand, managers may want to compare the relevant merits of two HRM policy alternatives, such as a work system with narrowly defined jobs versus one emphasizing whole tasks and team responsibilities. These managers can then attempt to forecast the differential effects of the two systems on the development of competence, the level of commitment, and the like. They can also attempt to extend the forecast another step by asking how good each policy is for the enterprise, the individual, and society. At either the first or second steps of these forecasts, the policy maker may decide that none of the policy alternatives being considered is satisfactory and return to the task of formulating another alternative.

The evaluation of given alternative policies and the formulation of new alternatives involve more than looking at the long-term consequences shown in Figure 2-1. Managers must also examine the question of *fit* among HRM policies—specifically the fit of the policy being reviewed with the other HRM policies and systems. For example, would a proposed approach to designing work systems require a change in the way employees are selected, and is such a change feasible? Managers must then return to an examination of situational factors. How does a proposed policy fit with each of the situational factors and stakeholder interests shown in Figure 2–1? We believe it would be a mistake to follow any analytical process mechanically. Thus we urge the reader to consider only the *spirit* of the foregoing description of analytical steps, and not to regard it as a procedural prescription. Ideally managers could simultaneously consider all of the above factors affecting both the feasibility and desirability of a policy alternative. The actual way a manager considers and reconsiders each of the relevant factors will vary from case to case and from policy maker to policy maker.

We turn now to an exploration of each of the elements in our analytical framework.

## EVALUATING HRM POLICIES IN TERMS OF THEIR CONSEQUENCES

We have proposed that the long-term consequences of HRM policies be evaluated in terms of their benefits and costs at three levels: the individual, the organization, and society. Let us elaborate.

It is almost tautological to argue that an organization's HRM policies should be evaluated in terms of whether they promote the organization's goal achievement and survival. An HRM policy may be important because it serves to increase the organization's efficiency or its adaptability, its service performance or its price performance, its short-term results or its long-term results.

It is insufficient to ask only about the organizational outcomes of HRM policies and practices, even if these include human outcomes such as turnover. The well-being of employees must be a separate and distinct consideration. Working conditions can have both positive and negative effects not only on employees' economic welfare, but on their physical and psychological health. The amount of weight managers will choose to give to such consequences, independent of their direct implications for the organization, will depend upon the managers' values and their own conception of the legitimacy of employee claims on the enterprise.

Evaluation of HRM outcomes can also be made on the *societal level*. What have management's past HRM practices cost not only the company and employees, but society as a whole? What are the societal costs of a strike or a layoff? Alienated and laid-off workers may develop both psychological and physical health problems that make them burdens to community agencies funded by the local, state, or federal government. Today employers pass on many of the costs of their management practices to society. Whoever bears these costs, they should be recognized as associated with the HRM policy decisions made by management.

In some areas there is a close coincidence of interests between corporations, individuals, and society. For example, the physical and psychological well-being of employees is gaining importance as a corporate concern. Employees' physical fitness and life-style (at work and away from work), as well as personal health habits with respect to tobacco, drugs, and alcohol are now recognized as contributing to the health care costs of the firm and to its productivity. Johnson & Johnson and Control Data, for example, have launched extensive programs to help employees diagnose their health and develop personal programs for improvements.

In considering whether an HRM policy enhances the performance of the organization, the well-being of employees, or the well-being of society, the four Cs can be considered in the analysis of these inherently complex questions:

1. *Commitment.* To what extent do HRM policies enhance the commitment of people to their work and their organization? Increased commitment can result not only in more loyalty and better performance for the organization, but also in self-worth, dignity, psychological involvement, and identity for the individual.
2. *Competence.* To what extent do HRM policies attract, keep, and/or develop people with skills and knowledge needed by the organization and society, now and in the future? When needed skills and knowledge are available at the right time, the organization benefits and its employees experience an increased sense of self-worth and economic well-being.
3. *Cost effectiveness.* What is the cost effectiveness of a given policy in terms of wages, benefits, turnover, absenteeism, strikes, and so on? Such costs can be considered for organizations, individuals, and society as a whole.
4. *Congruence.* What levels of congruence do HRM policies and practices generate or sustain between management and employees, different employee groups, the organization and community, employees and their families, and within the individual? The lack of such congruence can be costly to management in terms of time, money, and energy, in terms of the resulting low levels of trust and common purpose, and in terms of stress and other psychological problems it can create.

*The Problems of Measurement and Assessment*

The four Cs do not provide managers with actual measurement methods and data for assessing the effects of their firm's HRM policies. These methods are numerous, and they differ depending on the level of analysis chosen (individual, corporation, or society). Corporations gather data on the competence of employees through performance evaluation by managers and through third-party assessment of competence by personnel specialists, psychologists, other managers, or assessment centers. When such data are looked at in the aggregate, particularly when a company tries to determine the talent it has available for succession planning, a picture emerges of the depth in technical or managerial competence in the organization.

Data about employee commitment can be obtained by managers in any area of the organization by means of attitude surveys. These surveys can be conducted through interviews and questionnaires administered either by personnel specialists or by outside consultants. Open-door policies and observations of group meetings with employees can also keep managers in touch with their employees' attitudes. The key for any manager is to create conditions for expression of attitudes and open dialogue among various employee groups within the firm. Another source of data—personnel records about voluntary turnover, absenteeism, and grievances—can provide indirect evidence about employee commitment. Taken together, such data might fall short of providing managers with an absolute measure of commitment and congruence, but they can provide a useful overall picture.

Cost effectiveness may appear to be easier to measure, but that appearance can be deceiving. Wages are the easiest to assess, while the long-term costs of certain profit-sharing plans, pension plans, and cost-of-living adjustments are more difficult to assess because of future uncertainties. The cost effectiveness of recruitment and employee development is even more difficult to measure, yet both are an important part of the total employment cost.

Congruence of goals can be more easily identified, particularly when its absence results in an open conflict like a strike. Although the total costs of a strike are difficult to pin down, such an assessment can be part of a total assessment of HRM policies. The existence of more subtle forms of conflict, such as those between managers and subordinates or among various groups of employees, are more difficult to identify. Their costs are even harder to evaluate. Where employees are under union contract, the number of grievances is an indicator of conflict and the administrative costs of those grievances are measurable. But the impact of accumulated grievances on organizational performance is far more difficult to assess.

These difficulties in measurement are exceeded by the difficulties in making judgments about consequences of HRM policies on employee and societal well-being. Various governance mechanisms such as union-management task forces or employee committees (for nonunion employees) can provide important vehicles not only for gathering data about human resource outcomes, but for assessing the meaning of these outcomes for various stakeholders. Workers councils and collective bargaining are examples of legislated governance mechanisms that serve the same purpose. Only through participation of stakeholders in assessing HRM outcomes can managers obtain relevant data for an evaluation of the impact of HRM policies and practices on employee and societal well-being.

The problem of assessing HRM outcomes will not be solved easily. The desire to account for human resources as if they were in the same metric as financial resources (dollars) has led to experimentation with human resource accounting systems. These systems have tried to value a person by estimating his or her replacement costs and the investment the firm has made in that person's recruitment, training, and development. Such accounting efforts, while potentially very useful, have fallen short of their promise, at least judging by the fact that they are not widely used. An even more difficult task has been assigning a value to the commitment of employees or the climate and culture of the firm which encourage motivation and growth by its employees. These difficulties are not likely to be overcome soon. In the final analysis, assessment of HRM outcomes is a matter of judgment informed by data from a variety of sources and in a variety of forms (qualitative and quantitative) and evaluated by various stakeholders. A process of outcome assessment must, therefore, bring together a variety of stakeholders (employee groups, management, and union, for example) to discuss the data and to reach a consensus on its meaning.

## THE STAKEHOLDER INTEREST PERSPECTIVE

One way of viewing a company is as a minisociety made up of large numbers of occasionally harmonious, occasionally conflicting constituencies, each claiming an important stake in the way the company is managed and its resources are deployed. Central to the HRM approach of this book is the assumption that general managers must recognize the existence of the many stakeholders and be able to comprehend the particular interests of each stakeholder. In thinking about various HRM policies and practices, then, the general manager plays an important role in balancing and rebalancing the multiple interests served by the company.

Stakeholders in a given enterprise may include owners, government, host communities, workers, labor unions, and the managers themselves. The cases presented throughout the book, and not just in Chapter 3, provide ample illustration of the need for management to understand and deal with the concerns of all of these stakeholders. We will pay particular attention to workers as stakeholders. By "workers" we include blue-collar, professional, and other white-collar employees. Different employee groups can have different stakes in a particular policy matter. Younger and older workers might find their interests affected in very different ways by company policies relating to benefits and pensions. Black and white workers might feel differently about a company's promotion policies. So might male and female employees. In general employees and management will surely differ with some frequency over such matters as the amount and kind of pay, benefits, and conditions of work. While these are rewards to employees, they are costs to the employer—costs that reduce profits and investment funds.

Why are workers not as concerned as management about corporate profits? Why shouldn't they be more self-regulating in their expectations and demands for monetary and nonmonetary rewards? And why are managers not more understanding about worker needs and more concerned about worker well-being in their decisions? The answers lie, in part, in the different interests of the two groups. Those groups often have different views about the necessary but sometimes difficult trade-offs made within an organization—trade-offs between business goals of efficiency, growth, and investment on the one hand and employee needs for security, equity, job satisfaction, and economic well-being on the other.

Organizations constantly make trade-offs, either implicitly or explicitly, between the interests of owners and those of employees, as well as between various employee groups. Managers are not always aware, however, that such trade-offs are taking place, or even that different stakeholder groups may hold differing views of how those trade-offs should be made. Some managers may be lulled into believing that all stakeholders have the same interests and points of view because the organizational hierarchy has blocked stakeholders from expressing those interests or views. Other managers may be aware of the differences, but may deny the "legitimacy" of any viewpoint other than that of owners and managers.

The task of general managers is to recognize the potential for differing—even conflicting—points of view among the various stakeholders over how trade-offs should be made. They must develop a role and perspective that allows them to manage the trade-off process in such a way as to minimize differences between stakeholders and to contain conflict when it arises. For American managers (as contrasted with managers in Europe, for example) such a role represents quite a departure from the traditionally espoused shareholder perspective. While in actuality managers already manage in a way that recognizes shareholders as only one among many groups of stakeholders, conscious acceptance of the stakeholder perspective would put them in an even more neutral position with respect to shareholders to whom they traditionally have felt accountable. Given the make-up of boards of directors and the power of financial institutions, adopting a stakeholder perspective as opposed to shareholder perspective could be very difficult. Our HRM model suggests that changes in contextual factors such as society and legislation would be needed to support movement toward a stakeholder perspective.

## SITUATIONAL FACTORS

The HRM model suggests that HRM policies and practices must be designed and implemented to fit a variety of important situational factors. We do not want to imply that HRM policies should be *contingent* on situational factors, or that they become the dependent variable. To the contrary, we believe that in the long run, all situational factors are subject to some influence by creative HRM policies and practices. Some situational factors are subject to influence by HRM policies in the short to medium term. The use of the term "situational factors" should not imply that these factors are all "outside" the firm. Clearly, unions, laws, societal values, and labor markets are external to the firm in the sense that they are part of the organization's environment; yet they emerge, in part at least, from the human resource policies of the past. Management philosophy, work-force characteristics, task technology, and business strategy are "inside" the firm in the sense that they appear to be subject to more managerial control, yet they are also affected by external business and societal forces. The key point is that at any given point in time—for example, when a general manager is examining current human resource policies and contemplating making changes—all the factors are part of the situation, even the manager's own values and philosophy. More important, all the situational factors must be understood by the general manager as potential constraints created by the past unless specific steps are taken to modify them in the future.

The situational factors are discussed below, beginning with the most important and central of these: work-force characteristics.

*Work-Force Characteristics*

What is the nature of people at work? Managers at every level and in every function of the organization convey their answer to this question through their managerial actions: corporations convey their answer through their HRM policies and practices. These policies and practices reflect the *assumptions* of management about employee motivation, capacities, values, potential, and desire for personal development. If the assumptions are not consistent with reality or potential of the work force, HRM policies and practices will not fully utilize or develop employees, resulting in potential loss for both employers and employees. In addition, such policies may create conflict between employees and the organization. Thus, asking what is the nature of people at work may be the most important quesiton managers can address when formulating and monitoring their actions and the impact of those actions on their human resources. But like other important questions, this one has many, sometimes contradictory, answers which depend on the individuals under consideration and their development as human beings.

To simplify the problem of fitting policies to work-force characteristics, corporations typically develop different HRM policies and practices for different groups of employees. Administratively, the work force in most U.S. corporations is typically broken down into four identifiable aggregates: (1) hourly and blue-collar, (2) nonexempt salaried white-collar, (3) exempt salaried professionals, and (4) managers. Within these groupings, of course, there are many meaningful subgroupings such as engineers, clerical personnel, skilled tradespeople, younger and older workers, and so on.

Policy differences should be shaped by valid assumptions about the differences in background, needs, expectations, and educational qualifications that employees bring to their jobs. However, managers must be careful not to differentiate between groups on the basis of invalid assumptions. Distortions are most likely to occur with respect to people at lower levels of the organization. In part at least, policy differences between groups have arisen because managers make assumptions that lower-level people—who are different from them in terms of background, social skills, and values—lack the will and skill to contribute and the potential to develop. This distortion can happen easily because today's managers are often isolated from nonmanagerial employees by organizational practices, hierarchy, and bureaucracy. Managers are no longer promoted from hourly ranks as they once were. Rather, they are educated in business schools where their main contacts are with other prospective managers. The elimination of universal military training has also precluded an enforced opportunity for shared experience with dissimilar groups.

Because it is natural to assume the existence of differences, particularly when hierarchical levels and socioeconomic background make contact and communication difficult, it is especially important for managers to recognize the potential *similarities* between employees as well as the actual differences.

Firms that are effective in human resource management—such as IBM, McCormick Spice, Hewlett-Packard, Donnelley Mirror, and Lincoln Electric—explicitly or implicitly adhered to some fundamental assumptions about people when they developed their human resource policies, while also fitting them to more complex realities. For example, Charles P. McCormick, the architect of McCormick Spice's culture, assumed that all his employees had needs for equity, pay, participation, and security. This assumption guided the human resource policies of his firm in its early years.[1] The assumptions that people want autonomy, want a sense of accomplishment, want to identify with something, want meaning, and want to grow could be added to this list. The power in developing human resource policies in accordance with a few optimistic assumptions about people lies in the capacity of such policies to encourage the selection and development of employees who conform to them.

We do not propose that the list of assumptions above is right or complete. We do propose that effective human resource management involves a tension between some universal truths about what people want or might live up to if given an opportunity (the optimistic view or normative perspective) and the more complex realities of what people are capable of wanting and doing at any given point in time (the realistic view or situational perspective). The former perspective would lead to the view that employee groups are similar and that there are some human resource universals. The latter perspective would reflect the assumption that employee groups differ from one another and that human resource policies must be different for different groups and situations. Without the tension of *both perspectives*, human resource policies will fail to inspire the commitment and competence for which all employees have the potential and they will fail to be practical and workable.

The problem of emphasizing differences rather than similarities is most acute with respect to ethnic minorities and women in the work force. By 1985, women will outnumber men in the work force, and minority groups will be an even larger and more powerful constituency than they are now. Successful HRM approaches in the 1980s and 1990s will depend to a large extent on the ability of all managers in a firm to make valid assumptions about both differences and similarities of these various employee groups.

### *Business Strategy and Conditions*

An organization's HRM policies and practices must fit with its strategy in its competitive environment and with the immediate business conditions that it faces. If a manufacturing firm operates in a highly competitive environment in which cost effectiveness and efficiency in manufacturing are key, that firm needs to develop HRM policies and practices that encourage cost savings efforts by all its employees. If quality is a key success factor, then HRM policies and practices must encourage concern and involvement of employees with the quality problem. If a professional service firm depends on attracting, motivating, and keeping the best professionals in their field, then that firm must develop HRM policies that bring in the best people, develop their competencies, and offer rewards and other inducements that encourage the right people to join and stay with the firm. Such degrees of competency may be the main factor that differentiates one firm from another.

Unfortunately, the match between HRM policies and business strategy is often poor. One reason for this is that managers often develop business plans and make capital investments without adequate regard to the human resources needed to support those plans. For example, growth plans involving the building of plants or opening of branch offices may take inadequate account of a shortage of managers to run these facilities. The result can be lower returns on investment or even complete business failures. Managers, at least those outside the HR functional area, have typically assumed that human resources are not a constraint and will be available in sufficient qualtity and quality. With increasing managerial and technical complexity and a scarcity of talent, that assumption is often erroneous.

A second reason for the poor fit between business strategy and HRM policies lies in the human resource function itself. That function often develops activities and programs that are not relevant to line management's needs. This problem arises in part from the differences is perspective between short-term, profit-oriented line managers and long-term, people-oriented human resource managers. But the problem also stems from the fact that many HR activities are not developed in close coordination with business planning. HR executives are often left out of the business planning process, frequently because they do not occupy a high level in the organization. Just as regularly, these executives develop policies and practices based on general assumptions about the kinds of behavior and performance required rather than on a careful analysis of the strategy, the tasks that the strategy presents to the organization, and the competencies and involvement required from employees.

Business strategies can also shape the human resources of the firm, the types of people, attitudes, and commitment the firm is likely to obtain. If a company's success rests on promoting a relatively undifferentiated consumer product through advertising and promotion, for example, it needs to attract people whose skills are quite different from those of people in a firm where technology-driven products are clearly differentiated. The latter firm is likely to have longer-range goals, and needs to attract and keep people interested in contributing to these goals. The former is likely to set much shorter-term goals and rely on people attracted to quick results and personal gains. The competencies and commitments of the two employee groups are likely to be quite different. This does not suggest that one business is more desirable than another. It does point out that product/market strategies might constrain the kind of HRM policies and outcomes possible. Since these HRM policies must also fit with management's values, those values must be understood when managers make business strategy decisions. Ideally, then, business strategy should influence HRM policies and practices. At the same time, available human resources as well as managerial and societal values should inform decisions about business strategy.

### *Management Philosophy*

The HRM policies of an organization are shaped by the management philosophy of its key managers, just as the philosophy of these leaders is shaped by the historical pattern of HRM policies. The relationship between HRM policies and management philosophy is stronger in some organizations than in others, depending on the pattern of development of the organization. If, in the early stages of development, an organization has a powerful founder and leader with a clearly articulated philosophy and set of values, HRM policies are more likely to be internally consistent. This consistency will create a stronger and more pervasive culture with respect to HRM matters. That culture, if sustained over time, will mold new leaders who reflect its underlying values and style.

By "management philosophy" we mean the explicit or implicit *beliefs* of key managers about the nature of the business, its role in society, and how it should be run—particularly how it will treat and utilize employees. A manager's philosophy is shaped by his or her values or assumptions about the role of business in society and the role of people in the business.

In an earlier section on business strategy, we stated that a definition of the business itself may be related to the types of HRM policies and practices the firm can develop. That link is again evident if we inspect the relationship between business philosophy, which shapes strategy, and HRM philosophy and policies. The Lincoln Electric Company's philosophy that profits are a means to an end rather than an end in itself has surely shaped the longer-term strategy of the firm that has placed more emphasis on providing value to the customer than on a growth in sales and profits. This approach led naturally to HRM policies such as employment security, employee stock ownership, and a profit-sharing plan that doubles employee income and distributes to employees approximately half the profits of the firm.

There are numerous examples of corporations whose HRM policies have been shaped in accordance with their founders' business philosophies, among them IBM, Matsushita, Hewlett-Packard, and McCormick Spice. That these are successful companies with unique capacities to attract, keep, and involve their employees is not generally in dispute, though the direct link between their success and their HRM policies is more difficult to prove.

It is also not clear how long a philosophy of management and the corporate culture which it shapes can be sustained once the key leaders have departed the scene. For example, Konosuke Matsushita, Bill Hewlett, and Bob Packard are still alive if not very active in their firms. It is also not known how large or how quickly a corporation can grow before its philosophy is diluted and its human resource policies lose their internal consistency. Rapidly growing companies like Hewlett-Packard are facing these problems now.

These questions, while challenging the imagination of managers in diffusing and sustaining a philosophy, in no way weaken the known link between management philosophy and HRM policies. In fact, the importance of that link has been acknowledged in recent efforts to create innovative work systems at the plant level aimed at developing high commitment among employees. These efforts typically involve the definition, in advance of plant start-up, of a philosophy of management, that will guide the design of human resource policies and practices. This process not only helps lead to a consensus among the management team about what the philosophy should be, thereby socializing them into a common view, but it also provides a guideline for future action as new events and realities unfold. Without a stated belief system, short-term pragmatic consideration would dominate HRM policy decisions rather than simply influence them. The result would be inconsistent new policies and an erosion of the philosophy. Thus, a general philosophy allows lower-level managers and future managers to shape new HRM policies and practices that are consistent with the philosophy but pragmatic and relevant to the immediate situation.

If we were to examine the *Fortune* 500 companies, we would undoubtedly find many companies that do not have an articulated philosophy of management, though clearly their HRM policies are an implicit statement of philosophy. Lacking founders who articulated a philosophy, they probably tended to develop HRM policies on an ad hoc basis, with pragmatic considerations or values of the managers at the time dominating policy formulation. For this reason, their human resource policies may not be consistent and may be seen as inconsistent by employees. This lack of consistency probably makes it harder for employees to attach a meaning to their relationship with the firm other than one dominated by their own self-interest. Nor can these employees develop trust in the firm, since trust is based on consistent treatment. Instead, their basis of involvement with the firm will be utilitarian, based on an exchange of work or a service for certain rewards, as opposed to moral, based on their identity with a stated purpose or philosophy.[2] Finally, lacking a clear philosophy or strong culture, the future development of HRM policies is likely to be equally inconsistent and uncertain because key leaders with different philosophies will rise to the top.

Management's philosophy, whether stated or unstated, is not the only way managers shape HRM policies and practices. Their *style* of management—the way they behave, communicate, and interact with others—sends a powerful signal up and down the organization about what they care about. It also helps to shape the organization's HRM manager policies and practices. If managers state their philosophy that employees should be given the opportunity to grow and develop through participation in management, and then make unilateral decisions revising decisions made at a lower level, the credibility of policies that encourage worker participation may be undermined. Similarly, policies that encourage employee development through open and candid discussions of performance with subordinates are not likely to be implemented if upper level managers do not model this process through their own practices.

The lack of consistency between philosophy and policies can also undermine sustained implementation of HRM policies. Managers who have formulated a policy that conflicts with their own philosophy are not likely to sustain follow-up efforts to implement that policy. Only managers with convictions—those whose philosophy and style are both consistent with the policy—are likely to continue to implement and reinforce such a policy.

*Labor Market Conditions*

One measure of a firm's effectiveness is the ability of its managers to compete successfully with other firms for financial and human resources. With respect to human resources, that ability is determined by the attractiveness of the company to prospective recruits and current employees, as well as the condition of the labor markets from which the firm draws its supply of people. The boundaries that define the labor markets in which a firm competes may vary dramatically from one group of employees to another. For unskilled production employees, the labor market may be the surrounding community. For professionals and managers, the labor market may encompass all professionals in that category in the nation.

New hires will be motivated to come to work for a company and current employees will stay if they perceive the company's wages, location, organizational climate, advancement opportunities, job security, and working conditions as more attractive than those of other companies. Over a period of time, these factors combine to form a firm's reputation in the several labor markets in which it competes. That reputation becomes an asset or a liability in attracting and keeping employees. For example, a firm that has a reputation for periodic force reductions may have difficulty competing for employees, particularly for employees in scarce supply.

But the ability of managers to attract and keep the people they need also depends on the conditions of labor markets in which they compete, as well as on their firm's HRM policies. Shortages of people with given skills make it more difficult for a corporation to attract and keep people. In cases where it is extremely difficult to find people with the right skills (the current shortage of engineers and skilled blue-collar workers, for example), business plans and goals are affected. In tight labor markets, firms have to offer more inducements than they would otherwise in order to attract and keep people. Of course, the more a company is able to develop and keep its own professionals, managers, and other skilled employees, the less hiring of experienced personnel it has to do. The desire to reduce, as much as possible, the necessity of competing in a tight labor market has led some firms to consider an employment security policy. It has also led firms to intensify their efforts in training and developing their own employees. The shortage of skilled blue-collar workers in the machine tools industry recently caused one firm to reconsider its cyclical pattern of hiring and firing. It attempted, instead, to adopt an employment security policy accompanied by an investment in an apprentice training program.

Managers are well advised to track long-term trends in labor markets, since these trends indicate how difficult and/or expensive it will be to acquire people with the skills their business may require in the future. Information of this kind can help managers assess the viability of their long-term strategic plans. Perhaps more important, it can point to changes that will be needed in educational programming at colleges, trade schools, and professional schools [which will be needed] to assure employers themselves of an adequate supply of people with the right skills. When shortages are indicated, firms can attempt to influence educational institutions to modify their programs and recruit more students in an effort to influence the labor market. Or, business organizations can set up their own internal educational programs. Firms in high-technology fields have been doing both as they have come to realize that there will be a shortage of electrical engineers in the 1980s. Those that recognized the trends sooner and anticipated their needs more adequately will be able to compete more effectively in the labor market and the business.

Trends in the labor market include changes in the participation of women and minorities as well as changing values of the work force that make employees more resistant to arbitrary authority. And the movement of the post-World War II "baby boom" has created a gradual aging of the work force that will place changing demands on HRM policies, particularly in the areas of flow and rewards. These trends, if not anticipated, can present real problems to managers who have not adjusted their HRM policies and practices to fit them. On the other hand, organizations that effect changes in HRM policies and practices in anticipation of demographic trends can gain a competitive advantage by being better able to attract, utilize, and keep a new breed of employee.

In summary, a firm's ability to compete in its labor markets is dependent on its ability to anticipate trends in the labor markets and to prepare to take advantage of these trends through imaginative human resource management policies and practices.

### *Unions*

Historically, unions have served as a mechanism to provide a collective voice for nonsupervisory workers over such HRM matters as due process, the distribution of rewards, transfers and promotions, and working conditions. Even where employees are not unionized, unions can influence HRM policies. The perceived threat of unionization can lead employers to adopt HRM policies and practices that they might otherwise avoid. Within a company, wage increases negotiated by the union create pressures to increase wages for nonunion employees by a similar or slightly greater amount in order to avoid dissatisfaction that might lead to further union organizing. Firms without any union may feel forced to pay close attention to pay, fringe benefits, employment security, working conditions, promotion practices, and termination practices. If a corporation operates in a heavily unionized community, it must establish some degree of parity between its policies and those of unionized firms, or risk unionization. Nonunion firms like IBM have human resource policies and practices (including grievance procedures, open-door policy, and employment security) that are more generous and costly than those of many unionized firms. Undoubtedly, the desire to stay nonunion was a major factor in designing these policies.

Furthermore, unions influence HRM practices of nonunionized firms indirectly through their political influence. Legislation that has come about, in large part, because of the political clout of unions has imposed certain human resource standards on employers. Occupational health and safety, workman's compensation, and minimum wage legislation are just three examples. In France and Britain, where unions are more closely allied with political parties than in the United States, their influence is even greater and is felt not only in legislation but in government policy with regard to human resource practices. Even though only 35 percent of the U.S. work force was unionized at the peak of union power in the 1960s, unions have had an important effect on human resource policies and practices of all American businesses, unionized or not.

### *Task Technology*

By "task technology" we mean the way equipment (hardware or software) is arranged to perform a task. Historically, the technology used to produce a product or provide a service has had a powerful and pervasive effect on human resource policies and practices, particularly in manufacturing operations. It has been shaped by the engineer's view of what constitutes a rational and efficient operation. That rational view (heavily influenced by Frederick Taylor and other adherents of Scientific Management, which will be discussed in greater detail in Chapter 6) has traditionally dominated plant layout and the design of jobs. Similarly, the imperatives of technology itself often have determined the nature of work. The machine and the task have tended to constitute the independent variables, while human beings were left to be the dependent variable.

This view of technology has largely shaped the nature of work as we find it in the late twentieth century. It spawned the assembly line, as well as the division of work in which "planning" and "controlling" have been systematically split off from "doing" and assigned to higher levels or staff groups. Even "doing" has been divided still further with the goal of reducing the time and cost of employee selection and training. This trend has led to problems of depersonalization, boredom, and alienation. Such human problems may in part be responsible for the rise of unionization. They are partly responsible for the quality and productivity problems which have become concerns of most U.S. industries during the past decade.

Technology is now also transforming the office. The work of clerical employees, professionals, and managers will be affected as new information technology (minicomputers and word processing, for example) is introduced and becomes an integral part of the work system for these employees.

In the work systems section of the book, we will consider some of management's recent attempts to reverse the trends of the industrial revolution which has increasingly used the principle of division of labor to simplify and routinize factory work. We will also discuss the effect of this new technology on office work: Can it be developed in a way that enhances rather than degrades human commitment and organizational competence? A recognition of human needs has already prompted management to search for more socially sensitive options in job design and task technology in the plant, but it is still an open question whether these options will be extended to the new office technology, or whether an attitude of technological determinism will continue to guide its development.

### *Laws and Societal Values*

HRM policies and practices in various countries differ in accordance with the unique culture or ideology of each society. By culture, we mean the values or basic assumptions that people in a society or an organization seem to hold about how one ought to think and behave. These assumptions are often implicit and can be inferred from the standards of expected behavior that are informally enforced by the society, organization, or group. These standards of expected behavior are sometimes called "norms." Ideology is a dynamic framework of interrelated values and beliefs that emerges within a society and is used by that society to make its values explicit and give them institutional validity. Thus, ideology is more explicit than culture or norms and can be found in formal statements of beliefs provided by leaders and other prominent societal and organizational members. Ideologies are modified in response to changes in the nature of a society and in the real world in which that society exists.[3] For example, ideology is shaped by the unique historical and political development of the society, and that development is a function of realities such as geography, demography, resource availability, evolution of traditional institutions, and patterns of behavior and the collective experience of the society as it struggles to survive and prosper. The process of ideology formulation is, therefore, a dynamic one: Changes occur as the society is confronted with new realities. The importance of ideology is that it serves as a bridge between universally held values such as survival, justice, security, self-fulfillment, economic use of resources, and self-respect and the means by which those values are put into practice in a particular setting and at a particular time.

It should not be surprising that HRM policies and practices that express the ideology of an organization—which is itself a minisociety—are heavily influenced by the ideology of the larger society. Its managers and employees have been shaped by that ideology and are likely to develop and accept HRM practices consistent with it.

Likewise, it should not be surprising that HRM policies differ across societies because of explicit differences in government policies and legislation governing employer-employee relations. With the exception of Japan, where emphasis on informal understandings and relationships reduces reliance on legislation, most countries have developed extensive legal frameworks specifying the HRM policies and practices that firms are to employ. Legislation governing employer-employee relations develops out of negative experience of employees with HRM practices in the society. These result in political pressures on government to legislate or regulate HRM practices.

Legislation affecting HRM policies and practices includes the legal framework in which unionization and union-management relations occur, wage and hour laws which govern payment of overtime, laws governing occupational health and safety, equal employment opportunity legislation, legislation governing employee pension funds, and income maintenance programs like workers compensation. In Europe, more extensive legislation exists to govern employee relations, including strict rules that restrict the freedom of management to terminate employees and legislation which establishes the rights and framework for employee participation in an enterprise. As with other legislation, of course, the intent of this legislation is quite often not translated into practice. Managers who do not accept the right of employees to participate find ways to circumvent that legislated process, just as employee representatives who do not have experience in business have some difficulty participating meaningfully, even if they have been encouraged to do so. Thus, a society that seeks to influence HRM must, over time, transform the ideology and skills of both managers and employees if real transformations are to occur.

The extent of government influences over HRM practices often depends on the ideology of the political party in power. President Lyndon Johnson's concern for civil rights resulted in an executive order which prohibited federal contractors and subcontractors from employment discrimination on the basis of race, color, national origin, religion, and sex, and required larger employers to develop affirmative action programs designed to increase the representation of women and minorities in the company's work force. Under an administration that was less favorable to the ideology underlying such a program, enforcement obviously would be reduced, as would the effects on HRM practice.

It becomes obvious, then, that HRM policies and practices are not and cannot be formed in a vacuum. They must reflect the governmental and societal context in which they are embedded. For this reason, policies and practices that work in the United States will not necessarily work in Europe or Japan. Similarly, Japanese multinational firms have discovered that not all policies that have been effective in their home country are applicable in the United States. Company housing, slow promotion, or promotion based on seniority, for instance, may not have the same effect outside of the Japanese context. Managers both in and out of an organization's human resource function must understand the culture, ideology, legislation, and regulations of the society in which they operate before formulating HRM policies. A U.S. firm operating in Belgium recently learned that lesson when it discovered that its general manager, accustomed to great freedom in hiring and firing in the United States, cost the company a lot of money in severance pay as he tried to rid his subsidiary of managers he could not or would not learn to work with compatibly.

Just as important, variations in HRM policies and practices across countries offer useful alternatives for U.S. managers to learn from. This comparative perspective allows managers to examine and question the ideology and assumptions that underlie their own HRM practices. Looking at what managers in other countries do can also suggest alternative models for integrating people and organizations. The interest of American managers in Japanese practices and the stimulus for change provided by the success of Japanese management are the best examples of this phenomenon. However, wholesale application of HRM policies from another country must be avoided if good fit with situational factors is to be obtained. By studying other cultures, U.S. managers may also be able to discern long-term patterns that may engulf them in the future. The alternatives may also suggest strategies for dealing with these long-term changes. For these reasons, some cases and notes in this book deal with HRM in other countries.

## ORGANIZATIONAL ADAPTABILITY

Implicit in much of the discussion here and in later chapters of the book is the assumption that effective human resource management policies and practices lead to increased adaptability, a critical ingredient in the long-term survival of business organizations. This point is discussed more explicitly below.

In the long run, organizational effectiveness means that the firm has been flexible and responsive to its market and social environment. When the market demands lower costs, or product innovation, or improved service, the management of the corporation must sense the need for change and be able to mobilize the support of various stakeholders, employee groups, unions, government, educational institutions, suppliers, and the community to make adjustments in their own expectations and behavior. Effective HRM policies and practices are those that are designed and administered through a process of mutual influence between management and employees and that result in high levels of commitment, competence, cost effectiveness, and congruence. Here is how the four Cs can contribute to employee and organizational adaptability.

1. *High commitment* means that employees will be motivated to hear, understand, and respond to management's communications about changes in environmental demands with their implications for wages, work practices, and competency requirements. The mutual trust will be there to enable management's message to be more believable to employees and to enable management to be responsive to employee's legitimate concerns as stakeholders.
2. *High competence* means that employees in the firm will have the versatility in skills and the perspective to take on new roles and jobs as needed. Through a positive attitude toward learning and personal development fostered by policies that encourage and reward learning, employees will be more capable of responding to change.
3. *Cost effectiveness* means that the organization's human resource costs—wages, benefits, and indirect costs such as strikes, turnover, and grievances—have been kept equal to or less than those of competitors, while major adjustments such as the ones facing employees in the steel and auto industries have been avoided. Once again, only a continual process of mutual influence about the realities of the business and the needs of employees can bring about this outcome.
4. *Higher congruence* than competitors means that the firm has shaped work systems, reward systems, and flow policies so that there is a higher coincidence of interest among management, shareholders, and workers. Furthermore, a process of employee influence in the affairs of the company will also foster congruence. In such a climate, changes in policies and practices

> prompted by the external environment are less likely to be perceived by employees as not in their interest. Moreover, the inevitable differences between shareholder interests and employee interests that remain in even the most effective corporations will probably be easier to manage because an atmosphere of collaboration and mutual problem solving will have been developed between stakeholders. Adversarial relations are less likely to exist.

Effective organizations are also adaptive to changes in their social environment. Managers in adaptive organizations can sense changes in societal values and attend to the spirit as well as the letter of laws that operationalize these values. These changes begin to be reflected in their management philosophy and practices, particularly their human resource practices. Managers who see themselves as responsible for the well-being of the enterprise, its employees, and society—i.e., for long-term consequences as opposed to the more narrow outcomes such as profit or growth—are more likely to sense and incorporate changes in societal values into human resource policies. Their HRM policies are less likely to undermine their relationships with their employees, government, and community.

We believe that the relationship between employers and employees, and the attitudes and motivation of management and labor are very important ingredients in the process of organizational adaptation. Therefore effective human resource management as we plan to discuss it in this book is an important strategy for achieving an adaptive organization.

## SUMMARY

In this chapter we have provided a map of the key factors that have a strong influence on HRM policies and are in turn influenced by them. For example, we suggested that management's assumptions about work force characteristics influence human resource policies just as those policies affect work-force characteristics. Similarly management philosophy, business strategy, labor markets, laws and society, task technology, and unions affect HR policies and to varying degrees are affected by them. For many of these factors—business strategy, task technology, unions, and management philosophy—a two-way process of influence is possible and needs to be strengthened. That is, policies need to be forged with a clearer understanding of the constraints, just as those constraints may be seen as amenable to modification by progressive and well-articulated HRM policies. Other factors, such as laws, society, and labor markets, may be more immutable constraints in the short run, but even they are subject to influence and change in the long run. We characterized each of the situational factors interacting with human resource policies in the belief that a better understanding of their influence will allow managers to design policies that fit the situation and/or change the situation.

The interests of various stakeholders—shareholders, management, employees, government, the community, and unions—must also be an important factor in designing HRM policies and practices. Without attention to the perspectives of all stakeholders, HRM policies and priorities are unlikely to gain their acceptance. In the long run this is likely to result in the failure of those policies and in a loss of organizational effectiveness.

The well-being of the enterprise, society, and employees were suggested as long-term criteria by which general managers ought to evaluate the HRM policies of their organization. The clear implication is that general managers should search for policies that enhance the well-being of all three, not the enterprise alone, which has traditionally been the central consideration. Finally, commitment, competence, congruity, and cost effectiveness were suggested as specific outcomes that help define all three long-term criteria and that should be assessed explicitly in evaluating human resource policies. Innovative companies are explicitly shaping policies to enhance commitment, competence, and congruence, outcomes that in many companies are by-products of human resource policies rather than explicit goals. Such policy shaping increases an organization's capacity to adapt to changes in its environment.

The conceptual framework presented in this chapter offers *a way of thinking*, not a mechanistic tool for analysis. By adopting it, it is hoped managers will be able better to understand the historical roots of HRM policies and outcomes and to develop creative solutions to human resource problems that fit and influence the situation, satisfy the interests of several stakeholders, and reach for improved outcomes for the enterprise, society, and employees.

## NOTES

1. Charles P. McCormick, *The Power of People* (New York: Penguin Books, 1949).
2. This compliance framework has been suggested by A. Etzioni, "Compliance Structures," in A. Etzioni and E. W. Lehman (eds.), *A Sociological Reader on Complex Organizations*, 3rd ed. (New York: Holt, Rinehart & Winston, 1980), pp. 82–100.

3. The discussion which follows is based on George Lodge, *Context Ideology*, Harvard Business School Case Services No. 9-380-071 (1979). In the original, he uses the term *community* instead of *society* to indicate that any collection of people with a common need and purpose (factory, corporation, town, or union) develop an ideology.

CASE 1

# AIR TRAFFIC CONTROLLERS

*Bert A. Spector*
*Michael Beer*

On August 3, 1981, approximately 12,000 employees of the federal government went on strike. The strikers were air traffic controllers, employed by the Federal Aviation Administration (FAA) and members of the Professional Air Traffic Controllers Organization (PATCO), an AFL-CIO affiliate. Although the job action violated federal laws prohibiting strikes by government employees, the president of the union was on record as saying, "The only illegal strike is an unsuccessful one." Within hours, the President of the United States announced that any striking controller who failed to report back to work within 48 hours would be fired. Three days later, with 12,000 dismissal notices in the mail, the Secretary of Transportation announced, "As far as I'm concerned, it's a nonstrike situation. It's over. Our concern is rebuilding the system."

But the rebuilding task would not be an easy one. The *Los Angeles Times* estimated that the curtailment of air traffic necessitated by the severe reduction in the number of controllers was costing the economy anywhere from one to six billion dollars, with the number of layoffs in the airline industry expected to rise above 10,000. Then there was the problem of training qualified controllers to replace PATCO's members. The FAA's training center in Oklahoma City tripled its efforts despite a shortage of qualified trainers. Admission requirements were lowered for applicants, and the failure rate for trainees in the program shot up dramatically. Four months after the strike and layoffs, there were still lingering questions about how and when the system could be rebuilt to operate at full levels of efficiency and safety. Critics of the Administration's actions wondered out loud what the FAA was doing differently so that such problems would not recur sometime in the future.

## HISTORY

The FAA was established by an act of Congress in 1958 "to provide for the regulation and promotion of civil aviation." At that time, the Civil

---

Aeronautics Board was designated as the agency that would have jurisdiction over the establishment of air routes and review of tariffs, as well as responsibility for determining probable cause of air traffic accidents. The newly created FAA assumed responsibility over all safety rule-making authority. As such, the FAA trains, certifies, and employs all air traffic controllers in the United States. At the time, critics wondered whether the dual objectives of the FAA, to both look after safety *and* promote aviation, were not somehow contradictory.

### *PATCO*

In 1968, some controllers, dissatisfied with representation by the National Association of Government Employees, broke away to form PATCO as an independent union and elected John Leyden president. The main issues then were obsolete equipment and understaffing. Under the guidance of lawyer/pilot F. Lee Bailey, 450 PATCO members staged a two-day "sick-out" in June of 1969 to protest understaffing. A larger, three-day sick-out was held by some 3,000 PATCO members in 1970. Pittsburgh controller Carl Vaughn says of that job action: "We had no equipment. It was dangerous, dangerous. Little or no automation had been introduced, and near misses were a common occurrence." The FAA fired 100 controllers who were identified as leaders of the sick-out. A federal court issued a permanent injunction ordering PATCO never again to engage in a strike. In 1972 PATCO, by then an AFL-CIO affiliate, was officially certified as the exclusive representative for the FAA's air traffic controllers. Six years later, PATCO led a four-day slowdown, and was fined $100,000 for violation of the 1970 injunction. While the Justice Department found "sufficient evidence may exist to support criminal prosecution," the Department declined to prosecute because employees had not been notified in advance of such a possibility.

Throughout the 1970s PATCO grew at a steady rate. Because of shift work and the fact that controllers spend much of their workday away from radar scopes, controllers tended to socialize among themselves. They tended to become a strong, self-contained peer group both on and off the job. PATCO members could exert strong social pressure on their fellows to join the union and support job actions.

In April 1980 PATCO members elected Robert Poli to replace Leyden as president. Poli worked as a controller in Pittsburgh and Cleveland and had been a PATCO vice president since 1973. Of the change in leadership, Poli said, "It was a difference in philosophy. I guess I'm more militant than he is." The struggle between pro-Poli and pro-Leyden forces had been a bitter one, though, and ill feelings lingered into the summer of 1981.

*Public Employee Unions*

Public employees are the only sector of the work force in which unionization is increasing. In 1980, 43.4 percent of public employees were unionized as compared with 21.7 percent of the private work force.

As a public employee union, PATCO must work within the context of special laws. Public employees are specifically excluded from the protections of the National Labor Relations Act. In 1955 Congress outlawed participation in a strike by an individual who holds a position with the federal government, and the constitutionality of that law was later upheld by the Supreme Court. In 1962 John F. Kennedy issued an Executive Order establishing the right of federal employees to join a union.

The most recent law affecting unionization and collective bargaining among federal employees is the Federal Labor Relations Act. With public sector unionism growing rapidly, President Nixon had established a commission of union and management representatives to recommend new legislation. The resulting Act, which went into effect in January 1979, was designed both to define the scope of public sector collective bargaining, and to allow public employee unions some mechanisms of appeal. While allowing for collective bargaining, the Act specifically prohibits bargaining on any of the following matters: wages, job classification, benefits, work assignments, creation of an agency or union shop, and layoffs. Procedural matters can be bargained over. All other settlements between union and the government are not legally collective bargaining agreements, but rather are suggestions that must be approved by the responsible federal agency.

The Act also created the Federal Labor Relations Authority, a three-person board appointed by the President to rule on Unfair Labor Practices (ULP). It is considered a ULP, for instance, for the appropriate government agency to fail to bargain in good faith with the union. It is also a ULP for a federal employees' union to "call or participate in a strike, work stoppage, or slowdown, or picketing of an agency in a labor-management dispute if such picketing interferes with an agency's operations"; or for a union to either condone or fail to prevent a strike by its members.

If the FLRA finds that a union has committed a ULP, it must move to revoke a union's "exclusive recognition status" (decertification), or take "other appropriate disciplinary action." FLRA decisions may be appealed to the U.S. Court of Appeals and the Supreme Court.

Reinforcing the ban against federal employees' strikes is the oath taken by air controllers which reads, in part, "I am not participating in any strike against the Government of the United States or any agency thereof, and I will not so participate while an employee of the Government of the United States or any agency thereof."

Large strikes of federal unions are not unheard of. In 1970 approximately 175,000 postal workers went on strike. President Nixon called in 2,500 military personnel to move essential mail in New York City. Behind-the-scene negotiations between George Meany and Secretary of Labor George Schultz resulted in a return to work and resumption of negotiations. Of the 200 postal workers fired, all but 90 were returned to work.[1]

When taking over the presidency of PATCO in 1980, Robert Poli ruled out the possibility of future slowdowns, saying all that slowdowns accomplished was to inconvenience the public.

## AIR TRAFFIC CONTROLLERS

Prior to the automated air traffic control system implemented by the FAA in the early 1970s, flight progress data were compiled on plastic "flight strips" which were used by controllers to keep track of where the plane was supposed to be at any given time. Controllers moved plastic chips around on display screens to indicate which particular aircraft was in which position. Since the automated updating, high-capacity transponder equipment automatically provides a readout on the display screen of both the identity and altitude of all planes flying under instrument flight rules.

It is important to note that all planes fly under one or two sets of air control rules. Commercial airlines and some larger private craft use instrument flight rules (IFR). Most lighter-weight general aviation craft (private planes) use visual flight rules (VFR). VFR pilots are not required to file a flight plan; they are not restricted to any portion of the airspace save for very high altitudes; and they depend solely on pilot eyesight to maintain proper distance with all other planes, both VFR and IFR. In 1969, in response to a midair collision between an airliner and a VFR craft flown by a student pilot, the FAA designed 10 "hub" airports at which VFR planes must get ground clearance before landing. About 80 percent of all air traffic today flies under VFR.

There are controllers at work 24 hours a day. Individuals work eight-hour days, 40-hour weeks, and take a lunch break when their schedule allows. Most facilities rotate controllers between day and evening shifts on a weekly basis. Some facilities use a "2-2-1" rotation in

[1]In early August 1981 the two major postal unions—the American Postal Workers Union with 245,000 members and the National Association of Letter Carriers with 227,000 members—were scheduled to begin voting on a new contract.

which a controller works two 4:00 P.M. to midnight shifts, two 8:00 A.M. to 4:00 P.M. shifts, and one midnight to 8:00 A.M. shift.

There are two basic categories of controllers. Tower controllers work in a tower at or near an airport and, utilizing both radar and eyesight, bring planes in and out of that airport. En route controllers sit in isolated centers scattered across the country and guide IFR planes through their sectors. An en route facility tracks planes as far as 500 miles, and one en route controller may handle as many as 25 flights at a time. The nation's 17,000 air traffic controllers are divided about evenly between tower and en route controllers. (For a more detailed description of air traffic controllers' duties, see Exhibit 1-1.)

To be eligible to become a controller, an individual must be between 18 and 30 years of age, be a high school graduate, have three years' experience at any job, and pass aptitude and physical tests. In the past, about 50 percent of successful applicants have been former military air traffic controllers, and 15 percent were women. (Exhibit 1-2 provides a profile of the "average" controller at the highest-activity-level centers.)

As of July 1981 the FAA employed 17,275 air traffic controllers. Of that number, 3,063 were "developmental" controllers (at some level of training), 900 were staff, and the remaining were full performance-level controllers.

Training for air traffic controllers involves a 17-week training program at the FAA's training center in Oklahoma City. It is estimated that the cost of training each new controller at that center is $17,000. During the training (depending on the level facility the controller is training for), the controller is paid full salary and all benefits. For the next two to four years, the controller receives on-the-job training from journeymen controllers until rising to full performance level. The FAA estimates that in 1981 the direct and indirect costs of fully training a controller come to about $175,000.

Between 1968 and 1981 the salary for FAA full-performance controllers increased 120 percent on average. In 1977 the pay range for FAA controllers was $16,618 to $35,875; by 1981 that pay range was $20,467 for those operating in towers that handle light traffic to $49,229 for the most experienced controllers at the busiest airports (in 1981 there were about 100 controllers in the country at that level). At the busiest airports, like LA, JFK, or O'Hare, starting pay is $31,871 for full-performance-level controllers finished with all of their training. The average pay for a fully qualified controller is $33,000. (See Exhibit 1-3 for the government service (GS) level breakdown of controllers; Exhbit 1-4 for government service levels for some other occupational groups.) Because of a 10 percent night differential in pay, a 25 percent differential for nonovertime work on Sundays, and double pay for a regularly scheduled shift on a holiday, top paid controllers can earn as much as $50,112.50, which represents the legislated cap on pay for federal civil service employees.[2]

The FAA has devised no standard performance appraisal system for measuring the performance and proficiency of controllers. Instead, individual supervisors exercise their own criteria and judgment in approving controllers.

Controllers may retire at half pay at the age of 50 if they have worked for 20 years, and at any age if they have worked 25 years. By contrast, most other federal employees must be 55 with 30 years service, or 60 with 20 years service to get their full retirement rights of half pay.

## THE FAA AS EMPLOYER

One indication of employment conditions is a comparison between FAA controllers and controllers from elsewhere in terms of work week, vacation days, and paid sick leave days per year (Table 1-1). (Sick leave, vacation days, and work week for FAA controllers are the same as those for all federal employees. Because of the special characteristics of the job, however, special rules apply to controllers. Unlike other federal employees, for instance, controllers must take sick leave even for minor illnesses if they are on any type of medication.)

During the Presidential campaign of 1980 Republican candidate Ronald Reagan addressed a letter to PATCO's Robert Poli deploring the state of the nation's air traffic control system and pledging to take "whatever steps are necessary to provide our air traffic controllers with the most modern equipment available and to adjust staff levels and work days so that they are commensurate with achieving a maximum degree of public safety." (See Exhibit 1-5 for a complete text of the letter.) Candidate Reagan's letter did not refer to specific concerns with the FAA management and employment system. But controllers and outside consultants alike supplied their own list of concerns. Among the most frequently heard were:

### *Stress*

The FAA itself estimates that 89 percent of their controllers never qualify for full retirement benefits because medical disabilities force them to quit early (all controllers must pass a rigorous annual physical). Many controllers claim that the high attrition rate is due to the

[2]The Secretary of Transportation, like all Cabinet members, was paid $69,630 in 1981.

**TABLE 1–1 Comparative Employment Conditions**

| Country | Work Hours per Week | Vacation Days | Paid Sick Leave Days per Year |
|---|---|---|---|
| Eurocontrol[a] | 29 | 24–30 | Up to 180 |
| New Zealand | 32 | 23–28 | Up to 275 |
| Denmark | 33–34 | 24 | NA[b] |
| Australia | 35 | 30 | 15 |
| Sweden | 38 | 30 | NA |
| Austria | 38.5 | 37 | Up to 7 months |
| France | 32 | 56 | 90 |
| West Germany | 33 | 56 | 90 |
| Canada | 34 | 36 | 15 |
| Norway | 38 | 30 | Up to 1 year |
| Switzerland | 38 | 30 | Up to 1 year |
| United States | 40 | 19–26 | 13 |

[a]Private air control system for Belgium, the Netherlands, Luxembourg, and parts of West Germany.
[b]NA = not available.

stressfulness of their job. In 1977 Congressional hearing, John Cyrocki, the FAA's Great Lakes regional director, described the demands on an air controller this way:

> We estimate that a controller in any of our major facilities, such as O'Hare, for instance, has at least 50 variables affecting his or her air traffic control decisions.
>
> In making those air traffic control decisions, the controller is constantly integrating these variables and applying judgment, and because of man's ability to apply judgment, he can effectively cope with these variables which can result in a potential number of combinations on the order of magnitude that can best be expressed by the mathematical formula of 3.04 times 10 to the 64th power, or 3 with 64 zeroes behind it. This is really a mind-boggling number of most of us, and yet man is able to deal with these combinations very effectively, because he has the ability of applying judgment, and he eliminates, by use of judgment, most of the noncritical combinations in any one given situation and then focuses his attention on those combinations that are critical to the decision he or she is about to make.

Between 1967 and 1970 Dr. Robert Rose of Boston University, together with Dr. Sidney Cobb of the University of Michigan's Survey Research Center, surveyed the medical records of over 4,000 controllers. Rose and Cobb concluded that controllers suffered from significantly higher incidences than the general public of hypertension and peptic ulcers. They were significantly more likely to be heavy smokers and coffee drinkers, all of which indicates a higher incidence of heart disease. Their survey also showed that a significant relationship existed between the incidence of peptic ulcers and hypertension and the age of the controller as well as the traffic density with which that controller was working.

Rose conducted a separate study between 1973 and 1978 of 416 air traffic controllers. The study, sponsored by the FAA, involved interviews and extensive, regular physical examinations, and came to the following conclusions:

1. Controllers tend to be strong, emotionally normal, dominant, independent, highly motivated, self-confident, conscientious, and sociable.
2. Controllers have significantly higher intelligence levels than the national average.
3. Also, low morale and intense and chronic feelings of alienation from FAA management and the sense that the FAA makes them scapegoats when things go wrong are common to air controllers.
4. In a comparison with all other occupational groups, air controllers rank near the bottom on "social support" from supervisors and co-workers. Only unskilled and semiskilled blue collar employees rate lower.
5. While they are sober on the job, there tends to be considerable drinking among controllers off hours.
6. Controllers tend to have problems of self-control and minor scrapes with the law.
7. Great variability of blood pressure while on the job; 30 percent suffering from high blood pressure; risk of getting hypertension two to three times the national average. Hypertension, wrote Rose, "approached an epidemic proportion among air traffic controllers." There was, however, no evidence that hypertension led to poor job performance.

One PATCO member explained what he felt to be the personal costs of the job:

> I've lost partial hearing in one ear because the headset is such cheap equipment. I underwent a year of psychotherapy because of the stresses of this job. Some days I go home and walk in the door and my wife takes one look at my face—and my clothes, which are sweated through from the neck down—and she doesn't say a word, she sends my son to his room, and she makes me a drink, and we don't talk for two hours.

The FAA tends to downplay the stress associated with the job. Dr. Carlton Melton, chief of the aviation physiology lab at the FAA's Civil Aeromedical Institute, says that high incidence of hypertension is due not to the job but to the fact that the job attracts people who are already prone to hypertension. FAA spokesman John Leyden[3] says, "The job ranges from hectic to boring. In actual practice, a controller spends one hour at the console, one hour off." And President Reagan's Secretary of Transportation, Drew Lewis, says, "There is no more stress on this job than on a number of others: firemen, policemen just to name a few. I think maybe we've seen too many movies of pilots being brought in when someone has a heart attack.

Dr. Robert Rose reported that, when turning over his findings to FAA chief Longhorne Bond in 1978, he explained that the major problems with controllers were not economic, and that the FAA should work to improve its labor relations. "But," says Rose, "Mr. Bond did not seem to be interested."

### *Access*

Many controllers complain about the stress caused by the FAA's past policy of allowing private airlines virtually unlimited access to airports. That policy meant that more people were flying to the same place at the same peak times. That increased both peak activity and the gap between peak and valley activity. Controllers insisted that unlimited access increased the pressures of the job during peaks and the boredom of slow or idle time during valleys. Indeed, FAA data show that the size of the gap between peak and valley activity at air traffic facilities was strongly correlated to the number of grievances filed at a facility. (Later, a strong correlation would be seen between variability of activity and strike count at various facilities.)

### *Automation*

Computerization may be making the air controller job increasingly obsolete. Eventually, computers are expected to do what controllers routinely do now, leaving only supervisory and managing tasks to controllers. On August 7, 1981 (the fifth day of the PATCO strike), the *Wall Street Journal* reported that the FAA hopes to install, at a cost of $2.8 billion, computers which will alert pilots directly in case of problems and instruct them automatically on changing course. The FAA told the *Journal* that it hoped to use computers to grant clearance at the various flight stages. Such changes will have the effect of giving pilots more control over their in-flight operations. A spokesperson for Bendix, which will build part of the new system, noted, "We're building

[3]No relation to the former PATCO president of the same name.

elements of the ground system into the cockpit, making the pilot, in effect, a backup controller.'' The Air Line Pilots Association pushed for, and now applauds, a shift from a system relying on ground-based controllers to one which shifts some responsibility to pilots and computers.

Such automation, the FAA hopes, will enhance flight safety. It may also reduce substantially the number of air controllers needed to run the system. At a 1977 House hearing, Congressman Dale Milford asked Quentin Taylor, deputy administrator of the FAA, about the changing role of both controllers and pilots:

> MILFORD: Aren't we sort of moving into an era where both the pilots and the controllers are going to have to think of themselves more as systems monitors rather than individuals who previously controlled an airplane or a flight control sector?
>
> TAYLOR: I don't think there is any doubt about that. Certainly that is the state of the art with respect to automation, as it has progressed.

### *Overstaffing*

In the spring of 1979 the FAA's deputy associate administrator for engineering and development told a House committee that technological innovation would enable the air traffic control system to handle 50 percent growth in traffic over the next decade without a significant increase in the number of controllers. Two years later, the FAA's personnel analysis showed that the system could be maintained at *current traffic levels* with approximately 20 percent fewer controllers.

A recent report on the air traffic system in *Business Week* concurred with the assessment that automation would have a dramatic impact on work force levels:

> The most startling change in the air traffic control system of the future will be in labor savings. Each display screen, which tracks the traffic in a designated area, or sector, now is manned by two or three controllers. With the new system's advanced technology, just one controller will be able to handle each screen—and the sector it controls will be a wider slice of the surrounding air space.

Prior to the events of the summer of 1981, however, the FAA made no attempt to bring about a reduction in the work force. Explained Raymond Van Vuren, the FAA's head of control operations, ''I knew we had too many [controllers], but it was impracticable to attempt to streamline the controller force because of expected resistance from the [controllers'] union.''

### *Supervision*

Supervisors were people promoted from within the air traffic controllers' ranks. Because of that, most supervisors had no more than a high school education with no management training. There was no standard performance appraisal system and promotions seemed to be based more on the "buddy" system than on any plan for the development of human resources. In the past, the FAA sent personnel to management training school within 12 months of their appointment to a supervisory position. Budget cuts have eliminated such training, however.

One systematic study of controllers who became supervisors between 1973 and 1978 showed that, in general, those promoted were more satisfied with FAA policies, had higher amounts of personal job morale, and were more job-involved than those controllers not promoted. They tended to be older than those not promoted, more experienced, and more highly regarded for their skills by their peers.

Despite this finding, Robert Poli spoke of a good deal of resentment between controllers and their supervisors:

> First of all, controllers resent the fact that supervisors get paid the money they do because they're a [civil service] grade higher but don't work the airplanes. That's ridiculous. They get that for filling out schedules and sitting down there. They don't really provide supervision. There's no need for it. They have too many supervisors in areas where they could double the number of controllers the person supervises. . . . The FAA always fills those [supervisory] positions, but doesn't fill the controller positions.

Numerous internal studies conducted by consultants hired by the FAA agreed that management practices within the air traffic control system tend to reflect the military background of most controllers. The pervasive style is authoritarian, impersonal, and "by the book." Managers have little or no training, education, or experience in collaborative management skills, and evaluation and promotion policies within the system do not reward such skills.

### *Safety Responsibility*

One common complaint of air traffic controllers had to do with what they felt was their final responsibility for the safety of aircraft. They were solely responsible for safety, they felt, not pilots or supervisors, yet they could exercise only limited control over the operation of the air traffic system. Supervisors were interfering with their work, often telling them how fast to work and how their functions should be performed, and pilots did not always heed the advice of air traffic controllers.

The pilots themselves, however, disagreed with that assessment. John J. O'Donnell, president of the Air Line Pilots Association (AFL-CIO), says that federal legislation has placed "ultimate responsibility on the shoulders of the pilot." Robert Poli has conceded as much himself. When asked at a 1977 congressional hearing, "Isn't the pilot the ultimate person responsible for the aircraft?" Poli responded, "The pilot is the commander of the airplane. He is in command of the airplane and he is responsible for the ultimate safety of the airplane, yes, that is correct."

Studies have shown that air traffic controllers are cited as contributing factors in only a small number of aviation accidents (0.9 percent in 1980). They have also shown that most "system errors" by controllers occur during valley rather than peak periods and within the first hour on a position.

### *Pay*

Under the federal compensation system, air traffic controllers were well-paid federal employees who found themselves giving direction to people with greater prestige and higher salary: pilots. Observed 26-year-old controller Matt Blum, whose base salary was $27,000:

> You know how much pilots make [up to $115,000]. They're flying an airplane with 150 people on board and they're using automatic pilot. We're sitting at a scope working 10 airplanes at once with 150 on *each plane*. We have *more* responsibility and spend *more* time working.

As federal employees, controllers can, and do, rise to the top salary allowed by federal legislation ($50,112.50), the so-called federal pay cap. Because this cap applies to *all* federal civil service employees, the highest paid controllers earn as much not only as their supervisors, but as facilities chiefs and regional FAA directors. Also, the pay cap is administered in such a way that no federal employee can earn more than 1/26th of the cap in any two-week period. This rule applies even if a controller were to put in enough overtime hours during a two-week period to raise his or her pay (salary plus premium pay) above 1/26th of the cap. In such a case, the controller would be restricted to 1/26th of the cap, and the hours not compensated in that two-week period *could not* be applied to any other two-week period when the controller might fall below the 1/26th cap level.

## NEGOTIATIONS

With PATCO's three-year contract with the FAA scheduled to expire in March 1981, indications of an FAA-PATCO clash began appearing much earlier. Almost immediately after passage of the FLRA, for instance, in February 1979, the FAA filed an unfair labor practice charge against PATCO. The union had created a $600,000 Controller Benefit

Fund which, the FAA insisted, was really a strike fund, thus creating prima facie evidence that PATCO was not trying to prevent a strike. The FLRA ruled against the FAA, but agency executives were convinced that a strike was pending.

In January 1980, FAA head Langhorne Bond worked with the agency's former legal counsel Clark Onsted to draw up what Onsted characterized as an "incredibly detailed" legal strategy for dealing with a possible PATCO strike. The strategy included civil proceedings, court injunctions, citations for contempt, criminal proceedings, fines, threats of imprisonment for contempt of court, and decertification.

Bond also drafted contingency plans for operating airport control towers with supervisory personnel. In November he published the details of that plan, known as the "National Air Traffic Control Contingency Plan for Potential Strikes and Other Job Actions by Air Traffic Controllers," in the *Federal Register*. The plan called for "flow control," a computer-based system designed to get maximum use of air space with a severely reduced work force. Throughout the upcoming year, supervisors would be requalified to operate the system. Magnetic computer tapes containing all data necessary to implement the contingency plan were produced and locked into safes at each of the FAA's major en route control centers.

PATCO meantime was taking its own steps. Robert Poli's election as president in April 1980 was followed by PATCO's endorsement of the Republican Presidential candidate, Ronald Reagan. As such, PATCO was one of only four AFL-CIO affiliates to endorse the Republican over Jimmy Carter (the Airline Pilots Association was another).

Ronald Reagan, born in 1911, began his professional career in 1937 as a movie actor by joining the AFL-CIO-affiliated Screen Actors Guild. In 1964 he renounced his lifelong affiliation with the Democratic Party and became an active campaigner for the Republican's unsuccessful Presidential candidate, Barry Goldwater. After winning the governorship of California, Reagan sought the Presidential nomination himself, unsuccessfully in 1968 and 1976 and successfully in 1980. The Party platform on which Reagan ran that year "reaffirmed" the Party's standing support for states to pass laws outlawing union shops. In November Reagan received 43 million votes compared to President Carter's 35 million.

As PATCO entered the negotiations in the early spring of 1981, their bargaining position was spelled out in a House bill which included the following provisions:

1. An increase in the average controller's salary from $33,000 to at least $43,000.

2. A new maximum of $59,000 for experienced controllers at the busiest airports.
3. A reduction of the work week from 40 to 32 hours.
4. Full retirement benefits to be allowed after 20 years of service.
5. Cost-of-living adjustments to be made twice a year rather than once.

The FAA's negotiations were being handled at that point by Reagan's appointee to head the FAA, J. Lynn Helms. According to Helms's calculations, PATCO's package would cost the government $744 million for the first year. He countered with an offer he said would amount to $40 million the first year and $120 million over the three-year duration of the contract. His proposal, which would also need Congressional approval if accepted, included the following provisions:

1. Reduction of the work week to 37.5 hours.
2. Higher pay differential for night shifts.
3. Ten percent raise for controllers who do on-the-job training.
4. An average increase of $2,300 per controller in addition to the $1,700 increase all federal employees were scheduled to receive.
5. Elimination of the federal pay cap, allowing night, Sunday, and holiday pay to bring a controller's earnings above the cap.
6. One-year severance pay to experienced controllers forced to retire for medical reasons.

Helms accompanied his offer with a memo to all air traffic controllers warning about the possible consequences of a strike (see Exhibit 1-6).

PATCO rejected the FAA offer, and Poli called for a strike vote. PATCO's constitution requires a strike to be approved by a number equaling 80 percent of all 17,275 working controllers. PATCO's membership stood at about 16,200. The vote showed 75 percent of all controllers supported a strike, so Poli returned to the bargaining table.

At this point, Drew Lewis, Reagan's Secretary of Transportation, replaced Helms as the government's chief negotiator. Lewis, a graduate of the Harvard Business School, entered the weekend of June 20 and 21 prepared for further hard negotiations. Poli was already on record as saying that PATCO members would walk off their jobs on Monday, June 22 unless the government presented an "acceptable" proposal.

Over the weekend, Lewis remained firm on the $40 million cost of the package, but expressed a willingness to redistribute that money more to the union's liking. That Monday morning, Lewis and Poli emerged from their meeting room in the Washington offices of the Federal Mediation and Conciliation Services and announced a tentative pact. The contract provisions that had been accepted by both Lewis and Poli included:

1. Controllers would be paid "responsibility differential" of time-and-a-half for hours worked in excess of 36 during a 40-hour week. In effect, controllers would work 40 hours and be paid for 42 hours.
2. Night differential raised from 10 to 15 percent.
3. The federal salary ceiling was removed to accommodate premium pay for controllers.
4. There would be a guaranteed 30-minute lunch break per shift.
5. Controllers medically disqualified after five years of continuous service and not eligible for retirement would be given 14 weeks base pay for retraining.
6. An average increase of $4,000 per controller.

Lewis said of the settlement, "At a time when the President has called for reduced public spending and has asked all Americans to help control inflation, our proposal, I believe, represents an equitable package." Robert Poli commented, "I'm pleased with the settlement. We felt that, with the present economic conditions, it was a good package for us." Poli added that he expected no trouble with PATCO ratification. He pointed to certain nonwage concessions including the right of controllers to participate in the formulation of procedures to handle air traffic safety and efficiency and to make recommendations on new equipment.

## STRIKE AND TERMINATIONS

The situation remained relatively quiet for the next month. The day after the tentative agreement, FAA chief Helms did announce new moves toward computerization of the air traffic control system, specifically an automated "anticollision system" that would be in place by 1984 and eliminate the role of controllers in collision avoidance by alerting pilots directly when another aircraft posed a threat.

On Wednesday, July 29, after studying and debating the tentative settlement, the air traffic controllers voted 95 percent in favor of rejecting the proposal and going on strike. That Friday, Poli announced that he would again be willing to return to the bargaining table, and that PATCO would strike the following Monday, August 3, if the government had not made an acceptable offer. On Monday morning, August 3, in the absence of any movement in the talks, Poli announced that PATCO was on strike. Indications were that between 12,000 and

13,000 PATCO members were honoring the strike and staying away from work (see Exhibit 1-7 for profile of striking and nonstriking controllers).

*The Administration Reacts*

The Reagan Administration immediately began its own set of countermoves. Reagan ordered that all negotiations with PATCO come to an immediate halt, and stated that any striking air traffic controller who failed to report to work within 48 hours would be terminated. The government then successfully sought a court order barring PATCO from using any of its controller benefit fund for strike benefits, and at the same time lodged a complaint with the FLRA asking that PATCO be decertified for engaging in an illegal strike. Furthermore, the President issued a ban excluding striking air traffic controllers from *any* federal employment for the next three years. Public opinion polls showed strong support for the President's tough stand: 57 percent approved, 30 percent disapproved. On the other hand, a majority felt that the controllers must have had a legitimate reason for sacrificing their jobs (63 percent) and that controllers worked under undue stress (58 percent). The public was more evenly divided on whether the government should ever hire back the strikers (42 percent said should; 44 percent said should not).

On the evening of the Wednesday deadline, FAA director Helms suggested that if 1,000 or 2,000 controllers were fired, the system could operate without severe problems, but if the number was 10,000, "There's no question we're going to have difficulty, and we're going to have difficulty for a year." On Wednesday, despite court orders, heavy fines, and even scattered jailings of union leaders, only about 1,000 of PATCO's striking members returned to work. Drew Lewis informed the press that there had probably been a surplus of between three and four thousand controllers before the strike, and Helms explained that only 5,500 vacant controllers' jobs would be refilled. Poli responded by charging the government was using the strike "as an excuse" to fire employees they had intended to lay off anyway in revamping the controllers' system.

Organized labor found itself in a difficult position. While endorsing PATCO's actions with statements and denouncing the President as a "strike breaker" and a "union buster," to honor PATCO's illegal picket lines would itself have been a violation of the law. Also, there was some resentment against PATCO within the labor ranks both for crossing airport employee picket lines in the past and for not consulting with or keeping union leaders informed of their current plans. Still,

AFL-CIO president Lane Kirkland endorsed the right of all workers to strike:

> I respect the law. However, when working people feel a deep sense of grievance, they will exercise what I think is a basic human right, the right to withdraw their services, not to work under conditions they no longer find tolerable. I think that is a right that is inherent and one that's not adequately addressed by legislative remedies simply saying that it's against the law.

That Thursday, Lewis announced to the press, "As far as I'm concerned, it's a nonstrike situation. Our concern is rebuilding the system." With that statement, courts began dropping their contempt citations against strikers. It was clear from statements by Lewis and by FAA regional administrators that even if strikers wished to return to work now, they would not be allowed back.

The Sunday after the strike, Drew Lewis appeared on CBS TV's "Face the Nation." He conceded that the strikers probably had some legitimate grievances and that there was a need in the FAA for better communication with employees, improved equipment, and changes in work rules. When asked about the common charge that the FAA is a bad employer, he responded, "I think it's probably a legitimate charge." Lewis, however, insisted that the rejected contract would have corrected these problems.

In the following weeks, as periodic boycotts by sympathetic foreign air traffic controllers failed to disrupt the system for an extended time, Poli and other PATCO members used the press to charge that the system was in disarray and that safety was being sacrificed for expediency. During the early weeks, supervisors and nonstriking personnel were being supplemented by 370 air traffic controllers supplied by the military. The FAA reduced flights according to their early "flow control" plan to about 75 percent of normal. Helms admitted that supervisors were being asked to carry an extraordinarily heavy load. During the first week, most supervisors worked 60 hours. By the end of that week, Lewis could only offer the hope that they might be cut back to 48 hours soon. Still, the government, airline companies, and the airline pilots union insisted publicly that the system was as safe or safer than before the strike and layoffs.

## THE IMPACT

In the first weeks of the strike, as airline traffic stayed within 60 to 75 percent of normal, there were indications that the strike and subsequent layoffs would have some impact on the national economy. On August 5, the Air Transportation Association (whose members conduct 95 percent of scheduled airline flights in the United States) announced that the strike was costing the industry $35 million a day,[4] while the American Hotel and Motel Association estimated member losses to be $10 to $15 million a day. On that same day, Braniff announced its intention to lay off 1,500 employees. A week later, the president of the National Export Traffic League acknowledged, "There's a lot of trouble, and cargo is piling up. A lot of shippers are very concerned." By August 15 the total airline layoffs had reached 5,000 and that number doubled a week later. About half of those layoffs were attributed to seasonal adjustments, the other half directly to the strike. The first small airline to fold as a result of new restrictions on flights was Air New England, which announced its intention to lay off all 400 employees.

Shortly after the strike, two newspapers attempted to assess the economic impact of the events. *The Wall Street Journal* speculated that the strike would change the way airlines operate. Specifically,

1. One-stop trips might replace nonstop trips at greater cost to the customer.
2. Airlines could now ground less efficient craft and cut out some of the less profitable routes they had been forced to maintain by the Civil Aeronautics Board. In doing so, they could raise average fares.
3. The enforced curtailment of capacity would reduce competition in the airline industry.
4. Less need to fill empty seats would reduce offerings of discount fares.

At the same time, the *Los Angeles Times* estimated that the cost of the strike over a 60-day period could run between one and six billion dollars, not including the lost salaries of the controllers themselves. That figure was based on airline losses, the "ripple" effect on other industries, tax revenue losses, and the cost of training new controllers. The Commerce Department denied the *Times*'s estimate, arguing there would be no significant long-term economic impact, and that airline profits would in fact rise because of fuller planes and higher average ticket prices.

In the weeks and months after the strike and firings, many people talked about the broader implications of the actions by PATCO and the federal government. An editorial in *Business Week*, for instance, saw

[4]In its damage suit against PATCO, the Association settled on a figure of $28.9 million of damages caused by the strike for the first three days.

Reagan's tough stand as part of an administrative attempt to send signals to other unions, particularly public employee unions: "Reagan's attack on PATCO also completely undermines a recent strategy decision by the American Federation of Government Employees to adopt a 'confrontational' approach to the hiring freezes and layoffs planned by the Reagan Administration." A representative of the U.S. Conference of Mayors agreed that Reagan's stand "will reinforce the resolve of local elected officials to play it tough with unions"; while an expert in public employee labor relations for Columbia University noted that the Administration's handling of the strike would show all government employers how they could "seize control of labor relations instead of merely reacting to union demands."

Others talked about the impact technology had had on the strike and the handling of the strike. "This ability to fire a work force and run without it," noted one commentator, "has great implications not only for air controllers, but for a wide range of private and public employment."

The AFL-CIO's Lane Kirkland suggested what he saw as a basic inconsistency in the Administration's handling of the entire affair and offered a possible first step toward a solution:

> The air traffic control system is purely a subsidized service the government is providing for the private airline industry. Under the Reagan doctrine of getting the government off people's backs, you'd think they might try to turn the whole thing over to the industry to run instead of using the might and majesty of the government to suppress a strike.

### *Recruitment and Training*

Almost from the first day of the strike, the FAA was flooded with job applicants. The training center in Oklahoma City announced that, in order to fill 5,500 jobs within a year, they would have to change their operations in several important ways. First, they would offer around-the-clock training, allowing them to teach three classes at once. Two hundred additional instructors would be needed, to be recruited mainly from retired and medically disqualified controllers. Admission standards would also be lowered somewhat. The score on the paper-and-pencil aptitude test necessary for admission to the academy would drop approximately ten points, although academy spokespeople insisted that those certified would be of the same quality as before.

The academy soon ran into several problems. On August 7, 30 FAA instructors engaged in informational picketing to protest efforts to speed up controller training, expressing concern about the long-range safety of the system. And about three-quarters of the way through the first training period, the FAA estimated that there would be a failure rate among trainees about twice as high as was normal. At the end of November, the FAA announced that 44 students in the first class of 145 had failed. The failure rate in the second class was 31 out of 145, with an additional 17 dropping out before completion.

### *Decertification*

After weeks of delay, the FLRA announced its decision to decertify PATCO. The only dissenting vote came from Ron Houghton, FLRA chairman, who suggested that instead of decertification PATCO members be given five days to return to work.[5]

Drew Lewis reacted to the FLRA decision by saying,

> It reaffirms a basic principle of our democracy that no person or organization is above the law and that citizens of this country cannot be allowed to pick and choose the laws they obey.

William Ford (D-MI), chair of the House Committee on Post Office and Civil Service, offered his own assessment:

> It is unfortunate that the FLRA did not reach a solution that would have left room for a just resolution of the dispute between the government and the air traffic controllers. We have a combination of federal laws that provide no meaningful remedy for this kind of labor impasse, an impasse that adversely affects not only the economy, but the safety of the public and the defense of the nation.

Following that decision, Poli offered to order all PATCO members back to work, but the government declined the offer.

## AFTERMATH

Dismissed traffic controllers found their search for new jobs difficult, and the search for positions that paid as well as their past positions almost impossible. By year's end, as the country edged into recession, unemployment exceeded 8 percent. In early December, the President rescinded his three-year ban on federal employment for PATCO members, but insisted they would not be hired back as civilian controllers because to do so "would adversely affect operational efficiency, damage morale and perhaps impair safety." At that time, government unemployment stood at 5 percent, a 22 percent increase over the previous year.

[5]Earlier, the FLRA dismissed PATCO's ULP charge against the FAA for failure to bargain in good faith. The FAA's obligation to bargain with PATCO, said the FLRA, "was suspended on August 3 when the union began engaging in an unlawful strike."

In December 1981, a U.S. District Court in Denver dismissed criminal indictments against local PATCO leaders. The court found evidence that long before the strike, in February 1981 in fact, the FAA had aided the Justice Department in compiling a list of controllers to be singled out for prosecution should a walkout occur. Such a list had been developed and acted upon not on the basis of any criminal activity but on the basis of union leadership during a time period, said the judge, when the FAA was supposed to be negotiating with PATCO in good faith. The judge added:

> The selection of targets under these circumstances culminating in an ultimate hit list containing many top level union representatives is instinct with invidious motivations. . . . Accordingly, I conclude that the defendants were selectively prosecuted on the basis of their [constitutionally] protected activities as union presidents and representatives.

In January 1982, following an announcement by the Teamsters union that they were considering an organizing drive among air traffic controllers, Robert Poli resigned his position as president of PATCO. The way was thus cleared either for the FAA to negotiate with new PATCO leadership or for the AFL-CIO's American Federation of Government Employees to start from scratch with a new organization.

During the strike, Lewis announced that the government would still recommend passage of the same package that it had offered PATCO during the final weekend of negotiation. (Lewis estimated that the package would now cost $20 million rather than $40 million because of the terminations. As of May 1982, however, Congress had declined to approve those recommendations.) Saying "maybe we haven't done a good job in the past," Lewis also announced his intention to shore up labor relations and improve communication and the work environment. To that end, he announced the formation of a task force which would study all of the employment conditions of the air traffic controllers. The task force would make its recommendations directly to Lewis some time in the spring of 1982.

In early spring, as Lewis awaited the task force report, FAA officials conceded that as many as 700 striking controllers could be hired back into their old jobs as a result of official appeals of their dismissals. Three controllers had already been brought back into the system as a result of appeals to federal district courts, and government officials said the Reagan Administration might be willing to bring back those who could prove they had been intimidated by their colleagues or who had "legitimate reasons" for walking out. A poll of nonstriking controllers, however, showed that 58 percent thought none of the strikers should be hired back, 31 percent said some should be hired back, and 10 percent said they should all be hired back unconditionally. Drew Lewis responded by saying that because of the controller shortage and long hours still being worked by supervisors and nonstrikers, his life would be a lot easier if a couple of thousand controllers could be brought back. However, he added, government lawyers had assured him there was no legal way of screening out ''troublemakers'' while bringing back a significant number of controllers.

## EXHIBIT 1-1
## What Air Traffic Controllers Do

What follows is a step-by-step description of controllers guiding a flight from Chicago's O'Hare to New York's JFK Airport.

1. O'Hare departure gate—pilot confirms altitude, speed, route, and estimated flight time with controller at O'Hare tower. After clearance, pilot contacts a ground controller for taxiing instructions. Ground controller uses eyesight to direct pilot to proper runway.
2. On runway—using radar and view from tower, controller clears plane for takeoff.
3. One mile from Chicago—controller in Chicago tower transfers flight to departure controller, also at O'Hare, who directs pilot to proper course for first leg of flight.
4. Thirty-two miles from Chicago—departure controller transfers flight to Chicago Center en route controller located in Aurora, Illinois. That controller tracks plane on radar and automated readouts up to 23,000 feet.
5. One hundred miles from Chicago—plane is transferred to another Center controller when it reaches 23,000 feet, and that controller takes it up to 33,000 feet. The next handoff takes place from the Chicago Center to an en route controller at the Cleveland Center.
6. Two hundred miles from New York—as plane approaches Pittsburgh, it moves from airspace controlled by Cleveland Center to an area controlled by New York's en route center on Long Island. The Long Island controller grants clearance for the plane's descent to 24,000 feet.
7. One hundred miles from New York—the plane is passed to another controller at Long Island Center who gives clearance for descent to 15,000 feet.
8. Twenty-five miles from New York—Long Island Center tells pilot to contact terminal radar control at proper frequency. Pilots do not navigate on their own under this control system which provides radar vectors for all subsequent maneuvers. Pilot is given clearance for descent to 2,500 feet.
9. Six to eight miles from New York—as plane descends to 2,500 feet, it is handed off to the JFK tower which issues advisories on runway conditions and gives clearance for landing. The pilot now navigates with the instrument landing system which tells where the plane should be in order to land on the runway selected by the tower and alerts pilots to any changes.
10. The plane lands at JFK and ground control takes over.

**EXHIBIT 1–2**
**Profile of Average Full-Performance-Level (FPL) Controller—Level III Center[1]**

- **Age.** 37 years.
- **Education.** High school graduate (only about 15 percent of controllers have associate, undergraduate, or graduate degree).
- **Years of Service.** 15.
- **Salary.** FPL salary is GS-14 ($37,871 to $49,229). Average salary is $41,077, not counting overtime (time-and-a-half), holiday pay (double), night time duty between 6 P.M. and 6 A.M. (10 percent differential), and Sunday (25 percent differential).
- **Overtime.** Averaged 17 hours per controller in 1980.
- **Schedule.** Eight-hour shifts. However, half hour provided for lunch as well as routine breaks for coffee, rest, and other needs, plus time off for briefings and training sessions. As a result, controllers actually control traffic five hours a day or less. Moreover, contract stipulates no more than two consecutive hours at same position.
- **Qualifications.** Three years general experience plus written examination. Education may be substituted for general experience, which is defined as progressively responsible work which demonstrates potential for learning and performing air traffic control work.
- **Training.** Initial training of 17 weeks at FAA Academy in Oklahoma City. Then on-the-job training at the center as developmental controller under supervision. Most controllers reach full performance level within five years.
- **Retirement.** In fiscal year (FY) 1979, average age at time of retirement was 49.9 years.

[1]Level III: Highest activity category center. Must handle 275 or more IFR aircraft per hour. There are 15 centers in this category.
SOURCE: FAA.

**EXHIBIT 1–3**
## GS Levels for Air Traffic Controllers

| | No. Air Traffic Controllers July 1981 | GS Level | Waiting Period for Next Increase Within Grade | | | | | | | | | |
|---|---|---|---|---|---|---|---|---|---|---|---|---|
| | | | 52 Weeks | | | 104 Weeks | | | 156 Weeks | | | |
| | | | *Step* 1 | *Step* 2 | *Step* 3 | *Step* 4 | *Step* 5 | *Step* 6 | *Step* 7 | *Step* 8 | *Step* 9 | *Step* 10 |
| Trainees | 122 | GS-05 | 12,266 | 12,675 | 13,084 | 13,493 | 13,902 | 14,311 | 14,720 | 15,129 | 15,538 | 15,947 |
| Trainees | 0 | GS-06 | 13,672 | 14,128 | 14,584 | 15,040 | 15,496 | 15,952 | 16,408 | 16,864 | 17,320 | 17,776 |
| Trainees | 362 | GS-07 | 15,193 | 15,699 | 16,205 | 16,711 | 17,217 | 17,723 | 18,299 | 18,735 | 19,241 | 19,747 |
| | 0 | GS-08 | 16,826 | 17,387 | 17,948 | 18,509 | 19,070 | 19,631 | 20,192 | 20,753 | 21,314 | 21,875 |
| On-the-Job Development | 884 | GS-09 | 18,585 | 19,205 | 19,825 | 20,445 | 21,065 | 21,685 | 22,305 | 22,925 | 23,545 | 24,165 |
| On-the-Job Development | 757 | GS-10[a] | 20,467 | 21,149 | 21,831 | 22,513 | 23,195 | 23,877 | 24,599 | 25,241 | 25,923 | 26,605 |
| Full Performance Level Controllers / On-the-Job Development | 2,353 | GS-11 | 22,486 | 23,236 | 23,986 | 24,736 | 25,486 | 26,236 | 26,986 | 27,736 | 28,486 | 29,239 |
| Full Performance Level Controllers / On-the-Job Development | 3,283 | GS-12 | 26,951 | 27,849 | 28,747 | 29,645 | 30,543 | 31,441 | 32,329 | 33,237 | 34,135 | 35,033 |
| Full Performance Level Controllers / On-the-Job Development | 3,483 | GS-13 | 32,048 | 33,116 | 34,184 | 35,252 | 36,320 | 37,388 | 38,456 | 39,524 | 40,592 | 41,660 |
| Full Performance Level Controllers / On-the-Job Development | 6,019 | GS-14[b] | 37,871 | 39,133 | 40,395 | 41,657 | 42,919 | 44,181 | 45,443 | 46,706 | 47,967 | 49,229 |
| Full Performance Level Controllers / On-the-Job Development | 2 | GS-15 | 44,547 | 46,032 | 47,517 | 49,002 | 50,487[c] | — | — | — | — | — |

[a]Starting level for full performance level controllers at smallest airports.

[b]Starting level for full performance level controllers at largest airports.

[c]Basic pay for federal employees is limited to $50,112.50 in accordance with 5 U.S.C. 5303 and Section 101(c) of Public Law 96-369.

**EXHIBIT 1–4**
**GS Levels for Selected Occupational Groups**

| OCCUPATION | GS RANGE |
|---|---|
| Licensed practical nurses (Boston area) | GS-3 through GS-4 |
| Nurse | GS-4 through GS-5 |
| Veterinary medical officer | GS-9 |
| Professional engineer and architect | GS-5 through GS-11 |
| Coal mine inspector | GS-9 through GS-11 |
| Metallurgist | GS-5 through GS-11 |
| Mining engineer | GS-5 through GS-12 |
| Petroleum engineer | GS-5 through GS-13 |
| Printing management (with appropriate B.S. degree) | GS-5 through GS-7 |

**EXHIBIT 1–5**
**Text of Letter from Ronald Reagan to Robert Poli**

Robert E. Poli, President
Professional Air Traffic Controllers Organization
444 Capitol Street
Washington, D.C.

Dear Mr. Poli:

I have been thoroughly briefed by members of my staff as to the deplorable state of our nation's air traffic control system. They have told me that too few people working unreasonable hours with obsolete equipment have placed the nation's air travelers in unwarranted danger. In an area so clearly related to public safety the Carter Administration has failed to act responsibly.

You can rest assured that if I am elected President, I will take whatever steps are necessary to provide our air traffic controllers with the most modern equipment available and to adjust staff levels and work days so that they are commensurate with achieving a maximum degree of public safety.

As in all other areas of the federal government where the President has the power to appoint, I fully intend to appoint highly qualified individuals who can work harmoniously with Congress and the employees of the government agencies they oversee.

I pledge to you that my Administration will work very closely with you to bring about a spirit of cooperation between the President and the air traffic controllers. Such harmony can and must exist if we are to restore the people's confidence in their government.

Sincerely,

Ronald Reagan

**EXHIBIT 1-6**

**Memo from J. Lynn Helms to Air Traffic Controllers**

May 29, 1981

TO NONSUPERVISORY AIR TRAFFIC CONTROLLERS
IN CENTERS AND TOWERS

Dear Fellow Employee:

I am concerned about recent reports that you are being encouraged by your union to engage in a strike or work action against the Federal Government. You are being led to violate the law and the oath you took as a federal employee based on the assumption that the only illegal strike is an unsuccessful one. I feel obligated to take every step possible to ensure you are completely knowledgeable of the surrounding circumstances before you knowingly participate in such an action.

We are a government and a people of the law. Just as we expect our government to be bound by the Constitution and the law, we are also bound by the rules of law. We cannot pick and choose which laws we will obey based on personal judgment that a cause is just and deserving of action. No individual or group can claim justice by engaging in unlawful action to obtain it. If you believe your positions have merit, you can, of course, pursue them through the legislative process using lawful persuasion.

The course of action urged by your union can only result in harm to you, the public, and the government. The government will have no alternative but to vigorously pursue all remedies available to it to bring any unlawful action to an end. These remedies were spelled out by the Department of Justice in a letter to the FAA which is enclosed.[1] The most important message to you in this letter is to make you aware that the union officials <u>may not</u> suffer the consequences; <u>you</u> will bear the burden of violation in their behalf.

I am concerned about you personally and want to do everything possible to alert you to the potential consequences to you, your family, and your professional future, irrespective of employer, if your record includes conviction of violating a federal law.

J. Lynn Helms
Administrator

[1]The letter from the Department of Justice to Langhorne Bond, dated September 22, 1978, outlines a plan of injunction, fines, and criminal proceedings that can be used against both union officials and union members engaging in an illegal work action. The letter also states that, during the 1978 slowdown, the Justice Department found "sufficient evidence may exist to support criminal prosecution." Such actions, however, were not taken because the employees had not been notified of such a possibility in advance.

## EXHIBIT 1-7
## Profile of Striking and Nonstriking Controllers

- **Age.** Average age of strikers was 35 years versus 39 years for nonstrikers.
- **Length of Service.** Average length of service for strikers was 12 years versus 16 years for nonstrikers.
- **Retirement Eligibility.** At the time of the strike, 516 strikers were eligible for retirement versus 1,872 eligible nonstrikers.
- **Regional Distribution.** The distribution of strikers among regions was relatively even.
- **Facility Level.** Little difference in percentage of strikers versus nonstrikers among various facility levels.
- **GS Level.** A lower percentage of lower-graded personnel went out on strike as compared to higher-graded personnel.
- **Sex.** The percentage of women who went on strike was slightly less than men.
- **Race.** The percentage of hispanics, blacks, and Asians who went on strike was slightly higher than the percentage of whites.

*Chapter* 3

# Employee Influence

EMPLOYEES AND SHAREOWNERS are two important stakeholders in business enterprises. Typically, both groups share a stake in the survival and prosperity of the organization, but employees have an additional stake in the particular policies and other means employed by the organization in pursuing prosperity.

Employees' stakes are, in part, economic: What fraction of the economic pie will go to them as wages and benefits rather than to owners in the form of dividends, or be retained by the enterprise itself for capital investment? And who absorbs certain costs of uncertainty in the size of the pie—for example, employees through layoffs or shareowners through their financing of employment assurances? And how do these economic stakes differ from one employee group to another?

An employee's stake is also psychological: How much dignity is accorded the individual by management's policies and practices? How much status does one have as a factory employee, as a supervisor, as a division controller? How much intrinsic satisfaction does an employee derive from his or her assignments?

Employees also have a political stake in the enterprise. Unless people are self-employed, the work organization will be the setting in which they will spend about half of their waking hours during the 40 to 50 years of work life. What are an employee's rights and obligations within those workplace societies?

In the larger society in the United States, one has certain political rights: to vote on issues and to elect leaders. One is assured the rule of law, not rule by man. One is guaranteed certain rights of privacy, freedom of speech, and assembly. One is assured justice by due process. As citizens we take those rights for granted. These rights have never extended to corporate society. In many ways, employees are expected to leave their citizenship rights and responsibilities at the plant entrance each morning and pick them up again only when departing for the evening. Implicitly, if not explicitly, the employment relationship involves a contract in which an employee accepts a truncated set of political rights. But how truncated?

We believe the most central issue for employees as stakeholders is the question of *influence*: How can they act to improve or protect their economic share, psychological satisfaction, and rights? How is such influence to be exercised?

Management, of course, has a set of concerns different from the ones just expressed which leads them to a different view of the influence question. Top managers must act on their own judgment about the appropriate division of the economic pie, and that judgment often conflicts with employees' preferences. Managers are charged by stockholders with the efficient use of capital, people, raw materials, and energy. Efficiency involves control; control requires direction; direction requires authority. Management's policies and practices in service of efficiency and control may conflict directly with employee "political" rights and indirectly with their psychological needs. Not surprisingly, management historically has been attracted to their own version of political rights, i.e., "management prerogatives." Typically, they have regarded the idea of increased employee influence as subtracting from their ability to achieve efficiency and control.

Society's views of what employees are entitled to in terms of their economic, psychological, and political interests change over time. Indeed, employees themselves have shifting expectations, as do the unions who represent a segment of American workers. Finally, management's own values and their judgments about what is effective management involve shifting standards about how much the enterprise should accommodate employees' interests and especially how much employee influence is desirable. We will explore below how the direction of change has been toward an expectation of greater employee influence. We see no reason why that trend will not continue.

In this book we do not recommend specific answers to the question of how much influence employees should have over organizational objectives, policies, and practices, nor do we answer the question of what mechanisms should be provided to make possible the exercise of employee influence. Answers to these questions vary with circumstances and conditions. We do, however, take the position that managers should have a conscious and well-thought-out policy that addresses precisely these questions of how much influence and by what means. Policies in this area provide the cornerstone for the development of other policies regarding personnel flows, rewards, and work systems. We are confident that managers' objectives in this area are seldom simply to minimize employee influence. They are to provide for some optimum amount of influence. But how do managers decide what is optimal for their organization? What are the costs and risks associated with minimal employee influence? What costs and risks do managers have in mind when they think of "too much" employee influence?

We have used the phrase "employee influence" because it is a label not currently in widespread use by either practitioners or academics, giving us some freedom to offer a definition without contradicting already existing understandings. We should acknowledge, however, that it is related to "participation," as that word is used to describe a style of management in the United States and as it refers to codetermination and other forms of governance in Europe. "Employee voice" is another phrase we use occasionally, although it is not quite as descriptive as "employee influence." "Voice" says that employees' interests will be *expressed* (not necessarily heard and acted upon), while "influence" goes one important step further. Not only will their interests be heard, but there will be mechanisms which allow them to help shape their company's HRM policies.

Our concept of employee influence is intended to be the most generic formulation of the core HRM issue that underpins a number of different institutions or organizational practices, including collective bargaining in the United States, legislated works councils in Europe, Japan's *ringi* system of seeking consensus around management decisions through wide sharing of information, and a variety of other management devices for learning about and responding to the nature and strength of employee concerns.

This chapter will provide an historical and conceptual context for the employee influence issue. It will also outline some alternative ways corporations and societies have chosen to deal with the question of how much influence to give employees, what kind of influence to give them, and what mechanisms, legislated and nonlegislated, are to provide the vehicle for influence.

## THE CHANGING ROLE OF EMPLOYEES AND STAKEHOLDERS

To achieve its goals, a corporation must find some combination of motivation and control that will move people toward a common purpose. Historically, control has been exercised primarily through the authority of owner-managers, and later by professional managers representing shareholder interests. Organizations have historically been able to obtain effective control over operations through (1) division of labor intended to achieve efficiency, (2) a heirarchy of authority, and (3) rules and procedures designed to achieve coordination. In the early days of the industrial revolution such detailed control of employee behavior was considered completely legitimate. As George Lodge has pointed out, the legitimacy of such control rested upon an ideology derived from the British social philosopher, John Locke.[1] Lockean ideology placed primary emphasis on ownership of private property (a gift from God) and the unquestioned right of the property owner to exercise authority over how that property was used. The authority of managers, then, was bestowed down the hierarchical ranks from above, ultimately from property owners.

Given that ideological environment, the simple and routine tasks of early enterprises, and the labor market at the time, top-down control worked effectively. Prospective employees had few skills to offer factory employers, nor did these employers require many. Moreover, people lived much closer to the subsistence level than today. Thus, individuals did not have the power that comes from marketable professional and managerial skills which today give "knowledge workers" considerable power to negotiate conditions of work. In Europe a history of aristocracy and class structure conditioned employees to accept authority. In Japan employee compliance with hierarchical control was supported early on by Chinese Confucianism, which emphasized family hierarchy and responsibility to group, and military dictatorship which highlighted the warrior's code of "master above self."[2] In the United States a large immigrant population in the late eighteenth and early nineteenth centuries lacked not only skills and economic resources but also the power that comes from knowledge of language and culture. An implicit economic contract existed between employers and employees whereby employees accepted management's authority in return for the economic inducements of a job and pay. Employees were not in a position to talk of employment security or employee advancement and development. Furthermore, one worked under whatever conditions management specified, including long days, long work weeks, and sometimes unsafe conditions.

The virtually unchallenged authority of management had the apparent advantage of allowing rapid decision making and implementation. There was no time and energy spent in dealing with differences that existed between stakeholders. Employees dissatisfied with conditions of employment turned to labor unions. Some of these, such as Industrial Workers of the World, were militantly socialistic; others, such as the early American Federation of Labor, were interested mainly in increasing the economic share allotted to the craft workers they represented. But the numbers of unionized employees remained relatively small until the Great Depression of the 1930s, when the skilled, semi-skilled and unskilled workers formed industrial unions.

It was inevitable that unilateral management control would lead to problems. For one thing, such top-down controls allow a social and emotional distance to develop between powerful managers and less powerful employees. Those in power, therefore, run the risk of growing aloof and becoming even more insensitive in their relationships with employees. This gap can, in turn, lead to lowered trust and even less willingness to communicate with employees. This sequence of distance, aloofness, insensitivity, and distrust can develop between top management and middle management just as it can develop between a first-line supervisor and production employees. It can develop even more easily between top management and lower-level employees simply because the physical and hierarchical distance is so great and there are few, if any, opportunities for employees to voice their concerns and views about management's goals and means. Middle managers are distanced in the hierarchy from those both above and below them. Hence they are blocked from fully understanding the concerns and demands of employees below them, and from communicating upward the concerns and demands that they are aware of for fear of upsetting top management and being branded as disloyal. Add to these problems the different interests of management and employees that exist to begin with and it becomes clear that a potential for conflict is ever present.

Just as importantly, unilateral control can create dependence which in turn can increase resentment and distrust towards management and the organization itself. It has been argued that the developmental imperative for all human beings is to move from dependence (a condition of childhood) to independence and then interdependence (a condition of mature and healthy adulthood). Stated another way, human beings strive to be involved and to gain influence over their lives to the extent that they are psychologically ready to do so and to the extent that economic or organizational conditions enable them to do so. Hierarchical organizations have been said to impede this developmental process by placing too many controls on employees, thereby making them unnecessarily dependent.[3] The consequence of this dependency can be that employees are less willing to take responsibility for their work or the performance of the organization. Thus, with the exception of those who are rapidly promoted upward, bureaucracy may prevent the development of "involved" and "responsible" employees who would be assets to a corporation.

The limitations of hierarchical control have led naturally to a search for alternatives. Dissatisfied employees have sometimes attempted to gain some influence over their well-being by organizing unions. Spurred by dissatisfaction with the conditions of employment and the relative powerlessness of workers, societies have responded with legislation that enables employees to unionize more easily or that creates institutional mechanisms for worker representation on boards or councils. These mechanisms are intended to empower employees to influence affairs over which management has previously had more complete control. In other instances, societies have also legislated minimum standards for safety, employment security, employment opportunity, and other working conditions. Finally, spurred by the high costs of employee-management and union-management conflict, by increasing evidence that employees are now less willing to accept unilateral directives, by the desire to avoid unions and preclude further legislative initiatives by the society, or, in some cases, by progressive values, management itself has instituted reforms in its own practices. Corporations in Europe, the United States and Japan have experimented with a variety of innovations aimed at turning adversarial relationships with unions into cooperative ones and at giving employees more direct influence over their work and the human resource policies of the firm. Thus, a redefinition of management's prerogatives and employee rights has slowly been taking place in this century.

## LEGISLATED EMPLOYMENT STANDARDS AND EMPLOYEE PARTICIPATION

In democratic societies employees are also voters. When they are otherwise unable to satisfy what they consider to be legitimate aspirations for minimum wages, income security, safe working conditions, fair treatment, or equal employment opportunity, they have recourse through political means.

### *Legislation and Regulation*

European countries have enacted legislation to define minimum standards of employment more frequently than the United States or Japan. In many countries it is difficult to dismiss an employee without an extensive process of review by the government and the payment of high severance costs. Those requirements often in effect create an employment security policy. Only when whole industries or corporate survival is threatened are exceptions negotiated between companies and government.

In many western European countries, the national government legislates many of the matters that are dealt with by collective bargaining in the United States. After consulting with the affected parties, the national government legislates employee benefits including paid vacations, holidays, sick leaves, hospital and medical care, as well as payment for death, retirement, severance of employment, and increased size of family.

While in Europe national laws cover much of the substance of labor relations, United States collective bargaining law leaves a great deal to be determined in the bargaining process. Unlike European labor agreements, for instance, U.S. contracts usually include actual wage rates as opposed to minimum rates; benefit plans such as length of vacation, vacation pay, holidays and holiday pay, and supplementary unemployment benefits; and local plant and individual worker matters like discipline, promotions and demotions, layoffs, seniority rights, plant safety, and grievance and arbitration procedures. It can be said, then, that while U.S. laws tend to cover the *process* of labor relations, European laws often deal with the *substance* of that relationship.

Governmental legislation and regulation have increasingly been moving beyond the process of labor relations. Equal employment, health and safety, and minimum wage are some examples that have already been mentioned. Government regulatory agencies may lead companies to create their own influence mechanisms (job posting, for instance, which allows employees some influence over their career development, or affirmative action committees to which employees may appeal decisions on the basis of perceived inequities). These agencies also serve as external mechanisms to which employees may appeal as a means of influencing decisions.

### *Worker Representation on Boards or Councils*

Several European countries, including Norway, Denmark, and the Netherlands, have legally established a dual system of providing worker influence. Unions engage in collective bargaining and political lobbying, while elected workers councils are given certain governance powers—ranging from the right to be informed and consulted to the power of codetermination—over the workplace. Such councils are generally elected by employees of a particular plant, with larger multiplant companies having a central workers council as well.

A 1972 West German law, for example, requires that employees sit as representatives on permanent works councils that are granted legally defined rights such as the right to be thoroughly informed on human resource matters, the right to contest planned dismissals, and the right to advise and consent on such issues as employment, transfer, classification, and the wage framework. Other German laws call for labor codetermination by providing for worker representatives on supervisory boards (boards of directors) which meet a few times a year and have general responsibility for policy decisions. In large German steel companies, for instance, the boards consist of five representatives of employees, five of stockholders, and one neutral member elected by the rest of the board. The employee representatives include two members from the works councils and three from the union. In other German industries, codetermination grants just less than equal representation to employees on management boards. While supervisory boards do not run day-to-day operations, they do review corporate strategy and human resource policies, and appoint the management board, the top management group in German corporations.

Historically, unions in the United States have shied away from the notion of participation on corporate boards of directors, preferring to maintain an independent and adversarial position. An important exception to this rule is the agreement worked out between the United Auto Workers (UAW) and the ailing Chrysler Corporation to place then UAW president Douglas Fraser on the company's board of directors. Another exception is the agreement of several unions to make wage and work rules concessions to Eastern Airlines in return for employee stock ownership and four seats on its board of directors.[4] It is too early to tell whether these and other moves toward employee representation on boards of directors will be merely an exception or a trend forced upon seriously troubled companies seeking greater involvement of their unions and increased commitment of employees to reductions in labor costs.

How effective are legislated mechanisms for employee participation in giving employees real or "felt" influence? The degree of real influence is partially determined by legislation and varies from country to country. But it is also a function of how much management seeks to involve employee representatives actively in decisions, and here actual practice varies widely, from attempts to utilize participation mechanisms actively to efforts by management to minimize their power and influence. In addition, the business knowledge and group-process and decision-making skills possessed by worker representatives will affect their influence and, indirectly, the influence of employees.

As for the amount of "felt" participation by employees, some studies have shown that feelings of participation do *not* necessarily increase because legislated mechanisms for participation exist. Workers may feel as distant from their representatives as they are from managers. It turns out that skill in communicating with employees is as important for employee representatives as it is for management.

We can now return to the question of whether employee representation on boards of directors in the United States is an anomaly forced by economic crisis or a model that will be followed by less troubled companies. If these governance models are to be followed by other companies, they must provide those companies with a competitive edge by improving cost effectiveness, congruent (less adversarial) relationships, and commitment. These outcomes are likely only if management can develop a genuine stakeholder perspective and the skills to engage in a process of mutual influence. At the same time, union and employee representatives must acquire the requisite business knowledge as well as the process and political skills needed to manage their constituencies. The absence of requisite knowledge and skills by labor and a genuine stakeholder perspective and process skills by management underlies the problems sometimes experienced by legislated participation in Europe.

*Partial or Complete Employee Ownership*

In 1975 the South Bend Lathe Company was saved from closing when its 500 employees borrowed money from the federal government and bought shares in the firm through an employee stock ownership plan (ESOP). Such loans are possible under legislation aimed at making employee ownership easier. About 3000 firms, mostly small companies, have begun similar ESOP plans by turning some or all of their stock over to employees. A 200-employee picture frame factory in Somerville, Massachusetts operates under an employee stock ownership trust in which employees control all voting and nonvoting stock. More recently, General Motors' employees in Clark, New Jersey purchased a 43-year-old bearing plant from the company in order to prevent the plant from shutting down.[5] Unable to negotiate a 35-percent wage reduction with the union, management offered to sell the plant to employees under a plan that would loan employees money for the purchase and guarantee a specific order level from GM for three years. Only a third of the employees agreed to become owners, but they immediately took a 35-percent pay cut. Is the ultimate mutuality of interest between employees and shareholders made possible by employee ownership the only condition that enables such reductions in labor costs? What are the implications of this for corporate survival and responsiveness to competitive forces?

Partial or complete employee ownership theoretically allows employees the opportunity to exercise complete influence over the way the company is managed. Whether the shareholders will put mechanisms in place that allow various stakeholder groups to influence business goals or human resource policies is thus determined by the employees themselves. However, recent research suggests that employee ownership does not automatically lead to enhanced employee influence and labor-management cooperation.[6] A recent strike by the employee-owners of the South Bend Lathe plant provides dramatic real-world evidence that unless management possesses attitudes and skills in involving employees, and employees are willing and able to become involved, employee ownership will not result in greater influence. "Felt" influence does not increase with the increase in economic and legal power. Increases in congruity, cost effectiveness, employee commitment, and competence do not necessarily result.

## COLLECTIVE BARGAINING

Given the problems of unilateral control that were discussed earlier, it is not surprising that employees have attempted to protect their well-being through collective action. Feeling the inherent limitations of an "individual contract," employees organized into unions which served as a counterbalance to the dominant force of management. In the United States the modern trade union movement was born in 1886 with the creation of the American Federation of Labor (AFL). As president of the AFL from its founding to his death in 1924, Samuel Gompers indelibly marked and helped shape not only that union, but the entire labor movement. Gompers based his organizing efforts for the AFL on the tenet of "bread-and-butter" unionism. Others might talk about reforming the American economic system; it was the bread-and-butter issues of wages and working conditions that would propel the AFL. George Meany, who presided over the AFL when it merged with the Congress of Industrial Organizations in 1955 and who led the AFL-CIO through nearly the next three decades, agreed with Gompers's approach. "We accept without question," he said, "the right of management to manage with reasonable consideration, of course, for the rights of workers to a fair share of the wealth produced . . . . [T]he only reasonable difference of opinion between American labor and American management is over the share the worker receives of the wealth that he helps to produce. That, of course, is the simple basic reason for the trade union instrumentality. We want to have a say as to what that fair share for the worker should be."[7]

It was not until the Great Depression of the 1930s that political support developed for legislation that would protect a union's right to organize and collectively represent the workers. The National Labor Relations Act (1935) recognized workers' rights to bargain collectively over such issues as wages, hours, and conditions of work. It guaranteed covered employees complete freedom to select the bargaining agent of their choice. And it made any attempt by employers to dominate or otherwise interfere with the formation or administration of any labor organization an "unfair labor practice." Finally, the Act created the

National Labor Relations Baord (NLRB) as an independent federal agency to oversee the proper functioning of the law's provisions, and to issue rulings and directives.

It was this law, more than any other single act, that shifted economic power in the United States away from the exclusive domain of management to be shared by blue-collar workers. With the federal government as overseer, the law created three power bases—management, unions, and government—which would now act as countervailing forces. Management would speak for the interests of shareholders, unions would protect organized workers, and the government would attempt to seek a balance between the two on behalf of the "common good."

In the aftermath of severe labor disputes that followed World War II, Congress passed the Labor-Management Relations Act (Taft-Hartley), which defined unfair labor practices as applying to unions as well as management. Another provision allowed the president to issue a "cooling-off" injunction (a temporary back-to-work order) when a labor dispute in private industry imperiled the national health and safety. The law also specifically outlawed closed shops (an agreement that permits the hiring of only union members), and allowed individual states to pass their own laws banning union shops (an agreement which stipulates that while anyone may be hired, union membership is a requirement for continued employment). Since the passage of the law in 1947, twenty states, all of them in the South and the agricultural Midwest, have enacted laws to ban union shops.

The important point here is that U.S. society, along with other societies, has supported the institutional mechanism of collective bargaining by which employees can exercise influence. The collective bargaining process may take place at the plant, company, or industry level and even at the national level in some countries.

Representatives of management and those of the union sit across from each other at a bargaining table and hammer out agreements that provide for due process by specifying a grievance procedure, that define pay systems, and that establish procedures which govern transfer, promotion (usually by seniority), apprentice programs, and termination. Some unions have negotiated provisions limiting management's latitude with regard to contracting out work, introducing labor-saving technology, and transferring work from one unit to another.

In the United States, most contract negotiations cover a particular plant or company. Thus, the United Auto Workers negotiate separately with General Motors, Ford, and Chrysler. There are some exceptions to this; steel, for instance, negotiates as an industry. In the case of a large company like General Motors, the national contract is supplemented by local agreements between individual plants and their local unions which deal with the specific working conditions at that plant.

If management and union negotiators fail to reach an agreement, the union is free to strike and management is free to lock out employees. Because sit-down strikes are illegal, management personnel may enter a plant during a strike and attempt to operate the facility. The federal government can offer the assistance of trained labor mediators, but those mediators cannot impose an agreement. Once a contract is signed, both strikes and lockouts may be prohibited by that contract. There is always the possibility of wildcat strikes (local strikes unauthorized by the national union) or illegal lockouts of employees. However, nearly all contract disputes are settled through some sort of grievance or arbitration procedure. Unions and management typically write into their contract a provision for final and binding arbitration.

The National Labor Relations Act provided the NLRB with two main functions: to oversee free and secret elections by employees to determine their bargaining agent, and to prevent and remedy unfair labor practices by employers and unions. But before the NLRB ever becomes involved, unions must undertake a process of seeking support among the employees of a company or industry. During such an organizing campaign all managers, not just those specializing in labor relations, must be aware of the legal environment that governs their actions as well as the activities of the union.

The union organizer, with the help of some in-plant supporters, asks employees to sign a card authorizing the union as their bargaining agent. The union must secure the signatures of at least 30 percent of the employees before going to the NLRB with the request for a representational election. Many union organizers, however, will not seek an election until the percentage of employees who have signed cards is significantly higher than the 30 percent required by law. Those cards are not binding on the employee. In the election itself, employees who signed union cards are free to vote either for or against union representation.

Employers may waive the necessity of a representational election. If they wish to challenge the union's petition for representation, however, they must file their own petition so stating with the NLRB. The NLRB will then determine whether or not the employees are covered by its jurisdiction (government employees are excluded from NLRB coverage, along with agricultural laborers, domestic servants, and independent contractors). The NLRB then moves in to oversee the election.

One of the most critical early decisions to be made by both sides—management and union—is the definition of the bargaining unit. The Taft-Hartley Act prohibits the inclusion of supervisors. Beyond that, the employer and the union can reach their own agreement, or turn to the NLRB to make that determination. The NLRB has broad discretion to select an employer—or industrial—unit, a craft unit, a plant unit, or a subplant unit. The NLRB also sets the date for the election, usually 15 to 30 days after verifying the signatures.

During the organizing campaigns, employers are legally free to oppose the union's efforts (and they usually do mount a vigorous anti-union campaign). Employers may not, however, engage in any tactics which the NLRB determines would prevent employees from making a reasoned choice. Thus, employers cannot use economic power to coerce employees. They cannot threaten employees with reprisals like loss of job or benefits as an inducement for not supporting the union drive. Neither employers nor unions can make last-minute (24 hours prior to election) campaign speeches.

Studies indicate that employer campaigns against union representation are rarely effective when they engage in economic fear tactics. Such tactics rarely change attitudes, but rather tend to reinforce the pro-union attitudes of employees already convinced of their employer's hostility toward the employees.[8] A more effective tactic by employers emphasizes the uncertainties of union representation, and holds out the promise—vague, lest NLRB rules be violated—of improved and enlightened working conditions. Unions, on the other hand, often try to build on already existing dissatisfaction with working conditions, and work to reassure workers that they will not lose any benefits they have already won in changing from a nonunion to a union shop.

The NLRB-supervised election gives employees a choice between one or more bargaining representatives and no bargaining representative. Once an agent receives a majority of the valid votes cast, that agent becomes the *exclusive* bargaining agent for that unit. After the NLRB certifies the winner, the employer must bargain with that agent in good faith. (What constitutes "good faith" is sometimes difficult to determine.) Either side can appeal the results of an election, however, first to an NLRB regional director, then to the board itself. If the NLRB determines that an atmosphere existed in which it is reasonable to believe that the free choice of employees was interfered with, they may set aside the results and call for a new election. On the other hand, they may certify the results and order the parties to negotiate. If either party fails to comply, the board may seek an order from the United States Circuit Court of Appeals, at which time the contesting party may present its arguments to the court. Such appeals can be used as a tactic in the organizing campaign. By utilizing all available appeal channels an employer can drag out the organizing process for well over a year in an attempt to sap union strength.

Once the bargaining units are certified, the employer and the union must bargain in good faith over wages, hours, and other conditions of employment. Any dispute over the precise meaning of "other conditions'' will be determined by the NLRB. The National Labor Relations Board recognizes five broad areas of unfair labor practices by employers:

1. Interfering with, coercing, or restraining employees in the exercise of their rights to join (or not) or assist labor organizations.
2. Assisting, dominating, or contributing financially to labor unions.
3. Discriminating against employees in order to discourage union membership or encourage it, except as provided by a valid union security clause in a collective bargaining agreement.
4. Discriminating against employees because they have filed charges or given testimony to the NLRB.
5. Refusing to bargain in good faith with the representatives of the employees.

Likewise, the NLRB recognizes eight major areas of unfair labor practices on the part of unions:

1. Coercing or restraining employees in their choice of a bargaining representative.
2. Coercing or restraining employers in their choice of a bargaining representative in collective bargaining.
3. Causing an employer to discriminate illegally against an employee.
4. Refusing to bargain in good faith with an employer.
5. Engaging in secondary boycotts.[9]
6. Charging excessive or discriminatory initiation fees.
7. Engaging in featherbedding (receiving payment for work which is not performed).
8. Engaging in organizational or recognition picketing.

Unfair labor practices charges are filed with the regional NLRB director, and the ensuing appeals process is the same as that outlined above for the appeal of election results.

Though collective bargaining agreements provide influence mechanisms only for the workers who actually belong to the unions (a minority of the work force in the United States), they serve as an indirect mechanism for all employees. The perceived threat of unionization leads some employers to adopt human resource policies they might otherwise not adopt. Some nonunionized firms have grievance procedures, open-door policies, and employment security provisions that are motivated in part out of a desire to remain nonunion.

Unions also provide employees with influence over legislation. Unions support candidates and lobby directly for legislation favoring employee well-being. Many human resource standards, including occupational, health and safety, workman's compensation, and minimum wage laws, have been legislated partly as a result of union influence.

## MANAGEMENT INITIATIVES

Management's response to unions or legislation has typcially been resistance, since these mechanisms are usually seen as reducing management's freedom. But this response is not universal, and some managers today are looking for ways to make collective bargaining more constructive for all stakeholders. We will return to the alternative management policies toward unions after we examine some trends in direct employee participation.

### *Employee Participation in Work Itself*

In the past 20 years there have been an increasing number of managerial innovations in shop (and office) floor participation. Employees in such innovative organizations are given greater responsibility and authority for making decisions about the task itself than is common in most organizations. This involvement is accomplished by reversing the historical trend toward more division of labor and giving employees or groups of employees more responsibility for a "whole task." Thus, employees gain more control and influence over work goals and methods, a sharp reversal from the historical pattern of hierarchical control. Innovations in work systems have been applied in Europe and the United States. A variation of this approach, found most often in Japan, is to bring employees together in groups which identify prodution problems and make suggestions for solving them. Such groups are called "quality circles" or self-management groups and are increasingly finding their way into U.S. companies. This trend will be explored in detail in Chapter 6 on work systems, because these innovations also affect the content and organization of work.

Employees who are given increased responsibility for their tasks do not have more influence over corporate human resource policies such as pay or employment security. There may still be conflict between managers and workers over these matters, particularly if managers are making unilateral decisions. Employers hope that participative mechanisms will create a greater coincidence of interests between employers and employees, thereby increasing trust, reducing the potential for conflict, and increasing the potential for an effective mutual influence process on matters such as pay, employment security, and other working conditions.

Some companies introduce participative methods at the shop floor in the hope that a greater congruence of interest will make it less likely that workers will organize. However, when union avoidance is the objective to the exclusion of developing a genuine process of mutual influence between management and employees, participative methods are likely to fail. Similarly, in unionized shops work participation is unlikely to be effective if those unions are not involved. Unions will see such participation as a threat to their existence, while employees are likely to suspect that these developments are a management ploy. In short, worker participation in the task itself is likely to be a more successful nonlegislated mechanism for employee voice and influence if it is accompanied by union-management collaboration when a union exists.

### *Management Provisions for Employee Voice*

Some managers have unilaterally increased employee influence by creating mechanisms by which employees may have a stronger voice in the corporation's affairs. In the last decade Caterpillar Tractor, Northern Electric Ltd., IBM, Pitney Bowes, and McCormick, among others, have installed two types of mechanisms:

1. Ones that aim at ensuring due process for employees who have grievances.
2. Ones that enable employees to suggest changes and innovations in management practices which will increase fair treatment or enhance efficiency.

Such mechanisms can be seen as a way to balance the goals of justice and efficiency in the absence of a countervailing force such as a union. In effect, management creates a check-and-balance system over its own decisions in the conviction that checks and balances are needed over their natural tendency to take primarily the shareholder perspective or to emphasize business outcomes at the expense of human outcomes. Sometimes, management may create mechanisms for employee voice without being fully committed to the concept of greater influence for employees. Recommendations and suggestions are not acted on, or no provision is made for judicial review (that is, for review of grievances by third parties not involved in the dispute or otherwise biased in their perspective). In these instances the credibility of such mechanisms quickly erodes, creating a level of distrust that may be actually higher than it would have been without the installation of these mechanisms.

Mechanisms for employee influence may require direct contact between employees and managers or they may provide indirect information through surveys, ombudsmen, or employee relations personnel. While indirect means offer anonymity and protection to employees, they limit the ability of management and employees to understand first-hand each other's perspectives. Such mutual understanding has the potential for transforming the attitudes of both parties.

The following are examples of mechanisms for employee voice:

1. "Speak up" or feedback programs. Employees may telephone a special number to raise questions or voice concerns, or may write letters to a designated company representative.
2. Special councils where management and/or employees regularly get together to talk about problems. Agendas are submitted by employees and management.
3. "Sensing groups" in which managers meet periodically with small random samples of employees to hear their concerns or suggestions and to communicate company policy and goals.
4. Open-door policy and other formal grievance systems in which employees may complain to a manager who is not their immediate supervisor. Typically, a formal and preplanned process for review of the complaint is part of such a policy.
5. Task forces of employee groups (women or minority caucuses, for example). They can be commissioned to review corporate personnel policies including pay, affirmative action, promotion policies, and the like.
6. Employee relations personnel and ombudsmen located throughout the organization, accessible to employees to deal with grievance or concerns and to expedite their solutions.
7. Attitude surveys conducted by questionnaire or by an employee task force to diagnose problems and make suggestions to management. Management commits to respond publicly.

Historically, nonlegislated mechanisms for influence have been adopted by companies in order to avoid unions. There are instances of other companies, like McCormick Spice, that have adopted mechanisms for employee influence out of the deep convictions of their founders that employees have ideas that can contribute both to improved productivity and to employee satisfaction.

### *Union Relations Policy*

What policies do management in the United States adopt toward unions attempting to organize their workers and toward unions that already represent their workers? And what are the policies and preferences about relationships that union officials bring to collective bargaining?

Many of the companies in industries that have developed largely since World War II, such as the computer industry, have remained nonunion. They have adopted human resource policies and management styles that are relatively responsive to employee needs. Their history of growth has been an asset in this respect—producing both advancement opportunities and employment security. Other companies, such as Eastman Kodak, Delta Airlines, and Gillette have also been successful in keeping their work force nonunion, largely because of responsive human resource policies and practices. By and large, the companies that are today totally or predominantly nonunion intend to stay that way.

A very different pattern exists in most of the industries that developed before or during the 1930s and 1940s, when industrial unionization activity peaked. These industries include steel, automobile, rubber, glass, and mining. Almost all companies in these industries accept that they must deal with unions in their existing facilities. However, their actual labor relations may range across a spectrum from "conflict" or "containment-aggression" to "accommodation" or even "cooperation."[10] In these heavily unionized industries, when a company established a new plant in the 1960s or 1970s, it often considered the option of trying to keep the plant nonunion, and many companies have been successful in doing so. For example, the U.S. tire companies typically deal with the Union Rubber Workers in their older plants, but they also have several relatively new tire plants that have not been unionized. The labor relations dilemma for these managements is that if their collective bargaining relationship moves toward the collaboration end of the spectrum, the union appropriately asks, "If we can trust each other and solve problems to our mutual advantage in these older plants, why do you try to keep us out of the new plants?" Or more pointedly, they ask, "If you are so dedicated to keeping us out of the new plants, how can we trust you in the old ones?" This issue became increasingly salient in the GM-UAW relationship in the 1970s and was finally resolved by an agreement between the parties in 1979 which virtually assured the UAW that any new plants opened after 1979 would be union plants. How will this issue be handled by managements of other companies who, like GM in 1979, wish to evolve more collaborative relationships?

There is a third category comprising a small number of companies that have some unionized facilities but many more facilities that are not organized, and which have in recent years adopted a policy of converting unionized facilities to nonunion status whenever possible. They can do this legally only by implementing positive HRM policies and hoping employees will see the union as unnecesary or undesirable. The law precludes active encouragement to employees to seek a decertifica-

tion election. HRM policies that have decertification as their ultimate objective have met with very limited success to date, but a growing number of companies with a moderate fraction of their work force already unionized are considering this policy. Will this policy trend continue and become a major factor in the United States? Will it be successful? What revisions in their HRM policies will these managments regard as most instrumental to this labor relations objective?

A fourth, considerably looser grouping of companies fits into no convenient national pattern. Industries like supermarkets, building construction, maritime, and health care often involve multiple unions and follow regional or even local patterns. Public employment (except for federal employment) is sensitive to differing state and local laws. Employers in these industries, no less than in those industries with stronger national or industry-wide patterns, must make decisions on the nature and type of relationship they wish to see evolve from collective bargaining.

In general terms, it can be said that we are witnessing two opposing trends on the part of companies that currently are partly or predominantly unionized. On the one hand, a growing number of managements are attempting to structure a closer partnership with their unions—this involves accepting the legitimacy of the union role in a larger set of enterprise issues. On the other hand, a smaller number of companies are trying to decertify the unions they have whenever possible. Both sets of policy objectives are rationalized by their adherents in terms of increasing the competitiveness of the company through an increase in operational flexibility and a decrease in disruptive conflict.

That leaves a residual group of unionized companies—mostly those whose collective bargaining relationship can be characterized as containment-aggression or accommodation and who have no present plans to change their relationship pattern. Will these companies join one of the trends? How will they decide which?

How do the unions view efforts by management either to increase employee participation or to initiate more cooperative union relations?

In the United States, some union leaders are seeking influence over less tangible issues like the design of new technology, the design of work itself, relations between workers and their supervisors, and more broadly defined conditions of work. The president of the Communication Workers of America (CWA), Glenn Watts, believes that the time has come for unions to insist upon influence over the quality of working life for their members. "For many years there have been problems that we have not been able to take care of," Watts said. "Our members were expressing concern about things that went well beyond wages and benefits." The Teamsters are also beginning to reject the notion that management's participation and influence over non-bread-and-butter issues is inherently manipulative to the detriment of the interests of the workers. "The view that participative management is manipulative is old thinking," explained an officer of the Teamsters' Honeywell local in Minneapolis.

Not all union leaders accept the notion of increased influence in nontraditional areas. The independent United Electrical Workers (UE), for instance, say they "reject participation in any of these employer-generated groups which bypass our regular union structure with the goal of—by use of advanced psychological techniques—brainwashing workers into making suggestions that will result in speed-up, combination of jobs, downgrading and layoffs."

The UE's views of employee participation and union-management cooperation on noneconomic issues reflect the fears of some union leaders that cooperation with management will dilute the militancy of union leaders and rob members of a strong voice speaking for their own interests. Others may fear that employee participation will lessen the need felt by employees for a union and thus erode the union's base.

Traditionally, collective bargaining has been viewed as essentially adversarial in nature and distributive in intent. That is to say, two parties with inherently conflicting interests about how the economic pie should be divided—the key content matter of collective bargaining—engage in a show of power to determine the distribution of that pie. Necessarily, then, the more one side wins, the more the other loses. But, as the statements of union leaders cited above indicate, there are signs of interest in the United States on the part of some union leades as well as management in finding an alternative to such exclusively adversarial relationships and to engage in mutually beneficial problem solving. This urge, as we have already indicated, is especially apparent among companies facing a competitive crisis where joint problem solving may become a matter of survival. In such cases, joint union-management problem solving is acknowledged as a general goal by both union and management, but is engaged in separately from the collective bargaining process. This separation can reassure a union that its traditional role is not being threatened, while allowing them to participate in improvements in work life. Joint agreements between General Motors and the United Auto Workers (UAW), Ford and the UAW, and the Basic Steel Conference and the United Steelworkers of America all carefully separate quality of work life, employee involvement and labor-management participation activities—both in structure and content—from collective bargaining. Thus, collective bargaining deals with matters still considered to be distributive (wages, benefits, etc.), while joint committees composed of union officers and management representatives concern themselves with such matters as improving attitudes, sharing information about the competitive environment and the welfare and concerns of employees, redesigning the work environment, and—by implication at least—improving productivity and saving jobs.

General Motors structurally reflected this division between the cooperative quality of work life (QWL) approach and the more traditionally adversarial labor relations approach by placing QWL under its personnel function while keeping collective bargaining as part of labor relations. But an alternative pattern has already emerged within the auto industry. The cooperative initiatives with the union that Ford began in 1980, labeled "employee involvement," have been taken within the labor relations department itself. And the special collective bargaining in 1982 that led to a new contract first at Ford, then at General Motors, reflected an attempt to apply cooperative problem solving to the usually distributive bargaining process.

The movement from adversarial to cooperative relationship, which has affected a small minority of companies in this country, has gone further and affected more industries in Japan. During the post-World War II period, bad economic conditions, labor-management strife, and a desire to isolate radical factions within the trade union movement led to successful efforts by both moderate union leaders and management to cooperate. In exchange for employment security, many of these moderate labor leaders were willing to make concessions to management on such matters as flexible assignment of workers, worker involvement in problem solving, and other productivity-enhancing practices. Through extensive consultation on labor-management committees, many Japanese unions have exercised considerable influence on what has traditionally been viewed as prerogatives of management: quarterly production schedules, work-force levels for given jobs, and worker assignments, for example.[11] Different forms of worker and union influence that have emerged in Europe will be discussed below.

The high level of mistrust between managers and union officials in many American plants is one reason why managers prefer to have nonunion operations: it liberates the attention of supervisors for matters other than conflicts with the union. Historically, American unions have been too good at the adversarial role. When they meet management head-to-head in our industrial workplaces, the unions often prevail. As a result, management has tried to avoid the contest by being nonunion. The severe recession of the early 1980s, when many unions agreed to concessions, has resulted in a significant break with the general trend of unions winning higher wages through tests of strength with management. It is too early to know whether this experience will result in less adversarial relations or even cooperative union-management relations in the future. Much probably depends on management's posture toward unions whose bargaining power has diminished and on the capacity of union leaders to be creative in defining and selling to their members a new role for unions in a context of cooperative union-management relations. If management and unions seize the occasion to forge a new relationship, union-management cooperation of the type seen in Japan may well become the model. If union leaders continue to see an adversarial relationship over economic issues as the only role or if management uses its increased strength to weaken unions, then adversarial union-management relations will continue and management will continue to try to operate on a nonunion basis.

The desire to be nonunion is an aspect of American industrial relations that European (except British) and Japanese managers often fail to understand. American managers seem to them to be obsessed with being nonunion, when their own experience in Europe and Japan suggests that union relations can often be managed successfully just like other aspects of business. But European and Japanese managers by and large do not confront the presence of strong and militant unions on the shop floor as American managers do. Instead, the pressure of militant European and Japanese unions is felt primarily in the outside political environment, or at the industry-wide level in collective bargaining. The combination of militant trade unionism with a strong base is apparently unique to Great Britain and the United States.

The important point is that historically the emergence of unions and collective bargaining has, not surprisingly, resulted in an adversarial relationship and the use of power (strikes, walkouts, etc.) as the primary means of exercising influence. As the costs of this relationship to both parties begin to outweigh the gains, efforts begin toward accommodation and even cooperation, particularly on noneconomic issues that are more easily subject to problem solving. It is an open question as to how far this trend will go. Undoubtedly that will be determined by its utility to management, workers, unions, and society as a whole. A number of questions will be asked continually as this general trend continues:

1. Does cooperation enhance the influence of all parties? At what point, if any, does it erode the power of unions or management by coopting their perspectives to the point where their stakeholders' interests are no longer represented?
2. On what issues (pay, working conditions, supervision, business strategy, etc.) is cooperation and problem solving possible, even necessary? On what matters must union-management relationships continue to adhere to traditional negotiation and bargaining where economic power is the final arbiter?
3. If a mix of labor relations strategies (cooperation and adversarial) is necessary, how can such an inherently unstable mix be

managed? What structures and processes are necessary, and what skills do union leaders and managers need to possess to sustain a mixed relationship?

4. At what level in the hierarchy of the labor relations system—plant, corporation, industry, or national—should or can various issues be dealt with (for example, pay, economic security, supervision, and technology) and how will these choices affect the mutual influence process between unions and management?

### *Considerations in Developing an Employee Influence Policy*

There is a striking contrast between the employee influence practices of the 1800s and the practices that have emerged as a result of collective action by employees, government legislation, and management response and initiatives. While hierarchical authority representing shareholder and management interests continues to be an important source of social control in organizations, the limitations of hierarchy have forced a search for other mechanisms of social control, ones that recognize the legitimacy of other stakeholders. There is no reason to believe that the trend toward corporate governance which relies on mutual influence processes rather than hierarchical authority is likely to change. The success of Japanese companies and some companies in the United States and Europe in implementing a process of mutual influence adds weight to the hope that such shared influence may well help bring various stakeholders together in a mutual understanding of the realities facing each other and the enterprises as a whole.

Experience tells us, however, that mutual influence mechanisms do not always lead to desired outcomes. Highly participative mechanisms exact their own price from management and employees both. Managers may feel that their traditional prerogatives are being threatened, their authority over subordinates diluted. They may feel torn between the organization's long-range and often vaguely stated goals of improving productivity through participation on the one hand, and the short-term, more clearly defined and understood financial goals set by the organization on the other. Managing in an environment where employees are frequently consulted and involved can be tremendously costly in terms of time. Managers will find more and more of their work days being spent in committees or talking with union leaders, individual employees, or groups of employees. The skills demanded of a manager in such an environment differ considerably from those expected in a highly hierarchical setting. Supervisors become facilitators and decisions they previously made unilaterally become consensual. This lack of control and the high level of uncertainty and ambiguity make some managers feel uncomfortable. Others may need a significant period of time to adjust to the new demands being made upon them and to learn the new skills required. Still others may not be able to adjust at all. Companies may therefore face the dilemma of what to do with a manager whose economic performance in the past has been excellent but whose ability to function in a more participative environment is limited and whose limitations are blocking progress.

The impact of alienation, frustration, and boredom on employee well-being is relatively well-known. But systems that involve employees in decisions to which they have not previously been a party extract their own costs. Employees are required to shed their dependent role and become more interdependent. They must attempt to understand other stakeholder perspectives, acquire new knowledge about the business, and take responsibility for the enterprise as a whole. All of this requires employees to adjust and develop in ways that have the potential for adding stress, the kind of stress—uncertainty, ambiguity, complexity, and competing demands of company and family, for instance—more traditionally associated with management-level personnel.

Power and politics, too, may become a major barrier to greater mutuality in the stakeholder influence process. Because they want to retain their position of power, formal or informal leaders of stakeholder groups (managers, union leaders, etc.) may urge members of their group to hang on to older perspectives and block the development of new perspectives. Sometimes, aspiring leaders may "whip up" support for themselves by encouraging an adversarial relationship with other stakeholder groups. Changes in relationships and in the development of a mutual influence process between stakeholder groups may be blocked until circumstances reduce the appeals of such leaders or they have left the scene. Recognizing the political realities of various stakeholder groups and managing those realities become additional difficulties in implementing a process of mutual influence.

These potential barriers, and others, make any policy of increasing employee influence difficult to implement. Failure along the way, caused by the inability of stakeholder groups or their representatives to develop attitudes and competencies consistent with an emerging process of mutual influence, can cause major regression, higher distrust, and the reemergence of conflict. Indeed, as the organization depends more and more on an emergent culture which supports a mutual influence process and less on hierarchical control, managers fear that failures invite anarchy.

It is clear that managers' decisions about what employee influence policies to pursue must rest on balancing the opportunities of more participation by employees against the difficulties and risks of implementation. Ultimately these risks can only be reduced if the manager is persistent over time and willing to nurture a gradual evolution rather than a rapid revolution. That persistence will depend on the manager's own values and convictions.

If major change in an employee influence policy is dependent at least in part on management's values and convictions, a real dilemma is created, one that presents a major barrier to increasing employee influence. The willingness of managers to initiate and persist in such change efforts rests upon their assumptions about work-force competence and responsibility. If individual members of the work force are assumed by managers to be uninterested or incapable of making useful, intelligent, and informed decisions about the well-being of the organizations that employs them, then these managers are unlikely to want to initiate efforts to increase employee influence. Unfortunately, managers' assumptions about the capacity of employees to participate in decisions are likely to be pessimistic because their assumptions are shaped, in part at least, by their experiences in organizations that do not afford employees opportunities to participate and influence. Thus, a self-fulfilling prophecy develops in which employees are not offered an opportunity to influence because of pessimistic management assumptions, and those assumptions are formed by past practices which have left employees dependent and unskilled in the participative process.

This dilemma is one of the causes of the slow and uneven pace of change in employee influence. Organizations that have begun to transform their employee influence policies have typically started the process by allowing managers so inclined to experiment in outlying plants, branches, or divisions. By allowing them freedom to shape a new culture, models are created in the organization which can be used to educate other managers. That educational process can occur as less progressive managers visit the leading-edge organizational units or are transferred to them to learn by working in those units. In this way, change can be diffused to other parts of the organization as managers whose assumptions have been transformed by their experiences in model units are sent elsewhere in the organization. Because changes in employee influence involve a change in culture, experimenting in a few organizational units and diffusing change through socializing and transferring managers has been a part of most major change efforts. Of course if the changes start at the bottom or middle of the organization, there are potential conflicts between the emergent pattern of employee influence at these lower levels and more traditional values concerning employee influences that may remain among many top managers and staff groups. These conflicts in values can slow progress and cause regression.

Most organizations that are engaged in transforming patterns of employee influence create a network of change agents, whose full-time responsibility is to support the changes through consulting, teaching, counseling, and coaching their managers. These change agents may be personnel specialists, organization development consultants from either inside or outside the firms, or line managers who have been temporarily assigned to support the change. Ford Motor, for example, has assigned 150 individuals as full-time employee involvement coordinators. The theory underlying this approach is that individuals so assigned, properly trained and properly supported by higher level managers, can sustain a commitment to new values and assumptions more easily than managers who are embedded in day-to-day operations. By consulting with target organizations, they encourage managers to change because they represent living symbols that the organization is changing, and that new assumptions, values, and skills are called for.

Finally, transformation in employee influence policies has typically involved extensive educational programs for managers, supervisors, and employees. This investment in education has both real value in transmitting skills and symbolic value in serving notice that a change process is underway.

Implementing a change in employee influence typically involves several of these approaches, all of them aimed at creating new experiences for managers and employees and thereby changing assumptions and values.

## SUMMARY

Employees and employers will have different views on how to split the economic pie, on how much involvement employees should have, and about management prerogatives and employee rights. Originally employers had almost total authority over the disposition of these questions. But the trend in democratic societies has been toward more employee influence through collective bargaining, legislated mechanisms for worker participation, and management's initiatives to allow more employee participation. This trend has come about as employees, voters in democratic societies, exert political and social pressures to create more mechanisms of influence. Whatever the means, general managers should consciously decide what their employee influence policy is, and how much influence employees should be given.

Historically, aggrieved employees have organized themselves into unions to develop a collective voice about pay and working conditions. In the United States, the National Labor Relations Act and the National Labor Relations Board have empowered the government to maintain a balance of power between unions and management, making possible a process of mutual influence through collective bargaining. Management's approach to union relations can materially influence whether those relations are collaborative or adversarial, thus affecting employee influence. In many societies legislation specifies how much and what kind of influence employees should be given. In Europe, laws direct codetermination through employee and union representation on supervisory boards (boards of directors in Germany) and workers councils. In the United States, equal employment legislation gives employees a voice through regulatory agencies that enforce the law and through the threat of court action. The U.S. government has also enacted legislation which helps employees buy out their company's stock under certain circumstances, making it possible for them to become owners and elect board members. Though economic ownership would seem to make it possible for employees to have a lot of influence, in reality the extent of their influence is determined by management's and workers' skills in participation.

Unions and legislation have created pressures which have resulted in management initiatives to give employees more influence through involvement in decision making on the shop floor, through various task forces and committees, and through due process mechanisms. In some cases managers have initiated efforts to give employees influence because of their belief that this is the best way to maintain a competitive and adaptive corporation. General managers in these companies have developed a conscious policy to provide employees with more influence through participation and/or cooperation with unions.

Important questions remain about the future of employee influence in business organizations and about union-management cooperation. Does cooperation enhance the influence of all parties or can one party be coopted? Can cooperation in some areas coexist with competitive bargaining in others? Moreover, there are many problems in maintaining a process of mutual influence between employees and employers. Skills and competence of employees, union leaders, and managers are crucial to its success. The process is vulnerable to self-serving actions by leaders who can reduce trust and re-ignite suspicion and hostility. For this reason, most organizations engaged in the process of increasing employee participation and influence employ several approaches in concert to move change along. They develop model organizations, they create a network of internal and external consultants to support the change, and they invest in education and training.

## NOTES

1. George Lodge, *The New American Ideology* (New York: Knopf, 1975), pp. 9–11.

2. Stephen Marsland and Michael Beer, "Note on Japanese Management and Employment Systems," in Michael Beer and Bert Spector (eds.), *Readings in Human Resource Management* (New York: Free Press, 1985).
3. Cris Argyris, *Personality and Organization* (New York: Harper, 1957).
4. *New York Times*, 9 December 1983, p. 1.
5. *Buy Out: Hyatt-Clark Industries, Inc.*, Harvard Business School Case Services No. 9-383-122 (1983).
6. Joseph R. Blasi, Perry Wehrling, and William Foote Whyte, "The Politics of Worker Ownership in the United States," in Frank Heller et al. (eds.), *The International Yearbook of Organizational Democracy for the Study of Participation, Cooperation, and Power* (Sussex, England: John Wiley and Sons, 1981); and William Foote Whyte, *In Support of Voluntary Job Preservation and Community Stabilization Act* (Ithaca, N.Y.: Cornell University Press, 1978).
7. Quoted in D. Quinn Mills, *Labor-Management Relations*, 2d ed. (New York: McGraw-Hill, 1982), p. 195.
8. Writes Jeanne M. Brett, "Fear appeals are notoriously ineffective in changing firmly held attitudes and opinions. Employees who are basically fearful of retaliatory moves against them by an employer are not likely to have signed authorization cards in the first place. And in all probability, those who do sign authorization cards have already come to terms with their realization of the employer's hostility toward the union and his ability, allbeit illegal, to use economic power against them. . . . In fact, pro-union employees may view threatening employer behavior simply as confirmation of their poor opinion of him and as support for their previous decision that they need a union to deal with him." Brett, "Why Employees Want Unions," *Organizational Dynamics* (Spring 1980), pp. 53–54.
9. If, in furtherance of its actions against one company, a union were to take actions against a second company—say a customer or supplier of the first—in order to bring increased pressure against the first company, they would be engaging in a secondary boycott.
10. Benjamin M. Selekman, in fact, suggested eight varieties of bargaining relationships: containment-aggression, conflict, power, deal, collusion, accommodation, cooperation, and ideological. Selekman, "Variety of Labor Relations," *Harvard Business Review* (March 1949), pp. 177–185.
11. Marsland and Beer, "Note on Japanese Management and Employment Systems."

CASE 2

# FIRST NATIONAL BANK OF LAKE CITY (A)

*Thomas Kennedy*

On a Monday afternoon Wynn Evans, president of the First National Bank of Lake City, received a formal notice from the National Labor Relations Board (NLRB) that an election would be held at the bank's offices in 30 days to determine if the employees wished to be represented by the International Metalworkers Union (IMU). Evans arranged for a meeting to be held the following afternoon with the bank's labor attorney, Francis Grant, and a group of its executives including Paul Blanton, vice president of personnel. Evans indicated that the action taken so far by the bank and the union would be reviewed at the meeting, and that he would welcome recommendations concerning what further action management should take, if any, during the 30 days remaining before the election.

## COMPANY BACKGROUND

Located in an industrial state, Lake City had a population of approximately 70,000 which had remained relatively stable during the past 10 years. The economy of the community was completely dependent upon one large plant—an automotive parts plant—which was owned by one of the Big Three of the auto industry. When auto production was high the Lake City economy was high, and vice versa.

During the mid-1930s, Lake City had experienced some turbulent labor strife as representatives from the national headquarters of the International Metalworkers Union (IMU) tried to organize the workers in the local plant. In the late 1930s, however, the automobile company signed a national agreement with the IMU which included the Lake City plant. Since 1956 the agreement included a union-shop clause requiring all workers at the plant to be members of the union. The IMU had also been successful in organizing a number of machine shops and other types of small plants in the area. The IMU was very active in local politics; Lake City was sometimes described as a union town.

---

Most of the employees of the bank had relatives who worked at the auto plant and were members of the IMU. In fact, some of the bank's employees were closely related to the local IMU leaders. The IMU had made several unsuccessful attempts to organize the white-collar workers at the auto plant. Four years ago it had been successful in organizing the maintenance workers at one of the smaller banks. Unionization at that bank had not spread to the tellers or the other white-collar employees, however, and none of the employees in the other banks of the community were organized.

One group of professional employees in the community was represented by a union—the school teachers. Most of the grade school and high school teachers in Lake City had been members of the National Education Association (NEA) for many years. Until the 1960s, however, the NEA had been a purely professional society opposed to collective bargaining. In the late 1960s the NEA, pressed by the success of a rival organization—the American Federation of Teachers, affiliated with the AFL-CIO and a negotiator of sizable wage increases for teachers in some of the major cities—decided to support collective bargaining by its local groups. The business community of Lake City was surprised and disturbed when some of the local teachers, who were members of NEA, began to organize for bargaining purposes under the protection of the State Public Employees Relations Act. They were even more surprised when in an election the teachers voted to have NEA serve as their bargaining agent.

Following the election, the school board and representatives of NEA entered into collective bargaining. While it was six months before an agreement was reached on the first labor contract, it was generally agreed that the teachers had secured sizable economic gains as a result of unionization and bargaining.

The First National was the oldest and largest commercial bank in the Lake City community. It had assets of approximately $300 million—twice the size of the next largest of the other six commercial banks in the area. Founded in 1892, First National remained a single-unit bank until about 10 years ago when it began an expansion program by merging and acquiring a number of smaller banks in nearby communities. As a result, it had 16 offices by now, including two which had been opened recently in newly developed suburban shopping areas.

### *Working at the First*

Although the First National was the largest financial institution in the area, it was not the salary pacesetter in the community or even in the banking sector. First National salaries were generally 10 to 20 percent below those for comparable jobs at the auto plant, and one or two of the smaller banks had somewhat higher salary scales than the First. The First seldom lost employees to other banks, although recently there had been some movement of younger employees to the auto plant. This movement was especially noticeable among men and women whom the First had trained in data processing.

Everyone at First National, except the maintenance employees, was on salary. The bank had a formal salary evaluation program with ten classifications, each with a maximum and a minimum rate. The maximum of the range varied from 13 percent above the minimum for the lowest level classification to 30 percent above for the highest level classification. Within these ranges, increases were granted each year entirely on merit. All increases, whether as a result of a change of job or merit evaluation, became effective January first of each year. If an employee was promoted during the year, he or she received the new job title immediately, but a salary change frequently was not made until January first. Management thought that its somewhat lower salary scale was counterbalanced by its excellent working conditions, its job security, and its liberal profit-sharing plan.

The First National was looked upon by the employees as a prestigious place to work. The offices were clean and pleasant and the atmosphere was congenial and unhurried. Most of the employees were proud to say that they worked at the bank. The established work week was 38 hours during a five-day period; however, most employees averaged only 35 hours. For work between 38 and 40 hours, employees received additional compensation at straight-time rates; beyond 40 hours per week, a rate of time-and-a-half was paid.

The First was also viewed as a place where employees without college education, especially men, could rise to important positions. Practically all of the bank's employees, including all but two of its top officers, had ended their formal education upon graduation from the local high schools. After entering the First, many of them attended American Institute of Banking (AIB) courses at night, which the bank encouraged and financed. A job at the First represented an avenue for dependable young people without college educations to become important leaders in the community.

Jobs at the First were also valued because of their security. Employees were never laid off and discharge for poor work or offensive conduct was extremely rare. Once hired, persons could count on a regular paycheck for all their work life. In the past this job security had been very important in a community where the major industry was known for heavy overtime one year and heavy layoffs the next. In recent years, however, the security of working at the bank, compared to working at the auto plant, had largely disappeared as the union (in the

1950s and early 1960s) negotiated supplementary unemployment benefits (SUB). In 1967 it topped off its drive for income security by negotiating a Guaranteed Annual Income (GAI) which replaced the SUB. Under the GAI, employees at the auto plant with seven years of service were guaranteed 95 percent of their take-home pay for a period of 52 weeks. (Employees with less then seven years of service received the 95 percent guarantee, but for a lesser number of weeks.) Moreover, employees who were discharged at the auto plant could usually count on strong support from the union, including carrying the issue to the last step of the grievance machinery, which was arbitration by a neutral third party. One of the union leaders was quoted as saying: "Discharge is the capital punishment of labor relations, so we almost always walk the last mile with them."

### *Benefit Plans*

The bank's management thought that its profit-sharing plan was highly valued and appreciated, especially by its older employees. All employees became eligible for profit sharing after two years of employment, and percentage-of-salary participation was equal for everyone including officers. Under the plan, the bank contributed an amount each year that was equal to 7½ percent of its net operating income after customary reserves and dividends. The amount was then divided by the combined yearly salaries of the plan participants and that percentage was applied to each employee's base annual salary to determine his or her amount. During the 20 years that the plan had been in effect, it had never paid less than 10 percent of salaries and in recent years it had approached the 15 percent limit set on such plans by the Internal Revenue Service.

The payments from the profit-sharing plan were not immediately available to a participant; instead, they were held in a trust fund that earned income until the employee left the bank as a result of either quitting or retiring at age 65. At retirement the employee received 100 percent of the balance in his or her account. Employees who left the bank before 65 received less than the full amount depending upon the number of years they had been in the plan. It became 50 percent vested after 5 years and then increased 10 percent each year, becoming fully vested at the end of 10 years. The plan allowed employees to withdraw any amount in their balance which exceeded two and one-half times their annual salary. Likewise, if an employee died, the entire amount in the account was paid to the estate. The First was the only bank in the Lake City area that had a profit-sharing plan in effect. The IMU had tried to negotiate a profit-sharing plan with the auto company, but had not been successful. None of the other smaller industrial and commercial firms in the area had profit-sharing plans.

In addition to the profit-sharing plan, the bank also had a death benefit plan, a pension plan, and a salary continuation plan. The death benefit plan was intended to supplement the amount an employee's family or estate would receive at his or her death from the profit-sharing plan. It paid $3,000 to employees whose salary was $5,000 or less and dropped down in $500 units for each $200 increase in salary so that it paid nothing for salaries over $6,200.

The First's pension plan required an employee to have 15 years of service to be eligible for benefits. Retirement was mandatory at age 65, while early retirement was possible at age 55. In the case of early retirement, however, benefit payments were decreased on an actuarial basis unless the employee opted to have payments begin at age 65. The plan also provided for payment at any age after 15 years of service in case of total and permanent disability. Determining one's pension benefit under the plan was a complicated matter for it involved three separate calculations. Most of the employees had difficulty understanding it, although the bank had prepared and published an explanatory booklet.

Benefits under the pension plan were not as liberal as those provided under the union contract at the auto plant, especially for the lower-paid employees and for those who wished to retire early. However, they were as good or better than those paid by any of the other banks in the area. In fact, two of the other banks had no pension plans. Management thought that the pension plan and the profit-sharing plan had to be considered as a package; and that when this was done, the retirement benefits compared well, even with those of the auto company.

The First's salary continuance program, which became effective for employees immediately following the 90-day probationary period, provided one full week of sick pay during the first year and six full weeks of sick pay per calendar year thereafter. The six weeks were not cumulative. The weekly paycheck was decreased for any day of absence other than those covered by the salary continuance program.

The First's vacation plan provided two weeks of paid vacation after 1 year of service, and three weeks after 15 years of service. It was identical with the vacation plans of the other banks in the area, but not as good as the vacation plan at the auto plant. The First also paid for six holidays, which was the same as at the other banks in the area, but only about half the number given at the auto plant.

The First also permitted employees to borrow at reduced interest rates on mortgages, car loans, and personal loans. On mortgage loans, for example, the rate was reduced by .25 percent, thus enabling an employee to save a considerable amount over the property's purchase period.

The bank also enrolled all of its employees in the AIB, which conducted night courses in Lake City in bank accounting and numerous other subjects. The employees of the First could attend without cost, and approximately 25 percent of the employees took one or more courses each year.

Conspicuous by its absence in the bank's benefit package was an employer-paid hospital and medical care program. Such a program had been discussed by the management with Blue Cross–Blue Shield and several insurance companies and on several occasions proposals had been presented to the board. The proposals had been turned down each time, however, because of the vigorous opposition of Fred Savage. Savage, who was in his late seventies and controlled the largest block of stock in the bank, felt strongly that the good of the country would be served best if each person paid his or her own medical and hospital bills. He was able to bring enough pressure to bear on the president and the other members of the board to prevent adoption of any employer-paid hospital and medical plan.

The First did work out a group plan with Blue Cross–Blue Shield to be paid for entirely by the employees. Individual rates varied from $25 to $48 per month depending on the type of coverage. The bank agreed to deduct the amounts from paychecks, if employees so desired. The great majority of the employees participated in the group coverage; many of those who did not were covered elsewhere because their husbands or wives worked in other firms providing free family coverage.

The First was the only bank in the area that did not have a hospital-medical plan entirely or partially paid by the employer. At the auto plant, the union had negotiated a liberal hospital-medical plan, the cost of which was borne entirely by the company. Many of the other industrial and retail firms in the area also had plans where the employer paid all or part of the costs.

## THE ORGANIZING CAMPAIGN

The first indication of union activity at the bank occurred one Sunday morning. John Mason, a guard at the main office, discovered that IMU membership cards had been distributed to the various teller stations on the first floor, the desks in the bookkeeping department on the second floor, at the switchboard, and in the ladies' lounge. Mason reported the matter to his superior who in turn reported it to Paul Blanton, vice president of personnel. Blanton discussed the matter with the bank's attorney, Francis Grant, and upon his advice it was decided to collect and hold the cards.

On Monday morning Wynn S. Evans, president of the bank, called Blanton to his office. Evans, who was scheduled to retire in less than a year, had been president for 15 years. He had spent his entire working career with the First. Starting out as a clerk, immediately after graduation from Lake City High School, he had worked his way up through the ranks to his present position. He had good reason to be proud of the progress that had been made at the bank during his presidency. From a single office, it had expanded to the point where it now had 16 branch offices. Total assets and profits had increased far more rapidly than at any other bank in the area.

Blanton showed the cards to Evans and told him where they had been found. Blanton said that he and the other members of management with whom he had talked had no idea who might have been responsible for distributing them. Evans did not appear to be disturbed. Blanton was surprised when Evans said, "Paul, I don't think we should get too excited about this. After all, in a place like Lake City, I suppose it's inevitable that we will eventually have to deal with a union. Let's keep it all low key."

### *Union Letters Sent to Employees*

Management never was able to determine who was responsible for the distribution of the cards and the only action taken was to tighten security. Four months passed without any outward indication of further union activity, and management came to feel that the card distribution incident could be dismissed as the act of a single disgruntled employee. Supervisors who were in close touch with the employees who worked for them reported no evidence of any organizing activity. Then, one Monday morning a number of employees reported to their supervisors that they had received a letter from the IMU addressed to their homes (see Exhibit 2-1). It was soon learned that the letter had been sent to all of the employees. Evidently one of the employees had provided the union with a runoff of the names and addresses from the computer.

One of the employees gave Blanton a copy of the letter which he took to the president's office. Evans read it and discussed it by phone with Attorney Grant. Evans then scheduled a 1:00 P.M. meeting of the top management people and Attorney Grant to discuss the matter. At the meeting Grant explained that the union would have to get 30 percent of the employees to sign membership cards before the NLRB would hold an election. He said, however, that it was his experience that the IMU would not ask for an election unless it had at least 60 percent or 70 percent of the employees signed up. Among those present at the meeting, surprise was expressed that the union felt it had enough interest among the employees to warrant sending out the letter. On the other hand, there was a belief that only a very small number of the employees were involved and that the union had no chance of getting 30 percent to sign cards. For the time being, it was agreed that management would take no special action except to gather as much information as possible. Blanton was appointed by the president to serve as clearing house for any facts or rumors that they heard.

Approximately one month after the union's first letter, it addressed a second letter to the employees which read in part as follows:

> Your response to our first letter was very encouraging. As a result an informative meeting will be held next Thursday evening at the Lake City Hotel at 8:00 P.M. We will tell you what we believe we can gain through collective bargaining and will answer any questions you may have.

The meeting was held as scheduled, and management learned that between 75 and 100 of the bank's 350 employees attended. The group was made up largely of employees from bookkeeping, personal loan, and main office tellers, although some attended from other departments and from some of the branch offices. It was reported that not all those who attended appeared to be in sympathy with unionization.

Although salaries, individual grievances, and other matters were talked about at the meeting, the discussion centered on two major topics: (1) the pension and profit-sharing plans and (2) the lack of an employer-paid hospital-medical plan. Several of the older employees spoke favorably about the pension and profit-sharing plans and indicated that they were fearful that the First might decrease the pension benefits and eliminate profit sharing if it had to bargain with the union. The union representatives assured the employees that the union would never agree to changes in the pension and profit-sharing plans which would be detrimental to employees. Instead, they said that the union would insist that the employees receive even better pensions and a larger share of the profits—too much of which, they declared, now went to the owners and the management.

The issue that seemed to be of most concern to the majority of the employees at the meeting was the lack of an employer-paid hospitalization and medical plan. The union leaders played up this issue. They said they found it hard to believe that in this day and age a major bank like the First could be so little interested in its employees' welfare as to refuse to cover them with hospital-medical insurance. They pointed out that several of the smaller banks in the community did provide their employees with such insurance. They showed the employees a copy of the employer-paid plan which the union had negotiated for the employees at the auto plant. They also referred to a number of other contracts which the union had negotiated with other companies in the Lake City area, all of which contained employer-paid hospital-medical plans. They said they knew of no contract that the IMU had negotiated in recent years in which it had not secured an employer-paid plan. The union also assured the employees that if they chose the IMU as their bargaining agent, the union would insist that the First foot the entire bill for a good hospital-medical insurance plan. One of the union representatives stated that the value of this benefit alone would more than make up the cost of the union dues.

*The Bank's Response*

As the reports of the union meeting filtered in to Blanton, he became convinced that the bank was facing a serious unionization threat. Blanton had been appointed as vice president of personnel about 10 months earlier. Prior to that time, the personnel function had been handled by an officer of the bank who had other major functions; Blanton had no prior training or experience in personnel work. Among the bank officers he was relatively young both in age and service, having been hired only five years earlier. Prior to coming with the First, he had worked with one of the big Chicago banks. At the First, he had served as vice president of mortgages and manager of a branch before becoming vice president of personnel.

Blanton proposed to Evans and the other officers that the bank should engage in an active compaign to convince employees not to join the union. Attorney Grant urged an aggressive campaign including a series of letters by President Evans and a meeting of all the employees. It was decided that Blanton should work out a series of questions and answers with the attorney, and that Blanton should read these to the employees whom he would meet in small groups and then invite discussion (see Exhibit 2–2). Attorney Grant cautioned Blanton to be careful not to promise the employees anything as a result of not becoming unionized or to threaten them with anything if they did. ''If you promise them anything or threaten them with anything, the NLRB could find us guilty of an unfair labor practice and might even order us to bargain with them on the basis of their signed cards without ordering an election—assuming they have a majority of the employees signed up,'' Grant warned.

Blanton discovered that after he had read the questions and answers, the employees were primarily interested in discussing the bank's wage and benefit policies, of which (to his surprise) most of them had very little knowledge and appreciation. (The bank had never developed an employees' handbook or a pamphlet explaining the various wage and benefit policies.) The newer employees seemed to be better informed than many of the older employees because at the employment interview, the policies and plans were explained. Blanton believed that the meetings were helpful, but came away from some of them with a conviction that there was a sizable group that really wanted the union.

In several areas Blanton felt that he got a very cool reception. One of these was the data processing center. The center had been set up in the First's main office building six years earlier. In addition to the bank's work, it did some outside work for customers. Although a few of the bank's former employees had moved into jobs in the data center, the great majority of the 30 workers there were new employees. It was the only area in the bank that was on shift work. The 12 keypunch operators were on two fixed shifts and the computer operators were on three rotating shifts. Blanton had the impression that the employees here looked upon themselves as a group apart with very little loyalty to the bank. "Their loyalty," he said, "is first to the equipment, then to the system, and only after that to the bank. They are a lot closer to the data processing people at the auto company and other companies and banks in the area than they are to employees in the other departments here at the First." During the six years of its operation, there had been a considerably higher turnover of employees in this division than elsewhere in the bank, except in the consumer loans area. Blanton felt that the bank, to a considerable extent, served as a training school for employees in data processing who, once trained, moved to the auto company or in some cases even to out-of-town companies and banks.

Blanton divided the data processing employees into four meeting groups. At each of these meetings the question of wage rates for similar jobs at the auto company was raised by the employees. They seemed to be very well informed. Blanton admitted that the First's rates were not as high as those paid by the auto company, but he said that in some cases this was due to the fact that there was a difference in the skill requirements of the jobs. Moreover, he said that if they took into account the whole pay package, including the profit-sharing plan, he believed the pay was as good or better at the bank. However, Blanton left the meetings with the feeling that the employees were unconvinced. He thought that all of the data processing employees were interested in the union and that many of them were strongly interested.

Another area where the reception was quite cool was the consumer loans department in the main office. This division of the bank had been unusually successful compared with similar divisions in the other banks in the community, primarily because of the ability and drive of Frank Lockard, who had become vice president of consumer loans 10 years earlier. Blanton was aware that although Lockard's performance in terms of profit to the First was outstanding, he lacked skill and understanding in dealing with employees. In the short time that Blanton had been vice president of personnel, several of the 35 employees from consumer loans had discussed with him actions by Lockard which they believed to be very unfair and autocratic. On one occasion a female employee complained that she had been demoted from an interviewer to a loan teller without any explanation or warning. Lockard had simply attached a note to her time card which said, "As of today, you will work as a teller instead of an interviewer." Turnover in this department was higher than anywhere else in the bank, including the data center. In the past year 35 percent of the employees had quit or transferred to jobs elsewhere in the bank. Blanton had discussed the problem with President Evans and had recommended that some action be taken. Evans had replied, "I know Frank has problems with people, but with his performance on loans I think we'll just have to live with his people problems." Blanton came away from the meetings with the consumer loan groups convinced that 100 percent of them favored the union.

When Blanton returned to his office from one of the question-and-answer meetings, Harold Newton, vice president of branch operations, was waiting for him. Newton reported to him that a number of the branch office employees had informed him that the three assistant auditors were engaging in union-organizing activities in the branch offices. At the time, the bank was in the process of converting its saving accounts to a computer. As part of the conversion program, meetings were scheduled at all branch offices during which the internal auditors, as they were called, explained the new system. According to Newton's informants, the auditors spent only about 15 minutes explaining the computer printouts and the remainder of the two-hour session talking about the advantages of having a union. At the end of the meetings they had passed out union membership cards. By the time Newton received this information, meetings had already been held by the auditors at about half of the branches. Newton called off the other meetings.

The news that the assistant auditors were engaging in union-organizing activities came as a surprise and a shock to the officers of the bank, who had always considered them as part of the management team. It was agreed that Newton and the cashier would meet with the auditor and the three assistant auditors. At the meeting, the assistants admitted that they favored a union and had been trying to get other employees to join. Following the meeting, Newton discussed the matter with Attorney Grant, who said it was his opinion that the assistant auditors were a part of management and, therefore, that union activity by them was not protected under the National Labor Relations Act. Newton then recommended to President Evans that the three assistant auditors be discharged. Evans was of the opinion that the discharge of all three of the internal auditors would raise serious questions in the community regarding the integrity and soundness of the bank. As a result, no disciplinary action was taken. The meetings at the other branch offices were rescheduled at times when Newton could be in attendance and the assistant auditors limited their discussions to an explanation and discussion of the printouts.

### *Employees Sign Up with Union*

Two weeks following the union meeting at Lake City Hotel, Robert Marple, the international representative of the IMU, called on Attorney Grant and informed him that 80 percent of all the bank's employees had signed up with the union. He offered to produce the signed cards for signature comparison. Grant informed him that he would prefer not to see the cards, but had "an honest doubt" that the union really represented the majority of the employees. Marple then informed Grant that the union would petition the NLRB to hold a representation election.

One week after informing the bank's counsel that it had a majority of its employees signed up and wished to bargain for a contract, the union sent another letter to the employees (see Exhibit 2-3). Copies of the letter were given to management by several of the employees. A meeting of management representatives was then called by the president to discuss the letter and it was decided that the president should reply. Evans's letter, which was the first written communication from anyone in management to the employees on the union matter, is reproduced as Exhibit 2-4.

### *The First's Hospital-Medical Plan*

Two weeks after sending out its first letter to its employees regarding the union-organizing drive, the bank filed a request with the Internal Revenue Service to institute a hospital-medical plan, the costs of which would be paid entirely by the bank. (Fred Savage, a major stockholder who had opposed such plans, had died eight months earlier.) Following the filing, announcements were sent to all department heads, supervisors, and branch managers informing them that the bank was instituting a free hospital-medical plan, subject to approval by the necessary government agencies. No letter was sent directly to the employees on the hospital-medical plan at this time, but they were informed about it by their supervisors.

Two weeks after the bank announced its intention to assume the cost of a hospital-medical insurance plan, the union filed a petition with the NLRB requesting a representation election. At the same time, the union filed an Unfair Labor Practices (ULP) charge against the bank, claiming that the promise to institute a hospital-medical plan paid by the employer was for the purpose of avoiding unionization. The charge as filed by the union with the NLRB read as follows: "The above-named employer, by its officers, agents and representatives, has, by establishing a hospitalization plan for employees and their dependents and other acts and conduct, interfered with, restrained and coerced its employees in the exercise of the rights guaranteed in Section 7 of the Act." As a result of the filing of the ULP charge, the NLRB held in abeyance the union's request for a representation election.

Four weeks following the filing by the union, a hearing on the ULP charge was held before an officer of the NLRB. The First produced witnesses and correspondence to show that work on the hospital-medical plan had been undertaken before the bank was aware that the union was attempting to organize its employees. Attorney Grant argued that if the bank had not proceeded to develop the plan and try to place it into effect according to its original schedule, then indeed the bank would have been guilty of unfair labor practices. He requested that the hearing officer find that the union's charge was without merit.

### *Final Bank–Union Negotiations*

One month later the bank received a notice from the NLRB that the union had withdrawn the ULP charges. The president then addressed a letter to all the employees informing them that the new hospital-medical plan would become effective in two months (see Exhibit 2–5).

At about this same time, three employees at the bank's main office were observed by a supervisor in a part of the bank other than where they worked, handing out union membership cards to other employees during working hours. The officers of the bank were surprised when they learned that one of the employees was Esther Douglas, who had an excellent record of employment with the bank for the past 29 years. A review of her personnel record showed the following facts:

> unmarried and supports her mother; hired 29 years ago as a clerk upon recommendation of Wynn Evans who attended same church; excellent attendance record; very good ratings by her supervisors; interested in advancement, took AIB courses at night and worked hard; advanced over time to better and better jobs; eight years ago placed in charge of general ledger bookkeeping which required her to bring together all the data from the main office and the branches and deliver it to the president by noon each day; two years ago bank computerized the general ledger and Esther was moved to the savings department where she maintained controls over various matters; savings department job was important and bank maintained her prior salary; president still called upon her for data from time to time, but not every day; two months ago as a result of computerization of the savings department Esther was moved to the job of collection clerk with no decrease in salary; works with two other collection clerks who receive considerably less pay; still has desk at back of main floor, but no reason for president to see or talk to her now.

Two of the vice presidents discussed the incident with Esther. She admitted that she had passed out the cards and urged employees to join the union. She agreed with the officers that it was not fair to the bank for her to do this during working time and assured them that she would not do it again. Attorney Grant recommended that Esther and the other two employees who were observed passing out the cards be discharged. However, President Evans decided that it was better not to take any disciplinary action other than a warning. Esther continued to be interested in the union, but limited her activities to nonworking time.

Two weeks following the withdrawal by the union of the ULP charge, the NLRB informed the bank that it was proceeding with the union's request for a representation election. The bank refused to follow the informal procedure, but instead requested a formal hearing.

At the hearing, which was held a month later, the matter of the employees who should be included in the bargaining unit and therefore would be eligible to vote was discussed. Much to the surprise of management, the union did not ask to have the watchman and the other building and maintenance employees included in the unit. Management was happy to go along with their exclusion. Management argued also for the exclusion of the secretaries of the president and the personnel vice president on the grounds that they had access to confidential material. The union agreed to their exclusion. The greatest difference of opinion developed regarding supervisory employees. The National Labor Relation Act defines the term *supervisor* and provides that supervisors, as defined, shall be excluded from the bargaining unit (see Exhibit 2-6). Some of the employees whom the bank had given the title of *supervisor* did not meet the requirements as set forth in the Act. The bank argued that most of the branch managers, the assistant branch managers, and the purchasing agent should be included in the unit, but that the auditor and the assistant auditors should not be included. After discussing the content of the above jobs, it was agreed that three of the branch managers, three of the assistant branch managers, the three assistant auditors and the purchasing agent should be included and the others excluded. The election was delayed, however, because the bank challenged the validity of the union's signature cards and moved that the election petition be dismissed.

Following the hearing, the union sent another letter to the employees explaining the delay and assuring the employees regarding the profit-sharing plan (see Exhibit 2-7). Two weeks later, the hearing officer denied the bank's motion to dismiss and his decision was approved by the regional director of the NLRB. The bank then filed a petition for review with the NLRB which was denied two weeks later. The regional director of the NLRB then set a date for the election and sent formal notices to the bank and the union. The date was approximately one month later—almost exactly five months after the union had filed for an election. It was also a few days after the new hospital-medical plan became effective.

On the Monday afternoon on which the bank received the notice of the election date, Paul Blanton, vice president of personnel, discussed the matter briefly with Wynn Evans, president. They agreed it would be wise to have a meeting the next afternoon with their lawyer, Francis Grant, and the other executives of the bank in order to plan management's strategy and tactics during the 30 days remaining before the election. Evans informed Blanton that he would expect him to present a tentative plan of action that could form the basis for discussion and final decision.

## EXHIBIT 2-1
## International Metalworkers Union Local 76

To the Employees of First National Bank of Lake City
(Main Office and Branch Banks)

Greetings:

A considerable number of your co-workers have shown an extreme interest in the desire to unite for the good of all the First National Bank employees in Lake City and area branches.

You have the right by law from the National Labor Relations Act to self organize to form, join or assist labor organizations for the purpose of collective bargaining. This is exactly what your co-workers are attempting to do!

In order to petition the National Labor Relations Board (NLRB) for an election, we must have a sufficient number of the enclosed cards--signed! These signed cards are held in strict confidence and no one but a staff member of IMU or a field representative from the NLRB will see these cards.

No initiation fees or monthly dues are payable until an NLRB election is won. This is accomplished by each of you voting by secret ballot to accept IMU as your collective bargaining representative along with a committee of employees of your own choosing.

The professional employees of banking institutions are long overdue in exercising their right to self organize. You must realize that you are way behind professional employees pertaining to wages, vacations, pensions, paid hospitalization and accident and sickness insurance.

In just a few short years of self organizing, professional teachers of America have made substantial gains in all of the aforementioned benefits. You have that same privilege guaranteed by federal law. For your own benefit, take the first step as your fellow co-workers have and sign the enclosed card, which is held in strict confidence, and return it to IMU, Box 72, Lake City.

An extra card is enclosed for any of your fellow employees who wish to sign cards but did not receive a copy of this letter.

IMU Organizing Committee

## EXHIBIT 2–2
## Questions and Answers

A number of questions have been asked about what would happen if a union were to get in. Here are the answers:

1. **Question.** Is there any real reason why you need a union to speak for you and to pay dues to a union?
   **Answer.** No. You are always free to speak to any officer of the bank about wages, working conditions, or other conditions of employment without paying dues to a union.
2. **Question.** If the union wins, would there automatically be a contract with the union?
   **Answer.** No. The bank doesn't have to sign any contract that is not in the best interest of the bank. There is no law to force the bank to agree to anything the union asks and there can be no contract until we agree.
3. **Question.** Under a union, would you automatically get the things that the unions promise?
   **Answer.** No. The bank doesn't have to grant any request that the union makes. Our bank would agree only to those things that it is willing and able to grant which, in the bank's opinion, are in its best interests.
4. **Question.** With a union, would the employees go out on a strike?
   **Answer.** We don't know; but if the bank cannot agree to grant the things that the union has been promising or that the union wants for its own interests, the only way the union can try to force the bank to do these things is to get the employees to go out on a strike. It is easy for the union to make all kinds of big promises to you, but these are not always easy to fulfill.
5. **Question.** If the union calls a strike, can you be replaced?
   **Answer.** Yes. If the union makes you strike to try to force the bank to agree to the union's demands, under the law an employer is free to continue to operate and to replace the strikers. In addition, if our customers do not wish to be bothered with a strike, they can decide to end their relationship with us. Without customers where are we?
6. **Question.** Will you have to join the union if it gets in here?
   **Answer.** It is hard to tell what may happen if the union gets "in." Most unions try to force a company to sign a contract which requires all the employees to become union members or pay dues. Many strikes have been called to get just this kind of contract.
7. **Question.** If the union calls you out on strike, will you get paid while the strike is going on?

**EXHIBIT 2-2 (*Continued*)**

**Answer.** No. If you don't work, you won't get paid. An employer won't pay your wages and neither will the union.

8. **Question.** Why is it so often said that the employees lose by a strike even though they get a wage increase?
**Answer.** An employee who earned $100 a week loses $500 pay during a strike of only five weeks. If at the end of the strike he got a 5-cent-an-hour wage increase, how long do you think it would take to make up that kind of loss?
9. **Question.** If you did vote the union in and try it, and find that you don't like it, can you get rid of the union?
**Answer.** Not easily. It is a lot harder to get a union out than it is getting one in. If you vote the union in, you will probably be stuck with it as long as you work here.
10. **Question.** Would the union get us higher wages, additional benefits, and more job security, or is it possible that we could lose something we now have?
**Answer.** The union has probably told you that you have everything to gain and nothing to lose by voting it in. This is not true. The union can't guarantee you any new and additional benefits.
11. **Question.** Can a union do anything or punish an employee because he opposes it, speaks out against the union, or refuses to let them in his home?
**Answer.** No. It is a violation of the federal law for a union to even attempt to discriminate against an individual in his job or pay, or to attempt in any way to punish an employee because he opposed the union. The right of the employee to oppose a union is *guaranteed* by law. It is the employee's right and duty to make his own decision and make that decision known if he should so determine.
12. **Question.** If you signed a union card, can you vote against the union in an election?
**Answer.** Yes. If there is an election, you can vote against the union. It doesn't make any difference whether you signed a union card or went to the union meetings or even paid the union money. What you have signed or have told anyone would not count in an election. You would have an opportunity to vote *freely* and *secretly* under government supervision. It is illegal for a union to threaten or force an employee to vote its way.

**EXHIBIT 2-3**
**International Metalworkers Union Local 76**

To the Employees of First National Bank of Lake City--
June 2, 1972

For the benefit of the employees who were unable to attend our last meeting, I would like to point out the major questions that arose during the meeting, those concerning the current profit-sharing and pension program.

There is absolutely <u>no</u> way that you can jeopardize this benefit or any other benefits that you presently enjoy by self organizing. Your pension program is currently available to all employees of the Bank including some twenty (20) or so officers who are not eligible by law to join with you in a collective bargaining agreement.

The monies in this program have been set aside for pension benefits and your employer had already received a tax exemption by meeting Internal Revenue Service requirements. The pension money which has been set aside cannot be used for anything else but pension benefits. Furthermore, the federal law forbids your employer from reducing any of your present benefits for the reason you chose to self organize.

Organization can improve benefits in two ways. First, eliminate those not in the bargaining unit who take a lion's share from the fund, and second, negotiate higher benefits for those in the bargaining unit.

Unfortunately, a few employees at the First National honestly believe they can gain more on their own. Take a good look at these individuals and see where this has led them. What have they gained? Even your employer is distrustful of them. However, he would use them to his advantage. What happens when they are no longer useful to him? In unity there is strength and in strength and unity there are rewards at the bargaining table with the employer.

**EXHIBIT 2-4**
**First National Bank of Lake City**

To All Employees--June 7, 1972

I understand each of you received a letter signed by a stenographer in the name of an international representative of the IMU, which states as follows:

"Unfortunately, a few employees at the First National honestly believe they can gain more on their own. Take a good look at these individuals and see where this has led them. What have they gained? Even your employer is distrustful of them. However, he would use them to his advantage. What happens when they are no longer useful to him? In unity there is strength and in strength and unity there are rewards at the bargaining table with the employer."

The statement that we are distrustful of any of our employees is absolutely and unqualifiedly false and untrue. If we were distrustful of an employee, he or she would not be working for us.

You have the right to deal with us directly without the intervention of a union on any matter, both with respect to either present benefits or the consideration of any new or additional benefits.

It has certainly not been necessary in the past to have a union intervening on your behalf and we would hope that our past record would indicate that a union is neither needed nor necessary in considering future benefits.

The letter states that we would use employees so long as they are advantageous to us and asks what happens when they are no longer useful to us. All of our employees are valued by us and are useful to us. We do not use any of you in the manner suggested in this letter.

In fact, these statements are outrageous and show to what lengths this union will go to get you to sign cards.

We wish to make it perfectly clear, however, that you have the right to join a union. You have just as much right not to join. No union can guarantee you

**EXHIBIT 2-4 (*Continued*)**

economic benefits. If a union wins an election, the bank is not required to sign any contract that it feels is not in its best interest.

In their letter, the union refers to our profit-sharing plan. Both our pension and profit-sharing plans are purely voluntary on the part of the bank and, as you know, both are totally paid for by the bank. We hope to continue them, but there is nothing in the law to require us to do so if we feel economic considerations warrant a change. If you vote in favor of a union, all of these items are subject to negotiation.

I trust that each of you will give all these matters your serious consideration.

Wynn S. Evans
President

**EXHIBIT 2-5**
**First National Bank of Lake City**

To All Employees

We are writing this letter in order to report upon the progress to date of our efforts to install a fully paid hospital and major medical plan for all of our employees.

You will recall that you were advised of the bank having to obtain clearance from the Internal Revenue Service prior to the introduction of such a plan.

After consultations with appropriate Internal Revenue Service officials, it has been determined that the earliest date when such installation would be permissible is January 1 of next year. This year's salary increases already granted and the increases in profit sharing and pension allocations prevented any earlier implementation of the new hospital and major medical plan.

**EXHIBIT 2-5 (*Continued*)**

We are pleased, therefore, to inform you that we will be instituting a fully paid hospital-major medical plan covering both you and your dependents and under which you as an employee make no contribution, approximately two months from date of this letter.

Various proposals from insurance companies and Blue Cross-Blue Shield have been under study. As soon as complete details have been worked out, we will be sending them to you.

We are pleased that we are able to offer this protection to you because we recognize the pressures which unforeseen medical expenses can place upon family budgets.

Sincerely,

Wynn S. Evans
President

## EXHIBIT 2-6
## Provisions of the National Labor Relations Act Relating to Supervisors and Professionals

*Section 2 (3)*

The term "employee" shall include any employee, and shall not be limited to the employees of a particular employer, unless the Act explicitly states otherwise, and shall include any individual whose work has ceased as a consequence of, or in connection with, any current labor dispute or because of any unfair labor practice, and who has not obtained any other regular and substantially equivalent employment, but shall not include any individual employed as an agricultural laborer, or in the domestic service of any family or person at his home, or any individual employed by his parent or spouse, or any individual having status of an independent contractor, or any individual employed as a supervisor, or any individual employed by an employer subject to the Railway Labor Act, as amended from time to time, or by any other person who is not an employer as herein defined.

**EXHIBIT 2-6 (*Continued*)**

*Section 2 (11)*

The term ''supervisor'' means any individual having authority, in the interest of the employer, to hire, transfer, suspend, lay off, recall, promote, discharge, assign, reward, or discipline other employees, or responsibly to direct them, or to adjust their grievances, or effectively to recommend such action, if in connection with the foregoing the exercise of such authority is not of a merely routine or clerical nature, but requires the use of independent judgment.

*Section 14 (a)*

Nothing herein shall prohibit any individual employed as a supervisor from becoming or remaining a member of a labor organization, but no employer subject to this Act shall be compelled to deem individuals defined herein as supervisors as employees for the purpose of any law, either national or local, relating to collective bargaining.

*Section 9 (b)*

The Board shall decide in each case whether, in order to assure to employees the fullest freedom in exercising the rights guaranteed by this Act, the unit appropriate for the purposes of collective bargaining shall be the employer unit, craft unit, plant unit, or subdivision thereof: Provided, That the Board shall not decide that any unit is appropriate for such purposes if such unit includes both professional employees and employees who are not professional employees unless a majority of such professional employees vote for inclusion in such unit.

## EXHIBIT 2-7
## International Metalworkers Union Local 76

This letter will explain the delay in our organizing campaign and is also intended to let you know that the IMU is still very much interested in you as a member of our Union and as an employee of The First National Bank of Lake City.

I am sure the delay concerns you as much as it concerns me. I want you to know there is little the Union can do about the delay but I do want to explain the reason for it.

Recently a hearing was held before a Hearing Officer of the NLRB. Following the hearing, attorneys for the company and the Union were given twelve days to file post-hearing briefs. After the twelve days, the entire record is turned over to the Regional Director of the Labor Board. When he has completed his study he will then decide what jobs will be included in the bargaining unit, and will set the date for the election.

During the course of every union organizing campaign, many rumors, usually untrue, are circulated. These rumors are circulated, in most instances, by some supervisors or company propagandist who is taken in by the company's opposition to the Union.

Your company is no different. Our organizing committee has informed me that most of the present crop of rumors are so ridiculous that the men are laughing at them. However, there is one persistent rumor that the committee has asked me to put to sleep once and for all! These rumor mongers are saying you will lose your profit-sharing and pension benefits because you joined the IMU. Nothing could be further from the truth!

We challenge the company, its propaganda artists or anyone else to put in writing that you will lose benefits if the IMU wins!

Don't be taken in by these rumors that are intended to fool and confuse you.

Stick together and be part of the victory parade of the Union.

CASE 3

# BETHONEY MANUFACTURING (A)

*Amy Johnson*
*Michael Beer*

A group of strikers picketed the entrance of Bethoney's Farmington Plant G. It was January 3, 1977, the coldest day of the year. One month earlier, Plant Manager Arn Nelson had passed a rule banning coffee on the plant floor in an effort to improve cleanliness. The rule went into effect at midnight, January 3. Nelson remembered, "I got a phone call and they said 'you better give us our coffee and eating privileges back or we are going to walk out of here.' I said, 'Don't let the door hit you in the rear end as you do it.'" Encouraged by some of the more vocal members of the union, the A-shift (midnight to 8 A.M.) walked out. Other shifts refused to cross their picket line, and by morning the plant, normally in operation 24 hours a day, was shut down. The only department reporting for work was shipping and receiving. Nelson was faced with the immediate problem of getting the workers back to their jobs and explaining this work stoppage to his superiors in Los Angeles. He also had to consider the appropriateness of his management style, specifically his cleanup campaign, and what his stance would be once the wildcat strike was over. Good relations with the union membership were especially important because negotiations for a three-year contract were scheduled to begin in less than six months.

## ARN NELSON

In describing his background, Arn Nelson claimed to have spent 15 years going to school one place or another. After a year of studying the Bible and Philosophy at Wheaton College in Illinois, he completed a degree in mechanical engineering at Stevens Institute of Technology in Hoboken, New Jersey. He worked for RCA for five years and then studied electrical engineering while working in General Electric's aerospace program. He was hired by Bethoney in 1966 as a project engineer at the Riverton plant. Shortly afterward he became the produc-

This case was revised by Bert Spector under the direction of Lecturer Michael Beer.

tion superintendent, reporting to the plant manager. It was at Riverton that he met Jim Riley, who was acting personnel director.

The Riverton plant suffered from labor unrest and was plagued by wildcat strikes. After the employees walked out for the third time in two years in violation of the collective bargaining agreement, the plant manager, Nelson and Riley followed corporate instructions to fire them all and hire a new work force. Nelson related one particularly dramatic incident occurring during one of the wildcats. A striker on the picket line aimed a shotgun right at him at a range of about 50 feet. Nelson said:

> [The shotgun] was loaded and it was cocked . . . and I decided that this was one of those confrontation times. There was a whole group of picketers standing around watching, and I felt like I was representing more than just me. I was representing every manager and supervisor in that whole place. I starting walking towards him, and I said, "You only have one of two decisions: you either pull that trigger or I'll ram it down your throat." I got about half way towards him and he put the gun down. I said, "Don't you ever do that again."

In 1971, Nelson was transferred to Farmington as production superintendent at Plant B, one of the older, smaller plants in the division. Within a few months he was the manager of that plant. The 300 employees at Plant B constituted the most senior work force of the three Bethoney plants in Farmington. They were not likely to leave Farmington or Bethoney. Many had been with the company over 20 years. Plant B was well suited to Nelson's inclination to trust people and expect them to do their work with minimal supervision.

After contract negotiations in 1974, Nelson was transferred across town to Plant G, which was more than twice the size of Plant B. There he continued to operate in much the same way he had at Plant B. At Plant B, Nelson was personally involved in most decisions. Plant G was too large for this personal style of management. Some division people believed that he delegated too much responsibility without creating a mechanism for following-up on it. One said,

> I think Arn was fair in his position, enforcing rules and things like that, but I don't think he was kicking people in the butt and making them move. I think he was trying to use an approach that basically said, "We're all one happy family all with one objective, now let's get the job done." I don't think he would call a guy in and tear him apart for not doing his job right. I don't think he climbed all up and down his plant engineer the way he should have on maintenance problems in 1974 and 1975.

Nelson had a strong religious background which was reflected in his manner and his language. This made him different from other people in the plant and made some workers feel uneasy around him. One foreman said,

> He ran against the grain. His language was so pure, we thought he was too good to be true. In general he was a shock to the system. A guy who's out slinging mud finds it difficult to have a conversation with a guy who doesn't say "damn" or "hell."

Besides his religious differences, some people felt that Nelson's engineering degree put a gap between him and themselves. One said,

> I think Arn has trouble talking to people on the floor. He's from a different world. Everyone liked Ernie Bowen [Nelson's predecessor]. He wasn't afraid to get his hands dirty, but Arn is.

## THE CORPORATION

Bethoney was a diversified manufacturing corporation operating in six interrelated businesses. Most of its products were used in the building industry. It was publicly held and referred to as a "blue chip" company. (See Exhibit 3-1 for financial data.)

In mid-1976, the Board of Directors appointed Joseph Wheeler president and chief operating officer. He modified the organizational structure his predecessor had begun to implement, giving Bethoney the design appearing in Exhibit 3-2. Some functions, for example, marketing and labor relations, were carried out by a corporate department servicing all the divisions. The divisions had production responsibility, and plants were cost centers. Plant managers were not rewarded on profits, but on operating within their budgets.

The corporate labor relations department served all divisions employing hourly workers. Labor relations personnel acted as advisors during contract negotiations. They were responsible for maintaining consistency among all Bethoney contracts. They were present in arbitration hearings and counseled local plant employee relations managers on grievance handling at their request.

## THE GLASS DIVISION

### *History*

Bethoney's Glass Division began with the acquisition of the Brownfield Company in 1956. With this purchase, Bethoney acquired a going concern consisting of five plants (two in Farmington), a research center, and a warehouse (also in Farmington). Many executive positions in the Glass Division were filled by former Brownfield managers. The warehouse was gradually expanded into a production facility, Plant G. By 1977 it was the largest plant in the division.

Most products of the Glass Division were used in construction or automobile manufacture. Bethoney also produced specialty glass on a smaller scale.

For the ten years following Bethoney's entrance into the glass business, the division was only mildly affected by downturns in the economy. Concentrating on winning market share from large competitors, the division's sales grew more rapidly than its competitors throughout the 1960s (see Exhibit 3–3). In 1967, however, Bethoney's competitors began to respond to its success and tried to prevent any further erosion of their market share. In 1968 the division was affected by a mild recession and experienced idle capacity for the first time in its history. A recovery began in 1969, and by 1971 the division was in a sold-out position. This encouraged corporate management to invest in a major expansion of the division, enabling the division to capture an even larger share of the market. From that time until the middle of 1974, the division was producing at capacity and customers were on allocation. A recession beginning in late 1974 again idled equipment, and by February of 1975 the division was producing at only 50 percent of capacity. By the fall of 1976, though, the industry had recovered and the division was in a sold-out position once more.

Historically, the number of customer complaints about product quality increased in times of recession. When the supply of products was plentiful, customers could afford to be more demanding. At times when the division was producing at capacity, on the other hand, customers were willing to accept as much product as Bethoney could put out.

The end of 1976 brought some changes in the top management of the Glass Division as well as the corporation. Some managers from the old Brownfield Company were removed to make way for new blood. Ed Sherman was officially named vice president (V.P.) and division General Manager of the Glass Division. Sherman replaced the two group plant managers (from the old Brownfield Company) with one production manager who was responsible for production in all the plants in the division. Kevin Mallory assumed the position of production manager in early January 1977. Sherman also established the position of manager of organizational development, and brought Jim Riley over from another division to fill it.

Division management kept in contact with plant management by visiting the plants. Once a year an official group from headquarters toured each of the plants, reviewing production efficiencies and maintenance and inspection housekeeping. Plant personnel made presentations to division visitors on their areas of responsibility.

One division executive described the way the group plant manager, Dan Church, worked with the plants under this authority:

> Dan Church's method of operating was to establish an iron curtain around the plants for which he was responsible. There was no access from staff members into the plants. In fact, Ernie Bowen told me point blank at breakfast one morning, "I've been told not to talk to you about what goes on at this plant." Church believed the way to run his plants was to keep the problems hidden and he'd take care of them. Church was calling the shots at Plant G. Norris [manager of Farmington operations] was acting as a conduit; that's about all.

### *Control*

The performance of the plants in the division was measured by adherence to budget. The division reviewed performance against budget every month, and plant managers were expected to explain any variation. Part of the managers' annual compensation was tied to budget performance. Many felt the budgeted amounts were inadequate for long-range improvements and even regular maintenance. One plant manager said:

> When the money ran out, they'd stop fixing. They just did enough to keep up production. They'd allot such and such time [to fix it] and then the machine would go back up, ready or not.

### *Labor Climate*

The emphasis on growth throughout the 1960s made labor disturbances and consequent work stoppages highly undesirable. A high priority was placed on labor peace, an attitude carried over from the Brownfield Company. Before Ed Sherman became manager of the Glass Division, any manager with a history of labor strife was unlikely to be viewed favorably, so ambitious managers smoothed over difficulties when they could. Arn Nelson described the situation at Riverton in the 1960s this way:

> It was a kind of thing where they (the workers) would walk out because they wanted an extra three cents an hour, and the director of manufacturing would call from headquarters, "What's the problem now?" "They want three cents more an hour, and we wouldn't give it to them." "You wouldn't give them a lousy three cents an hour? Give it to them and get them back to work." It was that kind of philosophy.

## PLANT G

Farmington Plant G covered 13 acres under roof. The offices for the manager, employee relations supervisor, nurse, and other salaried personnel were in the front. Behind them, the production area covered over 137,000 of the plant's total 571,440 square feet. The production area was enclosed on two sides by warehouse space. Plant G was the largest manufacturing facility in Bethoney.

Plant G manufactured several products for both the construction and automotive markets. It was the primary production facility for automotive products in Bethoney. Most products used a similar process. Each had a hot end where the glass was melted in a furnace. The largest line had a hot end four stories high. The blasting and roar of its furnace made so much noise that ear plugs were required for anyone entering the area. The work area at the hot end remained hot all the time, summer and winter.

Several employees worked on each line, feeding in raw materials at the hot end or removing finished products and packaging them. They monitored the heat of the furnaces and the motion of the conveyor carrying the glass through. The operation of each machine was overseen by a machine chief, who reported any problems to his foreman. The foremen then arranged for maintenance assistance.

### *The Organization*

Plant G had 650 hourly employees. Seventy percent of them worked in the production department. The other 30 percent worked in shipping and receiving and maintenance. Maintenance workers were mechanics, welders, and electricians, responsible for keeping the machines running constantly. These employees were compensated on a straight hourly basis, with a premium paid for certain shifts and overtime.

Some 500 production workers who worked on the machines directly could earn an incentive bonus of up to $1.00 an hour based on production. This bonus had been negotiated with the union. Productivity was calculated by the pounds of finished product produced on a line less the reported scrap on the line. Scrap reports were obtained from the workers on the line. Large increments in productivity above a predetermined level yielded relatively small increments in the bonus. Thus, the bonus was essentially a payout for achieving productivity above a certain level.

The plant's 50 salaried employees worked in various functions, such as supervision, industrial engineering, quality control, and accounting. Quality control personnel checked density, thickness, and general appearance of the glass, and tested samples periodically.

Hourly employees with the least seniority usually worked the midnight to 8 A.M. shift, while senior employees worked the 8 A.M. to 4 P.M. shift. Foremen rotated shifts. This was to minimize favoritism and to discourage the incurring and trading of favors. Foremen reported to one of three shift foremen, who reported to the general supervisor for the shift.

The production superintendent was responsible for production in the plant, and shift foremen reported to him. The plant engineer was responsible for maintenance. He and the production superintendent reported to the plant manager. All three plant managers in Farmington reported to Carl Norris, manager of Farmington operations. Norris also supervised the employee relations manager and the employee relations supervisors at each of the three plants. (See Exhibit 3-4.)

### *The Community*

Farmington was a rural community in a midwestern state. Although industry had been introduced to the area in the 1950s, most people maintained at least a part-time farming interest in addition to their regular jobs. Many employees owned small farms or kept livestock.

Several companies had plants in Farmington. Bethoney was the second largest employer, with 700 employees at Plant G and between 250 and 300 each at Plants B and C. General Motors had the largest plant in Farmington: a foundry employing about 5,000 people. GM provided a standard for wages in other companies around Farmington. Some GM foremen belonged to a country club that Bethoney management personnel felt they could not afford. Bethoney employees believed that even broom-pushers at GM could earn $7.00 per hour. While the work at GM was harder and dirtier than at Bethoney, they were reputed to be more lax on attendance and discipline. One Bethoney employee relations supervisor said, "If GM was hiring at the same time we were, we would only get the people they didn't want."

Farmington was a union town. The three Bethoney plants were represented by Local 201 of the Glass Workers Federation (GWF). GM employees belonged to the UAW. Other industries in town were unionized and the unions were influential and well respected in the community.

### *The Union*

The GWF had its beginnings in the nineteenth century as a league of artisans and glassblowing specialists. By the 1970s the GWF represented 85,000 employees in industries making glass or plastic containers and products. Besides a national headquarters there were three regional offices. The International representative of the Farmington plants, Richard Evans, worked with all 23 locals in the state.

The seniority system extended across all three Farmington plants. Since the smaller, more established plants were viewed by many as more congenial places to work, employees with seniority took the opportunity to transfer there when an opening occurred. As a result, Plant G had the youngest, least settled work force of the three plants. These young employees were aggressive in voicing their opinions. Not surprisingly, the Local president, vice president, and secretary were all Plant G employees. The other plants were represented on the six-member union committee.

The Local president, Fred Saunders, worked in the production department and was serving his second term in office. He had been a union steward and even an acting foreman at one time. He represented the young, vocal element of the union. Saunders was in his mid-thirties and had been in Plant G 11 years. The vice president, Bob Graham, worked in the maintenance department. He had worked in Plant G since it had been a warehouse. Susan Fairbanks, the secretary, had just been elected to office in 1976. She was in her twenties and had less than five years' experience in Plant G. Her husband also worked at Plant G.

Richard Evans, the International representative, visited Farmington when he could, but his services were required all through the state. Therefore, his influence in Farmington was not as strong as the local union leaders'. He admitted that he was somewhat removed from the local union membership. He said, "I realize that some people may see me as more like management than union. . . . Maybe it's the necktie." Bethoney management perceived the International as being weak. They did not believe that GWF International had much power over the Local. This meant that the Local union committee was the dominant element in labor relations in Farmington operations.

There had not been a strike in Farmington over contract negotiations since a 17-day walkout in 1965. The contract was negotiated every three years and would be up for negotiation again in the summer of 1977.

### *Plant History*

Plant G was expanded from a warehouse shortly after its acquisition from Brownfield. One division executive remembered that it was equipped with the newest technology available at the time. Some of it did not start up well, resulting in the shifting of people from one machine to another. Workers were often frustrated by equipment failure and uncertainty about what job they would be doing each day.

The conversion from warehouse to plant created several new supervisory positions. Good machine operators were promoted to foremen with no formal supervisory training. They were left to rely on their own skills, without even the benefit of exposure to experienced foremen, since they were the first supervisors in the plant. This pattern was mirrored in the division's selection of plant managers. Most plant managers had good production records but received no management training when they moved into plant management jobs.

Arn Nelson's predecessor, Ernie Bowen, came to Farmington in the late 1960s. Having only a high school diploma, he worked himself up through the ranks of hourly employees in the Brownfield Company.

Bowen had a very warm, personable air about him. He spent most of his time on the plant floor, chatting with people. As one employee said, "Ernie was people-oriented and he was a good talker. He had a personal power that came from inside and not just from the position he held. He was a politician type. I would call him charismatic."

One machine chief commented, "Ernie could talk shop because he worked his way up from the bottom. You could talk to him and he would solve your problem. I wish he had stayed at Plant G. I liked him."

In the words of one foreman: "[Ernie] pictured himself as a very strong manager. He thought he could deal with the union and control morale. He thought of himself as an artist with people."

Bowen worked closely with union leaders to avoid any work stoppages. As one union member said, "He had to get the glass out, so he'd do anything to pacify you." The union vice president said, "He would give a lot of stuff away, but it always had strings attached. He traded favors." Bowen relied on these favors to circumvent the grievance procedure on occasion. For example, he might guarantee an employee overtime if, in exchange, the employee withdrew the grievance. He kept a looseleaf book containing a list of exceptions to the contract and special arrangements made with the union.

Bowen's relations with the plant foremen were not as close as those with the union. One foreman complained:

> Ernie did things that made it hard for a foreman to operate on the floor. Say a union guy was unhappy. The union committee and Ernie would get together and then the union official would pass on their decision to the foreman. Information about these decisions wasn't communicated to us officially. You had to check with Ernie to see if the union official was giving you accurate information. People wondered who the management really was.

An employee relations manager described the situation:

> A foreman could fire someone, and the next day the guy would be back at work. He would be reinstated by Ernie and employee relations, and no one would ever talk to the foreman who fired him in the first place.

Maintenance and housekeeping were not Ernie's strong points. As the plant grew from warehouse to factory, attitudes about cleanliness failed to mature with it. Ernie did nothing to proscribe the workers' habit of throwing their coffee cups and trash on the floor. One person claimed Ernie participated with the workers in chewing tobacco and spitting on the columns. Some employees became adept at frying hamburgers or steaks and warming chili at the hot end. Others used the special melting ovens to bake chickens and potatoes, removing products if necessary.

Machines were kept running at all costs. Bowen often made decisions to forego preventive maintenance procedures in order to keep machines in operation. He had no formal schedule of maintenance. Not only did this affect productivity but it also caused enormous frustration on the part of workers. For example, machines going out of control could cause larger amounts of broken glass to be strewn all over the plant floor. By the time he left Farmington, machine breakdowns were common.

When Arn Nelson arrived at Plant G in the fall of 1974, the economy was in recession and the Glass Division had idle capacity. Demand for glass was down, and the oversupply allowed customers the luxury of rejecting more product. Plant G received an especially high number of complaints and rejections because of its poorly maintained equipment. Thus, Nelson came to the plant with an emphasis on quality, while Bowen had always concentrated on volume.

With the end of the recession in 1976 and the resurgence of the construction and automotive markets, demand for glass was keeping the Glass Division running at capacity. While most indicators of Plant G's performance showed slight improvement (see Exhibit 3-5), the new division General Manager, Ed Sherman, was concerned that despite Nelson's efforts to introduce higher standards of discipline and performance, the plant was still not performing up to standards. Plant G was the largest plant in the division, but a very inefficient one. Maintenance and housekeeping were serious issues. In 1976, pressure was placed on Nelson by Sherman, to get the plant cleaned up no matter what it took. One executive described Nelson's reaction to these pressures:

> He got under tremendous pressures to improve the housekeeping and efficiencies, and he had to do something. He figured it was either going to be him or somebody else and it wasn't going to be him if he could do something about it.

At this point he started pressuring his production superintendent, even going to his home and bringing him back to the plant to correct problems he had left unsolved. He also began to be aggressive about cleanliness. One time he found a lunchroom janitor trying to clean up after an entire shift. He helped her push the tables to the wall and sweep the garbage to the middle of the room. Then he called the union leaders in to see the mess. He said later, "Of course, by the time that story got to the far end of the plant, it had me throwing over the tables in a rage!"

The arrival of a new plant engineer, Larry Johnson, in April of 1976 served to relieve some of the maintenance problems. Not only was he highly skilled, but his no-nonsense manner and willingness to work right on the floor with the maintenance crew improved morale significantly. By 1977 maintenance and efficiency had begun to improve.

## THE WILDCAT STRIKE

It was the winter of 1976–1977. Arn Nelson had been coming down hard on the workers on housekeeping for several months. Pressures to increase efficiencies made many workers feel that Bethoney valued them only as instruments of production and not as people. The atmosphere in the plant was tense, with departments blaming one another for slowdowns and equipment failures. The vocal union element at Plant G was convinced that Bethoney would do anything to prevent a work stoppage with demand so high, and threatened several times to walk out over minor issues.

When Nelson banned coffee, which employees insisted was necessary to keep their hands warm, the situation exploded. As one striker explained: "We were going to show them we weren't going to work that way!" On January 3, the midnight shift walked out and the workers on other shifts joined them. No one came to work on the third. The plant was idle again on the fourth.

Arn Nelson was in a quandary. On one hand he knew that a work stoppage at the largest glass plant at a time when customers were being put on allocation could have a serious effect on the division. On the other hand, the division had instructed him to get tough and get the plant cleaned up. What was more, contract negotiations would begin in six months, and if he gave in to the workers now, management would enter those negotiations with the image of being weak and easy to manipulate.

**EXHIBIT 3–1**
**Five-Year Summary of Operations**
*(All Figures Are in Thousands of Dollars)*

| Summary of Earnings | 1976 | 1975 | 1974 | 1973 | 1972 |
|---|---|---|---|---|---|
| Revenues: | | | | | |
| Net sales | $1,308,771 | $1,107,012 | $1,105,508 | $905,417 | $798,706 |
| Other | 12,388 | 10,005 | 12,359 | 10,089 | 8,426 |
| Total | 1,321,159 | 1,117,017 | 1,117,867 | 915,506 | 807,132 |
| Costs and expenses: | | | | | |
| Cost of sales | 983,431 | 852,786 | 838,462 | 674,130 | 586,007 |
| Selling, general, and administrative | 166,159 | 151,842 | 152,010 | 135,227 | 121,175 |
| Research, development, and engineering | 25,236 | 24,393 | 18,807 | 17,203 | 13,483 |
| Total | 1,174,826 | 1,029,021 | 1,009,279 | 826,560 | 720,665 |
| Income from operations | 146,333 | 87,996 | 108,588 | 88,946 | 86,467 |

| Results by Major Business Segments | 1976 | 1975 | 1974 | 1973 | 1972 |
|---|---|---|---|---|---|
| Net sales: | | | | | |
| Glass Division | $ 409,090 | $ 323,134 | $ 294,445 | $244,616 | $195,795 |
| Division V | 214,495 | 192,416 | 231,794 | 164,106 | 147,194 |
| Division W | 184,686 | 140,860 | 117,682 | 97,492 | 89,561 |
| Division X | 182,502 | 169,928 | 168,122 | 134,855 | 115,110 |
| Division Y | 174,372 | 166,462 | 172,773 | 167,073 | 162,777 |
| Division Z | 143,626 | 114,212 | 120,692 | 97,275 | 88,266 |
| Total | $1,308,771 | $1,107,012 | $1,105,508 | $905,417 | $798,706 |

| Results by Major Business Segments | 1976 | 1975 | 1974 | 1973 | 1972 |
|---|---|---|---|---|---|
| Earnings before income taxes and extraordinary items | | | | | |
| Glass Division | $45,629 | $23,098 | $15,273 | $24,827 | $23,092 |

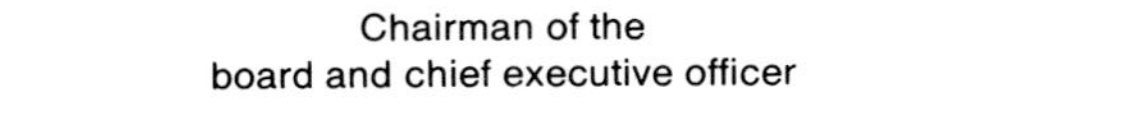

**EXHIBIT 3–2**

## Bethoney Organization Chart

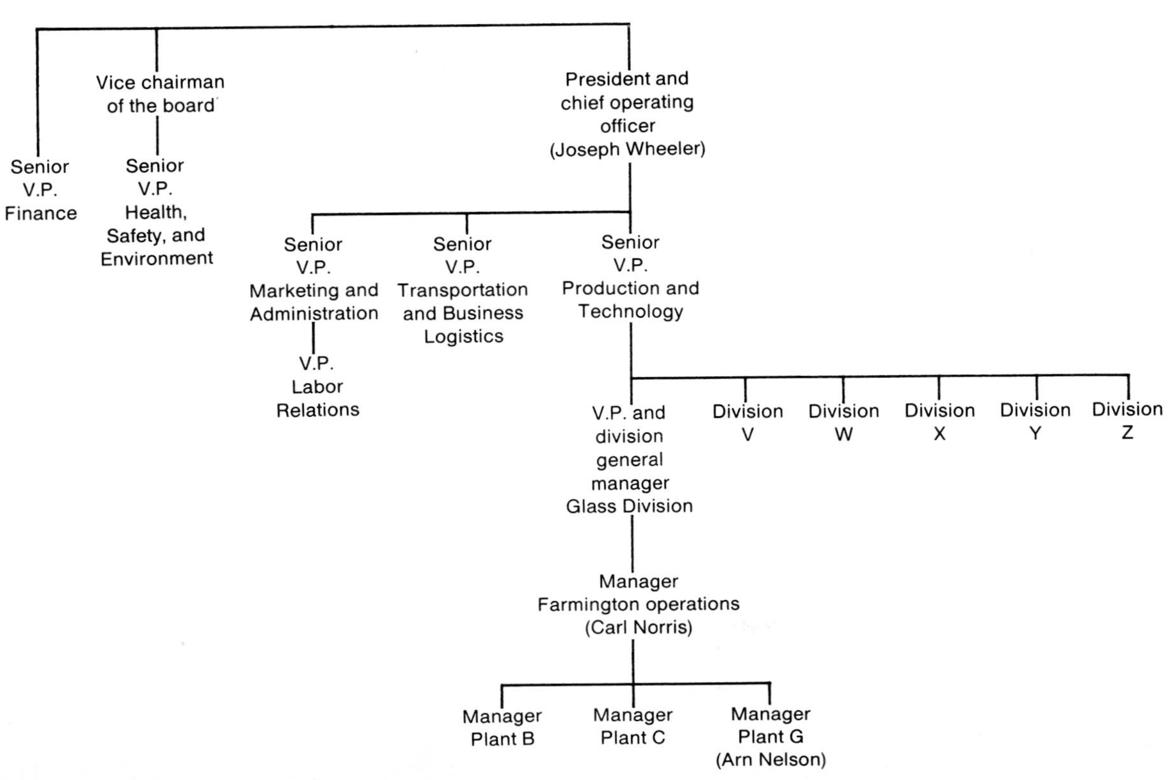

**EXHIBIT 3-3**
**Approximate Value of Glass Division Sales and Bethoney's Share** *(in Millions of Dollars)*

| YEAR | INDUSTRY TOTAL | BETHONEY'S GLASS DIVISION | % SHARE |
|---|---|---|---|
| 1950 | $ 68 | — | — |
| 1951 | 66 | — | — |
| 1952 | 71 | — | — |
| 1953 | 88 | — | — |
| 1954 | 93 | — | — |
| 1955 | 108 | — | — |
| 1956 | 110 | $ 13.6 | 12.4 |
| 1957 | 123 | 16.4 | 13.3 |
| 1958 | 124 | 20.3 | 15.1 |
| 1959 | 151 | 25.6 | 16.9 |
| 1960 | 163 | 25.0 | 15.3 |
| 1961 | 173 | 27.9 | 16.1 |
| 1962 | 187 | 29.7 | 15.9 |
| 1963 | 213 | 38.4 | 18.0 |
| 1964 | 226 | 42.5 | 18.8 |
| 1965 | 251 | 45.2 | 18.0 |
| 1966 | 282 | 50.0 | 17.7 |
| 1967 | 279 | 52.7 | 18.9 |
| 1968 | 312 | 64.4 | 20.6 |
| 1969 | 355 | 73.7 | 20.8 |
| 1970 | 356 | 80.9 | 22.3 |
| 1971 | 427 | 96.8 | 22.6 |
| 1972 | 487 | 109.9 | 22.6 |
| 1973 | 560 | 142.8 | 25.5 |
| 1974 | 648 | 161.1 | 24.9 |
| 1975 | 689 | 177.3 | 25.7 |
| 1976 | 860 | 232.7 | 27.1 |

## EXHIBIT 3–4
## Bethoney Plant Organization Structure

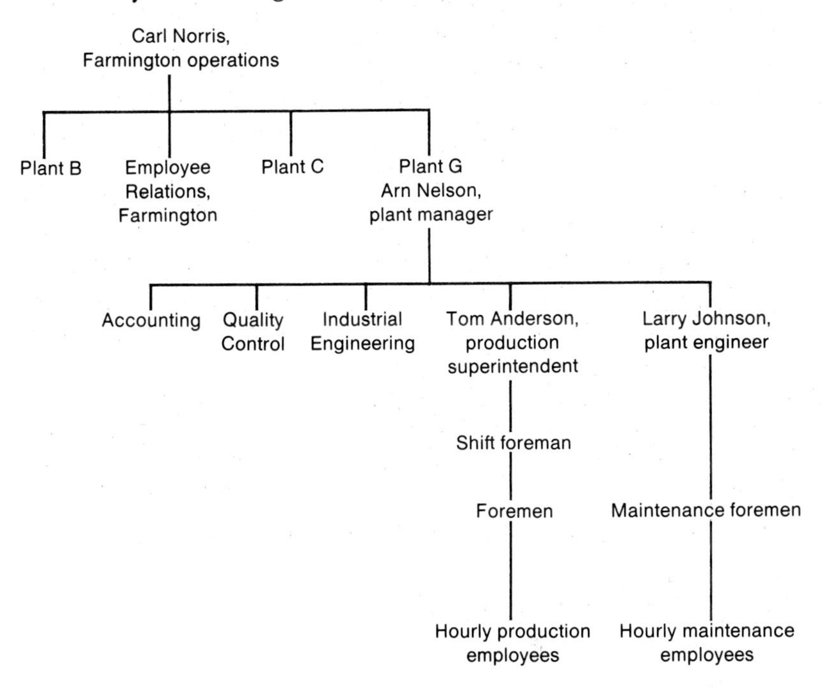

## EXHIBIT 3–5
## Indicators of Plant G Performance

The performance of plants in Bethoney's Glass Division was measured by deviation from standards. Following are some of the key indicators of the performance of Plant G.

| KEY PERFORMANCE INDICATORS | 1974 | 1975 | 1976 |
|---|---|---|---|
| OSHA injuries per 100 employees: | | | |
| U.S. manufacturing | 12 | 12 | 13 |
| Bethoney | 7 | 7 | 8 |
| Glass Division | 8 | 10 | 6 |
| Plant G | 10 | 13 | 11 |
| Shop expense controllables: | | | |
| Ratio of actual controllable[a] production expenses to budget production expenses | .99 | 1.13 | 1.10 |
| Plant expense controllables: | | | |
| Ratio of actual controllable[b] plant expenses to budget plant expenses | 1.19 | 1.05 | 1.04 |
| Direct material usage index: | | | |
| Ratio of direct material usage divided by standard material usage | 1.04 | 1.05 | 1.04 |
| Direct labor usage index: | | | |
| Ratio of direct labor usage divided by standard labor usage | 1.13 | 1.08 | 1.04 |
| Shop total variation: | | | |
| (% variation from standard) | 3 | 4 | 1 |
| Actual usage of direct labor, direct material, direct expense (electricity, gas), and indirect expense, divided by the standard for production | | | |

[a]Controllable shop expenses include overtime salary; labor premiums; special labor, i.e., cleaning, maintenance labor and materials; personal expenses; and so forth. Shop expenses are directly related to production.

[b]Controllable plant expenses include office supplies, purchased services such as telephone and postage, labor and materials for building maintenance, and so forth.

CASE 4

# BETHONEY MANUFACTURING (B)

*Amy Johnson*
*Michael Beer*

On January 3, 1977, Bethoney's Farmington Plant G lay idle. A rule banning coffee on the plant floor had taken effect at midnight, and employees reporting to work for the midnight shift walked out in protest. Workers reporting for subsequent shifts refused to cross the midnight shift's picket line; the plant was shut down by a wildcat strike. By the next night, only the shipping and receiving department was in operation. About midnight the picketers approached the plant manager, Arn Nelson, offering to come back to work if the coffee ban was lifted. Not only did he refuse to rescind the rule, but promised that each striker on A-shift would be given a day's disciplinary lay-off for every day they were out on strike.

The strikers, members of the Glass Workers Federation (GWF), appealed to Richard Evans, their International representative, for support. He informed them that the strike violated the contract and that the union could not sanction it. The issue should have been handled as a grievance. At the union's request, the strikers agreed to return to work. The first full shift reported at midnight, January 5. Thirty-six hours were required to return the plant to full production. The strike cost over $100,000 in lost production.

Arn Nelson held fast to the controversial rule that no coffee was allowed on the plant floor. Over the months that followed, each person on the midnight shift was sent home for a three-day disciplinary lay-off.

## DIVISION REACTION

Division management supported Nelson's clean-up campaign. Nelson described their attitude: "Nobody wants a dirty plant; there isn't any of the management that would condone a dirty plant, so I was told, 'Do whatever you have to do.'" However, when Nelson's actions resulted

---

This case was revised by Bert A. Spector under the direction of Lecturer Michael Beer.

in a strike, they were viewed less positively. Nelson said, "I would suspect . . . that if I had been relatively new in the management of Bethoney and had done what I did, I wouldn't be working here today. . . . Jim Riley was my advocate in Los Angeles . . . when other people were critical of the way I was behaving and managing the plant, [he] raised the question, 'Do you have someone else that you could recommend that would do it any better?' and they kept coming back to the same answer, 'We can't think of anybody.' "

Ed Sherman, General Manager of the Glass Division, described his reaction:

> I didn't feel that I was going to criticize him for the decision he made because we had told him, "You've got to get this place cleaned up. If you can't do it one way, perhaps you have to do it another way." I disagreed with the approach of discipline. It seemed to me that people walk out, and the discipline you give them is more time off, you're only adding fuel to their fire. On the other hand, I guess I didn't have any real good idea about how you should discipline people who do something like that.
>
> We concluded after getting the facts, that first of all the coffee cup situation was only a culmination of a lot of things. It brought to a head the fact that there was antagonism there, and that his [Nelson's] approach perhaps could have been different.

## ATMOSPHERE OF THE PLANT

Arn Nelson explained the feelings that prompted the walkout:

> They were convinced when they walked out over that coffee situation that not only were they going to get their coffee back, but that they would draw the attention of upper management to the fact that Nelson was abusing and persecuting them, and they were surprised that I was even around after they came back to work.

Having failed to bring back coffee or to intimidate Arn Nelson with their three-day walkout, the workers looked forward to the expiration of the contract on July 1 as an opportunity to demonstrate their power. One union leader explained, "After the coffee cup thing, they [workers] figured, 'We didn't get them in January, but we'll get them in July.' " A foreman remembered, "People who were normally levelheaded and calm were very belligerent." A management observer said of the workers' attitudes, "There wasn't any real confrontation. It was just that kind of lull before the storm. They took their free days, they took their lumps; they knew that we were going to get ours."

Bethoney employees were preparing for a strike. One couple paid up all their bills three months in advance. Unemployed spouses of workers sought part-time or temporary jobs. People saved money. Because the economy was good and unemployment low throughout the county that year, it was not difficult to find ways to supplement income.

## EMPLOYEE SURVEYS

Ed Sherman was concerned about performance and labor relations at Plant G. In March 1977, he sent the division's manager of organizational development (OD), Jim Riley, to Farmington to get an idea of what the climate would be for contract negotiations. For Jim, this was the first assignment as manager of OD in the Glass Division.

Riley used two survey instruments to get information on Farmington employees. One was an attitude survey in which employees indicated agreement with given statements. (See Exhibit 4–1.) Designed and administered by an independent consulting firm, this poll pointed up immediate trouble spots which would have an impact on contract negotiations. The responses indicated that the following issues were of greatest significance:

- Morale was very low among hourly employees.
- Working conditions were considered poor.
- Equipment was poorly maintained.

In their conclusion, the consultants advised, "In the event the union's contract is coming up for renegotiation any time in the near future, it is anticipated that the company is susceptible to a strike unless significant changes occur in the meantime."

The second instrument Riley used was a subjective values survey. He administered this survey to a group of foremen, a group of hourly employees, and several management personnel.

The values survey, created by the Center for Values Research, Inc., was designed to measure priorities. By defining the value an individual placed on an object or event in the work place, the researcher could categorize the individual according to needs, which could then be responded to by management. The survey was based on the ideas of Scott and Susan Myers.[1] They based their work on theories about the levels of psychological existence through which people progress as they mature. Each level had specific characteristics and needs, which are described in Exhibit 4–2. The Myerses found that groups of employees could be categorized, sharing the characteristics of one or more of these

[1]Their work is described in their article, "Adapting to the New Work Ethic," *Business Quarterly*, Winter 1973, p. 48.

psychological levels. For example, they found that a group of typical hourly employees whom they classified as "hourly traditional" scored lowest on tests measuring the existential level and highest on the conformist and tribalistic scales. They were able to draw profiles of other groups as well. (See Exhibit 4–3.) The purpose of the survey was to help managers recognize and cope with values systems that were different from their own.

Riley found that most respondents fell clearly into the categories described by the Myerses. Arn Nelson scored very high on the "existential" scale, which indicated a dislike for constraining authority and an ability to view things with a long-range perspective. The foremen were high on the "conformist" scale, which meant they had a low tolerance for ambiguity and were most comfortable in clearly defined roles. However, their supervisor, Production Superintendent Tom Anderson, rated high on "sociocentric," which indicated a dislike for control and directive management. One production worker explained, "Anderson didn't run the department. The foremen ran it." Riley realized that Anderson would have to change his easygoing approach in order to make the foremen effective on the plant floor.

Larry Johnson, the plant engineer, was quite different. He was defined as "egocentric," an aggressive, take-charge individual. Riley believed this was the ideal style for working with the maintenance department, whose employees closely fit the Myers's model of hourly traditional. Maintenance employees had high "tribalistic" needs, responding well to a strong dominant boss, or "tribal chief." In fact, most of the more senior employees in Farmington fit the traditional model closely. Jim Riley talked about these traditional employees:

> What we had is a traditional type of older employee, an employee that was relatively tribalistic; looked to a tribal chief. This is where the unions really came in pretty heavily. We had a conformist type of employee who wanted to be told . . . so chain of command was really appropriate for these people.

Not all employees fell into the hourly traditional category, however. To Jim Riley's surprise, about 30 percent of them, mostly younger employees, could be classified as hourly enlightened. He described them this way:

> What we had was a group of people, younger people, who were hourly enlightened. They were highly egocentric, which meant that they took things into their own hands. People who were not conformist, who did not participate in manipulation (and they thought Arn was very manipulative), who were highly sociocentric, and very frankly, who were damn high on the existential characteristic. They were really up on the issues (economic issues affecting the plant); they saw you needed to balance things.

Riley gave feedback on the findings of both surveys to each group. He was especially impressed that the hourly enlightened employees took great interest in the survey results. They asked questions about the implications of the findings for the plant and for their futures. Riley had the feeling that many of these people were more interested and capable of managing the plant than the supervisors were.

## TURNOVER IN THE EMPLOYEE RELATIONS DEPARTMENT

After taking the position of production manager for the Glass Division in January 1977, Kevin Mallory made a tour of the plants. While in Farmington, he learned from Carl Norris that the employee relations manager servicing all three plants was not performing adequately. Mallory said, "My first visit out there, Carl gave me quite a dissertation on his shortcomings, and the fact that he really wasn't doing his job, so he was taken off the job." He went on to explain how the new employee relations manager, Russell Waters, was chosen. "We normally go to our corporate labor relations people for recommendations and find out who we have as a candidate in the company. Russell's name came up and of course I didn't know Russell at all, but I talked to him. He came well recommended." Waters arrived in Farmington in March.

The division management decided that in addition to a central employee relations function reporting to Carl Norris, they also wanted employee relations supervisors on-site in each of the three plants. These supervisors would report to Waters, but they would provide services to the plant managers. Roger Atkins arrived in Farmington in April to take the position of employee relations supervisor for Plant G. Jim Riley and Arn Nelson had worked with Atkins in the Riverton plant, where he worked as an hourly employee and later a foreman.

As Waters began functioning in his new situation, certain problems began to appear. A division observer described him this way:

> He's a good man, he's a very intelligent, very honest person, very hardworking and did all the mechanics of the employee relations job in terms of handling compensation cases and benefits. But he had one basic problem. He couldn't establish rapport with people. That's kind of critical to that job. Some people just plain don't feel comfortable out talking to the folks out on the floor, and Russell was one of them.

One foreman called him, "a 5′6″ macho male with a swagger stick and boots style. He was dictatorial." A colleague said, "Russell was not effective at the plant level. He couldn't blend with either the hourly or salaried employees as groups. He'd walk out in the plant and people would turn their backs on him."

The timing of Waters' arrival in Farmington added to the animosity inspired by his personal style. One union official said, "People despised Russell Waters. He thought it was going to be his way or it wasn't going to be at all. People felt Waters and Atkins were brought in just to break the union. He was strictly company, and there was little give." A salaried employee commented, "He was pompous and he really didn't have any problems projecting that image. In fact he enjoyed it. . . . Salaried employees disliked him; the hourly employees hated him. But even if they hadn't, to take a guy and bring him into contract negotiations, just a couple of months before they were going to take place—that was insanity. That was absolutely pure insanity."

Roger Atkins had a different style. He had been an hourly worker in Riverton and had belonged to the same union as the Farmington employees. As a foreman he had learned how to communicate with people and knew how much contact people on the floor needed. Jim Riley said,

> He was just a natural for it. If you've been there [worked on the floor] and if you have any integrity at all, you usually have credibility. So he had credibility immediately. Roger has a way of talking with people that they like. That makes you want to be friendly.

## EXPANSION OF THE GLASS DIVISION

In the spring of 1977, the corporation announced plans to spend $250 million to expand the Glass Division. They had been running some small experimental plants and refining technology. Now they were ready to make large investments in new plants and equipment around the country. The Farmington plants, however, were not to be updated, but were to continue operating as they were. A supervisor described the impact this news had on the union. "They read in the paper about Bethoney's plans for expansion of the Glass Division—$250 million to be spent in other places. The union saw this year as the last good chance to get concessions from the company while the Farmington plant was still the key plant in the division."

## CONTRACT NEGOTIATIONS

In May, both the union and management geared up for contract negotiations. The employee relations department surveyed wages in the local area. Wage surveys were standard procedure for Bethoney before any contract negotiation. The company based its offers in part upon the prevailing rate in the area. Exhibit 4–4 shows the results of the Farmington survey.

Meanwhile, the International representative of the GWF was using resources provided by the AFL-CIO to collect data on wage and benefit packages awarded by other Bethoney plants in the division. This information would be used in framing an initial demand and in knowing how far the company would go.

With all of their research behind them, negotiating teams from both sides assembled in a hotel in a neutral city. Representing Bethoney were Russell Waters, Roger Atkins, and one salaried employee from each of the three plants in Farmington. These last three were selected because of their experience and credibility with the hourly employees. The plant managers themselves were not present at the bargaining table, but remained at their jobs in Farmington. Representing the union were Richard Evans, the GWF International representative, and Fred Saunders and Bob Graham, president and vice president of GWF Local 201. Also present was the union recording secretary, Susan Fairbanks.

In the past, contract negotiations had included quite a bit of fraternization between the parties. It was not uncommon for members of both negotiating teams to eat and drink together, and agreements were often reached over the dinner table to be formalized over the bargaining table. In 1977, however, Russell Waters would not allow any interaction of the teams outside of formal bargaining.

Roger Atkins claimed that the union team assigned members to sit across the table from specific people on the management team and observe their body language. Management frustrated the watchers one day by rearranging their seating after the union side was already seated. Richard Evans claimed that Russell Waters tried to confuse people by shuffling papers and burying negotiators in details. Neither side was prepared for the detailed questioning they received from the other side.

As a rule, contract negotiations began with a settlement of noneconomic issues, that is, contract wording on work rules and personnel procedures, before moving on to wages and benefits. In 1977, negotiations began in the usual way. The management team expected the discussion of noneconomic issues to last just a few days, but when it stretched out over a week, they became concerned. The union was having a national rally in June and negotiations would be suspended for a week while the union team attended it.

The management team decided to force discussion of economic issues by putting a wage offer on the table on May 25, even though the noneconomic issues had not been settled upon. Their first offer was voted on and soundly rejected by the union membership. At the same time the union voted to give their negotiating team the power to reject any contract of which they disapproved without putting it to a vote of the general membership. This gave the union negotiating team a large amount of authority and maneuverability.

The union did not make a counter offer until June 28. On that day they asked for an increase in wages, improved retirement benefits, and removal of the limit (cap) on cost of living increases. Throughout negotiations, retirement and cost of living remained key issues. Nothing was agreed upon before the contract expired on July 1, and the long-anticipated strike began.

## THE STRIKE

On July 1, 1977, nearly 1,000 Bethoney employees of the three Farmington plants went out on strike. Some machines at Plants B and C were kept in operation by salaried personnel, but Plant G was shut down completely. Arn Nelson and a few other management personnel stayed on the premises of Plant G to maintain security, but Nelson would not allow any of the machines to be started up for fear of vandalism.

Other unions in Farmington immediately expressed their support for the GWF Local 201. The UAW took out a large ad in the local paper backing the strike, and several other unions followed suit. On July 29 several unions and even some local businesses participated with the strikers in a parade through downtown Farmington. Some stores sponsored "strike sales" to cater to union members and many people offered odd jobs to strikers to help them meet financial obligations. One union member told the casewriter, "Most strikers didn't even have to look for other jobs. I got another regular job and my husband did a lot of construction and painting. I only went job hunting one day, but he never even had to look." The community continued to support the union through the summer. On August 8, Local 201 sponsored a pig roast at the UAW Park to boost strikers' spirits and keep them informed. Local companies donated hot dogs, corn and pigs for the event.

The mood of the strikers was easygoing at first. Newspaper pictures showed picketers dressed in cut-offs, sitting in lawn chairs under beach umbrellas in front of the plant. Many who had farming interests hoped the strike would last until the harvest was over. Union officials announced there were sufficient funds to support a strike of several months.

While some viewed the strike as an extended vacation, others accepted it as a normal part of union-management relations. One said.

> Sometimes you've got to have a strike to show the company that you're not scared of them. Here they are big, bad boys and people are scared of

the company. But if you just sit back and take it year after year after year, they'll think, "Well, they will just take anything."

However, as the negotiating teams became deadlocked, tensions began to build. When the strike stretched out longer than anyone had expected, these tensions began to be expressed physically. Vandalism was directed at the company and at individuals (see Exhibit 4-5). Non-union employees crossed picket lines and members of the Bethoney negotiating team often found their car windows broken.

The most dramatic event of the strike was a confrontation between picketers and sheriff's deputies. One night about 50 or 55 strikers tried to block the entrance of Plant B. They were confronted by about a hundred sheriff's deputies. They refused to leave the plant gate, when the garage door of a gas station across the street opened to reveal another contingent of deputies dressed in riot gear. The union crowd began to disperse, but the officers started swinging, according to union sources, and several people were hit with fists and sticks before they were able to get away from the plant gate.

### *Strikebreakers*

A week after the strike began, Russell Waters announced in the newspaper that Bethoney would bring salaried employees from other plants in the division to keep the operation going until the contract was settled (Exhibit 4-6). He also suggested that the company would consider hiring permanent replacements for the striking workers. Bethoney's salaried employees from all over the country were brought to Farmington to run Plants B and C. Plant G remained idle.

After a violent incident on July 20 (see Exhibit 4-5), a local judge issued a temporary restraining order forbidding the union to block the plant gates or to prevent nonstriking employees from entering the plants. Some union officials believed this injunction weakened the spirit and strength of the strike.

### *Mediation*

On July 28, a federal mediator was brought in. He continued to work with the teams for the duration of the strike.

Negotiations during the strike consisted of a series of package offers and counteroffers. The union would not consider wage offers unless they were accompanied by acceptable compromises on contract wording, retirement, and cost of living.

By mid-September, the GWF International was convinced that the company had made its best offer. The local leaders did not agree, however, and continued to try to negotiate a better one. Over the days that followed, union wage demands inched closer to the company's offer. Finally, on October 2, a compromise was hammered out. The union accepted the company's wage offer, the company met union demands on retirement, and the cost of living clause remained unchanged, with a limit on cost of living increases.

The union team took this contract back to its membership, which rejected it on their first vote. A second vote was taken a few days later, and the contract was accepted. Most union members attribute the success of the second vote to a letter sent to the families of striking employees from Bethoney President Joseph Wheeler. The letter claimed that Farmington was an unreliable labor market, and that Bethoney might be forced to relocate its plant in a more stable area. The letter had the desired impact.

Another factor affecting the union vote was the fact that the retirement issue had been settled. This was the most important issue to employees at Plants B and C, and once it was settled, they were unwilling to prolong the strike. Employees at Plant G knew they could not last long without support from the other plants, so the majority voted to accept the contract.

Bethoney employees began returning to work on October 11, more than one hundred days after the strike began. The strike cost Bethoney nearly $8 million in profits. Arn Nelson looked forward to their return with uncertainty about the future. How would the returning workers be treated by their supervisors, who had been doing their jobs? How could the tensions and hard feelings that existed before and during the strike be dissipated? How could he avoid the pitfalls into which labor relations had fallen in the past? He thought of his personal style; his insistence on cleanliness and on strict adherence to the rules. He wondered if that style would be effective in the plant once the workers came back. He knew that his actions over the next few days would set the tone in the plant for the next three years.

**EXHIBIT 4–1**
**Summary of Findings of Survey Conducted March 1977**

Sample: 162 hourly employees
(Note: The first column lists the company-wide average of hourly employees responding "agree" to each question.)

| | Agree Bethoney (Average) (%) | Agree (%) | Don't Know (%) | Disagree (%) |
|---|---|---|---|---|
| I feel responsible for my own work. | 83 | 89 | 5 | 6 |
| I enjoy working with the people here. | 83 | 75 | 16 | 9 |
| My job is secure at Bethoney. | 33 | 60 | 21 | 19 |
| I find my work satisfying. | 58 | 57 | 15 | 28 |
| I am proud to work for Bethoney. | 59 | 56 | 27 | 17 |
| My supervisor is fair in dealings with me. | 60 | 55 | 15 | 30 |
| I know where I stand—job performance. | 58 | 54 | 14 | 32 |
| My work gives me a sense of achievement. | 54 | 52 | 15 | 33 |
| I plan a career for working at Bethoney. | 50 | 48 | 32 | 20 |
| I look forward to coming to work. | 46 | 43 | 22 | 35 |
| My supervisor knows his or her job well. | 52 | 41 | 21 | 38 |
| My job allows me to improve my skills. | 45 | 41 | 13 | 46 |
| Promotions have been satisfactory for me. | 38 | 38 | 13 | 49 |
| My job makes good use of my skills. | 45 | 33 | 14 | 53 |
| I get enough information on how Bethoney is doing. | 36 | 32 | 12 | 56 |
| I get recognition when I do good work. | 37 | 31 | 15 | 54 |
| Bethoney's rules and policies help me. | 40 | 19 | 23 | 58 |
| Bethoney has good working conditions. | 29 | 17 | 16 | 67 |
| Overall percentage favorable | 50 | 44 | — | — |

**EXHIBIT 4–1 (*Continued*)**

The following questions were written specifically for the Farmington plants, and so have no company-wide responses.

| | Agree (%) | Don't Know (%) | Disagree (%) |
|---|---|---|---|
| With more training I could be more productive. | 56 | 17 | 27 |
| I am properly trained to do my job. | 48 | 13 | 39 |
| Bethoney is a good place to work. | 42 | 20 | 38 |
| Our safety programs work well. | 39 | 18 | 43 |
| I receive information to do my job well. | 35 | 14 | 51 |
| I get enough information about the plant. | 30 | 10 | 60 |
| My supervisor is interested in ideas. | 28 | 21 | 51 |
| Process and work methods are as efficient as possible. | 26 | 19 | 55 |
| Equipment is properly maintained. | 15 | 13 | 72 |
| Overall percentage favorable. | 35 | — | — |

SOURCE: Adapted from M. Scott Myers and Susan S. Myers, "Adapting to the New Work Ethic," *Business Quarterly*, Winter 1973, p. 49.

## EXHIBIT 4–2
## Levels of Psychological Existence

- **Existential (X).** High tolerance for ambiguity and people with differing values. Likes to do jobs in his own way without constraints of authority. Oriented toward broad goals and long time perspective.
- **Sociocentric (S).** High affiliation needs. Dislikes conformity, materialism, and manipulative management. Concerned with social issues and the dignity of man.
- **Manipulative (M).** Values higher status and recognition. May achieve goals through gamesmanship, persuasion, bribery, or official authority.
- **Conformist (C).** Low tolerance for ambiguity and different values. Attracted to rigidly defined roles, e.g., accounting, engineering, military. Tends to perpetuate the status quo. May be motivated by a cause, philosophy, or religion.
- **Egocentric (E).** Rugged individualism. Selfish, thoughtless, unscrupulous. Responds primarily to power.
- **Tribalistic (T).** Strongly influenced by tradition and the power exerted by the boss, tribal chieftain, policeman, school teacher, and other authority figures.

SOURCE: Adapted from M. Scott Myers and Susan S. Myers, "Adapting to the New Work Ethic," *Business Quarterly*, Winter 1973, p. 49.

## EXHIBIT 4–3
## Values Profiles Typical of Groups of Workers

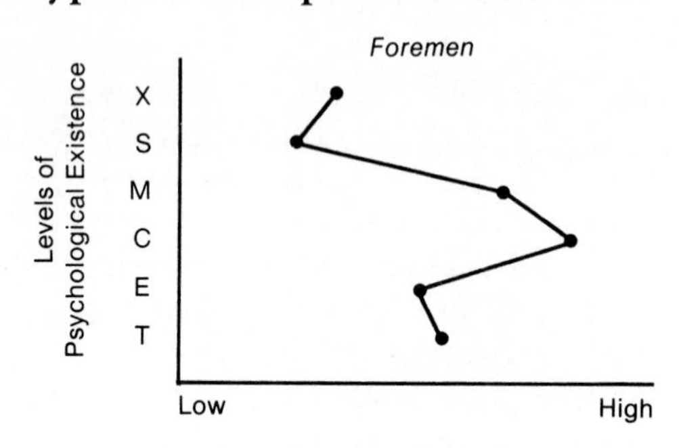


X = Existential
S = Sociocentric
M = Manipulative
C = Conformist
E = Egocentric
T = Tribalistic

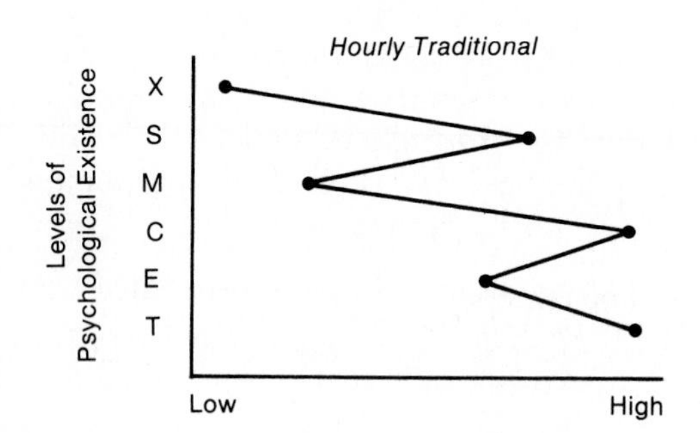


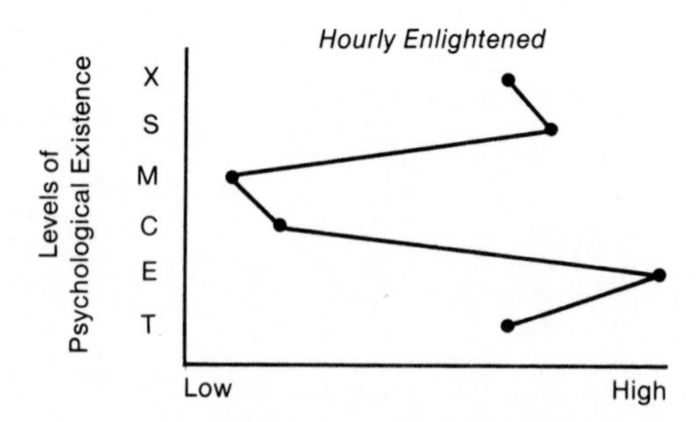

## EXHIBIT 4–4
## Results of 1977 Wage Survey

| Company | Straight Time Hourly Rate[a] | Cost of Living Allowance (COLA) |
|---|---|---|
| Bethoney | $5.47 | 1¢/hour for .4 increase in consumer price index, not to exceed 1¢ quarterly or 8¢ total for 3-year contract |
| Company A | 5.00 | No COLA |
| Company B | 7.05 | 1¢ for .5 increase |
| Company C | 7.90 | 1¢ for .4 increase, granted quarterly |
| Company D | 6.13 | No COLA |
| Company E | 7.09 | 1¢ for .3 increase, granted quarterly |

[a]Average wages for all hourly employees.

## EXHIBIT 4–5
## Strike Violence and Vandalism

*On July 20, 1977, the local paper reported:*

Fifty strikers, sweating in the sticky heat, had been blocking the gates to Bethoney's Plant C since 6:30 P.M. Farmington County sheriff's deputies stood quietly nearby or roamed the block in cruisers.

At 8:45 P.M. a line of pickup trucks and cars filled with company personnel turned and drove off, prevented by pickets from entering the plant.

Ten minutes later, a car drove up and stopped. Strikers surged around it, hitting the hood, occasionally kicking the doors, and shouting "Stop it there" and "You're not going in." The man inside, one of several Pinkerton guards hired by Bethoney to protect its plants, hesitated. Then he gassed the car and lurched forward, briefly pinning—but apparently not injuring—a half-dozen strikers between the car's grille and the gates.

As deputies ran forward, the surprised strikers pounded on the car. One kicked the car's side window, spraying shattered glass onto the street. Then, calmed by the deputies, the crowd parted and the car backed up and wheeled away.

*July 13, 1977: Bethoney Warehouse Blaze Under Investigation*

Farmington County sheriff's deputies are investigating a fire this morning which broke out in cartons in a warehouse at the Bethoney Plant C. A Bethoney official called it "arson."

**EXHIBIT 4–5 (*Continued*)**

The fire was reported at 3:15 A.M. and no damage was reported.

Russell Waters, manager of Bethoney employee relations, told the ____ News today that "there was no question in our minds" that arson was involved. "There was a break-in at our warehouse by an unknown individual who was seen fleeing from our warehouse after the fire was started."

"The company is simply trying to create an incident for us to react," responded union representative Richard Evans.

He said fires in exhaust ducts and fans are "a pretty common occurrence" and often not reported because they are extinguished by fire brigades comprised of hourly workers.

"I don't know how anybody could get in there," he said referring to the three Bethoney plants, which he said are surrounded by fences and have locked gates and security guards on the roofs.

## *August 18, 1977: Bethoney Claims "Saboteur" Cut Power to Plant*

A flash and a loud pop at 11:25 P.M. Wednesday and electrical power to about 2,500 customers, including the Bethoney Plant B, diminished.

Another flash and pop and the power was off.

"We intend to find the saboteur," said Russell Waters, Bethoney employee relations manager, about whoever opened a 138,000-volt power switch on ____ Street, cutting off the power for about 40 minutes.

Bethoney will offer "at least a $2,500 reward for information leading to the arrest and conviction of the saboteur," Waters said.

"It's hard to understand why anyone would risk their own well-being, inconvenience hundreds of friends and neighbors and cause hundreds of dollars in damage to Edison property," said ____, Farmington Edison district manager. Besides the obvious inconvenience of the power being off for about 40 minutes to over 2,000 homes, opening the power switch could also have injured or killed the person pulling the switch. "With that much voltage involved, if that wire falls, you're a dead pigeon," ____ explained.

Local 201 Vice President Bob Graham said, "We're peace-loving picketers. I don't know about any union people being involved. We're going to proceed as we have been, in a peaceful manner."

## EXHIBIT 4–6
## Strikebreakers

### *July 7, 1977*

As the strike by approximately 1,000 hourly workers at the three Bethoney plants in Farmington entered its seventh day, a company official said out-of-town workers may be brought in.

The official, Russell Waters, manager of Bethoney employee relations, added, "the company is also considering hiring permanent replacements."

He said, "In all likelihood, we will be receiving assistance from other Bethoney plants."

Bob Graham, vice president of Local 201 of the Glass Workers Federation, said comments and news given to this newspaper by Waters are "propaganda, news releases to excite the workers so they will want to buy a cheap contract.

"They're trying to get them (the workers) back to work under the present wages and break the strike," Graham said.

Today at approximately 10 A.M. the company began around-the-clock operation at Plant C with salaried employees. Plant B's Glass Department had been operated by salaried employees since the strike began at 12:01 A.M. last Friday.

A total of approximately 160 salaried Bethoney employees are now working at the three plants, including clean-up and security teams at each plant.

CASE 5

# THE COAL STRIKE OF 1977/1978 (A)(CONDENSED)

*Richard O. von Werssowetz*
*D. Quinn Mills*

On Wednesday, February 22, 1978, negotiators for the coal industry received word that the coal miners' union had rejected the industry's latest settlement plan. Leadership of the industry's negotiating team had recently moved to Nicholas Camicia, chairman of the Pittston Company (the largest independent coal company). Bruce Johnston, vice president of U.S. Steel, had led the industry bargaining group for the past month and still was an influential force. Now each of the members of the team considered what strategies to advocate that might win the contract improvements each thought were vital.

Negotiations had begun in October 1977. No agreement had been reached when the old contract had expired December 6, 1977 and the miners went on strike. The strike had now lasted 78 days. An agreement reached with the union's bargaining team in January 1978, had been rejected by the union's bargaining council. Recently, a smaller operator had settled independently of the industry association. Coal was in shortening supply and public attention was focused on the strike. President Carter had directed Secretary of Labor Marshall to personally intervene and there was intense political pressure to reach an agreement. Since the union had just rejected an industry offer to submit the dispute to binding arbitration, a new plan was needed.

## INDUSTRY BACKGROUND

Bituminous coal has provided a varying proportion of total U.S. energy consumption. Prior to 1900, coal made up as much as 90 percent of total U.S. energy. This proportion declined to 45 percent in the 1930s. After an increase to 52 percent during World War II, the increased availability of lower-priced oil and the switch of railroads to

---

This case was revised by Bert A. Spector, Research Associate, and E. Mary Lou Balbaky, Research Associate, under the direction of Professor D. Quinn Mills.

diesel locomotives dropped coal's share to 25 percent by the late 1960s. The United States' large coal reserves brought renewed interest in coal in the 1970s as the United States sought ways of reducing its dependence on imported oil (Exhibit 5–1).

Bituminous coal is of different grades. Much low-grade coal is burnt to create electrical power. But certain types of bituminous coal, called metallurgical coal, become raw material used in the smelting of iron ore. These coals are heated in the absence of air to form a hard, blocky substance called coke. Coke is required for use in blast furnaces. By-products of the coking process also provide raw materials used in making medicines, dyes, explosives, pesticides, and plastics. Total production of bituminous coal in the United States in 1977 was 688.6 million tons.

The most important coal-producing areas in the United States have been Pennsylvania, West Virginia, Kentucky, Tennessee, and Illinois. Recently, however, large coal fields in the Rocky Mountain States have been developed. (From 1973 to 1977 the number of mines in Colorado, Montana, North Dakota, Oklahoma, Texas, and Utah have roughly doubled. The number of mines in Arizona and Wyoming has tripled). Deposits of low-sulfur coal desirable in reducing air pollution are largely concentrated in the West, where many fields are yet to be developed. Metallurgical coals, in contrast, are mined primarily in the East.

Coal is obtained by either underground mining or by strip mining on the surface. Older fields primarily used the underground method which accounted for half of production as late as 1973. However, strip mining is especially important in the West, so that as Western fields have been developed strip mining has accounted for an increasing portion of total coal output (Exhibit 5–1).

Labor productivity in strip mines is far greater than in pit mines. U.S. Bureau of Mines statistics show that, on the average, strip mines are three times as productive as pit mines. The average production per man per day in 1977 was 8.7 tons for underground mines and 26.9 tons for surface mines. However, the range between the least and the most productive mines is far greater. It is alleged in the industry that the least productive pit mines produced only three tons per man-day worked while the most productive strip mines could produce over 150 tons per man-day. As an example, in 1976, Montana, with about 700 miners, produced 26 million tons of coal. West Virginia produced about 109 million tons with 56,000 miners.

Working conditions at a strip mine are similar to those at a highway construction site; conditions in a deep shaft mine are considerably different. Deep pit mining is often dangerous, unhealthy, and unpleasant work. Most miners are injured at some point in their careers. Most work considerable overtime in exhausting jobs. Black lung, a disease caused by inhalation of coal dust, can cause disablement.

*Industry Interest Groups*

Companies in the coal industry are widely diversified in size and type. Independent coal companies, many of them small operations, produce about half of the coal mined. The rest is produced by subsidiaries of noncoal companies, including some known as "captive suppliers" to coal users. Important groups were subsidiaries of oil and metal resource companies, steel companies, and electric utilities (Exhibit 5–2). Both steel and electric companies use coal as fuel and are heavily dependent on independent producers as well as their own captive mines.

Prior to the 1977 negotiations, different economic interests existed among three major ownership groups with different business motives. First, the independent coal operators were concerned primarily with the efficiency of mining, which was reflected in the price and profitability of coal. Second, the steel industry needed coal to make steel. Steel companies were less concerned with the price of coal in the coal market than with the impact of the price of coal on the price of steel. Their first concern was the price and profitability of steel in the steel market. Third, a group that had been called the "new breed," a group of natural resource-based companies, especially oil companies, although not new was rising in importance. This group was not as committed to coal, but would move their investment out of coal if returns were not adequate. These companie owned many of the undeveloped coal fields. They were interested primarily in alternative uses of capital.

*Industry Organization*

The Bituminous Coal Operators Association (BCOA) represented the industry in national collective bargaining. Within the BCOA attitudes towards labor relations were as diverse as the economic interests of the producers. The independent coal operators tended to view labor primarily as part of the production process. Few of these firms had labor relations professionals. The steel companies' need for cheap coal to help make U.S. steel competitive led them to press for low wage settlements. Nicknamed the "hardliners," they were influenced by their relationships with the sophisticated and fairly cooperative United Steelworkers who represented companies in the steel production process. The oil subsidiaries looked for return on investment. They considered themselves enlightened in industrial relations and had dubbed themselves the "liberals." BCOA's internal governance voting system based on tonnage produced, gave the few large companies, primarily hardliners, the greatest influence—despite the fact that the BCOA was overwhelmingly composed of small companies (Exhibit 5-3).

Despite these divergent interests, there were powerful incentives holding BCOA together. The companies preferred a united negotiation with the miners' union and had mutual interest in joint pension funding. And although not explicitly acknowledged, industry bargaining provided an industry forum for discussion of topics which otherwise might be prohibited by antitrust regulations. Nonetheless, many operators did not belong to BCOA. These nonmembers generally did not act as a group but acted independently.

## THE UNION

The United Mine Workers of America (UMW) represents employees in the coal industry. As an industrial rather than a craft union, it represents all workers at the mines, both skilled and unskilled. The UMW's membership in 1977 was approximately 150,000 active miners and 81,500 retired workers. UMW membership is now virtually confined to the coal industry.

### *Union History*

The hard, dangerous work in the deep pit mines where the UMW got its start bred tough, frequently violent men fiercely loyal to the union. Most miners lived in isolated communities where mining was a way of life. Early English immigrants to the coal fields, primarily Welsh and Scottish, brought a strong tradition of national unionism with them to the United States.

The UMW emerged from the merger of two early unions in 1890. Poor leadership and intense internal strife characterized its early years, but the union grew strong under the leadership of John L. Lewis. Lewis was president of the UMW from 1920 to 1959 and one of the most prominent men in the U.S. labor movement. Starting with World War I, years of often bloody organizing campaigns culminated in guarantee of the "right of labor to organize" included in President Franklin Roosevelt's National Recovery Act. In consequence, the UMW gained control of workers producing as much as 75 percent of the nation's coal. Membership soared to 515,000 in 1933.

World War II brought prosperity to the industry after the Great Depression. Lewis determined to win a $2 per day wage increase for miners. With a no-strike pledge, and during a period of governmentally imposed wage controls, Lewis resorted to a nationwide strike in 1943 at the height of World War II. Despite President Roosevelt's personal appeals to the miners to return to work and threats to draft the entire work force, the miners continued to strike. Federal courts ordered Lewis to sever communications with the union members. After settling the 8½-month battle the miners continued to refuse to return to work until the order was rescinded. The strike was successful in obtaining a substantial pay increase.

In the 1950s, competition from oil reduced the demand for coal. Production dropped from 631 million tons in 1947 to 392 million tons in 1954. Employment fell from 461,991 miners in 1942 to 169,400 in 1960. With this decline came a new era for the UMW and the coal industry.

In 1950 northern soft-coal operators, responsible for about 34 percent of industry production, formed the BCOA. In 1951 the first BCOA contract was signed. The Southern Coal Producers Association and Illinois Coal Operators Association joined in signing the pact simultaneously. The peaceful contract renewal had resulted from prior behind-the-scenes negotiations between industry leaders and Lewis. In fact, Lewis reportedly played an important role in establishing the BCOA.

The UMW's behavior during the 1950s demonstrated a concern for the problems of a declining industry. The union sought peaceful contract settlements and constant meetings with coal operators in order to sustain smooth, continuous production. The union also established stiff penalties for wildcat strikes. Union policy endorsed mechanization of coal production and the closing of smaller, inefficient mines even at the cost of higher unemployment. This policy was an effort to protect the industry from cheaper alternate energy sources.

Lewis retired in December 1959. In his 40 years of leadership, he had stamped union loyalty deep into the hearts of the miners. He left a legacy of union solidarity and absolute respect for a picket line.

### *The UMW Without John L. Lewis*

A contemporary of Lewis, Thomas Kennedy, was president for a brief period following Lewis's retirement. In 1963, the UMW presidency passed to W. A. "Tony" Boyle, picked as vice president and heir apparent by Lewis when he retired.

Boyle came from a career in the union Washington headquarters. Probably he did not know the miners well. Lacking the personal appeal of Lewis, Boyle resorted to other measures to retain his office. Union resources were used freely to promote Boyle and support his reelection campaigns. Dissident delegates in the 1964 and 1968 UMW national conventions were denied access to microphones. In December of 1969, Boyle engineered the murder of his political rival Joseph "Jock" Yablonski, a crime for which he has since been convicted. Yablonski had recently been defeated by Boyle in the UMW presidential election and was challenging the validity of that contest.

The recovery of the coal industry in the 1960s gave Boyle's administration an opportunity to press for contract improvements. Official UMW posture became increasingly militant. In 1968, contract negotiations brought on the first contract termination notice and first authorized national strike since 1952. The strike brought substantial gains in wages and fringe benefits. Contract negotiations in 1971 involving a 44-day strike brought further gains.

However, an increasing number of wildcat, or unauthorized strikes occurred during Boyle's presidency. Under Lewis, wildcat strikes had been a vehicle for promoting union policies. Under Boyle, they became a vehicle for the rank and file to express their discontent with union policies. A rebellious movement called "Miners for Democracy" pushed for improved mine safety and organized wildcat strikes for the settlement of local disputes.

Under pressure from the dissident movement, Secretary of Labor George Shultz decided to investigate the union. In May 1972, the U.S. District Court in Washington, D.C., declared the 1969 election void and ordered Boyle removed from office.

On December 22, 1972, Arnold Miller, the "Miners for Democracy" candidate, defeated Boyle in a hard-fought election. Miller's stated concept of union democracy was that all decisions should be made by the rank and file, free from any control, and should be implemented no matter how unreasonable.

In 1973 the union adopted a new constitution which contained numerous checks on the potential abuse of power. It guaranteed due process and the right of free speech to all UMW members.

A flood of new, young miners into the UMW had played an important role in the dramatic changes taking place. The rapid influx of returning Vietnam veterans, many of them political activists, dropped the average age of UMW members abruptly from the mid-50s to the mid-30s. Better educated than older miners, these new members demanded a more active role in decision making. Since earlier UMW leaders had discouraged the rise of rank and file leaders, few members had experience in managing the democratic process.

As a result of the changes in the union power structure and with the new procedures of the 1973 constitution, internal strife increased and the UMW became a chaotic world of bitter political struggles.

## THE GOVERNMENT

An important third participant in coal industry labor relations is the federal government, most importantly, the Federal Mediation and

Conciliation Service (FMCS), the Department of Labor, and the Office of the President of the United States.

The FMCS is an independent federal agency whose role is to reestablish and assist discussion between employers and employee representatives in the attempt to resolve labor relations disputes. The service is committed to facilitating the bargaining process and helping to achieve agreements. Wayne H. Horvitz, 56 years old, was appointed director of the FMCS by President Carter in May 1977. Prior to this appointment he had some 30 years of industrial relations experience, both in business and as a consultant. The FMCS director of mediation services was William P. Hobgood. Hobgood had participated in the 1974 UMW contract negotiations.

The Department of Labor is the principal federal agency responsible for helping the President to formulate and execute his labor policies. The Secretary of Labor in 1977, Ray Marshall, was appointed by President Carter after a career as professor of economics, most recently at the University of Texas in Austin. Marshall had little direct experience in collective bargaining. Marshall's record in 1977 as Secretary of Labor was acceptable to the unions generally. They felt affinity for his personal background of rural poverty.

Ultimately, severe national labor problems may involve the President of the United States. Presidential options for intervention in labor disputes include behind-the-scenes pressure, public pronouncements and pleas, use of court injunctions to stop strikes under the Taft-Hartley Act, and asking for the enactment of special legislation by the Congress. In some instances, simply implying that he would or would not use his powers to intervene could influence negotiations.

## THE CONTRACT

The contract between the UMW and the BCOA was complex. It had 30 major articles, covered 101 general job classifications and almost a thousand job titles. Compensation included wages and overtime premiums with cost-of-living adjustments (COLA) according to a formula tied to the Consumer Price Index.

Health and pension benefits were provided by a series of special trusts. The trusts were funded by contributions made by employers for each hour worked and for each ton of coal mined. Operators also made contributions to the trusts for each ton of coal used which had been mined by nonUMW workers.

Prior to the 1974 contract negotiations, all health and pension benefits were paid for by a single fund to which employers paid a royalty for each ton of coal produced. Strip mines produced far more coal per man-day than underground mines, yet employees of each type of mine drew equally on the benefits. This meant that strip mine operators were paying substantially more to cover each employee's benefits than underground operators. A dispute over this issue almost broke apart the BCOA.

As part of the 1974 negotiations, the employers developed a plan to restructure the trusts, which the union accepted. The 1950 Pension Trust would provide pensions for miners who retired prior to 1976. The 1950 Benefit Trust would provide health benefits to the same group. (About 82,000 miners and surviving widows were covered under these plans in 1977.) The 1950 trusts would be funded by royalty payments like the old funding method. Pension and health benefits for current miners and their families and miners who retired after 1976 would be funded by employer contributions made for each hour worked. These were the 1974 Pension Trust and 1974 Benefit Trust. Over a period of years the new funds would replace the old ones, with benefit costs being tied to employee hours worked.

The union constitution adopted under Miller also changed the way in which contracts would be negotiated by the union. Previously, demands were formulated in a policy committee under the total control of the International president. Now local unions would discuss their demands in detail and send representatives to a district conference. The district sent their proposed demands to the bargaining council, in which final demands for the national negotiations were formulated. The bargaining council was made up of elected representatives from the districts. Often, representatives simply pressed for demands reflecting the needs of their own district. Although the president of the UMW was responsible for negotiating the contract, the bargaining council had to approve it. Finally, the contract had to be ratified by vote of the rank and file before it could be signed by the union.

### *The 1974 Negotiations*

Events between September and December 1, 1974, when the first contract was negotiated under the new constitution raised many of the issues that were to influence the 1977/1978 negotiation process. The BCOA's stated major concern in the negotiation was to raise productivity, which had been declining for the last few years. Coal operators were prepared to yield a wide range of economic benefits with the condition that higher productivity be guaranteed. The operators considered government-mandated safety rules and wildcat strikes the cause of a 30 percent decline in productivity in underground mines since 1965.

The economic recovery of the industry which had started in the mid-1960s was accelerating in the 1970s. As the nation became increasingly concerned with developing a domestic energy supply, coal gained strategic importance as a major industrial fuel. The price of coal soared and coal company profits skyrocketed. However, although demand and prices showed an excellent rising trend, productivity did not. Productivity became the dark cloud on coal's future. The union's rank and file had responded to the new prosperity of the industry by becoming more militant in their demands.

Failure of the UMW negotiators and the BCOA to reach an agreement resulted in a nationwide coal strike which began on November 9, 1974. Ultimately, the parties agreed to a three-year contract which provided an economic package equaling an effective 49.7 percent increase in the miners' income, paid sick leave, improved safety standards, provisions for increased job security, and improved disability benefits. UMW negotiators submitted the proposal contract to the bargaining council for ratification on November 15. The bargaining council refused to ratify the contract.

Union negotiators returned to the table demanding higher pay, additional vacation, and reduced working hours. Faced with the intervention of the Federal Mediation and Conciliation Service, on November 23 the BCOA acceded to union demands for an improvement in the contract. When the second settlement was presented to the bargaining council on the morning of November 26, it was also rejected. However, that afternoon the council reversed its position and ratified the pact. Between November 27 and 30, the Miller administration conducted an extensive campaign to convince the rank and file to ratify the pact. On December 1 the contract was approved.

### *The Stage for Conflict*

Two major flaws in the 1974 contract became apparent in the summer of 1975. These concerned the grievance and arbitration procedure and the method of funding for the Pension and Benefit trusts.

The desire to eliminate wildcat strikes and resulting loss in production led to the inclusion in the 1974 agreement of a formal three-step grievance procedure followed by arbitration to resolve disputes. An arbitration review board was created as a level of final appeal of arbitration rulings.

This method of handling disputes was new to the coal industry. It required that miners continue working while resolution of a complaint was handled formally. Many coal operators refused to allow local managements to resolve grievances at the mine site. Instead, grievances were referred to higher levels of management for resolution. The union claimed this was "bureaucratizing" the grievance system. Some companies began to send every complaint through the time-consuming arbitration process. All levels of the grievance process became overwhelmed by the workload. The backlog of undecided cases grew. The miners lost confidence in the timeliness and even in the honesty of the process.

Dissatisfaction with the grievance procedure led to hundreds of wildcat strikes in 1975 and 1976. Mine operators turned to federal courts to obtain back-to-work orders enforcing the contract. Where violations occurred, fines and jail terms were assessed against striking miners. This created more ill-will and more "wildcats."

In Appalachia, a day seldom passed without a strike. The BCOA estimated that during the three-year term of the contract member companies suffered over 8,900 illegal wildcat strikes resulting in a loss of over 45 million man-hours of work and over 62 million tons lost production of coal.

Because the funding mechanisms for the trusts depended on hours worked and tons of coal mined, the plague of wildcat strikes was financially disastrous. Coupled with rapid inflation in medical costs and a crucial underestimation in the 1974 agreement of the number of eligible beneficiaries, the funds were on the brink of insolvency.

The financial plight of the trusts created serious problems for the miners. First, there was concern for the continuation of pension benefits provided under the trusts (and pensioners still voted in union elections). Second, the continued operation of the health insurance plan was jeopardized. The UMW health plan provided payment for full hospital and family medical care. The plan virtually supported medical clinics in much of the coal-mining region that provided the only care available in many areas. Monthly retainers paid to the clinics by the health plan accounted for up to 70 percent of their total revenues.

### *The Wildcat Strike in the Summer of 1977*

On June 20, 1977 the financial crisis came to a head. The trustees of the benefit trusts announced that starting July 1, miners would have to pay the first 40 percent of their doctor bills and the first $250 of hospital bills up to a maximum of $500 per family.

These reductions in financial coverage did not come without warning. Earlier crises in May and October 1976 had been averted only when the operators and the unions agreed to reallocate payments among the trusts. (Because the 1974 Pension Trust had a $310 million reserve, it could continue pension payments even if current payments due to the trust were diverted to the other trusts.) At that time the trustees calculated that wildcat strikes had reduced expected payments $65 million since the 1974 agreement. (Payments were made at $1.54 per hour plus $.82 per ton.) Harsh weather had cost $20 million more.

Now the operators refused to reallocate payments once again. They felt that to do so would expose them to additional liabilities under the Employees Retirement Income Security Act of 1974 (ERISA). As it stood, unfunded liabilities for past service were $4.0 billion. This enormous liability was due to the previous practice of funding only interest on the unfunded amount. (Prior to ERISA, current funding of such plans could be lessened by "borrowing" payments due to pay for future benefits and paying only "interest" on the unpaid amount to the funds. As long as current payments kept pace with current benefit needs, the principal would never need to be paid. The union had encouraged the practice as a means of winning larger benefits from the operators.) Should the plans be forced to terminate, up to 15 percent of the assets of the employers were subject to unfunded liabilities for each of the two Pension Trusts. The operators also felt strongly that to reallocate once again would be to condone the wildcat strikes.

Miller was incensed by this refusal. He contended that other reasons were more important than wildcat strikes in contributing to the problems of the trusts. He charged that the industry had failed to open new mines that had been contemplated during the 1974 negotiations. Furthermore, the wild inflation in medical costs could not have been foreseen. He pledged that he would win back from the companies and return with interest every single dollar coal miners were forced to pay. By June 24, wildcat strikes over the medical cutbacks had begun.

Meanwhile, the union was conducting a presidential election. On July 2, unofficial results showed that Miller had won the election. But his margin of victory was based largely on pensioners' votes and he had won with only 40 percent of the vote in a three-way contest.

After this narrow victory, Miller called a meeting on July 18 with the BCOA to reopen the contract. Joseph P. Brennan, president of the BCOA, agreed to meet but rejected the demand to reopen the benefits issue. Following this rejection, Miller considered a "ten-day memorial holiday" to protest the cutbacks. Some miners believed a strike had been called and went out. Despite rejection of the strike by vote of the UMW Executive Board and pleas by union officials, the strike spread.

Events unfolded quickly on many fronts. Over a thousand miners marched on Washington, D.C., to protest the cutbacks and to seek a promise from Labor Secretary Marshall to investigate. Lee Roy Patterson filed an official election protest to the Labor Secretary seeking to overturn Miller's election. As the strikes entered the eighth week, Marshall met with Miller and Brennan to seek a solution. (Horvitz and the FMCS continued to work actively behind the scenes to help effect an end to the strikes.) Marshall noted in a speech in West Virginia that since 1974, surface mines had produced over 50 percent of the domestic coal supply. Therefore, he argued, the wildcats in the east were no serious threat to the economy or energy supplies. Members of the UMW District 17, covering West Virginia, the largest UMW district with almost one-third of the UMW membership and Miller's home district, demanded Miller's resignation.

This latest crisis served to highlight Miller's ineffectiveness as a leader. Originally a compromise candidate, he was not articulate and had little patience. He suffered from black lung disease and hypertension. For days on end his own aides had no idea of where he was. He was suspicious of his own staff, changed locks frequently, and carried a gun for protection on his trips to West Virginia. He was the son of a union coal miner. He had been in the mines since he left school after the ninth grade at age 16, with a break for service in World War II. A personal back-to-work plea by Miller on West Virginia television during the 1977 wildcats was so rambling and ineffective that the strikes got worse after his appearance.

Finally, the trustees were able to negotiate a line of credit based on monthly fund payments receivable to assure continued payment of pensions. By the end of August, most miners were back to work.

### *A Weakening UMW*

Other problems beset the UMW as it prepared for the new contract negotiations. Its power was weakening by challenges across the country.

In the West, the International Union of Operating Engineers (IUOE) was agressively competing to represent employees at the strip mines and was winning a good share of representation elections. There were mines controlled by electrical workers; others by the independent Progressive Mine Workers Union; and, lastly, a substantial nonunion segment. While western coal accounted for 10 percent of U.S. coal production in 1975, government projections predicted the northern plains region alone providing 26 percent by 1985. The northern plains was the region in which the UMW had had the most trouble organizing. The UMW believed it represented about one-third of the western workers.

Although the availability of non-UMW western coal would affect the impact of a national UMW strike, little western coal could actually be used to buffer an eastern strike because of transportation problems. But the UMW had problems in its own backyard. There were large amounts of nonunion coal available in Appalachia. In recent years, the UMW share of coal production had fallen in Ohio from 75 percent to 50 percent, in Pennsylvania from 72 percent to 60 percent, and in Kentucky from 52 percent to 42 percent. In Tennessee the UMW represented only 2 of 60 deep mines yielding only 13 percent of production.

Thus, despite intense organizing efforts, the UMW was slowly losing its grasp on coal.

## SIGNIFICANT ISSUES FOR 1977 NEGOTIATIONS

Going into national contract negotiations on the heels of the wildcat strikes of the summer of 1977 served to highlight the issues that had to be faced. Among the major issues were:

Restoration of Benefits. The UMW's first priority was to restore the benefits which had been reduced. The UMW also sought to have employers repay the miners for the out-of-pocket expenses they had incurred and guarantee future benefits. In addition to the value of the benefits to UMW members, benefits were a major organizing weapon which the UMW used in many campaigns.

Stability. The operators' overriding goal was for a stable labor force and control on wildcats and absenteeism. Strikes and unexcused absences totaled 17.9 percent of all days that BCOA mines were available for work in 1976, a lost time rate ten times the average for all industries. But when one or two men were absent on a section (the mine work group), productivity plummeted.

In 1974, the employers had given a 54 percent compensation settlement in return, it thought, for stability measures that were not working. The employers were determined that something successful be done in 1977. They suggested a solution which included some type of penalties for wildcats, a no-strike clause "with teeth in it," a more liberal interpretation of safety rules, and the right of each company to install incentive/bonus plans to increase productivity.

Royalites on Nonunion Coal. BCOA members were required to pay royalties to the trusts on nonunion coal they bought. U.S Steel especially opposed this provision and sought to have it removed.

Wages. The UMW planned to seek wage increases from $64 to $100 daily and increased paid time off. On the BCOA side, the operators wanted elimination of the cost-of-living allowance (COLA), a provision the UMW had won in 1974.

Equalization of Pensions. Miners who retired prior to 1976 received $225 per month, miners who retired since 1976 received $400. Many miners felt this was unjust discrimination and wanted pensions equalized.

RESTRICTIONS ON OVERTIME. Miners were subject to compulsory overtime and could be forced to work six days per week. Increased absenteeism was one measure of the dissatisfaction with this rule. Many miners wanted this provision dropped, or wanted a work week of only four days.

## THE NEGOTIATION

### *Early Talks*

With the contract due to expire December 6, 1977, contract talks began on October 6 in Washington, D.C. The UMW negotiating team was headed by Arnold Miller and the BCOA team by BCOA President Joseph P. Brennan. The BCOA presented a printed pamphlet entitled "Will the United Mine Workers of America Play a Major Role in Coal's Future?" This paper summarized many problems facing the UMW segment of the industry. It challenged the UMW to help solve the problems together with the industry to permit future growth. It suggested that the alternative was the "decline and possible extinction of the UMW as a force in the national collective bargaining."

The UMW did not appear to be prepared to begin negotiations and another meeting was scheduled for October 13. However, the UMW did release a summary of contract demands to the press following the meeting.

During the next few meeting, the major UMW demands included a wage increase to $100 daily, added vacation time, the right to strike over local grievances, and restoration and guarantee of the health benefits which had been reduced. Counterproposals by the BCOA emphasized the need to promote labor stability and increase productivity. The operators wanted a provision that would fine those engaged in wildcat walkouts. The cash penalty would be used to replenish the health and benefit programs. In addition, the BCOA demanded elimination of COLA.

In mid-October, the trusts announced that a December strike would cause an immediate halt to all medical and health benefits and cancellation of pensions January 1.

On October 27, Miller suspended negotiations and accused the BCOA of refusing to discuss the union health and benefit proposals. The BCOA responded by stating that it would serve no meaningful purpose to isolate one problem. The BCOA felt that wildcat strikes, absenteeism, and declining productivity were equally as important.

At this time government interest, which had seemed to cool after an active role in settling the summer wildcats, became more evident.

Secretary of Labor Marshall stated that he was less optimistic about the possibility of averting a strike in December, but that such a strike would not be a serious economic blow. He said that the administration intended to follow a policy of nonintervention. He felt that a coal strike would not be considered a national emergency under provisions of the Taft-Hartley Act.

Wayne Horvitz of the FMCS had discovered that both the BCOA and UMW were very dissatisfied with the government's intervention in the 1974 bargaining when he had taken over as director in May. As a result, he had embarked on a program of "fence mending" to try to develop contacts and confidence among the involved parties with limited success. He had more successfully advocated an agreement not to intervene in the negotiations or possible strike with President Carter and Secretary Marshall.

*November Negotiations*

As formal talks resumed November 8, the BCOA warned that the union must back away from the demand that union locals be given the right to strike over local issues or else they wouldn't be able to meet the December 6 strike deadline. They emphasized that the BCOA had proposals on the table to provide a self-enforcing mechanism for stopping wildcat strikes. As the talks approached the effective deadline of November 25 (due to the ten-day minimum time for a ratification vote), Miller responded by accusing the industry of refusing to bargain in good faith. He said he was convinced that the industry wanted a strike. He predicted that if there were a strike that it would be "long and bitter."

On November 21, the UMW released an economic report to support its position. An analysis of labor costs applied the 1969 percentage of labor cost per dollar of sales (53.5 percent) to the 1977 price of coal per ton ($24.24) and production of coal per hour (1.54 tons/hour) to get an implied "equivalent" labor rate of $19.97 versus the actual 1977 labor rate of $13.08 per hour (Exhibit 5-4). Using this logic it contended that labor costs had fallen 35 percent since 1969, while the price of coal had risen more than 475 percent (see "Value/Average Per Ton," Exhibit 5-1).

Citing a Government Accounting Office (GAO) report naming coal mining as "the most dangerous occupation in the U.S.," the union contended that the combination of job hazards and industry profits justified a sizable boost in salaries, above workers in other industries. The UMW report contended that federal safety and health requirements were a much greater factor in declining productivity than wildcat strikes and were justified to limit the hazards of coal mining. It further noted that despite the substantial hikes in 1974, the general wage increases for general labor in the coal industry between 1957 and 1977 of 160 percent were "dwarfed" by those received by others: 266 percent for auto workers, 234 percent for steelworkers, and 201 percent for rubber workers.

Talks broke down on November 25. Miller charged that during the two-hour Friday meeting "the BCOA repeatedly threatened the UMWA [UMW], called it 'weak and divided' and stated the UMWA was 'on probation' and 'not the only game in town'." A strike was scheduled to begin at 12:01 A.M. December 6.

### *FMCS Enters as the Strike Begins*

On Sunday, November 27, the FMCS announced that the UMW and BCOA had agreed to resume talks November 29. The announcement stated: "It is the first time in this year's talks that the FMCS has become directly involved in the negotiations." With the aid of the FMCS, the BCOA accepted Harry Huge, not a union member but a Washington lawyer and recently resigned fund trustee, as part of the UMW negotiating team. He had a history of fighting for the miners, was articulate, and fully understood the crucial issues surrounding the funds' financial condition.

In separate meetings with the negotiators, Wayne Horvitz declared his intention "to remain personally involved in efforts to bring the parties back to the bargaining table." Attempts to get a contract extension to avoid the strike were rejected.

In an effort to resume fact-to-face negotiations, both parties agreed to FMCS's proposal to reduce the sizes of their respective bargaining teams. On December 5, the teams met again without UMW President Miller or BCOA President Brennan. Newspaper reports stated Miller had been edged out by all parties. He was described as "slow to grasp technical issues" and "unpredictable." Miller was "stunned and personally insulted" by the article. In any case, Harry Huge became the de facto lead negotiator for the UMW.

Brennan still led the BCOA although many in the industry felt he was "too soft" and indecisive. Even though Brennan had formerly been Research director for the UMW prior to joining the staff of the BCOA, he seemed to be unable to perceive the political situation in the union. By attempting to keep all members of the BCOA happy despite the evident factionalism he seemed unable to take the initiative.

### *Western Settlement*

As the workers went out on strike and negotiations prepared to resume, the UMW announced contract settlements concluded under separate negotiations with six western producers. The nonstriking workers would receive hourly wage hikes of 34 percent over the next 40 months. Under the western settlements comprehensive health coverage and pension benefits would be provided on an independent basis, separate from the existing UMW plans. Pensions for miners retired before 1974 would be raised from $250 to $300 per month. These agreements were based on the grounds that separate programs could be established at costs far below those paid to existing programs primarily covering the East.

Each company's settlement was slightly different because renewal of a multiemployer pact had been abandoned in favor of separate contracts with each company. Each settlement did include six guaranteed semiannual COLAs of $.20 per hour.

*Renewed Negotiations*

During the early negotiations, the BCOA's approach to the stability issue heavily relied on their idea of heavy penalties for those who initiated and participated in wildcat strikes. The union negotiators acknowledged that some method had to be found to handle the problem if they were to restore the health of the funds. However, they could not accept the BCOA idea of automatic discharge for those who initiated wildcats. And because of the tradition of violence in the coal fields which strongly influenced conformity, the UMW could not agree to discipline for those workers who "cooperated" in wildcat strikes.

Discussions continued haltingly through mid-December, trying to reach compromises on key issues. While the industry wanted an unconditional and absolute no-strike clause, the union, particularly Miller, supported a "limited right to strike." The UMW reasoned that the union could never completely prevent miners from walking out if they had a "beef" and that there would always be "pistols" eager to create real or imaginary problems. Therefore, Miller proposed a voting system that would provide a cooling-off period before the miners at the site voted. He believed that seven or eight out of ten times there would be a no-strike result. This would eliminate associated sympathy strikes and still leave the grievance procedure in place to settle the dispute.

Management, particularly steel, were appalled by this idea. Bill Miller of U.S. Steel flatly rejected this idea stating that he would never be able to face the United Steel Workers if the BCOA gave the UMW such a limited right to strike. The union responded that they couldn't possibly guarantee any absolute strike ban and they couldn't give into such a demand anyway for political reasons.

After many discussions around this impasse, the idea of a financial penalty for wildcat strikes resurfaced. The BCOA's original proposals in October 1977 had included this idea. They had suggested that "any employee absent from work because of an unauthorized work stoppage must repay the amount of the loss sustained by the programs as a result of his individual absence." This idea provided an area of compromise between the parties. The penalty would fine strikers engaging in wildcats and thereby, theoretically, discourage strikes. Progress seemed to finally begin.

As the negotiation break at Christmas approached, it appeared that most of the concepts needed for an acceptable package had been put together. The subcommittee on grievance/arbitration had developed adequate procedural changes. The absenteeism committee had negotiated a uniform national program. The whole group had agreed on a revised penalty clause for wildcats in return for an industry guarantee of a fixed contribution rate to the funds. Progress was avidly reported in the press based on the fact that William Hobgood of the FMCS was seen leaving the negotiation room whistling!

Leaked prematurely and incorrectly publicized by the press, the penalty concept caused mounting tension among the rank and file. There appeared to be two reasons why the concept could not be sold. First, the miners did not realize there had been a trade-off winning guaranteed financing of the funds for the first time in history. Second, the miners who understood they got a guarantee felt they were not getting anything new. After all, John L. Lewis had told them that the funds were "guaranteed" when they were set up 25 years ago.

### *Rod Hills Moves to Lead BCOA Negotiators*

When negotiations recessed December 23 for the holidays, the carefully developed concepts and the possibility of a contract once again appeared in serious trouble. Rod Hills, a former labor lawyer and arbitrator and ex-chairman of the Securities and Exchange Commission, as well as the new chairman of Peabody Coal Company, now moved to take a creative leadership role. Peabody, the nation's largest producer, was losing $1 million a day because of the strike and Hills badly wanted to settle.

During the recess, Hills arranged an informal meeting with Hartman, Horvitz, Huge, and Arnold Miller to consider other options and alternatives that might provide a compromise settlement. By the end of this meeting, a contract had virtually been put together which could be introduced into the formal negotiations. The key compromise was Miller's dropping the limited right-to-strike language and Hills' agreement to drop the absolute no-strike demand. Both sides accepted a plan which would include a fine to be paid by wildcat strikers. The money paid would go to the union trusts and not to the companies.

As negotiations resumed December 30, however, Miller would not be held to the informal agreement. Industry negotiators walked out for the first time since negotiations began October 6, claiming that the union had reneged on their agreement.

Talks resumed January 8, 1978 at the headquarters of the FMCS. The federal mediators had suggested moving the talks from the sixth-floor suite at the Capital Hilton to give negotiators more privacy and isolate them from reporters.

Negotiations broke down again January 17, generating predictions that the 59-day record for a UMW strike against the BCOA would be broken February 4.

Intense discussions over the weekend starting January 21 brought the parties to agreement. The outline required miners who engaged in unauthorized strikes to reimburse the funds for resulting income losses; if an arbitrator determined that an unauthorized strike was caused by the employer, the employer would be liable for the losses. The proposal also included guaranteed payments to the funds and a wage increase of $1.53 per hour over 40 months.

### *Union Bargaining Team Rejects Huge's Contract Proposal*

The proposal was presented to the full union bargaining team late January 23. The agreement had primarily been negotiated by Huge who thought he was acting with the concurrence of the entire union bargaining team. As it turned out, he was not and the team rejected the proposal. Whether to "punish" or embarrass Huge, or simply to reassert itself, the union team then presented a set of demands, which had already been discussed, to the BCOA in the early hours of Wednesday, January 24. The BCOA team felt insulted and decided to walk out. The talks collapsed.

Negotiations were now conducted at a distance. FMCS representatives shuttled between the groups. By February 2, Horvitz reported that after 14 hours of bargaining the issues had "narrowed significantly." Miller summoned the UMW's 39-member bargaining council to Washington for a meeting scheduled February 3. At the urging of Horvitz, President Carter requested that the meeting be postponed to allow more time to settle the few remaining differences at the bargaining table. The meeting of the bargaining council was rescheduled for February 7.

Arnold Miller had returned to his Charleston, West Virginia home for the weekend, so Brennan also stayed away while other negotiators met. Thus, negotiations continued without the presence of Miller or Brennan.

### *Negotiating Teams Agree to a Tentative Contract*

On February 6, Miller and Horvitz announced that the UMW and BCOA had come to terms on a three-year contract. Miller issued a statement saying:

> I am very happy with the tentative agreement we have reached today with BCOA. It is by far the best agreement negotiated in any major industry in the past two years. . . . The total package represents an increase of nearly 37 percent over the present level of wages and fringes. The health benefits program will be guaranteed for all active and retired members and their families. Pension benefits are restored and approved.
>
> In the interests of our members who have suffered so much during this long strike, I hope this excellent agreement is approved by the bargaining council and ratified by our membership.

An 18-page summary of the proposed contract was presented to the bargaining council February 7. members of the council met throughout the day and voted to defer their decision until they could study the full text of the agreement. One of the major concerns of many council members was the impact of the labor stability clause. Some council members were skeptical as to whether any contract that penalized miners who refused to cross picket lines would have any chance of approval by the membership. Yet the bans on participation in wildcat or sympathy strikes would require miners to cross picket lines set up by those who chose to ignore or disobey the bans.

Council members were also concerned over the settlement which would raise the wage of the average miner to about $84 a day. Many council members felt this would still leave them behind workers in other industries such as automobile and steel manufacturing. Some indicated they were expecting a figure much closer to the union's initial demand of $100 a day.

As news of the proposed settlement spread, many miners were upset by other concessions given to management. The operators won the right to change shift starting times, to mine coal on Sundays, and to implement a 30-day probationary period for new employees. The miners also would give up the cost-of-living adjustments and allowed individual company insurance plans. A contract provision that allowed miners to refuse to work in a case of "imminent danger" was modified. In the opinion of a local union president in Illinois, "All we're doing is going backward."

On February 10, several hundred angry miners demonstrated at the UMW headquarters in Washington to protest the tentative contract. The miners took over the first three floors of the building just prior to the scheduled meeting of the bargaining council. The council was unable to vote on the proposed agreement because Miller refused to attend while the miners protested. He accused the demonstrators of obstructing the union's constitutional process through "intimidation and threats of violence." He described the demonstrators as a "small irresponsible group."

Miller also told reporters that his life had been threatened and that he now carried a pistol in case he needed to defend himself. He added that he had received information that someone was going to hire a professional to kill him.

*Bargaining Council Rejects Contract Proposal*

On February 12, the bargaining council formally rejected the proposed contract by a vote of 30 to 6, with 3 abstentions. BCOA President Brennan said he was "appalled" at the council's rejection, which he said would have made coal miners the highest paid workers in any industry. Arnold Miller, interviewed on national television said:

> I think 90 percent of our workers want to work and they would have accepted this contract. If the membership had given an opportunity to accept or reject the contract I would have felt better about it.

When asked about the possibility of a back-to-work court order, Miller also indicated that he had been opposed to the Taft-Hartley law since its enactment and added that there was a "strong possibility" that the miners would ignore any government order to return to work. Some council members joined in demands from a number of district councils that Miller resign.

President Carter instructed Labor Secretary Marshall to become personally involved in the negotiations. President Carter also made moves to alleviate hardships caused by the strike in several mideastern states. These included development of plans to ship coal into areas where shortages occurred and transfers of electrical power to affected areas. Carter also relaxed federal air quality standards to permit utilities to burn high-sulfur coal. Administration spokesmen said they did not foresee a national emergency developing which would cause Carter to exercise his authority under the Taft-Hartley Act to seek an injunction ordering the miners back to work.

Marshall held a rapid series of separate meetings with representatives of the union and BCOA. Later on February 14, president Carter, in a televised announcement, asked negotiators to move their contract talks to the White House as "a final opportunity for the bargaining process to work." Officials of the BCOA first refused, expressing their pique at learning of the request "via television." The BCOA argued that collective bargaining had succeeded, but the agreement had been undercut by internal union problems.

### *Johnston Assumes Leadership of BCOA Negotiating Team*

Several changes in the negotiating teams took place at this time. For the BCOA, Bruce Johnston, vice president of U.S. Steel, and Bobby Ray Brown, president of Consolidation Coal (owned by Continental Oil), assumed leadership. Both were considered to be part of the hard-line faction within the BCOA. For the UMW, three new members were added to the negotiating team. All three were members of the bargaining council which had rejected the first contract agreement. Both parties finally agreed to a meeting. President Carter met with negotiators for about five minutes on the evening of February 15 at the White House. After about an hour and a half, Marshall moved negotiations to the Labor Department where they continued until 1 A.M. Marshall set a deadline of 48 hours for reaching agreement before resorting to some other, unnamed measures.

By Saturday morning, the BCOA had agreed to surrender the wildcat penalty provision, add a COLA in the second and third years, give up starting-time flexibilities which had been won in the first agreement and eliminate a dual seniority system created by provisions in the new strip-mining bill. In return, it also removed guarantees on the 1950 Benefit Trust.

The union either wanted or had been led to believe it had won another ten cents per hour the first year, wanted to scrap incentive provisions and insisted on guarantee of medical benefits. The many late night meetings over the previous days may have contributed to this confusion. The February 18 vote of the bargaining council was to reject the latest proposal, 37 to 0.

Marshall informed Carter that the union had rejected the companies' final offer. Some observers thought he acted too hastily. Because of his inexperience in collective bargaining, they felt, Marshall thought the latest BCOA offer was final. The BCOA said privately that it was ready to go on talking.

The next day, Carter met with Marshall, Secretary of Energy James Schlesinger, and other advisors to discuss ways of ending the coal strike. The three options discussed were use of a Taft-Hartley back-to-work injunction, seizure of the mines, and imposition of compulsory arbitration. The last two options would require congressional approval (during a time of intense debate over ratification of the Panama Canal Treaty). It was reported that Marshall favored seizure of the mines as the most neutral act. Other questioned that contention, believing that since seizure must impose some set of terms, it could not be neutral.

### *Pittsburg and Midway Settlement*

Several weeks prior to this time, Horvitz had Hobgood quietly approach UMW officials about conducting a separate negotiation with non-BCOA coal operators. After the latest contract rejection a UMW group led by Kenneth Dawes and including Tom Gaston agreed. Negotiations began with Pittsburg and Midway Company (P&M), a Gulf Oil subsidiary with operations centering in Gaston's western Kentucky district. Neither Arnold Miller nor Labor Secretary Marshall were kept abreast of these negotiations.

After a weekend of negotiations, an agreement was completed Sunday. By Monday night, February 20, Dawes had mustered enough political influence to obtain bargaining council approval of the P&M agreement, 25 to 13.

The major modifications to the rejected contract made in the P&M agreement were: a work stability clause which only penalized the instigators of wildcat strikes, removal of work incentives, reinstatement of COLA (netting these out of scheduled increases), continued prohibition of probationary periods for new miners and also of Sunday work, continued royalty payments for use of nonunion coal, and agreement to meet the BCOA's final settlement on benefit and pension funds. An additional five cents per hour was added to the wage settlement, resulting in a total of $2.40 an hour added over three years.

Some members of the BCOA balked at suggestions that the P&M settlement might be used as a pattern for their own agreement. One chief executive of a large BCOA member stated:

> Here's this silly little company that mines only 4 million tons a year, and in order to get a break in the market, they undercut us like this. I'd leave the BCOA before we'd agree to this deal.

### *Camicia New Leader of BCOA Team*

On Tuesday, February 21, the BCOA announced it had agreed to resume bargaining with the union. Johnston's influence over the industry group faded as Nicholas Camicia, who had been the principal BCOA negotiator in the 1974 contract discussions, now became the informal chairman of the BCOA negotiating team. Some industry leaders felt Johnston had taken intransigent positions which had been major obstacles to reaching agreement. Camicia was chairman of the Pittston Company, the largest independent coal producer. He had once been a West Virginia coal miner himself.

Late Tuesday, the BCOA suggested that both parties agree to voluntary binding arbitration. Under this plan, the miners would return to work immediately on the basis that both parties would agree to accept the award of arbitrators.

Kenneth Dawes of the UMW negotiating team complained that such an approach would take away the right of the UMW members to ratify the final agreement. He condemned the industry for using tactics designed to destroy the collective bargaining relationship and the union itself. (Some observers believed the BCOA call for binding arbitration was really designed to prevent Marshall from declaring a bargaining impasse. In theory, such a declaration might provide the basis for individual companies to leave the BCOA effort and begin negotiations on their own.)

Marshall warned that the administration must intervene by the week's end in the absence of a negotiated settlement, saying "We can't let it go on forever. . . . We must go on to our next step." President Carter continued a series of meetings with congressional leaders and other government officials to discuss ways of ending the strike.

On February 27, the bargaining council rejected the offer for binding arbitration and voted 25 to 13 to submit the terms of the P&M settlement to the BCOA as its "bottom-line offer." The council added that it would allow the P&M agreement to be used as a basis for settlement between individual companies and local UMW affiliates. The BCOA rejected this as the basis of renewed negotiations. When Marshall requested that face-to-face negotiations be resumed, the BCOA refused to participate. The BCOA's reason for refusing was that the UMW was standing "inflexibly" on the P&M terms.

**EXHIBIT 5–1**
**Growth of the Bituminous Coal Mining Industry in the United States**

| Year | Production[b] | Value[a] | | Men Employed | No. Mines | Average No. Days Worked | Net Tons Per Man | | Percentage of Total Production | |
|---|---|---|---|---|---|---|---|---|---|---|
| | | *Total* | *Average Per Ton* | | | | *Per Day* | *Per Year* | *Surface Mined* | *Mined Underground* |
| 1950 | 516,311,053 | 2,500,373,779 | 4.84 | 415,582 | 9,429 | 183 | 6.77 | 1,239 | 23.9 | 76.1 |
| 1951 | 533,664,732 | 2,626,030,137 | 4.92 | 372,897 | 8,009 | 203 | 7.04 | 1,429 | 22.0 | 78.0 |
| 1952 | 466,840,782 | 2,289,180,401 | 4.90 | 335,217 | 7,275 | 180 | 7.47 | 1,389 | 23.6 | 76.4 |
| 1953 | 457,290,449 | 2,247,828,694 | 4.92 | 293,106 | 6,671 | 191 | 8.17 | 1,560 | 23.6 | 76.4 |
| 1954 | 391,706,300 | 1,769,619,723 | 4.52 | 227,397 | 6,130 | 182 | 9.47 | 1,724 | 26.2 | 73.8 |
| 1955 | 464,633,408 | 2,092,382,737 | 4.50 | 225,093 | 7,856 | 210 | 9.84 | 2,064 | 26.1 | 73.9 |
| 1956 | 500,874,077 | 2,412,004,151 | 4.82 | 228,163 | 8,520 | 214 | 10.28 | 2,195 | 27.0 | 73.0 |
| 1957 | 492,703,916 | 2,508,314,127 | 5.08 | 228,635 | 8,539 | 203 | 10.59 | 2,155 | 26.8 | 73.2 |
| 1958 | 410,445,547 | 1,996,281,274 | 4.86 | 197,402 | 8,264 | 184 | 11.33 | 2,079 | 30.1 | 69.9 |
| 1959 | 412,027,502 | 1,965,606,901 | 4.77 | 179,636 | 7,719 | 188 | 12.22 | 2,294 | 31.2 | 68.8 |

| | | | | | | | | | | |
|---|---|---|---|---|---|---|---|---|---|---|
| 1960 | 415,512,347 | 1,950,425,049 | 4.69 | 169,400 | 7,865 | 191 | 12.83 | 2,453 | 31.4 | 68.6 |
| 1961 | 402,976,802 | 1,844,562,662 | 4.58 | 150,474 | 7,648 | 193 | 13.87 | 2,678 | 32.3 | 67.7 |
| 1962 | 422,149,325 | 1,891,554,474 | 4.48 | 143,822 | 7,740 | 199 | 14.72 | 2,935 | 33.4 | 66.6 |
| 1963 | 458,928,175 | 2,013,309,368 | 4.39 | 141,646 | 7,940 | 205 | 15.83 | 3,240 | 34.1 | 65.9 |
| 1964 | 486,997,952 | 2,165,581,847 | 4.45 | 128,698 | 7,630 | 225 | 16.84 | 3,784 | 33.9 | 66.1 |
| 1965 | 512,088,263 | 2,276,022,033 | 4.44 | 133,732 | 7,228 | 219 | 17.52 | 3,829 | 35.1 | 64.9 |
| 1966 | 533,881,210 | 2,421,292,716 | 4.54 | 131,752 | 6,749 | 219 | 18.52 | 4,052 | 36.6 | 63.4 |
| 1967 | 552,626,000 | 2,555,378,000 | 4.62 | 131,523 | 5,873 | 219 | 19.17 | 4,198 | 36.9 | 63.1 |
| 1968 | 545,245,000 | 2,546,340,000 | 4.67 | 127,894 | 5,327 | 220 | 19.37 | 4,263 | 36.9 | 63.1 |
| 1969 | 560,505,000 | 2,795,509,000 | 4.99 | 124,532 | 5,118 | 226 | 19.90 | 4,501 | 38.1 | 61.9 |
| 1970 | 602,932,000 | 3,772,662,000 | 6.26 | 140,140 | 5,601 | 228 | 18.84 | 4,302 | 43.8 | 56.2 |
| 1971 | 552,192,000 | 3,904,562,000 | 7.07 | 145,664 | 5,149 | 210 | 18.02 | 3,791 | 50.0 | 50.0 |
| 1972 | 595,386,000 | 4,561,983,000 | 7.66 | 149,265 | 4,879 | 221 | 17.74 | 3,989 | 48.9 | 51.1 |
| 1973 | 591,738,000 | 5,049,612,000 | 8.53 | 148,121 | 4,744 | 227 | 17.58 | 3,995 | 9.4 | 50.6 |
| 1974 | 603,406,000 | 9,486,209,000 | 15.75 | 166,701 | 5,247 | 206 | 17.58 | 3,620 | 54.0 | 46.0 |
| 1975 | 648,438,000 | 12,472,486,000 | 19.23 | 189,880 | 6,168 | 232 | 14.74 | 3,420 | 54.8 | 45.2 |
| 1976 | 678,685,000 | 13,186,850,000 | 19.43 | 202,280 | 6,161 | 232 | 14.46 | 3,355 | 56.6 | 43.4 |
| 1977 | 688,575,000 | 14,115,788,000 | 20.50 | 214,777 | 6,200 | 218 | 14.74 | 3,213 | 60.6 | 39.4 |

[a]In dollars.

[b]In net tons.

SOURCE: National Coal Association, *Coal Facts*, 1978.

**EXHIBIT 5–2**
## Industry Affiliations of Selected Coal-Producing Groups in 1974

| Coal Producing Group, Subsidiary, or Division | Parent or Controlling Company | 1974 Coal Output, Million Tons | Percentage of Industry Total | Industry Affiliations, Percentage of Total Industry 1974 Output | | | | | |
|---|---|---|---|---|---|---|---|---|---|
| | | | | *Coal* | *Petroleum* | *Metal* | *Steel* | *Utilities* | *Other* |
| Peabody | Kennecott Copper Corp.[a] | 70.7 | 11.8 | | | 11.8 | | | |
| Consolidation | Continental Oil Co. | 47.1 | 8.0 | | 8.0 | | | | |
| Island Creek and Maust | Occidental Petroleum Corp. | 22.8 | 3.8 | | 3.8 | | | | |
| Amax Coal | Amax, Inc. | 19.9 | 3.3 | | | 3.3 | | | |
| Clinchfield Coal | Pittston Co.[b] | 18.9 | 3.1 | 3.1 | | | | | |
| Captive | United States Steel Corp. | 16.4 | 2.7 | | | | 2.7 | | |
| Arch | Ashland Oil, Inc. | 14.3 | 2.4 | | 2.4 | | | | |
| Captive | Bethlehem Steel Corp. | 13.9 | 2.3 | | | | 2.3 | | |
| Westmoreland | Westmoreland Coal Co. | 13.2 | 2.2 | 2.2 | | | | | |
| A.T. Massey Coal Co. | St. Joe Minerals Corp. | 12.8 | 2.1 | | | 2.1 | | | |
| North American Coal | North American Coal Co. | 11.3 | 1.9 | 1.9 | | | | | |
| Eastern Associated Coal | Eastern Gas and Fuel Associates[b] | 10.4 | 1.7 | 1.7 | | | | | |
| Old Ben | Standard Oil Co. (Ohio) | 9.5 | 1.6 | | 1.6 | | | | |
| Pittsburgh and Midway | Gulf Oil Co. | 7.5 | 1.3 | | 1.3 | | | | |
| Navajo and San Juan | Utah International, Inc. | 7.1 | 1.2 | | | 1.2 | | | |

| | | | | | | | | | |
|---|---|---|---|---|---|---|---|---|---|
| Freeman and United Electric | General Dynamics Corp. | 7.0 | 1.2 | | | | | | 1.2 |
| Captive (7 units) | American Electric Power Co.[c] | 6.7 | 1.1 | | | | | 1.1 | |
| Joint Venture | Pacific Power and Light Co. | 6.5 | 1.1 | | | | | 1.1 | |
| Valley Camp | Valley Camp Coal Co. | 6.2 | 1.0 | 1.0 | | | | | |
| Pittsburgh and West Virginia | Industrial Fuels Corp. | 5.7 | 1.0 | 1.0 | | | | | |
| Rochester and Pittsburgh | Rochester and Pittsburgh Coal Co. | 4.6 | .8 | .8 | | | | | |
| Ziegler | Houston Natural Gas Corp. | 4.5 | .8 | | .8 | | | | |
| Falcon Coal | Falcon Seaboard Co. | 3.4 | .6 | | | | | | .6 |
| C&K | Gulf Resources and Chemical Co. | 3.2 | .5 | | | .5 | | | |
| Captive | Alabama By-Products Corp. | 3.1 | .5 | .5 | | | | | |
| Carbon Fuel | Carbon Industries, Inc.[b] | 2.8 | .5 | .5 | | | | | |
| Rapoca | Rapoca Energy Corp. | 1.8 | .3 | .3 | | | | | |
| Westrans | Westrans Industries, Inc. | 1.4 | .2 | .2 | | | | | |
| Appalachian | Appalachian Resource Co. | .8 | .1 | .1 | | | | | |
| Diamond Coal | Transcontinental Oil Corp. | .8 | .1 | .1 | | | | | |
| Total[c] | | 354.3 | 59.2 | 13.4 | 17.9 | 18.9 | 5.0 | 2.2 | 1.8 |

[a]Subject to Government Divesture Order. Request for reconsideration submitted.

[b]Holding company.

[c]Industry total = 603.4 million tons

SOURCE: 10K and U5S (Securities and Exchange Commission) of the companies listed and other related financial information. Industry affiliation based on primary line of business.

Of a total of 3,900 companies in production in 1974, 3,303 produced less than 100,000 tons. SOURCE: U.S. Bureau of Mines, Information Circular/1976, *The State of the U.S. Coal Industry*.

**EXHIBIT 5–3**

**Approximate Distribution of BCOA Membership and Voting Power**

| Member | Estimated No. Votes in 1978[a] | Parent or Controlling Co. |
|---|---|---|
| Peabody Coal Co. | 46 | — |
| Consolidation Coal Co. | 44 | Continental Oil Co. |
| AMAX Coal Co. | 15 | AMAX, Inc. (metal) |
| Island Creek Coal Co. | 17 | Occidental Petroleum Corp. |
| United States Steel Corp. | 13 | — |
| Bethlehem Mines Corp. | 11 | Bethlehem Steel Co. |
| Old Ben Coal Co. | 10 | Sohio Petroleum Co. |
| The North American Coal Corp. | 9 | — |
| Eastern Associated Coal Corp. | 8 | Pittston Co. |
| Freeman United Coal Mining Co. | 7 | General Dynamics Corp. |
| Westmoreland Coal Co. | 7 | — |
| American Electric Power Service | 5 | — |
| Drummond Coal Co. | 5 | The Drummond Co. |
| Southwestern Illinois Coal Corp. | 5 | Ashland Oil Co.<br>Arch Mineral Corp. |
| The Valley Camp Coal Corp. | 4 | Quaker State Oil Refining Corp. |
| Alabama By-Products Corp. | 4 | — |
| 6 members with | 3 each | |
| 8 members with | 2 each | |
| 126 members with | 1 each | |
| Approximate total votes | 366 | |

[a]According to the BCOA constitution, each member receives one vote for each million tons or fraction thereof of production. Coal produced in areas not under BCOA contract is excluded. These vote estimates were prepared using published membership lists and coal production information. Known associated companies are grouped together.

## EXHIBIT 5-4
## Labor Cost Analysis Prepared by the UMW—Labor Cost Per Dollar of Sales for the UMWA-BCOA Sector of the Bituminous Coal Industry *(Using Estimated Average BCOA Price[a])*

| | 1970 | 1969 | 1976 | 1977 | 1977 Adjusted[b] |
|---|---|---|---|---|---|
| 1. Price of coal per ton | $4.68 | $5.08 | $22.56 | $24.24 | $24.24 |
| 2. Employee total compensation per hour | $4.06 | $6.13 | $12.55 | $13.08 | $19.97 |
| 3. Production of coal per hour (tons) | 1.45 | 2.25 | 1.61 | 1.54 | 1.54 |
| 4. Labor cost per ton of coal—(2) ÷ (3) | $2.80 | $2.72 | $ 7.80 | $ 8.49 | $12.97 |
| 5. Labor cost per dollar of sales—(4) ÷ (1) | 59.8% | 53.5% | 34.6% | 35.0% | 53.5% |

[a]Average industry prices for underground and surface, weighted two-thirds and one-third, respectively, to reflect distribution of BCOA output.

[b]Assumes labor cost per dollar of sales of 53.5 percent.

Source: The Bureau of National Affairs, Inc., *Daily Labor Report*, November 21, 1977

| Average Hourly Earnings | |
|---|---|
| Bituminous coal | $7.91 |
| Steel industry | 7.68 |
| Auto industry | 7.10 |
| Chemicals | 5.89 |
| All manufacturing | 5.19 |
| Textile mills | 3.67 |

Source: National Coal Association, *Coal Facts*, 1978.

CASE 6

# WORKERS' COUNCILS: HOBBEMA & VAN RIJN, N.V. (A)

*Dwight R. Ladd*

In October 1974, Dirk van Berkel, Chairman of the Management Board of Hobbema & van Rijn, N.V., was reviewing his experiences in dealing with the Central Workers' Council which had been functioning in the company since January 1974. Van Berkel was concerned about several general issues which appeared to be involved in working with such a council, and with a very specific issue which was emerging. This latter involved the sale of the company's Amersfoort Division, which was currently being negotiated by management, and which would have to be presented to the Central Workers' Council for the latter's advice before final consummation. (See Exhibit 6-1 for a summary of the Council's powers.) Dirk van Berkel anticipated that this issue could cause a good deal of difficulty in the months ahead, and that it could well have a good deal of influence on future functioning of the Council.

## HOBBEMA & VAN RIJN, N.V.

Hobbema & van Rijn, N.V. was engaged in the layout design and furnishing of offices—primarily for business, government and institutions such as schools and hospitals. The company had a large staff of designers, architects, decorators, and so forth, whose services were available on a contract or consulting basis. The company also manufactured certain lines of office furniture and equipment—primarily filing cabinets and other stamped metal items. These were sold directly to institutional clients and through a number of retail shops which the company operated in major Dutch cities. These shops sold a complete line of of-

---

The case has been revised and edited by Bert Spector, Research Associate, under the direction of Michael Beer, Lecturer, Harvard Business School.

fice supplies. In addition to the Dutch operations, the company had sales offices and design staffs in West Germany, Belgium, Switzerland, and the United Kingdom. In 1973, total company sales were about Dfl. 285,000,000 and profits were Dfl. 9,700,000.[1]

Contract sales and design work accounted for about 60 percent of sales, manufacturing for about 35 percent and retail shops for about 15 percent. In terms of employees, between 45 and 50 percent were employed in manufacturing operations. The company had some 3,400 employees working in 60 separate operating units. Overall, about 60 percent of the employees were in managerial, professional, or clerical positions, with the remainder being production and maintenance workers. About 50 percent of the total work force was unionized. For management purposes, the 60 operating units were grouped into ten divisions such as retail stores, commercial contract sales, and so forth. The Amersfoort Division, which manufactured filing cabinets and similar items, was one of the ten divisions. It employed about 650 people and accounted for about one-half of the company's manufacturing turnover.

### *Worker Participation*

Since World War II various European countries have passed legislation which makes it mandatory for larger companies to create formal structures and mechanisms by which elected worker representatives can have a say with respect to a variety of corporate policies and practices. The formal mechanisms for worker participation differ between countries, as do the issues that are subject to review and approval by workers. Likewise, there are differences between countries in how workers are elected as representatives and in the role of unions in the process. In many cases, the laws are vague about what workers should have a say over, leaving the nature of participation within a firm to evolve from management's and workers' interpretations and initiative.

Broadly speaking, there are two approaches in Europe to structuring worker participation. One, practiced in West Germany under the label of code termination, requires worker representation on existing management decision-making bodies such as the supervisory board (board of directors), and the management board (an executive committee in U.S. firms). In West Germany, worker representatives have over half the seats on the supervisory board.

The other approach has been to create structural overlaps called workers' councils to which workers are elected. Workers' councils usu-

[1]For comparative purposes, these were equal, in January 1975, to about U.S. $112 million and U.S. $3.5 million, respectively.

ally exist at the corporate, divisional, and plant level, and are involved in reviewing actions, in some cases approving or rejecting management plans which affect the interests of employees. This is the approach in the Netherlands. Changes in the law since 1974 have excluded the chairman of the management board from chairmanship of and membership on the workers' councils.

At least in part, it could be said that the drive for legislated participation by workers in Europe grew out of the absence in traditional European labor relations of worker influence over the structure of working conditions through the collective bargaining process. In Canada and the United States, labor unions bargain with management over working conditions and rules, hiring and firing, social services, and so forth. This practice is rather different from continental Europe where union-management negotiations are limited almost exclusively to wages, and where bargaining is national and industrywide.

### *Van Berkel's Approach to the Council*

The broad underlying issues which concerned van Berkel were centered around a conflict between his views of the roles of business and of management on the one hand, and the purpose of a workers' council on the other. The Dutch government had first passed a law calling for worker participation in management in 1956, but that law was permissive rather than mandatory, and under it, very few workers' councils were established. In 1971, the government enacted a new law which made such workers' councils mandatory in all concerns employing at least 100 people. The law stated that the workers' councils were to be established "in the interest of the correct functioning of the enterprise in all its objectives, and in behalf of the consultation with, and representation of the persons employed in the enterprise." During the debate over the law there was a good deal of conflict over whether the councils should function as pressure groups for workers or as broadly based supervisory boards. The ambiguous language of the law made it clear that the conflict over purpose was not resolved. In effect, companies and their councils were left with the task of setting their own direction, and in his opening remarks to the Central Workers' Council, van Berkel addressed this problem directly:

> I regret that I cannot give you a watertight formula for the task of the Council. The law under which we have been established, describes a twofold function. On the one hand, we must contribute to the successful functioning of Hobbema & van Rijn. On the other hand, the Council is charged with being the representative of the workers in Hobbema & van Rijn. From our preliminary discussions, I have the distinct impression that, for you, the second function weighs much more heavily than the

first, and in the circumstances I regard this as extremely desirable for Hobbema & van Rijn. Nevertheless, I must ask for your understanding that as your chairman and as a member of the management of Hobbema & van Rijn, I see my task as one of maintaining equity among all groups—employees, investors, management, customers, suppliers, Dutch society—that are essential to the successful functioning of Hobbema & van Rijn. It is clear that an area of tension exists, but that will merely give a greater challenge to us in our discussion.

The basic idea of a workers' council did not entirely fit this view of the enterprise. While it did give workers a status within the company, more or less equal to that of investors, it also gave them a rather special status as compared with the other groups. On the other hand, Dirk van Berkel and his colleagues in top management had entirely rejected the traditional view that workers were simply suppliers of labor, believing, as he put in his opening remarks to the Council, "that employees are joint players of leading roles in the game called enterprise." These somewhat conflicting views could lead Dirk van Berkel to attempt to minimize the role of the Council, or to attempt to make it into an important force in the company. Based on his experience with the Council since January, he felt that he could have considerable influence over the direction the Council took.

Beyond these basic questions of approach and attitude, van Berkel faced an important tactical question. The Amersfoort Division had been losing money for some time, and a potential buyer for it had been found. If the sale were negotiated, the law required that the matter be referred to the Workers' Council for its advice to management. The Council could not veto such a sale, but could have a good deal of influence over workers' response to it. Two members of the Council were employees of the Amersfoort Division (see Exhibit 6–2). Since the possible sale had thus far been discussed only by a few members of top management, there was a distinct possibility that supervisors in the division would learn of the impending sale from subordinates. On the other hand, van Berkel realized that if the matter were carefully handled, the two employees could be very helpful in disarming opposition to the sale in the division. It was also possible, of course, that the two members would attempt to forestall or sabotage the sale. Van Berkel recalled the recent instance where workers in AKZO, the large Dutch chemical combine, had effectively blocked the closing of a plant even though the union involved had initially agreed to the closing.

### *Makeup of the Council*

The Central Workers' Council at Hobbema & van Rijn consisted of Dirk van Berkel who was its chairman by law and 19 members elected by employees. (Everyone except the three members of the management board was considered to be an employee.) The number of members was specified by law and was based on the number of employees in the company, though councils were never larger than 25. Members of the Central Workers' Council were elected by local councils from among their own members.

The law required that every division or branch of a company with more than 100 employees must have its own workers' council, though if there were several divisions in the same community they could have a single joint council. There were 12 local councils in Hobbema & van Rijn which were somewhat smaller than the Central Workers' Council, ranging in size from 5 to 11 members. For the most part, their development had followed the pattern of the Central Workers' Council described in this case, though, as might be expected, they tended to concentrate on local matters.

Representation on the Central Council reflected the relative size of the divisions. All persons who had been employees for at least one year were eligible to vote in the election of local council members. Unions with members in a company or division had the right to nominate candidates, and candidates could also be nominated by at least 30 nonunion employers.[2] Council members, who had to have been employees for at least three years, were elected for three-year terms and were eligible for reelection. (Exhibit 6–2 shows the members of the Hobbema & van Rijn Central Workers' Council, where they worked, and their relative status in the company.)

The law required that the manager of the company or his representative be the chairman of the Council, a stipulation which had continued to be a matter of controversy. The Socialist unions were advocating a shift to an elected chairman not from management, while the

[2]Dutch unions, like most Dutch institutions, reflected the so-called "three pillars of society." There were Catholic unions (NKV), Protestant unions (CNV), and neutral unions (NVV), the latter being basically Social Democratic in ideology and practice. (This means that for every industry or trade there were three unions. For example, a printing plant would have the Catholic Printers' Union, the Protestant Printers' Union, and the Neutral Printers' Union.) In general, the unions were closely affiliated with political parties: the Labor Party, the Catholic Party, or the two Protestant Parties. The Labor Party, as noted above, was Social Democratic in its policies while the religious parties were generally Conservative. During the late 1960s and 1970s there began to be a significant shift away from the traditional religious/class basis of Dutch society by both unions and voters in general. In 1974, the Dutch government was a coalition of left-of-center parties without formal connections with either church or organized labor.

The existence of the three groups of unions does not complicate things so much as it might appear to some. In the Netherlands, as in most continental countries, collective bargaining is done nationally and industrywide and is confined almost entirely to wages and related issues. Hobbema & van Rijn employees who were union members belonged to one of nine unions.

Christian unions were advocating that the councils be changed into something like the German supervisory boards with an outside or neutral chairman.

### *Council Procedures*

The law required that each workers' council meet at least six times a year, and that council members be furnished with annual and semi-annual financial reports. Hobbema & van Rijn actually planned to have seven or eight meetings a year, and van Berkel gave Council members quarterly financial reports for each division within Hobbema. The company annual budget was also discussed with the Council, though the law did not require it. The Workers' Council had a secretary elected from among its members, and a four-member agenda committee of which van Berkel was chairman. The agenda committee met at least once before each Council meeting. In addition, the elected members (everyone except the chairman) met together at least once before each formal meeting. Council meetings generally took about one-half a day. Van Berkel estimated that each meeting required about two days of his time, a good deal of which was involved in preparation, since he felt it necessary to try to be prepared to deal with any issues which might come up. Council members were reimbursed for any expenses in traveling to and from meetings. They received their regular pay while attending meetings, but were not compensated for any overtime involved. Van Berkel said complaints had been received from the supervisor of the Council secretary to the effect that the secretary's work took so much time that he was no longer able to do his regular job properly.

### *Information*

Early operation of the Workers' Council had raised several issues in connection with information. Under the law, all information given to the Council was supposed to be confidential unless it was agreed to disseminate it. Van Berkel stated that thus far there had been no unauthorized leaks of company information though he added that most of the information given to the Council was no longer "hot."

A somewhat more difficult issue had to do with the relationship between the Workers' Council and the regular formal channels of communication within the company. Van Berkel observed that since he seriously tried to involve the Council in company decisions, it was virtually impossible in the give and take of discussions, for him to avoid referring to facts and opinions that had not been made public in the company. This meant that Council members might be in possession of information not yet known by their superiors, a possibility not without serious consequences for established relationships within the company. This problem had been part of van Berkel's concern about the upcoming discussion in the Council of the possible sale of Amersfoort Division.

Finally, there was a problem of communication between the Workers' Council and the rest of the employees they represented. An agenda for each Council meeting was posted on all official notice boards throughout the company, and official summaries of each meeting were similarly made available. At van Berkel's urging, Council members from two of the operating companies arranged plant meetings in their units to discuss the agenda of the Council. Attendance at these meetings, however, was very small.

*Relationships Between Council and Unions*

The law which mandated the creation of workers' councils made special provisions for unions in the election of members and, in effect, protected any prior rights of unions under collective bargaining agreements. At the same time, the councils were given very extensive powers under the law and a potential for conflict between councils and unions was present. As a general rule Dutch unions had not been enthusiastic supporters of the establishment of workers' councils. They felt that if the councils developed into effectively functioning bodies under management chairmanship, their influence with workers would be undermined. They were further concerned about the possibilities of open conflict between two groups representing workers. Van Berkel described one instance where just such a conflict had developed.

Early in 1974, Hobbema & van Rijn decided to discontinue one of its minor product lines, a move which would eliminate the jobs of about 75 employees. About 35 of these could be given comparable jobs elsewhere in the company, but the remainder would have to be let go. Hobbema & van Rijnn prepared a "social plan" required by union agreements in such cases, which provided that if these latter employees had to take jobs at lower pay, Hobbema & van Rijn would make up the difference on a sliding scale ranging from 6 months for workers under 29 years old to 5 years for workers over 60. The unions involved had agreed to this social plan, but just before the discontinuance was to take place, the elected members asked to have the matter put on the agenda of the Central Workers' Council. The plant manager who negotiated the agreement with the union was entirely opposed to discussion by the Central Workers' Council on the grounds that the agreement might be upset. Council members felt equally strongly that this was precisely the sort of question with which the Council should deal. In legal terms, discussion with the local workers' council was required but it was not at all clear that this issue had to be brought before the Central Workers' Council, and van Berkel was rather sure that it did not. However, because he felt that the Council should develop as a collaborative and significant part of the organization, he decided to accept the question as an agenda item, but only for purposes of "advice" to management and not for "consent" by the Council. Council members agreed to this format, and, after discussion, accepted the decision already negotiated. However, the Council did insist on publication of a special report on its deliberations and conclusion. Van Berkel felt that this was a reflection of the Council members' desire to establish some visibility and importance vis-à-vis the unions and the local council.

### *Council Business*

After several meetings of the Workers' Council in 1974, it had not become clear with what kinds of issues the Council would concern itself. In his role as chairman, and given his knowledge of company affairs, van Berkel really controlled the agenda and observed, late in 1974, that he had been more concerned with getting things on the agenda than with keeping things off. (A summary of the agenda of the first few meetings of the Hobbema & van Rijn Workers' Council is included as Exhibit 6-3.) On the whole, Van Berkel felt that the Workers' Council did not really get at important issues, but tended to focus on trivial things or on matters which came up accidentally, and to do so without much systematic analysis.

For example, the first issue that the Council wanted to discuss was payment for members of the Board of Directors. (Annual compensation of Hobbema & van Rijn board members amounted to about Dfl. 20,000. Total operating expenses were Dfl. 263,000,000.) On another occasion, Council members questioned the policy governing use of company cars. This had been recently studied by management but the Council insisted on studying it for themselves anyway, assigning the task to one member. That member eventually reported that there was no really good policy so that the present company policy, developed by management, should be left undisturbed.

One of the statutory powers of the Dutch workers' council is approval of appointments to the company's board of directors. Under Dutch law, shareholders of public companies do not elect board members. In effect, board members appoint their own successors, though shareholders do have the right to appeal appointments through the courts. If appointments are made without approval of the workers' council, the latter also has the right of appeal to the courts. Dutch law also requires that directors of public companies must retire at age 72.

Just prior to the first meeting of the Hobbema & van Rijn Workers' Council the board chairman reached that age. On behalf of the board, van Berkel proposed as new chairman a former university professor who was widely regarded as a very able man, but who had been an active member of one of the right-wing political parties. This, not surprisingly, made his candidacy very unpalatable to the Workers' Council. Because of the recognized ability of the nominee, van Berkel was anxious to have him appointed, and so he proposed a compromise to the Council. He pointed out to them that because of the mandatory retirement age, several other board seats would soon become vacant. He proposed that the next board vacancy[3] would be filled by a nominee of the Workers' Council with the provision that the appointee would function as a regular board member and not as a designated representative of the workers. The Workers' Council quite readily accepted van Berkel's proposal and the issue was resolved. However, Dirk van Berkel realized as a result of the discussions that his colleagues on the Council had very little idea of the functions of a director or any idea of whom to select—even though the law permitted them to do so.

Van Berkel felt that this general failure to probe into more significant issues reflected a lack of sophistication and experience on the part of most Council members. All of the Council members had gone through one of the three-day training programs sponsored by the Dutch unions. These programs involved instruction in such things as financial statements, organization structure, company law, and so forth, and devoted about an equal amount of time to the techniques of participating in and conducting meetings. The training programs were put on for the members of specific councils and there was a good deal of emphasis on group dynamics and team building. Because the manager/chairman of each council was also a member, the union programs had agreed to include him for the last evening and final day of the program.

*Future Possibilities*

After four meetings of the Workers' Council of Hobbema & van Rijn, Dirk van Berkel felt that the institution had been introduced into the company without major difficulty, and that its impact had thus far been quite limited. From the point of view of management, it meant that greater care had to be exercised in making decisions and publishing them, and van Berkel felt that the upcoming discussion of the proposed sale of the Amersfoort Division would put that care to the test. It

[3]Under Dutch law, directors serve three-year terms and must be formally renominated for a subsequent term.

did not appear to Mr. van Berkel that the Council had as yet contributed much to the quality of decision making at Hobbema & van Rijn, though he felt that as members became more knowledgeable and experienced, their contributions might increase.

Van Berkel's concerns about the Workers' Council encompassed three different time dimensions:

1. **Short-run.** His immediate concern was the discussion of the potentially touchy issue of the sale of the Amersfoort Division.
2. **Medium-run.** The outcome of that discussion would influence the somewhat longer-run question of whether to try to minimize that role of the Council or to try to make it into a positive and important force in the company.
3. **Long-run.** Van Berkel felt that the powers of the Council would increase, partly because of greater strength resulting from experience, but mostly because the Dutch government was actively pushing to expand those powers.

Van Berkel foresaw that the distance between the members of the Council and their constituents would increase, and that the Council would become increasingly like a parliament. He felt this tendency would be an inevitable result of increasing Council activity. As noted above, the supervisor of one Council member had already complained about time away from the job, and van Berkel felt that eventually Council membership would be a full-time job. The inevitable result of this, van Berkel felt, would be to make the Council increasingly political, and that ambiguity of purpose contained in the law would willy-nilly be resolved in favor of political bargaining as opposed to collaboration.

Dirk van Berkel hoped that his dealing with the Council in the near future would not accelerate this trend.

## THE AMERSFOORT DIVISION PROBLEM

The Amersfoort Division of Hobbema & van Rijn had been acquired by a previous management several years prior to 1974, and had operated at a loss since then. The division, which manufactured filing cabinets and other stamped metal items, had considerable excess capacity, a situation which was made worse, in 1974, by the decision to discontinue a line of metal desktop items which the plant had manufactured. It was apparent to both management and workers that continuation of the operation would require a significant reduction in the size of the work force. In these circumstances, the management of Hobbema & van Rijn was delighted to be approached with an offer to buy the Amersfoort Division. The offer came from a relatively large company which manufactured a wide range of stamped metal cabinets and housings for such things as machinery and furnaces. The potential buyer operated through the European Economic Community. The offer was at a price attractive to Hobbema & van Rijn, and while it did not include any guarantees that jobs would not be eliminated, the buyer did believe that because of his much broader market, he could utilize the facilities more effectively than could Hobbema & van Rijn, thus minimizing the number of necessary lay-offs. The buyer also agreed to maintain the same employment conditions for those employees who were kept on.

### *Van Berkel Negotiates with Central Workers' Council*

As soon as the buyer and Hobbema & van Rijn reached general agreement on the terms of the takeover, management reported that fact to the unions in the Amersfoort plant as was required by labor agreements. This was done on November 7. At the same time, management, with the agreement of the unions, called a special meeting of the Central Workers' Council of Hobbema & van Rijn for November 8. Under the law a matter such as this had to be brought before the Workers' Council for its "advice," though the Council did not have the legal right to veto the sale. There was, however, some difficulty over the questions of jurisdiction. Since the sale of such a major division would affect the entire company, the law gave jurisdiction to the Central Workers' Council. However, the workers' council of the Amersfoort Division argued that since they were the ones who would be sold, they should be able to advise management. The Central Workers' Council asserted that the function of the local council was to provide information and judgments, and that this could be done through the two members of the Central Workers' Council who were representatives of the Amersfoort workers' council.

Management attempted to resolve this issue by agreeing to accept advice from both councils, and the Amersfoort council countered this with a proposal that, on this matter, the two councils meet jointly. The Amersfoort council feared that if they gave negative advice while the Central Workers' Council gave positive advice, management could go ahead with the sale and state it did so with worker approval. Because it wanted to preserve its position in such an eventuality, the Central Workers' Council rejected the proposal for joint meetings, and since the law supported its position, joint meetings were not held. Management's commitment to accept advice from both councils remained in effect.

Dirk van Berkel was chairman of the Central Workers' Council and was the member of management most directly involved in the sale.

However, he had no official relationship with the Amersfoort workers' council whose chairman was Jan Sonneveldt, manager of the Amersfoort Division. Sonneveldt reported to, but was not a part of top management of Hobbema & van Rijn.

NOVEMBER 8: CWC HEARS VAN BERKEL'S PLAN. At the meeting on November 8, the Central Workers' Council heard Dirk van Berkel outline the plans for the sale, and describe management's reasons for believing that it was good for the company as a whole. While most Council members seemed initially to understand management's position, van Berkel felt that the open and strident hostility of the two members from Amersfoort tended to diminish the support of the other members for the sale. The Council decided to exercise its right to present formal questions to management about the latter's views on the sale. These questions were drafted.[4]

The first of these questions to be presented to management concerned finances. The workers asked about the general financial position of the new owner, about how he would finance the purchase, and what would be his likely financial position after the takeover. The second question concerned the commercial future of Amersfoort under the new management. The Workers' Council wanted to know how the buyer saw the future of his business in Europe and specifically how the Amersfoort Division would share in it. Finally, the Workers' Council asked about social policy—specifically about working conditions, pension rights, and promotion and retention policies.

Van Berkel had the controller of the company and the prospective buyer prepare the details of the answers to these questions. Van Berkel suggested to the controller that he approach the financial question from a more or less neutral stand, i.e., that he take neither the role of the buyer nor that of the seller. In its own prior thinking, of course, Hobbema & van Rijn management had thought only as sellers—sellers who were anxious to get rid of a poorly performing division. The data which had been prepared for van Berkel did not, he felt, provide a basis for very reassuring answers to the members of the Workers' Council. For one thing, it was not at all clear from the financial statements that the buyer did have the financial resources necessary to purchase and integrate the Amersfoort Division into his own company. Further, van Berkel felt that the information on commercial prospects provided by the purchaser was obviously optimistic as well as extremely offhand

[4]The elected members of the Workers' Council had the legal right to meet separately in order to draw up these questions, but they specifically asked Mr. van Berkel to assist them. He, of course, was put into the somewhat unique position of helping to frame questions which he would have to answer.

and superficial. It indicated, he felt, that the management of the buyer did not take the ability of the Workers' Council very seriously.

While van Berkel wished that the answers to the questions posed by the Central Workers' Council offered more convincing support for management's position, he retained his conviction that most members of the Central Workers' Council did accept the validity of the argument that Hobbema & van Rijn would be better off without the ailing division. It was with these somewhat conflicting thoughts that he contemplated his strategy for the meeting next morning.

NOVEMBER 15: FORMAL MEETING OF THE CWC. On the morning of November 15, van Berkel convened a formal meeting of the Central Workers' Council. The meeting had two items of business on the agenda: an interview with a nominee for the company's Board of Directors, and consideration of the proposed Amersfoort sale. The latter question would be the first item discussed. Van Berkel anticipated a good deal of controversy, but as management's answers to the questions posed by the Council on November 8 were reviewed, it appeared to van Berkel that the Central Workers' Council (with the exception of the two members from the Amersfoort Division) generally accepted management's conclusion that Hobbema & van Rijn would be strengthened by divestiture of the Amersfoort Division. The two members from the Amersfoort Division indicated opposition because they had not been convinced by management's analysis of the financial strength of the purchaser, nor about how the Amersfoort Division would fit into and fare within the purchaser's European operations. They feared that the profitable parts of the operation might be transferred elsewhere and the balance eventually shut down.

As the discussion went on, the opposition of the Amersfoort group became more open and more strident, and Dirk van Berkel felt that the initial support for the sale was slipping away and that the members of the Central Workers' Council were moving toward a negative position based on support of fellow-workers. He concluded that if the meeting took a formal vote it would result in the Central Workers' Council advising management against the sale.

However, before a vote could be proposed, the meeting had to be adjourned so that the Central Workers' Council could interview the candidate for the Board of Directors. The Amersfoort representative announced that their council was going to prepare its own advice to management. The Central Workers' Council then agreed to postpone further discussion of the proposed sale until the Amersfoort workers' council had prepared its advice. It seemed likely that this would take several weeks.

DECEMBER 2: THE AMERSFOORT COUNCIL GIVES ITS ADVICE. On December 2, the Amersfoort workers' council presented its advice to management in the form of a 65-page printed and bound report. (The report was sent to the Board of Directors, the Management Board, the Central Workers' Council, and to the Minister of Social Welfare in the Dutch Cabinet.) The elected members of the Council had exercised their legal right to meet without the Chairman, Jan Sonneveldt, being present, and as a result, no one in management really knew what to expect from the report.[5]

The report was a rather thoroughgoing condemnation of the proposed sale and of the management of Hobbema & van Rijn. It reviewed the uncertainties about the purchaser's financial strength and about his market prospects, and pointed out that these uncertainties had not been diminished by the discussions which Council members had had with the management board of the purchasing company. In short, the report constituted a negative advice to management, though at one point it did suggest that the workers might look somewhat more favorably on a partial sale which would leave Hobbema & van Rijn with a 49 percent interest in the division.

DECEMBER 10: THE CWC EVALUATES ITS POSITION. The Central Workers' Council scheduled a meeting for December 10 to discuss its own position in light of the advice from the Amersfoort worker's council. The hostile tone of the Amersfoort report influenced the Central Workers' Council which demanded that the meeting not be held in the usual meeting place in company headquarters, but on "neutral" ground. Thus, the meeting was held at the Holiday Inn in Leiden. The day of the meeting all of the members of the Amersfoort workers' council showed up and demanded to be heard. The Central Workers' Council refused to admit their colleagues from Amersfoort, either as participants or as observers, arguing that the two Amersfoort members could adequately present the point of view of the others. The latter remained in the motel throughout the meeting.

The meeting went on for several hours. As a result of the aggressiveness of the two Amersfoort members and the aggressive tone of their report, the meeting moved steadily away from support of management's position. A draft of a recommendation to management

[5]Sonneveldt's position was extremely difficult. He was not a part of, and could not speak for, top management. Furthermore, he would continue as plant manager if the sale were made, and hence did not wish to alienate his fellow-workers. As a result, the elected Council members felt that they were neither getting a hearing with those who counted nor getting very convincing answers to their questions.

which was essentially negative in tone was slowly put together. Since the meeting had been going on for several hours, it was decided to adjourn temporarily. The meeting was officially adjourned until the next afternoon, this time to be held in the usual meeting place in company headquarters, but to be held without the Chairman, Dirk van Berkel.

### *Van Berkel's Concerns*

As he left the meeting, Dirk van Berkel sensed that things were going rather badly. He felt quite certain that without some new input, the adjourned meeting would produce a negative advice and that in that event, the sale would collapse. The buyer might withdraw. Even if he did not, the unions which had initially accepted the sale would now oppose it. Van Berkel realized that he now had to deal with both councils, and wondered if the partial sale referred to in the report of the Amersfoort council provided a basis for negotiating with that group. In the case of the Central Workers' Council, he wondered if the members were not operating on the assumption that management would go through with the sale whatever advice they gave, and thus felt that they could show support for fellow-workers without losing anything. These thoughts ran through Dirk van Berkel's mind as he headed for what promised to be a long evening of discussion with his colleagues on the management board.

## EXHIBIT 6–1
## Summary of Statutory Powers of Dutch Workers' Councils

1. (Sec. 24) *Discussion* of general course of the affairs of the enterprise at least twice annually. Appropriate financial statements including net profit before creation of reserves must be furnished. In the case of a workers' council for a subunit of a larger concern, "an insight into the extent to which the relevant subunit has contributed to the results of the enterprise as a whole" must be furnished to the council.
2. (Sec. 25) *Advise* management on:
   a. Transfer of the control over the enterprise or any division thereof to another employer
   b. Discontinuance of the activities of the enterprise or any division thereof
   c. Considerable curtailment, expansion or other change in the activities of the enterprise
   d. Considerable changes in the organization of the enterprise
   e. Change of the place where the enterprise carries on its activities
   f. The entry into or severance of permanent cooperating of the enterprise with other enterprises

   If management feels that the "weighty interests" of the company should preclude open discussion of any of these matters, it must give the council a statement of what these interests are. If the action entails the discharge of "considerable number of persons" the unions must be given prior notification.
3. (Sec. 26) *Advise* management on the establishment or modification of:
   a. Any scale or other scheme of remuneration
   b. Any measure in the field of training
   c. Any standard of judgment
   d. Any of the main lines of appointment, discharge, or promotion policy
   e. Any measure in the field of industrial social work

   These requirements do not apply if the issue is covered by a collective labor agreement.
4. (Sec. 27) *Agree* to the adoption or modification of pension plans, profit sharing, working hours, or holidays, and "any measure in the field of safety, health or hygiene."

   These requirements do not apply if the issue is covered by a collective labor agreement. If employer and council do not agree, the issue is referred to the Trade Commissions. (Trade Com-

**EXHIBIT 6–1 (*Continued*)**

missions are labor-management bodies appointed by the government to deal with disputes relating to workers' councils.)

5. (Sec. 28) Promote *consultation* "as to work, as well as the allocation of competencies within the enterprise, in order that the persons employed in the enterprise will to the extent possible be associated in the arrangement of the work in the branch of the enterprise where they are employed."
6. (Sec. 29) *Appoint* members to the boards of "institutions formed in behalf of the persons employed in the enterprise" (e.g., pension funds).
7. (Secs. 30, 31) Except in the case of "weighty interests" to the contrary, *to be informed* about personnel policies, (appointment, remuneration, discharge, and so forth) and about the intended appointment or intended dismissal of managers.

SOURCE: *Statute Book of the Kingdom of the Netherlands 54*, Workers' Council Law, Chapter IV, Secs. 23–32.

**EXHIBIT 6–2**
**Members of the Central Workers' Council**

| MEMBER | POSITION | SALARY INDEX | AGE | JOINED COMPANY |
|---|---|---|---|---|
| J.F.B. | Machine operator | 100 | 42 | 1965 |
| P.J.E. | Draftsman | 140 | 42 | 1956 |
| P.L.B. | Manager, Accounting Dept. | 400 | 53 | 1948 |
| J.S. | Draftsman | 140 | 44 | 1945 |
| G.B. | Sales Clerk | 175 | 41 | 1955 |
| M.A.R.[a] | Designer | 300 | 35 | 1972 |
| M.S. | Foreman | 150 | 52 | 1960 |
| K.J.S.[b,c] | Blueprint maker | 175 | 39 | 1966 |
| W.J.C.[c] | Maintenance manager | 200 | 47 | 1953 |
| H.J. | Designer | 200 | 34 | 1963 |
| M.A.M.[a] | Chief accountant | 300 | 37 | 1957 |
| P.J.W.C. | Architect | 300 | 34 | 1971 |
| H.J.K.S. | Order clerk | 175 | 61 | 1967 |
| D.P.S. | Accountant | 200 | 44 | 1972 |
| G.V.O. | Decorator | 200 | 35 | 1964 |
| M.H. | Assistant decorator | 175 | 39 | 1971 |
| L.A.B. | Chief accountant | 250 | 57 | 1946 |
| M.P. | Foreman | 150 | 31 | 1969 |
| G.M.V. | Clerk | 175 | 25 | 1972 |

[a]Female.

[b]Secretary of Council.

[c]Members from Amersfoot Division.

**EXHIBIT 6–3**
**Agenda of Workers' Council Meetings**

| Topic | Initiated by | Disposition |
|---|---|---|
| *First Meeting* | | |
| 1. Appointment of secretary | Routine | Done |
| 2. Preparation of by-laws (largely by statute) | Routine | Done |
| 3. Communication between council and rest of organization | Van Berkel | Not resolved, but see text of case for steps taken. |
| 4. Appointment of board chairman | Statute | See text of case. |
| 5. Payment of travel expenses and overtime for council meetings | Council member | See text of case. |
| 6. Training for council members | Van Berkel | Not resolved |
| *Second Meeting* | | |
| 1. Training for council members | Van Berkel | Not resolved |
| 2. Introduction of Hay system for management compensation | Van Berkel | Information only |
| 3. Request for employee discount on purchases from company | Council member | Referred to local councils |
| 4. Elect agenda committee | Statute | Done |
| 5. Makeup of board of directors | Van Berkel | Report presented primarily for information |
| 6. Policy for use of company cars | Council member | See text of case. |

**EXHIBIT 6–3 (*Continued*)**

| Topic | Initiated by | Disposition |
|---|---|---|
| *Third Meeting* | | |
| 1. Retroactivity of extra pay for statutory holidays | Council member | Extra pay had been agreed to by company, but held up by temporary government wage freeze. Company agreed to retroactivity when freeze lifted. |
| 2. Group insurance for private cars of employees | Council member | Investigation showed that there was no benefit, but council made report to all company, showing its initiative. |
| 3. Announce takeover of a small retail store | Van Berkel | Council members wanted to consider such issues before decision, but agreed that it would be too difficult in light of negotiations involved. |
| 4. Presentation of annual report and budget | Statute | Two weeks before publication. New board chairman present for discussion at request of council. |
| *Fourth Meeting* | | |
| 1. Report from council member present by invitation at shareholders' meeting | Council member | Information only |
| 2. Pension fund direction | Council member | Law requires pension fund directors to be three from management and three from employees participating in fund. Law also gives "responsibility" for pension matters to council. Conflict resolved by having council member be one of participant directors. |
| 3. Product line discontinuance | Council member | See text of case |

CASE 7

# NOTE ON WORKER PARTICIPATION

*Dwight R. Ladd*

The idea that workers should have some control over their work and have some voice in the operation of the enterprise in which they work is at least as old as the beginning of the Industrial Revolution and modern capitalism. In recent years, especially in continental Europe and some of the developing countries, a variety of schemes for creating such control and such a voice have been enacted into law. The general intent of all of these enactments has been to provide for the "participation" of workers in the development of policies which directly affect them, and in the general development of the enterprise. As with most intentions—good or bad—there are a number of theoretical and practical issues which are not automatically resolved by the intention. Several of these are discussed below.

## WHO ARE WORKERS?

A decision to make provision for worker participation immediately requires another decision about who are workers. In virtually all cases, it has been decided that the members of management boards or committees (top management) are not workers. As the Hobbema and van Rijn case shows, the Dutch approach has been to define everyone else in the company as workers. (This is not quite accurate because in the case of a single plant in a large corporation, the "top manager" in that plant would be management rather than worker, yet in the overall corporate hierarchy he might rank well below headquarters officials who would be considered workers.) In Germany, however, a three-way division has been practiced. "Management" is defined in conventional terms as top management, but in between top management and workers is a class of "leitenden Angestellten" (literally, leading employees) who are not represented in the organs of participation. German law left the definition of leading employee to individual companies, and some chose to adopt a very narrow definition while others created a very large class of "leading employee." The latter approach presumably reflected an at-

 Harvard Business School case 9-481-108.

tempt to isolate those who might be expected to oppose management most effectively. In 1974, however, there was strong political pressure to provide for special representation of leading employees. If carried into law, this would, of course, increase the representation of "non-management" in those companies which had opted for a broad definition of leading employee.

## MANAGEMENT ROLE

An issue related to the foregoing concerns the role of management (however defined) in the operation of "workers' councils." In the Dutch case, the president or equivalent is by law both member and chairman of the council. In Germany, the top manager is specifically excluded from membership, and a similar change was recently made in Yugoslavia. The principal rationale for excluding the top manager is that in the nature of things, he will have to be in constant contact with the council, and thus membership would tend to give excessive influence. This issue is rather closely related to the issue of whether the process of "participation" is to be negotiation or collaboration, a matter discussed below.

## STRUCTURE FOR PARTICIPATION

Broadly speaking, there are two approaches for structuring participation. One is to add workers to already existing bodies with established powers and roles in the overall policy and decision-making system of the organization. This approach has been followed by the Germans in their coal and steel industries, where workers' representatives have one-half the seats on the supervisory boards (i.e., boards of directors) of the companies. In many other countries, workers are given a minority of seats on the board. In other cases, such as the Netherlands, workers do not have specific seats on boards of directors, but do, along with shareholders, have veto power over appointments to boards—appointments which are made by the boards themselves.

The other approach to structuring participation is to create new bodies—primarily made up of workers' representatives—which are grafted onto the companies' preexisting management system. This is the approach illustrated in the Hobbema and van Rijn case. When this approach is adopted, the governments have attempted to define the powers of these "extra" bodies in some detail, but inevitably there is a good deal of ambiguity which has to be worked out in actual practice. How this is done depends a good deal on the form of participation and the related matter of power discussed below.

## FORM OF PARTICIPATION

Meaningful "participation" in the industrial context involves some sharing of power between managers and workers and thus some limitations on the prerogatives of managers and owners. Put in a different way, it involves the creation of a new influence bloc in the decision-making structure. How far the sharing of power goes, how much impact the influence has depends, in the first instance, on the form which "participation" takes—for that term can mean many different things. There are at least four distinct forms found in practice. The most limited form of participation is the right *to be informed* about actions taken or contemplated and about results. This right to be informed probably involves the minimum sharing of power. A somewhat greater share of power probably goes along with the right *to advise* or *to be consulted* which is another form of participation. The right *to give consent* (or conversely to have a veto) is a form of participation which involves a still greater share of power. In theory, the maximum sharing of power is the true codetermination practiced in the German coal and steel industries where workers and shareholders have equal representation on supervisory boards (boards of directors).[1] The reality is somewhat different, however, because the jurisdiction of those boards is extremely limited—primarily to choosing members of the "Vorstand" (management board) which really runs the company.

Of course, real sharing of power or real influence does not necessarily follow upon the creation of workers' councils. The workers' representatives must want to share power and wield influence and usually must learn how to do so. At the same time, management generally has a good deal of control over the situation because of far greater knowledge and much more experience, and at least, in the short run, probably has the ability to minimize the impact of the councils by minimizing the effective sharing of power. Given that ability, management also has a choice of strategy.

## PROCESS OF PARTICIPATION

Any degree of participation in whatever structure can take the form of collaboration or it can take the form of negotiation. There is perhaps a rather general feeling among most people that collaboration somehow defines a more meaningful participation, but there is not objective sup-

[1]German workers are also represented through works councils which function much like similar groups in other countries. Equal representation on the board of directors is unique to the German coal and steel industry, but in other German industries and in many other countries, workers have been given minority representation on boards.

port for this conclusion. Collaboration may somehow seem "friendlier" or "nicer" but the purpose of participation is that one have an influence on the outcome of the development of a policy or the making of a decision, and there is no intrinsic reason why that influence need be any greater or lesser if the participation is in the form of negotiation rather than collaboration, or as is probably true in most actual organizational situations, some of both.

This point can be illustrated by a broad comparison of American and Canadian practice with that on the continent. If an objective of participation is the sharing of power between management and workers—the limitation of management prerogatives—a good deal of "participation" may be said to have been achieved by Canadian and American workers through collective bargaining. It has long been North American practice for management and labor to bargain over working conditions and rules, hiring and firing, social services, and so forth. This is rather different from continental Europe where union-management negotiations are limited almost exclusively to wages and where bargaining is national and industrywide. Indeed, it may be supposed that part of the drive for workers' councils in continental Europe is a result of the absence in traditional European labor relations, of this influence over the structuring of working conditions.

## YUGOSLAVIA

Because the Yugoslav experiment with workers' councils has been so widely discussed, it seems appropriate to point out that the Yugoslav situation is not really comparable to any others. In that country the workers own the business in the full sense of the word. (This is not state ownership in the classic socialist or Marxist sense. The state does control most funding and economic plans. It exercises control over the whole economy as in most industrialized countries of whatever political faith, but within those constraints individual business is owned and operated by the workers.) Yugoslav workers do, in effect, share power with managers, but the managers are employees of the workers and are accountable to them. Obviously, managers have a certain amount of power accruing from greater knowledge and experience and in this sense, the relationship between workers' councils and managers has many similarities with those in ostensibly capitalist countries. One interesting feature of Yugoslav practice is that members of workers' councils may not be immediately reelected. This means that a very large number of persons have experience in council works, and also tends to prevent the development of self-perpetuating power groups. On the other hand, it tends to tip the experience balance more in the direction of managers.

*Chapter* 4

# Managing Human Resource Flow

THE MORE DYNAMIC the environment (rapid changes in market and technology), the more a corporation must be concerned with managing the flow of people *in, through,* and *out* of the organization. Growth requires recruitment, development, and promotion of an expanding pool of competent managers and technical specialists. Increasing competition in mature industries may require fewer employees—ones with a different mix of talents, capable of responding to different environmental demands. Strategic decisions concerning how an organization will respond to its environment must be matched by equally strategic decisions concerning how the organization will manage the flow of employees. Not having the right skilled workers or managers when they are needed can seriously undermine the success of strategic business choices. Just as damaging is a surplus of human resources which can be costly to the corporation and potentially damaging to the sense of well-being of employees. Unfortunately, the problem of ensuring that the right people are available is not merely a problem of forecasting personnel requirements, difficult as that task is. The availability of needed talent is also a function of the corporation's capacity to attract, keep, and develop the people it needs. These tasks require that management adopt a social capital perspective (see Chapter 1). Employees are treated as investments which if properly supported and developed can yield a long-term stream of benefits to the organization, not as variable costs to be hired when the organization is growing and laid off when the organization is retrenching (though clearly cost effectiveness must be of continuing concern).

A corporation's continually changing requirements for types and numbers of people are sometimes poorly matched with concurrent employee needs for stability and opportunity. The objective of human resource flow policies is to meet the corporation's current and future force requirements and employees' career needs at the same time. Obviously, these objectives may be in conflict. Unions are often formed as a result of conflict between employers and employees about these very issues. Therefore, human resource flow policies must reflect management's values about the relative importance of organization and employee needs.

## THREE PERSPECTIVES IN MANAGING FLOW

We are suggesting that flow policies can be approached from the point of view of the *individual* employee and of the *organization*. Increasingly, these policies must also reflect the interests of yet another stakeholder: the organization's host *society*. These interests are imposed upon the organization through government legislation and regulatory agency policies concerned with such matters as employment, promotion, termination, and retirement. Though the role of government differs from country to country, its involvement reflects the fact that corporate policies on human resource flow have a profound effect on people's economic and psychological well-being, and therefore have an effect on the economic and social well-being of society as a whole. Thus, flow policies can be examined and evaluated from the perspective of the *individual*, the *organization*, and *society*.

### *Individual Perspective*[1]

The term "career" is too often seen as applicable only to the lives of managers and professionals, and not to the lives of nonexempt white- or blue-collar workers. Typically, the term connotes upward mobility and aspiration. From that perspective, an assembly line worker or a restaurant waiter is not thought of as having a career. As a result, corporations focus career development efforts on their professionals and managers, while ignoring blue-collar workers. Since human resource management applies to *all* employees, a broader concept of career seems to be in order. From this broadened perspective, careers may be viewed as "a series of separate but related experiences and adventures through which a person, any person, passes during a lifetime.''[2] Careers can be long or short, and an individual can pursue multiple careers either in sequence or at the same time. In this sense, the concept of career becomes a shorthand notation for a particular set of activities with a natural, unfolding history—involvement over time in a given role or series of roles. Moreover, career includes both an individual's work and family experiences, as well as the interaction between the two.

An individual attempts to gain control of these ''separate but related'' experiences so that they fit an emerging self-concept (self-perception of unique competence and values). At the same time, that self-concept is progressively shaped by work and family experiences. Central to this broader definition of careers is the component of identity. As Erik Erikson has said, identity is never gained once and for all, but is achieved throughout life.

Individual careers develop from an interaction between the competencies and career goals an individual brings to the organization and the work experience the organization provides. To the extent that the organization provides opportunities for the individual to use and develop his or her personal competence while moving through various jobs, functions, and levels, the individual will grow and experience career satisfaction.

Organizations may respond to strategic requirements for certain skills by altering the types of opportunities they provide. For example, a strategic decision to develop more generalists rather than functional specialists must be accompanied by human response policies that provide opportunities for and encourage multifunctional experiences. Multifunctional experiences also provide an opportunity for individuals to clarify their career goals and to decide whether this developmental direction is personally satisfying. Thus, varied experiences act to clarify a person's career goals as well as develop them.

It should be clear that career development is an organic, unfolding process rather than a mechanistic, preprogramed one. Each career experience leads to a new understanding of self as new successes or failures redefine how individuals see themselves, their potential, and their limitations. Each experience therefore reshapes an individual's career aspirations. Major failures can lead to career crises which arise from job choices that do not fit the individual's core competencies and personality. Understanding and managing a process that avoids major failures but makes possible personal learning and growth is critically important if organizations are to develop their employees while at the same time giving them career satisfaction. It is generally accepted that the more control an individual has over career choices, the more the individual is likely to choose a career path that fits his or her core competencies and values, thereby ensuring satisfactions and growth. Historically, individuals had little control over their life's work. Career choices were determined by one's station in life, one's family, and one's society. Most organizations gave employees little control over their careers, preferring to make placement and promotion decisions without consultation. It has become increasingly clear that this practice cannot continue, given the desire and power of today's employees to exert more control over their careers.

One example of this desire and expanding power to control one's own career can be seen in today's "knowledge workers." With marketable skills gained through education rather than through apprenticeship, they have the ability and the interest to exercise substantial control over their careers. With the growth in demand for knowledge workers (skilled labor, professionals, and managers), these individuals will have to be allowed increasing control over the entire course of their working lives, such as becoming established, being promoted, undergoing job changes, reaching a leveling-off point, being fired or laid off, and facing eventual retirement. As we shall see, organizations, too, want control over these events and for this reason a continual tension exists.

This broad concept of career implies that it is impossible for organizations to apply a single definition to what desirable career development is. For managers and professionals, it may be an opportunity to develop and advance, though advancement may be defined differently by an engineer and an achievement-oriented business school graduate. For many blue-collar and white-collar workers, employment security and stability may be more important, while security may be of lesser importance to managers and professionals. Further, assessments of career needs are complicated by changes in career aspirations that take place throughout a person's life.

Effective human resource flow policies and practices must allow a continual process of *matching* individual career needs and organizational requirements. Of course, to the extent that an organization develops an interactive process, it not only allows individuals who want to exercise career choices to do so, but it also arouses desires to make career choices in employees who may not otherwise have thought they had such control their lives. In this regard, such policies can shape the amount of influence employees may come to want over their careers.

It is important to note that employees' perspectives may differ between cultures. Do Japanese workers have different career needs with respect to rapid promotion and do they desire less control over their careers than American workers? We do not know the answer to this and other specific questions about cultural differences, but we do know that cultural and organizational forces shape views of careers just as personal forces do.

### *Societal Perspective*

It is no longer possible for managers to develop human resource flow policies and priorities without considering the societal perspective. That perspective can be said to impose itself on the organiztion in one of three ways: through the shifting values of the work force, through the impact of outside institutions, and through regulation and labor union policy.

SHIFTING WORK FORCE VALUES. Complicating the problem of managing human resource flows is an apparent shift in social values away from a view of work as the single most important aspect of life, and toward a view that work is only one of many facets of life. Strategic decisions concerning internal movement and career development of employees can no longer be made without taking into account this growing emphasis on both self-development and family development. Employees no longer automatically accept job assignments that their employers consider important for their development if these assignments conflict with personal and family needs. Similarly, blue-collar workers no longer accept as given the fact that they must and should work overtime. As educational levels increase, blue-collar workers may grow dissatisfied with the same routine job for the duration of their careers. Flow policies that give these workers opportunities for career progress will become more important. These trends probably apply most to economically developed countries where standards of living are high and security needs have been met, freeing individuals to seek fulfillment of other needs. However, good cross-cultural data are not available.

OUTSIDE INSTITUTIONS. The emergence of knowledge workers as a growing proportion of the work force makes organizations increasingly dependent on educational institutions. Not only do these institutions control the number of people that will be available to corporations, they often create and define career paths in society through program decisions. These institutions also socialize people within particular career paths. The expectation and values of the students they turn out may or may not mesh with organizational realities. When they do not, frustration and turnover are often the result. The current shortage of engineers in high-technology companies, and the frustration of pharmacists with their roles in large pharmaceutical chains are only two examples of such mismatches between the programs of educational institutions and the needs of business. An interactive process between educational institutions and business is required so that educational institutions will be able to shape and modify their programs to business needs so that corporate human resource flow policies will mesh with educational realities.

GOVERNMENT REGULATION AND LABOR UNION POLICY. Government bodies and labor unions are increasingly responding to the needs of people for employment security. There is growing research evidence that the unemployment that results from corporations that treat labor as a variable cost creates psychological stress and social dislocation. Losing one's job can increase family problems, endanger emotional health, and increase the likelihood of alcoholism, drug abuse, psychiatric disorders, cardiovascular disease, and even suicide.[3] In Europe, high severance pay requirements and other legislative restrictions on an employer's freedom to terminate employees have resulted, in part at least, from an awareness of such negative costs. Under the restraints imposed in many European countries, managers will have to manage in a way that stabilizes employment and offers more security. An American firm operating in Belgium recently found that it could no longer afford to tolerate its subsidiary manager's policy of terminating employees he perceived to be ineffective. The costs of termination were just too high. Instead, that manager had to learn to obtain effective performance through better selection and management methods.

As the cost of termination increases, or the flexibility of management decreases—through either government legislation, social pressures, collective bargaining agreements, or explicit unilateral policy decisions by employers—management will have to give increasing attention to deciding which employees to hire in the first place and efforts to train, retrain, or otherwise develop their already available human resources. This has been true for some time in Japan, where approximately 30 percent of the work force—those in large corporations—have lifelong employment, and it appears to be the direction in which some United States corporations are also going.

On the other hand, legislation is often used to open career paths that historically have been available to only a privileged few. Workforce, welfare, and unemployment policies affect the careers of people and the supply of people available to firms. Similarly, licensing and standardization of occupations in various states and industries affect corporate selection and training policies. In the United States, equal opportunity legislation has and will continue to have significant effects on hiring, internal placement and promotions, and termination practices. Selection methods and performance evaluation systems are being challenged in the courts on the grounds of their validity and objectivity. Class action suits, brought against companies by the Equal Employment Opportunity Commission (EEOC) on behalf of groups of employees, can end in settlements worth millions of dollars. The most celebrated of these suits, involving the EEOC and AT&T, ended in a consent decree costing the company $33 million. There has also been an increase in the number of lawsuits that employees in the United States are bringing against corporations claiming unjustified discharge.[4]

The emergence of legislation and regulations governing flow policies reflects the recognition by society that corporate actions have profound effects on the well-being of people and society as a whole. Layoffs, for example, have economic consequences for the communities in which they occur. Because of strong family and community ties, some unemployed workers will remain in their city or state instead of looking for work in other sections of the country. Layoffs thus often place the greatest financial burdens on the communities that can least afford to carry it.

When social and government agencies are burdened by the social and psychological problems resulting from layoffs, *all* citizens end up paying an economic and social price. Though less dramatic, flow policies that do not allow personal development and utilization of employees' talents also reduce the quality of life and have social consequences. For example, Kornhauser found that employees in dull jobs are less involved in family and community affairs.[5]

We may say, then, that human resource flow policies can have significant negative social consequences. On the other hand, they can contribute to the career development and life satisfaction of employees, thereby enhancing societal well-being.

### *Organizational Perspective*

Managing human resources flow has historically *not* been a major strategic consideration in running a business. Many of the jobs required in business organizations were unique to individual companies and could be acquired only through experience within those organizations. Because of the relatively slow pace of change, skill requirements did not change much over time. Many jobs such as accounting or management had not yet emerged as professions, and there were few technical and professional schools to supply needed talent. Government was relatively uninvolved in employment issues. There was also a large supply of labor willing to move from agriculture to the factory and office.

All of these factors have changed. The emergence of the knowledge workers in the labor force, rapid changes in technology and business practices, the increasing need for generalists, more complex organizations, the emergence of minorities and women, mobility of the work force, and the greater involvement of government have made the management of human resource flow policies a more important consideration. Rapid change can result in costly excess work force, while rapid growth can mean insufficient workers. The unavailability of an experienced plant manager is clearly as critical to the success of an operation as the unavailability of capital resources. From the organization's perspective, effective flow policies should lead to the following outcomes:

1. Availability of the right number of personnel with the needed mix of competences in the short and the long term.
2. Development of people needed to staff the organization in the future.
3. Employee perception of opportunity for advancement and development consistent with their needs.
4. Employee perception of relative security from termination due to factors beyond their control.
5. Employee perception that selection, placement, promotion, and termination decisions are fair.
6. The lowest possible payroll and people-processing costs possible to meet the objectives above.

Finally, it should be understood that policies concerning recruitment, selection, promotion, and termination of employees are the means by which institutions can shape a philosophy of management; they are often the implicit means by which a corporate culture is formed. Not only do people become socialized through their experiences with flow policies, they also come to recognize the qualities of behavior that will be rewarded with promotion, and they come to form views about management's concern for their well-being.

## HUMAN RESOURCE FLOW POLICIES, SYSTEMS, AND PRACTICES

As the discussion so far has indicated, human resource flow must be managed strategically so as to match organizational needs with the career aspirations of employees. This must be done within the constraints imposed by social institutions, and with the well-being of society in mind. At best, managing human resource flow is imperfect. Some people will always be insecure or unhappy with the opportunities afforded them. Every organization has considerable "noise levels" associated with these issues. Similarly, the best personnel planning process may not deliver the people needed by the firm because employees do not grow as expected or because business projections do not materialize. However, major discontinuities can be avoided and employee satisfaction can be increased by more deliberate planning and examination of particular policies, practices, and systems and their relationship to each other. We now turn to a discussion of some of the strategic issues that general managers must consider in managing human resource flow.

### *1. Managing Inflow*

Recruitment decisions about where and how to recruit can have an important impact on the composition of the work force, its ultimate fit with the corporation's needs and culture, and employee turnover. These decisions affect all of the four Cs: competence, commitment, congruence (conflict), and cost effectiveness.

Problems in recruiting, particularly for certain professional and technical talent, arise when educational institutions fail to yield an adequate flow of qualified graduates. The recurring shortage of engineers, for example, results from fluctuations in the supply of engineering graduates and experienced engineers (which in turn are related to demographics and past educational patterns), and from fluctuations in the overall demand for engineers.[6] While it is not our purpose to present a detailed discussion of the identification and selection of recruits, we can point to several methods that organizations can use to ensure an adequate supply of talent:

1. A decision to locate facilities in the proximity of educational institutions that graduate people with the needed competencies or in industrial centers that already employ such people can increase the availability of talent.
2. Human resource functions can provide schools, particularly schools from which they recruit, with forecasts of future personnel needs.
3. Corporations can develop their own educational institutions, as Wang Laboratories and General Motors have done.
4. An organization that develops a good reputation as an employer in such areas as employment security, compensation, employee relations, and opportunity for challenging work and growth can increase its capacity to attract recruits.
5. Corporations can establish ongoing relationships with universities by assigning key executives to coordinate recruiting and by donating time, equipment, and people to those schools.
6. Corporations can use visits and summer jobs as a way of identifying talent and involving students early in their schooling, perhaps several years before they are ready to enter the job market.

#### *Criteria for Judging Recruiting Effectiveness*

Recruitment policies need to be considered as part of an organization's overall strategy for two reasons. The first and more obvious reason is that recruitment seeks to provide the organization with people who have the talents needed to achieve strategic goals. But recruitment will also have significant impact on long-range employment stability and turnover. Employee turnover is both disruptive and costly. It is well known that the most important reason for turnover within the first several years of employment is unmet expectations, and these disappointments are often a function of the recruitment process itself. Managers motivated to attract scarce talent tend to discuss only positive elements of the job and company while glossing over less attractive realities. They do not help the prospective employee to assess realistically the fit between personal skills and goals and the job and the organization. A more open process of communicating organizational realities would yield employees who were satisfied with their careers. New hires would be more highly motivated to adapt themselves to organizational realities. The likelihood of fit in expectations, skills, and core values between themselves and the organization would be higher because more self-selection would take place. Some companies have found that training line managers to conduct recruiting interviews can improve the effectiveness of recruitment. The interviewee can also take some responsibility by asking hard questions and testing for fit between him- or herself and the organization.

The discussion above suggests that the recruitment and "joining up" process should not be looked at only from the point of view of its impact on cost effectiveness and congruence or conflict. Recruiting can be an important strategy for shaping the culture of the organization. It is at the time of recruitment and entry into the organization that an implicit "psychological contract" begins to be formed between employee and organization. Prospective employees receive many signals about what the company expects, just as company recruiters make many judgments about the fit of the prospective employee with the company.

Understanding these transactions can help general managers understand the culture of their organization. Reshaping these transactions can help them develop their organization in desired directions. For example, the choice of which managers in the corporation will recruit and make final selection decisions will affect who enters the organization, and what their competencies, predispositions, values, and expectations will be. It is for this reason that key line managers often involve themselves in recruitment interviews. They want to influence the inflow of personnel because they know it is a major lever for shaping the company.

### 2. *Managing Internal Flow*

Once employees have been recruited, their flow through the organization—transfers, job assignments, promotions, and demotions—

must be managed so that their competence is developed to meet corporate needs, while at the same time they satisfy their own career aspirations. We will now discuss key considerations in managing internal flows: the velocity of personnel flow, the assessment and measurement of performance effectiveness, and the development of employee skills and competencies. Each of these considerations must be viewed in terms of its impact on organizational effectiveness and employee and societal well-being.

### *Velocity of Personnel Flow*

By velocity of personnel flow, we mean the rate at which employees move from job to job. Velocity may be examined for horizontal movement (lateral transfers) and vertical movement (promotions). It varies widely between different employee groups in the corporation. Historically, middle and upper middle managers have moved from job to job rather frequently; the average time in a job being as low as two to three years in some corporations. Among clerical workers or technicians, the average time in a job may be far higher, say five to ten years. Similarly, managers in mature industries are likely to be in their jobs far longer than managers in growth industries like high technology or health care. Finally, velocity for different employee groups will vary across time periods. For example, the postwar baby boom will lead to a large population increase in the 35 to 50 age category between 1980 and 1990. That increase will be accompanied by a relatively slower growth in middle management jobs, resulting in fewer opportunities and slower upward movement.

Corporate Strategy and Velocity. Any given velocity may have positive and negative outcomes with predicatable benefits and costs, and these must be balanced by the general manager. The important point is that velocity is part of managing human resource flow and it warrants monitoring. Naturally, flow velocities are sometimes beyond control of management—demographics, for example, will affect velocity. But managers make some decisions that have consequences for human resource flow velocities but are not immediately recognized to have such effects. For example, strategic decisions concerning how rapidly a corporation grows will affect flow velocities. Too often, market opportunities are considered far more important than human resource considerations in determining a growth strategy. The potential consequences of insufficient human resources on profitable growth and the effects of rapid growth on quality of life need to be weighed.

Decisions about how many employees are to be recruited each year also affect velocity, as well as the availability of trained personnel in the future. Uneven recruiting from year to year, often brought on by economic cycles, can force rapid movement and promotion for one cohort of entering employees and too-slow movement for another. Such uneven recruiting patterns result in an uneven supply of talent to replace retiring employees or feed growth. Companies with lifetime employment that promote only from within have learned that steady recruitment is necessary to assure a balanced distribution of age and skill in the work force.

In evaluating the strategic impact of velocity decisions, managers can consider the impact of their decisions on the following HRM outcomes:

1. *Satisfaction and commitment.* Satisfaction of employees with career development will increase if upward mobility in the corporation becomes more rapid. Lateral transfers also seem to have a similar effect. These in turn are likely to increase commitment to the organization because employees see a bright future in terms of personal rewards.
2. *Competence.* A curvilinear relationship probably exists between velocity and the development of employee competence. That is, slow movement of personnel (laterally or vertically) is likely to result in too few opportunities for employees to broaden their skills and their perspective of the enterprise—that is, to develop as generalists. On the other hand, the type of very rapid personnel movement that is experienced in rapid growth companies can easily result in individuals progressing faster than their capacity to develop and demonstrate skills. The result can be failure for the individual (the well-known Peter Principle) and a resulting loss of investment by the company.
3. *Motivation.* There is also a curvilinear relationship between velocity and motivation. Too many years in the same job will reduce motivation, as the challenge that comes from efforts to master a new task declines.[7] On the other hand, insufficient time to master a task not only leads to the inadequate development mentioned above, but may prevent individuals from developing a sense of competence and a continued desire to achieve.
4. *Congruence.* Slower advancement can lead employees to question the fairness of the decision-making process in the corporation. The consequence can be litigation by employees, particularly women and minorities. On the other hand, high velocity can be so demanding that quality of life suffers, particularly in relationships with family. Personal stress and higher divorce rates are not uncommon among employees in rapidly growing high-

technology companies. Similar symptoms have been found among blue-collar employees in new plants that are attempting to increase commitment by having employees rotate jobs, take more responsibility, and assume accountability.

5. *Costs.* High flow velocities are more costly. An employee who has been on the job a short time is less effective. Also, the costs of training and transfers are high and getting higher. Finally, the risks of employee failure and costly mistakes resulting from inexperience must be considered.

### *Defining and Evaluating Employee Effectiveness*

The management of personnel flow through the organization requires continual judgments by managers about potential effectiveness of recruits and employees. Poor judgments translate into failure for the individual, immediate costs resulting from poor performance, and long-range costs associated with missed opportunities to promote employees who have potential. Too many bad personnel decisions can leave an organization without adequate backup personnel to fill openings created by promotions or retirements. The cumulative impact of poor individual judgments will ultimately impair the ability of the organization and its subunits to meet their strategic and business goals.

The biggest problem in selecting and evaluating effective employees is the subjective nature of the process. Except for education, academic performance, and specific technical skills, it is hard to measure the characteristics that are assumed to be predictive of performance: motivation, cooperation, ability to make decisions, initiative, ability to work under pressure, capacity to develop, and capacity to supervise. Even when attempting to be objective about whether a candidate possesses certain qualities, a manager sees the candidate through his or her own personality, past experiences, and values. Managers tend to hire people in their own image. While such an approach may ensure smooth boss-subordinate relationships, it may not ensure effectiveness, particularly if the biases imposed on the selection process—temperament, dress, social mannerisms, etc.—are not in actuality related to performance. Since managers' values and predispositions are subtly shaped by the culture of the organization, the potential for systematic bias throughout the organization is high.

One of the by-products of managers hiring in their own image has been systematic discrimination against minorities and women. Government has responded to this discrimination with legislation such as the Civil Rights Act of 1964, requiring employers to hire and promote women and minorities in proportion to their presence in the larger population. If they cannot do this, employers must prove that their personnel decision-making process is baed on job-relevant selection criteria. While some corporations have always had an interest in developing good and fair selection and evaluation procedures, government legislation and the potential for costly court decisions have stimulated a wider concern about this problem.

Unfortunately, efforts to develop objective employee evaluation procedures have not met with great success. To be sure, psychological testing, assessment centers, and improved performance appraisal systems have contributed to some improvements in the judgments that can be made. But these methods have not changed the fact that it is fallible human beings who fill out appraisal forms or integrate information from tests and third-party assessments into their decision-making process. We suggest that the task of evaluating performance be approached with realistic expectations. Countless corporations have experienced a common pattern when new procedures for selecting and evaluating employees are established: an initial period of enthusiasm is followed by general disillusionment as problems become evident. Finally, another new method is developed to solve those problems, and the whole pattern repeats itself.[8]

At best, the *methods* of selection and evaluation will be imperfect in their capacity to measure performance and potential and in their capacity to meet tests of objectivity and fairness. This suggests that more emphasis be placed on the *process* of selection and evaluation and how it is embedded in the larger organization, and on the amount of influence employees have on that process. Such influence can come through the participation of employees in the definition of effectiveness and through their direct involvement in evaluating prospective employees, peers, and bosses. Employee effectiveness traditionally has been defined and evaluated exclusively by management, but consultation with employees can give managers the opportunity to improve their own judgments with relevant information and improve employee perception of fairness.

With this perspective in mind, we now proceed to a discussion of two major questions that must be addressed in managing the selection and evaluation process: what is effectiveness and how will effectiveness be evaluated?

WHAT IS EFFECTIVENESS? That question must be addressed at two levels of analysis: the immediate job for which a person is being considered, and the culture of the organization in which that job is situated. Except for some blue-collar, clerical, and technical positions that are relatively easy to define, insufficient attention has been given to identifying the requirements for job success. As a result, typical specifications call for certain academic standing and work experience. These specifications have the virtue of being measurable. Unfortunately, they may not be relevant. Most selection processes, particularly those for higher-level jobs, tend to be based more on general parameters and subjective assessments than on defined characteristics that are assessed with objectivity.[9]

A clear statement of job responsibilities is also not entirely helpful because these cannot always be translated into the skills, abilities, and knowledge that the individual must possess. Managers concerned with improving selection and promotion decisions must invest time and energy, both of which are quite costly commodities, in specifying the task segments of a job and translating these into the specific skills and knowledge required to perform the job. Personnel departments can help. But if the resulting definition of effectiveness is to be truly relevant to the organization's task, managers must be involved in the definition process.

Effectiveness, particularly in managerial positions, is also a function of the organization's culture. Over time, many characteristics and ways of doing things come to be valued by the organization and are implicitly or explicitly taken into account during selection and promotion processes. General managers must attempt to define as explicitly as possible what individual characteristics are valued. Personnel specialists can help by researching the characteristics that distinguish effective and ineffective performers as defined by judgments of the corporation's managers. This research process makes it possible for managers to examine these characteristics for their relevance to business strategy and organizational effectiveness and helps them identify irrelevant biases or important omissions. It allows top management to determine if their philosophy is adequately represented in personnel decisions and to take appropriate action if it is not.

Organizations that rely on a strong culture of shared traditions and beliefs for achieving employee commitment must be especially concerned about selecting and promoting individuals with characteristics that fit that culture. Such organizations can sustain their culture only if they maintain a fairly high degree of homogeneity of values. They are, therefore, likely to emphasize personality and management style as significant dimensions, perhaps more than technical skill. Of course, by doing so they may discriminate against certain employees, and take the risk that their biases violate legislative guidelines or society's values.

So far, little has been said about results—sales, costs, profits, market share, number of units produced, etc.—as a criterion of effectiveness. This is not because we believe that the attainment of results is irrelevant, but because results are not the *only* criterion of effectiveness, even when they are espoused to be the primary criterion for promotion and compensation decisions. When first introduced, quantitative measures of results were thought to be the way to make performance evaluations more objective. However, such measures do not always reflect important dimensions of performance nor are they always within the control of employees. Thus, "process" dimensions of effectiveness (those having to do with *how* the job is done) are often introduced in personnel decisions. Furthermore, the accomplishment of results at one level is not always a good predictor of whether an employee will be able to function effectively at higher levels in the organization.

Figure 4–1 illustrates this point. Individuals who achieve results *and* exhibit the behaviors, attitudes, and characteristics that experience suggests are effective and/or that managers believe to be effective are clearly effective performers and possess the potential to rise in the organization. Individuals who do not obtain results and do not fit are rarely retained by organizations because they do not appear to have the potential to succeed. It is the individuals in the other two quadrants who present dilemmas for organizations. Those who do not achieve results but do fit behaviorally are sometimes promoted well beyond their level of competence. Organizations that attempt to identify high-potential employees early in their careers are subject to this error. These individuals may be promoted so rapidly on their *assumed* potential that they never master either the business management or technical task. On the other hand, some employees are not promoted despite a consistent record of results because they are not judged to possess the skills required for higher-level positions and/or because they do not fit the culture. For example, some successful plant managers or successful deal-makers in banks do not understand how they could have been passed over for promotion, given their job performance. What they do not understand, and what has not been made explicit by their organizations, is that certain behavioral skills and personal styles are as strategically important to the organization as are quantifiable and measurable technical skills. Because they do not know what these behavioral skills and style characteristics are or how strategically important they are relative to results, these individuals are unable to develop them or make the decision to seek other employment—an argument for explicitly defining and communicating behaviors associated with effectiveness.

If behavior is to be a criterion, attention must be given to the question of fairness as viewed by employees. Employees who do not believe that the criteria being utilized are relevant will either leave the organization or protest by seeking legal redress or union protection. In the past, management has dealt with this problem by commissioning personnel research studies to establish the objectivity of effectiveness criteria. But this approach still leaves the power for defining effectiveness

| | | Results: High | Results: Low |
|---|---|---|---|
| Behavioral fit | High | Effective performer | ? |
| | Low | ? | Ineffective performer |

**FIGURE 4–1 Effectiveness Dimensions**

with management. An alternative approach may be to allow employees more influence in selecting managers or peers as a way of giving them influence in the definition of effectiveness. Peer ratings, which have been shown to be good predictors of effectiveness, probably gain their validity because peers possess information about each other that superiors may not possess. Some of the most innovative work systems in the United States involve members of work teams in the selection of new employees, although getting employees to rate their peers is difficult and requires extraordinary maturity and interpersonal competence. Employee task forces may be involved in defining effectiveness for their group, department, or plant, creating the standards that will guide personnel decisions in the organizations as a whole. Employee influence in defining effectiveness can only work, however, if employees and management share common goals.

HOW WILL EFFECTIVENESS BE EVALUATED? Organizations face two sets of evaluation problems: evaluation of *prospective* and of *current* employees. Even if effectiveness has been adequately defined, managers must still assess the extent to which individuals possess certain characteristics. The most common methods for doing this are the employment and performance appraisal interviews. Because both methods have been shown to be subject to bias, they have been supplemented with other methods:

1. Structured interviews
2. Interviews or performance evaluations by multiple managers/evaluators
3. Checklists of derived characteristics as guides to the employment and performance appraisal interview
4. Paper-and-pencil tests of ability, intelligence, personality, and interest

5. Clinical assessments by psychologists or consultants
6. Internally administered assessment centers and performance tests that ask individuals to perform tasks under simulated conditions

These methods structure the assessment process so that information gathered is more reliable (less subject to errors in measurement) and more valid (the information is relevant and predicts effectiveness with greater accuracy) than is the information collected in employment and appraisal interviews alone. The predictive power of these additional assessment techniques is established by one of two types of validity studies. Either the characteristics being measured have been shown to be correlated with the present performance of current employees (concurrent validity), or scores on tests or evaluations are correlated with later performance on the job or advancement in the organization (predictive validity). Another method for determining the validity of an assessment procedure is to examine whether the knowledge and skills being assessed represent adequately the actual content of the job (content validity). These methods of validation have all been subject to challenge in the courts. Of the three methods, content validity is most likely to be upheld by the courts. If more than one of the approaches to validation described above have been used, the organization's assessment methods have generally been upheld.

Many corporations prefer not to use either paper-and-pencil tests or assessment centers during recruitment for fear that applicants will resent being subjected to such an evaluation process. Some companies use these methods to help evaluate the potential of existing employees, while others may attempt to increase objectivity (validity) through multiple appraisals, checklists of relevant characteristics, and the use of in-depth clinical interviews by psychologists or personnel specialists. Self-selection by prospective and present employees is a method that is underused by corporations. If employees are informed candidly and in some depth about the characteristics that are required for success, they will eventually select jobs or career tracks that are realistic given their talents and aspirations.

Discussions about the validity of various testing and measurement tools have usually been the province of staff specialists. However, we are suggesting that general managers need some familiarity both with the general concept of validity and with the specific applications within their organization. More structured and well-researched methods of assessment can improve the organization's probability of selecting the right people for specific jobs when effectiveness has been defined. What is less clear is the impact of these methods on the relationship between the individual and the organization. Do applicants or existing employees who are subjected to the various impersonal selection procedures resent them and, as a result, decide to go elsewhere? If so, what kind of people are alienated by these procedures, and how do they differ from those who are not? Would an emphasis on self-selection as opposed to formal selection procedures demonstrate an organization's commitment to informed choice and self-control over career? If so, how would this emphasis affect who decides to take a job and how that individual subsequently relates to the corporation? These are all questions that general managers, as well as testing and measurement staff specialists, must weigh.

The challenge to managers is to take advantage of available measurement and testing technology, while not losing sight of its effects on how recruits perceive and later relate to the organization. The companies most successful in their use of sophisticated assessment methods have usually avoided using results in a rigid manner. It is important to recognize that the more openly and regularly assessment results are discussed with inside or outside candidates, the more trust candidates have in those results.

Evaluations of employee effectiveness and potential are usually performed by supervisors and then used by management to make personnel decisions. An enormous amount of time, money, and energy has gone into the development of different performance appraisal systems. While improved appraisal systems may better reflect job content, successful implementation still rests largely with the managers involved in the process. And a significant number of managers resist evaluating their subordinates. When controls force them to evaluate, they provide ratings of questionable validity. In response, some corporations have adopted forced distributions in rating employees. Quotas mandate a fixed percentage of employees that will be placed in each of the rating categories from poor to excellent. This type of forced distribution, however, is resented by managers and subordinates alike. It has the potential for damaging the self-esteem of individuals, particularly since studies have shown that a disproportionate percentage of employees rate themselves as high performers.

Research evidence and experience suggest that managers assign more accurate performance ratings when those ratings are not used to make personnel decisions and/or when they are not made available to subordinates. Because evaluations of performance are a matter of judgment, managers are naturally concerned about negative impacts on pay, promotion, and job security. They also prefer not to discuss these ratings with subordinates, because they do not want to damage relationships. If they have to justify the ratings or if personnel decisions about pay, promotions, or terminations are to be made as a result of their judgments, ratings tend to be less valid.

For this reason, it has been recommended that evaluation for administrative purposes (pay and promotion) be kept separate from evaluations for career development purposes. Developmental evaluations should be performed at different times from pay and promotion assessments, and the results should not be placed in personnel files. By separating these two evaluation processes, it is hoped that evaluations for administrative purposes will be more accurate, while performance feedback discussions will be open, but not overly evaluative.

There are no easy solutions; it is unlikely that the evaluation problem will ever be completely resolved. The most creative solutions have concentrated on the *process* rather than the *method* of appraisal and on *developing manager ability and motivation to evaluate accurately and communicate* this evaluation openly to subordinates.

### *Employee Career Development*

There are really two major concerns that a human resource flow policy must address when considering ways of managing internal flow. The first, addressed above, is the question of how to define and evaluate performance effectiveness. Consistent with the social capital perspective of HRM introduced in Chapter 1, we would also suggest that internal flow policies need to address the matter of employee and career development. After selection, employee development is one of the key methods available to corporations for ensuring the mix of skills needed to be competitive in the future. It is a form of investment which is directly related to the corporation's capacity to be flexible and adaptable to changes in its environment. In short, employee development is a key strategy for organizational survival and growth.

Far from taking a coherent and strategic approach to employee development, many corporations engage in scattered, uncoordinated, or even inconsistent developmental activities that are poorly suited to the developmental needs of individuals or to the corporation's strategic needs. Training departments plan programs and market them internally in accordance with their perceptions of developmental needs, which do not always coincide with the strategic goals of the company or individual employee needs. Employees are often transferred or promoted on a timetable dictated by organizational needs, not by their own readiness. Participation in a training program may not coincide effectively with the need for education created by a job transfer or promotion. Assessment, feedback and counseling methods are rarely coordinated to maximize the learning and development of the individual. This lack of coordination between centralized practices and the individual's needs can reduce development, because as we stated at the beginning of this chapter, individual development is an organic unfolding process, not a mechanistic one.

The challenge, then, is to *stimulate* and *guide* an essentially individual developmental process in a way that is consistent with corporate needs. Some corporations operate with few centrally planned career development programs, while others have chosen to centralize and control the process to the detriment of individual choice, growth, and career satisfaction. The most effective approach is for general managers to create a context that encourages employee development in directions that meet corporate needs but does not overdetermine the speed or direction of any given individual's development.

We have said that the *career development* process encompasses *a series of experiences* that stretch individuals to learn new knowledge, attitudes, and behavior. Through this process, employees can determine if they have the core competencies to master the task. If they do not, they obtain feedback that the career directions chosen are not the right ones. If they do master the new experiences or jobs, the resulting sense of accomplishment confirms the direction chosen and sustains it as long as the experience continues to be satisfying. Employees must, of course, stay in their jobs long enough to obtain closure, to see the results of their efforts. This cannot happen when the velocity of movement in the firm is too rapid.[10] It should be clear that the most important developmental experiences are job and task experiences. This fact is not always reflected in the mix and sequence of developmental tools used by corporations. Education and training, which are not always sequenced to complement a special assignment, seem to work best when job experiences have motivated an individual to learn needed knowledge, and when they are accompanied by feedback on performance and counseling from a respected supervisor.

When the slow growth of a firm precludes promotions as a means of providing growth experiences, job enrichment—the redesign of work to include more responsibilities—is used increasingly to stimulate development and reduce costs. Enrichment is usually applied to traditionally fairly narrow blue-collar jobs, but it can also be applied to middle management, where too many jobs and levels have increased costs and reduced opportunity. Lateral transfers are another method of providing an opportunity for development and growth short of promotions.

Figure 4–2 illustrates the multiple tools that must be properly mixed and sequenced by the supervisor and employee working collaboratively to enhance the employee's development. Organizations need to inventory these tools in order to make them known to managers and to develop plans to help managers use them. Education programs are easier to inventory than job enrichment programs, which is why they are more frequently used. But it is the competence of supervisors in performance appraisal, coaching, counseling, modeling, and supporting that is the key to a program's success. Therefore, if career development is to occur in an organization, general managers must find ways

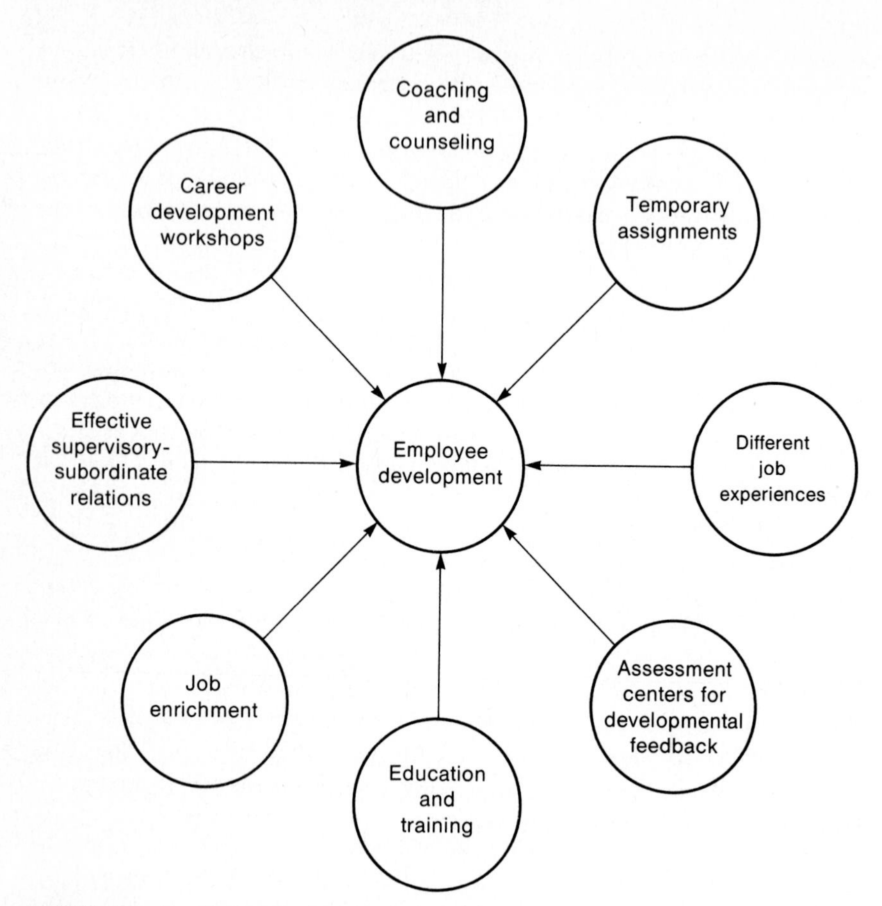


**FIGURE 4–2 Tools for Employee Development**

to select, train, and reward so as to build these elusive developmental skills. Some corporations are supplementing the supervisor's role in coaching and counseling with a staff of personnel specialists trained in this task. Career development workshops and assessment centers are also utilized to provide participants with a guided experience in exploring their interests and aspirations.

Perhaps the most important but underutilized part of the developmental process is follow-up. When developmental plans are created by a supervisor and submitted to the personnel department, it is essential that the company follow up to determine what the result has been. As we shall see, the key to follow-up is a continuous forum for discussing the potential of employees and their developmental needs.

We now turn to a brief examination of the context that general managers might create to encourage employee/career development, and discuss some of the elements of that context.

PHILOSOPHY AND REWARDS. In some companies few resources are available for education and career development, and supervisors do not spend much time discussing performance or doing career planning. In others, such as AT&T, Exxon and IBM, considerable emphasis is placed on these activities. Exxon's chief executive officer, Clifford Garvin, meets frequently with the corporate compensation and executive development committee to discuss the top 250 executives in the company.[11] For a career development process to be encouraged centrally but not overly controlled, managers throughout the corporation must share a belief that employee development is important and will be rewarded. This shared belief must be articulated by the organization's leaders. They must provide a model for effective career development in their relations with subordinates and they must explicitly and visibly reward managers for developing people.

CAREER OPPORTUNITY INFORMATION. In order to ensure that employee development is successfully meshed with an organization's strategy, it is essential that the organization encourage employees not just to develop, but to develop in directions required by that strategy. Are technical skills likely to become less valued in the next five years as compared with general management skills? Will the company be placing more emphasis in the upcoming years on the interpersonal and behavioral skills of its managers? Is it likely to need a more aggressive sales force? Will competitiveness hinge on low costs, efficiency, and productivity? It is not only important for organizations to be able to answer such questions, but the answers must also be *communicated* to employees. Only through such communication will employees have some idea of what skills will be valued in the future and what experiences are considered important in developing those skills.

To do this well, corporations should project the types of jobs and skills requirements they estimate will exist in the future given their business strategies. Will the competitive edge in the future be obtained through production, sales, or technical work? What mix of skills is likely to be valued, to fit evolving corporate strategy and culture? Just as important, what have been the career paths to general management or technical management in the past? Estimates of future growth can never be totally accurate, but employees should be encouraged to think about what paths successful people in various careers have followed and how these paths might change in the future. Information can be disseminated through publications, training programs, and the audiovisual medium.

CAREER PATHS. The career paths a corporation makes available to its employees have an important influence on the extent and nature of their development. One way to characterize career paths is in terms of whether they encourage functional or technical specialization, or whether they encourage cross-functional mobility. Investigations of companies that have not adapted well to competitive pressures, those in the steel industry for example, show that these companies have developed few generalists capable of becoming general managers, product managers, or program managers. Individuals were brought in at the bottom of a function and promoted within it, causing them to retain a specialist's view.[12] A strategic emphasis on adaptation to new competitive demands might suggest an emphasis on cross-functional mobility in order to break down barriers between functions, develop individuals who understand the views of other functional specialists, and develop employees committed to the solution of business problems.

We are not advocating that all firms adopt cross-functional career paths, nor that all individuals be encouraged to take them. Along with the benefits described, there are some costs. Some depth of functional and/or technical expertise may be sacrificed. It is important, however, for corporations to make conscious policy choices about how much cross-functional or divisional mobility they desire, consistent with other strategic choices concerning the direction of the corporation.

In each organization, there are some career paths that are more valued than others. The valued track can be managerial (referred to as cross-functional above), or it can be technical. Typically, managerial jobs are more valued for the status, power, and monetary rewards associated with them. Attracted by these rewards, individuals in technical or sales jobs often attempt to switch careers and seek managerial positions despite the fact that their skills and/or interests may lie in their technical specialties. A firm needs to examine the career decisions that its internal job market encourages to determine if these decisions are consistent with its strategy and needs for employee competence.

Traditionally, blue-collar workers and white-collar clerical and technical employees have not had much opportunity to progress to more challenging jobs. Locked into their stations, their on-the-job enthusiasm and capacity for learning and growth declines. In response, some companies have attempted to stimulate growth and commitment through job rotation or job enrichment. Others have designed skill-based pay systems that align rewards with learning and development. We will explore some of these efforts in later chapters.

Companies also need to consider the opportunities for upward mobility that they provide to blue-collar and white-collar clerical and technical employees. A two-class society has been created in many companies, lowering cooperation and commitment to common goals. The removal of artificial barriers to advancement such as the requirement of a college degree is one method of increasing employee competence and commitment. Other ways of increasing the corporation's human assets include providing education and training (or the opportunity to seek it), and providing job experiences that allow lower-level workers to gain the knowledge, attitudes, and behavior required to join the managerial class.

CAREER AUTHORITY AND CONTROL. We discussed earlier the importance of individual control over the developmental process. There are three principle means by which the corporation can provide individuals with control over their careers.

First, a company can develop a cadre of *personnel development specialists* to whom employees may go directly to discuss their career goals and receive information about realistic career possibilities. These specialists typically are involved in helping managers find candidates for open positions, so they are aware of opportunities. They provide an employee with an alternate route for career management if his or her boss is ineffective or too controlling. But these specialists also serve the corporation, which means they play the difficult role of representing both employees *and* the company in personnel transactions.

Second, employees can be asked to fill out an *inventory of skills and job preference*, which can be cross-referenced for use in job searches.

Third, a system of *job posting* allows employees to apply for other positions in the company when they become vacant. An increasing number of companies are using this method in an attempt to give more direct career control to employees. It calls for employees to respond to announcements (postings) of positions and to be considered just as if they were external job applicants. The personnel department may screen applicants for a job before giving the hiring manager a list of potential candidates. The hiring manager interviews applicants, decides who to hire, and provides feedback to successful and unsuccessful applicants. Job posting has been adopted widely, particularly for lower-level jobs, because it appears to solve the problems of control. The courts and regulatory agencies such as the EEOC have looked favorably on job posting as in indication of affirmative action and nondiscrimination, one reason why an increasing number of corporations are adopting the system. However, job posting does not ensure fairness. In some cases, supervisors have decided who they want to hire before posting, making the interview a sham. Furthermore, the screening process is subject to bias. Finally, unless the company is willing to explain to employees why they have been rejected, the system may simply raise expectations and then dash them. Despite its weaknesses, job posting has potential for giving individuals some control over their careers, provided the corporation is open and willing to invest in the method by giving supervisors the proper training.

These three approaches to managing internal flow are not mutually exclusive. Together they offer an opportunity for giving an increasing amount of career control to employees; but that control will not be felt until corporations are able to change the paternalistic attitudes of managers concerning employee influence over their careers.

### *3. Managing Outflow*

A company may attempt to improve its mix of competencies rapidly by increasing the outflow of personnel through early retirement programs and/or layoffs of the lowest performers. Early retirement increases the percentage of younger personnel who management often believes are more flexible in adjusting to a changing business future than older, more entrenched employees. At the same time, personnel reductions allow for a rapid lowering of payroll costs, which can improve profitability in the short term. In the United States, this scenario has been used by companies in many industries as a response to recession and competition. Pressured by the quarterly earnings expectations of investors, corporate management has used work-force reductions as a major strategy for maintaining earnings and dividends expected by investors, stock analysts, and financial institutions. It has been one of the primary means by which mature industries such as autos, steel and rubber have attempted to cope with international competition in the early 1980s.

As we have already mentioned, legislation in some European countries and a social contract between unions and management in Japan have placed significant constraints on layoffs in those countries. Some restrictive legislation on terminations and layoffs is also beginning to be seen in the United States, suggesting that American managers will find it increasingly difficult to use personnel outflow as a strategic response to competitive pressures. Individual rights and the welfare of society will become more important considerations. Under the Age Discrimination in Employment Act of 1967, as amended in 1978, older employees are protected from forced retirement prior to age 70. In some states there is no upper limit. "There is a tremendous increase in employee lawsuits, particularly over age, sex and race discrimination and unjustified discharge," says Robert Conken, president of the American Arbitration Association.[13] These pressures will modify the policies of U.S. firms toward more caution in layoff and terminations, ultimately moving them closer to the full employment model.

The *central strategic dilemma* for managers is how to balance the needs and rights of employees for employment security with the requirements of the corporation to use personnel outflow as a means of cost reductions and renewal. Research evidence and experience demonstrate that employees who become insecure because of work force reductions are less productive and less committed to the organization.[14] The best tend to leave after the economy turns around. On the other hand, unless corporations take extraordinary care in the selection, training, and internal movement of personnel, legislative barriers to outflow can erode competitive position. How can corporations and society obtain the benefits of employee security without incurring the costs of overstaffing and stagnation?

LIFELONG EMPLOYMENT/TERMINATION FOR POOR PERFORMANCE. Lifelong systems, such as those at IBM and Hewlett-Packard, guarantee employment only if performance is maintained. If performance declines, so does pay, and employees are pressured either to improve their performance or to reexamine their relationship with the company. Terminations occur for poor performance on a case-by-case basis and not when a recession and profit squeeze provide a convenient excuse. This policy requires continual attention by management to performance and a willingness to confront problems.

LIFELONG EMPLOYMENT FOR A CORE GROUP. If a corporation cannot offer employment security to all of its employees, it may still choose to offer it to some of them. The number of employees is based on the lowest employment level economic circumstances are likely to force on the corporation. Ford Motor and the UAW agreed in their 1982 contract to institute such a policy at two experimental plants, subject to worker approval, for the life of the contract. The assumption is that it is better to remove job security as an issue for a core group (at these two Ford plants, 80 percent of the work force) who can then be asked to waive restrictive work practices and to participate in improving productivity. This policy does not deal with the potential obsolescence of the core group nor is it known what effects the policy will have on relations between protected and unprotected employees.

DOWNWARD AND LATERAL CAREER MOBILITY. One means of achieving a better balance between required job skills and job holders without termination is to utilize downward and lateral mobility, particularly late in a person's career. A division manager may move down to head a function from which he or she came, or a salesperson who has been promoted to management may welcome returning to sales again if he or she is given proper status and recognition. Companies that deemphasize hierarchical position and emphasize professional competence as a source of power are more able to move employees out of managerial positions with dignity.

CAREER RENEWAL. Companies can encourage individuals to leave oversupplied positions and move to undersupplied positions through effective training and development programs. Job retraining for laid off employees is a variation of this concept. Both Ford Motor and General Motors have negotiated with the UAW to undertake an extensive job retraining effort for laid off employees; the programs will be managed and funded jointly as part of the 1982 contract.

EARLY RETIREMENT. By offering special financial inducements, many companies have increased the outflow of personnel they consider unable to adapt to a realignment of the firm. Usually the inducement is retirement at an earlier age without a reduction in pension. The employee is able to retire at age 55, but will receive benefits he or she would have received at 62 or 65. The individual is then free to pursue a new career if he or she so chooses, and the firm can offer promotions to those they believe to be more competent to perform in the future. This is the single most popular option for managing outflow used today by American firms to revitalize themselves in the face of international competition.

WORK-FORCE REDUCTION THROUGH ATTRITION. Given the short-term severance and outplacement costs of work-force reductions, the savings in salaries are often overstated, particularly if cuts are not assumed to be the only way of eliminating poor performers. If one adds the costs of lower productivity and commitment, a case can be made for reducing the work force through attrition in conjunction with training and lateral or downward mobility.[15] The attrition alternative is not sufficiently considered, because a cost-benefit analysis is rarely conducted (particularly with regard to the impact on organization effectiveness). In times of adversity, finance and control functions, with their relatively short-term focus on quarterly earnings, gain power at the expense of the human resource function which takes a long-term perspective.

OUTPLACEMENT. A recent survey[16] found that 40 percent of the companies in its sample use outplacement firms that take over immediately after a person has been terminated and help him or her launch a job search. While outplacement service is typically offered only to higher-paid executives, there are examples of firms providing extensive outplacement counseling for a broader spectrum of employees terminated in a work-force reduction. Providing outplacement services demonstrates a sense of responsibility by the firm to those terminated, to the public, and to the remaining employees. In moderate recessionary periods, outplacement can result in better adjustments to termination and even salary increases in new positions.[17] If individuals are supported economically during the unemployed period, they may find their way to satisfying second or third careers or to organizations that fit them better. If outplacement works in this way, it can provide firms with a less costly alternative to guaranteed employment while still offering *career security* to individuals.

CRITICAL POINT REVIEWS. If an effective outplacement process allows separation without severe psychological or economic trauma, then why not induce employees to reexamine their places in the firm periodically instead of waiting for an economic downswing to force reexamination? This is the approach taken at Corning Glass Works. Every five years, bosses and personnel development specialists conduct reviews to determine whether it makes sense for an individual to remain with the firm given his or her needs, available opportunities, and the firm's view of his or her potential. A joint decision to stay or leave is agreed upon. Since both parties are presumably committed to the decision, separation, if it occurs, is less painful and more amicable. The firm's reputation in its labor markets is not damaged and it can go on to provide opportunities for other employees.

In summary, policies affecting personnel outflow need to be considered as part of an organization's overall strategy, since they will have a major impact on the commitment of employees and on the ability of the firm to be competitive. A combination of the policies and practices outlined above may make it possible for firms in the United States, where legislation has not yet restricted managerial freedom with respect to layoffs and termination, to find a path that balances employees' needs for reasonable employment security with the corporate need to maintain a quality and quantity of personnel consistent with being competitive.

## FAIRNESS IN MANAGING HUMAN RESOURCE FLOW

Every society must deal with the problem of justice. Unless citizens believe they are treated fairly and have the opportunity for their grievances to be adjudicated, they will not be committed to that society; conflict and disintegration will result. Corporations as mini-societies are not exempt from the need to deal with the problem of fairness, particularly with respect to managing personnel flow. There are few issues on which employees or prospective employees feel more strongly than unfair practices with respect to hiring, promotion, and termination. The perception of the fairness of these policies is thus as strategically important to the organization as the particular system and procedures selected to implement the policies. For that reason, we suggest that general managers, as well as staff specialists, need to give careful consideration to the fairness of their human resource flow policies.

Unfortunately, attitude surveys taken over the last 25 years show low employee satisfaction with advancement and a dramatic and consistent decline in feelings of fair treatment.[18] Barely 50 percent of managers and less than 25 percent of hourly and clerical workers felt that their chances of getting ahead were good. When combined with the dramatic decline in perception of fairness by employees (less than 25 percent of clerical and hourly employees rated "fairness" as good or very good while less than 50 percent of managers did), major problems are indicated.

Why is there such a decline in employee perception of fairness? It is quite likely that company practices have not gotten worse; indeed, they may even have improved. With the passing of equal opportunity legislation and greater emphasis in society on the rights of membership, employees are more sensitized to their basic rights and more willing to articulate them. The ever increasing number of legal suits being brought against companies with regard to hiring, promotion, and termination supports this and makes it quite evident that management cannot ignore the fairness issue.

### *The Legal Side of the Problem*

In the United States, employers must comply with two major sets of regulations governing equal employment practices: Executive Order 11246 (as amended) and Title VII of the Civil Rights Act of 1964 (as amended). These provisions establish criteria by which discrimination is judged, notably comparing the selection ratios of minorities or women with those of whites or males and comparing numbers of minorities and women in the work force with their representation in the population of the community. Thus, intent to discriminate does not necessarily have to be proven (although recent Supreme Court rulings have made proof of intent a more important factor). In many other instances, the government can require employers to develop affirmative action programs (AAPs) aimed at redressing imbalances. It is not our intent to go into the details of these laws or the means by which the government enforces them. The reader can go to other sources for a complete discussion of these specific issues.

### *Due Process Mechanisms*

It *is* our intent to emphasize the importance of equal employment opportunity laws and regulations in the United States and to point to the consequences of their existence and of noncompliance with them. The consequences are not only financial, though the $33 million consent decree between AT&T and the federal government illustrates that a great deal of money can be at stake. These laws represent a new standard by which employees and the community can judge a corporation. If management calls itself an equal opportunity employer, employees will feel more unjustly treated if they perceive discrepancies in actual practice than if management had not made such a claim. Under these circumstances, employees will feel much more strongly that changes must be made, and they will feel empowered to confront management directly, knowing they have legal recourse if no action is taken.

Management must create a mechanism for determining if complaints are valid and for resolving the problems if they are. This calls for an industrial jurisprudence, a process management can create for resolving grievances before grievances get to a court of law. David Ewing, who has studied how companies handle disputes, found few have appropriate means through which nonunion employees can voice a complaint or file a grievance.[19] There are several types of complaint resolution processes that seem to work in the few companies that have them. Control Data and Polaroid use panels of managers and/or employees, who hear both sides of the case and decide what correction if any must be made. Bank of America, General Electric, and Massachusetts Institute of Technology employ trained investigators or ombudsmen to work out solutions. Donnelly Mirrors and Pitney Bowes use elected employee councils to discuss problems and devise solutions. Companies without due process mechanisms run the risk of expensive legal suits and of arousing distrust among employees. A perception is created, whether justified or not, that management does not value fairness. With that perception comes dispute and legal action, beginning a vicious cycle.

### *Management Enforcement and Organizational Culture*

There is little doubt that fair treatment of employees cannot spring from legal constraints alone, though these have provided the pressure for change in standards of fairness. (Prior to regulation in the United States, most corporations did not have effective affirmative action programs.) Nor can fairness be obtained by the written policies of top management that have followed legislative pressures. Only the sincere belief of management in certain standards of fairness for all can result in a persistent top-down effort to enforce the standards and thereby change the values of managers throughout the corporation. The following strategies have to be employed in concert to achieve the needed changes in attitudes and behavior throughout the corporation.

1. *Clear articulation of top management values and philosophy* on fairness issues. What is meant by fairness? In particular, what constitutes a fair process?
2. *The setting of clear goals* for hiring and promoting women, minorities, and other underutilized groups. Achievement of the goals must be rewarded and nonachievement must have negative consequences. Experience suggests that only companies that have such goals have had some success in enforcing standards of fairness.
3. *The creation of corporate policies and systems* that encourage fairness. These might include information systems to track the number of women and minorities who were hired, promoted, terminated, and who left voluntarily. They might also include performance appraisal and bonus systems that incorporate fairness considerations.
4. *The development of due process systems* for resolving complaints about hiring, performance evaluation, promotion, and termination decisions. The more power employees or their representatives are given to help adjudicate disputes (for example, the elected committees of Pitney Bowes), the more likely it is that change will occur and that perceptions of fairness will result.
5. *Awareness training* for employees, particularly women and minorities, which helps them clarify and articulate their career goals and teaches them how to utilize due-process mechanisms.
6. *Training and development* for managers and supervisors aimed at helping them understand the characteristics of a fair process and developing their skills in managing fairly a number of critical processes, including selection interviews and decisions about performance appraisal, pay, promotion, and termination.

Fairness cannot be measured by results alone, since various stakeholders in the corporation will apply different values in defining a standard. Therefore, efforts to institutionalize fairness must concentrate on defining an open and participative *process* for making human resource flow decisions and resolving disputes that will surround them. Ignoring or suppressing different views or disputes will have a negative impact, leading inevitably to dissatisfaction, turnover, low commitment, a poor public image, and lawsuits. If feelings of unfair treatment are widespread in a democratic society, they will result in legislation that further reduces managerial freedom and flexibility.

## MANAGING FLOW STRATEGICALLY

There are many systems and practices that must be orchestrated to manage the flow of human resources (see Figure 4-3). The personnel function plays a central role in designing and administering many of the practices, but general managers are the only ones who can be responsible for articulating the philosophy that must guide the design

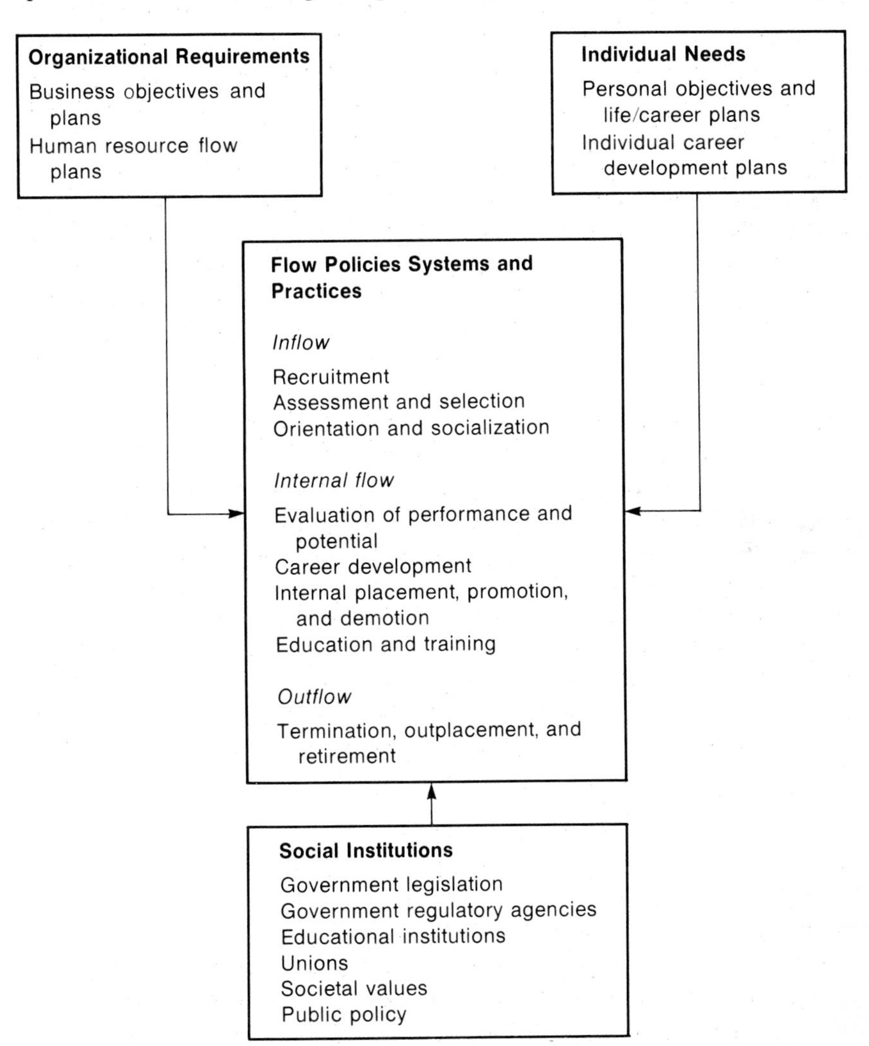


**FIGURE 4-3 Human Resource Flow**

SOURCE: Based on ideas from James Walker, *Human Resource Planning* (New York: McGraw-Hill, 1980).

and administration of these systems. Without such an articulation, human resource flow practices will not be internally consistent, nor will they support the firm's strategy or culture.

At the beginning of this chapter we made the point that personnel flow patterns *into, through*, and *out of* the organization can have a profound impact on the security and career development of each employee, on the competence level and mix of talents of employees in the aggregate, and on the well-being of the community and society as a whole.

It is a general manager's responsibility to take a leadership role in deciding on a flow pattern and designing policies and systems that take these three areas into account. It is in this sense that we refer to human resource flow as a policy area. The process of continually discussing and monitoring who is being hired, transferred, promoted, terminated, or retired and the way these decisions fit the needs of the individual and the company are also responsibilities of the general manager.

### *Alternative Flow Patterns*

There are three basic types of human resource flow patterns that may exist in an organization, and a fourth type that is a mix of the first three. Each of these patterns has different effects on employee well-being, organizational effectiveness, and the role of the corporation in society. The four types of flow patterns are:

1. *Lifelong employment system.* People usually enter the organization at the bottom and stay with the organization throughout their careers. The bottom may be defined differently for different employee groups. Blue-collar employees enter at the lowest job classification in the company, while MBAs are hired for entry-level exempt positions. No one is laid off as a result of economic cycles, but people may be asked to leave because of poor performance, depending on the company and on national practices. Large companies in Japan operate under this system. A select group of their employees are not discharged because of poor performance; instead, they may be sidetracked to less important jobs.[20] Hewlett-Packard, IBM, and some other high-technology companies have a lifelong employment system, but poor performers can be terminated on a case-by-case basis. In Europe, companies are forced to operate under this type of system because legislation makes the costs of termination prohibitive, particularly for older employees.
2. *Up-or-out system.* Employees enter at the bottom and move up through the organization through predetermined tracks until

they reach the top rank, which offers full partnership in the organization and usually tenure. Inability to be promoted through any of the ranks along the way or to the highest rank usually means that the person must leave. This system has high levels of turnover at the bottom and relative stability at the top. Big Eight accounting firms, law firms, some management consulting firms, and university faculties are examples.

3. *Unstable in-and-out system.* Employees enter at any level in the organization, depending on the organization's need, and may be asked to leave at any level or point in their career because of economic conditions, poor performance, or lack of fit with new management. Sometimes, employment contracts exist for given periods to ensure individuals some stability. While this type of system is not restricted to any industry, it tends to be found in industries where performance is thought to be a function of the individual (rather than the group) and is highly variable (often due to factors outside the control of the individual). The entertainment industry (sports teams and network television) and many retailing organizations are examples. In-and-out patterns are found in the blue-collar work force where poor economic conditions trigger layoffs and good economic conditions result in hiring.
4. *Mixed patterns.* There are few corporations that are clear-cut examples of one of the above. Large Japanese companies have lifelong employment for their core employees while using an in-and-out system for temporary workers and women. Some companies operate a lifelong employment system for top management, but an in-and-out system for middle and lower management. Furthermore, flow patterns shift over the life cycle of an organization. In the United States, mature companies under competitive pressure from Japan have moved from de facto lifelong employment for management to an in-and-out pattern in an effort to revitalize. Big Eight accounting firms, also under competitive pressures, are outplacing low-performing partners and hiring experienced professionals, thus moving towards an in-and-out system.

In most cases, the choice of patterns selected by an organization is less reflective of a coherent set of management attitudes and values than it is of the economic environment in which that organization operates. If demand for a company's products is subject to severe economic fluctuations, the company is more likely to adopt an in-and-out flow pattern, subjecting employees to layoffs when poor economic conditions prevail. On the other hand, a company in a rapidly growing industry may adopt a lifelong employment policy simply because it has never had to face severe economic decline. If the labor market has a large supply of needed talent, in-and-out flow patterns develop since they allow the firm to replace employees relatively easily. Choices about flow patterns also reflect societal values which can be imposed through legislation restricting the freedom of managers to terminate. Finally, flow patterns may be shaped by the philosophy of a corporation's founders. The belief of James Lincoln that workers should not suffer for the mistakes of management resulted in his adoption of well-known lifelong employment policy at Lincoln Electric.[21]

### *Strategic Implications of Flow Pattern Choices*

The situational factors that have shaped successive managerial decisions about hiring, promotion, and terminating employees also shape the ideas of the corporation's managers. Over time, a human resource flow pattern is institutionalized. Managers who know they will be asked to reduce employees at some point may be more careless about who they hire and how tightly they control headcount. They may purposely build a reserve of excess employees as a buffer against eventual cuts; this decision, in turn, makes reductions inevitable. The problem with this process is that it does not take into account the effects that institutionalized flow patterns have on the relationship between the organization and its employees or the relationship of the corporation to society. A more strategic approach to human resource flow patterns would suggest that an organization's general manager, supported by the expertise of his or her human resource staff, should weigh carefully the impact of such choices on a broad spectrum of key strategic outcomes, including employee commitment and competence, organizational adaptation and culture, the impact on interdependence and cooperation, and the relationship between the organization and its host society.

EFFECTS ON EMPLOYEE COMMITMENT. Employees who know that terminations or layoffs may come any time the economy takes a downturn will think differently about their relationship to the organization than employees who know they have a job until retirement. Stories about "bloody September" or the "guns of August," when large numbers of employees were terminated, shape employee expectations and commitment. Insecure employees are likely to be more calculating about the relationship, deciding to stay only so long as their career needs are met quickly. Employees who expect to be with the company until retirement are likely to take a longer-term view of their relationship to the organization. They may be willing to accept slower promotions or temporary setbacks in their career aspirations without lowering commitment. Up-and-out firms may be successful in obtaining high levels of motivation from younger employees who seek promotion, but are likely to incur problems of motivation or "burnout" among senior employees. Thus, different flow patterns and the policies about employment security, advancement, or demotion that shape them cause employees to develop different rationalizations for why they are working and why they are working for a particular company. Are they working to accumulate rewards such as money and promotion that they can take with them to another company or are they working to contribute to an institution from which they will retire? Different flow patterns create quite different "psychological contracts" between the individual and the organization.

We are *not* saying that flow patterns themselves can create high commitment in an organization. We are saying that some flow patterns (notably in-and-out and up-or-out patterns) make it difficult for employees to develop long-term commitment to an organization, even when other factors such as satisfaction with work, pay, and working conditions may make commitment desirable. Thus, some flow patterns may make it more difficult for managers to develop commitment and competence in employees. Lifelong employment creates a base for building commitment and competence, assuming management can develop effective policies in the areas of employee influence, rewards, and work systems.

EFFECTS ON EMPLOYEE COMPETENCE. The flow pattern of an organization affects how its managers think about the general task of managing. An in-and-out system fosters an emphasis on *selection* as opposed to *development*. If there are no constraints or identifiable costs to hiring and firing, why invest efforts in developing employees? On the other hand, if firing employees is difficult or costly, managers will become more careful in selection and will invest more in development. That developmental approach may increase the competence of employees as well as change the relationship between the organization and the employee. Employees who believe they are receiving an opportunity for development often feel a greater sense of commitment to the organization.

EFFECTS ON ORGANIZATIONAL ADAPTATION. Flow patterns may also affect the organization's adaptive capacities. Some American managers argue that periodic work-force reductions force managers to weed out dead wood, and provide opportunities to reshape the organization with a new breed of employees. This is one method for managing change. The argument suggests that organizations with in-and-out flow patterns are likely to have more diversity among employees. It is generally accepted that diversity contributes to innovation. Newcomers, not yet socialized by the organization, see old problems in new ways and propose different solutions. It is widely speculated that Japanese companies may not be as innovative as American companies, because of their lifetime employment system. Diversity can, however, be built into firms with lifetime employment if they systematically recruit people with different backgrounds and traits. On the other hand, in-and-out and up-or-out systems are likely to experience problems with adaptation because new people moving rapidly through lower levels do not have the power or network of relationships to create major changes or cannot afford to take risks.

EFFECTS ON CULTURE. Each organization has its own cultures, a set of shared beliefs and values that guide employee behavior. However, organizations differ in the strength of their corporate cultures. Culture is so pervasive in some organizations that it is an extremely powerful force in shaping behavior, while in other organizations values are not as widely shared and have less of an impact on employee behavior.

Flow patterns affect the *strength of a culture* because they determine how long employees will be with the organization, learning and transmitting a set of beliefs. In an in-and-out system, turnover may be so high that employees do not stay long enough to be fully socialized, or there may be an insufficient number of long-time employees to transmit traditions. Developing a culture in an organization with an in-and-out system is like trying to fill a can with water when it has holes in it. Without employment stability it is difficult, perhaps impossible, to maintain a strong culture.

Strong cultures develop more easily in lifetime systems because employees are more likely to identify with the organization and want to become socialized. Furthermore, a stable pool of senior employees can help with the socialization of new members. An up-or-out system can also develop a strong culture, but the burden of maintaining the culture falls on a relatively small number of senior employees. Managers of high-commitment work systems who want to use culture as a means of social control and want to develop a clan-like organization will have to consider these factors in choosing a human resource flow pattern.

Flow patterns can also influence *the type of culture* that an organization develops, particularly with respect to how power is distributed. An up-or-out system is likely to develop two cultures: senior partners who have made it and have the power, and juniors who have not, the latter being dependent on seniors for approval and ultimate promotion. In a mixed system, employees who have lifetime employment will have more power than those who are not expected to stay or be promoted.

Effects on Interdependence. Cooperation in organizations may occur because formal structures direct people to work interdependently. Matrix structures, task forces, special coordinating roles, and reward systems can be used to encourage collaboration between interdependent groups and individuals. But interpersonal relationships can be a more powerful means than formal structures for encouraging cooperation. Senior employees in lifetime employment systems and partners in up-or-out systems develop a network of relationships that make it easier to coordinate interdependent parts of the organization. In Japanese companies cooperation is achieved in the absence of many formal structures because their lifetime employment system allows relationships to develop. Thus, organizations that rely on interdependence to achieve their goals might consider how their human resource flow patterns contribute to this objective.

Role of Corporations in Society. In-and-out flow patterns reflect different assumptions about the role of the corporation in society than do lifetime employment systems. The former assumes that employees exist for the purpose of helping the corporation make a profit. The latter assumes that the corporation exists to provide stable employment and a meaningful existence for workers. These assumptions are usually implicit. Only occasionally do managers explicitly ask what the purpose of the corporation in society is. Are profits an end or a means to some other end? James Lincoln, the founder of Lincoln Electric, and Konosuke Matsushita, the chairman of Matsushita, were explicit in their beliefs that profits were merely a measuring device, and that the corporation had a higher purpose in society—that of providing a useful product of service to customers and meaningful employment to labor. Lifetime employment fits that concept. Similarly, European legislation regarding the termination rights of employees reflects the implicit belief of those societies that the purpose of the corporation is to provide employment and that profit is not an end, but a means. American managers, on the other hand, usually operate under the assumption that profits are the primary goal of the corporation. Not surprisingly, systems have been developed to fit that belief.

It remains to be seen what impact more intensive international competition will have on the corporation's role in society and on employment security. Will competition force companies and societies to reexamine lifetime employment systems and move closer to the American model? Or will they find ways to remain adaptive while maintaining lifetime employment? What will happen to the predominant American models of in-and-out systems? Can they be adapted to meet the employee's needs for security and the corporation's needs for higher commitment and lower employment costs in recessionary periods?

DECIDING ON A FLOW PATTERN. The discussion above suggests that human resource flow patterns can affect employer-employee relationships in several important ways, just as they reflect management's implicit assumptions about the purpose of the corporation. However, in many corporations, flow patterns are shaped in a reactive way by the situational forces in the history of the company. This suggests that general managers would be well advised to examine their human resource flow pattern, the rationale underlying it, and its consequences for some of the variables we have discussed. A strategic decision to change the flow pattern might then follow, and that decision could contribute significantly to reshaping all four HRM outcomes: commitment, competence, congruence, and cost effectiveness.

Examination of flow patterns could lead to policy innovations that combine the advantages of both lifetime employment and in-and-out systems and nullify the disadvantages of both. For example, if lifetime employment provides a sense of security for employees but could lead to an obsolescent work force and high costs in a recessionary economy, might it not be possible to obtain both psychological security and the flexibility that management seeks by providing *career*, not *job* security. Company outplacement support, discussed earlier in this chapter, reflects such a strategic decision.

### *Designing Flow Policies/Systems*

The choice of a flow pattern will probably emerge from a careful examination and discussion of many of the policies and issues discussed in this chapter. When and how should recruiting be done? How should employee effectiveness be defined and evaluated? How should this information be used in personnel decisions and career development? What systems and practices should the company adopt for developing employees, and what philosophy should guide this process? What philosophy and policies should guide outflow?

These are questions that should be answered explicitly by general managers with the help of key managers and human resource specialists. When a system for examining and shaping flow patterns is lacking, an organization's history and its immediate problems will shape these patterns in ways that may not fit the company's strategic needs.

There is no magic system for designing flow policies. General managers must orchestrate an ongoing process of discussion with key line managers and human resource staff executives about what policies are needed. This dialogue should be based on the following:

1. A data base of information providing some indication of how the flow system is working; for example,
   - Number of qualified ''backups'' for each management position
   - Turnover rates (voluntary and involuntary)
   - Average tenure in a job
   - Average number of functional experiences of key executives and high-potential middle managers
   - Sales dollars or profit per employee
   - Amount of dollars spent in training and education
   - Types of education programs
   - Compliance with affirmative action goals
   - Employee satisfaction with advancement, personal development, and influence on career decisions
   - Number of hourly and salaried nonexempt employees promoted one, two, or more levels.
2. Appraisal of the values that managers have about employee development, security, and effectiveness.
3. Clarificaiton of corporate strategy—what kind of a firm have we been and will we be in the future? What are the implications for types of people, functions, specialties, and roles we will need?
4. Ongoing dialogue with stakeholders, employee groups (i.e., blacks, women, production employees, managers), union leaders, community social agencies, and federal equal employment compliance agencies about hiring, promotion, and outflow patterns.
5. Task forces of employees assigned to study specific flow issues (e.g., employment security, development of engineers, image of the company at key universities, and so on).
6. Analysis of characteristics, functional competencies, values, and management style of those being promoted most rapidly in the company. Do these fit management's vision of the company 15 to 20 years from now?
7. A similar analysis of those who are leaving the firm voluntarily. Are these people the company can afford to lose given its values and its vision of the future?

A top management group should take time periodically to examine the type of information described above to answer the questions suggested. Some companies have commissioned audits by outside consultants. The consultants collect information by examining records and conducting interviews, then report to top management. Some of the data can be supplied by the human resource function, particularly by a competent personnel research department. With this type of information in hand, top mangement and key line managers should engage in a dialogue to clarify for themselves corporate strategy and philosophy. In the final analysis, flow policies reflect the assumptions of top management about human competence and development in the context of business reality.

### *Planning Human Resource Flow*

If you are the general manager of a rapidly growing, high technology company, your continued concern is that an adequate supply of managers and engineers will be available to allow the company to expand to the potential created by the market. How would you determine numbers and types of employees? How would you determine who stays and who goes? The answers to these questions can only emerge from a flow planning process, which may be formal or informal, quantitative or judgmental, long- or short-term. The plan may be aimed at assuring a supply of employees in all categories (i.e., engineers, production personnel, secretaries, managers), or it may be aimed at only one or two critical groups such as engineers and managers. Finally, the planning process may encompass the entire company or just a smaller group of key executives and technical personnel. Regardless of the focus, the process encompasses the same basic steps.[22]

1. *Forecast* the number and types of employees that will be needed (labor demand) and the number and types of employees that will be available in the organization (labor supply) assuming certain rates of turnover, transfers, and promotions.
2. *Program* recruiting, employee development, and/or outplacement to deal with anticipated shortages and surpluses.
3. *Evaluate* the effectiveness of personnel programs in dealing with surpluses and shortages, and revise the plan where necessary.

A quantitative forecast of demand can be made by using certain leading indicators that have a demonstrated relationship to personnel requirements (for example, ratio of sales to sales personnel). The problem with this approach is that it assumes the future to be an extrapolation of the past, an unwarranted assumption in a rapidly changing environment. Alternatively, management can try to project the implications of changes in markets, technology, and strategy for the structure of the organization and the strength and size of certain functions and roles. From this, a forecast of personnel needs can be developed, particularly one that highlights changes in requirements. Management groups that engage in this qualitative forecasting process often find many side benefits such as a clarification of strategy, changing functional roles and relationships, and emerging structural arrangements. The demand forecasting process can lead management to address difficult organizational issues before serious problems develop.

Effective demand forecasting requires a blend of quantitative and qualitative approaches, using each to check and inform the other. Table 4–1 illustrates a typical format for forecasting labor supply, whether arrived at quantitatively or judgmentally.

While the procedure for forecasting supply is well established, the effectiveness of the procedure depends heavily on good personnel data. Even when performance evaluation data are obtained, managers may not always report accurately their assessments of subordinates or their intentions to fire or promote if they don't know how this data will be used. Nor do companies know exactly who is planning to quit. Through an examination of historical patterns, some estimates may be made but these are highly problematical. This is why *aggregated forecasting*, which projects supply for a group of employees using sophisticated models, does not usually yield very useful information, though it may be of some value as a check on a *disaggregated approach to forecasting supply*. This approach, commonly referred to as succession or replacement planning, relies on the personal knowledge of managers to estimate who might quit or retire and who should be promoted or terminated. In replacement planning, managers are asked to designate individuals whom they regard as *backups* for their or other key jobs. Individuals are chosen on the basis of their experience and evaluation of performance and potential. By comparing demand estimates and supply estimates, a shortage or surplus may be identified for each category of employee within the company to which the process is applied. Action plans are then devised by line managers to deal with filling gaps or terminating employees.

The critical link in the flow planning process is *follow-up*. Even after managers have established procedures, development programs do not always follow. If individuals who were to receive specific training or job experiences do not, the company will find itself lacking the needed technical and managerial talent. These are "soft" programs that are difficult to define, preprogram, and measure. Increasingly, corporations are finding that flow planning needs to be tied to the strategic planning process. These corporations will not accept a business plan from a manager unless it provides a flow analysis. When these

**TABLE 4–1 A Forecast of Labor Supply**

| | | Losses | | | Gains | Internal Moves | | |
|---|---|---|---|---|---|---|---|---|
| | (1) | (2) | (3) | (4) | (5) | (6) | (7) | (8) |
| Job category | *Beginning inventory* | *Retirements* | *Quits* | *Others* | *Transfers in* | *Promotions out/in* | *Demotions out/in* | *Anticipated internal supply* |
| 1 | 136 | 4 | 0 | 11 | 3 | 0/13 | 0/0 | 137 |
| 2 | 255 | 2 | 18 | 0 | 3 | 13/26 | 0/0 | 251 |
| 3 | 291 | 1 | 29 | 0 | 8 | 26/39 | 0/0 | 282 |
| 4 | 357 | 0 | 36 | 0 | 0 | 39/0 | 0/0 | 282 |
| | 1,039 | | | | | | | 952 |

Source: Adapted from Herbert G. Heneman, Donald Schwab, John A. Fossum, and Lee D. Dyer, *Managing Personnel and Human Resources: Strategies and Programs* (Homewood, Ill.: Dow Jones–Irwin, 1981), Fig. 7–2, p. 13.

plans are reviewed periodically and managers are rewarded for their accomplishment, they are more likely to be implemented. If the corporation wishes to reward managers who successfully develop people, it is important that follow-up include not only a monitoring of activities (training programs, recruitment programs, etc.) but also developmental results (the number of successful technical or managerial personnel promoted from a unit).

In addition to its analytic nature, succession planning is also a *consensus-building process*. Employees who are candidates for promotion in the eyes of one manager may be viewed negatively by other managers applying different standards. In any case, succession in a corporation must be agreed to by a number of key managers, all of whom will have to work with the person in question. For this reason many companies (for example, Hewlett-Packard, GM, IBM, and GE) have developed a committee process for reviewing key managerial personnel at every level of the organization. At Exxon, as mentioned earlier, the chief executive officer heads a compensation and executive development committee which meets frequently, sometimes once a week, to review development of top Exxon executives. Composed of Exxon board members, the committee discusses each executive's performance and examines developmental needs. To insure continual flow of managerial talent, the committee compares the performance and potential of all executives and makes decisions about who are the most likely successors to key jobs and what experiences they need to succeed. The same development committee system is replicated at each subsidiary, where the president of that subsidiary has his or her own committee. At Hewlett-Packard, the top management group uses three-day sessions more than once a year to discuss each key executive in the company. At General Motors ten vice-presidents and group executives also meet regularly to probe the effectiveness of each executive in a pool of 600 managers. Does the executive seem to be developing at the rate expected? What is the job contributing to the person's ability? Is it rounding out the person as intended? Should an individual be given more responsibility or be moved to another division? If so, who would be put in that executive's place?[23]

A succession review process for key managerial and technical personnel can be established at every level of the organization, starting at the bottom and moving up. If such a process is led by line managers and is regularly scheduled, the message to managers is clear: Flow planning and human resource development are important in this organization! When combined with information from more quantitative aggregate planning, a flow planning process can be developed that will insure the numbers of people and talent mix that the company requires to be competitive in the future.

## SUMMARY

Managing the flow of people *in*, *through*, and *out* of the corporation is a human resource policy area of strategic importance to corporations. Policy decisions in this area require that general managers adopt more than just an enterprise perspective. They must also understand the perspective of the individual, particularly in regard to what constitutes career development and satisfaction. Additionally, they must develop a societal perspective, which involves an understanding of changing worker values, educational institutions that supply prospective recruits, legislation, government regulatory agencies, and union policy.

To assure the right numbers of employees with a mix of skills required to implement corporate strategy, corporations must design appropriate policies and practices for managing employee inflow, internal flow, and outflow. A number of important questions and issues must be addressed to develop effective flow policies. How can employees be recruited that will fit the corporation's needs and culture? What is the optimum velocity of personnel flow through the corporation consistent with good employee development and the strategic needs of the corporation? How is employee effectiveness defined and how shall it be evaluated? How can an organizational context be created that will encourage employee development? What mechanisms and processes can corporations install to meet employee expectations for fairness in connection with hiring, promotion, and termination decisions? Finally, should the company terminate, retire early, or otherwise encourage employees to leave when profits drop? What alternatives exist to this policy?

The sum total of flow policies and practices create a flow pattern. We have identified four types of patterns: lifelong employment, up-or-out, in-and-out, and a mixed pattern of all three types. Each has a quite different impact on important outcomes such as commitment, competence, and organizational culture and adaptibility. General managers must make strategic choices about the flow pattern they want and the policies and practices that will be needed to support their choice. Such strategic choices will be a function of competitive realities, stakeholder interests, and management's values with regard to employee development and security. A continuous process of examining values, the effects of current flow policies, and the future goals of the firm will allow managers to shape flow patterns and policies.

One ongoing responsibility of general managers is to be involved in planning and managing personnel flow within the context of existing policies. How many managers, professionals, specialists, or skilled workers will the firm require to meet its business goals? What mix of recruiting and employee development programs will be needed to serve those needs? Who are the managers and professionals with the highest potential to succeed incumbents in key positions? These are questions that should be addressed as part of the business planning process. Many corporations create special forums where key managers at each level of the organization discuss key people, their potential, and their developmental needs. General managers who create such forums for discussion signal their own concern for developing the corporation human assets and encourage a social capital perspective throughout the corporation.

## NOTES

1. This section draws on the work of John Van Mannen and Edgar H. Schein, "Career Development," in J. R. Hackman and L. J. Suttle (eds.), *Improving Life at Work: A Behavioral Science Approach to Organizational Change* (Santa Monica, Calif.: Goodyear Publishing, 1977), pp. 30–95.
2. Van Mannen and Schein, "Career Development," p. 31.
3. Ramsey Liem and Raymar Ponla, "Health and Social Costs of Unemployment," *American Psychologist* 37 (October 1982), pp. 1116–1123.
4. "Bosses on the Barricades," *U.S. News and World Report*, December 20, 1982.
5. A. Kornhauser, *Mental Health of the Industrial Worker* (New York: Wiley, 1965).
6. James Walker, *Human Resource Planning* (New York: McGraw-Hill, 1980).
7. Ralph Katz, "Job Longevity as a Situational Factor in Job Satisfaction," *Administrative Science Quarterly* 23 (1978), pp. 204–223.
8. Conference Board Report on performance appraisal cited in R. Landsbury, *Performance Appraisal* (South Melbourne: Macmillan of Australia), 1981.
9. Walker, *Human Resource Planning*.
10. Edgar Schein, "Increasing Organizational Effectiveness Through Better Human Resource Planning and Development," *Sloan Management Review* 19 (Fall 1977), pp. 1–20.
11. Noel M. Tichy, Charles J. Fomburn, and Mary Anne Devanna, "Strategic Human Resource Management," *Sloan Management Review* 23 (Winter 1982), pp. 47–62.
12. Paul R. Lawrence and Davis Dyer, *Renewing American Industry* (New York: Free Press, 1983).
13. "Bosses on the Barricades."
14. Leonard Greenlaugh, "Maintaining Organizational Effectiveness During Organizational Retrenchment," *Journal of Applied Behavioral Science* 18 (1982), pp. 155–170.

15. Greenlaugh, "Maintaining Organizational Effectiveness."
16. Lawrence J. Styble, "Matching Those Pink-Slip Blues," *Industry*, January 1983.
17. This conclusion is based on an internal company study conducted at Corning Glass Works during the 1974–75 recession.
18. M. R. Cooper, B. S. Morgan, P. M. Foley, and L. B. Kaplan, "Changing Employee Values: Deepening Discontent?" *Harvard Business Review*, January-February 1979.
19. David W. Ewing, *"Do It My Way or You're Fired!": Employee Rights and the Changing Role of Management Prerogatives* (New York: John Wiley and Sons, 1983).
20. Marsland and Beer, "Note on Japanese Management and Employment Systems."
21. See Lincoln Electric, Harvard Business School Case Services #9-376-028.
22. Parts of this next section are based on "Personnel Planning," in Herbert G. Heneman, Donald A. Schwab, John A. Fossman, and Lee A. Dyer, *Personnel/Human Resource Management* (Homewood, Ill.: Richard D. Irwin, 1980).
23. The Exxon and GM examples are taken from Tichy, Fomburn, and Devanna, "Strategic Human Resource Management."

CASE 8

# NIPPON STEEL CORPORATION

*Stephen Marsland*
*Michael Beer*

Nobuo Somemori looked up from his desk. It was nearly midnight, and from the seventeenth floor of Nippon Steel Corporation's (NSC) headquarters he could see the neon signs of Tokyo flickering in the distance. In front of him were two sets of data. One related to NSC's financial pro formas for the coming years. The other set of data related to union proposals to move back the retirement age for NSC employees from age 55 to 60 years.

In mid-1979 NSC's financial future did not look good. NSC was burdened with 3,500 excess personnel costing (with fringes and bonuses) some ¥50 million per day. Steel demand was stagnant—NSC faced crude steel shipment projections of 32 to 34 million metric tons per year for the next five years. The realized price per metric ton of crude steel was forecast to rise 0 to 6 percent per year (from ¥75,000 a ton)[1] for the next several years, while costs for materials, depreciation, and operating expenses (including the effect of mill shutdowns, but excluding personnel, interest, tax, and miscellaneous expenses) were expected to begin to climb at about 5 percent a year from their current plateau of ¥57,000 per metric ton. Interest, local tax, and miscellaneous expenses were expected to stabilize at ¥250 billion a year. This left employment costs, now running at ¥350 billion a year (including the cost of excess personnel), as the key variable. Any increase in the retirement age, Somemori knew, would mean that NSC would have to live with its 3,500 excess personnel that much longer, since the plan to reduce the work force relied primarily on retirement.

Was it time, Somemori wondered, to change NSC's personnel policies? NSC had always tried to provide employment until retirement for each employee it hired. NSC had also tried to provide superior wages and benefits, relying extensively on its work force for process improvements. Yet the real cost of this approach was finally beginning to hit home. Could NSC afford to continue its old policies?

[1]NSC sells many grades and finishes of steel, and this price per crude ton simplifies pricing for the purposes of this case.

## HISTORY OF THE JAPANESE STEEL INDUSTRY

Mr. Ikeda, section manager in NSC's Planning Department, commented on the growth of the Japanese steel industry:

> The Japanese steel industry surpassed the French in 1959, the British in 1961, and the West Germans in 1964. From 1965 to 1973 our output tripled to 120 million metric tons of crude steel, making us the third largest steel-producing country in the world, close behind the United States (which is a distant second behind the Soviet Union). And we achieved this without any sizable domestic production of coking coal or iron ore.

The Japanese steel industry had emerged from World War II badly damaged and operating well below capacity. Until the Korean War Allied policy favored a small Japanese steel industry, but after 1950 the Japanese government was allowed to begin to rebuild the country. Through government-allocated loans and credits, particularly in the early phase of growth (1950–1955), the steel industry was made the foundation of national economic recovery along with coal.

But government involvement in steel did not stay at the same level in later phases of the industry's development. Mr. Manita, section manager in NSC's Finance Department, commented:

> In the early fifties the government set up a plan to assist in managing the economy and rationalizing industry. Government involvement was very important in the first phase of rationalization. Once the major steel firms were back on their feet, however, they began to make their own plans. Government involvement was substantially less in the second phase, and virtually disappeared in the third phase. We in steel say that MITI (the Ministry of International Trade and Industry) was one step ahead of us in the first phase, was running even with us in the second phase, and ever since the third phase they haven't been able to keep up with us!

Exhibit 8–1 shows how steel output in Japan grew rapidly up to 1973—and the dominant role played by Japanese domestic steel demand in the growth. Nevertheless, exports were important to the industry. Not only was Japan the world's largest steel exporter throughout the seventies, but 20 percent of domestic steel demand was exported in the form of ships, automobiles, and electrical appliances.

## HISTORY OF NSC

NSC traced its history back to 1901, when the Japanese government set up Japan'e first steelworks. Through World War I this government-owned enterprise produced 70 percent of all Japanese steel output. Although a number of smaller private steel firms were set up during the war and the 1920s, in 1934 the Japanese government consolidated these into the government-owned steel firm, forming a new company which was one-half private and one-half government-owned. This enterprise, the Japan Steel Corporation, was the mainstay of the Japanese steel industry throughout the war.

After the war, the Allied powers split up the near-monopolistic Japan Steel Corporation into two smaller firms—Yawata Steel and Fuji Steel. These companies were Japan's largest and second largest steel firms, respectively, for the period 1950–1970. In 1970 they merged to improve the operating efficiency and international competitiveness of Japanese industry, thus forming the NSC.

NSC was viewed as one of Japan's most progressive employers. For years Japan's top university students had ranked it among the top ten employers in Japan. Its wages and benefits were among the best in Japan, and it had a reputation of being one of Japan's best-managed firms (see Table 8–1). In Japanese society, being hired by NSC was viewed as having been elected to join an elite group.

Managers and blue-collar employees at NSC expected continuous employment through to retirement, without layoffs or discharges. On the other hand, employees recognized that changes in jobs and locations might be required as the firm grew and steelmaking technology changed. Managers viewed blue-collar workers more as technicians than laborers, and this view was reinforced by extensive company training for blue-collar personnel.

Employees entered an almost-closed world when they entered the firm, since NSC sponsored its own company sports teams and clubs, tour groups and trips, and social events. This close-knit group spirit was fostered through company housing—company employees lived together in the same apartment complexes and neighborhoods. The company promoted social interaction between blue- and white-collar groups by sponsoring company-wide sports and cultural activities. NSC employees thus spent their time almost exclusively with other NSC employees.

Management of the company seemed to have a fervent dual allegiance—to the company and to Japan itself. The company's success was perceived as contributing to Japan's ability to compete internationally. Maintaining national employment levels and combating unemployment were perceived to be company responsibilities. The company's prominence in the public eye led it to adopt a socially responsible position on pollution, working conditions, and benefits, often to the detriment of its financial position. NSC thus often led the private sector in responding to social criticism.

**TABLE 8–1 Employment and Wages at Nippon Steel Corporation, and Inflation and GNP Growth for Japan, 1970–1979**

| Year | Employees (Thousands) | | | Average NSC Blue-Collar Employee's Monthly Wages[a] (¥ Thousands) | Inflation Rate (%) | Real GNP Growth (%) |
|---|---|---|---|---|---|---|
| | *White Collar* | *Blue Collar* | *Total* | | | |
| 1970 | 22.2 | 59.6 | 81.8 | 90.0 | 7.3 | 10.2 |
| 1971 | 22.8 | 61.8 | 84.6 | 95.1 | 5.7 | 5.6 |
| 1972 | 22.7 | 60.0 | 82.7 | 107.5 | 5.2 | 10.4 |
| 1973 | 22.4 | 58.0 | 80.4 | 126.5 | 16.1 | 6.5 |
| 1974 | 22.7 | 57.4 | 80.1 | 161.9 | 21.8 | 0 |
| 1975 | 23.1 | 57.3 | 80.4 | 176.3 | 10.4 | 3.2 |
| 1976 | 23.3 | 55.8 | 79.1 | 189.2 | 9.4 | 5.9 |
| 1977 | 23.5 | 54.3 | 77.8 | 205.9 | 6.7 | 5.6 |
| 1978 | 23.5 | 52.6 | 76.1 | 212.8 | 3.4 | 5.5 |
| 1979 | 23.0 | 50.7 | 73.7 | 228.4 | 4.9[b] | 6.0[b] |

[a]Excludes bonus.
[b]Estimate.

## COMPETITIVE POSITION

NSC, as the world's largest producer of crude steel, was clearly the industry leader. NSC was 2.5 times larger than its largest domestic competitor, and offered the broadest and most complete product line, both directly and through its many subsidiaries. NSC's position relative to major U.S. and Japanese steelmakers is shown in Table 8-2.

Mr. Manita of NSC's Finance Department pointed out:

> Nippon Steel has always acted to stabilize the market. During the period 1963-1966 Nippon Steel was holding back its investment despite aggressive investment by its competitors. This was because steel demand was not growing very fast and overcapacity threatened to be a real problem. Once demand took off in 1967 NSC pushed forward aggressively to bring capacity in line with demand. Again, today, since steel demand is sluggish, NSC is holding back its investment—it is less than depreciation—at the expense of market share so as to bring order into the market.
>
> Our leadership role doesn't preclude competition, though. Nippon Kokan has just started a one trillion yen modernization of one of their facilities to make it the most efficient steelmaking operation in the world. Competition is stiffer due to the government's recent emphasis on parks and roads which has helped the small steelmakers—who specialize in smaller production runs, special shapes, and custom orders—to gain market share at the expense of the majors. Competition also takes place on a subtler level, as each steelmaker tries to build the best reputation for always delivering, on time or faster, at a competitive price, steel that meets specifications and exceeds quality standards. Uniformity, speed, and reliability are as important as price in the steel industry.

## HISTORY OF LABOR RELATIONS

Nippon Steel[2] had encountered difficult problems in the immediate postwar period. Thanks in part to the Allied policy of promoting unionism and releasing all political prisoners (including communists), Nippon Steel's plants were quickly organized by communist unionists. Under conditions of rapid inflation and mounting unemployment, unions took an aggressive stance against rationalization and layoffs, and pushed hard for large wage increases. The steel companies, facing slack demand and spiraling costs, pushed back equally hard for rationalization and no wage increases. Confrontation was the result.

[2]Although really two different firms from 1950 to 1970, and known by a different name prior to 1950, for convenience all of NSC's predecessor firms will be referred to as "Nippon Steel."

**TABLE 8-2 Crude Steel Output, in Millions of Metric Tons, for Major U.S. and Japanese Steel Firms**

| Company | World Rank 1978 | Country | Output | |
|---|---|---|---|---|
| | | | *1977* | *1978* |
| Nippon Steel | 1 | Japan | 32.4 | 31.2 |
| U.S. Steel | 2 | United States | 26.1 | 28.4 |
| Bethlehem Steel | 3 | United States | 15.1 | 17.1 |
| Nippon Kokan | 5 | Japan | 13.8 | 13.4 |
| Sumitomo Metals | 7 | Japan | 12.5 | 12.0 |
| Kawasaki Steel | 8 | Japan | 12.5 | 12.0 |

In 1950 Yawata Steel experienced a 20-day strike protesting abolition of the piece-rate system and reduction in incentives. In 1952 the steel industry was disrupted by four brief strikes and a lockout[3] over the steel companies' offer of a zero wage increase. Strikes continued annually through to peak in 1957 with 11 separate strikes at Yawata Steel over another zero wage increase for the year, and a massive 49-day strike in 1959 at Fuji Steel and Nippon Kokan. During this period the steel industry developed its tradition of "one offer"—a single response to union demands which the union has never been able to improve through negotiation or strike action. The offer, explained carefully to the work force, is usually a fair offer in management's eyes and applies to both blue- and white-collar employees. The tradition of "one offer" still determined company responses in 1979.

Mr. Okamoto, Industrial Relations section manager for NSC's Yawata Works, explained how union-management relations changed:

> This period of labor unrest led both sides to the realization that something had to be done. The rank and file wasn't getting anywhere by striking. The company lost customers during strikes that couldn't be lured back once the strikes were over. A moderate faction began to develop within the union, arguing that more concessions could be gained from the company through cooperation rather than confrontation. Meanwhile, the company began to adopt new policies to promote good relations between management and the rank and file.
>
> Starting in 1958 the old system was revised to allow blue-collar workers promotions into management, and more authority was given to the foremen and assistant foremen. A new position was created—"senior foreman"—and these spots were filled with blue-collar workers who were given significant authority. This system was based on the U.S. foreman system. Furthermore, management began extensive efforts to improve

[3]A lockout is a physical shutdown of a business by the employer, denying employment to all employees, with the aim of obtaining concessions from or resisting demands by the work force.

> interpersonal relations and communications between management and the rank and file. The company sponsored social events and sports activities, and encouraged management to take time out to talk to the men and go drinking with them.
>
> Also, a new pay system was devised in 1962. Until then, the entire wage was pretty much determined by seniority. We made 15 percent of the pay a function of the difficulty of the job. We also made the annual seniority wage increases a function of effort on the job. Under the new system a slack person would get a smaller seniority increase (say, a 1.5 percent increase instead of 2 percent) than someone who was industrious. All these innovations were modeled after successful job rating programs and incentive systems in the United States.

Labor unrest began to diminish due to the combined efforts of union moderates and management. After 1959 the number and intensity of strikes began to decline, and moderates began to win more and more union elections. After 1965, Nippon Steel experienced no more strikes. In 1968 union moderates gained control of the Nippon Steel union with 52.7 percent of the vote, versus 47.3 percent for the leftists. Moderate control of the NSC union increased to the point where 81.6 percent of vote went to moderates in 1978.

Mr. Kobayashi, general manager of the Industrial Relations Department, explained:

> We have placed great importance on anticipating problems and solving them before they arise. We meet often with union officials in order to avoid strikes. We find that this method of meeting often and working out problems in advance is very effective.

Moderate unionists felt they had achieved a great deal for their members. Although their tactics were not spectacular, moderates argued that the union membership consistently voted for moderates because the moderates delivered results. Mr. Eto, union branch secretary at NSC's Yawata Works, explained:

> Both the union and the company know they must reach agreement. The question is how quickly and fairly agreement can be reached. Japanese unions in the private sector have already graduated from the immature "strike, take what you can, and show it off to the membership" stage. No matter how good you are at presenting yourself to the rank and file, they look at the bottom line to see what you've really done for them. So we don't bolster appearances by striking—we go for the reality of good wages, hours, and working conditions.
>
> The facts bear this out. Our union, without striking, has done as well for its members as those unions that *do* strike. Steelworkers are among the best-paid workers in Japan. Steel sets the standard for the country. We have achieved things radical unions could never have attempted—after

1974 we negotiated pattern[4] settlements which, when followed by the other national union federations, resulted in stopping the wage-price spiral in Japan. By holding down our demands, we cut the inflation rate so far that we got a real wage increase.

Management felt that moderate rather than leftist leadership of the NSC union was very helpful. The NSC union was the leading union in the steel union federation. The steel federation, in turn, was the largest private-sector federation in the national left-wing labor confederation. This confederation, called Sohyo, was mainly composed of leftist public-sector unions, and had been the leading proponent of militant strike action for wage increases and union rights. Management felt that a strong voice for moderation within this left-wing union confederation was important for the country. Management also felt that union-management cooperation had been essential in solving labor relations problems before they became serious, and in successful implementation of new management systems and technology. One such innovative management system was the concept of ''self-management'' (*Jishu Kanri* or JK in Japanese). One of the originators of the concept explained:

> Groups of blue-collar workers work after hours to develop safety, energy, and process improvements. They conceive and carry out their own projects, calling on white-collar staff and their foremen for help. Each group contains seven to nine workers who work together during the same shift. Nearly all blue-collar workers participate, and each work group undertakes two or three projects a year. Work groups present their projects to plant and company conventions, and compete for awards. The main incentive for these groups is prestige, not cash, since awards are at most equivalent to $30 for the group, although workers are paid for the extra time they put in. Since ''self-management'' was started in 1965, it has saved NSC a total of ¥400 billion—and this year's savings alone are some ¥50 billion.

One blue-collar worker presented a different view:

> If it really were ''self-management'' that would be great, but in my group most of it is just appearances. Even if one person does the whole project it is announced as a group effort. You know how it is—when it's quitting time some guys just go home and won't stay for group meetings. It's tough when all the work has to be done after hours. I'd like to try self-management but. . .

[4]A pattern settlement is a collective bargaining agreement between a prominent union and company which becomes a reference point for later settlements between other unions and companies. These later settlements closely resemble the initial pattern settlement.

Another blue-collar worker presented a positive outlook:

> My wife sometimes asks me to get home earlier than I do, but I find the self-management meetings very challenging. Not only does self-management allow me the chance to make use of skills and abilities not called on in my regular job, it is also good training—it will serve me well in my new job if I am promoted.

Self-management projects involved many different areas. One self-management group found a way to cut heat loss when opening reheating furnaces by hanging steel chains outside the furnace door. The chains absorbed heat when the door was opened, and thus radiated heat back into the furnace and cut air circulation without interfering with steel billets as they came out of the furnace. Another self-management group had found a way to replace several workers with TV cameras. Another group developed a safer technique for doing a particular manual operation.

Management at NSC believed that self-management had significantly improved NSC's operating performance. It had not only improved profits but also made middle management more effective by allowing lower levels to contribute technical and system innovations. Self-management also improved relations between blue- and white-collar personnel, since blue-collar self-management group leaders or group members could call on white-collar staff specialists for advice.

## TECHNOLOGY AND BUSINESS STRATEGY

Significant economies of scale exist in steelmaking, and Nippon Steel and the rest of the Japanese steel industry tried to take full advantage of these. One NSC manager pointed out:

> The Japanese penchant for scale economies can be seen in the size of blast furnaces. Of the 20 largest blast furnaces in the world in July 1978, 15 were Japanese. NSC owned six of these, including the largest blast furnace in the world. By comparison, not a single one of the 20 largest blast furnaces was American.

## WORK FORCE STRATEGY

A flexible, skilled work force was a central component of NSC's strategy. Making quality steel, even with computerization, still required a certain knack in some operations. Keeping down scrap required attentive and careful operation of equipment. Process improvements and automation could best be implemented when the people who had been working with existing methods had an opportunity to give their opinions about how to make changes. The cooperation of the work force was essential so that there was minimal downtime and waste when methods were changed.

NSC's approach to managing growth also required a flexible, adaptable work force. As NSC built new ''greenfield'' facilities, thousands of veteran blue-collar workers were transferred to help start up operations and then man the new facilities.[5] NSC sought to minimize hiring needs through scale economies and rationalization, which meant that workers had to keep up with constant job changes.

The Japanese steel industry was able to maintain stable employment and efficient scale operations by turning to exports when the domestic market faced a downturn (see Exhibit 8-1). This allowed growth in capital investment and output to proceed without interruption despite fluctuation in domestic demand.

Stagnant demand in the late 1970s caused elements of NSC's strategy to be modified. Since new economies of scale could not be achieved due to lack of demand, there was an increased emphasis on cost-cutting through careful management and efficient work methods. New investment in equipment could not earn a sufficient return, so investment in capital equipment had been cut back below the level of depreciation. New technology was also de-emphasized because NSC had sometimes moved too quickly to implement a new process, only to find that it was substantially out of date a few years later, or that the same thing could have been done much cheaper several years later. Mr. Manita of NSC's Finance Department explained:

> There is such a thing as overinvestment in new technology. Look at our Oita Works—our newest facility. Seven years ago, in 1972, when the facility was coming on-stream, we put in five state-of-the-art continuous-casting lines. The continuous-casting process has been improved so much that today we are closing down two of those lines—the remaining three lines have increased in speed to the point that they can handle all of Oita's output. The investment in the other two lines need not have been made—we've moved one line to another facility and we're using the other for experimental purposes.

NSC managers were concerned, however, about competition from the rapidly growing Korean steel industry. If NSC cut back investment, it might lose its ability to compete. Would NSC become another U.S. Steel, following a short-run profit strategy and losing long-run competitiveness?

[5] A ''greenfield'' facility is the term applied to a new plant built in a new location.

## NSC's 1979 SITUATION

Although Japanese steel output reached a peak of 120 million metric tons in 1973, the "oil shock" of that year pushed the industry into a recession from which it had not recovered by 1979 (see Table 8-3).

Despite the recession's impact, NSC did not begin to trim its work force until 1977. Mr. Tashiro of the Industrial Relations Department explained:

> Looking back on those few years after 1973, it's hard to understand why we didn't let our work force begin attrition right away. But we felt that steel demand would rebound to its old levels once the economy had adjusted to the oil shock. We also expected some growth each year once the economy was back on the track, although not, of course, like the growth that had taken place from 1965 to 1973. So we felt we couldn't afford to let our work force levels decline, and we continued to rationalize by cutting the labor required for operations. For a while we tried to keep up output by exporting at a high rate. Then the European Economic Community set up import quotas and the United States put its trigger price mechanism in place. That meant we had to again rely primarily on the Japanese domestic steel market for growth. It was still stagnant in 1979.

In 1979, in spite of stagnant demand, NSC was operating all its facilities, though some were operating at only 40 percent of capacity. Even with this policy, only 70,500 personnel were needed to actually meet projected demand, leaving 3,500 employees as excess work force. The financial effects on the firm may be seen in Exhibits 8-2 and 8-3—1975 and 1977 had seen dividend cuts, accounting changes, and sale of securities holdings. Mr. Tashiro of NSC's Labor Relations Department explained:

> Although we may have delayed more than we should have in starting, we can still adjust to these excess work force levels. We are looking at shifting our production so that we can shut down several rolling mills and cut out fixed costs. No one need be laid off. We will transfer the personnel at these mills to fill vacancies created through retirement at all our other mills, and reduce hiring somewhat. It will take several years to bring our excess work force levels fully into line, but by 1982 or 1983 our work force levels and manpower requirements will be in balance.

## PRESSURE TO INCREASE THE RETIREMENT AGE

Complicating NSC's already difficult employment situation was the government's announced intention, during the summer of 1979, to in-

**TABLE 8-3 Nippon Steel Corporation Outlook, 1973-1979**

| YEAR | NSC OUTPUT | NSC EMPLOYMENT (THOUSANDS) | INCOME FROM OPERATIONS (¥ BILLIONS) | INDUSTRY CAPACITY UTILIZATION (%) |
|---|---|---|---|---|
| 1973 | 41.0 | 80.4 | 131.4 | 93.0 |
| 1974 | 36.9 | 80.1 | 67.5 | 81.6 |
| 1975 | 32.3 | 80.4 | - 22.7 | 71.6 |
| 1976 | 34.4 | 79.1 | 57.7 | 74.2 |
| 1977 | 31.7 | 77.8 | - 18.4 | 65.4 |
| 1978 | 32.0 | 76.1 | 81.6 | 68.7 |
| 1979 | 33.0[b] | 73.7 | NA[c] | NA |

[a]Output in millions of metric tons of crude steel.
[b]Estimated.
[c]NA = not applicable.

crease the retirement age of government employees from 55 to 60 years. The standard mandatory retirement age throughout the civil service and most of private industry had been 55 up to that time. A government white paper advocated a mandatory retirement age of 60 for all civil servants. Private-sector unions immediately pushed for parity with the civil servants, demanding that companies move ahead mandatory retirement to age 60.

The debate on mandatory retirement had begun in the early 1970s, as Japan's demographics began to change noticeably. After the war, the birth rate had dropped steadily until 1965, when it stabilized at slightly over two children per family. Meanwhile, average male life expectancy rose from 50 years in 1947 to 70 years in 1973. Japan had begun to "age" rapidly. In 1950, only one Japanese in nine was over 55, while in 1979 one person in five and one adult in three was over 55.[6] The Japanese social security system, meanwhile, did not adequately provide for the increasing number of elderly people. To make things worse, private-sector pensions were nonexistent—companies preferred to pay employees a lump-sum retirement bonus of ¥5 to 12 million.

Most "retirees," therefore, could not afford to retire at 55. They found low-paying jobs and continued to work until 60 or 65. This had become an issue for three reasons. First, lower wages meant lower contributions to the social security system. Second, due to their lower wages "retirees" were less able to support themselves when they stopped working. Third, most people felt a 55-year-old was still capable of doing his old job, and so shouldn't have been retired in the first place. Public opinion, public-sector union agitation, and the eco-

[6]Masao Ueda, *Population Problems in Japan* (Tokyo, International Society for Educational Information, Inc., 1975), pp. 15, 20, 25-26, and 51-52.

nomics of social security combined to push the government to recommend retirement at 60 for public-sector employees.

NSC's union had pushed hard for retirement at 60. The NSC union, leading the steel union federation, had gone to the public arguing that the only responsible solution to the national social security problem was retirement at 60. The steel federation received wide acclaim. It was already well regarded for helping to stop Japan's wage-price spiral over the previous several years. Hailed as "labor statesmen," the leaders of the NSC union turned to labor-management negotiations holding public opinion as their trump card.

NSC labor relations officer Tokumitsu pointed out:

> The union's plan of action of the retirement question was masterful. The union knew that the company was in tough financial condition so that simply negotiating wouldn't be enough. So the union went out and used its national stature to mobilize public opinion in favor of retirement at 60. This was very clever because NSC is a leading national firm and the steel union federation is a prominent moderate national union. The company doesn't want to be seen as falling behind or opposing Japan's move toward becoming more of a welfare society. Also, since the union leaders have staked their political lives on getting a concession on retirement, the company might end up toppling all the moderates (who led the country down from high inflation) if it refused any concession. Then radicals might gain control of the union. It certainly looks like the union has the upper hand.

## NSC'S MANPOWER PLAN PRIOR TO EMERGENCE OF THE RETIREMENT ISSUE

Nippon Steel's plan to adjust to stagnant demand had evolved since 1977. Once corporate staff saw that steel demand had still not recovered in 1977, they proposed that staff at the various steel works examine ways to reduce fixed costs and work force levels. Each facility submitted proposals for itself and suggestions for the entire company. These proposals were developed by task forces made up of low-level staff at the various facilities. Headquarters staff saw, once the proposals were consolidated into two alternative companywide plans, that consensus was developing for the shutdown of four or five rolling mills which had been operating at well below 60 percent of capacity. Upon resubmission to the various facilities, the facilities approved a plan which called for gradual shutdown of four mills over the period 1980–1982. Personnel from these mills were to be transferred to other NSC facilities to fill vacancies created by turnover and retirement. Exhibit 8-4 shows NSC's plan, which projected balanced work force levels by 1983.

Despite consensus on the need for mill shutdowns by management staff, these shutdowns were not always readily accepted by the workers and the union. At NSC's Kamaishi works, townspeople and employees were firmly opposed to the shutdown of one of the two mills there. Kamaishi had grown up around the steel mills after steelmaking operations first began in 1874. There was no other major employer besides NSC in Kamaishi. Townspeople were afraid the town would die. Employees, most of whom were over forty and who had worked at Kamaishi since the 1950s, were opposed to uprooting their families, selling their homes, and leaving their friends. After the plan to close the mills was announced, demonstrations broke out in the city. NSC labor relations officer Tashiro pointed out:

> It has become much tougher to transfer people between facilities these days. In the past, nearly all transfers between facilities involved the start-up of a new facility. In these cases, a younger veteran who was, say, number three in his old mill was given the chance to be number one at the new mill. His pay and status rose with the transfer, and since he was still relatively young, he was willing to settle in with his family at a new spot. Today, transfers between mills don't mean better pay or a promotion—sometimes pay falls (due to loss of shift premium, or change of job content). And the men being transferred are often older, even though we try to transfer the youngest people we can.

Union and management were deadlocked over the Kamaishi mill shutdown. In some 35 separate joint consultative committee meetings, union appeals were met by management's tough financial arguments. The Kamaishi mill was old and uncompetitive, and the entire firm was suffering financially. When NSC management softened the blow by making informal promises not to shut down the remaining mill unless "absolutely necessary" and took special care in making transfers, the union and the townspeople finally gave up. Labor relations officer Mr. Tashiro explained:

> The shutdown at Kamaishi will allow us to transfer production to newer, more efficient mills that are operating below capacity. It will also allow us to cut overhead since the mill no longer has to have lighting, heat, and so on.

Although transfers between mills were proving more difficult, management maintained that transfers within existing facilities could be made fairly easily. Since an employee expected "lifetime" employment, he realized that during his working life things would take place which would require him to change jobs, or work places, or both. Blue-collar workers were not reluctant to learn new jobs if they were assigned to them. A union official stated the union position on transfers:

> We recognize that transfers must be made. But our position is that transfers must never be made at the expense of the employee. When a transfer requires that an employee go to a new job, we try to protect him from downgrading of his working conditions and wages. We have recently negotiated an increase in the retraining period (for a transfer) from two to six months. We have obtained a new one-week orientation period, and have set up a "coach system" where an experienced man at the new work place takes the transferee under his wing. Starting this year the company has begun to take the wishes of each individual into account—he still has to be transferred but has some say over where he will go. Finally, we've negotiated a step-down system where a worker's pay is gradually reduced over one year rather than all at once when he has to take a pay cut (usually due to the loss of his shift premium when he's transferred). We still feel that the retraining period is too short, though. It should be two years long, not six months, and no worker should have to take a pay cut when he transfers.

When asked about refusing to transfer, a worker responded:

> You just don't. If you object, your foreman asks you to go. If you tell him no, then the senior foreman asks you. If you still refuse, the assistant manager politely asks you to go. If you are still stubborn, the mill manager asks you to cooperate. If you don't give up then, they order you to go. Disobeying an order means discharge.

## MANPOWER FLOWS—CONSTRAINTS AND OPTIONS

With NSC's plan to shut down rolling mills in full swing, NSC manpower planners had to examine the impact of various solutions to the problem of retirement at 60. Some alternatives being considered were: (1) an immediate move to retirement at 60; (2) moving back the retirement age one year at a time (either 1982, 1984, 1986, 1988, and 1990 or 1981, 1983, 1985, 1987, and 1989); (3) waiting several years and moving to retirement at 57, then to retirement at 60 four or five years later; (4) moving to retirement at 60 in two or three years; and (5) staying at retirement at 55.

In order to determine the match between manpower requirements and personnel available (and thus excess personnel levels and associated costs), Nippon Steel's planning staff had to take account of five decision areas: (1) anticipated personnel outflows (including retirement), (2) rationalization, (3) hiring (personnel inflows), (4) stopgap placement measures (temporary methods of saving on costs for excess personnel), and (5) other short- and long-term adjustments of the work force.

For NSC's planning purposes, an average nominal increase of 6 percent a year in the average wage per person was assumed for the next five years. Planning was required only for the blue-collar personnel, which numbered 51,000 in 1979, since the white-collar staff was only slightly too large for the required work load. In 1979 the blue-collar manpower requirements were 48,000 employees, leaving 3,000 blue-collar personnel in excess.

### *Anticipated Personnel Outflows*

Turnover, promotion, and retirement constituted the major source of outflows of personnel. Turnover had historically been one-half of 1 percent of the work force. Two hundred blue-collar personnel were promoted to white-collar positions each year, on average. Without moving back the retirement age, scheduled blue-collar retirement for the next five years was as follows:

### *Rationalization*

One key determinant of the number of excess personnel was the number of people actually required for operations (excess personnel equals the number of people available minus the number required for operations). The 1979 manpower requirements for an output level of 33 million tons of crude steel per year was 48,000 blue-collar workers with current capacity utilization of facilities.

NSC had reduced this number in past years at the rate of about 700 jobs per year, primarily by automation, reorganization of work methods, and allocation of work between facilities to increase capacity utilization. Such rationalization was relatively cheap (a one-time cost of ¥1 million per man).[7] The future maximum rate of rationalization was expected to decline to 500 jobs per year as fewer and fewer opportunities for rationalization presented themselves. If rationalization were stopped, it would result in a modest cash savings (of rationalization costs) and would help ease the problem of excess personnel. However, if rationalization were skipped for a year it could not be "doubled up" the following year—only the annual maximum rate of rationalization could be undertaken in any one year since rationalization beyond that point threatened to disrupt steelmaking processes. Rationalization did not affect the number of people on the payroll—just the number of people required for operations.

[7]This includes training and other miscellaneous costs.

| YEAR | SCHEDULED RETIREMENT |
|---|---|
| 1980 | 1,400 |
| 1981 | 1,400 |
| 1982 | 1,600 |
| 1983 | 1,600 |
| 1984 | 1,000 |

### *Hiring*

Mr. Sasaki, General Manager of NSC's Personnel Department, explained:

> Since we have more people on the payroll than we need, it would seem that all we have to do is reduce hiring. Well, compared with 1400 blue-collar workers hired each year on average in the past, in 1976 we hired only 600. In 1977 it was only 500. In 1978 it was 300. This year we're not hiring any. On the surface, this looks great—we're cutting back our work force levels. But it's not that simple. Smooth, steady hiring is much better than ''off and on'' hiring—better for training, better for filling vacancies, and better for administration. And if we don't hire any new recruits each year, what's going to happen to us in 1995? We won't have any young, experienced people, aged 28 to 38, to form the backbone of our productivity and become our first-line foremen. All we'll have is kids and old men! And how are we supposed to keep our work force up to date if we don't bring in young people familiar with computers and flexible about learning new techniques and systems? Besides, we're not saving much money when we cut hiring—a new hire makes only ¥90,000 a month plus four months' salary in bonuses each year.[8]

NSC's long-range forecasts (to 2000 and 2020) showed that a steady annual hiring rate of 700 men a year would provide the best future balance, flexibility, and manpower age structure.

### *Stopgap Placement Measures*

NSC had five ways to temporarily assign excess blue-collar workers so as to reduce costs and/or give these employees meaningful tasks to perform. These five methods were accelerated career training, ''loaning'' workers to other firms, ''restructuring'' work assignments given to subcontracting companies, transfers of personnel to help start up a new venture, and early placement of workers in their postretirement jobs.

[8]These bonuses are part of compensation and are paid each year—they are relatively unaffected by company performance. Such bonuses are common throughout Japanese industry.

Acceleration of scheduled training was an important temporary measure to assign personnel. Since at NSC each blue-collar worker received, on average, five years of training during his career, such mid-career training could be moved up in hard times or delayed in good times. This gave NSC the option of accelerating up to 200 man-years of training in each slack demand year. Such accelerated training did not actually save any wage expense, however.

"Loaning" workers was another option. Although the Japanese steel industry was in a slump, the Japanese automobile industry was booming. NSC was sending some of its employees to work at a major Japanese auto company.[9] The auto firm paid the men its going rate, and NSC made up the difference between that and what the men had been making at NSC. This saved NSC about 70 percent of the average wage costs of these men (the average wage was ¥230,000 per month plus four months' bonus each year), but none of the costs of fringe benefits. NSC had "loaned" about 300 men at a time in 1979, but since the men disliked living in the auto companies' dormitories and working at less-skilled jobs, NSC sent men on only two- or three-month assignments, and then replaced them with new men. NSC estimated that perhaps as many as 400 men could be "loaned" at a time, but men did not like leaving their friends and families for several months. Morale was hard to maintain in the face of heavy "loaning."

"Restructuring" work assignments given to subcontracting companies was another method of reducing the cost of having excess personnel. This restructuring would allow NSC to redefine the services performed by its subcontracting firms so as to cut back on payments to them and provide jobs for its excess work force. NSC's subcontracting firms exployed some 40,000 blue-collar people. Some managers estimated that if NSC restructured over one-half of 1 percent of subcontracting work some subcontracting firms might go out of business—with serious consequences for NSC's relations with such firms. Such restructuring would save 60 percent of the wage costs of an average NSC employee (excluding fringe benefits) for each job restructured.

If NSC started up a new venture, it could transfer personnel into it to assist in the start-up. Such personnel could be kept at the new subsidiary indefinitely, or could be brought back to NSC proper at any time. NSC had one such opportunity to start a viable subsidiary and transfer out 100 people, which would be available in 1980. Such a transfer would save all of the wage costs of an average employee (ex-

[9]These workers generally took low-skilled work except where their skills were directly applicable.

cluding fringe benefits) for each person so transferred. Such opportunities were rare, and another such opportunity would probably not appear for four or five years, given the current bad economic climate.

Another safety valve for NSC was early placement of older workers in the jobs they would hold once they retired. NSC tried to place its retirees with subcontracting firms that did business with it. Men aged 53 or 54 would be encouraged to "try out" the jobs they would have once they retired. While the men "tried out" their jobs, NSC paid them. The subcontracting firms would pay NSC for the labor of NSC employees working for them at the subcontracting firm's usual rate—about 60 percent of the rate of pay at NSC. Subcontracting firms did not cover the cost of NSC fringe benefits, however, which NSC continued to pay. The salary for 53- or 54-year-olds averaged ¥300,000 per month plus four months' salary as a bonus each year. NSC was already making maximum use of this option—some 200 men had been sent out in 1979.

### *Short- or Long-Term Adjustments to Work Force Levels*

If NSC had excess personnel it wished to keep on the payroll who could not be absorbed by stopgap measures, such personnel could be assigned to make-work projects to keep them occupied. No savings would result from such make-work projects, however. Of course, Western-style adjustments to the work force were not unknown in Japan. Lay-offs, early retirement, and discharge had been used in tough situations. Mr. Ikeda of NSC's Planning Department explained:

> If we don't get some kind of financial relief, we're going to begin to look like the shipbuilding industry. They've watched demand drop 50 percent in the past two years, and firms have begun to take drastic measures. Some have resorted to voluntary retirement—they announce that 1,000 individuals must leave, but don't actually ask any one individual to leave the firm. Within a few weeks those people who feel best able to endure unemployment voluntarily retire, and retirements continue until one thousand people have left. A small monetary incentive is usually given—a retirement bonus some ¥2 million larger than it otherwise might be. Other firms have laid off employees—employees are sent home at 90 percent of their base pay. This layoff pay is paid by the company. Many firms have been forced to discharge employees, however. It's the only way they can survive. Firms near the brink of bankruptcy which hesitated to fire people found themselves out of business before they knew what hit them. Things haven't looked this bad since those chaotic years right after World War II.

## ALTERNATIVES FOR REDUCING EMPLOYMENT COSTS

NSC's personnel planners could cut costs by cutting employment costs per employee instead of by cutting personnel. Employment costs per employee could be reduced via lower wages (including bonuses), fringes, retirement bonus, or seniority increase. Each area offered potential for savings, although the threat was that established union relationships and employee morale might be damaged.

The most substantial area for saving was in wages. NSC could decide to begin to take a very tough stand against wage increases in the future. Since the average wage was ¥230,000 a month plus four months bonus, the difference between a 6 percent increase and a 3 percent increase for 51,000 employees was ¥5.6 billion per year. This, while clearly the fastest way to cut employment cost increases, might result in the moderates in the union being voted out, and a breakdown of management-union cooperation and communication.

Fringe benefits, while only ¥50,000 per month per employee, could also generate substantial savings. A 10 percent cut of fringe benefits, either by charging more for company meals and housing, or providing fewer services (such as company-operated recreation facilities), could save ¥3 billion a year. This took aftertax benefits away from NSC employees, however, and also could give employees the impression that NSC was getting "cheap."

The retirement bonus seemed a particularly attractive place to cut compensation costs. In 1979 NSC was paying ¥9 million to a blue-collar worker who retired with 30 years of service. If employees were going to work for the firm longer, it made sense that they would have less of a need for such a large retirement bonus. If one thousand men retired and the bonus were cut by ¥2 million per man, then the savings would be ¥2 billion. Of course, savings from this cut could be realized only in those years when employees actually retired. Furthermore, the level of the retirement bonus was negotiated each year with the union, and so could not be unilaterally cut by management.

The annual seniority-based increase offered several different options for reducing employment costs. Each year NSC gave a seniority increase to each employee. In 1980 this increase, which was independent of the union's negotiated wage increase, was expected to average ¥42,000 per year per employee. If this seniority wage increase were not given one year, it would save some ¥2.5 billion per year from then on. Eliminating the increase across the board would not change existing seniority differentials, since it would only keep the seniority-based wage from climbing. Another option was to stop or reduce all seniority increases for employees aged 50 or older. This would save about ¥500 million per year every year such increases weren't given. Some NSC executives were arguing for a "step-down" seniority adjustment for employees older than 55. Instead of wages going up, they would be stepped down by ¥42,000 per year until the employee retired. This was designed to ease the impact of the cost of moving retirement to age 60, and also to try to match the wage to the work done (since older workers were expected to be less productive as they aged). Savings were difficult to estimate since they depended on whether and how the retirement age was moved back. Compared to the normal system of "step-up" seniority increases, however, this option would save NSC an average of ¥240,000 each year for each employee over age 55 on the payroll that year.

## IMPLEMENTATION IMPLICATIONS

Even with a workable manpower and retirement plan, several important implementation issues stood out. These were how to make the decisions about retirement, and what to tell the work force about these decisions.

NSC headquarters normally asked the concerned functional department in each of the eight steel works for its proposals as to what should be done. A low-level manager in that department, or a task force of several such managers, got the job of coming up with an idea of how to handle the situation. Their proposals were passed up through the ranks and approved or modified at each level, until they were sent to headquarters. At headquarters the proposals were consolidated into two or three plans and then resubmitted to the various steel works, which selected the plan they liked best.

In the case of the retirement question, however, it was unclear whether the normal procedure should be followed. The decision would have long-run implications for either the financial health of the firm, or its industrial relations policies, or both. The recommendation would affect the wages and retirement age for the managers who made the recommendations, since NSC had a policy of extending benefits won by the union to management personnel. A low-level manager would thus be making recommendations about not only retirement for the blue-collar people, but for himself and his supervisor as well. This argued for departing from established procedure in this case. Yet this would mean that lower-level managers would be shut out from their customary decision-making role, which would adversely affect their morale and future decision making.

Another consideration was how the decision, once made, would be presented to the work force. Normally, all aspects of a decision were presented, along with relevant facts. Yet if NSC opted for any strategy which delayed retirement at 60 some managers felt it might be better not to do this. They argued that since the company strategy, in that case, was to delay as long as possible, it would hardly do to reveal the company's plans to the employees. Furthermore, the company might be trying to get concessions such as a lower retirement bonus or elimination of the seniority wage increase. Informing the employees in advance would undermine their morale. Other managers argued that to depart from past policies of being open with employees would undermine morale to an even greater extent. They felt that it would be better to be open with the employees and try to sell them on the company's position.

Mr. Somemori glanced at his watch. It was one o'clock in the morning. He wondered if he could develop a manpower plan out to 1985 that would be acceptable to the work force and the union, maintain operating efficiency and morale, and still meet the company's financial constraints.

**EXHIBIT 8–1**

**Japanese Steel Industry Production, Exports, and Domestic Demand, 1958–1978** *(in Thousands of Metric Tons)*

| Good Years | Poor Years | Output | Steel for Use in Japan | Change (%) | Steel Exports | Change (%) | Exported Steel/Output (%) |
|---|---|---|---|---|---|---|---|
| 1958 | — | 12,773 | 10,856 | — | 1,917 | | 18.1 |
| 1959 | — | 18,247 | 16,420 | + 51.3 | 1,827 | – 4.7 | 12.3 |
| 1960 | — | 23,161 | 20,495 | + 24.8 | 2,666 | + 45.9 | 14.5 |
| 1961 | — | 29,399 | 26,778 | + 30.7 | 2,621 | – 1.7 | 11.3 |
| — | 1962 | 27,250 | 22,458 | – 16.1 | 4,792 | + 82.8 | 22.3 |
| 1963 | — | 34,080 | 28,537 | + 27.1 | 5,543 | + 15.7 | 20.7 |
| 1964 | — | 40,532 | 32,814 | + 15.0 | 7,718 | + 39.2 | 24.6 |
| — | 1965 | 41,296 | 31,194 | – 4.9 | 10,102 | + 30.9 | 31.4 |
| 1966 | — | 51,898 | 42,242 | + 35.4 | 9,656 | – 4.4 | 22.9 |
| 1967 | — | 63,777 | 53,949 | + 27.7 | 9,828 | + 1.8 | 19.1 |
| 1968 | — | 68,987 | 55,130 | + 2.2 | 13,857 | + 41.0 | 24.9 |
| 1969 | — | 87,026 | 70,226 | + 30.2 | 16,800 | + 21.2 | 24.0 |
| 1970 | — | 92,406 | 73,653 | + 4.9 | 18,753 | + 11.6 | 25.1 |
| — | 1971 | 88,441 | 64,192 | – 12.8 | 24,249 | + 29.3 | 32.0 |
| 1972 | — | 102,972 | 80,214 | + 25.0 | 22,758 | – 6.1 | 26.2 |
| 1973 | — | 120,017 | 93,983 | + 17.2 | 26,034 | + 14.4 | 25.7 |

**EXHIBIT 8–1 (*Continued*)**

| Good Years | Poor Years | Output | Steel for Use in Japan | Change (%) | Steel Exports | Change (%) | Exported Steel/Output (%) |
|---|---|---|---|---|---|---|---|
| — | 1974 | 114,035 | 79,700 | – 15.2 | 34,335 | + 31.9 | 34.6 |
| — | 1975 | 101,613 | 70,232 | – 11.9 | 31,381 | – 8.6 | 35.6 |
| — | 1976 | 108,326 | 71,809 | + 2.2 | 36,517 | + 16.4 | 38.7 |
| — | 1977 | 100,646 | 66,047 | – 8.0 | 34,279 | – 6.1 | 38.8 |
| — | 1978 | 105,059 | 73,778 | + 11.7 | 31,281 | – 8.7 | 34.1 |
| Compound growth rate 1958–1973 | | + 20.5% | + 19.7% | — | + 24.3% | — | — |
| Compound growth rate 1973–1978 | | – 2.6% | – 4.7% | — | + 3.7% | — | — |
| Compound growth rate 1958–1978 | | + 11.1% | + 10.1% | — | + 15.0% | — | — |

Source for all figures is company documents.

**EXHIBIT 8–2**

**Nippon Steel Corporation Income Statements Fiscal 1972–1978** *(¥ Billions)*[a,b]

| | 1972 | 1973 | 1974 | 1975 | 1976 | 1977 | 1978 |
|---|---|---|---|---|---|---|---|
| Net sales | 1,418.7 | 1,855.7 | 2,287.0 | 2,101.2 | 2,506.1 | 2,326.2 | 2,412.5 |
| Other income | 49.5 | 68.8 | 64.9 | 48.5 | 67.4 | 59.8 | 48.3 |
| Yen appreciation gain | — | — | — | — | 11.2 | 33.2 | 19.1 |
| Total income | 1,468.2 | 1,924.5 | 2,351.9 | 2,149.7 | 2,584.7 | 2,419.2 | 2,479.9 |
| Employment costs | 185.2 | 235.2 | 298.1 | 301.8 | 319.4 | 346.1 | 347.8 |
| Materials, depreciation and operating expenses | 1,071.4 | 1,392.8 | 1,818.1 | 1,670.0[c] | 1,971.4 | 1,824.9 | 1,832.3 |
| Interest on debt | 98.1 | 99.3 | 116.7 | 141.5 | 165.0 | 158.1 | 142.6 |
| Local and misc. taxes | 17.6 | 17.1 | 17.9 | 20.3 | 33.0 | 30.6 | 44.9 |
| Misc. expenses | 38.2 | 48.7 | 33.6 | 38.8 | 38.2 | 77.9 | 30.7 |
| Total expenses | 1,410.5 | 1,793.1 | 2,284.4 | 2,172.4 | 2,527.0 | 2,437.6 | 2,398.3 |
| Income from operations | 57.5 | 131.4 | 67.5 | (22.7) | 57.7 | (18.4) | 81.6 |
| Reserves | (32.3) | (43.3) | (13.2) | (17.2) | (19.7) | 2.7 | 14.1 |
| Loss reserve | — | — | — | 15.0 | 9.5 | — | — |
| Sale of securities gain | 2.4 | .2 | .5 | 39.4 | 1.3 | 35.5 | .5 |

**EXHIBIT 8–2 (*Continued*)**

| | 1972 | 1973 | 1974 | 1975 | 1976 | 1977 | 1978 |
|---|---|---|---|---|---|---|---|
| Income before tax | 27.8 | 88.3 | 54.8 | 14.5 | 48.8 | 19.8 | 96.2 |
| Corporate income tax[d] | (8.6) | (37.5) | (25.0) | 0 | (20.0) | (4.0) | (51.0) |
| Net income after tax | 19.3 | 50.8 | 29.8 | 14.5 | 28.8 | 15.8 | 45.2 |
| Dividends | 17.3 | 23.1 | 23.1 | 25.5 | 32.4 | 19.4 | 26.0 |
| (Dividends per share) | (¥3.75) | (¥5.00) | (¥5.00) | (¥5.00) | (¥5.00) | (¥3.00) | (¥4.00) |
| Retained earnings | 2.0 | 27.7 | 6.7 | (11.0) | (3.6) | (3.6) | 19.2 |
| Year-end exch. rate $1 = | ¥265.9 | ¥273.8 | ¥293.8 | ¥299.7 | ¥277.3 | ¥222.4 | ¥209.3 |

[a]Fiscal year runs April 1 to March 31; fiscal year 1972 runs from 4/1/72 to 3/31/73, and so forth.

[b]Figures may not add exactly due to rounding. Source for all figures is company documents.

[c]This figure reflects change from last-in, first-out (LIFO) method to averaging method in accounting for inventory.

[d]This income tax figure is the amount actually paid. Since income reported for tax purposes does not match income reported in financial statements, income tax figures do not reflect the appropriate tax for the income shown in financial statements.

**EXHIBIT 8–3**

**Nippon Steel Corporation Balance Sheets Fiscal 1972–1978** *(¥ Billions)*[ab]

| | 1972 | 1973 | 1974 | 1975 | 1976 | 1977 | 1978 |
|---|---|---|---|---|---|---|---|
| Cash | 153 | 178 | 205 | 309 | 248 | 247 | 243 |
| Receivables | 174 | 225 | 182 | 240 | 389 | 332 | 372 |
| Inventory | 300 | 318 | 449 | 636[c] | 701 | 740 | 632 |
| Other current assets | 104 | 174 | 183 | 313 | 280 | 264 | 290 |
| Total current assets | 731 | 895 | 1,019 | 1,498 | 1,618 | 1,582 | 1,538 |
| Net fixed assets | 1,196 | 1,153 | 1,256 | 1,439 | 1,535 | 1,569 | 1,542 |
| Investments | 168 | 197 | 230 | 262 | 300 | 285 | 250 |
| Other assets | 18 | 26 | 26 | 8 | 7 | 7 | 6 |
| Total fixed assets | 1,382 | 1,376 | 1,512 | 1,709 | 1,842 | 1,860 | 1,798 |
| Total assets | 2,113 | 2,271 | 2,531 | 3,207 | 3,460 | 3,455 | 3,336 |
| Accounts payable | 382 | 461 | 611 | 728 | 756 | 702 | 658 |
| Debt due in one year | 218 | 186 | 181 | 306 | 379 | 468 | 483 |
| Other current liabilities | 136 | 202 | 186 | 216 | 237 | 221 | 293 |
| Total current liabilities | 736 | 849 | 978 | 1,250 | 1,372 | 1,391 | 1,434 |

**EXHIBIT 8–3 (*Continued*)**

| | 1972 | 1973 | 1974 | 1975 | 1976 | 1977 | 1978 |
|---|---|---|---|---|---|---|---|
| Long-term loans | 741 | 720 | 794 | 922 | 1,022 | 965 | 861 |
| Corporate bonds | 152 | 123 | 131 | 271 | 255 | 271 | 271 |
| Special reserves | 154 | 230 | 267 | 292 | 317 | 341 | 220 |
| Other long-term liabilities | 32 | 24 | 29 | 58 | 82 | 78 | 9 |
| Total long-term liabilities | 1,079 | 1,097 | 1,221 | 1,543 | 1,676 | 1,655 | 1,471 |
| Total liabilities | 1,815 | 1,946 | 2,199 | 2,793 | 3,048 | 3,046 | 2,905 |
| Capital stock and paid-in capital | 249 | 249 | 249 | 342 | 344 | 344 | 347 |
| Retained earnings | 49 | 76 | 83 | 72 | 69 | 65 | 84 |
| Total equity | 298 | 325 | 332 | 414 | 413 | 409 | 431 |
| Total liabilities and equity | 2,113 | 2,271 | 2,531 | 3,207 | 3,461 | 3,455 | 3,336 |

[a]Fiscal years run April 1 of year listed to March 31 of following year.

[b]Figures may not add exactly due to rounding. Source for all figures is company documents.

[c]This figure reflects change in method of accounting for inventory from LIFO to averaging.

**EXHIBIT 8–4**
**NSC's Original Manpower Plan to Adjust to Excess Work Force Levels[a]**

| | 1980 | 1981 | 1982 | 1983 | 1984 |
|---|---|---|---|---|---|
| Work force at start of fiscal year | 51,000 | 49,900 | 48,800 | 47,500 | 46,200 |
| Less retirement | – 1,400 | – 1,400 | – 1,600 | – 1,600 | – 1,000 |
| Less turnover | – 200 | – 200 | – 200 | – 200 | – 200 |
| Less promotion to white collar | – 200 | – 200 | – 200 | – 200 | – 200 |
| Plus hiring | + 700 | + 700 | + 700 | + 700 | + 700 |
| Work force at end of fiscal year | 49,900 | 48,800 | 47,500 | 46,200 | 45,500 |
| Less work force required for operations (reduced annually due to rationalization) | – 47,500 | – 47,000 | – 46,500 | – 46,000 | – 45,500 |
| Excess work force | 2,400[b] | 1,800 | 1,000 | 200 | 0 |
| Less stopgap measures | | | | | |
| Accelerated training | – 200 | – 200 | – 100 | 0 | 0 |
| "Loaning" workers | – 400 | – 400 | – 400 | – 200 | 0 |
| "Restructuring" subcontracting | – 200 | – 200 | – 200 | 0 | 0 |
| Transfers to new firm | – 100 | – 100 | – 100 | 0 | 0 |
| "Job trials" at subcontractors | – 200 | – 200 | – 200 | 0 | 0 |
| Excess work force assigned to make-work projects | 1,300 | 700 | 0 | 0 | 0 |

[a]Blue-collar personnel only.

[b]The discrepancy between the 3,000 figure in the case and this 2,400 figure is accounted for by the fact that the 3,000 refers to 1979 and outflows continued throughout the year.

CASE 9

# WEBSTER INDUSTRIES (A)

*R. Roosevelt Thomas, Jr.*

On Friday, October 17, 1975, Bob Carter, a 32-year-old graduate of the Amos Tuck School, was observing his first anniversary as manufacturing manager in the Fabrics Division of Webster Industries. Except for 2 years spent earning his MBA, he had been with the company for 10 years and he was very satisfied with his Webster experiences. Before being selected for his current position, he had spent 2 years as a plant production superintendent, 3 years as a plant manager, and 2 as assistant to the president, Abe Webster. On a day that should have been one of celebration, Carter sat at home in a very somber mood and started on his third martini of the afternoon

Earlier in the day Ike Davis, head of the Fabrics Division, had told Carter that Fabrics would have to reduce its personnel by 20 percent and that the manufacturing department, in particular, would have to make a cut of 15 percent at the managerial level. This meant that Carter would have to trim his 289 managers by 43 individuals. Davis's request stemmed from reduction plans presented to him by Abe Webster. Because Abe had set the following Friday as the deadline for the submission of termination lists, Davis wanted his top divisional managers to begin a review as a group on the preceding Wednesday of all proposed Fabrics separations. Davis concluded his conversation with Carter by listing the five guidelines that Abe Webster had provided:

1. No one with over 20 years of Webster service and 50 years of age should be terminated without a review by the president.
2. Since the last reduction (approximately one year before) had affected primarily hourly and weekly workers, this go-around was to focus on managerial levels.
3. Seniority was not to be a major determining factor as to who would be separated.
4. Early retirement should not be relied on as a mechanism for meeting reduction targets.
5. Blacks, women, and other minorities were not to be terminated more aggressively than other employees.

---

After speaking with Davis, Carter went home to ponder the situation.

Carter spent the afternoon in his den thinking about the task before him. He remembered the first time he had terminated an employee. Early in his career he had fired a secretary—it had taken him a week to muster enough courage to do it and a week to recover. Since that experience, however, he had found each successive termination increasingly easy. But never before had he been involved in releasing so many individuals at once, especially so many people with whom he had worked and developed social relations. Though he had been in his present position for only a year and had no previous experience in the Fabrics Division, Carter knew most of his managers by name and considered several to be friends. Furthermore, he and his family dealt with many of these individuals and their families in various community and civic activities. In addition to the likelihood of having to recommend the termination of personal and family friends, Carter worried about the possibility of having to release employees with significant lengths of service. He knew that any person with over ten years of Webster employment would be very surprised by termination. While pondering the possible consequences of the reductions, Carter became more and more anxious as he realized that he had few firm ideas on how the cuts should be made. The only certainty was that he must conform to Abe's guidelines.

## GENERAL INFORMATION ON WEBSTER INDUSTRIES

### *Location*

Located on 17 acres of rolling red Georgia hills on the northern outskirts of Clearwater, Georgia, Webster's headquarters resembled a college campus with plantation-like buildings. Top management was housed in the refurbished "Big House" of the old Webster Plantation, while middle-level corporate managers were situated in a modern three-story office building that was known as the "Box." Built a thousand yards from the Big House, the modern structure appeared out of place in the plantation setting. The Big House and the Box were the heart of one of America's most successful textile companies.

Clearwater was unabashedly a company town. Of its population of about 35,000, one-half of the employed residents worked for Webster, one-third engaged in serious farming, and the remainder labored in several small factories around the town. Not only was Webster the dominant employer, Websterites held all important community positions. The company stressed community involvement and encouraged its people to accept civic responsibilities.

Because Webster attracted highly educated employees from a variety of places, Clearwater differed from the typical small, rural Georgia town. For example, Georgia educators ranked its school system ahead of Atlanta's The town had experienced much success in attracting quality teachers by offering generous salary schedules and excellent facilities. Another unique feature of the town was a thriving set of cultural and entertainment events, from regular appearances by the Atlanta Symphony and various theater groups to exhibition games featuring the Atlanta professional athletic teams. As one Clearwaterite put it, "Clearwater is not your run-of-the-mill mill town."

*Company History*

Colonel Jeremiah Webster, an officer in the Confederate Army, founded the company after the Civil War. When the colonel retired from the operations, his youngest son assumed the leadership. He in turn was followed by his oldest male offspring, Mark Webster, who presided over the company from 1941 to 1960. Under Mark's tenure, Webster grew and branched into other fabric markets. By 1960 the company produced fibers for carpeting and for home and industrial furnishings. Sales rose from $150 million in 1941 to approximately $900 million in 1960. During this period Webster opened its first plants outside of Clearwater. Growth and geographical dispersion of operations greatly strained the company's management.

In the 1950s Mark Webster recognized his company's need for skilled management. Convinced of management's importance for the future of Webster, he set out to attract MBAs to his organization in 1955. Though trained as a lawyer, he had considerable respect for professional business education. This respect had been fostered by consulting relationships with professors from some of the leading national and regional business schools. Mark also encouraged his son, Abe, to attend the Wharton School.

After earning his MBA at Wharton, Abe served five experience years before assuming the presidency. Until that time, Webster's president had also served as chairman of the board of directors. After Abe's five years of experience, however, Mark decided to split the jobs. Abe became president and Mark concentrated on the chairmanship. Mark still kept regular hours, but emphasized that Abe was running the business. Under Abe the company continued to grow, primarily through diversification by acquisition of several small furniture and carpet manufacturers. Following these acquisitions, Webster's management adopted a divisional structure (see Fig. 9–1). Despite its diversification, Webster was very much a textile company. Of its 1974 sales of approximately $1.7 billion, 70 percent came from the Fabrics Division. The carpet and furniture lines each accounted for 15 percent.

The Fabrics Division's products were categorized as fibers for apparel, home furnishings, carpeting, and industrial furnishings. Organizationally, the Fabrics Division had a functional structure of sales, manufacturing, distribution, and research. Within sales, the organization was by markets; the sales force was organized around the different fiber classifications. Comparable to sales, the manufacturing plants were grouped by markets with three in apparel and two in each of the other areas. Each group reported to a production manager, who in turn reported to the assistant production superintendent, Cecil Stevens (see Fig. 9–2).

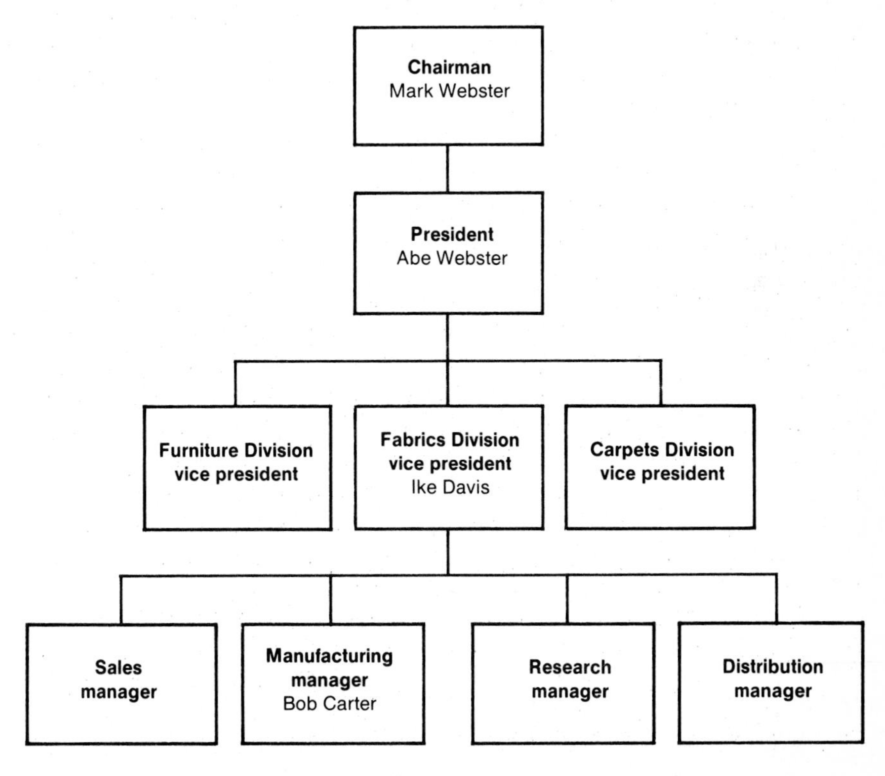


**FIGURE 9–1 Webster Industries, Partial Corporate Organization Chart**

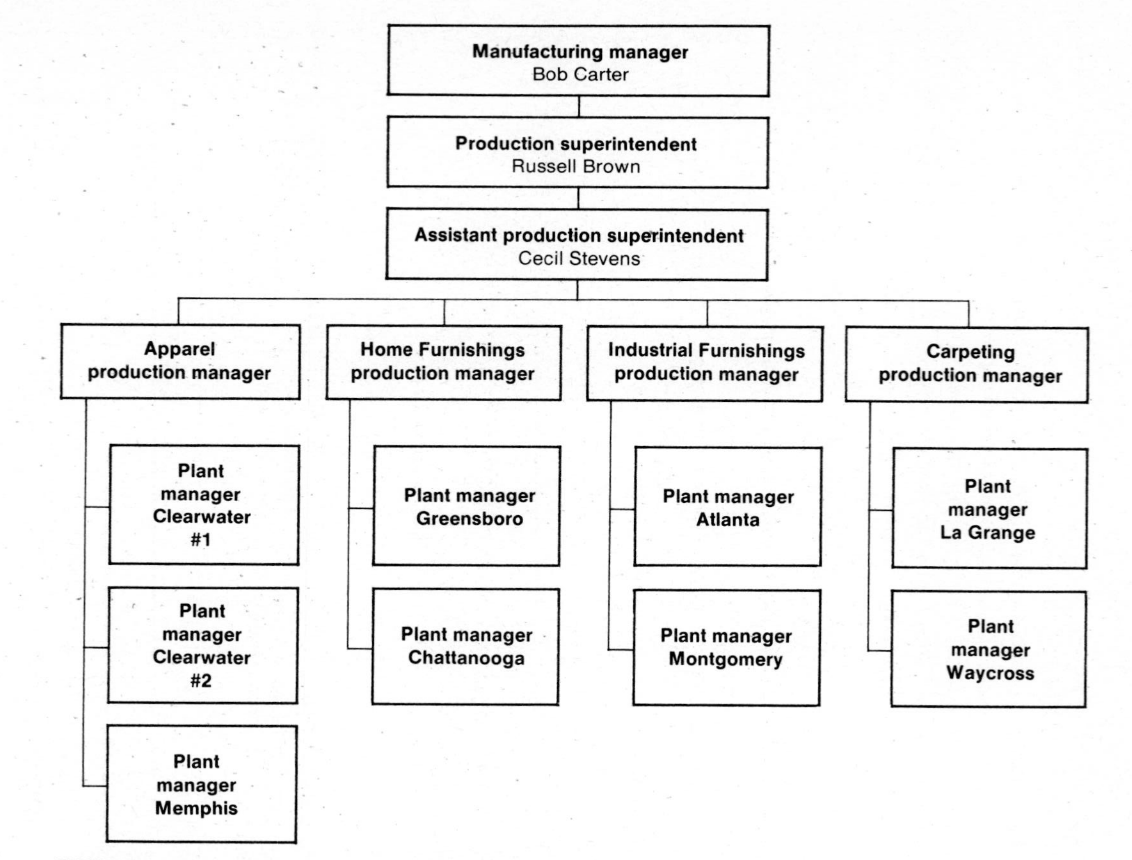


**FIGURE 9–2 Fabrics Division Organization Chart**

*Organizational Climate*

Websterites described the company as a first-class place to work. Employees took great pride in the company's nationally known products and frequently remarked, "You can tell Webster fabrics from a mile away!" The organization consistently won industry awards for superior products which were displayed in the Big House lobby. Webster also maintained excellent relations with its employees.

Management spared little in its efforts to make work at Webster rewarding *and* productive. The organization's facilities and working conditions excelled those of its competitors. Webster's pay and fringe benefits systems offered attractive financial packages and served as models for several firms located throughout the country. Further, because of its rapid growth, Webster had been able to provide its people with challenging work and opportunities for advancement. The company pioneered in establishing a Human Resources Division which performed the regular personnel functions along with a number of activities intended to facilitate the employees' growth and development. As part of its development projects, the Human Resources Division designed both a performance appraisal system (PAS) and an information system capable of tracking each employee's career and development. Top management gave the division much credit for the fact that no Webster plant was unionized.

Company officials also pointed to the firm's paternalistic culture as another factor contributing to good employee relations. They used the term *constructive paternalism* when describing the organization's attitudes and activities. For example, there were the annual company picnics, luncheons, dinners, and parties centered around special occasions. The employees' belief structure also reflected paternalism. Typically, the Webster employee believed, "If you make it through the tenth year, you can be reasonably assured that Webster always will have a place for you." Many employees expected this reciprocal agreement to hold even for individuals who had developed drinking and/or emotional problems. In more than one instance, Webster had kept an employee long after alcoholism had impaired his or her effectiveness, primarily because of top management's feeling that the person had no other place to go. Similarly, the company had paid the psychiatric bills of several employees rather than dismiss them as ineffective performers. Some viewed the open-door policies of the chairman and the president as another illustration of paternalism. All decisions could be appealed to the highest levels. A few managers expressed concern that employees with the appropriate connections had tended to use the open-door policies to secure undeserved promotions. Finally, the company on several occasions had financed the education of local youths—obviously with hopes that they would return to Clearwater and Webster, but with no strings attached. Two benefactors of this practice were the present Montgomery plant manager (Harvard B.A. and MBA) and the chief corporate counsel (Yale B.A. and J.D.). Neither had ever worked for any other organization than Webster.

Clearwaterites openly spoke of the firm's paternalism, as shown here in the words of one plant controller:

> There is a sense of family here. An expectation that if you are loyal to the company, it will be loyal to you. An expectation that if you have a problem, you can take it to Papa Webster [the company] and it will be at least seriously considered. Twelve years ago, a tornado came through and fiercely hit Clearwater. Those new houses you see along Webster Drive are a result of the company's generous response.
>
> I could go on and on. Fringe benefits also reflect how the company takes care of its people. The whole fringe benefits package is oriented toward taking care of the employee's family. We were the first to insure the education of a worker's children should he or she die. We continually upgrade retirement benefits to offset inflation. The company's hiring and promotion practices are also paternalistic. The offspring of employees always have first shot—if they are qualified—at openings. Webster—along these same lines—promotes from within. Rare is the case of someone being hired from the outside for a top position. What more is there to say? Webster is a darn good company.

### *Webster's Employees*

Webster's managerial employees came from several areas of the United States. Typically, they had received degrees from schools on the East Coast. The MBAs were from the top national and regional schools. Managers without MBAs had sophisticated technical training. The backgrounds of Webster's managers differed significantly from those of its typical plant laborers, who tended to come from the area around the plant and to have at least a high school diploma or at most an associate degree from a community college. Despite these differences, Webster had experienced little class conflict. Most attributed this harmony to the Human Resources Division, the many opportunities for advancement, and Webster's practice of having MBAs (especially those in manufacturing) spend some time in low-level plant positions.

Manufacturing in the Fabrics Division had 1,787 people located at headquarters and in nine plants. Of these, 289 served as managers. Managers worked either at corporate headquarters on the manufacturing manager's staff, or functioned in a managerial, supervisory, or staff capacity at one of the plants. The background of manufacturing managers was similar to that described above for Webster managers in general. Of the 289 managers, 160 lived in and around Clearwater.

## WEBSTER'S TROUBLES

The symptoms that set off the alarm at Webster were second-quarter earnings of less than 50 percent of 1974 earnings and a threatened cash position. The economy and Webster's sloppy growth habits contributed to each of these difficulties.

The economy, especially the slowdown in the construction industry, hit Webster's furniture and carpeting businesses hard. The softening of the demand for furniture and carpeting caused Webster's sales to decline from a 1973 peak of $2.1 billion. Simultaneously, inflation exerted upward pressure on costs. The dips in sales and earnings reduced Webster's cash flow considerably, so much so that money became extremely tight for the first time in 35 years. Though Mark and Abe Webster had expected the current earnings and cash troubles, they were unnerved by the extent of the problems. In addition to the troubled economy, the firm's phenomenal growth had complicated matters further.

The production manager in the largest Clearwater plant offered the following observations:

> We grew too fast. We wanted diversification but were not ready to handle it. With the acquisitions of the 1960s we became a different company almost overnight. Truthfully, we definitely were not prepared to break the billion-dollar level in sales. We grew too fast to consolidate. Only now are we learning the basics of managing a multibusiness enterprise. Controls were poor, especially in some of the plants we acquired. Staffing was done sloppily, so we ended up with a lot of fat. Plus we were—in my opinion—lax in our evaluation of performance.

The economy and the problems of diversification combined to slow Webster's growth and to threaten its financial integrity.

## BOB CARTER'S EVENING

By 6 P.M. Carter began to overcome his initial shock and to realize that, while painful, the reduction was probably needed and probably best for the company. He had known for some time that his department had fat at the managerial levels. Just six months earlier he had sought to demote three individuals—including his second in command. In denying his recommendation, Ike Davis had told Carter, "These men have too much service to be treated as you have proposed." So Carter was stuck with them; at least that had been the case until then. Carter reasoned that one benefit of the reduction in force would be an opportunity to make some long-needed changes. He saw his task as that of making the best reductions possible in the least painful manner.

After dinner Carter returned to his den to address the issue of how to cut 43 individuals from his managerial payroll. Because of his relatively brief tenure, he wanted to consult at least one other individual. The logical choices were the number two and three persons in his hierarchy; however, Carter wanted to demote the production superintendent, Russell Brown, and to promote the assistant production superintendent, Cecil Stevens. He had been impressed with Stevens and had decided some time back that he should have Brown's job. The reduction presented an opportunity to make the change.

Carter concluded that Stevens should be involved initially and perhaps others later on some basis. At 8:30 P.M. he called Stevens, who lived four miles away, and asked him to come over to discuss the critical situation. Cecil arrived an hour later. Carter informed him of the reduction plans and of his intention to recommend him for promotion to production superintendent. Stevens was both delighted by his promotion and shocked by the magnitude of the proposed separations. After relating details of his session with Davis, Carter asked Stevens to aid him in developing a strategy for determining the individuals to be released. Specifically, he requested that Stevens be prepared by Monday morning to identify and discuss issues that should be considered in formulating a reduction plan.

Carter and Stevens spent another 45 minutes discussing their perceptions of the company's situation and the need for the reduction. They also raised some questions about Webster's PAS. Stevens wondered how much weight should be given to performance ratings. Carter admitted that he had not gotten around to using PAS on a regular basis, but indicated that he would be interested in hearing Stevens's views of the system and its usage in the department. Stevens asked if they should consider inviting others to the session on Monday morning. After some discussion, they agreed to invite the production managers with the exception of the home furnishings manager, who was a likely candidate for demotion or termination. Carter and Stevens ended their meeting by agreeing on a timetable: Monday, 8 A.M.—develop strategy; Monday, 1 P.M.—begin to implement strategy; and Wednesday, 2 P.M.—present list to divisional managers.

## THE MONDAY MORNING MEETING

On Monday morning Carter, Stevens, and three of the four production managers met as planned. Stevens began the meeting by presenting his thoughts on possible criteria for developing a termination list:

> The following represents my thinking on possible options open to use. I see five.
>
> The first is *seniority*. Though guidelines prohibit much use of this criterion, there are a few individuals who might be receptive to offers of early retirement.
>
> The second is *fairness*. Should this be a criterion? Operationally, I do not know what it means except that we would not do anything that would be perceived as grossly unfair. I do know, however, that our people will expect fairness.
>
> The third is *fat*. The list would be determined by the elimination of "fat" or excess positions. This approach has legitimacy. The difficulty, however, is that some good people are in "fat" positions. The use of this criterion alone could result in a net quality-downgrading of manufacturing personnel.
>
> The fourth is *performance*. The basic question here is, "How do we measure performance?" How much weight do we give to PAS data? Some individuals feel that the PAS data are hopelessly biased, because of the managers' tendency to give everyone good ratings. How much weight do we give to the personnel audit data?[1] If we were to give significant weight to the audit data, would we be compromising the future effectiveness of the auditor? When making field visits, the auditor not only gathers data on performance from managers but also talks to individuals about their careers and problems. Many employees have been very frank with the auditors. If we use audit data as input in making termination decisions, the employee may feel betrayed and become reluctant to trust the auditors in the future. This would be especially likely if managers tried to make the auditors scapegoats. I can hear a manager telling a terminated employee, "I wanted to keep you, but our auditor Jack had too strong a case against you."
>
> Additionally, to what extent are we constrained by past practices? In the past, few managers have been diligent and responsible in talking with their people about performance; as a consequence, many employees are not aware of their relative standing with respect to performance. If these individuals are terminated, they will likely be shocked and feel that they have been treated unfairly. Can we fairly terminate on the basis of performance?

[1]Personnel auditors from the Human Resources Division visited each manager at least once a year to discuss his or her employees' performances. During these discussions they obtained a performance rating for each employee. This process was separate from Webster's performance appraisal system (PAS).

The fifth is *potential*. Again, the basic questions are around measurement and the weights to be given to PAS and audit data. How do we measure potential? How much weight do we give to PAS data? Audit data? Should we terminate an individual with little potential but capable of doing his or her present job fully satisfactorily? I am thinking about one plant controller in particular. He is an excellent assistant plant controller, but he does not have the potential to advance further. Would he be a candidate?

I consider this large reduction to be a one-shot deal. As such, the reduction represents a beautiful crisis opportunity to make moves that would be difficult under normal circumstances. We can seize the opportunity not only to meet our termination target but also to upgrade our department. Other divisions are releasing competent people. Some will be better than those that we will propose to keep. This means that we could upgrade by reducing a larger number than our target, and then hiring replacements from our sister divisions' terminations. For example, our target is 43. If after meeting this target we identified 5 available individuals who were better than persons we were planning to keep, we could terminate 48 and hire the 5 former employees of the other divisions. However, if we are to seize this opportunity, we will have to develop sound ways of evaluating performance and potential.

A lively discussion of PAS and the personnel audit followed Stevens's remarks. During these deliberations the group relied heavily on Stevens's memorandum on performance appraisal at Webster (see Exhibit 9-1).

**EXHIBIT 9-1**
**Memorandum**

---

To: Bob Carter

From: Cecil Stevens

Re: Performance Appraisal at Webster

Date: October 20, 1975

Since leaving your home on Friday evening, I have had an opportunity to talk with a number of individuals. Specifically, I saw Ed Johnson, the designer of our PAS system, at the club and had a good conversation; talked with Jack Bryant, our personnel auditor, about his work with the division; and spent two hours after church discussing the reduction with the manufacturing managers of the other divisions. Immediately below are my impressions of PAS and also the personnel audit function of the Human Resources Division.

PERFORMANCE APPRAISAL SYSTEM (PAS)

Bob, PAS was designed three years ago and has been used primarily on a voluntary basis. My discussion of the system is based primarily on conversations with its designer, Ed Johnson.

Purpose

The system is intended to help the manager act as a:

Manager responsible for attaining organizational goals
Judge responsible for evaluating individual performance and making decisions about salary and promotability
Helper responsible for developing subordinates

**EXHIBIT 9-1 (*Continued*)**

One problem in the past has been a failure to recognize the three roles cited above or a tendency to emphasize one over the others. PAS is based on the assumption that each role is equally important and is intended to help the manager do justice to each.

Components

PAS components are three in number: management by objectives (MBO), a developmental review, and an evaluation and salary review.

Management by objectives. This component focuses on results and is intended to help the manager realize organizational goals. Though each manager is expected to adapt management by objectives (MBO) to his or her situation, there are typically six steps.

1. Identification of objectives. Here, objectives are identified and prioritized. Also, review periods are set.
2. Establishment of measurement criteria. The basic question here is, "What monetary measures, percentages, and/or other numbers will be used to measure the achievement of objectives?" For example, if we in manufacturing were to establish "greater production effectiveness" as one of our objectives, we would have to decide how to measure the extent of achievement. Total unit costs? Total direct labor unit costs? Total production?
3. Planning. Plans are made for achieving the identified objectives. What is to be done? Who is to do it? When is it to be done? How is it to be done?
4. Execution. Plans are implemented.
5. Measure. Secure actual monetary figures, percentages, and/or other numbers so that results may be reviewed.
6. Review results. Compare actual measurements to plan. The frequency of measurement and review will depend on the number of review points within a year. Typically, the entire MBO cycle is repeated once a year, with intermittent reviews in between.

MBO is essentially a system for identifying what is to be done and ensuring that it is done. As such, MBO has a major weakness in terms of the managerial role: It does not aid the manager in observing, evaluating, or improving the behavior of subordinates. If the manager is to help his employees improve their behavior, he will need a behavior-oriented tool. The developmental review was designed to meet this need.

The developmental review. As indicated above, the review is intended to help the manager observe, analyze, and improve subordinate behavior. There are three subcomponents: the performance description questionnaire, the performance profile, and the developmental interview.

1. Performance description questionnaire. The questionnaire contains 70 behavioral statements, each describing a behavior determined through research to be indicative of effectiveness. Supervisors are asked to rate the extent to which the subordinate exhibits the behavior described. The 70 behavioral statements are grouped into a smaller number of dimensions such as openness to influence, priority setting, formal communications, organizational perspective, decisiveness, delegation/participation, support for company, unit productivity, and conflict resolution. The manager is asked to complete a questionnaire for each subordinate. He or she is asked to indicate on a six-point rating scale how descriptive the statement is of the employee's actual behavior. Also, under each statement is space for recording of any critical incidents supporting the manager's judgment. (See Attachment 1.) The performance profile is produced by computer from the questionnaire data.
2. Performance profile. The profile is intended to serve as a tool to help managers discriminate among a subordinate's performances on a number of performance dimensions. An individual's profile shows net strength or weakness for each dimension in terms of the person's own average. The profile line represents the average of the employee's ratings on all performance dimensions. The number and location of X's show the extent to which the

**EXHIBIT 9-1 (*Continued*)**

employee's score for a particular dimension is below or above his or her average for all dimensions. Dimensions with X's to the left of the profile line are those where the individual is relatively weak (compared to his or her average). Dimensions with X's to the right are those where the subordinate is relatively strong. The number of X's indicates the extent of the weakness or strength. (See Attachment 2.) The tool is designed to facilitate analysis of a subordinate's performance and is not valid theoretically for comparison of individuals.

3. Developmental interview. The purposes of the developmental interview are to provide the subordinate with a performance analysis based on the performance questionnaire and profile, to identify areas of weaknesses, and to translate these weaknesses into an appropriate developmental program. Tools are available to help the manager and subordinate in designing developmental plans.

The reasoning behind the design of the developmental review was a hope that the performance description questionnaire and profile would help the manager and his subordinates distinguish development from MBO and evaluation, and thereby reduce subordinate defensiveness that typically characterizes feedback sessions where developmental and evaluative issues are handled simultaneously.

Evaluation and salary review. This review is separate from the MBO and developmental reviews. Its basis is a form which asks the manager to rate the employee's overall performance and his or her potential. (See Attachment 3.) The overall rating should reflect the MBO sessions and the developmental review data and interview. In short, the two other components of PAS provide important inputs for the evaluation review. Possible overall ratings are unsatisfactory, fair, fully satisfactory, excellent, and outstanding.

Once the overall rating has been given, the salary matrix may be used as a guide in determining recommendations for salary adjustments. The matrix approach is straightforward and used by several organizations. Under this method salary adjustments are a function of the subordinate's rating and the relative standing of the employee's salary within his or her pay range. (See Attachment 4.)

Usage of PAS

Bob, as I indicated earlier, the system has been used on a voluntary basis so far. In the corporation as a whole, the usage rate is 29 percent; in manufacturing it is 40 percent. The only group using it 100 percent is the Fabrics Division's sales force.

THE PERSONNEL AUDIT

In addition to PAS the Human Resources Division is also responsible for conducting the personnel audit. The purposes of the audit are to secure performance data that will facilitate corporate manpower planning, to encourage and improve communications between superiors and subordinates, and to provide career development counseling. There is a potential conflict among the purposes in that the auditor is required to perform both evaluative and counseling roles. Some individuals who "pour out their souls" to the auditors are unaware of their evaluative function.

Our auditor, as you know, is Jack Bryant. At least once a year Jack visits all managers and talks about their subordinates. He also talks with subordinates about their development and perceptions of where they stand. Where there are discrepancies between a subordinate's perception and what his or her manager has said, Jack works with the manager in developing a plan for correcting the employee's misperceptions. Jack, however, has no enforcement power; consequently, some managers fail to give accurate--if any--feedback to their employees. The audit has been very successful in securing information for the central corporate data bank, but has had somewhat less success in getting managers to be honest with subordinates. Though individual employees may see their central file, few avail themselves of the opportunity; consequently,

**EXHIBIT 9-1 (*Continued*)**

many subordinates remain in the dark as to how they are actually perceived by their bosses. I, however, understand that a computer-based system capable of providing each employee with performance data has been designed and implemented below managerial levels. Reportedly, the system annually provides each employee with a printout showing--among other things--performance ratings and career history. April 1, 1976, is the target date for full implementation in the managerial ranks.

Currently, the form used by the auditors asks for a rating of the individual's performance and potential. There also are sections dealing with the employee's strengths and weaknesses and the manager's recommendations for future reassignments. (See Attachment 5.)

I have checked with Jack, and he has assured me that there are audit ratings on file for at least 97 percent of our personnel.

Bob, hopefully these remarks on PAS and the personnel audit will stimulate discussion leading to an appropriate reduction plan.

**Attachment 1 Sample Items from Performance Description Questionnaire**

1. Involves subordinates in decision-making process ______
2. Makes a special effort to explain Webster polices to subordinates ______
3. Molds a cohesive work group ______
4. Fails to follow-up on work assignments given to others ______
5. Works closely with subordinates who lack motivation ______
6. Selects and places qualified personnel ______
7. His or her subordinates accomplish a large amount of work ______
8. Objects to ideas before explained ______
9. Is accurate in his or her work ______
10. Gives poor presentations ______

Ratings

| Number | Definition |
|---|---|
| 1 | Strongly agree |
| 2 | Agree |
| 3 | Somewhat agree |
| 4 | Somewhat disagree |
| 5 | Disagree |
| 6 | Strongly disagree |

**Attachment 2 Sample Profile Interpretations**

| *Dimension* | *A*[a] | | *B*[b] | | *C*[c] | |
|---|---|---|---|---|---|---|
| 1. Openness to influence | xx | | xxxxx | | | xx |
| 2. Priority setting | | xx | | xxx | | xxxxxx |
| 3. Formal communications | | xx | | xxx | xxxxxx | |
| 4. Organizational perspective | xx | | xxxxxxxxxx | | xx | |
| 5. Decisiveness | | xx | | xx | | xx |
| 6. Delegation participation | xx | | | xx | xxxxxx | |
| 7. Support for company | | xx | xx | | | xxxxxx |
| 8. Unit productivity | xx | | | xxx | xx | |
| 9. Conflict resolution | | xx | xx | | xx | |
| 10. Team building | xx | | | xxx | xx | |
| 11. Control | | xx | | xx | | xxx |

[a]Implication is that manager is well-balanced dimensionally.
[b]Implication is that this manager has one very significantly weak dimension and another relatively weak dimension, contrasted to the remaining favorably balanced dimensions.
[c]Implication is that this manager has two relatively weak dimensions and two relatively strong dimensions, with remaining dimensions relatively balanced.
CAUTION: Remember that you are only comparing the individual to himself and *not* with other people. *If* an individual is "well balanced dimensionally," it means there is not much difference between what he does best and what he does the poorest; it does *not* necessarily mean he is a "well-balanced manager."

## EXHIBIT 9-1 (*Continued*)

**Attachment 3**

Detach and send to: Private

*Position Preference* Date ____________

Employee name ____________ Employee number ____________

Division ____________ Location ____________

Position ____________ Supervisor ____________

Supervisor and subordinate develop *together.* Indicate below subsequent positions for your subordinate *that you both can agree* are realistic, appropriate, and interesting. Specify both functional area (e.g., sales, personnel, and so forth), and, whenever possible, type of job.

Order of preference for next jobs:

| Short-term | Long-term (within next 5 years) |
|---|---|
| First choice: | First Choice: |
| Second choice: | Second Choice: |

*Supervisor's summary:* Supervisor fills in by himself *after* the developmental interview. The subordinate should be shown these ratings after the supervisor has coordinated the rating with the *second*-level supervisor.

A. *Change of status:* Indicate by your choice of the statements below (check one) the change of status you recommend for this person during the next twelve months.

_____ Should be separated as soon as possible (SEP)

_____ Should be reassigned to position with a decreased responsibility (DEM)

_____ Should be reassigned to a position with a similar level of responsibility (LAT)

_____ Needs more experience before reassignment can be considered (EXP)

B. *Career potential:* Based on current knowledge, indicate in the spaces below (check one) the level this person has the greatest probability of achieving. Note: Potential ratings do *not* imply a person's readiness for promotion now.

_____ Potential division manager or equivalent. (Must be Group 50 or above.) (BLUE)

_____ Potential to higher supervisory/managerial level (GREEN)

_____ Potential is best utilized within a specialty or as an individual performer (BROWN)

_____ Good performer; no indication to date of potential for a higher level (YELLOW)

______ Should be reassigned to a position with more responsibility (RDY)

______ Should remain in present position (STA)

______ Questionable performance (RED)

C. *Overall job performance* during the past 6 to 12 months may be characterized as: (Check scale)

| Unsatisfactory | Fair | Satisfactory | Excellent | Outstanding |
|---|---|---|---|---|

D. *Comments:*

- - - - - - - - - - - - - - - - - - - - - - - - - - - - - - - - - - - - - - - -

*Endorsement of second-level supervisor*

______ I agree with all of the above recommendations.

______ I disagree with some (or all) of the above recommendations and would make the following recommendations:

______________________

Signature

## EXHIBIT 9–1 (*Continued*)

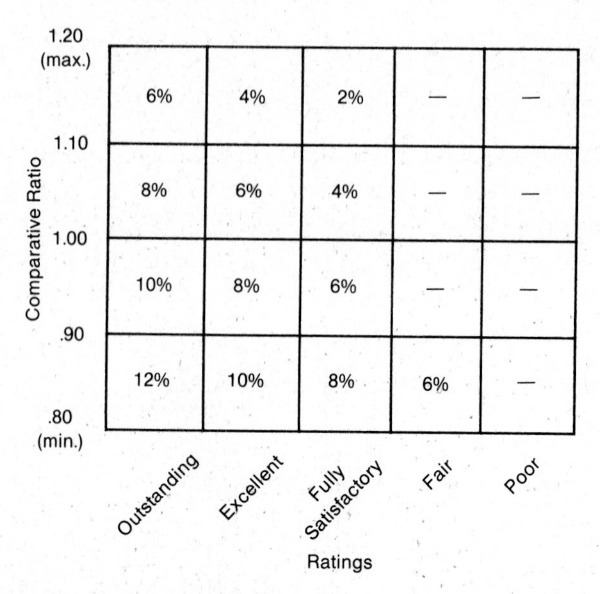


**Attachment 4 Salary Matrix.** *Note:* Comparative ratio equals actual salary divided by the midpoint of the individual's salary range. Salary adjustment was a function of the individual's ratio and rating. An employee with an .85 ratio and a rating of excellent would receive an adjustment of 10 percent.

**Attachment 5**

Employee name ________________ Supervisor ________________ Date ______

| Performance | Potential |
|---|---|
| 1 2 3 4 5 NR (Circle one) | (Circle one) 1 2 3 4 5 NR |

*Comments:* [Supervisor should define significant strengths and weaknesses (development needs) and accomplishments.]

*Change of status:* (for the next 12 months) (Check one)

| | | |
|---|---|---|
| 1. ______ | Should be separated as soon as possible (termination) | |
| 2. ______ | Should be reassigned to a position of decreased responsibility (demotion) | Which function(s) (comment) ______ |
| 3. ______ | Should be reassigned to a position with a similar level of responsibility (lateral move) | Which function(s) (comment) ______ |
| 4. ______ | Needs more experience before reassignment can be considered (not ready) | Which function(s) (comment) ______ |
| 5. ______ | Should be reassigned to a position of more responsibility (promotion) | Which function(s) (comment) ______ |
| 6. ______ | Will probably remain in present position indefinitely (leveled) | |

Performance

| Number | Definition |
|---|---|
| 5 | Outstanding |
| 4 | Excellent |
| 3 | Fully satisfactory |
| 2 | Fair |
| 1 | Unsatisfactory |

Potential

| Color | Number | Definition |
|---|---|---|
| Blue | 5 | Potential division manager or equivalent (for individuals currently at the ''A'' payroll level) |
| Green | 4 | Potential to higher supervisory position |
| Brown | 3 | Potential is best utilized within a specialty or as an individual performer |
| Yellow | 2 | Good performer; no indication to date of potential for a higher level |
| Red | 1 | Questionable performer |

CASE 10

# COLONIAL FOOD SERVICES COMPANY

*James Clawson*
*Michael Beer*

Colonial Food Services Company (CFS) provided food and refreshment to a variety of customers across the country. In its mid-Atlantic states region, the company's primary clients were colleges and prep schools where CFS operated hot food services, cafeterias, and vending machines under contracts which were renewable every one to three years. To have contracts renewed, it was essential to maintain good customer relations; indeed, CFS placed a great deal of value on the interpersonal skills of its employees. The company was proud of its ability to recruit, train, and develop new managerial talent.

## THE MID-ATLANTIC STATES REGION

The mid-Atlantic states region of CFS was headed by Vice President James Cranston, who was responsible for serving approximately 80 customers. These 80 accounts were grouped into eight food districts[1] and two vending districts. Each district was supervised by a district manager who reported either to Cranston or to a regional operating manager who in turn reported to Cranston. (An organization chart for the region appears in Exhibit 10–1.) Each of the food districts contained from 1 to 14 client accounts which were supervised by unit managers and assistant managers; the vending districts were also administered by district managers. It was Cranston's custom to travel to the various cities in the region and spend a day or two working with the local district managers as they, in turn, visited their unit managers.

*Note*: This case provides background information for "James Cranston," Case 11, and "Eugene Kirby," Case 12. Taken together, these three cases describe a situation in which a manager approaches a performance appraisal interview with a long-time employee. The names in all three cases have been disguised.

[1]A food district involved the cooking and serving of food by hand. Sales in Cranston's area were about $35 million in 1976.

## CFS PERFORMANCE APPRAISAL SYSTEM

The central feature of the company's performance appraisal system was an annual interview. Managers were expected to sit down with each of their employees at least once a year (or more often if appropriate) and review their performance. The company had recently introduced a new form to facilitate planning and conducting these interviews. (See Exhibit 9-2.) These forms were to be filled out in advance by the person conducting the appraisal. During the interview, salary considerations for the coming year were to be discussed and the decision about the employee's raise communicated. Copies of the form were to be signed by the employee after the performance appraisal interview as an indication that he or she had seen the appraisal. Each appraisee then had the opportunity to add any additional comments that he or she felt should be included in the personnel file. The forms were then sent to the interviewing manager's immediate superior for review. When the supervisor had signed the forms, a copy was sent to the personnel files and a copy was sent back to the interviewing manager.

## EVENTS PRECEDING CRANSTON'S INTERVIEW WITH KIRBY

Jim Cranston had made plans to conduct performance appraisal interviews with each of his district managers during 1977. He arranged to have such an interview with Eugene Kirby, one of the district managers, in the latter part of June.

Around that time, Cranston had decided to reactivate the position of regional operating manager. While this position had always been in the region, the responsibilities associated with it had declined to almost nothing over the years. After some deliberation Cranston had assigned Mike Mason, a good friend of Gene Kirby's, to the position. Mason supervised five food service district managers.

Cranston's interview with Kirby was scheduled once and then postponed for a week to accommodate an unexpected change in Cranston's itinerary. Kirby traveled two hours by car to a city where Cranston was working with another district manager. Kirby arrived on time but had to wait two hours while Cranston finished his business. The two men then drove together to a nearby conference room where they sat down for the interview.

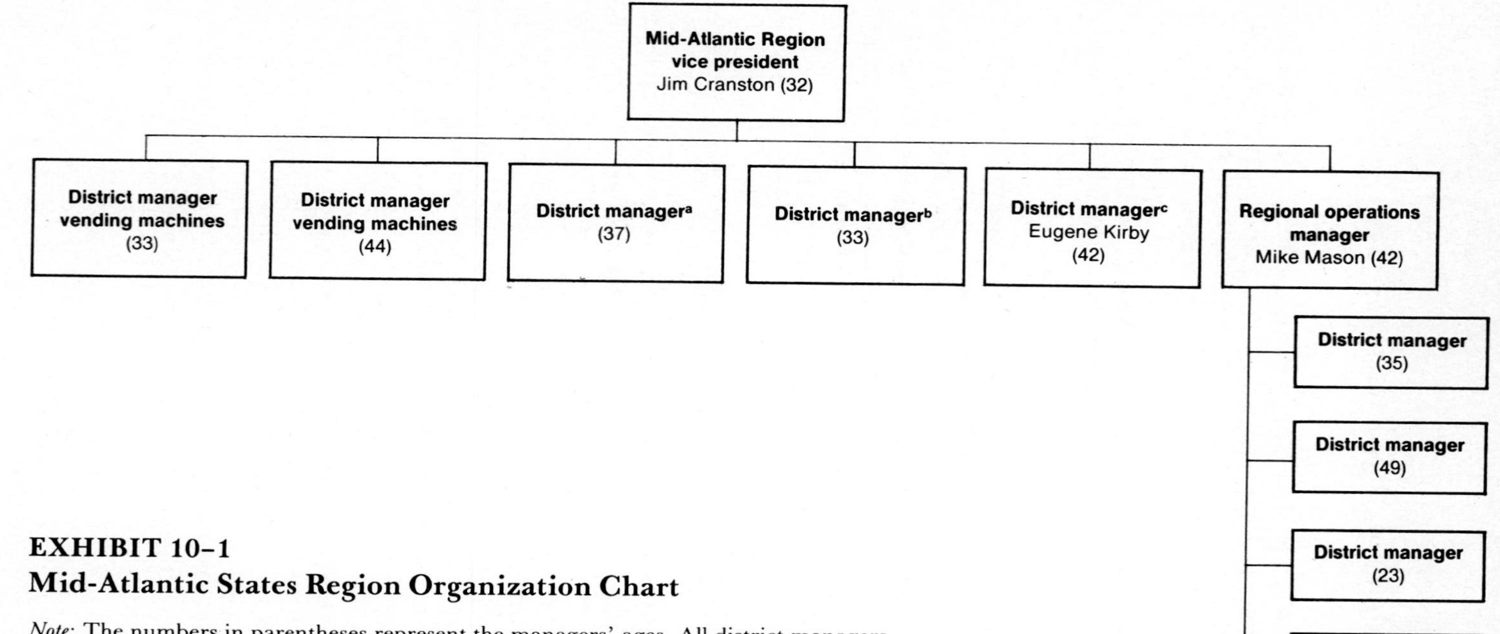


## EXHIBIT 10–1
## Mid-Atlantic States Region Organization Chart

*Note*: The numbers in parentheses represent the managers' ages. All district managers had several food unit managers reporting to each of them, and they in turn had people working for them who operated these units. The vending districts and food districts were structured differently.

[a]Ten managers reported to this district manager.

[b]Seven managers reported to this district manager.

[c]Eight managers, with a total of 227 personnel, reported to Eugene Kirby.

## EXHIBIT 10–2
## Performance Appraisal Form

Name ______________________________ SSN __________

Position title ______________________ Present grade __________

Component number ______________ Component name ______________

Months in present position ______________ Months in CFS ______________

Appraisal period: From ______ To ______ Date of last appraisal ______________

Scale values for describing characteristics and applications:

A. More than needed for job requirements
B. Fully meets job requirements
C. Moderately meets job requirements
D. Does not meet job requirements

Characteristics:

1. Technical knowledge (information and skills required to fulfill the functions of the job) ☐
2. People knowledge (understanding of individual and group behavior and awareness of others, self-awareness) ☐
3. Administrative knowledge (information about company procedures, policies, directives, and requirements) ☐
4. Physical energy (level of dynamics, vitality, activity) ☐
5. Mental energy (level of intellectual force, creativity, comprehension, and conceptualizing) ☐
6. Factor "X" (Designate: ______________________________ ☐
   ____________________.) (This is to be used for any factor the rater believes essential to the job that cannot be rated in the above.)

Applications:

7. Planning (setting goals and objectives, forecasting, establishing programs, scheduling, allocating time.) ☐
8. Structuring (initiating activities, controlling, coordinating, events communicating, directing) ☐
9. Motivating (providing personal support, use of rewards, encouraging development, appraising, and coaching) ☐
10. Decision making (problem solving, resolving conflict, using feedback to improve situation and self) ☐
11. Factor "Y" (Designate: ______________________________.) ☐
    List any action believed important to conduct the job not rated under items 7 through 10.)

**EXHIBIT 10-2 (*Continued*)**

Overall rating: This rating should reflect the overall performance of the individual, taking into consideration all factors. Check one block. (Percentage figures indicate the probable dispersion of ratings.)

| 1 | 2 | 3 | 4 | 5 | 6 | 7 | 8 | 9 |
|---|---|---|---|---|---|---|---|---|
| ☐ | ☐ | ☐ | ☐ | ☐ | ☐ | ☐ | ☐ | ☐ |
| Unsatisfactory (5 percent) | | Acceptable 15 percent | | Fully satisfactory 60 percent | | Superior 15 percent | | Exceptional 5 percent |

Comments: (Note important or additional factors affecting the overall rating.)

______________________________

______________________________

______________________________

______________________________

Development:

1. Suggestions for personal development in present position:

______________________________

______________________________

2. To what position (2) might this person be promoted in the future? When?

______________________________

______________________________

3. Appraiser's name (print) ______________ Date ________

Title ______________ Signature ______________

Review by appraisee:

Comments: ______________________________

______________________________

Signature ______________ Date ________

Review by endorser:

Comments: ______________________________

______________________________

______________________________

Signature ______________ Date ________

Title ______________

CASE 11

# JAMES CRANSTON

*James Clawson*
*Michael Beer*

James Cranston, vice president for the mid-Atlantic states region of Colonial Food Services (CFS),[1] leaned forward in his chair as he spoke with the casewriter about his upcoming interview with Eugene Kirby, one of the district managers. He emphasized the man's capacity, ability, and great sensitivity. The district manager was a man of experience, a man of many talents—and a few faults. Cranston was convinced that Kirby was a valued employee, but a few of his characteristics made Cranston wonder if the man had reached a plateau in the company. As he contemplated the upcoming performance appraisal interview with his district manager, Cranston grew quiet and reflective.

## THE MID-ATLANTIC STATES REGION VICE PRESIDENT

Cranston was 6′2″ and athletic. He was impatient with rambling conversations, and when the speaker seemed unsure of his direction, Cranston tried to help him find his words or conclusions. Commenting on his own style, he remarked, "I like to get the floor. I like to talk. I'm a very bad second man. It is hard for me to listen to others when they're not getting to the point."

As Cranston talked about Gene Kirby, his comments were a curious mixture of impersonal assessments of Kirby's relative strengths and deficiencies, as well as concern for his feelings and personal problems. This readiness to entwine both impersonal and personal comments, and to express both the positive and negative sides of an issue, made it difficult sometimes for the casewriter to understand just where Cranston stood on a particular point.

[1]Background for this case is provided in "Colonial Food Services," Case 10. The perspective of the employee involved in this description of a performance appraisal interview is contained in "Eugene Kirby," Case 12.

Cranston graduated from the Air Force Academy where he played varsity baseball and soccer. While serving his five-year obligation in the air force, he earned his MBA at the University of Denver. Upon leaving the air force in 1972, Cranston accepted a position in sales at Colonial Food Services. After 15 months, he applied for an opening as executive assistant to the president and was selected. Two years later, at age 30, he became vice president of the mid-Atlantic states region. Cranston described the area as being very flat at the time:

> Sales had tapered off, the personnel did not seem motivated and lacked spirit. You could tell it as soon as you walked into an account. CFS is very people-oriented and encourages frequent visits to the operations. My predecessors made infrequent visits. You have to go out at least two or three times a week. I go in with the district managers, look around, sit down with the manager and the assistant manager over a cup of coffee, and talk about their problems. They know the individual client situation better than I do, but in the end I'm responsible for the financial considerations. I talk with these district managers three or four times a week on the phone.
>
> There are about 80 accounts in my area. As a company, we do not operate cheaply. We work on client and customer satisfaction. We have to maintain our existing accounts. We are not geared to simply work for less money, but rather to high performance standards. Our clients expect dependability and quality for our prices, and we have to deliver. We're in demand, so there's something in that strategy.

## THE CFS PERFORMANCE APPRAISAL SYSTEM

Colonial Food Services had recently instituted a new performance appraisal form as a part of its overall performance appraisal system (see Exhibit 10–1). Cranston commented on the overall performance appraisal system:

> We have a new form out now. We have interviews once a year formally, but I meet with my managers informally every three months. Some of the older guys say they've never been interviewed. We usually just gave a manager his increase and did not talk much in depth. Now, we evaluate them on initiative, leadership, development of their subordinates, cost control, profits, forecasting, and delegation of responsibilities.

CFS employees were given a bonus if they were able to make profits higher than their forecasts, but base salary increases were made on a superior's judgment of merit. Cranston remarked:

> Profit performance figures into the performance appraisal process but not so much in terms of a percent increase. There's a great deal of emphasis around here, of course, on making money, but that's not all of the story. I gave the guy with the best profit performance last year the lowest merit

> increase. He did great on bonus which depends primarily on profits. A person's management future is correlated with the merit increases because they address the development of management skills. This individual lacked the people skills needed to develop his own career growth. The forecasting process and the achievement of profits are important in an individual's annual review, but many additional factors are also weighed heavily. We have to stress interpersonal skills—they are the basis of our business.

Cranston was also acutely aware that as a young manager he had to be careful of his own interpersonal relationships with older, more experienced subordinates. As Cranston talked about the upcoming interview with Gene Kirby, he touched on many aspects of Kirby's personality and performance. What he said has been organized into the following six major themes.

## PERSONALITY AND SENSITIVITY TO FEEDBACK

Cranston was concerned as he thought about the upcoming performance appraisal interview with Gene Kirby. He had mixed emotions about Kirby's ability to deal with negative feedback. On the outside, he felt that Kirby was a strong, forceful, and toughened manager, but on the inside, he felt that Kirby was a fragile person who needed a great deal of positive reinforcement and who reacted defensively to negative feedback. Cranston felt that he would have to be very careful not to hurt Kirby's feelings, if he talked about the employee's shortcomings. Cranston said:

> He is a most sensitive, emotional person—*the* most sensitive and emotional manager I have. He's a very proud person. He seems to take criticism pretty well, but underneath he's basically an insecure person. You just can't go in and tell him to stop bullying people. Telling him that makes him defensive and protective. You have to be careful. Gene reads things into the discussion. Somebody came to him with a job offer recently, and he was all upset thinking that we had arranged it and were trying to transfer him. This was when he had his back problem. Gene needs to listen longer and not get so defensive. He gets red and then he really starts to come back at you. I wouldn't question his loyalty, yet I know if CFS shafted him, he'd confront me. He's no wallflower.

## PHYSICAL CONDITION

Kirby's physical condition was also a matter of concern to the vice president. Cranston felt that Kirby just did not have the physical energy and endurance to handle the demands and stresses of a higher position. Kirby had had a small heart attack several years before, and more recently he had been laid up in bed for three weeks with a bad back. In fact, Cranston felt that Kirby's struggling to keep up with the physical demands of his job had been so much of a source of frustration to Gene, that it had contributed to the interpersonal difficulties Kirby had been experiencing recently. Cranston surmised that Kirby had tried to compensate for his own frustrations by bullying people, particularly colleagues and staff personnel at company headquarters. Kirby had an excellent knowledge of the headquarter's staff assignments and was able to use that knowledge to try to get what he felt he needed. Sometimes Kirby offended people at company headquarters with his aggressive style and this bothered Cranston. Speaking about Kirby's physical condition, Cranston said:

> Gene has had one major heart scare. He's very overweight and smokes to excess. He is in poor physical condition, and he's worried about that. He has endurance limitations. He's well groomed, well dressed, and very conscious of his physical appearance. In short, he looks like a professional. Lately, he's been down a while with a bad back.

## DECISION-MAKING INITIATIVE

Cranston also felt that Kirby called on the telephone too often to discuss problems in his district. It was irritating to Cranston that Kirby did not take greater initiative in solving these problems on his own. He made the following comments:

> He's a good company man. He really supports the next level of management. He's very good at keeping me informed, *but* he calls too frequently. He *needs* stroking at times.

## RELATIONS WITH OTHERS

Cranston felt that Kirby's temper had recently created a number of problems in his relationship with peers and with headquarters. Cranston was very concerned about these problems and talked about them:

> He loses his temper and talks when he should be quiet. He tends to be an island unto himself. He has a very short temper. He blows up. He creates malice that I have to clean up. He *causes* problems.
>
> For instance, not all of our employees have responsibility for operations. Most of our line people can deal with the staff when we have problems. Gene often feels that responsibility very heavily and often goes right for the jugular. One time, we had a contract problem with a client, and

we were working with a new lawyer in the legal department. The guy was slow, and we had to have the new contract immediately. After several revisions the new lawyer sent a copy of the *original* draft directly to the client instead of routing it through Gene as he should have. The client was surprised and called Gene and said, "Wait till you see what they're sending me now." Now, rather than *talk* to the lawyer, Gene called him on the phone, gave a tirade, and wiped him out, I mean *wiped* him out—over the phone. So I had to get involved to patch things up with the legal department. The lawyer later left the company.

## MANAGING AND DEVELOPING PEOPLE

Cranston was convinced, however, that Kirby was an asset to the company. Kirby's experience, technical competence, ability to meet his forecasts, and ability to train people were all valuable items in his present job, although Cranston had some concerns about the way Kirby communicated with his managers and the way he moved his people around from client to client. Cranston commented prior to the interview on his assessment of Kirby's performance.

Gene is very good with people. He has good patience. He's very protective of his boys. He won't list the bottom third on his regular evaluation sheets. He creates this halo effect around his personnel that they're all so good there is no bottom third.

He's a very good teacher. He's a *tremendous* developer of people. He's very good with the this-is-how-you-do-it part of management. But he opens his mouth and doesn't know when to shut up. Gene is very vocal. It is one of his overwhelming pluses and minuses. He makes the expedient comment and then does not or cannot follow through because of company policy limitations. These expedient remarks are often not well received by his managers. They begin to think that he's blowing smoke at them.

He's good with clients, very innovative, and good on working out new contracts. He's a fox. But that can work against you, too. They can think he's a "shrewdy" and manipulative. But he doesn't always see how others perceive him. He's able to squirrel people away to other institutions for later use elsewhere in the company as they grow. But that can make people mad. My two predecessors both had negative input to me about Gene's shrewdness. Some clients said they didn't want Gene back as their account manager. We try to group accounts around a guy's home so it will be both convenient and efficient. Gene's clients were mostly small prep school accounts in his area. They are a great training ground for new employees. They run a seven-day operation, and if you can get a promising assistant manager in them, they are a fine place to train people. So, the idea is that you train several assistants like this and then shoot them out to more complex situations with a wider range of services, or more consumers, or have them assume the managerial function at one of the smaller accounts. Our region is raided a lot because we have such good training grounds. Well, these schools complained about getting all of these new assistants and having such a high turnover. They desired a greater degree of stability. They felt like there was too much movement, too much shifting of the deck.

## OPERATIONS MANAGEMENT AND RESULTS

Gene has a very strong operations background. He knows his stuff, and he's a very hard worker. Gene was given two big problem accounts, accounts that other people just couldn't manage. They were supposed to be unworkable. Gene made them work.

Gene can go in and put on an apron if he has to and teach the chef; he just has all of the technical skills. He can help with the customer counseling if he has to, and he can talk to the students in the dining room. He can organize the kitchen. He's a very observant guy, too; he looks around him. He's shrewd with the finances; he has an outstanding profit performance record. With profits, Gene always tracks right on his forecast from way back. When he tells me he's going to bring in *X* dollars, I put it in the bank right then. I believe his forecasts.

Often he runs his district out of his home. He needs to get out and get more new accounts. He's never had an account terminate, though. Operationally, he does almost everything right.

## POTENTIAL FOR PROMOTION

As Cranston considered his upcoming performance appraisal interview with Gene, he knew the promotion issue would come up. Cranston believed that Kirby wanted to continue to rise in the organization, but he had ambivalent feelings about Kirby's potential in the company. He wondered what he should say in the interview and how that might help Kirby to develop. He commented:

Gene has been a district manager for five years. His potential to go up in the organization is limited. He might have regional operations manager potential. Gene desires advancement; he wants more. He has a strong tie to his community. His current income is about 30K with bonuses. The regional operations manager's job is about 36K. Gene could live at any level of income. He appreciates the finer things of life and could find use for the money.

A few days before his interview with Gene Kirby, Cranston filled out the corporate performance appraisal form indicating his assessment of Kirby's performance and potential.

On the day of the interview, Cranston was visiting another district manager in a city approximately midway between his regional office and Kirby's home. Kirby had agreed to drive to this city to meet Cranston for the interview. The local district manager had a problem, thus Cranston was delayed two hours in meeting Kirby. When Cranston arrived, the two men drove together to a nearby conference room where they sat down for the interview.

## EXHIBIT 11–1
## Performance Appraisal Form

Name *Eugene Kirby* SSN ________

Position title *District Manager* Present grade ________

Component number ________ Component name ________

Months in present position *60* Months in CFS *156*

Appraisal period: From *3/76* To *6/77* Date of last appraisal ________

Scale values for describing characteristics and applications:

A. More than needed for job requirements
B. Fully meets job requirements
C. Moderately meets job requirements
D. Does not meet job requirements

Characteristics:

1. Technical knowledge (information and skills required to fulfill the functions of the job) — B
2. People knowledge (understanding of individual and group behavior and awareness of others, self-awareness) — B
3. Administrative knowledge (information about company procedures, policies, directives, and requirements) — A
4. Physical energy (level of dynamics, vitality, activity) — B
5. Mental energy (level of intellectual force, creativity, comprehension, and conceptualizing) — B
6. Factor "X" (Designate: *anticipation of client situation; briefing superiors on client situations*.) (This is to be used for any factor the rater believes essential to the job that cannot be rated in the above.) — A

Applications:

7. Planning (setting goals and objectives, forecasting, establishing programs, scheduling, allocating time.) — B
8. Structuring (initiating activities, controlling, coordinating, events communicating, directing) — B
9. Motivating (providing personal support, use of rewards, encouraging development, appraising, and coaching) — A
10. Decision making (problem solving, resolving conflict, using feedback to improve situation and self) — C
11. Factor "Y" (Designate: *development of subordinates*.) List any action believed important to conduct the job not rated under items 7 through 10.) — A

Overall rating: This rating should reflect the overall performance of the individual, taking into consideration all factors. Check one block. (Percentage figures indicate the probable dispersion of ratings.)

| 1 | 2 | 3 | 4 | 5 | 6 | 7 | 8 | 9 |
|---|---|---|---|---|---|---|---|---|
| ☐ | ☐ | ☐ | ☐ | ☐ | ☒ | ☐ | ☐ | ☐ |
| Unsatisfactory (5 percent) | | Acceptable 15 percent | | Fully satisfactory 60 percent | | Superior 15 percent | | Exceptional 5 percent |

Comments: (Note important or additional factors affecting the overall rating.)
Gene has excellent understanding of company policies and procedures and successfully implements this knowledge in the majority of situations. Gene often becomes frustrated with administrative entanglements and it shows often with adverse effects on subordinates.

Development:

1. Suggestions for personal development in present position:
Gene needs additional exposure in other market groups as well as more exposure to company headquarters. Any management program on an in-house or university level.

2. To what position (2) might this person be promoted in the future? When?
Senior District manager
Regional operating manager

3. Appraiser's name (print) JAMES CRANSTON Date JUNE 30, 1977
Title VICE PRESIDENT Signature James Cranston

Review by appraisee:

Comments: ______________________________

Signature ______________________ Date __________

Review by endorser:

Comments: ______________________________

Signature ______________________ Date __________

Title ______________________

CASE 12

# EUGENE KIRBY (A)

*James Clawson*
*Michael Beer*

Eugene Kirby was one of several district managers who reported to Jim Cranston, the mid-Atlantic states region vice president for Colonial Food Services (CFS).[1] His accounts included three prep schools, one hospital, and four colleges. These accounts were operated by 28 unit managers and assistant managers and 227 staff personnel.

Gene Kirby was about 6′2″ tall and robustly built. Although he carried a noticeable paunch, his 250 pounds sat comfortably on his large frame. He dressed and groomed himself meticulously. Kirby was fond of wearing double-knit leisure suits and an occasional white belt. His clothing was always neat and clean.

Kirby had attended but never graduated from college and this was a source of concern to him. Part of the concern was a feeling that the new college graduates coming into the company had a better career future, even though they did not have the experience and interpersonal know-how or, as he put it, "street savvy." Another part of his concern was a dislike for being graded. While Kirby did not mind discussing his performance with other people, he genuinely disliked having another person affix a scaled grade to his work. This aversion had kept Kirby from attending continuing education courses, even though he thought them desirable and necessary.

Kirby was proud of his ability to train and develop managers, and he often noted the people in management positions who had once been under his supervision. He had organized training programs in the past for his employees, and he wished to continue this practice although funds were not always available for such activities.

When Gene Kirby spoke to the casewriter about his background, his soft but husky voice contributed to the aura of precision surrounding him:

> I'm 42, married, and have twin boys who are 14. I was a preministerial student majoring in psychology. I'm an evangelistic type; I like preach-

[1]See the following cases for background: "Colonial Food Services," Case 10; "James Cranston," Case 11.

ing. But I didn't finish college. I'm really close to my community, served on the school board and the zoning board of appeals. There isn't anyone in this town of 18,000 that doesn't know me.

I don't embarrass easily. I'm at home in front of a group—a natural ham. For instance, I gave a speech in 1969. We opened up a large prep school, and the headmaster asked me if I wanted to have the chapel to speak in, and I jumped at the chance. It was during an economy drive when we were concerned about waste and so on, so I piled up the equivalent of one week's wasted food from the food service in the middle of the room, and told them that it was costing them at the rate of $32,000 a year. I gave my little 25-minute speech on food management and waste and all. Later, the headmaster told me it was the first time he'd ever heard a sermon on food! I believe in it very strongly. I'm not shy about that. I'm not bashful.

I have spent 20 years in the food industry—7 with Universal Hotels in New York City and 13 with CFS. The last 5 years as a district manager [DM]. The time has gone by very quickly and has been very productive. The last 5 years have given me as much satisfaction as anything I've done. I've never regretted this profession; I would recommend it to my kids. Being a district manager gives you opportunity to impact on people's lives, opportunity to interject, to suggest recommendations, and to pursue change in higher management. I liken the district manager to master sergeants—they run the army. They have so much input both downward and upward.

Three years ago I had a coronary and had to slow down for a while. It happened at an employee's Christmas party. The next day my two strongest managers—I had 16 units then—divided up the district and visited or called the other managers to say that they were taking over while I was out. They called the vice president [James Cranston] and told him that things went very smoothly. I was out for three months, but it was very gratifying to see those managers take over like that. It showed the value of our training skills.

Then Kirby began to describe his current job:

As district manager, I get things done *through people*. There are pages and pages of job description for the DM, and when you read it, it seems like you own the world.

There are subtle changes when you have to go from unit manager to a district manager; you have to work with people differently.

I am defensive about my people, like a white knight on a charger if I don't think someone is helping my people. That's a big part of my job—to take care of my people.

I'm a trainer; that's my job. I get people ready to take other jobs. We have training programs with a regular chef and dietician which we provide for young folks after they have had a year with us. We have had flat sales in our area so these young men were "in grade" (that is, in the same lower-level job) for a long time. Last year, however, sales were good and promotions were good. There will be more opportunity to move this year, so I'm concerned about preparing these men quicker than in the past. I'm doing some little training modules—a day on food production, a day on management technology, giving them time in other units, some time with our chef and chief dietician, and some short one- or two-day training programs.

But there is no typical day. I lay out a weekly schedule on Sunday or earlier where I'm going to be. I'm not an early riser like Jim Cranston, who gets up at 5:45 A.M. I'm on the road at 7 or 8 o'clock. I try to see one unit a day, not like when I was young and stupid five years ago and tried to see two units a day. I have eight units with about $4.5 million in sales. These units cover two marketing groups, plus the education division, and the hospital division. In two of these units we have senior citizen programs and in one unit a summer lunch program.

Part of my job is dealing with higher management. By *higher management*, I mean at the corporate level. Our organization begins with the assistant managers at the bottom, or rather, at the *top*, then unit managers, district managers, vice presidents, then the president of CFS; and all the corporate structure backing us up. I find the corporation easy to work with, although more complex recently. There never seems to be enough time. Your control keeps broadening. One of my peers used to say, "There used to be an awful lot of time to laugh in this business, but now there's only a few minutes to giggle."

This is the most enlightened company in the industry. We are far ahead of the others, and we can offer more opportunity because of our broad market base. This is a people company; there is a high degree of job security. We are five years ahead of the other companies in the industry.

When I first became a DM, I went through the National Training Laboratory (NTL)[2] workshop in Washington, D.C. It was a group training session for four days. It was the first chance I'd had since school to be with my peers and to exchange ideas and opinions. I started polling my managers after that to see what kind of manager they thought I was. I thought that I was supportive in the field, but the managers thought that I was a control taker. It was disturbing that I had a different perception of how I was. I get my managers to rate me every year now. It's a three-page questionnaire similar to one that NTL created in their Management Climate Assessment Program. Now Sam [the corporate level officer in charge of organization development] feels that I'm blocking out the results from these questionnaires because I've done it so much. The ratings are low in some areas, and he thinks I should be working on them harder.

[2]The National Training Laboratory is a private institution that regularly conducts laboratory training sessions for the public. Laboratory training or T-groups are essentially small, unstructured groups where the members are encouraged to learn from the natural evolution of their own interactions. The first NTL program was held in Bethel, Maine, in 1947.

My usual working day is spent with my managers and clients. I review with the manager any problems he may have, let him get his problems off his chest first, and then I walk through the unit on a cursory sanitation check. Sometimes I call the client directly in advance to set up an appointment to talk with him in person. I don't make a production out of coming to the unit; I don't let them know my schedule. I just drop in to see how things are *really* operating. But I don't kid myself. There's a grapevine out there, and they can tell generally when I'm in the area.

I'm an everybody-knows-me type. I don't operate under the I'm-the-boss philosophy; that's plain stupidity. I talk to the employees and review the accounting, which is becoming more complex, more of a system-management process. The company is more focused on concern for client relations. That was interesting because I was on the task force for input into the new system. Trying to sell a new project to your peers, getting involved in trying to find easier ways to get the job done, was very interesting to me.

I have the authority to transfer people within my district. I can determine who should be in what slot. I call Jim [Cranston] and talk to him, and he has always concurred. Sometimes, when you have such a strong training ground, they like to get your people out to use elsewhere. I haven't had much of a problem with that. And I don't mind if it's for the good of the man. But we can block some moves up to a certain point. For instance, if a man has personal reservations about moving from his community, we can try to find an arrangement agreeable to us both.

For moves within my district you have to be careful because the clients can get upset about transfers. You can jeopardize the account and cause a schism. You don't want to cause client dissatisfaction. One of my managers is being promoted, and I've had the replacement on board for six months so the client gets used to him. That's the way to make those transfers. It's part of my job to handle accounts with that kind of concern for them.

It's a 24-hour day. The world and the needs of people generally get more complex every day. It just gets harder and harder to meet all of those needs at the same time. In some ways this industry is protected from this growing complexity. Like a former boss of mine once said, "There is nothing new in the food business except new ways to do old things." The basic problems are the same here as in any other industry. How can you make a profit? How can you get things done through other people? What are the alternative ways to get things done if one way collapses?

When Gene Kirby was asked about his strengths and weaknesses, he responded:

I'm a very sensitive person, sensitive to other people's needs. My strongest suit is in the selection and training process. I have turned out three district managers and two more are ready to go in about a year. I push my people hard to develop pride and individualistic interest in their work.

You have to get a manager to believe that his unit is his own little business in order to get the excellence you want. I enjoy being the mentor. I get my stroke by watching people grow, and I'm proud of that. In a world of structure, I try to get as unstructured as possible so they feel they're their own man. I don't try to insulate them from above; they know the problems that we face as a part of the larger corporate entity. I teach, lecture, and philosophize with these managers. I spend an hour or more with each manager talking about philosophy. Each visit, you have to bring the world down to the personal level of the manager to get him to reveal his personal philosophy. You can't go in and rap a guy every day all day; you have to address broader ideas because the manager will make or break the unit, and he has to be highly motivated. He's an extremely important person, and this is a way of getting him to feel that his view of the world counts for something.

On the other hand, I'm my own worst enemy. I'm a charger. If I can't get my thing by asking, I start charging. If I can't get it then, I go and do it myself, if possible. Sometimes you step on people's toes. I don't know if that has hurt me in advancement.

If I know what I want, I don't mind attacking and knocking heads. If I need to do something to meet the needs of the people, I try to get it done. I keep coming back at them, and a little aggravating, until they say, "Look, Kirby, there's no way!" and then I can handle that because I know I've done all I could. I ran a seven-day training school with my regional chef and regional dietician. Of the 25 hourly chefs who attended, 12 were moved up into administrative positions and to this day they attribute their moves to that program getting them energized. Now I can't get the dollars to run the seminar again, but I can live with it. I charged on that for a while, but couldn't get it done. But generally, the corporation is very supportive. And Jim Cranston is the best VP I've ever worked for. So far no one has told me to shut up and that's nice. It's a supportive company. I'm a corporate animal. I enjoy getting up in the morning. I used to be *very* volatile; now I'm *mildly* volatile. I get frustrated at situations. But even now I don't walk away from an argument. I like to use the "Yes sir, but . . ." or the "Yes sir, why?" approach.

I worry about this education thing. Some of these new managers come in and are very bright but they don't have a lot of street sense. I didn't finish college but I figure my 20 years of experience is the equivalent of a college education. I've thought about going back to school—but that would be hard for me. I know I could do it, but I hate being in a situation where somebody's going to put a grade on my performance. I don't mind talking about how I've done, but as soon as I know they're going to put a number on it, I freeze up. I have this hangup about education. Although it's better now. The college grads have a brighter future—but they really don't understand what's going on. They need "street savvy." And I have that. Maybe I should go back to school.

At the close of the interview, Kirby commented on Jim Cranston and the upcoming performance appraisal interview:

> This will be my first rating. I had one three years ago, done in pencil with no indication of what areas I needed to improve, but this will be my first formal performance appraisal interview. I have a high degree of respect for Jim. He's a super human being. He's always accessible, always able to listen. He's 10 years my junior, you know, but he has an unbelievable mind. As far as working with people under him goes, he earns his respect and trust. When it comes down to it, you know he'll fight for you. That's important.
>
> Jim is shrewd. He doesn't set goals with me. He believes you leave the sky open to let a guy go as far as he can. If you're reaching it, OK; if you're not motivated to work for that naturally, you shouldn't be in this job. I'm looking forward to being rated by him, to finding out what he will say. But Jim knows my weak and strong points. He'll tell me what I have told you. And I'll tell Jim how I see the industry going. We're getting more new graduates, and I want to make sure that I'm equipped to deal with this type of person. You develop a management style which is good only for the time being. You have to constantly update yourself to new tools of management, new instruments to use, or else you fall by the wayside. I don't ever want to get to that point. I don't feel that way now. It's like being a doctor—I have to keep myself abreast of new surgical techniques.

On the day of the interview, Kirby drove two hours to a city where Cranston was working to have the interview. It was to be the first personal, formal performance appraisal interview Kirby had had in five years. Cranston was busy when Kirby arrived, so he had to wait approximately two hours. When Cranston was available, both men rode in the same car to a nearby conference room where they sat down for the interview.

CASE 13

# Assessing Managerial Talent at AT&T (A)

*Emily Stein*
*Michael Beer*

On August 21, 1978, Walt Jackson and Donna Lawrence boarded airplanes bound for Atlanta, Georgia. For 3½ days, beginning that Monday evening, these American Telephone and Telegraph (AT&T) middle managers were to participate in the company's first Advanced Management Potential Assessment Program (AMPA). Walt Jackson and Donna Lawrence, like the other participants, had been nominated to attend by their telephone company based on the belief of their supervisor and vice president of personnel that they had the potential to advance to higher levels in the company. The program was designed to investigate their individual potential for top management positions. Before heading for Atlanta, Walt and Donna were each briefed by their own phone company's personnel vice president about the purpose and process of AMPA. Each individual, however, was somewhat unsure about exactly what the assessment technique would entail. Both hoped for a positive experience and were concerned about performing well as the assessment results would most likely have a major impact on their futures in the Bell System.

## BACKGROUND OF PARTICIPANTS

Walt Jackson graduated from high school and went to work as an errand boy for a large machinery manufacturing organization. After several years he enlisted in the Navy, served for four years, and then returned to his original employer. He continued to work for that company for 20 years. During that time he completed a college degree, got married, and had a family. He joined the Bell System in 1968. Since coming to the phone company he has had three different middle management positions. All have been district manager positions within

---

This case was edited by Bert A. Spector, Research Associate, under the supervision of Michael Beer, Lecturer. The help of Joel Moses in completing this case is gratefully acknowledged.

the network operating department. Exhibit 13–1 provides his last performance appraisal before going to the assessment center.

Walt was recommended for assessment by his vice president of personnel because "he is an intelligent, articulate manager who had demonstrated the ability to learn and perform in several areas of business."

Donna Lawrence came to work for the Bell System after graduating from college with a B.A. in engineering in 1970. Since joining the company she has had four different management jobs, each as an engineer in the network department. Each job has represented a step up the management hierarchy. In 1978 her title was district staff supervisor of budgets and results. This is a middle management position (third level). Exhibit 13–2 provides her last performance appraisal before going to the Assessment Center.

Donna was recommended for assessment by her vice president of personnel because "she has intelligence, drive, and desire to advance in the business. She is quick to learn and has proven her ability to take on new assignments, learn quickly, and make a contribution by effectively supervising her subordinates."

## THE AT&T ORGANIZATION

AT&T is the parent company of 23 operating telephone companies which provide service to the continental United States.[1] AT&T has a majority of full ownership in these companies and sets standard policy according to governmental regulations in a variety of areas. However, each of the companies has its own board of directors and, within the boundaries of corporate policy, operates quite autonomously. According to Joel Moses, manager of human resource development at the corporate level, "This relationship between corporate and the independent companies is an interesting one. We [at corporate located in Basking Ridge, New Jersey] manage cooperatively, not coercively. Yet, operations across companies are quite consistent."

AT&T and its 23 companies are organized similarly. Each is comprised of six major functional units including business, residential, network (operations), finance regulatory, and another department which includes a diverse group of functions including personnel. At the independent company level, these departments are divided geographically into divisions which are subdivided into districts.

Management structure at AT&T follows a ten-level pyramid pattern which applies both to corporate and each of the telephone companies. Each level represents a distinct step towards increased managerial responsibility. Titles are one tool used to differentiate between levels.

Although they differ across departments, typically foremen are considered level 1 managers, supervisors are level 2, and district managers level 3. It should be noted that the company considers level 3 "middle management."

Division heads are level 4 and department heads are level 5. Level 5 individuals represent the bottom rung of top management and are considered primarily responsible for business operations. Level 6 employees are vice presidents and are viewed as policy makers. AT&T's highest level of top management, company presidents and the very top executives at corporate, are between levels 7 and 10. Of the management personnel in the Bell System, 138,000 are at level 1; 51,000 at level 2; 12,000 at level 3; 3,100 at level 4; and 1,100 at level 5. Four hundred people hold managerial positions at levels 6 and 7. Approximately 9,300 people considered managers hold level-unspecified positions.

There is a great deal of interaction between AT&T and its phone companies, particularly in the area of personnel. Middle and top level managers from the various companies rotate into corporate for several years of service and are sent back to their home organizations for the balance of their careers. This aids management development and increases communications between the parent and independent companies. Lower level managers are both selected and trained by the companies themselves.

### *Manpower Planning and Development at AT&T*

Manpower planning and development is a high corporate priority at AT&T. The Human Resources department at headquarters in Basking Ridge has been responsible for conducting research which aids the corporation in analyzing specific manpower needs, and developing and implementing programs designed to meet these needs. One major tool the Human Resource function has supplied is the assessment center technique. At AT&T this method has been used for the past 20 years as one tool in predicting management potential and identifying the strengths and weaknesses of individual employees.

ASSESSMENT CENTERS. The history of assessment centers can be traced back to World War II. The Office of Strategic Services (OSS) of the United States government had a great need to select capable individuals for hazardous and unusual assignments. After recruiting a large number of people who turned out to be "misfits," the OSS sought professional assistance in designing a more effective and reliable

[1] *Editor's note*: This description applied to AT&T prior to court-ordered divestiture.

selection process. A group of psychologists hired by OSS designed and, by late 1943, had implemented the first assessment center employed in the United States.

The center required its "assessees" to enact a variety of on-the-job situations. As a result, the OSS was able to select personnel who performed more effectively than those previously selected. The element which seemed to account for the success of the new method was the behavioral element of the design. Essentially, performance during simulated "spy-type" assignments allowed OSS to predict, with some accuracy, on-the-job ability. Once the OSS experience was publicized, an interest in the assessment center technique began to develop in the American business community. AT&T was the first organization to research and actually apply the technique to personnel practice.

In 1956 AT&T launched a longitudinal management research study. Specifically, their research was designed to find characteristics which were associated with upward mobility in management or which were developed as a result of movement up the management ladder. The company utilized a "tailor-made" assessment center as a major measurement tool for the study. Managers were assessed for three days when the study began, and again eight years later. Research findings to date, available in *Formative Years in Business* (Bray et al., 1974),[2] indicate the method's validity and reliability over time as an aid in management selection.

Across the Bell System, many managers who participated in the study early on expressed an interest in adapting assessment centers for practical, as opposed to research, purposes. In 1958 AT&T developed such a center to aid in selecting first-line supervisors from the hourly ranks. Subsequently, other large organizations began to utilize the assessment technique not only as a selection tool, but also as a tool for promotion and development decisions. Companies which adopted the method include Standard Oil of Ohio, Sears, IBM, and General Electric. As of 1977, at least 30,000 individuals are assessed yearly in well over 1,000 organizations.

The set of qualities or dimensions which are measured at any assessment center is a vital element of the entire technique. The center's validity greatly depends upon the degree to which the dimensions are representative of what is required for the position or level in question.

AT&T AMPA contains several elements common to most successful assessment centers:

*A series of exercises or simulations* is a standard part of any assessment center. Although the nature of the exercises will vary according to the

[2]Douglas W. Bray et al., *Formative Years in Business: A Long-Term AT&T Study of Managerial Lives* (New York: Wiley, 1974).

objectives and dimensions inherent in the center, certain types of exercises are used in most working centers. Such simulations include group exercises, "in-baskets," individual problem-solving exercises, work simulations, interviews, and individual exercises. Each exercise or simulation stimulates behavior relevant to several assessment dimensions. Paper-and-pencil tests may also be used in an assessment center.

*The assessment staff* coordinates, administers, supervises, and carries out the assessment process itself. To function effectively the staff, comprised of one director and several assessors, who are often managers in the organization, must be well trained in the process of assessment.

Typically, assessment directors are trained professionals working out of the human resources area who may themselves have been involved in the development and design of their centers. Specifically, a director must manage a center's facilities, assessors, participants, and process. He or she generally supervises assessor training, administers exercises, chairs assessor discussions, writes up the final assessment report and recommendations, and carries out or delegates the feedback process. Organizations utilize directors either on a full-time or special-assignment basis.

One facet of the director's job is to supervise assessor training. To assure accurate, objective participant assessment while providing a truly developmental experience for assessors, a substantive staff training program must be included in the design and process of any assessment center.

*A preestablished evaluation technique which includes a standardized rating scale* is an essential part of any assessment center regardless of objectives, dimensions, or exercises employed. Such a technique is important because when it is understood and used correctly it assures the reliability and validity of the evaluations.

*A feedback session and report* is extremely valuable for the assessee's "back-home" manager, but can be especially valuable for the participants themselves.

The data collected by means of the assessment process describe an individual's strengths and deficiencies and can be quite useful as an aid in the selection of candidates for promotion. Because the process provides managers with a detailed and objective picture of the assessee, managers can also utilize this picture to understand developmental needs, and coach subordinates to establish appropriate training programs or job progression plans.

Assessment centers can be a valuable training method for managers acting as assessors. Observational and evaluation skills are required of these assessors. Managers who participate as assessors are asked to identify assessee strengths and weaknesses, understand the way these characteristics contribute to job success, and integrate observations about individuals and established job requirements in developing recommendations for promotion and development experiences. Assessors are trained, during the week preceding the assessment center, to observe behavior in assessment exercises carefully, relate observed behavior to the appropriate dimension, and select the behavioral anchor on each scale which most closely described the observed behavior. According to Joel Moses, when assessors scrutinize participants, rate characteristics, and make developmental recommendations, they improve their own evaluation and interpersonal management skills.

ASSESSMENT AT AT&T. AT&T's first assessment program, initiated in 1958, was directed at hourly workers with 10 to 12 years of company experience, and was used to identify individuals for level 1 managerial assignments. Since its inception approximately 100,000 individuals, representing 18 Bell System companies have participated in this two-day program. In 1968 AT&T instituted a second program, also two days long, which was used with level 1 personnel to assess potential for level 2 and level 3 positions.

Assessment programs at AT&T are typically designed by corporate staff and made available to the independent companies. Each company participates voluntarily. Apparently, the two assessment programs described are widely accepted across the organization as valid and reliable tools for decisions about management's development and promotion, although the results are used differently by different companies and managers. According to Joel Moses, AT&T maintains a constant and growing interest in the assessment process as evidenced by increasing numbers of program participants. Also, according to Moses:

> We have been very successful at meeting our organizational needs for low-level managers. In recent years, however, our needs have shifted. There is a real concern here now to identify talent for succession purposes. We need to be sure we are preparing people early in their careers for higher-level management positions, now more than ever before.

## AMPA PREPARATION AND IMPLEMENTATION

AT&T conducted the first AMPA during July and August 1978. Seven programs took place that summer. They accommodated a total of 77 level 3 participants who usually came in groups of 12. Fifteen assessors, level 5 managers, served the center for three to five weeks at a time in groups of six. On board permanently in Atlanta were the center director, Joel Moses, three part-time clinical psychologists, and two secretaries.

Since 1976 formal efforts had been made to design an assessment tool which would look at promotability and developmental needs of level 3 managers for level 5 assignments. Extensive research was conducted and, by the spring of 1978, the program design was established (see Exhibit 13–3).

Having designed the program, Moses set out to manage the process of recruiting participants. On May 3 and 4 he held a meeting with the assistant vice presidents of personnel from interested Bell System companies. At this session he explained the intent of the program, its content, and the desired participant population. He explained that the company was interested in assessing third-level individuals who had been in-grade for a couple of years and who were considered likely candidates for promotion by back-home companies. (Most company personnel departments kept promotable lists so there was no problem in identifying capable people.)

By the end of June, phone company personnel vice presidents had identified candidates for AMPA, contacted them, filled out nomination forms on their behalf, and supplied AMPA applications to be completed by candidates themselves. By the end of June the 77 participants had been selected. Simultaneously, Moses was devoting energy to the process of selecting and training assessors. Assessors were drawn from the population of fifth-level managers in the seven Bell companies which elected to participate in AMPA that year. Once assessors and assessees were selected, care was taken to mix the participants according to sex, location, and functional area, and to mix assessors and participants so assessors would not have to assess individuals they knew.

On July 10, 1978, about one week before AMPA began, the 15 fifth-level managers came to Atlanta to participate in a six-day assessor training program. The training included long hours of explanation meetings, observing simulations of exercises with local graduate students acting as assessees, rating their behavior according to established dimensions, and report-writing and critique feedback sessions. The training program was demanding but was devoted to preparing assessors to be as knowledgeable about the process and competent with their tasks as possible. It was characterized by two major design elements for this purpose including: (1) extensive practice in actually rating behavior and (2) feedback and critique from very experienced assessors from AT&T's corporate Human Resources staff.

Walt Jackson and Donna Lawrence began their AMPA program by attending an orientation meeting conducted by the center director. In this session the goals of the program and the various elements of the 3 ½-day assessment process were explained. Specifically, AMPA was designed (1) to identify individuals for placement in a pool as potential officers of the company, (2) to examine the individuals in existing pools as potential officers of the company, (3) to identify individual developmental needs, and (4) to closely examine managers to understand more clearly the company's human resource strengths and weaknesses. Specifically, these goals were to be met by putting candidates through a series of exercises and tests, during which time assessors would observe participants, take careful notes, and later rate the behavior according to a set of dimensions which were associated with high-level management behavior.

Walt and Donna spent the next three days going through the six major assessment tools that were used at AMPA and which had been designed specifically for the program. Those tools involved two group exercises (Riverview and Investment Problem), and four individual activities (In-basket, Problem-Solving Exercise, Personnel Interview, and Paper-and-Pencil Tests).

Each exercise is described below, with sections of the assessment reports on Walt and Donna presented in smaller-size type.

### *Group Discussion (Riverview)*

In this exercise, six participants role-play members of the Riverview city council. They are meeting to decide how to allocate a three million dollar federal grant to improve various services in their city. Each participant represents an elected member of the council for a different district, and is trying to obtain a portion of the grant to improve their district. Since it is an election year, there is considerable pressure to represent the needs of their districts in allocating the money.

This is a complex exercise, with a considerable amount of back-up information and data which candidates must sift through in arguing their proposals. The exercise consists of a one-hour preparation period, a one-hour oral presentation phase, and a one-and-a-half-hour group discussion phase. It is a primary source of information for evaluating interpersonal and communication skills.

*Walt Jackson's Performance.* Walt began his seven-minute presentation by assuming a standing position near the map. He used the map effectively as he acknowledged the previous proposals, recognizing overlap and potential conflict. At this time he appealed to the group with the question, "How much is life worth?" This emotional plea seemed to be his theme as he proceeded to describe his proposed traffic study.

During his presentation he spoke slowly and clearly. His voice was solid and he effectively used inflections as he made his key points. He had good audience eye contact and seemed to hold the group's attention well throughout. He used a prepared chart as he discussed proposal components. He had no distracting mannerisms.

In summary, Walt delivered an interesting, convincing proposal. His use of visual aids, speaking technique, and little dependency on notes added to his effectiveness.

Walt's group worked at dividing the funds allocated on a "top-down" basis with little attention paid to specifics or what the money could do. Compromise was involved.

Most of the participants had prepared handouts before the exercise but none were used. Coalitions were formed during the hour but they were passing in nature and seemed to be more self-serving than cooperative efforts.

Walt was an energetic and confident member of the group. He had done his homework and was prepared to fight for his proposal.

He suggested a strategy for disseminating the funds by using a top-down approach. This was made after a number of participants made presentations which were self-serving and indicated an unwillingness to compromise. Walt seemed to be able to size up the group and was able to develop a strategy for compromise. Instead of attacking an individual's idea he helped the group focus its actions on its overall task of distributing funds.

Walt was quite active and took on a directive role, clarifying issues, questioning members, challenging ideas and probing for compromise. He was able to elicit good cooperation from a group of individuals who were basically unwilling to compromise.

He sensed that a number of coalitions had formed and obtained agreement from members before attacking another idea. He went to the easel and directed the group's attention to his summarization of the distribution of funds. Although not given the title, he clearly was the chairman of this group.

*Donna Lawrence's Performance.* Donna Lawrence participated consistently throughout this exercise although she lacked skill during both oral and discussion periods. She seemed to have spent a lot of time preparing her case and demonstrated a good grasp of the problem. She interacted with others in the group in a supportive manner, a challenging manner, and a consoling manner when appropriate. During the discussion period she was challenged by the group but eventually got what she asked for. She ranked herself the second-best performer and gave herself a very good rating.

Donna was the last member of her group to make a presentation. She made a brief presentation using the city map (premarked to indicate dams and flood areas) as an aid. She was very soft-spoken and had minimal eye contact with the group because she frequently referred to her hand-held notes. At several points she actually read her presentation. She presented numerical data verbally without using the easel or handouts. She included pertinent facts in her presentation but it was brief. She did not seem very poised or self-assured when making her presentation.

Donna asked one question of each "council member" during the oral defense phase. During her own defense she made little or no reference to notes and seemed more sure of herself and less tense than during the presentation.

Donna was the first to speak up during the group discussion. She used the easel and showed how the previous days' requests were well over the allotted funds. She proposed cutting her own request as a means of achieving her goal within the stated budget. She also summarized each candidate's proposal. Each member of this group had also prepared a compromise and she was asked to post these. She did so while continuing to actively participate in the discussion.

While presenting her summary of overnight work, she relied heavily on notes and spoke so rapidly that she lost the group's attention at times. She did speak extemporaneously in pleasant conversational style during parts of the summary and made references to comments made by others. On two occasions she encouraged the group to discuss a subject she wanted discussed. As noted, she was able to get the funds she requested for her project.

In summary, while an active participant, Donna's role was to summarize others' positions. While able to get her project funds, she did not challenge others, nor did she really attempt to lead the group to accomplish its tasks.

### *Complex Business Game (Investment Problem)*

Six participants work as the Board of Directors of the Ajax Fund, a small mutual fund investment company, in this two-and-a-half hour exercise. During four trading periods, the directors buy and sell stocks based upon price quotations which change every five minutes during the period. A news ticker indicates "developments" which may affect certain stocks, and there are advisory services available for purchase which provide timely information about stock trends. Scheduled "breaks" for Board of Director meetings allow participants to negotiate and renegotiate strategies. The participants' objective is to maximize profits of the Ajax Fund (which starts with $10,000) through careful planning and trading of stock. Like the Riverview exercise, the Investment Problem is a primary source of information on interpersonal skills.

*Walt Jackson's Performance.* Walt's group made an effort to establish direction early in the exercise by immediately discussing objectives, ideas, and approaches. Most candidates participated in the initial discussion but no leader emerged. After several minutes of floundering conversation, the group sensed a need for structure, and role assignment was attempted. Roles were accepted but did not restrict out-of-role behavior. During the exercise candidates were reluctant to fully support the position of any one participant and, as a result, did not agree on much. Candidates did not listen well or respond to each other's suggestions.

Walt jumped into this exercise early, attempting to assume a leader role, and stayed highly verbal. He attempted throughout to delegate work to others. He was persistent in his opinions and equally persistent in his approach. He never actively sought collaboration or compromise.

Walt remained active throughout. He made numerous suggestions to purchase and sell various stocks. On a number of occasions, he persistently argued for his point of view and was able to sell his ideas. As noted, this was a competitive group with little support for individual ideas. Jackson was able to get his recommendations accepted more often than others. In part, this was a function of his persistence. In part, it was his good sense of timing. In part, it was his desire to win. All contributed to his performance here.

*Donna Lawrence's Performance.* Donna's group began with an attempt to organize themselves which was not very effective. They began to discuss what to buy, how much to invest, and whether to be risk or dividend oriented. Everyone participated and generally two or more candidates were always talking at once. Throughout the exercise the group members were friendly and social, frequently laughing as they handled their task.

After a period of initial discussion the group unknowingly divided itself into two groups: one group stayed at the table, the other moved toward the ticker. Finally, one member called the group back together successfully and began to emerge as chairman of the group. The group remained disorganized and independent. However, they were able to realize a moderate profit. In summary, this disorganized, talkative group remained cooperative with a mutual desire to "win the game."

From the beginning, Donna did not contribute very much to this group. Although many opportunities arose, she offered only infrequent suggestions but instead kept records of news releases and stock purchases. When she did contribute verbally, her comments seemed calculated and very well thought out. In general, Lawrence was a quiet, attentive observer. Her substantive contributions were sparse. Regarding her own performance, she commented "[I had] some suggestions with a conservative outlook" and that "[my] contribution would have been greater given the time to plan and analyze. I tend to be more confident of decisions with thought behind them but will take a risk if there is justification." This final comment seems to capture her performance during this exercise. Donna ranked herself the third best performer [out of six] and rated herself "very good."

### *In-Basket*

This is a three-hour exercise where participants role-play an assistant vice president (AVP)-traffic generation and operations for the Midland Central Railroad Company. The Midland Central has four divisions covering much of the central United States, and is a close affiliate of two other railroad companies with which it coordinates long-distance service. The AVP position has responsibility for a number of functional areas, including transportation, sales, marketing, industrial development, and public relations and interacts with peers responsible for finance, personnel, physical plant, and legal matters. The participant must work through a substantial amount of letters, memos, reports, and other written materials, making decisions on a variety of complex issues. The materials represent a mixture of short-term problems as well as longer-term concerns which require effective planning, analytical, and administrative skills.

After completing the exercise, participants are interviewed by a staff member who role-plays the incumbents' supervisor, the vice president. During this interview, the participant has an opportunity to review the decisions made and explain the rationale behind the action taken. The In-Basket is the primary source of information for administrative skills.

*Walt Jackson's Performance.* Walt began the In-Basket problem by reviewing his material package. He studied the organization and oriented himself to superiors, peers, and subordinates. He then, in sequence, scanned each item for critical dates and key players in various problems. At this point he spent approximately one-and-a-half hours reading the material in greater detail and relating common issue items. He then "prioritized" the items for action based on urgency and importance. All items were effectively related and prioritized.

Walt felt a major time constraint during this exercise as evidenced by the fact that he finished only half of the items. He had a good understanding of all issues and good recall of facts for those items where action was not taken. He felt a need for additional information for most items and planned to get that by requesting investigations. His overall view of the In-Basket was that it was tough, demanding, and comprehensive. If he had the opportunity to repeat the problem, he would allocate more time for taking action and would write out thought processes instead of letters.

In summary, Walt understood the content of the In-Basket well. His written actions were thorough and complete. Although he deferred most final decisions, the material was well organized, related, and prioritized but his use of time was a deterrent. When given some additional time by this assessor, he described intended actions and solutions clearly. His written output did not capture his total understanding and given the opportunity to discuss items during the interview, he demonstrated a good grasp of the materials and his strategy for action.

*Donna Lawrence's Performance.* Donna began this exercise by looking for information to orient herself to the organization, its functions, and its territory. She reviewed all items, looking for those requiring special attention, and then proceeded to work on them in their existing sequence. She skimmed items and then reread those which seemed to require more attention. All items were not read, however.

Because she did not at the outset organize the In-Basket items in terms of their potential interrelationships, Donna was on more than one occasion unaware of the impact of unread items on the issues she chose to address. In one instance, an important item which could substantially alter the company's relations with a major client was overlooked. She did state that she would approach the In-Basket by searching for "themes" were she to go through the exercise again. Nevertheless, Lawrence did do a thorough job on a number of items, attempting to tie in relevant background information and additional items where she saw fit.

Donna felt a definite time constraint and deferred two issues of lesser importance. The easiest matter for her to handle was one that had to be referred back to a subordinate. The most difficult item was one characterized by a multitude of related problems. The most important items were viewed this way because of their close time deadlines.

Donna appeared to be a bit nervous during the first few minutes of the interview and on the few occasions where she realized that she had overlooked a key piece of information, but otherwise was calm yet quick to respond. She was able to answer all questions asked and had good recall of the items, including some which she had not read in detail.

### *Problem-Solving Exercise*

This exercise involves selecting, analyzing, and recommending a program of stress management in order to meet an objective set by the company president. Participants must work through and arrive at a solution to this problem by gathering facts from written material and questioning a staff analyst, and then analyzing the information obtained and presenting the recommended course of action to the president. There is no one ''best'' solution; participants are required to select from several possible options and to defend their decisions.

The exercise takes three hours to administer, and consists of four major parts: an initial preparation period; a fact-finding interview; a final preparation period; and an oral presentation, discussion, and defense period. It is a primary source of information for the analytical skills.

*Walt Jackson's Performance.* Walt began his interview by stating the purpose of his visit and that he had eight questions that were applicable to each of the three possible options. He said he wanted to cover these questions and then he might have additional questions. He was very organized. He controlled the interview and did not let the assessor delay on items that he did not consider important. He remained calm throughout even when he thought assessor-given information was meaningless.

Although he followed a general plan, he did not hesitate to do additional probing when necessary. He accomplished his plan within the time allotted. In summary, Walt was poised, well organized, and in control at all times. Essentially, he got all important information. All questions were probing, open, and logical.

Walt began his presentation by revealing an easel with a thorough outline concerning the three possible programs to deal with stress. He covered each in detail but did not waste time on the two programs he did not recommend. He had sufficient notes but did not seem to need them. He used a pointer as he discussed information on the easel. He maintained a good pace and enunciated well. He reached his recommendations within the allotted time.

Walt presented his recommendations in a clear, concise manner following an outline depicted in a second chart. He outlined his program's positive points and defended it with solid evidence.

When challenged by the assessor, Walt argued well. He responded to direct questions logically. He went directly from a defensive to an offensive position, restating the benefits of the program he recommended.

In summary, Walt had prepared well. His presentation was logical; he had integrated material well. He spoke clearly and used easel and notes effectively but not in excess. He seemed at ease and was not disturbed by challenges. He met time requirements.

*Donna Lawrence's Performance.* Donna seemed very relaxed in her information-gathering role. She was able to obtain information on each of the three possible programs. She pressed the individual she was interviewing for facts, and for his opinions, but accepted his unwillingness to give them. All of her questions were stated clearly and a great many were open-ended. She was able to generate many questions and seemed adept at keeping the interviewer talking.

Donna began her presentation in an almost apologetic tone. She claimed that she had limited information to work with but proceeded to review each of the three programs being considered. She asked the assessor his opinion concerning which program he wanted and seemed unable to give her own recommendations or conclusions. She frequently sought his reaction to what she had said.

Her presentation was not organized and was delivered in a monotone. She frequently spoke so softly that she was difficult to hear. She gave the impression that she really did not want to recommend anything but instead wanted the recommendations and decisions to be made by the president.

In summary, Donna gathered data effectively but seemed almost apologetic when asked to defend her position.

### *Personal Interview*

The personal interview is designed to provide information on a number of career orientation variables, as well as several personal characteristics. It is the only formal opportunity during the assessment week for the participants to discuss themselves, their experiences, and their careers with a member of the staff. The interview briefly covers their general background and early academic and work experience, and then progressively probes in greater depth the participant's feelings about his or her Bell System career—major assignments, career progress, career orientation, financial concerns, and major problems. The final portion covers the participant's perceptions on a number of self-development related areas—hobbies, interest, plans (short- and long-term goals), strengths, and weaknesses.

The interview takes a little over one hour, and is conducted by a clinical psychologist.

*Walt Jackson's Interview.* The psychologist who conducted this interview reported, "Walt is an extremely pleasant and self-assured individual who is in touch with his feelings and at ease with himself. He appears self-confident and happy. He is quite articulate."

Born in the South, Walt worked while attending high school to help support his family. (Walt's father died when Walt was in elementary school.) Hard work and achievement are dominant themes in this man's life. He has always worked hard and is proud of his accomplishments. He is a self-reliant individual.

Today, Walt is not as achievement oriented as in the past. Because he is in his mid-forties he feels that his opportunities for promotion are limited. He feels that he could possibly get one more promotion but doubts whether he can advance beyond that.

Walt has some very active outside interests. He owns and manages a 10-unit apartment building. This takes 10 to 15 hours per week. He has studied real estate and reads related books for pleasure. He used to be very active in the community and has earned 12 credits toward his master's degree. In 1970 he was hospitalized and now has tried to slow down. He plans to take early retirement in 15 years. He has no major goals for advancement but would like to have a different job within the next few years in personnel or labor relations.

Overall, Walt is an ordered and planned individual. He is pleased with his accomplishments, family oriented, well adjusted, and satisfied with himself.

*Donna Lawrence's Interview.* Donna was interviewed by one of the center's clinical psychologists, who submitted the following report:

Donna is 29 years old, has been married 8 years, and has no children by choice. While growing up, Donna attended 12 schools in 12 years as her family moved a great deal. Donna reports that this experience helped her learn how to meet people, become involved in activities quickly, and how to be self-reliant.

After graduating from college she was pleasantly surprised to find a job she liked which offered good money and that was future oriented. She had expected that she would marry, have kids, and publish scientific articles in between housewifely duties. She came to Bell with hopes that she would have the opportunity to use her mathematics skills and be with people. In terms of her career at Bell she enjoyed her jobs as manager and district manager between 1974 and 1976 most, because in those positions she had the opportunity to learn about the company and learn how to supervise. She was least excited about her job between 1970 and 1974, as plant engineer, which she found repetitive and boring.

To date, Donna is satisfied with her own career growth and has progressed faster than both male and female peers. She expects her next promotion to come within 2 years but if that does not materialize she will be patient for a while. She hopes future assignments will move her out of technical assignments and into supervision.

Donna wants very much to work with people but she is somewhat reserved and feels that maintaining personal privacy is very important. Typically, she will work through lunch and does not have a lot of friends now. She misses "grapevine information" this way and admits to being unaware of certain aspects of company politics. She is logical, tenacious, works hard, and has a desire to succeed but is unsure about whether, as a manager, she can convey a feeling of success to subordinates.

### *Paper-and-Pencil Tests*

In addition to the set of exercises just described, a series of tests are administered to participants during the three-and-a-half day program. These tests are much less significant as assessment tools than are the exercises described previously. They are used only if they support behavioral data based on performance during the exercises. If they do not support such data they are ignored. Two kinds of tests are used including:

A. **Projective Tools**
   1. **Sentence completion tests.** A sentence completion test consists of a few words which are presented to the assessee to stimulate the formation of a sentence.
   2. **Thematic Apperception Test.** In the Thematic Apperception Test (TAT) the candidate is shown a series of pictures and asked to write a story about what is happening in the picture, what led up to the events described, and what the outcomes will be.

B. **Bell System Qualifying Test (BSQT).** This is an in-house instrument, developed by Educational Testing Service for the Bell System, which measures mental ability.

*Walt Jackson's Performance.* The psychologist's report of Walt's projective tests indicated that he is an open, realistic, down-to-earth kind of person. He is neither "driven" nor complacent but instead has established a comfortable balance between these two characteristics. Doing his best and living up to his potential are important to him. He is comfortable with competition but not highly competitive himself. He seems to prefer a cooperative approach but can be competitive on occasion. He likes people and is friendly and optimistic. He is accepting of people, values them for their individual qualities but is not a "do-gooder." He has a healthy interest in knowing himself better and working toward self-improvement. He views failure as an opportunity for growth. He doesn't expect to win every time but does want to always do his best. He is optimistic about his future although in the past he has had family and monetary problems. Money is important to him now. He regrets having gotten a late or slow start in his career. In general, he takes a sensible, realistic approach to life, work, and interactions with others.

On the BSQU Walt received a much higher percentile score on verbal (78) than quantitative (10).

*Donna Lawrence's Performance.* The psychologist's report of Donna's projective tests indicated that she is an independent thinker, is very analytical in her approach to problem solving, and organizes and plans actions carefully. She is not afraid to state opinions which are positive or negative but relies heavily on others for support. She tends to be a perfectionist who values excellence in herself and others and consequently is seldom satisfied with an end product. She gets great satisfaction from performing well but can be somewhat intolerant and impatient.

Donna values honest, hard work, and "people relationships." She relates effectively to authority. She enjoys excitement, challenge, and even potentially threatening situations. She reacts well to stress and sees herself at her best when under pressure.

Donna has a good self-concept and self-respect. She works hard to increase her competence and increase working opportunities. At work she seeks support, acceptance, and recognition. She seems to relate easily to people and treats them as individuals. She is a relatively open person with a sense of humor. Her view of herself seems fairly objective and relatively accurate.

Donna likes to minimize boss/subordinate roles and prefers a more equal relationship. She is uncomfortable "bossing" and "being bossed" because she feels that is overbearing and demeaning. Since she is her own worst critic she resents further criticism. She feels she is regarded as a self-starting, energetic, bright, and competent person.

On the BSQT, Donna scored in the 95th percentile in verbal and the 97th percentile in quantitative, for a total score in the 98th percentile.

## EVALUATION AND FEEDBACK

Following the three-and-a-half-day period, assessors were divided into two teams to evaluate candidates' performances. Teams were headed by the center director or one of the psychologists. Each evaluation took approximately two hours and was divided into three phases: (1) dimension ratings, (2) overall rating, and (3) developmental recommendations. In preparation for the evaluation meetings assessors wrote one- or two-page descriptive narrative reports about the candidates' behavior during each assessment activity. In the meeting their reports were read aloud and then they proceeded to individually rate 24 dimensions of behavior divided into six categories (see Exhibit 13-4 for a sample form).

To rate candidates, assessors assign a number between 1 and 5 for performance on each dimension. Each number is assigned a meaning which is behaviorally anchored and described clearly in an assessor manual. A behaviorally anchored rating scale is one in which each numerical point on the scale is explicitly defined by a description of the behavior an individual must display to receive that numerical score. Such scales are generally acknowledged to increase the reliability (consistency over time) of ratings and therefore their predictive validity and validity of the assessment.

A rating of 1 indicates that a low amount of a behavior was observed and a 5 indicates that a high amount of that behavior was observed. Thus, 1 generally indicates poor performance and 5 indicates excellence. When rating candidates on various dimensions such as energy, decisiveness, or problem solving, assessors do this in relation to their extensive knowledge of other Bell System executives. That is, individual ratings are done in the context of Bell System executives in general, not just other assessment center participants. This is thought to increase their objectivity.

During evaluation meetings assessors do differ in their rating of a candidate on given dimensions. When ratings with a one-point spread are given, they are recorded without much discussion. The rating most often given is the final assigned rating. For instance, if three assessors assign a rating of 4 to the fact-finding dimension and the fourth assigns a rating of 5, a rating of 4 is the final rating given. In the event of a tie the team leader makes the final decision. If, however, there is a two-point spread, discussion is required to eliminate the spread. After all of the dimensions are rated, then and only then are overall ratings assigned. Candidates receive an excellent, good, moderate, or low rating to indicate level of assessed promotability. These scores are based on performance during the exercises but are also influenced by assessor understanding of what is required in a top management job.

After arriving at an overall rating, assessors make developmental recommendations which are based upon all pertinent information gathered during the three-and-a-half-day period, the back-home personnel vice president's nomination form, and the candidate's application. These recommendations are shared with the personnel vice president and the candidate as feedback.

Two specific feedback mechanisms were employed by the center. The first was a written report to be sent to the vice president of personnel of each candidate's Bell System company (company coordinator) prepared by the center director. The report, which might be used by the vice president for staffing decisions consisted of (1) an overall rating of potential; (2) a description of candidate performance; (3) an overview of strengths and weaknesses in each dimension area (personal characteristics, communication skills, interpersonal skills, administrative skills, analytical skills, and career orientation); and (4) suggested developmental assignments and activities. The vice president of personnel was the only recipient of this report. It was stored in a private personnel file and was not part of the individual's general personnel record.

Assessment center performance makes up only part of a promotional decision. One personnel vice president spoke for his own company and some of his peers in other companies when he commented upon how the AMPA results are considered:

> At lower levels, if we are confident an individual is promotable, we may put aside or ignore negative recommendations. However, at higher levels competition is greater and, I suppose, it would be difficult to promote someone who did poorly at AMPA. Still, AMPA results just can't be the only tool. They shouldn't wipe out an individual's future. As I said before we *do* take results seriously, and we *certainly* take developmental recommendations seriously. . . . But if our own perceptions are not confirmed we owe it to ourselves and the individual we sent to think twice.

The second feedback mechanism was a one-to-one meeting between an AT&T staff psychologist and the candidate. Wherever possible, this meeting was scheduled within two weeks of the actual assessment. The meeting consisted of an in-depth discussion of performance, self-perceptions, and developmental needs as discovered during the assessment process.

Although many candidates leave Atlanta already having learned a great deal about themselves, the feedback provides an objective view of performance and an additional opportunity for increased self-understanding and career or personal counseling.

When the assessors for AMPA 1978 met to evaluate Walt and Donna they had a tough job ahead of them. Both candidates demonstrated a variety of strengths and weaknesses. They were viewed positively by some and negatively by others. As the assessors began their meeting they knew lively discussion would follow.

## LEAVING AMPA

Walt and Donna left AMPA with mixed feelings. They were in some ways relieved it was over. In other ways they were excited about the experience. Both were curious about the way in which they performed, looked forward to the feedback they would receive, and wondered about the impact such feedback would have on their careers.

**EXHIBIT 13-1**
**Assessment of Walt Jackson**

**Management Performance Appraisal System**

Performance Summary

Employee's name Walt Jackson Title District manager--plant

Area ________ Department ________

Supervisor's name ________ Title Division manager--plant

Date 10-24-77/Date of last performance summary 3-23-77

Reviewed by________ Title ________
(Appraiser's supervisor)

Performance: Keeping in mind the individual's major objectives, how well did he/she perform? Support your appraisal by citing specific instances of outstanding or deficient performance.

This year has been an unusual one for Walt Jackson, in that consolidation of the Dorman and Peabody plant districts caused him to be reassigned three times. He started the year as district manager in Peabody. On June 1, after the decision to consolidate was made and after he was selected to be the manager of the new district, he was transferred to Dorman. Following two months of becoming familiar with Dorman, the consolidation was announced and he was appointed district manager--plant--Peabody/Dorman. Then, as part of the corporate reorganization, Walt and his district were reassigned to South Area on October 24.

Because of these changes, it would be difficult, and perhaps unfair, to attempt an evaluation of performance after June 1. An outline of performance during the first five months at Peabody follows:

**EXHIBIT 13-1 (*Continued*)**

Maintenance:

Peabody's performance in the Exchange Maintenance Service Results index was especially strong through April, and continued the fine improving trend of the last two years. The Records Quality component averaged 98.9, or well above the 97.5 objective. The Report Rate component averaged 98.6, reflecting the substantial reduction of 13.7 percent in the customer report rate over the comparable period in 1976.

Subsequent reports, Found-OKs, and the PBX report rate also were improved over 1976 performance and well ahead of their respective objectives. The Public Coin rate, while slightly worse than objective, was one of the lowest in the Operations.

Repeated reports proved to be a serious problem, as scoring accuracy improved and the absolute number of "Repeats" was not significantly reduced. Total Upkeep productivity ran some 0.8 percent behind the annual commitment through May.

Installation:

Customer Installation Service Results performance was uneven through the first five months of the year, with a monthly low of 91.8 recorded in January and a high of 97.8 in February. The Customer Service Comments and Requests Not Complied With components of the index were troublesome during this period, but missed appointments (Not Met) were the major problem. A special effort to reduce "Plant Other" misses eventually arrested a poor trend in this result.

Despite a great deal of attention to Outward Movement Control, Peabody had disappointing results in "Telephone Sets Removed on the Disconnect Rate." Through May, the result was 54.2 percent, or roughly three-quarters of the objective. Total C, X, and M productivity also proved difficult through the period, with performance at 9.05 work units per hour, or well behind the 9.76 objective. Two components of this result looked weak through the month of May:

- Straight-line performance was 6.6 percent under objective, and had not met the objective in any month.
- Assignment was 10.0 percent under objective.

Installation Sales continued to be Peabody's real claim to fame. While another district won the President's Plaque in the first quarter, Peabody was easily the top district in the company in consistency through the first five months.

General:

The last five months surely have been difficult for Walt, and yet he never let frustration show in public. Managing "around" preparations for the consolidation and deciding on a myriad of detailed questions were special burdens. When morale problems developed after the consolidation was announced, he worked with them directly. Later, when the corporate reorganization raised tough questions from management people, as well as craft, Walt chose to work on a personal basis again. In both instances, he was most effective--his people were not necessarily happy, but adjusted to the changed conditions.

Overall, Walt Jackson had made a substantial contribution to the business this year. He should take pride in a job well done under adverse conditions.

He is familiar with the Affirmative Action objectives of the company, and has actively taken part in their implementation this year. In a recent internal compliance review, he made it quite clear to his subordinates that he supports the corporate commitment to equal employment opportunity (EEO).

Management methods: Describe the management techniques used by this employee in achieving his or her objectives.

**EXHIBIT 13-1** (*Continued*)

Walt Jackson is an especially mature individual, who uses his experience to good advantage. He is thoughtful and deliberate; and evaluates as many aspects of a problem as possible before taking action.

He is very sensitive to "people problems," and has confidence that he can work effectively with them.

During the last year or two Walt has become much more of a "field manager," in the sense that he spends much of his time asking questions, following-up, analyzing details and observing work operations first-hand. In the process, he has become increasingly well grounded in the fundamental aspects of the plant job.

Strengths: In what way is this manager especially competent?

Walt is a highly competent communicator, both orally and in written form.

He has a very broad background in business, and is seldom surprised when some "new" problem turns up. He tracks a large number of operating results, and challenges his subordinates when poor trends develop.

Areas requiring improvement: What aspects of the job performance should receive attention?

He must continue to be alert to subordinates who respond to problems with "pat answers" and "quick solutions."

Development needs: List specific action that should be taken to aid this manager's growth.

The newly consolidated district he is managing should be sufficiently challenging to continue to develop Walt's management skills over the near-term future.

Employee response: How does the employee feel about the performance summary?

I appreciate the balanced perspective reflected in this performance summary. It is always gratifying when real understanding of one's efforts is displayed.

The problem areas discussed are, with one or two exceptions, less of a problem now than at the five-month mark. Of particular note is Total CXM productivity, where substantial gains have been made. This, I think, is a tribute to the people working in the district and their will to try.

I shall continue to put forth my best effort to become all that a field third-level manager should be.

Employee's initials W.J.
Date 11/7/77

**EXHIBIT 13-2**
**Assessment of Donna Lawrence**

**Management Performance Appraisal System**

Performance Summary

Employee's name Donna Lawrence Title District manager--switching services

Area ______ Department Switching services

Supervisor's name ______ Title Division manager--switching services

Date 2-4-77 Date of last performance summary 9-75

Reviewed by ______ (Appraiser's supervisor) Title General manager--switching services

Performance: Keeping in mind the individual's major objectives, how well did he/she perform? Support your appraisal by citing specific instances of outstanding performance.

**EXHIBIT 13-2 (*Continued*)**

For approximately the first three quarters of 1976, Mrs. Lawrence was responsible for all switching maintenance and dial administration in the Southwest District. Her productivity and service performance during that period was as follows:

CO Service Index

| Bev XB | | Por XB | | Pro XB | | Pul XB | |
|---|---|---|---|---|---|---|---|
| Obj. | Act. | Obj. | Act. | Obj. | Act. | Obj. | Act. |
| | | | | 97.1 | 96.6 | | |
| 98.5 | 98.6 | 97.4 | 96.5 | 97.2 | 95.9 | 98.2 | 98.6 |
| | | | | 96.5 | 96.6 | | |

| Sou XB | | Bev ESS | | Pul ESS | | Por ESS | |
|---|---|---|---|---|---|---|---|
| Obj. | Act. | Obj. | Act. | Obj. | Act. | Obj. | Act. |
| 93.3 | 94.4 | | | | | | |
| 96.6 | 96.6 | 97.3 | 97.5 | 97.3 | 97.8 | 96.7 | 96.7 |

District Productivity

| | 17R | 47R | 77R | Tot R | 603-04 | Upkeep | M | Mtce |
|---|---|---|---|---|---|---|---|---|
| Obj. | 25.88 | 7.35 | 14.00 | 9.78 | 34.26 | 11.386 | 7.95 | 10.838 |
| Act. | 30.49 | 7.63 | 15.83 | 10.21 | 37.17 | 12.020 | 8.53 | 11.542 |

All service objectives with the exception of Por XB and Pro no. 1 XB were met or exceeded. Of particular note is the outstanding accomplishment in productivity increases. The actual productivities achieved in every code not only greatly exceeded objectives, but were high in comparison with productivities achieved anywhere in the company for like codes and/or work unit composition.

During 1976, ESS operations presented Mrs. Lawrence with a particularly difficult set of problems: With three small offices she was forced to curtail the size of her work force to just eight craftsmen to meet her stringent productivity objectives; she had just three ESS foremen, two of whom split their time for nearly the entire year between ESS class at BSCTE and field operations, to cover the three offices and the SCC (this left her with effectively less than two foremen). Yet, in spite of these two fundamental handicaps, she met both her service and productivity goals, while reorganizing her ESS operations to full SCC mode.

On October 1, 1976 the responsibilities of the district switching managers in North/South Division were realigned, with the result that Mrs. Lawrence assumed responsibility for all ESS switching maintenance, Sanborn and Portland XB maintenance, the Sanborn, South Cincinnati, and all succeeding cutovers, the implementation of the TASC and ATA systems, and the creation of the EM-SCC.

This combination of duties represents an unusually heavy assignment requiring not only extensive and detailed follow-through, but the development of new procedures, methods, and organizational interfaces and arrangements.

Many difficulties in connection with ESS maintenance and cutover operations were encountered and overcome during the year: a severely compacted schedule of growth and change jobs in the three control groups (including a major trunk frame rearrangement preparatory to the Sanborn cutover) to be done with a force barely adequate for normal maintenance; a continuing series of frustrating, time-consuming, and penalizing delays and errors by the Western Electric forces; despite an exceeding shortage of people, the Sanborn scrub is complete and the South Cincinnati

**EXHIBIT 13-2 (*Continued*)**

scrub is proceeding in excellent fashion; with an inexperienced (but intelligent and well-motivated) switching manager responsible for cutovers, she has been involved in the development of exhaustive, detailed cutover planning, including interfacing with many peers and second-level managers in other groups on a most intensive scale to win their concerned involvement and successful assistance. As a result of her personal effort, all projects have been completed, or are proceeding, successfully on schedule.

Crossbar operations have also proceeded under difficult circumstances: Sanborn XB was reduced to nine craftsmen in 1976 (from 14 in 1975) with two foremen, and is presently operating with six craftsmen and one foreman (meanwhile service continues at a high level); and Portland has shown decided improvement in both service and productivity.

The TASC project has been faced with delays in preparation of space for the computer (therefore, delivery of the computer), and errors and delays in both Western Electric wiring and circuit design. Nevertheless, while the project is behind original schedule due to these WECO and building delays, the exceedingly detailed preparations necessary for implementation, which required creating and training an entirely new group, are proceeding excellently.

Typical of Mrs. Lawrence's work is her approach to the Sanborn scrub. She located a Western Electric mechanized scrub program (TES) which could take the FRA output and perform a complete scrub on all but about 6,000 lines, and automatically assigns the lines in accordance with established balance and short jumper parameters. In addition, it will provide stick-on labels for Repair line cards. The process also produced direct savings of $20,000 over any other scrub methods. Furthermore, her search for a mechanized scrub method which would interface with FRA led the BIS people to uncover the DENS system, which has been accepted for a trial in Cincinnati and Suburban Switching and promises to produce a 50 percent reduction in dial administration clerical forces.

Mrs. Lawrence is familiar with Affirmative Action goals and rigorously implements them.

Management methods: Describe the management techniques used by this employee in achieving his or her objectives.

Mrs. Lawrence learns the work and is intimately acquainted with its progress, plans with great thoroughness, analyzes problems and conditions extensively, interacts intensively with subordinates and coordinates, develops new methods to deal with problems, and confronts all problems (machines, methods, and people) forthrightly and positively.

Strengths: In what way is this manager especially competent?

She is quick to adapt to new situations and learn new technologies; very adept at analyzing problems and coming up with creative solutions. She is quietly determined in her dealings with others, yet completely flexible to alternate options that will produce comparable results. She is highly achievement motivated and is completely comfortable in an open and forthright relationship with her colleagues and subordinates, with a streak of genuine compassion toward others.

Areas requiring improvement: What aspects of the job performance should receive attention?

Donna has been learning the need to develop a certain degree of wariness and toughness in her dealings with others. She has managed to develop these characteristics remarkably during the past year and apply them as needed with no loss of her excellent trust-building ability.

Development needs: List specific action that should be taken to aid this manager's growth.

Continue in her present assignment.

Employee response: How does the employee feel about the performance summary?

*Editor's note*: Employee response was not available to the casewriter.

## EXHIBIT 13-3
## Advanced Management Potential Program Design

| | | |
|---|---|---|
| Monday | P.M. | Candidates arrive for social hour, orientation, meeting, and discussion. |
| Tuesday | A.M. | Group exercise (Business Game—explanation to follow). The candidates were divided into two groups of six. Each group was observed by three assessors who took notes on the total activity and two individual participants. |
| | P.M. | 1. Individual interview with clinical psychologist<br>2. Psychological testing with candidates for assessment information and research purposes |
| | | Free evening |
| Wednesday | A.M. | Individual exercise (In-Basket) |
| | P.M. | 1. Interview regarding In-Basket performance<br>2. Additional testing<br>3. Group exercise (Riverview) |
| Thursday | A.M. | 1. Continuation of Riverview<br>2. Problem-solving exercise |
| | P.M. | Free time to complete unfinished testing or interviewing, "decompression," "debriefing," and "reentry" work. |
| | | Assessees leave. |
| | Evening | Assessors work on writing two- to three-page narrative report based on observations of participants. |
| Friday | | Assessors meet in teams of three with a psychologist to rate and evaluate participants and prepare developmental recommendations. |
| Postprogram | | Feedback given to at-home officer and candidate (to be explained in depth subsequently) |

## EXHIBIT 13–4
## Variable Rating Form—Individual[1]
## AMPA

Code no. ________
Date ________
Staff member ________

*Personal qualities*

1. Energy .......... ______
2. Self-objectivity .......... ______
3. Tolerance of uncertainty .......... ______
4. Resistance to stress .......... ______
5. Range of interests .......... ______
6. Scholastic aptitude .......... ______

*Communication skills*

7. Oral presentation .......... ______
8. Oral defense .......... ______
9. Written communication .......... ______

*Interpersonal skills*

10. Leadership .......... ______
11. Impact .......... ______
12. Behavior flexibility .......... ______
13. Awareness of social environment .......... ______
14. Autonomy .......... ______

*Administrative skills*

15. Decision making .......... ______
16. Decisiveness .......... ______
17. Organizing and planning .......... ______

*Analytical skills*

18. Fact finding .......... ______
19. Interpreting information .......... ______
20. Problem solving .......... ______

*Career orientation*

21. Inner work standards .......... ______
22. Goal orientation .......... ______
23. Need advancement .......... ______
24. Development orientation .......... ______

*Overall rating* Indication of potential to perform effectively at fifth level is:

Excellent ________
Good ________
Moderate ________
Low ________

[1]Each quality or skill is rated by assessors on a five-point scale with each point on the scale illustrated by a descriptive statement which defines the extent to which the person demonstrated the behavior.

CASE 14

# HIGHLAND PRODUCTS, INC. (A)

*Richard O. von Werssowetz*
*Michael Beer*

The envelope was marked "PERSONAL AND CONFIDENTIAL." Ray Kirk took out the letter and began to read what the morning's mail had brought this February 11, 1980.

February 7, 1980

Messrs: John A. Robie -- Chairman and Chief Executive Officer, Highland Products, Inc. [HPI]

Raymond S. Kirk -- Vice President and General Manager, Hampton Division

George D. Wilkes -- Corporate Vice President of Personnel

Corporate Policy Statement on Equal Employment Opportunity

Re: John A. Robie's letter of January 7, 1980 [Exhibit 14-1]
Raymond S. Kirk's letter of January 14, 1980 [Exhibit 14-2]

The opening statements in both reference letters state "We will continue to recruit, employ, train, and promote individuals without regard to race, color, religion, sex, age, national origin, physical or mental handicap, or status as a disabled veteran or veteran of the Vietnam era. In other words, all applicants will be judged on the basis of their ability and skills alone."

I am a woman, and as a woman, I thought I should fit into one of the above-mentioned categories; but the North Haven plant personnel have found many loopholes in this statement.

I am writing to say that I am a minority who is "mad as hell." The discriminating practices that are practiced at the North Haven, Connecticut, plant against women are barbaric. Do you Messrs. Robie, Kirk, and Wilkes just issue these corporate policies to pacify the branches of governments who set these guidelines (federal, state, and local), thinking that your responsibility ends by issuing this type of letter once a year? You gentlemen certainly can't be naive enough to think that because it is a corporate policy, signed by yourselves, that it then becomes a standard operating procedure. Because here in the North Haven plant your letters on equal opportunity are known as the "joke-of-the-year."

How can an organization that employs approximately 1,375 employees, 390 of them women, justify itself as an equal opportunity employer to government-regulated agencies, when there are no women in any supervisory positions? There also are no women in any training programs for supervisory positions. The same old excuse is always applied: "We just don't have any qualified women." Of course the women aren't as qualified as the men, because the men are given all the opportunities. I am attaching a copy of the last wonderful opportunity that was offered to the women here. [Exhibit 14-3] If you read it, and don't see that it is a sham, and one of the most hypocritical actions that could be practiced, then I know what actions will have to be taken.

The real farce of the attached opportunity was that the position was filled before the job was posted. Naturally, the position was filled by a man who is overqualified for the position, and naturally he is no level 4.

The women here in the North Haven plant are told, "You must have a technical degree in the specialized field you wish to enter, if you want anything other than secretarial-related jobs." But, many of the men are holding prominent jobs--some are even in supervisory positions--and they do not possess a degree. They may be in the process of getting their degrees, but they certainly didn't have them before they entered their positions. Upon questioning the personnel manager about this I was told "That may be what was said, but it certainly wasn't meant that way." Well, the women have been told this for years, and will continue to be told this lie and many, many more of the deceitful practices that go on around here unless Baltimore HPI personnel or a federal labor group comes in here and straightens this mess out. Of course, we are also told that they are only following orders that Baltimore has issued.

The women in union jobs, who wish to come into the office and work, they tell me that they are told the same thing, and also they are told that should they become a salaried employee instead of union, they stand to lose as much as $400 per month in income. Well, I don't need a degree in math to figure that what they stood to lose in a year was more than 1/2 of what I make a year. So, if you feel that this feeling of unrest and unfairness exists just within the office areas, again you are being blind to a fact. It is plant-wide.

We are told "No lateral moves." So, if you are unhappy with your job, supervisor, or etc. "tough luck"! You can either leave the company, hope that your supervisor gets transferred, or learn to enjoy being treated without respect, like an indentured servant or a second-class citizen. If you apply for a job that has the same level rating as yours, the personnel department takes it upon themselves to see that you do not receive an interview for the job. But, the men are moved in lateral moves all the time. Almost like checkers on a checkerboard, sometimes to block a job that a woman might want to enter. But, the personnel department will leave no stone unturned to find a more "qualified" man to fill the higher-paying positions. The men also receive a pay raise when they make a lateral move, because they must learn a new job. One woman told me when she had to take a lateral move, that she had to wait till the following year when her annual raise was due and then got no more than what her normal raise would have been. Another woman who was willing to drop a level rating to get away from her supervisor had to take a cut in pay.

Also, when men are hired into the company they do not hire in at the minimum of their level-rate pay scale, but 20 out of 20 females when asked where they started in their job's group rating pay, started at the minimum or below minimum. The men start at midpoint, or somewhere in between minimum and midpoint. One woman told me that she and a man both started a new job at the same time, he was a level 4 and she was a level 5, he was started at midpoint in his pay range and she was started at minimum. When she questioned this, she was told that he is a man and that he needs more money because he has a family. Of course, he has since been promoted out of his lowly level 4 job, and into greener pastures. The woman who didn't get the job he now holds would also like to speak to someone who will listen.

The highest-paid female here in this office, when she was promoted to her new job (previously held by a man), was told that she would not receive a promotional raise because she had just received a yearly raise three months before in her previous job. Therefore, she worked one (1) whole year at below the minimum at her new job. When she found out that her supervisor had lied to her, it came down to this--that's the breaks, take it or leave it! Naturally, she had no choice, and he knew it: she needs her job.

Why is a woman told, who has gone to night school for many years, and has finally gotten her degree in English, that Highland Products doesn't need English teachers. But the plant manager's degree is in sociology, the superintendent of technical products has his degree in elementary education, and the previous plant manager has his degree in English. How did these men ever get to these positions? The reason is, the company was willing to take a chance on them, work with them, train them, and promote them. These men all have been an asset to the company, without a technical degree before they came to work here. Why can't the same thing be done for the women? Why? Why? Why? Are men so immature and insecure in their positions, their knowledge, and their qualifications that got them their positions that they fear women? I was told that even if I changed my career objectives and got a technical degree, that I probably wouldn't get promoted, because women do not excel or succeed in technical fields. I would love to have you hear what position he holds with this organization. If you are a woman, to get anywhere in this company, you must think like a man, act like a woman, and be willing to work like a dog!

Why must there still be "double standards"? Why the lies? Why the deceitful practices? Why motivate by fear? Why not equal pay for equal work? Instead it is who you work for not what you do that determines your pay. Why is it that if there is a change in personnel, and your new supervisor is not as high-ranked as your old one, the secretary's job is re-evaluated and downgraded, but the men in the department, their jobs and pay rates remain the same. Why is it that if a man retires from a good-paying job, and they know that the women will be applying for the job, they immediately downgrade it, and also heap on more requirements and responsibilities?

Why are the women employed here forced to live by a federal freeze on their wages, but Highland Products doesn't have to promote women? Just because there are lots of women in the office is no defense against having none in higher-paying supervisory positions and production-line jobs.

Well, as you can see I have been questioning the system, demanding and seeking answers, and wanting to know the how's and why's of the system. Then I was told what happens to women who question the happenings around here. I was told that should I continue my raises and promotions would be affected, the company would be looking for any reason to fire me. Also, I was asked about how I would feel about character slander. My husband, I was told, is promotable material and how will I feel and more importantly, how would he feel when he is not considered or passed over because of my actions? His raises could also be affected, we both would be made to suffer. I was also told that the company is too big to try to fight them, I couldn't possibly win! Upon reporting this threat, I was told, "Yes, this will probably happen."

Well, gentlemen, you are now reading a letter from a woman whom you cannot motivate by fear. If I have nothing to gain as a Highland Products employee, then I certainly have nothing to lose. Should your actions be to fire me, that doesn't worry me either because I can make almost as much in the unemployment line as I make working here. If you are thinking of ostracism, you are too late. The latest one I just heard about was--the supervisor who told his female employees to stay away from me, because if they didn't they would be known as troublemakers also, and that he didn't need to tell them what happens to troublemakers. He also told them that associating with me could harm their chances for promotion. This one still has us laughing. Chances for promotion--the women in this department average 30 years of service, at the same job in the same level rating! Come talk to them about equal opportunity.

Should you start to harass my husband, who is a blue-collar supervisor, who has worked for Highland Products for almost 15 years, please remember that none of the college boys employed here are willing to work and report for work 24 hours a day, seven days a week, or to be on call and willing to report for work every day of the year. He spends approximately 55 to 60 hours a week at his job, brings work home with him, and works with conditions and heat that he does, for the wages that he is paid. New industrial engineers, whose value to the company is still trying to be decided, are hired in fresh from college at $100 less a month than he now works for. Then after they have been on the job six months they receive a promotional raise.

Well, Messrs., I have been warned not to proceed with this, but proceed I must, and proceed I will. Therefore, my first attack is launched--this letter to you. What can we expect from the corporate leaders of this organization? Are corporate policies and federal laws going to be initiated and upheld? Or are they the "joke-of-the-year"? Do you truly represent the corporation and <u>all</u> employees or are you too just figureheads, collecting large incomes, totally unconcerned and uncaring about the women employed here? I think not, I hope not, because within one (1) week of my sending this letter, step #2 will be taken, if I have not heard from you. (Step #2 attached [Exhibit 14-4].) The women employed here are a force that must be recognized sooner or later; and being as the Civil Rights Bill was passed in 1964, you have gotten away with and ignored the fact for 15 years. There once was a President of the United States and his staff, who thought they were above the law also.

As you can see, gentlemen, after reading step #2 and giving a little thought to what I have said, and wondering what I have left unsaid, you will decide that I am a woman who will take no more of this. I am asking you, your staff members and the people that you employ in the positions to see that I am given equal rights and equal pay, to investigate the procedures here. It has become a situation that I cannot put aside and be content with. So, what action is taken depends upon you. See, I believe in equal opportunity, I'm willing to give you a chance to prove yourselves! That is all that the women of HPI have asked for. The women of Highland Products are tired of being oppressed.

Looking forward to hearing from you,

Susan E. Lesley

## COMPANY BACKGROUND

Highland Products, Inc. (HPI) is a large, U.S.-based manufacturer of a wide variety of low-technology products. Sales for 1979 totaled over $2 billion, with about 20 percent of sales from non-U.S. subsidiaries. Corporate headquarters were located in Baltimore, Maryland, but management was strongly decentralized with HPI's 97 U.S. plants organized into six major divisions by product groups. Most of these divisions competed in maturing markets that were often regional and usually very price competitive. A number of these divisions sold to U.S. military and civilian agencies.

The Hampton Division had 10,000 employees in seven manufacturing plants located in the eastern United States. These included almost 3,000 women and 2,000 members of minority groups. Hampton's plants made standard rubber, plastic, and metal fixtures used in commercial and institutional kitchens and food processing areas. Each plant had product sales and marketing support groups, and product development, plant accounting, and plant engineering staffs.

The North Haven, Connecticut, plant made metal components, primarily from sheet metal and wire stock. An assortment of punches, presses, lathes, welders, and grinders were used in the process, including some computer-driven numerically controlled machines. The production work force was represented by the United Engineering Workers Union. This relationship was one of long standing and was generally cooperative and cordial. Michael Benson, the plant manager, was 54 years old and was a long-time HPI employee. He had been plant manager for nine years, was active in the local community, and had not been a strong supporter of social change.

## AFFIRMATIVE ACTION AT HAMPTON

As Ray Kirk finished reading Susan Lesley's letter, he began to consider what it meant and what actions he should consider. First Ray recalled a briefing of affirmative action requirements that had been prepared by HPI's corporate legal staff (Exhibit 14-5). There was no question that there were serious responsibilities in this area. Each of the plants and the division had had affirmative action programs (AAP) for some time. However, Ray knew that his plant's AAP hiring performances were only modest at best. North Haven's latest Affirmative Action Goals for salaried personnel showed considerable progress to be made (Exhibit 14-6). Although Ray knew he had several women managers and foremen at other plants, Susan's assertion about North Haven supervisors seemed to be correct.

As Ray Kirk thought about North Haven, he felt that one of the factors slowing their progress might be the values of the community. The plant work force was drawn heavily from several strong ethnic communities that had culturally defined roles for men and women. Ray's new personnel manager, Alfred Kraft, had put it this way:

> At home it's Mama in the kitchen and Papa head of the household. Mama serves Papa dinner. The people bring these attitudes to work. Many employees of both sexes relate to male and female jobs. The manager's job is a male job.

This bias was no excuse under the law, but the attitudes did help to explain some "footdragging" he had felt from the plant management.

Susan Lesley's comments about the posting program were especially disturbing. Posting of hourly job openings under union labor agreements had been common for years in many HPI plants. It seemed to work quite well. Posting of office and clerical jobs was more recent, starting in the late 1960s. In the mid-1970s, posting was extended to include the lower-level specialists, analysts, and coordinators. (Candidates for management, supervising, engineering, and other professional jobs were identified by management recommendations, internal salaries, advertising, and employment agencies.) One of the important objectives of the posting program had been to open up opportunities within the plant for minorities and women.

## THE CHAIRMAN'S MESSAGE

One thing was certain: John Robie was not going to be happy to receive Susan's complaint. The board of directors had recently been shocked by the major risks and exposures companies faced in light of a number of highly publicized multimillion dollar judgments in such areas as corporate political activity, product liability, antitrust, and discrimination. This was just the kind of problem they wouldn't want.

As Ray began to develop a plan of action, the telephone rang. It was the chairman of the board. John Robie too had gotten Susan's letter that morning and was very disturbed. He said that George Wilkes and his staff were at Ray's disposal to use as Ray saw fit. But the message was clear: "Fix it."

**EXHIBIT 14-1**
**Corporate Policy Statement on Equal Employment Opportunity**

January 7, 1980

Corporate Policy Statement on Equal Employment Opportunity:

This will reaffirm that Highland Products is strongly committed to a continuing policy of equal employment.

We will recruit, employ, train, and promote individuals without regard to race, color, religion, sex, age, national origin, physical or mental handicap, or status as a disabled veteran or veteran of the Vietnam era.

To insure full compliance with this policy, all applicants for employment and all current employees will be judged on the basis of their ability and skills alone. The only criteria for evaluating applicants and candidates for promotion are those basic qualifications which bear a direct relationship to job performance. Consideration of any other criteria is inconsistent with our merit employment policy.

We will reevaluate and monitor our policies, practices, and procedures to comply with the applicable laws and to guarantee that all positions within our organization are open to qualified women, minorities, veterans, and handicapped individuals.

Further, the Company will continue its Affirmative Action efforts in seeking and recruiting women, minorities, veterans, and handicapped applicants both internally and externally for positions at all levels and in all career disciplines within the company.

All officers, managers, and supervisors will be held responsible for the application of this policy. This includes initiating and supporting programs and practices designed to develop understanding, acceptance, commitment, and compliance within the framework of this policy.

The corporate manager of Equal Opportunity Programs is responsible for developing, coordinating, and

**EXHIBIT 14-1**
**(*Continued*)**

directing programs of equal opportunity throughout Highland Products and will report to me on a quarterly basis. But every employee is obligated to make equality of opportunity a reality in Highland Products.

John A. Robie
Chairman and
Chief Executive Officer

**EXHIBIT 14-2**
**Divisional Policy Statement on Equal Employment Opportunity**

January 14, 1980

Divisional Policy Statement on Equal Employment Opportunity:

I want to reaffirm that Hampton will continue to recruit, employ, train, and promote individuals without regard to race, color, religion, sex, age, national origin, physical or mental handicap, or status as a disabled veteran or veteran of the Vietnam era. In other words, all applicants for employment and all current employees will be judged on the basis of their ability and skills alone.

While all Hampton managers and supervisors are responsible for implementing this policy, Nancy Hobbs, salaried personnel administrator for the Hampton Division, will continue to be responsible for coordinating and monitoring our program. Please give her any assistance she needs in this extremely important area.

I want to make additional progress in 1981 in hiring and promoting females and minorities. It is morally and legally right to do so and it also makes good business sense.

Raymond S. Kirk
Vice President and General Manager,
Hampton Division

**EXHIBIT 14-3**
**Job Posted**

Highland Products — Career Opportunity

Date: January 15, 1980

Job title: Technician--technical service department

Hampton Engineering

Description
- Prepare samples for durability tests
- Prepare samples for particulate and flake tests
- Make physical measurements
- Make hydraulic tests on vials or bottles
- Run moisture permeation tests
- Test ampules for break force characteristics
- Prepare materials for factory use
- Run thermal shock tests
- Prepare sketches as needed
- Perform other miscellaneous tasks as needed

Requirements
- Associate Science Degree preferred
- Manual dexterity desirable
- Knowledge of Hampton products and plant processes desirable

Contact: Fred Strapp--Personnel

Rate level 4

**EXHIBIT 14–4**
**List from Susan Lesley**

*Step #2*

Letters are prepared for mailing to:

- Members of the Board of Directors, Hampton Products, Inc.
- The President of the United States
- The Attorney General of the United States
- Federal Agencies
- Federal Committees on Equal Rights
- Senators
- Congressmen
- Assemblymen
- The Governor of Connecticut
- State agencies
- Labor departments
- Wage and Hour Control Boards (both federal and state)
- Connecticut Civil Rights Bureau
- The Attorney General of Connecticut
- Local mayors
- Local civic leaders
- Local civil rights agencies
- The National Organization for Women, Washington, D.C.
- The National Organization for Women, Connecticut branch
- N.A.A.C.P.
- Chair of the Equal Employment Opportunity Commission
- Project Manager of Equal Employment Opportunity Commission
- Director of the Office of Affirmative Action at the University of Washington, D.C.
- U.S. Assistant Attorney General
- President of the National Organization for Women
- The Department of Health, Education and Welfare
- *The New Haven Register*
- *The New York Times*
- *The Wall Street Journal*
- *The Hartford Courier*
- *The Boston Globe*
- *Working Woman* magazine
- *New Woman* magazine
- *Newsweek* magazine

- Area colleges and universities
- Labor Department's Office of Federal Contract Compliance
- The Federal Trade Commission

All above agencies were asked to have the words "Equal Opportunity Employer" removed from HPI advertising, and so forth.

## EXHIBIT 14-5
## Affirmative Action Requirements

The HPI staff summarized several areas of employment law:

### *EEO Distinctions*

Equal Employment Opportunity (EEO) involves two distinct, though occasionally overlapping, concepts: nondiscrimination and affirmative action, the former encompassing a set of "passive" obligations and the latter requiring certain "active" responsibilities.

Congress has prohibited employment discrimination through the enactment of several laws: the Equal Pay Act of 1963 (equal pay for equal work for men and women); the Civil Rights Act of 1964 (equal opportunity in all aspects of the employment relationship without discrimination because of race, color, religion, national origin, or sex); the Age Discrimination in Employment Act of 1967 (protecting persons between ages 40 and 70); and statutes protecting handicapped persons and Vietnam Era veterans enacted in the early 1970s. Parallel laws exist also in most states.

President Johnson promulgated Executive Order 11246 in 1965 to require employers who contract with the government to adopt "affirmative action programs" (AAPs) designed to improve the *utilization* of minorities and women without regard for whether or not discrimination had ever occurred against them.

While achievement of affirmative action programs will generally eliminate exposure to claims of discrimination, "underutilization," i.e., failure to achieve fully AAP objectives, does *not* amount per se to discrimination.

**EXHIBIT 14–5 (*Continued*)**

*EEO Litigation Timetable*

Since July 1, 1979, The Equal Employment Opportunity Commission (EEOC) has had enforcement authority over discrimination claims under the Equal Pay, Civil Rights, and Age Discrimination Acts. The date on which an EEOC discrimination charge is filed by a complainant establishes the parameters of discrimination litigation:

1. Only employment actions which occurred within 180 to 300 days before the charge was filed will be ''actionable.''
2. Back pay exposure is limited to the period two years before the charge was filed (or three years for ''willful'' violations of the Equal Pay and Age Acts) until the personnel action is corrected.
3. EEOC has exclusive control over a charge for at lest 180 days (60 days for an Age Act charge and none for an Equal Pay Act charge) following its filing, before which time EEOC may sue but a private complainant may not sue.

In the event a private party is dissatisfied with EEOC disposition of the charge, the complainant may request a ''right to sue'' letter after receipt of which suit must be filed in Federal Court within 90 days or it is barred as untimely. The earliest date by which a suit will come to trial is generally from two to five years after it is filed.

AAP performance, on the other hand, is solely the responsibility of the employer subject to ''compliance review'' (usually every three years) by the U.S. Department of Labor, Office of Federal Contract Compliance (OFCCP). Private complainants may *not* sue to enforce an AAP. In the event OFCCP determines, after a compliance review, that an employer has failed to achieve its AAP ''goals'' within a reasonable time frame, OFCCP will issue a ''show cause'' notice whereupon the employer may voluntarily correct the deficiency by conciliation agreement. Should no agreement be achievable, OFCCP then may institute a debarment proceeding—an administrative trial. Back pay is restricted to a period two years before the date of the compliance review.

Private claimant suits may be filed as individual actions or as ''class action,'' i.e., on behalf of claimant and others ''similarly situated.'' Class actions are not permitted under the Equal Pay or Age Discrimination Acts (EPA or ADEA). EEOC, which has enforcement authority for all federal law discrimination claims since July 1, 1979 can sue on behalf of ''similarly situated'' persons, however, making a government action somewhat like a private class action. Because class action suits can result in damages to all affected individuals, judgments in these cases can be large.

Substantial concern has arisen over what is often referred to as "reverse discrimination." In a series of decisions since 1971, the U.S. Supreme Court has intimated how it will decide the "reverse discrimination" issue. First the Court held:

> Congress did not intend by Title VII, however, to guarantee a job to every person regardless of qualifications. In short, the Act does not command that any person be hired simply because he was formerly the subject of discrimination, or because he is a member of a minority group. Discriminatory preference for any group, minority or majority, is precisely and only what Congress has prescribed. What is required by Congress is the removal of artificial, arbitrary, and unnecessary barriers to employment when the barriers operate invidiously to discriminate on the basis of racial or other impermissible classification.

Later Court decisions held that race discrimination prohibitions protected whites as well as minorities but did allow numerical quotas based on race in certain *very* limited situations. These required manifestly imbalanced ratios in traditionally segregated job categories, a voluntary plan enacted by private parties, no displacement of nonminorities from their jobs, no exclusion of nonminorities from participation in such a program, no setting aside of existing job expectations of nonminorities, and a temporary nature that would end when parity is met. The Court held that Title VII imposes no obligation to "maximize" the utilization of minorities, only to refrain from discriminating. However, federal contractors are required to improve statistical "underutilization" by executive orders.

Two important concepts emerged:

1. "disparate impact" occurs when any "systemic" personnel practices, e.g., hiring, initial job assignment, seniority systems, access to apprenticeship programs and salaried job vacancies, testing, or job evaluation systems uniformly applied, adversely affect minorities or women to a disproportionately greater extent than whites or males;
2. "disparate treatment" occurs when an individual is intentionally victimized because of race, color, religion, sex, or national origin, e.g., a "pretextual" discharge.

The complaining party must prove discriminatory motive to prevail in a "disparate treatment" case, but need not prove motive, only effect, in a "disparate impact" case.

The Court also sanctioned the use of statistical proof in employment discrimination litigation so that a complaining party may establish a prima facie case for relief on the basis of the absence of minorities or women from particular job classifications. The burden then shifts to the employer to come forward with a nondiscriminatory reason for the

**EXHIBIT 14–5 (*Continued*)**

particular personnel action or "system" based upon safety or efficiency. The employer must prove that it could have used "no other reasonable alternative" system.

Based upon the evolution of the foregoing Supreme Court precedents, Highland Products believes that equal employment opportunity is not to be measured on the basis of equality of results or statistical parity: "goals and timetables" realistically sought to be achieved through nondiscriminatory "affirmative action" designed to improve "underutilization" of *qualified* minorities and women is the proper objective.

Enforcement of "affirmative action" obligations is a three-phase program. Phase I requires the employer to:

1. Promise, as a condition of eligibility to contract with the federal government, to engage in "affirmative action" with respect to employment practices so as to improve the "utilization" of minorities, women, and the handicapped
2. Develop a written "affirmative action plan" (AAP) which includes at least:
   a. Written "affirmative action" policy statements by appropriate management officials
   b. Work force composition analysis by department, job classification, race, and sex
   c. Job grouping of work force by EEO categories
   d. Statistical comparison of existing work force utilization corresponding to "availability" in the "relevant labor market with requisite qualifications" to determine areas of "underutilization" and explanations of those areas[1]
   e. Projections of anticipated vacancies in "underutilized" areas and good faith "goals and timetables" for improvement over the next 12 months and 5 years
   f. Identification of "problem areas" expected and plans to overcome them.
3. Consult the AAP goals and timetables *before* any vacancy is filled which presents an opportunity to improve "underutilization"
4. Periodic internal audit procedures to review AAP performance

[1] "Relevant labor market" refers essentially to the source from which persons are generally selected to fill vacancies in particular jobs, i.e., within the existing work force, from the local labor market, or on a national basis.

Phase II requires submission of the AAP plan to audit, including on-site compliance reviews with access to all personnel files, records, and interviews of supervisory personnel and hourly employees.

Phase III involves conciliation or litigation of AAP deficiencies found during the review process.

The use of a job posting system is often an excellent component of an AAP. Not only is it a good management tool that benefits *all* employees, but the discipline and documentation imposed by such a procedure can be very useful. Such a procedure shifts to the complaining party the burden of proving discrimination where he or she failed to apply for the vacancy, rather than requiring the company to reconstruct years later its reason(s) for a particular personnel action. It also compels the selecting supervisor to substantiate his or her selection *before* the vacancy is filled. In the hourly unionized jobs, this procedure has long worked well; and, where we have been challenged in EEO litigation, we have won largely on the basis of posting evidence. In fact, improvement to and extension of posting systems has been the major remedial action required by several court decisions to correct instances where discrimination had been found.[2]

---

[2]*Editor's note*: Exhibit 14–6 appears on p. 782.

CASE 15

# NOTE ON JOB POSTING

*Bert A. Spector*
*Michael Beer*

In 1973 Sun Company introduced an internal placement system under which 6,500 of the company's professional and managerial positions would be advertised internally. Each week Sun distributed a listing of open positions and encouraged employees to apply for those jobs which met their desired career plans. Sun explained the implementation of this open posting system by saying,

> It is based on the principle that the employee must share in shaping his or her own career path. It recognizes that as employees' career/life needs change over the years, they should have a way to express that change at their work location. A closed promotional system assumes that every employee is in the department or division he or she wants to be in, and that given the opportunity, promotion to a higher level or a different location will always be welcomed.[1]

Simply stated, job posting is a system that considers an organization's internal staff to be an important labor market, and advertises open positions within that internal market either just as it would on the outside or by giving some preference to internal employees. Open posting has been adopted widely, particularly for nonmanagerial, salaried positions like office and clerical workers as well as for administrative and technical positions.

In recent years, some companies have adopted open posting as a way of increasing access to information about job openings and career development for women and minority employees. In such a case, open posting may, if done right, help overcome organizational barriers to equal employment opportunity.[2]

[1]Quoted in Paul Pigors and Charles A. Myers, *Personnel Administration: A Point of View* (New York: McGraw-Hill, 1981), p. 80.

[2]See Gloria J. Gery, "Equal Opportunity—Planning and Managing the Process of Change," *Personnel Journal* (April 1977), p. 188.

In a 1967 article, Theodore M. Alfred[3] compared an open posting system which, he says, creates an environment of *choice*, to a closed system in which the individual employee does not participate meaningfully in organizational career decisions. In a closed system, Alfred suggests the "Checkers" analogy as more appropriate. Without an open posting system, decisions as to which employees will be considered for certain jobs are left to the discretion of management. Such "unnecessary authority," asserts Alfred, creates certain problems, both for the organization and the individual employees:

1. Because individual supervisors may be unaware of the available talent pool within an organization, good candidates can be overlooked. Since the primary objective of staffing is to get the right person for the right job at the right time, a closed system may interfere with organizational effectiveness.
2. In a closed system, career development is considered the responsibility and function of the supervisor in particular and the company in general. "It is impossible for employees to feel responsible for their own development," writes Alfred, "when the chances of being considered for a job to which they might aspire are a function of their present supervisor's opinions and knowledge of job openings in the company."
3. Because employees do not know whether they have been considered for promotion and what the reasons were for not receiving a promotion, employees may become disenchanted with the way their organization handles staffing, discouraged because they do not know where they stand in the organization in terms of a career path, and perhaps tempted to look for career opportunities elsewhere.

In what ways, then, can a system of open posting enhance organizational effectiveness and employee satisfaction? Alfred suggests four broad points:

1. Open internal job advertisement allow individual employees to assume some responsibility for their own career development.
2. Open posting minimizes the role of chance, prejudice, and power factors in career advancement by disseminating knowledge of job openings on a systematic basis throughout the organization.
3. Open posting may allow employees to take their own initiative in moving out of their current department because of an unfavorable work or supervisory climate and laterally into another

[3] "Checkers and Choice in Manpower Management," *Harvard Business Review* (January-February 1967), pp.157–167.

department. Thus, open posting may help alleviate one reason for personnel turnover.

4. Furthermore, the practice of occasionally applying for internal jobs provides the organization and the individual employees with a regular, natural forum for performance and career prospects review.

That last point about regular performance review depends, of course, on the extent to which managers have the willingness and competence to adhere to the rules of the system, and the system has the processes by which employees are given open feedback about why they did not get the job applied for. Alfred, in fact, suggests that such a feedback interview is a critical part of an open posting system. He also urges the development and use of both internal and external training opportunities for those within the organization who wish to prepare for future job openings; as well as the compilation of data indicating to employees how often openings have occurred in particular jobs and into what kind of a career path such jobs might fit.

While the theory of open posting may seem attractive, there are certain limitations that should not be overlooked. Job posting, for instance, is an inherently time-consuming and costly process. Applicants will be given time off their jobs for interviews; supervisors need to take time to do the interviewing; and the feedback process adds further to time away from the job. Travel expenses can become a significant additional cost in multilocational companies. The cost of transporting employee applicants from one location to another can mount quickly, so most companies limit job posting to within a geographical area or severely restrict the number of jobs that will be posted across locations. Also, job posting can set off a chain reaction of personnel shifts within the company that management is unable to anticipate and plan for much in advance.

Many of the limitations of a job posting system derive from implementation problems. The administration of such a system requires a certain set of skills, competencies, and even values on the part of managers which are different from the skills, competencies, and values used in a more traditional system. Managers will need to possess skills not only in judging potential but in explaining what is finally a subjective judgment to the people involved. Poor skills in communicating how and why a decision was made can increase disappointment on the part of employees who were turned down for a job. And the supervisor, feeling either unsure about his or her judgment or defensive about the necessity of explaining that judgment to the job applicant, may feel more comfortable falling back on criteria like seniority that can be more objectively explained. The task of a manager telling a senior employee that he or she has been turned down for a promotion in favor of a junior person deemed to have greater potential can be a difficult and uncomfortable one. Perhaps this difficulty can be lessened or even overcome by training in appraisal and communication skills. Or perhaps such a difficulty is inherent in an open posting system. That question is still an open one. It does seem fair to say that the extent to which an organization teaches or encourages the acquisition of such skills will help determine the extent to which a job posting system can be successfully implemented.

Open posting implies some changes in the organizational power structure. Supervisors are relinquishing some of their authority to determine the career paths of subordinates to those subordinates themselves. The unwillingness of supervisors to do this may work against implementation of a job posting system. Job posting may become a sham in which promotional decisions are, in fact, made prior to the posting, or in which cronyism rather than qualifications determines the success of an application. The theoretical free flow of individuals throughout an organization, in which employees may use job posting to determine where and for whom they would like to work, can be halted by supervisors who intimidate employees into not applying for open jobs. Such limitations may be mitigated by an organizational culture that places value on sharing power over career and job decisions and that encourages the acquisition of skills to implement such a system. Companies must weigh these limitations against not only the potential benefits but also against their optimism about their ability to overcome limitations and their willingness to commit time and resources to implementation before deciding to undertake such a shift in the manner in which they manage their own staffing needs.

CASE 16

# MEDICAL AND ENVIRONMENTAL ELECTRONIC DEVICES CORPORATION (A)

*Constance Baher*
*Richard O. von Werssowetz*
*Michael Beer*

In January 1980, Barbara Hamlin, newly appointed manager of Human Resource Development and Planning (HRPD), put together a population profile for the Integrated Circuit Group (ICG) of Medical Environmental and Electronic Devices Corporation (MEED). That profile showed clearly that ICG faced a major challenge in meeting its fiscal year (FY) 1980 and FY 1981 needs for engineers, managers, technicians, and production workers (see Exhibit 16-1). ICG had been growing rapidly and was projected to continue this growth in the next several years. Currently, ICG had 623 employees (plus 8 staff personnel), and 106 open positions to be filled. If the projections were correct, ICG would grow to a total of 946 people by the end of FY 1980 and 1,429 people by the end of FY 1981, a 51 percent growth in personnel. Projections through FY 1985 called for more than 9,000 new hires (see Exhibit 16-2).

The IC group represented MEED's efforts to assure itself of an adequate supply of large-scale integrated circuits (ICs) through purchase of standard ICs from outside suppliers and through design and manufacture of unique ICs required for new product designs. Tom Douglas, manager of the group since 1977, was pleased that ICG was successfully meeting MEED's needs through purchase from outside vendors, but he was concerned about slower-than-expected progress in gearing up internal design and manufacturing operations for unique ICs so critical to MEED's current and future success. Several specific problems seemed to be responsible for the slower progress.

---

This case was revised by Bert A. Spector, Research Associate, under the direction of Michael Beer, Lecturer.

1. The Jackson, Michigan, manufacturing plant, which began operation in July 1979, was still experiencing difficulties in start-up and it was now the beginning of 1980.
2. Design projects were not being completed on time or within projected budgets. In part, this had been attributed to a lack of know-how in project management.
3. Annual turnover, while not high by industry standards, was running close to 10 percent among exempt employees and 20 percent among nonexempts; forecasts predicted higher rates in the future unless specific corrective actions were taken.
4. The labor market was exceedingly tight for exempt employees, especially the highly trained engineers critical to ICG's work.
5. Managerial talent was also a pressing need; ICG had little management depth. More and better managers needed to be found and developed.

Because of these problems, some of Douglas's managers strongly urged him to establish a new position concerned with people planning and development. Attracting, training, developing, and retaining the right people in the right numbers, particularly salaried technical and managerial personnel, some felt would be essential for the success of the IC group. In response to his own concerns and that of his managers, Douglas created the new HRDP position Barbara Hamlin now occupied. Her charge was to forecast the IC Group's human resource needs, with special attention to professional and managerial personnel and to design and implement programs to meet those needs.

The forecast of staffing needs which Barbara Hamlin developed raised more questions than it answered. Nonexempt employees were not that difficult to hire, but where should ICG look for its engineers and managers? What kind of programs should be developed to recruit and/or develop the needed technical and managerial talent which ICG lacked? Once designed, how should a human resource program be implemented? What should Barbara's role in all this be and what should be the role of key managers, especially Tom Douglas? Their support, she knew, was the key to success.

## MEDICAL AND ENVIRONMENTAL ELECTRONIC DEVICES CORPORATION

MEED was founded in 1959. Originally exclusively involved in new applications in medical device technology, the company had expanded its sights to environmental control applications and adopted its current name in 1964. By 1979, MEED had achieved an overall 31 percent market share in its market area (a market expected to grow at more than 30 percent annually during the 1980s). MEED's closest direct competitors had only 20 percent and 11 percent shares, respectively.

MEED now designed, manufactured, sold, and serviced complex medical and environmental control systems. MEED sold direct to major end-users, provided some controls for OEMs, and provided equipment to smaller end users through an international force of marketing representatives. With headquarters in Westland, Michigan, MEED had facilities in 21 countries throughout the world.

Sales, growing at more than 30 percent per year for the last five years, topped $1 billion in 1979; profits for 1979 were $107 million (see Exhibit 16–3). The average number of employees for 1979 totaled 24,900 and another 7,000 were expected to be hired as MEED continued its rapid growth during FY 1980.

Over the past 20 years, MEED had developed its own highly distinctive set of values and modus operandi. As described by a company handbook, "MEED culture" is:

> . . . a catch-all phrase attempting to describe norms peculiar to the company. Words or expressions associated with "MEED culture" can be:
>
> - Unstructured
> - Make it happen
> - Positive approach toward people
> - Informal
> - Rapid growth

Hallmarks of the MEED culture were ambiguity, freedom, flexibility, risk-taking, and a supportive attitude toward employees.

One MEED general manager wrote in a memo to incoming employees:

> You must be a self-starter and self-director. Only you can really decide what is the right thing to do. If you really believe in doing something, do it, even if you are told no. Be prepared to get killed if you are wrong. Tell the right people what you are going to do even if they say no and disagree.
>
> Get accustomed to radical changes in organization and jobs people are doing, including your own. Be prepared for surprising and unpredictable changes every couple of years.

President Dave Bertram once explained how to succeed at MEED:

> There are no rules. Do a good job. It may take a while before people appreciate and notice what you're doing, but in the long run it's the job that counts. . . . Sometimes we move people so fast that they don't gain any experience. You should really stay in an area long enough to live with your mistakes. The biggest thing to learn is the results of your mistakes.

In line with many tenets of the MEED culture, the company had not placed great emphasis on formal planning. While not all agreed, it was not uncommon for people at MEED to express little faith in plans. As one manager put it, "The planning process is just beginning to take hold." In light of the company's remarkable history, it was not surprising that some MEED oldtimers felt that if things had worked out before without much long-range planning, they would again.

While planning had previously been done within various product lines, the first, loosely coordinated companywide plan for MEED was undertaken by FY 1980.

While planning had previously been done within various product lines, the first, loosely coordinated companywide plan for MEED was undertaken in FY 1980.

## THE IC GROUP

Integrated circuits represented vast advances over earlier generations of electronic technology. First transistors replaced vacuum tubes. Then in the early 1960s, via large-scale integration (LSI), thousands of tiny transistors were combined in integrated circuits, placed on tiny chips (so small they fit on a fingertip) of semiconductor material (notably silicon), and the semiconductor was born. Under extreme magnification, a semiconductor chip looks like New York City might from 50 miles out in space with thousands of intersecting lines for streets and small blocks for buildings. These lines and blocks, which exist at several levels within the silicon chip, is the complex circuitry which has been etched into the chip. The lines on a 64,000 bit memory chip are 3 $\mu$m wide, roughly 1/10,000th of an inch. In earlier generations of electronic technology this circuit would have been represented by thousands of transistors connected by wires.

The development of an integrated circuit requires electrical engineers and technicians with specialized skills (often in short supply) to design the circuitry according to product requirements, draw it up in large scale and shrink the drawing photographically so that the resulting transparent film may be used as a mask in etching and plating operations. Manufacturing requires engineers and technicians to design a complex and unique process which includes radioactive doping, metal plating, and etching process among approximately 300 steps. Because of the microscopic dimensions of the chip, mistakes might not be detected until final test, at which time 6 to 12 weeks of work might have to be scrapped. All this required unique technical and managerial skills.

In what has been called the third computer revolution, the central processing unit itself was miniaturized onto a chip, called a microprocessor, and this made possible the minicomputer used in MEED's many medical and environmental control products. The next step is a further reduction in size, very large-scale integration (VLSI), in which "superchips" contain hundreds of thousands and ultimately millions of parts. This advance requiring design and miniaturization techniques unavailable today promised to shrink the large computer down to about the size of a match head and to increase MEED's flexibility in applying computer technology to its products. Therefore, the IC Group worked in both LSI and VLSI technologies.

Like many manufacturers whose products were or contained minicomputers MEED decided to backward-integrate in semiconductor development and manufacture. A primary reason was the semiconductor industry itself. While demand was growing, the number of independent vendors was shrinking. As the IC Group's January 1980 five-year plan explained:

> MEED's integrated circuit requirements will grow from 0.9 percent of the industry output in FY 1980 to 2.5 percent by FY 1985. The number of suppliers external to MEED for these needs is actually shrinking by acquisition, redirection, or noninvestment. The capacity currently on-line is not enough for comfortable supply and the number of potential large customers for that limited supply is growing. These bleak facts drive much of the ICG strategy.

Nonetheless, ICG was never envisioned as a major supplier for MEED. Through larger, longer-term, and admittedly less flexible arrangements, MEED would continue to buy 80 percent of its semiconductor parts from outside. At most, ICG was expected to produce 20 percent of MEED's needs.

ICG would be MEED's "laboratory" for IC design, the development of new manufacturing processes, and the quick execution of prototypes. New custom-integrated circuits would be produced by ICG and, if capacity permitted, additional chips for use in MEED's equipment assembly operations.

## SEMICONDUCTOR CULTURE

In starting its own semiconductor operation, MEED's IC Group needed the expertise of experienced engineers and managers from the semiconductor industry. Managers in ICG felt that semiconductor people, and the technology of semiconductor design and manufacture, brought the IC Group face-to-face with a culture significantly different from what most at MEED were accustomed to.

An IC Group engineer who had been with MEED for 18 years, characterized the two cultures:

> In the traditional semiconductor company, people have often been treated harshly: laid off or fired on short notice. At MEED we've prided ourselves on treating people like people.[1] Once we know someone is competent, we tend to let them alone to do their job. If they are failing, we work with them a long time if necessary.

By contrast, the culture of the semiconductor industry was seen by people at MEED as unforgiving, coldly results-oriented, and sometimes unscrupulous as well. Kenny Lash, ICG operations manager, described the contrast by saying "Relative to the semiconductor industry, there is less structure, regimentation, or discipline at MEED than I am used to."

An IC engineer traced the culture difference to differences in basic technology:

> We've never scrapped a whole equipment system just because somebody goofed. We diagnose and fix the problem and ship it.
>
> But there is usually no way we can diagnose and fix and ship a wrongly processed wafer. Once the mistake is made, and for as long as it goes undetected, all further work is scrap.
>
> There is no place else in MEED like this. In our history, we have never had a manufacturing, engineering, selling, or administrative technology so unforgiving of mistakes.

The differences in culture created an assimilation problem for experienced semiconductor people. According to one manager, "Semiconductor-trained people get rejected, just like a heart transplant."

MEED was determined not to run its semiconductor business the way it was run on the outside, but clearly there were challenges in applying the MEED culture to this new and demanding technology, or, as one engineer suggested, inventing a new culture midway between both traditions.

### *Organization*

Starting as an idea and a group of people in 1972, ICG had 66 people in 1975, but began its real growth in 1977, reaching 448 employees at the beginning of FY 1980 (see Table 16-1). The group was organized functionally into these subunits: Advanced Design (AD), a circuit design group, a manufacturing plant, and Materiel, which provided the link between ICG manufacturing and the volume assembly

[1]The company has not yet laid off workers, despite recessions. MEED employees are not unionized.

**TABLE 16–1 ICG Population** *(at Fiscal Year End)*

| *1972* | *1973* | *1974* | *1975* | *1976* | *1977* | *1978* | *1979* | *1980*[a] |
|---|---|---|---|---|---|---|---|---|
| 5 | 12 | 28 | 66 | 110 | 232 | 360 | 448 | 946 |

[a]Forecast.

operations of MEED. Materiel was responsible for all semiconductor components used by MEED. Following the production goals set for ICG, Materiel was expected to buy 20 percent of MEED's semiconductors from ICG Manufacturing (at a transfer price of cost plus 15 percent and the rest from outside suppliers. In addition to purchasing, Materiel's other major function was to assure the quality of components through the use of carefully developed, complex testing procedures.

Materiel was headed by Les Hogan; Advanced Design was headed by Dom Raffaelli; and Tom Douglas, adding to his responsibilities as group manager for ICG, was also plant manager of the Jackson plant. Several group staff functions also reported to Douglas, including program management, planning, and personnel. Barbara Hamlin, as director of HRDP, reported to the IC Group's personnel manager, Tim Ott. Each of the ICG subunits also had a personnel manager, who reported both to the head of that subunit and to Tim Ott. (See Exhibits 16–4 through 16–6 for ICG organization charts and additional information on the backgrounds of key ICG managers.)

Douglas ran the IC Group primarily through informal contact with his staff and top line managers, rather than through regularized meetings. Tom was one of the MEED oldtimers, having been with the company since 1962. A systems engineer by training, he was new to semiconductors. He had also never run a plant before, and was finding the experience so stimulating that he sent a memo to other senior managers recommending that they all consider the value of tours of duty "down in the trenches."

### *Performance*

One measure of ICG Manufacturing's performance was yield: good chips as a percentage of chip starts. Manufacturing yields frequently ran 10 to 20 percent. Many wanted to see these figures improved, although others noted that, with new custom chips, yields of even under 10 percent were to be expected, especially when a chip first went into production. In one instance where others in the industry were producing chips similar to ICG's, industry yields were running 71 percent and the Jackson plant 65 percent.

Expenses in the manufacturing operation for the current fiscal year were running $11 million more than forecast. When asked whether any pressures had been applied from the corporation, Douglas replied that while his boss in corporate manufacturing had shown great understanding, he and his managers felt great responsibility for this overrun.

Although the goal was to meet vendor cost standards, ICG-produced components cost approximately twice as much as components bought from the outside. Furthermore, ICG was only manufacturing 5 to 8 percent of MEED's semiconductor needs instead of the 20 percent planned. Materiel had been able to make up the difference from outside, and although there had been at least one close call, no line in the volume assembly plants had been shut down because of a lack of parts. Characteristically, MEED remained tolerant of ICG's growing pains and committed to the principles behind its establishment.

## ISSUES FOR ICG

Performance problems were clearly of major concern to Tom Douglas, but there were also other issues which demanded attention.

Scheduling was such an issue. Delays in delivering parts to volume assembly meant unrecoverable losses for MEED. According to the head of the Advanced Design group, the critical problem was that life-cycles in the semiconductor business ended abruptly when new technologies obsoleted a given device. Every week ICG had to wait to get a chip into production meant delays for volume assembly, and at least several days lost from a life span that would meet an arbitrary cut-off point at some time in the future. A week lost could mean approximately $100,000 lost in profit before taxes for MEED. Right now, Advanced Design had $2 million worth of design work that he couldn't get into production.

Understaffing and a lack of management depth had added further complications to Douglas's task. The most prominent example involved Douglas himself. Kenny Lash had been plant manager. Kenny came from the semiconductor industry; he talked with a Southwestern twang and wore Western clothes to work. (In general, dress at MEED was casual; managers rarely if ever wore suits.) Encountering overwhelming difficulties in the startup of the Jackson plant, Kenny asked to be relieved of his responsibilities so that he could fill the open position of operations manager. He became manager of operations, and Tom took over as plant manager.

Throughout the IC Group, other people as well were holding down two and sometimes three jobs, often acting in both supervisory and technical capacities. Douglas was well aware that filling the 106 authorized but still open positions would not be easy.

*The Labor Market*

While direct workers and other nontechnical employees could be hired and trained relatively easily, there was a significant problem in attracting engineers capable of the state-of-the-art work that ICG technology demanded.

As one engineer at the IC Group explained, "In the whole country, there are 2,000 electrical engineers who can do the work we need. MEED has 160 of them now. If we increase our numbers to 300 or 400, we have to take them from somebody else."

Taking them from somebody else generally meant hiring experienced engineers from the semiconductor houses. Most of them were located in California's Santa Clara Valley, nicknamed Silicon Valley. Many of the manufacturers had developed out of or alongside university programs at Stanford, the University of California at Berkeley, and Caltech. A few semiconductor houses were located in Arizona, Texas, Colorado, and Massachusetts; MEED's entry into the business represented the first major semiconductor effort in the Midwest.

Attracting semiconductor engineers to the IC Group meant, in many cases, luring them from California to Michigan. Companies vied with one another to offer the most enticing tangible and intangible rewards (see Exhibit 16–7); it was well known that an experienced engineer could get a 30 percent raise simply by moving from one company to another. For ICG, there were also relocation costs; the group estimated that it cost $5,000 to bring a West Coast semiconductor engineer to Michigan. Despite the salary increases and other benefits ICG offered, the group found that semiconductor people felt uncomfortable in the MEED culture, disliked the Michigan weather and nonurban environment, and felt uncomfortable with the midwestern life-style. A few left the company within three months.

Recognizing the high cost of attracting experienced engineers from outside the IC Group, Douglas sought to reorient ICG recruiting toward meeting needs with existing employees and recent college graduates. In 1979, he created a new College Relations department for the group; in particular, ICG sought to build relationships with the University of Michigan, the University of Illinois, Michigan State, Purdue, the Illinois Institute of Technology and Wayne State, and five other schools in the Midwest and East. It took about three years of work at ICG for a college graduate to be fully trained, but by working with these colleges to develop programs and by providing equipment and dollar donations, ICG hoped to shorten on-the-job training to 1½ case years. The goal was to ensure that by FY 1985, 50 percent of professional hires would be new college graduates.

Even among the college graduates, however, the numbers were not that favorable. According to the planning manager for the IC Group, "there are 20,000 electrical engineers graduating, but 40,000 are needed."

Furthermore, engineering graduates often lacked competencies required by companies like MEED. Faculty at large nationally known institutions designed curriculum in accordance with their more theoretical perspective of a field. Responding to practical needs of local businesses was generally not seen as the role of a nationally known educational institution. Recently, Wang Laboratories, a computer company headquartered in Massachusetts, had established the Wang Institute, an independent high-technology graduate school which expected to train its students for work in many high-technology companies, including Wang (see Exhibit 16-8). Although MEED thinking was in the formative stages only, some saw this kind of school as an ideal additional source of highly trained manpower.

### *Employee Development*

The other notable source for employees was within ICG or MEED itself. While some managers, such as Dom Raffaelli had come up through the ranks, Douglas felt this source of engineers and managers could be considerably improved.

MANAGERS. There was no formal program of management development at ICG. Job searches were concentrated on ICG's very pressing need for engineering talent; the group had no formal program for recruiting MBAs. The general pattern was that engineers moved "up" into management. "A good engineer wants to be a supervisor," explained an employee relations specialist for Advanced Design. "That's where the power is."

In some cases the transition worked, but in many it didn't. "Engineers don't care about managerial tasks like reporting. They want to know, is there going to be a juicy project for me?" Despite chronic understaffing, they often failed to follow up on recruits. The Employment staff's role was only to assist the line managers; it was the managers who actually did the hiring. "There's a manager of an engineering group who is excellent technically," said one personnel manager, "but when Employment people give him the name of a job candidate, he doesn't even call the guy."

As one engineer who tried management and went back to engineering put it, the fallacy was "that being a 'good engineer' said something good about my management potential.'' Other engineers simply found themselves saddled with management tasks (such as budgeting, scheduling) in addition to their engineering assignments. As a result of all this, said an employee relations specialist, ''The least amount of expertise *looks* like management. . . . There are no models. People don't know what a good manager looks like.''

ENGINEERS. If an engineer didn't move into management, he or she could follow the engineering path: a junior engineer could aspire to become a senior engineer, principal engineer, and finally consulting engineer. Technical training, which many viewed as a major need at ICG, had received some attention, but many thought there should be more training (for example, design and process courses), especially to provide career tracks and development for the engineers. As it was, the engineering career path played second fiddle to the path leading to management. ''We want dual career paths,'' said an employee relations specialist, ''but we don't have them.''

*Opportunities and Stresses*

For some, ICG's human resource needs were a benefit. Said an employee relations specialist:

> We hired a technician fresh from school and after his first six to nine months, he wound up acting as a circuit designer, one of the most highly paid and highly regarded positions in the country. . . . he was doing more technically than his boss's boss.
>
> Because we are stretched, people with talent get sucked up. They're given opportunities they wouldn't otherwise get.

However, Barbara Hamlin estimated that the IC Group's exempt attrition would rise to an average of 15 percent per year, and nonexempt to 35 percent unless the group improved its recruitment, career development, performance appraisals, and promotion practices.

Personnel turnover was only complicating the group's needs for more employees. Including estimated attrition, the IC Group would need 241 hires just to bring the employee total up to the target for the end of FY 1980. Another 364 hires would be needed by the end of FY 1981. With or without the necessary people, the jobs still had to get done.

One ICG engineer took terminals home so that he could work on weekends. The ''MEED way of doing things,'' said one manager, was that people put out 150 percent. ''With years and years of experience,'' he said, ''you get to know how to handle pressure.'' Others saw more difficulties; the manager of product engineering: ''We're not the kind of top-down organization where you can pass your troubles up the line."

## THE ICG SUBUNITS

Within the IC Group, the different subunits faced different tasks and responded in different ways to these problems.

### *Materiel*

Materiel was well regarded within ICG as was its manager, Les Hogan. It was generally thought of as the most top-down of the three subunits; it was a disciplined organization which consistently met its goals.

Materiel's acquisition function was divided into two groups: an operations group that focused on such functions as production purchasing, and a strategic group that dealt with commodity management (including 5-year planning, make/buy decisions, engineering relations), IC Group manufacturing, and custom projects.

The operations group was the hectic side of the business; before division into two groups, current purchasing and longer-range planning had been combined, with the need to "meet the numbers" forcing out strategic planning, and vice versa. The strategic group now provided a focus for the longer-term planning, away from the day-to-day pressures of operations.

According to the Acquisition manager the strategic group was a major factor in Materiel's low turnover rate. It provided new career paths: In the past a buyer (in the operations group) could become a supervisor in operations or else would leave the company to work the other side of the desk as a salesman for a vendor. Now the buyer had the additional option of staying within Acquisition but moving to a job in the strategic group. In the last 15 months, Acquisition had lost only one buyer.

### *Advanced Design*

AD was headed by Dom Raffaelli, a young and energetic manager who rode his motorcycle to work (as did many of his staff). Raffaelli had started as a technician in Corporate Research and Development in 1965. Earning his engineering credentials through MEED's in-house accreditation program, Raffaelli worked as a systems design engineer, joining ICG in 1974. Named manager of AD in 1978, Raffaelli had made a number of changes that were serving the organization well. (Concerted attention to turnover problems had reduced attrition from a high of 17 percent in one quarter to virtually zero in the first two quarters of FY 1980.)

AD had two primary tasks: circuit design and the development of CAD (computer-aided design) tools.

AD's engineers worked on a contract basis, competing with outside semiconductor houses to design the chips for MEED's products. The contracts were awarded by MEED's R&D group. Annual budgets had varied considerably (for example, from $5 million to $2 million), since design tended to be needed on a cyclical basis: design work was needed for the introduction of new products, there was little need while the life cycle played itself out, and then design would be needed for the next round of products.

The peaks and valleys in design needs made it difficult to attract and keep engineers in Advanced Design and led to what Raffaelli called a "tincupping" approach to R&D: AD was always having to hold out its tin cup and beg for contracts to achieve stability in its budget and staffing from year to year.

To smooth out the cyclicality and reduce the need for tincupping, Raffaelli worked his contacts at corporate R&D, sat in on their planning, and reoriented the business from service to product development. "We're now chartered to be innovative, to plan forward." AD now got a lump sum budget in advance, and worked from rolling five-year plans. This meant that engineers could be hired, trained, "so they are on board when we need them."[2]

While Raffaelli felt he needed "a critical mass of talented senior people," a year ago AD had also initiated a college relations program; young college graduates could be "sewn up" early, came with no previous bias, and, especially if they had been at midwestern schools, were already used to this part of the country. Given the geography of the semiconductor industry, there was also less competition for college graduates at the midwestern schools.

AD sought to help focus and influence program directions at midwestern technical schools ("help get them up to speed"), and to develop cooperative programs that would bring students to the IC Group during their college years. While current goals called for 50 percent of new professional hires from colleges, Raffaelli wanted to see the figure ultimately 60 percent or 70 percent.

[2]As chips became more complex, they also took much longer to design. Raffaelli's technology manager felt that he was forced to plan ahead by lead times now running as long as two years (and likely to run longer in the future).

The third source he saw was the pool of device designers at MEED: "You have to coerce them into becoming semiconductor people." He had two or three such people already at AD and felt they were working well.

THE CAD GROUP. The CAD group was a vital part of AD. Formerly, chips were designed manually. Now, with the increasing density and complexity of chips, CAD tools had to be used.

When Bill Ambrose took over the CAD group, some slots had been open for many years. He immediately set recruiting as a top priority (and evaluation criterion) for his managers. He defined a middle layer of supervisors, and beneath them, group leaders. All were given recruiting responsibilities as Ambrose set up what he called his "recruiting machine." He also drafted a recruiter from AD's personnel organization, Charlie Polk. "Charlie is like a member of our team. He comes to our staff meetings. He goes on recruiting trips and drives the effort."[3]

The selection process began with an applicant's resumé book that was reviewed by supervisors and group leaders. Following this resumé screen was a telephone screening, an invitation to meet with the appropriate CAD people, a review of the interview, and a decision on further action; if an offer was made, a reply date was specified for the applicant. A flow chart tracked each prospect so that, as Ambrose said, "Nobody falls through."

As of the beginning of 1980, Ambrose's group had openings for two out of five supervisory positions, and 13 of 37 subordinate engineering slots. He expected to fill these positions in the next three to six months but also to add five to ten new positions.

### *Manufacturing*

Until the time Douglas took over as plant manager, Manufacturing had gone through five plant managers (all of them from the semiconductor industry) in four years. A first plant had been set up in Lansing, Michigan. Plagued by high turnover and increasing expenses, the plant was eventually closed and its operations were being transferred to the manufacturing plant now headed by Tom Douglas in Jackson, Michigan.

[3]As a member of the AD staffing unit, Charlie was also working with Dom Raffaelli on other college recruiting programs. Orry Nickols, who headed Institutional Relations, had no recruiters assigned to him; he worked, via dotted-line relationships, with recruiters such as Polk. Both Polk and Nickols reported to an employment manager, who in turn reported to Matt Terry, the personnel manager for Advanced Design and Manufacturing (see Exhibit 16-6).

Tom Douglas talked about the Jackson plant: "Three-quarters of the people in this facility didn't work for MEED a year ago. . . . In the plant, of the top 12 managerial people, 5 have been with MEED less than four months."

While Douglas's dual role as group manager and plant manager was taking its toll (he was constantly preoccupied with the problems at work and wasn't sleeping well), Douglas was nonetheless enjoying this opportunity immensely. "I've never been a plant manager," Douglas explained. "I love it. You forget what it's like to do things." Characterizing himself as a firefighter, he said of MEED, "We've trained and hired and rewarded firemen. We have a lot of people who love to fight fires all over the place." Barbara Hamlin had urged Douglas to begin actively looking for a new plant manager (such a search could be expected to take six to nine months), but, according to Douglas, the urgent problems of current operations had to be addressed first.

Some thought Douglas should never have taken the plant manager job and saw him being "sucked down into the day-to-day." Different people within ICG offered different diagnoses of the problems in Manufacturing.

Dom Raffaelli felt that the plant needed someone who knew how to operate within the MEED culture: "They need a MEED manager to run Jackson, somebody who can develop relationships with other key groups, to protect them from hassle and give them clear priorities. . . . Tom Douglas has a track record. He can go to his friends and take the heat off, he can bargain for all the right things."

The manager of circuit design in Advanced Design, a semiconductor man, insisted that Manufacturing had to be run by someone who understood the technical detail. "We're operating close to the vanguard of knowledge. This work involves optics, thermodynamics, polymer chemistry, physics of materials, metallurgy, ceramics, computer instrumentation, purity of materials, crystallography. . . . We know more about silicon by two orders of magnitude than anything else on earth. . . . Managers don't need detail? Bullshit."

## POTENTIAL BARRIERS TO HUMAN RESOURCES DEVELOPMENT AND PLANNING

Barbara Hamlin knew that certain aspects of the MEED culture and of present human resources policies and procedures would have to be taken into account as she sought to formulate and implement human resources plans.

### *Planning*

To begin with, planning per se was relatively new to ICG, as it was to MEED as a whole. According to one staff member of the IC Group, "We couldn't spell 'Planning' around here five years ago." Some even speculated that greater attention to manpower planning might have led MEED to locate ICG closer to the major sources of trained engineers, or perhaps even to recast its plans to enter the semiconductor industry.

It was hard to forecast accurately the shape of the organization five, three, or even two years from now. Thus, starting the HR planning process by projecting future organization charts was seen by some as too fraught with uncertainties. Another option was to proceed by creating individual career paths for those within ICG, but this option was discounted by those who felt that such paths might only raise expectations that might not be fulfilled. The option of simply hiring in good people now (so there would be enough on board as ICG expanded) met resistance from those who pointed out that there were no slots for these people until the growth actually took place.

While some urged that, nonetheless, ICG should be looking ahead, identifying slots that needed filling, and planning to get the right people into those slots, there were others, mindful of ICG's needs to meet present operating goals, who felt it was imperative to get the group on its feet before diverting attention to human resource development and planning (HRDP).

### *Employee Mobility*

Employee mobility at MEED also made planning difficult. As growth created opportunities within the firm, people became accustomed to moving themselves rapidly into new positions. Many joined MEED with expectations that such mobility would be possible. According to personnel policy, an exempt employee was considered movable after he or she had been in a job for one year; for nonexempts personnel, the period was six months.

Employee mobility caused particular problems for Program Management, a staff unit created in FY 1979 within ICG. The IC Group was organized primarily on a functional basis. Program managers gave the group a matrix configuration, since they were to track groups of custom chips (ultimately intended for given MEED products) across all the functions, including design, manufacturing, and procurement. This period could run from three years to as long as 15 years, from the placement of design contracts through ultimate phase-out of a given component. Given the MEED culture, it was also unreasonable to expect that any one program manager would remain long enough to see one component through its entire life.

### *Performance Appraisals*

Bosses and subordinates found it difficult to conduct regular performance appraisals; they were supposed to be conducted at least once a year as part of an employee's salary review. Elizabeth Harris: "I had five different jobs in three years. I had one performance appraisal in that time, and six weeks later I was out of that particular job." Another ICG manager had had four bosses in three months, and held five jobs in five years.

It didn't make much sense to appraise the performance of someone who had just come into one's department, or was just about to leave it; the boss-subordinate relationship changed so frequently that it often was hard for a boss to have enough information at any one time to properly evaluate all of his or her subordinates. Efforts were underway to improve the appraisal process, but the quality of the appraisal discussion sometimes left something to be desired.

Only in Materiel had performance appraisals become routine. Les Hogan, head of Materiel, had required his managers to conduct semiannual performance appraisals and made this one of his criteria in evaluating their own performance.

### *New Hires*

A number of ICG managers agreed that, despite the limited labor pool, recruiting was not the real problem; it was assimilating the new hires. They observed a high failure rate among those who couldn't cope with the MEED environment.

"We don't have mentors here to help people start out," said one manager. "It's not part of our philosophy."

### *Compensation*

ICG faced a potential problem with salary compression; incoming senior engineers might be paid more than those who had been with the group for some time. (And senior IC Group engineers were frequently raided, bid away by other companies.)

Some at ICG felt that more than salary was involved in attracting engineers. Fran Haeuser, manager of an advanced process engineering group in AD, kept salaries in line by stressing the additional benefits of working for ICG. "Engineers can make $5,000 more on the West Coast, but they like what they're doing here, they like the growth potential and the stability." She was also aware of needs to motivate and challenge them. "They should have 10 to 15 percent of their time to sit and think, to work on their own projects. They need time for creativity. You have to be supportive, you have to be flexible with time and money. Encourage them to go to meetings, technical seminars, talk with others in their field."

### *The Future of HRDP*

Given the newness of the HRDP function, Barbara Hamlin was uncertain about the role, power, and jurisdiction of HRDP. Some line managers thought of HRDP primarily as a provider of training. Some emphasized recruiting and college relations. Some expected HRDP to focus on management development, although Barbara felt that not all managers recognized the lack of management talent in ICG nor its importance.

Barbara thought of her role as a more encompassing people planning and development activity which included many of these specific personnel activities with a good dose of coordinated planning added. But this view raised several new questions. How could ICG attract and keep the technical and managerial talent needed? Should planning be at the aggregate level (i.e., types and numbers of people needed and sources where they would be obtained) or should it deal with specific people within ICG who were candidates for promotion, their current performance and specific plans for development? If planning involved the latter, was it her job to develop such plans for line managers, many of whom did not have the skills, or was it her job to help them develop individual development plans? If development planning was to occur at the individual level how many such plans would it be reasonable to expect managers in ICG to develop and implement?

A broader HRDP role also raised several potential implementation problems within the personnel department. Human resource planning would require a change in the reactive and decentralized personnel function in ICG. Institutional relations (Orry Nickols) was part of Matt Terry's organization yet it was critical to human resource planning. Barbara had a management development manager reporting to her, but a similar position had recently also been created by Matt Terry. Equally important personnel people had learned to respond to managers' needs but were not comfortable with the initiating role human resource planning required. Finally, the managers reporting to Douglas did not understand or agree on what the HRDP role should be or its value. For that matter, Barbara was not clear on how Douglas conceived of the role when he created it or if he understood many of the issues with which she was beginning to grapple.

While Barbara was developing a human resources plan for presentation to Douglas, the staffing problems being experienced by ICG were being complicated further by the resignation on April 18 of Kenny Lash, the manager of operations for the plant. Having come from the semiconductor industry, feeling ill at ease in ICG, and under pressure to improve plant performance, Lash left to take a job back in the semiconductor industry after 13 months at MEED.

Lash's resignation left Tom Douglas with two key openings in the Manufacturing hierarchy—plant manager and operations manager. Now, de facto, Douglas was doing both jobs in addition to carrying overall responsibilities for ICG as group manager. Barbara Hamlin wondered what effect this would have on her recommendations to initiate a human resources planning process.

**EXHIBIT 16-1**
**ICG Population Profile[a,b]**

| | Advanced Design | | | Manufacturing | | | Materiel | | | Total | |
|---|---|---|---|---|---|---|---|---|---|---|---|
| Employee Category | *Current* | *FY 1980* | *FY 1981* | *Current* | *FY 1980* | *FY 1981* | *Current* | *FY 1980* | *FY 1981* | *FY 1980* | *FY 1981* |
| Managers | 6 | 7 | 7 | 11 | 13 | 30 | 6 | 10 | 10 | 30 | 47 |
| *Exempt* | | | | | | | | | | | |
| Supervisors | 10 | 11 | 13 | 32 | 42 | 62 | 12 | 16 | 16 | 69 | 91 |
| Consultants | 3 | 4 | 6 | 2 | 2 | 2 | 1 | 1 | 1 | 7 | 9 |
| Engineers | 40 | 45 | 61 | 50 | 79 | 77 | 22 | 30 | 51 | 154 | 189 |
| Other exempt | 6 | 8 | 10 | 39 | 48 | 58 | 25 | 37 | 91 | 93 | 159 |
| Subtotal | 59 | 68 | 90 | 123 | 171 | 199 | 60 | 84 | 159 | 323 | 448 |
| *Nonexempt* | | | | | | | | | | | |
| Technicians | 25 | 32 | 43 | 91 | 120 | 157 | 22 | 30 | 52 | 182 | 252 |
| Secretarial | 7 | 9 | 10 | 24 | 26 | 26 | 23 | 32 | 36 | 67 | 72 |
| Production | 0 | 0 | 0 | 38 | 180 | 314 | 75 | 90 | 148 | 270 | 462 |
| Other nonexempt | 0 | 0 | 0 | 35 | 54 | 128 | 18 | 20 | 20 | 74 | 148 |
| Subtotal | 32 | 41 | 53 | 188 | 380 | 625 | 138 | 172 | 256 | 593 | 934 |
| Total | 97 | 116 | 150 | 322 | 564 | 854 | 204 | 266 | 425 | 946 | 1,429 |

[a]Includes no temporary employees.

[b]Figures for current employees come from personnel office records. Figures for FY 1980 are aggregates of positions budgeted and approved for that year. Figures for FY 1981 are aggregates of employee forecasts prepared by planning managers for each of the ICG subunits.

## EXHIBIT 16–2
## ICG Hiring Requirements Projection[a]

| EMPLOYEE CATEGORY | 1980 | 1981 | 1982 | 1983 | 1984 | 1985 |
|---|---|---|---|---|---|---|
| *Advanced Design* | | | | | | |
| Exempt | 35 | 56 | 88 | 142 | 226 | 363 |
| Nonexempt | 18 | 31 | 56 | 90 | 144 | 229 |
| *Manufacturing* | | | | | | |
| Exempt | 40 | 73 | 117 | 187 | 322 | 554 |
| Nonexempt | 147 | 151 | 245 | 393 | 629 | 1,006 |
| *Materiel* | | | | | | |
| Exempt | 47 | 66 | 105 | 167 | 267 | 587 |
| Nonexempt | 102 | 149 | 238 | 382 | 610 | 976 |

[a]Hires per year including attrition

SOURCE: Draft of Human Resources Strategy for Five-Year Plan, Barbara Hamlin, October 11, 1979.

**EXHIBIT 16-3**

## Ten-Year Financial Highlights

| | 1970 | 1971 | 1972 | 1973 | 1974 | 1975 | 1976 | 1977 | 1978 | 1979 |
|---|---|---|---|---|---|---|---|---|---|---|
| Sales[a] | 79 | 86 | 117 | 161 | 256 | 321 | 440 | 637 | 856 | 1,083 |
| Net income[a] | 8 | 7 | 9 | 14 | 25 | 28 | 42 | 64 | 86 | 107 |
| Total assets[a] | 70 | 89 | 116 | 170 | 265 | 336 | 523 | 647 | 893 | 1,109 |
| Stockholders' equity[a] | 44 | 74 | 86 | 130 | 209 | 238 | 366 | 473 | 541 | 668 |
| Stockholders' equity per share[b] | 1.88 | 2.96 | 3.35 | 4.86 | 6.80 | 7.91 | 11.26 | 13.54 | 15.97 | 19.86 |
| Net income as a percentage of average stockholders' equity (%) | 23.8 | 10.6 | 11.2 | 12.7 | 15.9 | 12.6 | 14.8 | 16.3 | 17.2 | 17.5 |
| Net income as a percentage of average total assets (%) | 16.4 | 8.1 | 9.0 | 9.9 | 12.2 | 9.3 | 10.2 | 11.4 | 11.0 | 10.5 |
| Average number of employees for year | 3,100 | 3,700 | 4,000 | 6,100 | 9,200 | 11,000 | 13,300 | 18,200 | 22,400 | 24,300 |

[a]Millions of dollars.

[b]Dollars.

## EXHIBIT 16–4 ICG: Partial Organization Chart

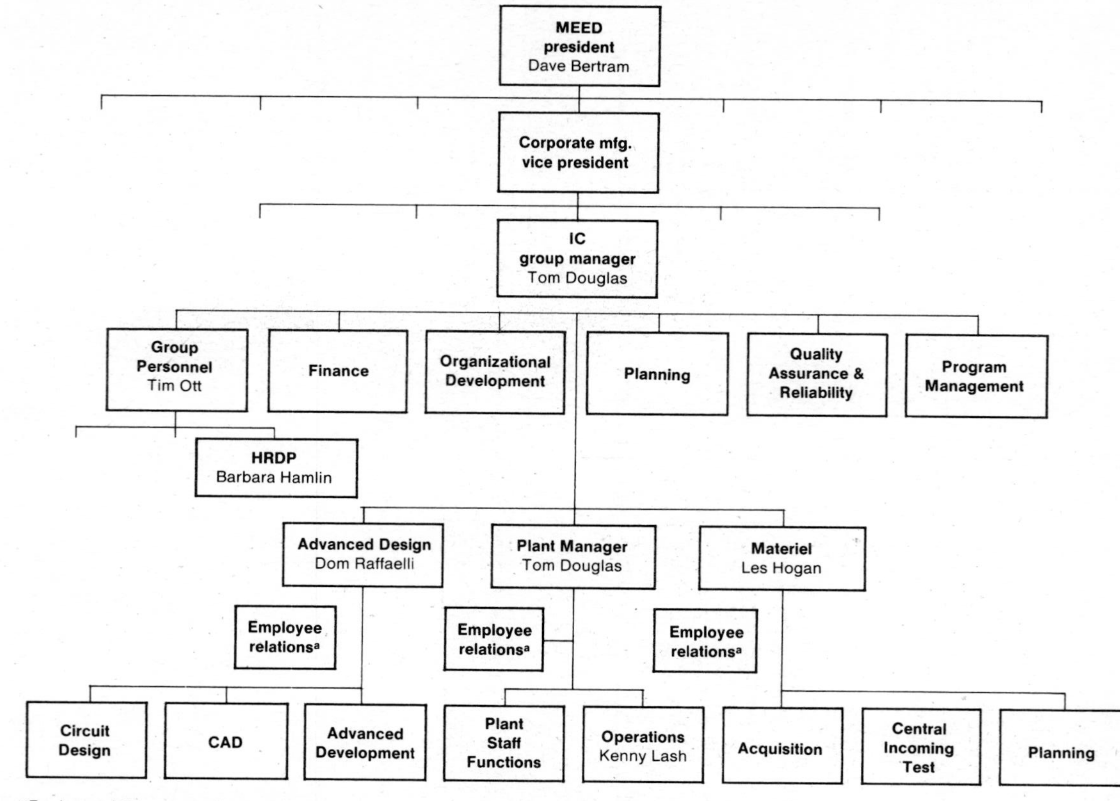


[a]Employee relations managers reported both to their respective line managers and to the IC Group Personnel manager, Tim Ott. Relationships within the personnel function are shown in Exhibit 16-6.

## EXHIBIT 16–5 IC Group Personnel—Partial Organization Chart

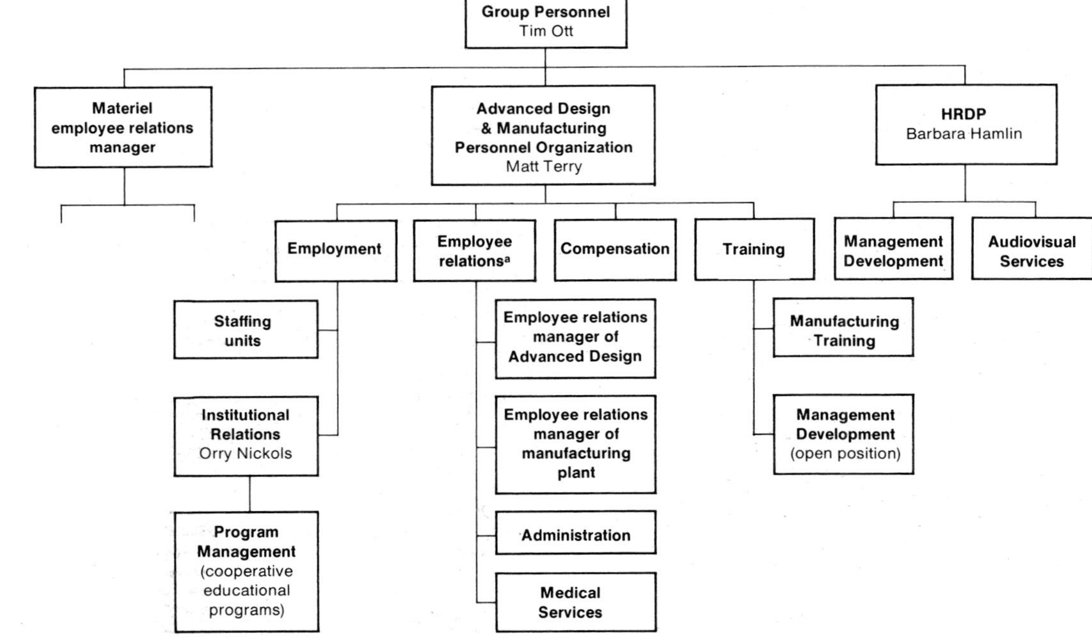


[a]Employee relations managers in Materiel, Advanced Design, and the plant, plus Matt Terry, also reported to their respective department managers. All others on this chart reported only to Tim Ott and served the departments through the employee relations managers.

**EXHIBIT 16-6**
**Biographical Information**

| Name | Position | Age | Education | Joined MEED | Job Experience |
|---|---|---|---|---|---|
| Tom Douglas | Group manager, ICG; manager, ICG Plant | 41 | B.S.E.E., Wayne State University, 1960; advanced management course, University of Detroit, 1971 | 1962 | MEED: systems engineer, manager for Quality Control, Manufacturing Engineering, Test Equipment Manufacturing; joined ICG 1977 |
| Dom Raffaelli | Manager, ICG Advanced Design | 34 | Associate in E.E., Oakland Community College, 1965; engineering certification from MEED's Engineering Review Board,[a] 1967 | 1966 | MEED: systems technician and design engineer; joined ICG in 1974 as manager, Central Incoming Test; 1978 to present, manager, Advanced Design |
| Les Hogan | Manager, ICG Materiel | 41 | B.S., University of Minnesota, 1961 | 1968 | Honeywell, Inc.; MEED: Finance manager, MEED manufacturing; marketing manager, product lines; joined ICG in 1979 as manager, Materiel |

| | | | | | |
|---|---|---|---|---|---|
| Kenny Lash | Manager of Operations, ICG plant | 46 | B.S., physics, Texas Tech; M.S., physics, Rice University, 1966 | 1979 | Texas Instruments Product Design manager, 1976–79; MEED: March-Dec. 1979, ICG Manufacturing manager; Dec. 1979-present, manager of Operations, ICG Manufacturing |
| Barbara Hamlin | Director, Human Resource Development and Planning | 32 | B.S., Ohio University, 1970; M.A. University of Chicago, 1971 | 1976 | Public school administrator; MEED: joined ICG in 1976 in Employee Relations; 1979 to present, director, HRDP |

[a]Employees who satisfactorily completed examinations and MEED coursework in engineering could be certified by the company's Engineering Review Board, which qualified them for engineering positions.

**EXHIBIT 16-7**
**The New York Times, April 30, 1980**

# Companies Compete To Lure Employees

*California Computer Suppliers Trying Novel Incentive Plans*

**By PAMELA G. HOLLIE**

Special to The New York Times

SUNNYVALE, Calif.—The airconditioned lobby of Advanced Micro Devices Inc. is decorated for Christmas, complete with a shimmering Christmas tree and posters that proclaim "Christmas in May."

The display is part of A.M.D.'s innovative employee incentive program, under which the company will pay $20 million to its 6,000 workers this year. W.J. Sanders 3d, the president of A.M.D., will be playing Santa Claus next week because the manufacturer of integrated circuits for computer equipment surpassed its sales and profits goals in its latest fiscal year.

"We are going to give away $1,000 a month for 20 years," he said. "That's $240,000 to one employee; no strings attached."

That kind of program to keep employees happy is no longer a luxury for companies here—it is a necessity. At a time when a recession is beginning to take hold and employment in the auto, steel, forest products and other sectors is falling, the high-technology companies, particularly those in California, are begging for workers, paying top dollar for recruits and doing everything they can to keep the workers they have in order to supply the semiconductors and other computer components that continue to be in great demand.

## High Turnover Rate

"There was a time when the most innovative thing a company did was have a sack race at a picnic," said Charles Elkind, vice president of the American Electronics Association, an industry trade group based in Los Angeles. "But there is a shortage of workers in our industry and the turnover is high, especially in California," he said. "The competition is tough. It's hard to keep employees from going across the street for a higher-paying job."

Nationwide, 30 percent of high-technology workers left their jobs in 1978, with the rate at companies with fewer than 500 workers at more than 50 percent, and that at concerns with more than 1,000 at about 22 percent. In May, the American Electronics Association will announce the 1979 figures, which are expected to show an increase in turnover.

Complicating the situation for companies like A.M.D. is the critically tight housing market along the 20-mile corridor south of San Francisco known as Silicon Valley. In what is the largest concentration of high-technology companies in the United States, dozens of concerns make their headquarters in communities like Sunnyvale, Palo Alto, Mountain View and Santa Clara.

As the nation's ninth-largest manufacturing center, Silicon Valley generates one out of every five new jobs in the United States. For the last three years, the valley has been adding as many as 50,000 jobs a year. One study of the employment needs of the area projected a 57 percent growth in manufacturing employment by 1985.

## Difficulty With Recruitment

But the valley, which since 1963, has become an endless freeway lined with low-rise buildings, has not been able to keep pace with the needs for schools, housing and other facilities. And now, despite such incentives as free orthodontia, trips to Tahiti and Mexico, country club memberships, help finding housing and bonuses of up to $7,000 to employees who bring in recruits, new workers are difficult to woo.

Companies big and small have vacancy rates of 10 percent in every job category. And, because tight housing has reduced additions to the employee pool, those who already live in the valley have been characterized as children in a candy store, faced with a bewildering array of opportunities.

The competition for engineers, technicans, accountants, programmers, secretaries and janitors is fierce, and payrolls are high: an unskilled production trainee starting at $4 an hour will make $10,000 after the first year, and, once eligible for profit sharing and other bonuses, can make more than $15,000 after the second year.

''In the valley, even a janitor makes $20,000,'' quipped one vice president of a large computer components company, who said that, despite the high salaries, people do not stay in their jobs long. ''I've had four secretaries in three years,'' he said. ''Each one left about the time when things started running smoothly.''

**Worries Over Job Experience**

With the high job turnover, companies worry that the experience needed to produce their high-technology products will suffer if workers do not stay on the job long enough to become proficient.

''Every executive in our industry is worried about maintaining quality,'' said a spokesman for American Microsystems Inc., which has geared its incentive programs to reward its long-time employees. ''A long service employee is five years,'' he added.

Nearly all the companies in Silicon Valley have stock purchase plans, good medical benefits, and profit sharing. Some have programs that focus on the employees' physical health, their mental health or their wealth.

In 30 days, the Rolm Corporation will have completed construction on a new employee recreation facility that will include racquetball courts, a swimming pool, sauna and running track. The Signetics Corporation hopes to have its ''individual accountability program'' in full swing soon. The company has done away with time clocks, unnecessary work classifications and a rigid bureaucracy.

''We are using very, very subtle techniques to improve the way workers feel about their work; we are moving toward systems where workers manage their own work,'' said Gerald R. Pieters, an industrial psychologist who is vice president of management and organizational development at Signetics.

**Money Seen Bringing Results**

At Advanced Micro Devices, Mr. Sanders believes money will bring the results in productivity and employee longevity he seeks. His employees already receive twice-yearly cash bonuses of up to 13 percent of their salaries and other incentives. The company's vice presidents drive leased Mercedes-Benz cars and hourly employees get paid up to $1.50 a day as a bonus just for showing up for work.

Next week, in addition to the $240,000 grand prize, the company will give away a new diesel-powered Cadillac Seville and a five-foot-high home television system to winners of the ''Christmas in May'' promotion. In addition, because profits improved from the third to the fourth quarter, the company will give away a second Cadillac Seville and another television system to two other employees.

In the last five years, A.M.D. has been the industry's star performer, a fact that Mr. Sanders attributes to his incentive program.

''We share the results of the enterprise with the employee,'' Mr. Sanders said. ''Every employee wants a return on his effort. Every employee wants to make more money.''

---

## EXHIBIT 16-8
## The Wang Institute

### A unique institution for high-tech training
*Wang graduate school could become 'another MIT'*

By Margaret A. Bengs
Special to The Globe

Lest anyone fear that California is usurping the Massachusetts high-technology industry's lead in innovation, he must now think twice.

Massachusetts is about to acquire a first in both the high-technology industry and in the field of education. There's nothing like it in California and, despite acute demand, very little like it in the country.

According to B.J. Rudman, a spokesman for the Massachusetts High Technology Council, the Wang Institute of Graduate Studies could become a "magnet, drawing people into the state—another educational resource like MIT."

The Wang Institute will initially offer a master's degree in software engineering from its School of Information Technology in Tyngsboro. It is a non-profit institution, and although the initial endowment came from Dr. An Wang, president of Wang Laboratories of Lowell, and his family, it is an independent school, run separately from the company. It is designed for qualified students and its graduates may go to any company they choose—no strings attached.

The institute's opening comes at a time when many companies, according to Joseph Cashen, vice president of engineering at Prime Computer, are looking for "creative ways to get the technical manpower we need. Any time an event like this happens, it's a spur to the thinking of companies like ours."

Massachusetts companies are particularly pleased because, where most schools focus on theory, the Wang Institute will focus on the practical, as well as theoretical, training in software engineering, whose needs are fast eclipsing even those of hardware. (Software specialists design and program a system.)

"There are two bottlenecks to industrial growth in this country," according to Dr. Ugo Gagliardi, president of General System Group in Nashua, who is taking a leave of absence as Gordon McKay professor of the practice of computer engineering at Harvard University to become the institute's first dean. Those are oil and software, he says.

Why, in a state noted for the quality and quantity of its academic institutions, is the Wang Institute opening?

No. 1: need.

The need for computer specialists and technicians in this state is now so acute that many companies are finding it difficult to justify their personnel offices. "I get the impression today that we hire just about anyone who comes in to apply," quips William McMillan, president of Computer Fulfillment in Winchester. McMillan suggests that part of the staggering demand today is due to the increasing "sophistication" of the industry.

Needs, McMillan says, have become increasingly "exotic." His company, for example, is handling a case for a major printer who's trying to decide whether to build a new plant. "We have to identify which magazines would be attracted to the plant. We figured out that the plant would need to attract 1¾ trillion pages. . . . but that's not all they need to know. We have to tell them the average number of pages each magazine published, the type of paper, its color, how it's distributed, whether it's in tabloid or digest form . . . and that's not all. Before they decide whether to build the plant, they have to know the profile of the press—how much paper, how much ink—how many forests to buy . . ."

Yet, for all the innovation and sophistication of its high-technology industry, and for all its highly acclaimed colleges and universities, New England seems to be having a tougher time adjusting its educational establishment to the market. "Advertising for computer specialists in other regions of the country has dropped, but not here," says Howard Morrison, president of Arthur D. Little Systems in Burlington. Massachusetts is having a lot of problems, says Morrison, because unlike San Francisco, Los Angeles and New York—other centers for high-technology—Boston offers a relatively small population base.

Also, according to Morrison, "We have an ineffective state college system. The University of Massachusetts," he says, "turns out so few computer science majors and electrical engineering majors, it's startling. Schools here are the most expensive in the country, and we just don't have the kind of innovative programs we should—so a lot of bright people are leaving to go to school. We just don't have a base."

The University of Massachusetts counters that it has made several grand efforts in the last few years to start or expand programs in computer science and engineering. It points to an 85 percent increase in the number of engineering graduates expected this year over last. Ten percent of the entire enrollment at Amherst—or 2400 students—are enrolled in the School of Engineering, according to UMass spokesperson Carole Cohen. the Amherst campus has just graduated 20 students from its first undergraduate computer science program, in addition to 50 from its graduate programs. The Boston campus has 35 students enrolled in its first computer science program, and the university expects the number of both its computer science and engineering graduates to double or triple within the next few years.

Yet, despite many recent efforts to redirect some of the state's nearly $300-million higher education budget, to train students as technicians, engineers and computer scientists, placement records show that only 3 percent of them went into a computer-related field. By contrast, more than 25 percent went into teaching. The community college system, also, has graduated few technicians, according to a recent Technical Marketing Associates report commissioned by the state. Yet, according to the report, "local industry faces a recruiting challenge of major proportions over the next five years, as at least 6500 and possibly as many as 12,000 technicians will have to be added to the high-technology work force in Massachusetts."

The High Technology Council, furthermore, predicts a 25 percent growth in demand for electrical engineers and computer scientists.

One of the problems of traditional universities in trying to meet this increased demand, according to Professor Thomas Cheatham, chairman of the Computer Sciences Department at Harvard and a member of the Wang Institute's National Academic Advisory Committee, is "inflexibility" when it comes to new ventures.

Another problem, according to Cheatham and Dr. Edmund Cranch, president of Worcester Polytechnic Institute and also a member of the advisory committee, is that many universities are geared for research and are "not professionally oriented to equip people to work in a practical way in industry." Very often, in a traditional computer science program (which, he adds, may be only five or six years old), the projects and theses are strongly mathematical, "without the constraints and limitations of the real world. You can make assumptions, you can make equations, but to actually put the components in place and build a machine is different," he says. "The machine doesn't know your equations."

The directors of the Wang Institute plan to alleviate part of this problem by "blending" formal academic methods with real-life projects. "When you train doctors, you let them work with real patients," says Dean Gagliardi. "When we train students, we want them to work with real systems." From running his own company, Gagliardi finds: "It takes two years of on-the-job training, which

## EXHIBIT 16-8 (*Continued*)

we have to pay for, before an employee becomes good. A lot of these people," he says, "just aren't familiar with the complexity of real software applications."

This complexity is almost impossible to simulate in a traditional classroom. It often takes about two years for several practitioners to write a compiler (which translates information into language a computer can understand) for a company, according to Dr. Caroline Wardle, former chairperson of the Computer Science Department at Boston University's Metropolitan College and a UN expert in language processor design, who is now the institute's associate dean. "But in a classroom, you might have 25 students, each working on a single project." In a typical semester, says Wardle, the student spends the first six or seven weeks learning theory. The next two months are spent working on the project. Schools are, therefore, forced to make up a miniature version of the problem, she says. They make up a fictitious project with a fictitious company about a fictitious problem. They create a small prototype, "but the real world of large production offers more complex problems." At the institute, says Wardle, "we'll be working on real projects."

Another feature which will differ from the traditional curriculum is the emphasis, in Gagliardi's words on "discipline and a sense of responsibility—on all the ethical aspects." Just as ethics is a major part of a doctor's training, so it must be for a computer specialist, he says. Because computers bear an ever greater responsibility for the smooth functioning of people's lives and organizations."

The institute plans to enroll 30 to 40 full-time "equivalent" (full and half-time) students, but because it is directing its efforts to train project leaders, who then will eventually direct a subgroup, institute planners feel its impact will reach close to several hundred persons a year. Tuition will be $700 per course, or $5600 for two full-time semesters. The institute, which is applying for degree-granting authority from the state Board of Higher Education, estimates it will cost approximately $20,000 to educate one full-time student per year. The difference will be picked up by its endowment fund and other contributions.

Institute directors are confident that many of its graduates will stay in New England. "Most people don't realize," says Gagliardi, "that the computer industry is not headquartered in California. "The total number of computers shipped out of Massachusetts is much greater than out of California. The most-expanding companies in the mini-computer field are on Rte. 128."

Since it is unique and since it will be taking dramatic steps to improve "the state of the art," the institute's directors envision that those practitioners with a serious interest in advancing themselves will be more willing to come to Massachusetts once the "fringe benefit"—the Wang Institute—is established.

The institute, in fact, has already been contacted by New Hampshire's Sanders Associates, whose engineers, according to Lewis Jamison, manager of technical development and manufacturing training, are interested in going on to a graduate program but who, because of gasoline prices, traffic, and inconvenience, don't want to drive.

Although graduates from the institute may end up working for competitors of Wang Laboratories, An Wang says that doesn't concern him. "I think competition is healthy," he says. Wang, in fact, hopes that the institute will educate leaders who might someday start their own companies, thus stimulating the state's economy even further. "We want to generate people who are good for the industry," he says. "Massachusetts has to do something to attract people into this state."

"This is a charitable institution," Wang says. "I want it to be for the community."

---

SOURCE: *The Boston Globe*, March 2, 1980. (Reprinted courtesy of *The Boston Globe*.)

*Chapter* 5

# Reward Systems

THE DESIGN AND management of reward systems constitute one of the most difficult HRM tasks for the general manager. Of the four major policy areas in HRM, this is where we find the greatest contradiction between the "promise" of theory and the reality of implementation. Organizations sometimes go through cycles of great innovation and hope as reward systems are developed, followed by disillusionment as these systems fail to deliver. Organizations must reward employees because in return they are looking for certain kinds of behavior: they need competent individuals who agree to work with a high level of performance and loyalty. Individual employees, in exchange for their commitment, expect certain extrinsic rewards in the form of promotions, salary, fringe benefits, perquisites, bonuses, or stock options. Individuals also seek intrinsic rewards such as feelings of competence, achievement, responsibility, significance, influence, personal growth, and meaningful contribution.

Employees will judge the adequacy of their exchange with the organization by assessing both sets of rewards. The attention of both employees and employers tends to focus on extrinsic rewards, because these rewards are easily defined, measured, and compared across people, jobs, and organizations. Intrinsic rewards, on the other hand, are less clearly definable, discussable, comparable, and negotiable. Union-management negotiations, for instance, rarely deal with intrinsic rewards even though these intangible rewards are often at the root of the conflict between management and labor. Workers who have routine jobs may feel powerless to influence their work or the conditions of work. Wage demands can mask this fact, so that increased pay serves to compensate for the inadequacy of intrinsic rewards. Likewise, the dissatisfaction of a manager or a professional with his or her progress up a pay scale may reflect a deeper dissatisfaction with growth in responsibility, career, and power. Increases in compensation may reduce conflict for a while, but they will not resolve the fundamental problem.

Complaints about compensation and other extrinsic rewards may thus mask problems in the relationship between employees and their organization: the nature of supervision, the opportunities for career development, and employee influence and involvement in work itself.

When conflict over pay erupts, general managers would be well advised to undertake their own careful diagnosis of the situation, rather than assuming that the problem should be "handled" by staff specialists in compensation. Such a diagnosis may well point to problems in the other three HRM policy areas. If this is the case, an increase in compensation and the resulting increased cost to the organization will not resolve the underlying conflict. We are not saying that conflict over wages does not have validity or that money is unimportant. We are saying employees sometimes compensate for their dissatisfaction with intrinsic rewards by demanding improvements in extrinsic rewards, particularly pay.

The capacity of an organization to deliver intrinsic rewards through innovations in work systems, employee influence, and human resource flow policies may have marginal effects on the negotiation of extrinsic rewards. Delivering intrinsic rewards through innovative policies will probably not lower compensation costs; in fact, it may call for higher compensation. However, it may stimulate employees to increase commitment and develop their competence, leading to positive effects on effort, indirect labor costs, innovation, and flexibility in the work force. The net benefits of such outcomes to the organization can be quite high even when considered against the cost of higher compensation.

Tying pay and other extrinsic rewards to performance may *reduce* the intrinsic motivation that comes when individuals are given freedom to manage and control their jobs.[1] By making pay contingent upon performance (as judged by management), management is signaling that it is they—not the individual—who are in control, thus lowering the individual's feelings of competence and self-determination. Intrinsic motivation decreases when a person's behavior becomes dependent on a reward that someone else controls, or on the threat of sanctions. Intrinsic motivation also decreases when pay decisions provide individuals with negative feedback about their performance on an intrinsically interesting activity. Therefore, managers must decide whether intrinsic or extrinsic reward systems are to be the primary means for motivating employees. Moreover, managers must be careful to prevent pay and other extrinsic rewards from interfering with intrinsic motivation.

This chapter will deal primarily with the design and management of compensation systems. Intrinsic rewards will be discussed in Chapter 6 on work systems, where we will explore in some detail how work may be organized to stimulate intrinsic motivation. In this chapter intrinsic rewards will be discussed only as they interact with the design of compensation systems. These systems warrant specific attention because they present difficult choices to general managers. Furthermore, compensation systems are the primary subject when employees or unions negotiate with employers. Finally, money is important to employees. Dissatisfaction with pay can easily lead to negative effects on employer-employee relations in other policy areas.

The central thesis that we will put forward is that while compensation systems can be managed to improve cost effectiveness and avoid conflict, they have only limited potential for developing commitment and competence. On the other hand, compensation systems can and sometimes do interfere with innovations in the other HRM policy areas. Our point of view runs counter to much of management theory and practice in the United States (though not in Europe and Japan). We are suggesting that the design of a compensation system should rarely be the place to start in solving business and human resource problems, though it will always be an area that will have to be managed to complement other HRM changes. Top-down design of reward systems, particularly those systems aimed at controlling behavior through pay-for-performance incentives, can often hurt an organization's HRM efforts more than it can help. (We are not talking here about participative approaches to designing new pay systems which, in effect, are changes in employee influence.)

## THE REWARD SYSTEM CHALLENGE

In manufacturing firms, payroll costs can run as high as 40 percent of sales revenues, while in service organizations payroll costs can top 70 percent. It is not surprising, therefore, that general managers take a great interest in payroll costs and how these dollars are spent. In the steel and automobile industries for example, payroll costs for production, clerical, and management personnel are generally regarded as one of the factors affecting the competitiveness of these industries. Comparing a firm's total payroll costs to the payroll costs of the competition is one way to assess the competitive position of the firm. It can and should guide management in its policies regarding compensation levels and its positions in collective bargaining.

Despite the enormous amount spent on wages, commissions, cost of living increases, bonuses, and stock options, many studies have shown that in most organizations 50 percent or more of the employees are dissatisfied with pay, and that this percentage is increasing. In 1973, 48 percent of a representative national sample of employees felt they received "good" pay and fringe benefits; by 1977 the percentage had declined to 34 percent.[2] Pay is a major problem in many organizations and there is a continual "noise" level about its adequacy and equity. A recent summary of survey findings by a major opinion polling organization concluded that a majority of employees come to work each day believing that their wages are unfair, that pay increases are unfair, and that any improvement in their performance is unlikely to result in better pay. This is somewhat less true of managers than of clerical, professional, and hourly employees. Satisfaction with fringe benefits is typically higher, but even that dropped in the 1970s to a rate slightly better than 50 percent.[3] These findings are particularly disturbing when one considers that pay has been consistently found to be one of the most important job factors to individuals, usually ranked first or second among all levels of employees. Thus, employees are dissatisfied with the very reward that appears, based on their stated preferences, to have the potential to influence powerfully their willingness to work and to stay with a company. Not surprisingly, the tremendous amount of time and energy expended in dealing with dissatisfaction with pay systems represents a major administrative cost to organizations.

The source of the problem seems to be a contradiction between the *theory* of pay systems and the *reality* of pay practice. Managers in the United States (not so much in Europe and Japan) espouse the importance of paying for individual performance. Similarly, research has shown that employees are more satisfied with pay when it is based on performance.[4] With the exception of those who are unionized and perhaps those who work for the government, American employees seem to accept pay for performance as a basic principle which should govern the distribution of money. The belief in pay for performance is undoubtedly rooted in national culture, which stresses individualism. Yet there is considerable evidence that in many organizations pay is not based on performance. For example, a survey of *Fortune* 500 companies showed that 42 percent used no formal system for assessing the performance of professional and technical personnel, while 41 percent used single rate compensation systems for blue-collar workers so that wage increases could not be based on individual performance but only on general increases, job promotions, or on subjective performance judgments.[5] Without a formal appraisal system it is inevitable that employees would question the equity of pay decisions. Other surveys have indicated that at top management levels, company *size* (measured by sales volume) is the primary factor in determining the pay of the top executive and that pay differentials are then built downward to determine wages of lower-level executives. Corporate performance such as return on equity seems to have no relation to compensation rates for chief executive officers.[6] The gap between espoused beliefs of managers and employees and actual practices undoubtedly causes some of the general dissatisfaction with pay.

Even in firms with a pay-for-performance system, there seems to be a large gap between the promise of these systems and the reality of practice. The most sophisticated pay-for-performance systems designed specifically to motivate employees often end up with significant flaws. Either they do not motivate employees, or they bring about unanticipated and dysfunctional behavior. A frequent consequence of individual pay-for-performance systems is competition between employees when cooperation is desired. In other instances, the measure of performance is invalidated by changes in the firm's business environment. Sales volume may become less important and return on equity more important as a firm moves from an environment of market expansion and resource slack to one of fierce market share competition and scarce resources. In still other situations, the chosen performance criteria may be subjected to the influence of environmental forces beyond the individual's control, or the performance may be negatively affected by interdependence with other individuals and departments. Inflation may erode the value of a merit increase; or increases may be based on performance criteria that are never explained to subordinates.

Some well-designed pay systems simply fall prey to low trust between supervisors and employees or to inadequate communication skills by managers. Employees may discount or even resent merit or bonus awards if they do not believe in the fairness of decisions. The level of pay itself, or its equity with the labor market, may be questioned because employees do not know enough about how the organization has determined pay grades. The result is potential conflict betweeen human resource personnel who are attempting to enforce the pay system and line managers who want to pay salaries which they believe are appropriate.

The still strong support for individual pay-for-performance systems in the United States is based on more than the lingering belief on the part of managers and workers that pay should be based on individual performance. The potential of rewards for motivating behavior, substantiated by many examples where its absence has caused lower performance or its introduction has temporarily improved performance, provides the impetus for a continued search for better reward systems. The remainder of this chapter will discuss the theory of reward systems and a review of the problems. The final section will discuss the policy implications in the rewards area.

## THE THEORY OF PAY AND BEHAVIOR[7]

A body of experience, research, and theory has been developed about the way in which money satisfies and motivates employees. These theories seem to validate the general assumption of managers that money can be used to motivate employees, but they also suggest cautions, limitations, and contingencies that are often either forgotten or are difficult to implement in practice. Some of the problems described above are the result.

### *Pay Is Important to Individuals*

Virtually every study on the relative importance of pay to other potential rewards (extrinsic and intrinsic) has shown that pay *is* important: it is consistently ranked among the top five rewards. In fact, in more than one-third of 45 studies conducted, pay was ranked number one as a valued reward. An opinion polling organization, reviewing data from the past two decades, found that pay and benefits were ranked first or second in importance by employees in every job classification (see Table 5-1). Because it is so important, pay has power to influence people's membership behavior (where they go to work and whether they stay) and their performance.

However, the importance of pay and other rewards is affected by many factors. Money, for example, is likely to be viewed differently in early, middle and later career because needs for money versus other rewards (status, growth, security, etc.) are different in each stage. Another imporatnt factor is national culture. United States managers and employees apparently place much more emphasis on pay for individual performance than do their European counterparts. European and Japanese companies, on the other hand, rely more on slow promotions and seniority, as well as some degree of employment security. Even within a single culture, shifting national forces may alter people's needs for money versus other rewards. High inflation tends to encourage people to emphasize the importance of money, while periods of slow growth or unemployment place a greater premium on intrinsic rewards or employment security.

**TABLE 5-1 Top Five Work Values**

| RANK | MANAGERS | PROFESSIONALS | CLERICAL | HOURLY |
|---|---|---|---|---|
| 1 | Pay & benefits | Advancement | Pay & benefits | Pay & benefits |
| 2 | Advancement | Pay & benefits | Advancement | Security |
| 3 | Authority | Challenge | Supervision | Respect |
| 4 | Accomplishment | New skills | Respect | Supervision |
| 5 | Challenge | Supervision | Security | Advancement |

SOURCE: From William A. Schiemann, "Major Trends in Employee Attitudes Toward Compensation," in Schiemann (ed.), *Managing Human Resources/1983 and Beyond*. Printed with permission from *Managing Human Resources/1983 and Beyond*. Opinion Research Corporation, Princeton, NJ. © 1984.

*Rewards and Employee Satisfaction*

There are some general conclusions to be drawn about the relationship between rewards and employee satisfaction. Since dissatisfaction among employees can lead to turnover, absenteeism, and withholding of effort, organizations seek employee satisfaction to maintain or improve organizational effectiveness. But employee satisfaction with pay is not a simple matter. Rather, it is a function of a number of factors which organizations must learn to manage:

1. The individual's satisfaction with rewards is, in part, a function of *what is expected and how much is received.* Feelings of satisfaction or dissatisfaction arise when individuals compare the nature of their job skills, education, effort, and performance (input) with the mix of extrinsic and intrinsic rewards they receive (output).
2. Employee satisfaction is also affected by *comparisons with other people in similar jobs and organizations.* In effect employees compare their own input/output ratio with that of others. People vary considerably in how they weight various inputs in that comparison. There is a tendency to weight more heavily those things in which they excel, certain skills or a recent incident of effective performance.[8] Individuals also tend to overrate their own performance compared to that of their supervisors. For example, it has been found that many employees rate their performance in the eightieth percentile.[9] Given the fact that an organization cannot pay everyone at the eightieth percentile, it is not surprising that many employees feel they are being underpaid relative to others in the organization. The problem of unrealistic self-ratings exists in part because supervisors in most organizations do not communicate a candid evaluation of their subordinates' performance to them. Unless supervisors have exceptional communication skills, such candid communication to subordinates seriously risks damaging their self-esteem. The real dilemma is that failure to communicate a candid appraisal of performance makes it difficult for employees to develop a realistic view of their own performance, thus increasing the possibility of dissatisfaction with the pay they are receiving.
3. *The misperception of the rewards of others* is a major source of dissatisfaction. There is evidence that individuals tend to overestimate the pay of fellow workers doing similar jobs while underestimating their performance (a defense or self-esteem building mechanism). Misperceptions of rewards and the performance of others also occur because organizations do not generally make available accurate information about salaries or performance levels of their employees. Managers are understandably

reluctant to publish information on individual salaries and performance appraisals. Such information is likely to reveal some inequities in the pay system, and could also lead to dysfunctional competitiveness between employees. Nonetheless, it is not surprising that, given the known tendencies toward misperception, the lack of such information leads to the perception of inequities.

4. Finally, overall satisfaction is *the result of a mix of rewards*, rather than any single reward. The evidence seems to be clear that intrinsic rewards and extrinsic rewards are both important, and that they are not directly substitutable for each other. Employees who are paid well for repetitious, boring work will be dissatisfied with the lack of intrinsic rewards, just as employees paid poorly for interesting, challenging work may be dissatisfied with extrinsic rewards.

### *Pay and Membership Behavior*

Companies that give the most desirable rewards will be best able to attract and keep people, particularly the better employees. Substantial rewards lead to higher satisfaction, which is generally associated with lower turnover, though turnover is also a function of the labor market and the economy. It is for this reason that companies like IBM intentionally position their total compensation packages at the high end of the market range. High total compensation does not, however, ensure that the best employees are retained. To do this, a company must also pay its better performers more than it pays poorer performers; and the difference must be significant (recognizing that the significance of the difference is a subjective judgment on the part of individual employees).[10] A less than significant differential will result in feelings of inequity when better performers compare their input-output ratio with that of poorer performers. A well constructed and administered pay-for-performance system will then result in retention of better performers, and the turnover of the poorer performers—those the organization may want to lose despite the significant replacement costs incurred. An operational test of a company's success in doing this is to correlate individual employee satisfaction with performance ratings. A low correlation or a negative one indicates problems. The problem may be in the design of the pay plan; it may also be in the administration of that plan. Later in the chapter we will examine some of the problems that can occur in administering a pay-for-performance system.

### *Pay and Motivation*

From the organization's point of view, rewards are intended to *motivate* certain types of behavior. But under what conditions will rewards actually motivate employees? Important rewards must be perceived to be tied to effective performance in a timely fashion. In other words, individuals will behave in a way that will lead to rewards they value. Motivation depends on the situation and how it is perceived by employees, but the needs people do or do not possess will make them more or less susceptible to motivating situations. For example, individuals with a high need for achievement are more likely to be motivated by situations that provide them an opportunity to satisfy that need than individuals whose need for achievement is low. A person who has a high need for money or advancement will be more motivated to perform in a situation that provides monetary rewards or promotions than an individual who is low in these needs.

An expectancy theory model (Fig. 5–1) has been developed to suggest the conditions necessary for employee motivation:

1. Employees must believe that effective performance (or certain specified behavior) will lead to certain rewards: for example, at-

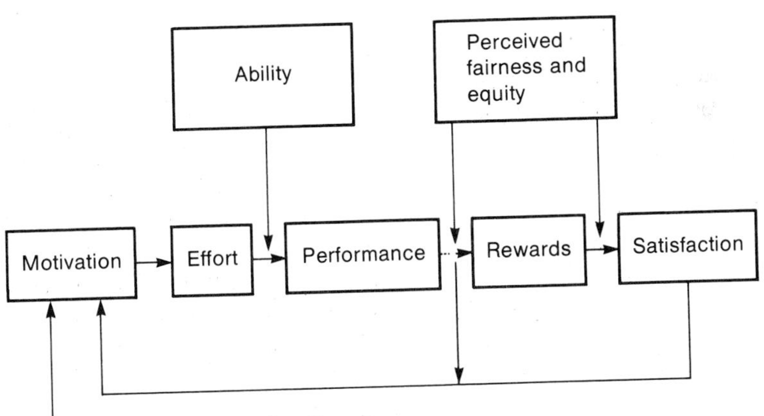


A person's motivation is a function of:

1. Effort to performance expectancies
2. Performance-to-reward expectancies
3. Perceived attractiveness of rewards

**FIGURE 5–1 The Expectancy Theory Model**

SOURCE: Adapted from Edward E. Lawler, *Pay and Organization Development*, ©1981, Addison-Wesley, Reading, Massachusetts. Pg. 21, Table 2.2. Reprinted with permission of Addison-Wesley.

taining certain results will lead to a bonus, or a certain performance will lead to approval or disapproval from peers or supervisors.

2. Employees must feel that the rewards offered are *attractive*. Not all rewards are equally attractive to all individuals because of differences in needs and perceptions. Some employees may desire promotions because they seek power while others may want a fringe benefit such as a pension because they are older and are concerned about retirement security.
3. Employees must believe that a certain level of individual effort will lead to achieving the corporation's *standards of performance*. Unless employees believe that their efforts can have a reasonable probability of affecting performance—e.g., the profit level of a factory or the introduction of a product—they see no reason to exert the effort.

The expectancy theory model's conditions for motivation are shown in Figure 5-1. The model suggests a highly instrumental view of motivation. Motivation to exert effort is triggered by the prospect of desired rewards: money, recognition, promotion, and the like. If effort leads to performance, and performance leads to desired rewards, the employee is satisfied and motivated to perform again. Motivation can be sustained over time only if successive experience in the organization leads the person to believe that this sequence is repeatable (that is, to *trust* the reward system), that his or her efforts can affect certain performance outcomes, and that the organization will reward these achievements. The dotted line between performance and rewards and the feedback loop to motivation are intended to show that motivation is a function of the performance-reward relationship.

It should be noted that the "ability" box between "effort" and "performance" is intended to indicate that performance is a function of ability as much as effort. Ability reflects not just the individual's skills and talents, but also the training and information provided by the organization. Effort thus combines with ability to produce a certain level of performance.

As we have already mentioned, rewards fall into two categories: extrinsic and intrinsic. *Extrinsic rewards* are provided by the organization in the form of money, perquisites, or promotions or from supervisors and co-workers in the form of recognition. *Intrinsic rewards* are those rewards which accrue from the performance of the task itself: satisfaction of accomplishment, sense of influence, sense of competence, or self-congratulation on a job well done. The process of work and the individual's response to it provide the intrinsic reward. But organizations seeking to increase intrinsic rewards must provide a work environment that allows these satisfactions to occur. This is why more organizations are redesigning work and delegating responsibility to enhance employee involvement. (We will discuss ways of enhancing intrinsic rewards and motivation in Chapter 6.)

In the expectancy model, satisfaction is a *result* of performance, not a cause of it as is often thought. Satisfaction does influence motivation indirectly, however, because satisfaction that follows rewards for performance strengthens the employee's belief in the linkage between effort, performance, and rewards. Satisfaction of certain needs can also heighten or reduce those needs. For example, the experience of promotion or achievement may heighten the need for further advancement and achievement. On the other hand, already having a lot of money could lessen the satisfaction derived from yet another incremental increase in pay.

The implications of the expectancy model for the use of pay as a motivator are not simple. The model could lead to the erroneous conclusion that an organization need only relate pay and other valued rewards to achievable levels of performance. First, this is not the only factor an organization needs to control in order to motivate employees. Management-worker relationships, the opportunity to develop, and a sense of contribution to meaningful goals are all very important ingredients in motivation. Second, the linkage between rewards and performance is a difficult one to achieve. It is not easy to develop good measures of performance, to communicate a performance evaluation to subordinates so they will accept it, to identify which rewards are important to employees, or to control the distribution of rewards so that better performers obtain more than poor performers. Yet all of these factors directly affect employee perception concerning the linkage between rewards and performance. Judging by a national survey of randomly selected individuals, a majority of workers fail to see a direct linkage in their organization: only 27.2 percent of those surveyed said they were likely to get a pay increase or bonus if they performed well.[11]

There are numerous reasons for the apparent difficulty organizations have in linking pay to performance. The lack of visibility of pay increases or bonuses makes it difficult for employees to judge if a relationship exists between these rewards and performance. Furthermore, there is the issue of trust and credibility. For individuals to exert effort in anticipation of rewards, they must believe that the rewards will follow. If the organization has not established trust and credibility that belief will be eroded.[12]

Finally, basic questions have been raised about the extent to which pay-for-performance systems reward for effort or reward for ability. If the organization has succeeded in hiring individuals with high need to achieve and contribute (a need that theorists such as Douglas McGregor argue is present in the majority of people), and it has provided a work environment that allows employees to contribute, then pay for performance is pay for ability. All employees are motivated, and the differential in performance is a function of innate ability and/or skill and competence obtained through training and experience. In this instance, pay-for-performance does not motivate; it merely rewards differentially for ability. This is not necessarily bad, but it changes the conception of what pay is doing. It creates an argument for training low performers in skills they need to perform. Such a policy is not likely to be established if the assumption is that motivation is the problem, and that pay for performance will motivate low performers. Therefore, it is important to diagnose correctly whether differential performance is a function of motivation or ability. If it is a function of the former, a pay-for-performance system may be called for if all conditions specified earlier can be met to make it workable. If low performance is a function of inadequate ability, a pay-for-performance system may still be warranted to pay equitably; however, improved selection or training will be needed to obtain better performance.

### *Rewards: Equity and Participation*

As previously noted, the motivational and satisfactional value of a reward system is a function of the perceived equity of the reward system. Without the perception of equity, trust in the reward system will be low and the contingent linkage between performance and pay will not be accepted. But the motivational and satisfactional value of a reward system is also a function of *who influences* and controls the design and administration of the new reward system. Even though there is considerable evidence that participation in decision making can lead to greater acceptance of decisions,[13] participation in the design and administration of reward systems is rare. Such participation is time consuming and thus costly. But probably a more important road block to participation in the design and administration of a reward system is that pay has been one of the last strongholds of managerial prerogatives. Concerned about the effect of self-interest on compensation system design and compensation costs, corporations do not typically allow employees to participate in pay system design or decisions. Thus, it is not possible to test thoroughly the effects of widespread participation on acceptance of and trust in reward systems.

Experience and research suggest that more participation in pay system design, is desired by employees and that such participation in a limited number of experiments, has generally led to higher satisfaction and acceptance.[14] The desire for participation is especially high when rewards are perceived to be inequitable. Collective bargaining is an outgrowth of dissatisfaction and perceptions of inequity in pay administration. By establishing their influence on pay system design and pay levels, workers feel more assured that they are equitably treated (leaving aside for the moment the problems that occur in large unions where workers are far removed from the bargaining process). Both union and management, particularly those parties directly involved in the negotiation process, are more likely to be committed to some degree to the reward decisions reached when they have participated in the process. Furthermore, survey data suggest that employees want more influence over pay raises than they get, though they do not want as much influence over these decisions as over how to carry out or schedule their work.[15] Finally, a limited number of studies that have examined the effects of participation in decisions about pay system design and pay raises have shown that employees' self-interest does not lead to irresponsible design or pay-level decisions. Later in this chapter we will return to the possible role that participation can play in solving reward system problems.

### *Summary of the Theory*

The discussion above suggests that pay is generally important to people, that it is related to satisfaction, and that satisfaction or the prospect of satisfaction with pay will influence people to come to work for a company and to stay with it. Pay can also be used to motivate job performance, provided certain conditions are met: employees must believe that acceptable levels of performance can result from their efforts and that important rewards will follow achievement of those performance levels. Both satisfaction and motivation can be eroded by perceptions of inequity in pay system administration. We now turn to a discussion of contemporary compensation practices.

## COMPENSATION SYSTEMS: THE DILEMMAS OF PRACTICE

Companies have developed a wide variety of compensation systems and practices in order to achieve employee pay satisfaction and employee motivation. These systems and practices have tried to take into account, in one way or another, the major factors affecting employee satisfaction and motivation which we discussed in the previous section. Company efforts to keep employees satisfied are reflected in decisions about where to peg the company's compensation with respect to the market; for example, at the fiftieth or seventy-fifth percentile. Those choices have an obvious impact on cost effectiveness. Thus, cost effectiveness and conflict over pay are inversely related. Satisfaction and potential motivation are also reflected in the mix of cash versus fringe benefits. The importance of equity is reflected in a choice of a job evaluation system to identify objectively contribution to the overall organization. Finally, decisions about whether pay should be tied to performance and how that linkage should be accomplished are critical to satisfaction and motivation. Choices such as those inevitably result in consequences for satisfaction, turnover, and motivation.

Experience with compensation systems and practices quickly leads to the conclusion that many of them are flawed in some major way, and generally cannot meet the conditions that research and theory specify are necessary for satisfaction and motivation to occur. One response to flawed compensation systems has been the design of new and presumably better systems. In some cases, this has led to some interesting alternative systems. In this section we will describe the major compensation system choices available to general managers and discuss the problems associated with each. Because many excellent full-length books have been written on the subject, we will not discuss the systems and techniques in depth here. Consistent with our belief that new systems typically hold out more promise in theory than in practice, we will suggest caution in relying primarily on compensation to achieve human resource goals. The traditional emphasis of managers and compensation specialists seems to be that if the right system can be developed, it will solve most problems. We do not think this is a plausible assumption—there is no single right answer or objective solution to what or how someone should be rewarded. What people will accept, be motivated by, or perceive as fair is highly subjective. Rewards are a matter of perceptions and values and it often generates conflict.

If system design is not the ultimate solution, then what is to be done? Communication of pay policies and their intent, participation in pay system design, and trust between management and workers are all key ingredients in making flawed compensation systems more effective. Communication, participation, and trust can have an important effect on people's perceptions of pay, the meaning they attach to a new pay system, and their response to that system. In short, *the process may be as important as the system*, and it should be taken into account when the system is designed and administered.

### *Management's Influence on Attitudes Toward Money*

Many organizations are caught up in a vicious cycle that, in part at least, is of their own making. Firms will often emphasize their compensation levels and their belief in individual pay for performance in recruitment and internal communications. In doing so they are likely to attract people with high needs for money and to heighten that need in those already employed. Money, which is already a symbol of status, power, and esteem in our society, will become even more so. That is because the significance employees attach to money is partly shaped by the manner in which management communicates about it. If merit increases, bonuses, stock options, and perquisites are held out as valued symbols of recognition and success, employees will come to see them in this light even more than they might have at first. Having heightened the importance of money as a reward, management must then be responsive to employees who may demand more money or more elaborate pay-for-performance systems. The development of such systems serves to further underline money as the measure of contribution, success, and worth.

There are understandable forces that push management in this direction. They may indeed believe that money is a very important motivator and yardstick. That belief may come out of their own experience or it may be absorbed from the ideology of the larger society. As we discussed in Chapter 2, that ideology in the United States (as compared with Europe and Japan) has placed great emphasis on individualism and free enterprise in which money plays a very important symbolic role. Furthermore, in some industries compensation plays an especially important role in attracting and keeping employees, thus "forcing" management into an emphasis on money.

Firms must start their thinking about the design and administration of a reward system by considering *a philosophy about rewards* and the role of pay in the mix of rewards. How should money be used? To recognize performance stimulated by other means? To provide direct incentives for performance? What other tools does the organization have at its disposal—tools that might, in fact, be less costly and less troublesome to administer—in order to achieve those outcomes? Unless these issues are addressed up front, the compensation practices which happen to be in place will continue to shape the expectations of employees, and those expectations will sustain the existing practices.

We are not suggesting that money is unimportant, only that its degree of importance and its centrality in the meaning people make out of their work experience is influenced by the type of compensation system and philosophy management adopts. Moreover, we believed that any given company can differentiate itself somewhat from the prevailing industry pattern with respect to the role of compensation in attracting and keeping employees. It can do this by attracting employees whose reward needs are compatible with the philosophy of the company or are subject to the influence of the company philosophy. Unfortunately, many general managers have not examined their assumptions about compensation or have not examined compensation systems for their fit with those assumptions.

*Fringe Benefits as Part of the Compensation Mix*

Though fringe benefits are part of the mix of almost every reward package, organizations differ in the percentage of total compensation costs allocated to cash versus fringe benefits. There are wide individual differences in the preference of people for cash and fringe benefits, depending on age and background. There are also differences in which fringe benefits individuals prefer. Thus, a standardized benefit package designed for all employees is likely to satisfy few individuals completely, so that overall satisfaction will be relatively low despite the high costs of such packages. Fringe benefits can be an inducement to motivate employees to join a company, though it is not clear how important minor differences between companies are. Fringe benefits do not, however, meet the criteria for motivating performance, since there is virtually no linkage between performance and the reward.

While fringe benefits may not be cost-effective, they are offered by all large companies and most small ones. Thus, they become a competitive tool for attracting prospective employees, making it difficult for any one company to make radical reductions in these benefits. Perhaps employees really prefer the security of fringes despite their espoused desire for higher pay for performance.

A typical fringe benefit package for employees might consist of one or more of the following items:

1. Extra pay for time worked on holidays, weekends, and shifts.
2. Nonproduction awards and bonuses such as safety awards, and Christmas and year-end bonuses.
3. Payments for time not worked such as sick days, vacations, and religious holidays.
4. Payment for employee health and security such as insurance, pension fund contributions, and payments and supplements to workman's compensations.
5. Perquisites for top executive such as bigger offices, reserved parking, and expense account arrangements.

As extensive as that list may seem, fringe benefit packages in the United States are far more limited than they are in other countries. Large companies in Japan, for instance, offer benefits that include subsidized food and vacations, company housing, and cost-free loans. (It is this dramatic variance in fringe benefit packages that often makes cross-national compensation comparisons difficult or misleading.)

The cost of fringe benefits in the United States has grown rapidly in recent years. In 1968 the fringe benefit package for an average organization amounted to about 21 percent of the total compensation cost. By the late 1970s, many companies were putting 40 percent of their compensation cost into fringe benefits. There are some estimates that the average organization could be spending 50 percent by 1985,[16] further reducing the compensation dollars available for motivation and forcing companies to find other rewards that will motivate—recognition, work itself, and so on.

A typical aspect of most fringe benefit packages is that the benefits offered differ for different groups of employees. These variations occur, however, not because of differing individual or group preferences, but rather because of hierarchical status within the organization. Thus, hourly workers often receive one benefit package, salaried workers another, and top management personnel still another. Since reward systems can serve as a visible statement about the organization's view of its employees, such differences in fringes reinforce the hierarchical notion of the work force. Companies that are experimenting with new forms of work organization, particularly those attempting to create an atmosphere of cooperation and shared responsibility, have occasionally tried to change this approach. By offering the same fringe benefit package to all their members, they have attempted to eliminate at least one symbol of inequality. At the same time, by eliminating one incentive for climbing the corporate ladder they must find other rewards to motivate employees to take more responsibility.

The possiblity that fringe benefits might be used to motivate employees within a certain organization has been eliminated in some countries by government legislation. In France, fringe benefits such as holidays, sick leave, medical care, retirement, and severance pay are legislated by the national government. The government has also moved to eliminate at least some of the differential in fringe benefit packages between blue-collar and white-collar workers.[17] While such legislation prevents an organization from using fringe benefits to attract people or motivate upward mobility, it does hold some advantages for the organization. Because fringe benefits can differ only slightly from company to company, organizations can turn to other, more flexible and *less* costly rewards to attract and keep employees. Of course with the rise of international competition, national differences in the cost of fringe benefits affect each country's ability to compete, requiring countries that legislate fringes to examine their costs in comparison to other countries.

Cafeteria-Style Benefit Packages. Typical fringe benefit packages are aimed toward a working man with a dependent wife and children, but by 1981 such employees constituted less than 15 percent of the work force. In 1974 one American company—the Systems Group of TRW Corporation—experimented with a way of increasing the cost effectiveness of fringe benefits as a satisfier. What they offered their 12,000 employees was a form of cafeteria-style fringe benefit planning. Employees were told how much the company would spend on them individually in fringe benefits. While all employees were required to take a minimum level of certain important benefits (there would be no such requirement under a pure cafeteria-style program), each was allowed to select individually from a list of remaining options until they had spent the total individual package cost. The year the plan was first introduced, over 80 percent of the employees indicated at least some dissatisfaction with their previous fringe benefit packages by asking for changes. Each year thereafter, the requirements became fewer and the options greater. More recently, the American Can Company moved to a cafeteria-style plan with similar results.

Such an approach obviously helps to individualize fringe benefits, thereby increasing congruence. The cafeteria approach, according to the management of TRW, has also increased the company's ability to retain people, an indication of increased *commitment* and resultant increase in *competence*.[18] It would appear that the cafeteria approach to fringe benefits is a more cost-effective approach to spending compensation dollars. It also creates certain problems. It requires additional bookkeeping for the salary administrators. In small companies particularly, it could create problems because the cost of many benefits (like health insurance) depends on participation by a certain number of people. In the two cases cited above, the problem of insurance rates has been dealt with by the requirement of a minimum core of fringe benefits. There are ways to manage the other problems raised by a cafeteria-style plan, and each organization must find appropriate methods to cope with the problems in order to obtain the potential for greater employee satisfaction and commitment.

### *Payroll Stratification: A One- or Two-Class Society?*

When an organization develops different fringe benefits, pay-for-performance rewards, and administrative procedures for different levels of the organization, it is sending a message to employees beyond the specific behavior these compensation systems are intended to reward. That message is that there are differences between hierarchical levels in their commitment, role, and the degree to which they are full and responsible members of the organization. In many organizations this is the case.

There are several understandable reasons for these differences. To get around the intended effects of progressive tax laws, corporations pay higher management levels in a different form than lower levels. Deferred compensation, stock options, and various perquisites protect executives from taxation that reduces the value of their reward. In the

United States, all organizations must make a distinction between *exempt employees* (those who, according to the wage and hour laws, have significant decision-making responsibility—typically managers and professional employees), and *nonexempt employees* (all other regular members of the organization—typically clerical white-collar and hourly blue-collar employees). Nonexempt employees are covered by federal law requiring that they receive overtime pay for a work week that exceeds 40 hours; exempt employees are, as the name implies, exempt from such legislative protections. Because of this legal requirement organizations must maintain records of time worked by nonexempt employees, which often results in the use of time clocks. Different payroll labels are given to these groups: salaried payroll for exempt employees and hourly payroll for production employees, creating a two-class language. It also means that a nonexempt employee cannot demonstrate spontaneous commitment to the organization by offering to stay after regular work hours. This can only be done within the law by negotiating overtime pay with the organization, a process that immediately sets the nonexempt employee apart from the exempt employee. Otherwise, this spontaneous commitment results in collusion between the employee and the company in breaking the law, something that happens quite frequently.

Federal law governing overtime pay for nonexempt employees was created in the 1930s to protect employees from exploitation by management. It can, and often does, have the unintended result of creating or reinforcing certain assumptions made by managers about their employees' commitment to the organization. It might also affect employees' perceptions of their role in the organizations and thereby alter their commitment. In a subtle way, a two-class society is created within the organization.

ALL-SALARIED SYSTEM. One way that some organizations have attempted to overcome this legislated division of the work force is through an all-salaried compensation system. Workers traditionally paid by the hour now join management in receiving a weekly or monthly salary (nonexempt employees are still paid on an hourly basis for overtime work). Such a system has been in effect in several large nonunion companies (such as IBM and Gillette) for decades. More recently, the United Auto Workers have encouraged America's Big Three automobile makers to consider it. While an all-salaried system cannot eliminate the legislated distinction between exempt and nonexempt employees, it can at least remove one symbolic, but nonetheless important, difference. Workers then join managers in having more flexibility. Time can be taken off from work with no loss in pay. Workers can be given more responsibility. Such treatment, in turn, can increase their commitment and loyalty to the organization. The fear that such flexibility will lead to greater absenteeism does not seem to have been established. However, there is no solid evidence that such a system in fact increases commitment.[19]

It is not surprising that the all-salaried payroll together with other approaches to standardizing the forms, but not the amount, of compensation cannot of themselves improve commitment. If accompanied by other efforts to create a more egalitarian atmosphere and increase commitment (see Chapter 6), the all-salaried payroll can reinforce these efforts. Just as we have seen overreliance by managers on pay-for-performance systems (which we will discuss later in this chapter), so we have seen a tendency to rely too much on a change to an all-salaried payroll as the means for improving commitment. Though it may be an important symbol needed to sustain changes in the employee influence and work system policy areas, an all-salaried payroll by itself cannot change a two-class company into a one-class company. Nevertheless, as part of an overall shift in corporate philosophy and style, this is a compensation system innovation that can play an important supporting role. Companies such as Hewlett-Packard, IBM, and participative nontraditional plants at Procter and Gamble, Dana, TRW, and Cummins Engine have successfully used the all-salaried payroll in this way.

### *Systems for Maintaining Equity*

In order to maintain employee satisfaction with pay, corporations have developed systems that are intended to maintain pay equity with internal- and external-comparison persons and groups.

The consequences of inequity in employee pay with respect to external labor markets are potentially severe for a corporation. One result might be an inability to attract and keep the talent required. However, the costs of maintaining pay equity are also high. If a company were to offer to meet all competitive wage offers obtainable by employees—the extreme form of maintaining external equity—employees would search for the highest paying job offers to convince management to increase their pay. This would result in a market system for determining compensation, much like the free agent system in sports, and would be a time-consuming and very expensive proposition for employers which could lead to internal inequities. It would also lead to a self-centered orientation toward career and pay, rather than a primary commitment to the organization and a secondary commitment to pay.

The potential consequences of internal pay inequity are employee dissatisfaction, withholding of effort, and lack of trust in the system.

Internal inequity can result in conflict within the organization which consumes the time and energy of managers and personnel people. However, maintaining high internal equity can result in overpaying some people compared to the market—a competitive cost disadvantage to the organization—and underpaying others, thus destroying external equity.

As we shall see, there is continual tension in an organization between concerns for external and internal equity. Line personnel are willing to sacrifice corporate internal equity (never equity within their departments) to attract and keep the talent they want for their own departments. The human resource personnel, who must maintain a corporate view, are placed in the position of opposing such efforts by line managers; they perceive efforts to pay whatever is needed to attract a candidate as a threat to internal equity. They insist on the integrity of the job evaluation and wage survey systems in order to avoid the costly conflicts that they fear will inevitably follow if a large number of exceptions to the job evaluation system are allowed. There is no solution to this dilemma; no new system will eliminate it. The balance must be continually managed to reduce problems and maintain a pay system that yields congruence and cost effectiveness.

JOB EVALUATION. In this country, the most common method of determining pay level is to assess the worth of a job to the organization through a system of job evaluation. About 75 percent of United States firms utilize some form of job evaluation. Simply put, job evaluations begin by *describing* the various jobs within an organization. Then jobs are *evaluated* for their worth to the company by taking into account a number of factors: working conditions, necessary technical knowledge, required managerial skills, and importance to the organization of the results for which the job incumbent is held accountable. A rating for each factor is made on a standard scale, and the total rating points can be used to *rank jobs hierarchically*. Once that is done, a *salary survey* is taken to learn what other organizations are paying for similarly rated jobs. A company must identify comparable jobs in other organizations. The salary survey, together with considerations such as legislation, job market conditions, and the organization's willingness to pay, lead to the establishment of *pay ranges* for jobs. (The tighter the labor market, the more closely wages will be tied to the going rate. In a loose labor market, the other factors will tend to dominate.) Jobs may then be grouped into a smaller number of classifications, with each assigned a salary range. The level of the individual employee within his or her particular range is determined by some combination of job performance, seniority, experience, or any other combination of factors selected by the organization.

Job evaluation plans in combination with wage surveys have been used in wage and salary administration for more than 50 years. They have proven a useful tool for maintaining internal and external equity. The basic premise of such plans is that the relative value of a job can be established objectively, even scientifically, by formulating a careful description of an individual job and then comparing it with other jobs or assessing the degree to which certain "job worth factors" are present. The assumption is that a system can be worked out for getting managers to describe jobs accurately. A factor rating system can be developed that will allow personnel analysts, presumably objective parties in the process, to rate jobs and rank them. Pay ranges can then be determined accurately by finding comparable jobs in other companies. It is generally assumed that an objective, scientifically determined system will help create employee trust in the ranking and pay range of jobs, thus insuring perceptions of internal equity. Unfortunately, this assumption is not entirely valid.

Fifty years of new and better job evaluation systems have not completely solved the internal and external equity problem. There are always unhappy people in organizations, both workers and managers, who claim inequity in the job evaluation system and attack the personnel department for its inadequacy. Given their current level of sophistication, it would seem that more refined job evaluation systems and better analysis by personnel departments or outside consultants will be able to offer only marginal improvements. "Employee perceptions of the process will ultimately determine its success or failure," Howard Risher has noted. If employees believe that salaries and salary grades are inequitable, the system has failed to achieve the primary objective: increased satisfaction with pay. Management might consider its evaluation system fair and valid, but employees tend to view their jobs somewhat differently from management or personnel specialists."[20] The misperceptions of self and others that we discussed earlier are the root cause.

There are several potential approaches to these problems. First, general management and personnel departments should *reduce their expectations* for solving the problem and claim less inherent validity for their job evaluation systems. This can significantly reduce the expectations of managers and workers. Secondly, *more participation* in the design and administration of job evaluation systems is required. A number of companies have set up job evaluation committees (some with hourly production employees as members) to agree on factors and to be involved in evaluating jobs, at least for "benchmark jobs." Involvement provides more understanding and acceptance of the system by the very managers who may argue for a higher salary for their departmental employees at the expense of internal equity. Broader involvement of employees at all levels, including unions, may help. Thirdly, a company could provide *more information* about pay grades and ranges and about the results of salary surveys, thus reducing misperceptions. Salary survey results are often not shared with employees. Finally, a representative committee of *employees might review* the evaluation system periodically and inform the employee population at large about their findings. These steps will not solve the problem, but they can help manage it.

Even if these steps are taken, no job evaluation system can solve the problem of salary inequities that inevitably occur when new employees are hired or experienced employees are brought in. To recruit successfully in the labor market, firms must offer competitive wages, and this sometimes creates inequities (salary compression) with the salaries of employees who have been with the firm for some time. This occurs because corporations typically do not raise the salaries of incumbents automatically when salary surveys result in an upward movement of the salary range. To do so would be very costly. Not doing so also allows the firms to keep the pay of poorer performers behind the market by denying merit increases. The compression problem is thus created by the desire to reduce costs and to discourage poor performers. It has been argued that companies should solve inequities due to compression by regularly raising wages for everyone when salary surveys so indicate and to manage poor performers through other means. Some companies ask supervisors to position their subordinates within their pay ranges according to performance. Over the years, larger increases are provided for good performers so they will be near the top of their range, while poor performers receive lower increases or no increases to keep them at the bottom of the range. We can see that conflicting objectives—keeping costs down and rewarding good performers—not the job evaluation system itself are the cause of inequity and dissatisfaction. Of these objectives, cost effectiveness is the critical factor that managers must consider, since performance can be rewarded and poor performance discouraged in other monetary and nonmonetary ways. They must decide if the cost of across-the-board increases is worth the benefits of more perceived internal and external equity. To solve the equity problems, general managers must clarify their philosophy and make choices between objectives of cost and equity, a process that is determined more by values and financial constraints than by systems.

Job evaluation systems have created other problems. Salary ranges associated with jobs limit the pay increases an individual can obtain. Thus, significant advancements in status and pay can only come through promotions. This need for promotion can cause technical people to seek promotions to management positions, even though their real skills and interests might be in technical work. If no promotions are available, individuals' needs for advancement and progress are frustrated. Additionally, job evaluation systems cause a certain loss of flexibility in transferring people within an organization. If that transfer is to a job with a lower pay grade, a fear of lower pay and status will reduce the individual's willingness to transfer. While companies usually "red circle" that individual's pay by making an exception and maintaining the individual's salary above the range of the new job, the perception of loss and the reality of actual pay loss over time make transfer difficult.

To solve the problems of job evaluation systems, some companies have come up with an alternative: a person- or skill-based evaluation system. These systems promise to solve the problems of inflexibility and limited growth, but they do not solve all the equity problems discussed above.

SKILL-BASED EVALUATIONS. Person- or skill-based evaluation systems base a person's salary on his or her abilities. Pay ranges are arranged in a hierarchy of steps from least skilled to most skilled. Employees come into the organization at an entry-level pay grade and move up the skill-based ladder after they have demonstrated competence at the next level. This system encourages the acquisition of new skills and should lead to higher pay for the most skilled individuals. Skill-based systems are generally thought to allow more flexibility in moving people from one job to another and introducing new technology. A skill-based compensation system can also change management's orientation. Instead of limiting assignments to be consistent with job level, the emphasis must shift to utilizing the available skills of people, since they are already being paid for those skills. Moreover, a skill-based evaluation system's greatest benefit is that it communicates to employees a concern for their development. This concern is consistent with the social capital perspective of human resource management discussed in Chapter 1, leading management to develop competence and utilize it, and resulting in greater employee well-being and organizational effectiveness.

Skill-based evaluation systems have been applied to technical personnel in R&D organizations, and are often called technical ladders. They could also be applied to other technical specialists such as lawyers, sales personnel, and accountants. Their use might encourage good specialists to stay in these roles rather than seek management jobs which pay more but for which they may not have talent. The organizations would thus avoid losing good technical specialists and gaining poor managers.

Skill-based pay systems have also been applied to production level employees in the past decade. Companies such as Procter & Gamble, General Motors, and Cummins Engine have introduced plans that pay for the skills that workers possess and utilize rather than for the jobs they hold. The benefits of flexibility and employee growth and satisfaction, which were mentioned earlier, have been experienced in these plants. But it is important to note that many of the plants have adopted skill-based systems to *support*, not *lead*, a change in management philosophy—one that emphasizes employee responsibility and involvement in work. Again, a compensation system is an essential support, but we wonder whether merely changing the compensation system will in fact foster flexibility and employee growth.

There are some problems to be considered in a skill-based approach, however. For one thing, many individual employees may, after several years, reach the top skill level and find themselves with no place to go. If nothing is done by the organization, there will be no pay incentive for employees to continue acquiring new skills. At this point, the organization might consider some type of profit-sharing scheme to encourage these employees to continue to seek ways of improving organizational effectiveness. A skills evaluation program also calls for a large investment by the organization in training, since pay increases depend upon the constant learning of new skills. Furthermore, the matter of external equity is more difficult to manage. Because each organization has its own unique configurations of jobs and skills, it is unlikely that individuals with similar skills can be found elsewhere, particularly in the same community, which is where production workers typically look for comparisons. This is less of a problem for professional employees whose jobs are more similar across companies. Because skill-based systems emphasize learning new tasks, employees may come to feel that their higher skills call for higher pay than the system provides, particularly when they compare their wages to workers in traditional jobs. Without effective comparisons, expectations could rise unchecked by a good reality test.

Since there are incentives for learning new jobs, it is conceivable that employees will want to progress to these jobs before they have mastered their current jobs. If this occurs widely, the organization will have many employees who are barely competent to perform their jobs and will never benefit from full mastery by long-term incumbents. If not managed skillfully, this problem will clearly reduce organizational effectiveness.

By far the most difficult problem facing a skills evaluation plan relates to its administration. In order to make the system work properly, attention must be paid to the skill level of each and every employee.

Some method must be devised *first* to determine how many and what new skills must be learned in order to receive a pay boost, and *second* to determine whether or not the individual employee has in fact mastered those new skills. The ease with which the first point is achieved depends on how measurable or quantifiable the necessary skills are. Identification of particular skills is more easily accomplished for lower-level positions than for top-management or professional positions.

Some companies have tried to meet the second point by asking co-workers to pass judgment on their colleagues. But there can be some pressure to award pay increments independent of actual skill acquisition. That pressure may come not only in the form of peer pressure, but also from the fear that an honest evaluation of a co-worker might affect negatively one's own evaluation by that co-worker. If that kind of pressure comes to dominate, then skills evaluation will quickly become a seniority-based system. The success of such an evaluation system depends on a number of factors: an overall organizational culture that encourages cooperation, mutual help as well as openness in peer evaluation, realistic self-appraisal for all members of the organization, and a shared commitment to the well-being of the organization.

Skill-based pay systems hold out some promise of improving competence in a cost-effective way and enhancing both organizational effectiveness and employee well-being. They are not right for all situations, however. Because they depend heavily on solving the problem of measuring and assessing skills or competencies, only an organization with the right climate of trust and an effective process of evaluation is likely to use the system successfully. Without the appropriate culture and process, even a new and innovative compensation system will not work. Moreover, skill-based compensation systems are only right for those organizations in which skill requirements are high and are undergoing constant change. They are also hard to introduce in existing organizations where a traditional job evaluation system already exists.

SENIORITY. It is also possible to base pay solely on seniority. Seniority has been accepted as a valid criterion for pay in some countries. Japanese companies, for instance, use seniority-based pay along with other factors such as slow promotion to help achieve a desired organizational culture.[21] In the United States, the major proponents of a seniority-based pay system tend to be trade unions. Distrustful of management, unions often feel that any pay-for-performance system will end up increasing paternalism, unfairness, and inequities. For those reasons, unions often prefer a strict seniority system. To many managers in the United States, however, seniority seems to run contrary to the country's individualistic ethos that maintains that individual effort and merit should be rewarded above all else. Therefore, most American companies prefer to make performance a major factor in their pay systems. The notion of pay for performance should be carefully scrutinized both for its advantages and its shortcomings.

### *Pay for Performance*

There are many good reasons why organizations should pay their employees for performance:

1. Under the right conditions, pay-for-performance can motivate desired behavior.
2. A pay-for-performance system can help attract and keep achievement-oriented individuals.
3. A pay-for-performance system can help to retain good performers by satisfying their needs and will discourage the poor performers. By not giving poor performers increases or by giving them only small increases, their pay relative to good performers and the labor market will decline.
4. In the United States at least, most employees, both managers and workers, prefer a pay-for-performance system, although white-collar workers are significantly more supportive of the notion than blue-collar workers. Therefore, a pay-for-performance system should lead to higher perceptions of equity and feelings of satisfaction.

For all these reasons, many organizations employ some type of pay-for-performance system for their employees, with unionized and government workers by and large excepted.

Despite the obvious benefits of pay-for-performance systems, there is plenty of evidence that they do not always achieve the motivation and satisfaction they promise. For example, far more management employees express a belief in some sort of pay-for-performance system than believe they are actually operating under a system that does pay for performance.[22] There is a gap, and the evidence indicates a wide gap, between the desire to devise a pay-for-performance system and the ability to make such a system work in practice.

PAY-FOR-PERFORMANCE SYSTEMS. There are numerous forms of pay-for-performance systems, and organizations can select one or more of them. The most important distinction between them is the level of aggregation at which performance is defined. Are we talking about individual performance, group performance, or organization-wide performance? Under each of these three broad categories, there are a number of possible options which are summarized in the chart below:

**Pay-for-Performance Systems**

| INDIVIDUAL PERFORMANCE | GROUP PERFORMANCE | ORGANIZATION-WIDE PERFORMANCE |
|---|---|---|
| Merit system | Productivity incentive | Profit sharing |
| Piece rate | Cost effectiveness | Productivity sharing (Scanlon plan) |
| Executive bonus | | |

Historically, pay-for-performance has meant pay for *individual* performance. Piece-rate incentive systems for production employees and merit salary increases or bonus plans for salaried employees have been the dominant means of paying for performance. In the last decade, there has been a dramatic decline in piece-rate incentive as managers have discovered that such systems result in dysfunctional behavior: low cooperation, artificial limits on production and resistance to changing standards. Similarly, more questions are being asked about individual bonus plans for executives, as top managers discover their dysfunctional effects. At the same time, organization-wide incentive systems are becoming more popular, particularly as managers are finding that productivity and innovation suffer due to lack of cooperation. In fact, one recent survey of large American companies found that nearly one-third are engaged in some type of organization-wide incentive plan.[23] However, for these plans to work, certain conditions must also exist. In this section we intend to review the key considerations when designing a pay-for-performance plan and the problems which arise when these considerations are not taken into account.

LEVEL OF AGGREGATION.[24] At what level should the pay-for-performance plan be aggregated: the individual, group, or organizational level? Organization-wide plans motivate cooperation, and teamwork can improve significantly. However, the individual is further removed from the level of performance being measured and rewarded. Consequently, the perceived connection between pay and performance is diminished. One of the reasons that individual pay-for-performance systems are so popular is that the linkage between individual effort and the performance being measured and rewarded is tighter. Organization-wide plans may be introduced to increase the perception of a linkage between individual effort and organization performance and to increase the incentive for cooperation. If the trade-off between individual and organization-wide pay-for-performance systems is recognized, managers can take action to minimize the dysfunctional effects of each plan. They can rely on other motivational methods (involvement in work, for example) when using organization-wide plans, or they can urge cooperation in nonmonetary ways when individual bonus plans are used. Alternatively, individual and organization-wide pay plans can be used simultaneously, communicating that both individual performance and cooperation are important. In our experience competition can arise when individual bonus plans are introduced without corresponding communication about cooperation, particularly if the bonuses are substantial. Similarly, organization-wide plans require effective supervision to maintain high individual performance.

NATURE OF THE TASK. The design of a pay-for-performance system requires an analysis of the task. Does the individual have *control over the performance* (results) that is to be measured? Is there a significant effort-to-performance relationship? For motivational reasons already discussed, such a relationship must exist. Unfortunately, many individual bonus, commission, or piece-rate incentive plans fall short of meeting this requirement. An individual may not have control over a performance result such as sales or profit because that result is affected by economic cycles or competitive forces beyond his or her control. Similarly, an individual may depend on other functions and employees to achieve performance outcomes like sales, cost savings, or profits. Sales volume, for example, may depend more on good products developed by the R&D function, or on advertising by the marketing function, than on individual sales ability. There are few outcomes in complex organizations that are not dependent on other functions or individuals, fewer still that are not subject to external factors.

So long as employees continue to receive bonus payouts, these interdependencies do not become an issue. When performance drops and payouts are reduced, employees begin to point to interdependencies and lack of control over results as flaws in the system. Commitment to the system and trust in it then drops, as does its capacity to motivate and satisfy. Similarly, if individual incentives are offered but cooperation between individuals is required, the seeds for potential conflict are planted. Individuals will blame others for their poor performance and lower pay when these occur.

In our experience, there are few jobs that meet the conditions of individual control and independence; therefore, few individual incentive plans do not fall prey to these problems. Interdependence with other functions or employees and lack of control over aggregate results such as profit lead managers to consider group or organization-wide pay-for-performance plans. These plans communicate to employees their dependence on others in achieving a result; say lower costs or profits. Problems with individual bonus systems also lead managers to introduce subjective judgments into performance ratings. Supervisors are expected to look not just at bottom-line results, but also to make judgments about behavior and to factor out poor results which were beyond the individual's control. This type of system eliminates the problems associated with result-based individual bonus plans, but introduces a new problem: the credibility of the subjective judgment.

MEASURE OF PERFORMANCE. Choosing an appropriate measure of performance on which to base pay is a related problem incurred by individual bonus plans. For reasons discussed above, effectiveness on a job can include many facets not captured by cost, units produced, or sales revenues. Failure to include all activities that are important for effectiveness can lead to dysfunctional consequences. Because pay is an effective motivator, singling out one measure of performance for financial reward leads employees to give that measure disproportionate attention at the expense of other facets of the job that may also affect short- and long-term performance. For example, sales personnel who receive a bonus for sales volume may push unneeded products, thus damaging long-term customer relations; or they may push an unprofitable mix of products just to increase volume. These same salespersons may also take orders and make commitments that cannot be met by manufacturing. Why not then hold salespeople responsible for profit, a more inclusive measure of performance? It should be clear that the problem with this measure is that sales personnel do not have control over profits.

These dilemmas are constantly encountered and have led to the use of more subjective but inclusive behavioral measures of performance. Why not observe if the salesperson or executive is performing all aspects of the job well? Most merit salary increases are based on subjective judgments, as are some individual bonus plans. Subjective evaluation systems, though they can be all inclusive if based on a thorough analysis of the job, require high levels of trust in management, good manager-subordinate relations, and high levels of interpersonal competence. Unfortunately, these conditions are also not fully met in many situations, though they can be developed if judged to be sufficiently important. Even objective measures of performance require some trust and good relations if a pay-for-performance system is to be perceived as fair and credible. Thus, management is well advised to give considerable attention to how to measure performance, or no pay-for-performance system will work.

A final measurement problem typically encountered with bonus plans is that they are often tied to performance measures that are appropriate for one type of business or economic condition—growth, for instance—but not another. When the business environment changes, managers no longer receive a payout even though their effort has been high. If, as often is the case, they have come to expect and rely upon that bonus, dissatisfaction occurs. Organizations often respond with some modification in their bonus system. The problem, however, results from a more fundamental flaw in the bonus plan: the performance outcomes measured were not a function of effort from the beginning. They were a function of external factors such as growth or decline. The lack of linkage between individual effort and results was not apparent or questioned so long as a payout occurred.

AMOUNT OF PAYOUT. For a pay-for-performance plan to motivate, the amount of the pay increase or bonus tied to good performance needs to be perceived as being *significant*. Significance is obviously a subjective matter that varies from individual to individual. Typically, merit salary increases range from 5 to 15 percent of salary. Since fringe benefits constitute about 40 percent of total compensation, a 5 or 10 percent increase in salary represents a small amount (about 3 to 6 percent) of total compensation, particularly after taxes. It has been argued that these amounts are much too small to have motivational impact,[25] particularly given the potential of pay-for-performance systems for damaging self-esteem. As we mentioned earlier, most people perceive themselves in the eightieth percentile with respect to performance and expect merit raises consistent with their self-perception.[26]

The importance of a large payout makes individual bonus plans based on results more attractive since they typically pay out a higher percentage of base salary. Unlike merit pay, bonuses do not become part of base pay the following year. Thus, unlike salary increases which become annuities, bonuses can result in a decline in the individual's pay. However, the attractiveness of delivering large bonuses based on performance is undercut by the problem of measuring performance.

It is more than likely that the amount of payout is also a function of whether the increase is publicized within the organization. If the payout is public, it affects reputation, status, and pride. Thus, the rewards of recognition and increased prestige are added to the monetary reward. If pay increases are kept private, the dollar amount must carry the motivational message alone. In this case, the monetary amount needs to be large. Most organizations do not publicize payouts for merit or bonus because employees do not want this information known. So the small amounts given in merit increases probably do not motivate. However, organizations might experiment with providing information about the average salary increase or bonus so that individuals can gauge the meaning of their own increase or bonus. Of course, this might lead employees to question their evaluations, putting more pressure on the evaluation system. Because of the necessity of justifying the equity of an open system, managers may hesitate to make discriminatory comparisons about employee performance. For that reason, management often opposes publicizing such information. Nevertheless, more information about the meaning of a pay increase, whether communicated by the supervisor or by general comparison information, is critical to making merit and bonus systems more effective.

Another reason merit salary increases have questionable motivational value is that the amount of the increase is judged by the employee against factors *unrelated* to performance: the rate of inflation, increases negotiated by a union, and the movement of salaries in the market. If salaries in the labor market go up 7 percent during a given year (due to inflation or other supply and demand forces) a 10 percent increase includes only a 3 percent merit increase, a rather small amount. Moreover, individuals often do not know what part of the increase is tied to merit, and organizations are reluctant to communicate this since the sum is insignificant. Without explicit knowledge, feedback is blurred and individuals may actually underestimate the merit component of the increase. It has been argued that organizations should separate salary adjustments from merit increases, providing yearly salary adjustments to everyone but giving merit increases only to a few high performers. Of course, this is more costly and prevents the organization from putting pressure on low performers by actually letting them lose ground relative to inflation.

To deal with the problem of payout amount in merit systems, some organizations have instituted the option of *lump sum salary increases*. Individuals may choose to receive their increase in one or two installments rather than having it buried in their paycheck over a whole year. The advantage is that the salary increase becomes more visible, has more motivational value, and the employee is given some choice.

Organization-wide pay-for-performance plans are not exempt from the problems of payout. Unless the amount received every month is significant, the pay itself has little motivational value (although, as will be discussed below, the *process* of administering such a plan may, in fact, be a motivating factor).

THE PAY-FOR-PERFORMANCE DILEMMA. The problems of pay-for-performance systems we have discussed have led some observers to suggest that these systems should be discontinued. The costs of dealing with many of the problems cited simply outweigh the limited motivational benefits they offer, according to these observers. Indeed, some organizations have done this. Digital Equipment Corporation, for example, does not use a bonus system to reward its salespeople, a group typically thought to put a high value on pay for performance. European and Japanese organizations use virtually no pay-for-performance systems, so they have to find other ways to motivate. Participation, involvement, and communication are used by the Japanese in place of individual pay for performance to motivate their employees.

Despite many potential problems, pay for performance remains popular in the United States. In order to maintain external equity so as to attract and keep high performance individuals, some organizations feel compelled to offer some sort of bonus or incentive regardless of their potential for motivating dysfunctional behavior. Still others insist that, despite all the potential dangers, it is proper and sensible to pay for performance. To pay on some basis other than performance risks overcompensating poor performers and undercompensating good performers, which in turn could lead to the loss of the very individuals the organization wants most to keep. That fact, plus the benefits of being forced to define what constitutes good performance, providing a realistic individual performance measurement, and encouraging exactly the kind of behavior the organization seeks are all advantages to the organization that are not to be given up lightly. The difficulties of implementing individual pay-for-performance plans are not easily overcome, however. This may account, in part at least, for a growing interest in some sort of organization-wide pay system.

### *Group and Organization-Wide Pay Plans*

Organizational effectiveness depends on employee cooperation much more frequently than is realized. An organization may elect to tie pay, or at least some portion of pay, only *indirectly* to individual performance. Seeking to foster team work, perhaps, or even organization-wide cooperation and commitment, a company may tie an incentive to some measure of group performance or it may offer some type of profit- or productivity-sharing plan for the whole plant or company. We will discuss only organization-wide pay plans since group plans are relatively rare and are subject to some of the disadvantages of individual plans, such as problems caused by interdependence between groups.

Gains-sharing plans have been used for years and there are many varieties. In many cases, they are simply economic incentive plans and are not part of a broader management philosophy regarding collaboration and participation. In these instances the plan may have some marginal value in encouraging cooperation among people. The real power of a gains-sharing plan comes when it is supported by a climate of participation and when various structures, systems, and processes involve employees in decisions that will improve the organization's performance and result in an organization-wide bonus. The Scanlon plan, for example, involves more than a bonus based on company-wide savings in costs. The plan also calls for the creation of management-labor committees and demands cooperation with workers and unions (if there are unions). The committees seek and review suggestions for reducing costs. Payout is based on improvements in the sales-to-cost ratio of the plant compared to some agreed-upon base period prior to the adoption of the plan. Organization-wide incentive plans that are part of a philosophy of participation require high levels of labor-management cooperation in design and administration (the Scanlon plan requires a direct employee vote with 75 percent approval before implementation). Without that joint participation, commitment to the system will be low, as will its symbolic and motivational value.

There are several critical decisions that influence the effectiveness of any gains-sharing plan.[27]

1. Who should participate in the design and administration of the plan and how much participation will be allowed by management and union?
2. What will be the size of the unit covered? Small units obviously offer easier identity with an organization's performance and the bonuses which result.
3. What standard will be used to judge performance? Employees (union) and management must agree on this for commitment to be high. There are inevitable disagreements.
4. How will the gains be divided? Who shares in the gains? What percentage of the gain goes to the company and what percentage to employees?

When management and employees have gone through a process of discussion and negotiation, allowing a consensus to emerge on these questions, a real change in management-employee and union relations can occur. A top-down process would not yield the same benefits. Gains sharing approached in a participative way can create a fundamental change in the psychological and economic ownership of the firm. Therein lies its primary motivational and satisfactional value. However, only a management that embraces values consistent with participation can make it work.

## IMPLICATIONS FOR THE DESIGN AND ADMINISTRATION OF COMPENSATION SYSTEMS

It should be clear to the reader that the theory of compensation is extremely difficult to translate into practice. A solution to one problem inevitably leads to another problem. What are the implications of these difficulties for the design and administration of compensation systems?

### *The Role of Compensation*

We do not believe that pay can or should be abandoned as a motivator. It is simply too important to people and has enormous symbolic value beyond its obvious material value. But we do believe that the role of pay in the enterprise needs to be rethought substantially so as to reduce some of its dysfunctional effects. Compensation should be used far *less* frequently as a leading policy area in human resource management, and should be thought of rather as a policy designed to support policies in the other HRM areas: employee influence, human resource flow, and work systems. For example, instead of rushing into the design of a new incentive system for production workers or executives, it might be wise first to discover whether employees are clear about goals, if they received information and feedback, if they have sufficient influence over getting jobs done, if there is adequate collaboration with other functions, and if there is adequate education and coaching to develop needed competencies. Lacking such an analysis, managers often install compensation systems without paying appropriate attention to what *they* must do as leaders to effect changes in employee behavior.

Compensation systems should be designed so that behavior and attitudes which are to follow from policy decisions in the other HRM areas are reinforced rather than contradicted. Money should be used to reward behavior stimulated by other policies, thus becoming primarily a means for recognizing performance and ensuring equity. The approach we are suggesting places much less burden on the compensation system to directly stimulate behavior and attitudes. Thus, pay typically needs to be *less tightly tied* to specific results or behavior, reducing the probability of dysfunctional behavior. Moreover, when compensation is not the leading variable in HRM, managers can be less ambitious in their claims of validity or equity for the system (claims that few systems can meet anyway), resulting in lower, more realistic expectations by employees. More realistic expectations by employees will mean less focus on compensation and less disappointment and dissatisfaction when experience shows these systems to be flawed.

We are arguing for less reliance on elegant compensation systems, particularly pay-for-performance systems, to satisfy and motivate and *more reliance on intrinsic rewards*. Compensation should be used less to initiate behavior and attitudes and more to reinforce behavior and attitudes which are stimulated by other means: involvement in work, identity with the company, and influence over the task. Of course, this approach demands greater management skill and competence. Some of the problems with compensation systems arise because managers do not want or cannot motivate other human beings through leadership and the development of a good work environment. All of this requires that general managers start by defining their *philosophy of rewards*, particularly with regard to the relative role of intrinsic rewards and compensation, but also with regard to where salaries should be pegged and what kind of pay for performance systems will be used.

### *Participation in Pay System Design and Administration*

Participation in pay system design and administration is a second major way in which the motivational power of compensation can be retained while reducing problems. High levels of participation by employees and unions in the design and administration of the compensation system undoubtedly result in a pay system that fits the needs of employees and the reality of the situation better than the top-down design of compensation systems. Even aside from experience with the Scanlon plan, there is evidence that employees can be involved in designing and administering compensation systems in a responsible manner. Donnelly Mirrors has employee job evaluation committees that rate jobs. Employees in other companies have designed pay-for-performance systems and conducted salary surveys. The result seems to be high satisfaction, effectiveness, and longevity for the compensation system when compared with identical pay-for-performance systems where employees were not involved.

Despite this evidence, pay systems are one of the last vestiges of traditional managerial values regarding authority. Managers protect their prerogatives in this area more closely than any other, believing that employee self-interest precludes participation. This view is understandable, particularly if levels of distrust and hostility are high, or if management, employees, and unions are not willing to take the enormous amounts of time needed to participate in reward system design and administration. We believe that if the conditions and process are right, participation can be a major tool for improving the design of pay systems. It can result in higher commitment of employees to pay systems and a corresponding reduction of dysfunctional behavior, particularly if employees continue to be involved and influence administration of the system. Equity problems can be reduced by such participation, but management must be willing to cede its unilateral power in these areas. One legal caveat is necessary in the case of nonexempt employees: when there is no union, employee influence must be limited to recommendations, since participation could constitute negotiation with nonunion employees, a possible unfair labor practice which could lead to automatic recognition of employees as a collective bargaining unit.

*Communication*

Pay systems can be made more effective by more and better communication about their intent. What behaviors and attitudes does management expect employees to exhibit, and how do these behaviors and attitudes support business goals? Too often, employees are left to interpret the meaning of the compensation system on their own. Communication about intent can prevent employees from overfocusing on certain goals or behaviors to the exclusion of others, a frequent by-product of pay-for-performance systems.

Open information about the pay system can also be an important factor in determining its effectiveness. For understandable reasons (employee desires for privacy and management's fear of opening up a Pandora's box of questions and challenges concerning equity), companies are hesitant to provide too much information about compensation systems. Not only are others' salaries, bonuses, and increases kept secret, but so is information about pay ranges and salary survey results. However, the natural tendency of people to misperceive both the pay of others and the value of their own contribution to the organization can actually reduce the power of these systems to satisfy and motivate. A closed system tends to undermine perceptions of equity; and equity, as we discussed earlier, is a critical ingredient if a reward system is to satisfy and motivate.

We do not suggest that all compensation systems should be totally open, or that moves toward openness can or should occur overnight. We do suggest that more openness is possible. Companies should strive to be as open as possible, consistent with their culture. That openness could extend at least to announcing information about the system: for example, pay ranges and the average merit increase or bonus awarded employees in a given year. Organizations that allow some degree of participation in the design and administration of reward systems will be sharing information about that system as a necessary by-product of the participation process. Corporate culture is critical to the development of openness, particularly managers' beliefs about the right of employees to challenge pay decisions.

Manager-subordinate relations and interpersonal competence in handling performance appraisal discussions are key to pay system success, particularly when the pay system is open. Unless these are effective, managers cannot help subordinates understand the meaning of pay decisions, leaving much room for misperception and ambiguity. Pay increases or bonuses under these circumstances simply do not work well and can create unexpected problems.

*Multiple Systems*

Since pay systems are limited in the messages they send, and since it is nearly impossible to predict precisely how the message of any single pay system will be interpreted by employees, managers should use multiple systems to avoid narrow, dysfunctional behavior aimed at increasing individual pay rather than at enhancing organizational effectiveness. An organization-wide incentive system may be used to encourage cooperation while an individual pay-for-performance system can be used to stimulate individual motivation. Some organizations accomplish both these objectives by stipulating that bonuses will not be paid until the total corporation's earnings reach a certain level. Similarly, a merit salary system can be anchored to a set of broad, inclusive behaviors thought to contribute to overall organizational effectiveness, while a bonus is paid on top of the salary for achieving certain clearly identifiable and measurable results. In this way, the bonus motivates the short-term performance, while the salary rewards behaviors required for success of the enterprise as a whole. Organizations can then manipulate the richness of the salary component versus the bonus in the total compensation package to avoid overemphasis on short-term performance versus behaviors thought to enhance long-term effectiveness. Another application of multiple systems would be to use a job evaluation plan for one group of employees where jobs can be clearly defined and segmented, while using a skill-based system where greater flexibility and growth is desired. Organizations should weigh the complexities and sometimes contradictions of multiple systems against the potential benefits to the organization of not having to put all their "eggs" in one pay system basket.

*Symbolism*

Managers should not lose sight of the fact that compensation systems, because of their importance to employees, are powerful symbols. They communicate, beyond their instrumental value, management's philosophy, attitudes and intent. For this reason, managers must examine the implicit meanings employees are likely to derive from a pay system, as well as its implicit messages. For example, what messages are sent to employees when different systems are designed for the top, middle, and bottom of the organization? What messages are sent when top management pays itself a bonus or goes off to a resort for a conference, while lower-level employees do not receive pay increases? A recent example of the symbolic importance of rewards was the announcement of a new executive bonus plan at General Motors on the same day that the United Auto Workers signed a wage concession agreement for their members. The symbolism of that announcement led to a degree of deterioration of trust between workers and top management. It also led to a decision by top management to rescind the executive bonus plan, a powerful reminder that even in the area of executive compensation employees have increasing influence if management requires their commitment. Unfortunately, the belief in the legitimacy of hierarchy in the United States is emphasized clearly in a symbolic way by the wide gap—a much wider gap than in Europe or Japan—between the amount and kind of rewards offered to top executives and to employees at lower levels.[28]

### *Loose Coupling*

The validity and viability of any given measure of business performance to which pay is tied has a limited lifetime. Business and business environments simply change too frequently. It is probably better, therefore, to tie pay to judgments of performance by others, while specifying clearly what the criteria for judgment are during any given year. Experience suggests that companies spend enormous amounts of time designing and redesigning pay systems because a given measure of performance to which they are tied becomes less relevant over time. Of course such an approach requires a high level of trust and probably a good deal of participation, a condition we have said is important for almost any type of pay system to be effective.

## SUMMARY

We began this chapter by stating that the rewards policy area presents the general manager with one of the more difficult HRM tasks. there are numerous dilemmas and contradictions inherent in the reward system area which make it difficult to design and administer with predictable outcomes. There is the question of how important intrinsic rewards are relative to pay and other extrinsic rewards. What should be the relative emphasis on these rewards, and what effect do policies regarding one set of rewards have on the other? There are questions about what systems are most effective for maintaining internal and external equity with respect to pay, and about how employee perceptions of equity and trust can be enhanced. We also raised numerous questions about-pay-for-performance systems, their efficacy and role in the enterprise. At the same time, we indicated that process may be as important as the design of the system when it comes to compensation. How much participation and communication went into design and administration of the pay systems? How does that amount fit with the culture of the organization? What message has the organization sent about how much influence, involvement and development employees will receive? There is an inevitable need for fit between reward systems and other policy areas. We concluded that reward system policies should, in most instances, follow rather than lead other human resource policies, unless, of course, participation in compensation system design is the guiding philosophy in the rewards area.

## NOTES

1. E. L. Deci, "Paying People Doesn't Always Work the Way You Expect It To," *Human Resource Management* 12 (Summer 1973), pp. 28–32.
2. R. Quinn and G. Staines, *The 1977 Quality of Employment Survey* (Ann Arbor, Mich.: Institute for Social Research, 1979); Edward E. Lawler, *Pay and Organization Development* (Reading, Mass.: Addison-Wesley, 1981).
3. William A. Schiemann, "Major Trends in Employee Attitudes Toward Compensation," in Schiemann (ed.), *Managing Human Resources: 1983 and Beyond* (Princeton, N.J.: Opinion Research Corporation, 1983).
4. Edward E. Lawler, *Pay and Organizational Effectiveness: A Psychological View* (New York: McGraw-Hill, 1971).
5. William J. Kearney, "Pay for Performance? Not Always," *Compensation Review* (1979), pp. 47–53.
6. *Fortune*, July 12, 1982, pp. 42–52.
7. The discussion in this section is based on the work of Edward Lawler, a leading theorist in the rewards area, particularly Lawler, "Reward Systems" in J. R. Hackman and J. L. Suttle (eds.), *Improving Life at Work: Behavioral Science Approaches to Organizational Change* (Santa Monica, Calif.: Goodyear Publishing, 1977), pp. 163–226 and Lawler, *Pay and Organization Development*.
8. Edward E. Lawler, "Managers' Attitudes Toward How Their Pay Is and Should Be Determined," *Journal of Applied Psychology* 50 (1966), pp. 273–279.
9. H. H. Meyer, "The Pay-for-Performance Dilemma," *Organizational Dynamics* 3 (1975), pp. 39–50.
10. L. W. Porter and Edward E. Lawler, *Attitudes and Performance* (Homewood, Ill.: Richard D. Irwin, 1968).
11. Quinn and Staines, *The 1977 Quality of Employment Survey*.
12. Meyer, "The Pay-for-Performance Dilemma."
13. V. H. Vroom and P. W. Yetton, *Leadership and Decision Making* (Pittsburgh: University of Pittsburgh Press, 1973).

14. Lawler, "Reward Systems."
15. P. A. Renwick and Edward E. Lawler, "What You Really Want from Your Job," *Psychology Today* 12 (1978), pp. 53–66.
16. Some of the technical data in this chapter comes from D. W. Belcher, *Compensation Administration* (Englewood Cliffs, N.J.: Prentice-Hall, 1974).
17. Thomas Kennedy, *European Labor Relations* (Lexington, Mass.: Lexington Books, 1980), pp. 52–57.
18. Lawler, *Pay and Organization Development*.
19. See R. D. Hume and R. V. Bevan, "The Blue Collar Worker Goes on Salary," *Harvard Business Review* 53 (1975), pp. 104–112; Lawler, *Pay and Organization Development*, pp. 62–64; and J. H. Sheridan, "Should Your Production Workers Be Salaried?" *Industry Week* 184 (1975), pp. 28–37.
20. Howard Risher, "Job Evaluation: Mystical or Statistical?" *Personnel* (Sept.-Oct. 1978), pp. 23–36.
21. Marsland and Beer, "Note on Japanese Management and Employment Systems."
22. Lawler, "Managers' Attitudes Toward How Their Pay Is and Should Be Determined."
23. *People and Productivity: A Challenge to Corporate America* (New York: New York Stock Exchange Office of Economic Research, 1982).
24. This discussion is based on Lawler, *Pay and Organization Development*.
25. Meyer, "The Pay for Performance Dilemma."
26. Meyer, "The Pay for Performance Dilemma."
27. Adapted from Lawler, *Pay and Organization Development*, pp. 134–140.
28. David Kraus, "Executive Pay: Ripe for Reform?" *Harvard Business Review*, September–October 1980, pp. 36–48.
29. Marsland and Beer, "Note on Japanese Management and Employment Systems."

CASE 17

# ALCON LABORATORIES, INC. (Condensed)

*Paul H. Thompson*

In the summer of 1966 George Leone, national sales manager of Alcon Laboratories, initiated an appraisal of the organization and morale of his 70-member sales force. Leone expressed particular concern over the high turnover in the sales force (28 percent in the fiscal year 1965–1966). He had considered a number of changes that might reduce the turnover but was unsure as to just what action he should take. While he was willing to make any changes that might improve the situation, he felt it would be better to do nothing than to attempt changes that were inappropriate to the needs of his organization.

## COMPANY HISTORY

In Fort Worth, Texas, two pharmacists founded Alcon Laboratories in 1947 on the principle that more accurate, sterile, and stable pharmaceutical compounds could be manufactured by Alcon on a large-scale basis than was possible in retail drug stores, where most prescribed drugs were being compounded at that time.

In early years Alcon management decided to achieve growth by concentrating its marketing efforts in specialty fields. The field in which Alcon first specialized was ophthalmological drugs (drugs used in the treatment of defects of the eye). In 1947, 85 percent of all eye-care drugs were being compounded in drug stores.

As doctors became familiar with the company's products and their quality, they prescribed them more and more, and Alcon prospered. By 1957 a sales force of 30 people was promoting the company's eye-care products nationally, and sales had grown to nearly $1 million.

Alcon Laboratories continued to grow both domestically and internationally. In fiscal 1966 total sales were $9.1 million. Domestic sales of 33 products were about $6 million and were promoted by a 70-member sales force. In addition, by purchasing another small specialized pharmaceutical firm, Alcon entered a second specialty field. Further-

---

This case was condensed by Joseph Seher and John P. Kotter.

**TABLE 17-1 Highlights of Operating and Financial Data ($ thousands except E.P.S. and current ratio)**

| | 1966 | 1965 | 1964 | 1963 | 1962 | 1961 | 1960 | 1959 | 1958 |
|---|---|---|---|---|---|---|---|---|---|
| E.P.S. | 1.30 | 1.05 | 1.20 | 0.86 | 0.66 | 0.50 | 0.40 | 0.30 | 0.13 |
| Current ratio | 3.24 | 3.06 | 2.39 | 1.96 | 1.87 | 1.31 | 2.25 | 2.03 | 2.02 |
| Net sales | 9,114 | 8,749 | 8,697 | 7,718 | 6,392 | 3,057 | 3,094 | 2,035 | 1,347 |
| Net income | 821 | 663 | 750 | 534 | 404 | 268 | 215 | 163 | 69 |
| Working capital | 3,262 | 2,448 | 1,846 | 1,065 | 734 | 186 | 532 | 381 | 169 |
| Total assets | 7,016 | 6,007 | 5,426 | 4,413 | 3,648 | 2,606 | 1,810 | 1,478 | 545 |

**TABLE 17–2 Income Statement ($ thousands)**

| | Year Ended April 30, 1966 |
|---|---|
| Net sales | 9,114 |
| Costs and expenses | |
| Costs of goods sold | 3,129 |
| Selling, general, and administrative expenses[a] | 4,411 |
| Total cost and expenses | 7,540 |
| Income before provision for federal taxes | 1,574 |
| Provision for federal income taxes | 753 |
| Net income | 821 |

[a]R&D represented a significant portion of general and administrative expenses.

more, the company had achieved some backward integration by purchasing a manufacturer of plastic containers for pharmaceutical products. Alcon manufactured and sold its product line internationally through foreign subsidiaries and joint agreements. Table 17–1 shows selected historical operating and financial information for the period 1958–1966. Table 17–2 gives the consolidated income statement for 1966.

## ALCON'S EYE-CARE PRODUCTS—USE AND DISTRIBUTION

Alcon manufactured products for a wide array of eye problems, ranging from treatments for serious eye diseases to less serious infections and cleansing agents. Similarly, Alcon sold products used in diagnostics and for surgical assists. These products were available either directly or through wholesalers, both to hospitals and to retail drug stores. Ninety percent of total sales were prescribed by one of the 6,000 ophthalmologists (medical doctors specializing in the treatment of eye diseases and defects) or by one of 2,000 eye-ear-nose-throat doctors who practiced in the United States. Alcon salespeople regularly visited these doctors.

## THE MARKET AND COMPETITION

In 1965 total retail sales of ophthalmological drugs in the United States were $30 million. Alcon Laboratories' share of the total domestic ophthalmological drug market was nearly 20 percent. Small, specialized manufacturers like Alcon, which attempted to find a niche in the total market by catering specifically to the ophthalmic market, competed directly with Alcon. The company also competed with large, diversified drug manufacturers for whom certain segments of the ophthalmic market were large and lucrative enough to warrant attention. Alcon management stated that in 1966 two large drug manufacturing firms controlled about 30 percent of the domestic ophthalmic market.

The active chemical compounds used in various ophthalmological preparations were essentially the same, regardless of manufacturer. Competing products were differentiated primarily on the basis of their form[1] and vehicle.[2] Competing manufacturers were constantly looking for new preparations that would have performance superior to existing ones. While Alcon was interested in developing compounds of active ingredients, the major thrust of its research was to improve the performance of existing compounds by developing better or new forms and vehicles.

## MARKETING DEPARTMENT

### *Organization*

The marketing department of Alcon Laboratories was under the direction of the marketing director, who was also a vice president of Alcon and a member of the company's executive management group. Ed Schollmaier, who currently held this position, was 32 years old and had risen rapidly at Alcon. After receiving his MBA at the Harvard Business School in 1958, he had started as a salesman with Alcon and in a short time he had been promoted to district sales manager. After less than two years with Alcon, he had been called into the home office to assist in directing the sales effort. In 1963 he was appointed director of marketing. Reporting to Schollmaier were the national sales manager, product managers (marketing responsibility other than direct sales), and the director of market research.

The primary responsibility of the marketing department was to assure the success of the sales effort. The home office was responsible for the design of the sales program, while the field sales organization was responsible for the program's execution. A great deal of time and effort were typically spent on both areas. According to a 1965 study, drug

[1]*Form* referred to whether the compounds came in solution, ointment, cream, pill, and so forth.

[2]The *vehicle* comprised the inactive ingredients that were important in determining such product qualities as the stability of the product, how well the product stayed in the eyes (instead of "sweating out"), the irritation and/or side effects of the product, and so forth.

and pharmaceutical firms' selling costs were twice those of U.S. industry as a whole. The survey showed that in 1964 the cost of selling pharmaceuticals amounted to 30.5 percent of gross sales revenue. This study included as selling costs such items as seminars held for doctors to acquaint them with new drugs, and samples sent out as part of a product's introductory stage. Other industries did not have such expenses to the degree that the drug industry had, and some companies included similar costs in R&D for accounting purposes. Another factor to consider in comparing drug industry costs with those of other industries was that most consumer goods manufacturers shared costs of advertising with retailers; drug companies, on the other hand, bore most of these costs alone. In addition, allowances for returned merchandise were higher in the drug industry, since companies regularly took back unopened stock that was out of date. The study presented the following breakdown of total selling costs (see Table 17-3). Between 1961 and 1966 Alcon's total annual expenses for advertising, merchandising, and promotion increased from $90,000 to $750,000.

The central activity of the marketing department was the planning of promotion programs, a joint responsibility of the product managers and the national sales manager. Prior to the beginning of each fiscal year, the product managers would meet with George Leone, the national sales manager. This group would draw up a list of the particular products to be promoted in the coming year, on the basis of the size of the total promotion budget, the length of time since a product had been actively promoted, Leone's estimate of market potential, the current share of market held by the products involved, and competitive activity. Products on the list were then assigned specific dates for promotion. This promotion schedule was then approved by the marketing director.

**TABLE 17-3 Total Selling Costs**

| | Drug Industry (%) | Average (All Industries) (%) |
|---|---|---|
| Sales force | | |
| Compensation | 37.3 | 45.2 |
| Travel and other expenses | 13.6 | 12.8 |
| Sales management costs | 14.0 | 16.2 |
| Advertising, merchandising, and promotion | 29.9 | 14.2 |
| Servicing | 3.0 | 7.4 |
| All other costs | 2.2 | 4.2 |
| Total | 100.0 | 100.0 |

The promotional campaign was developed by the product managers, who first consulted with the national sales manager for his ideas on market positioning. After the campaign had been designed, the national sales manager and his subordinates taught the sales force how to carry it out. To provide the sales force with the information that was desired by doctors, the marketing department needed the aid of the medical department and research department.

The medical department was responsible for professional contact with members of the medical profession. Through a clinical liaison group the medical department engaged physicians doing clinical research to conduct studies to test the uses or find new uses for Alcon's products. These findings were frequently used in the form of professional articles, technical bulletins, or promotional campaigns. It was not uncommon for a member of the marketing department to ask the medical department to help in developing some technical data to support particular claims for a product.

Alcon's R&D department was also important to the marketing effort. The development of new chemical compounds, new uses of existing compounds, and improvements in existing compounds, were all considered to be of prime importance. Introducing new and improved drug preparations was considered to be one of the most effective ways to increase sales and enhance the company's reputation in the medical community. Sales of various ophthalmological preparations tended to be more stable than the sales of the pharmaceutical preparations in general, which were characterized by extreme volatility due to the frequent introduction of new chemical compounds that made existing compounds, in all types of forms and vehicles, obsolete. Alcon management stated, however, that "the impact of new products (i.e., new formulations of existing ophthalmological compounds) since 1960 accounted for more than half of Alcon's growth, and half of that growth was attributable to innovations in the steroid product category in particular."

The mutual interests of the marketing, medical, and R&D departments were coordinated through meetings of the product committee whose members included Ed Schollmaier, marketing vice president; Dr. Earl Maxwell, medical director and director of R&D; Frank Buhler, director of international operations; and William Conner, chairman of the board and president. For example, through the product committee the time and resources of the R&D department might be allocated to fill gaps in the product line, as determined by sales management and product managers. The need for providing technical data from the medical department was also coordinated through the product committee.

*National Sales Manager*

George Leone headed the 70-member sales force in 1966. He had been with Alcon since 1950, when there were only six salespeople in the company. After doing an outstanding job as a salesman, he was made a district sales manager in 1955, a regional sales manager in 1961, and national sales manager in 1963.

As national sales manager, Leone was responsible for the overall administration and performance of the sales force and for coordinating the activities of the sales force with other groups in the marketing department. In his administrative capacity, Leone was primarily concerned with the establishment of company programs in the areas of recruitment and selection, training and development, supervision, standards of performance appraisal, and compensation and benefits. He was also responsible for identifying and developing field sales managers.

Leone directed three groups of personnel: regional managers, district sales managers, and medical sales representatives. The latter were more commonly known within the industry as salespeople, and were frequently identified by physicians as "detail men." Figure 17-1 shows a chart of the sales organization.

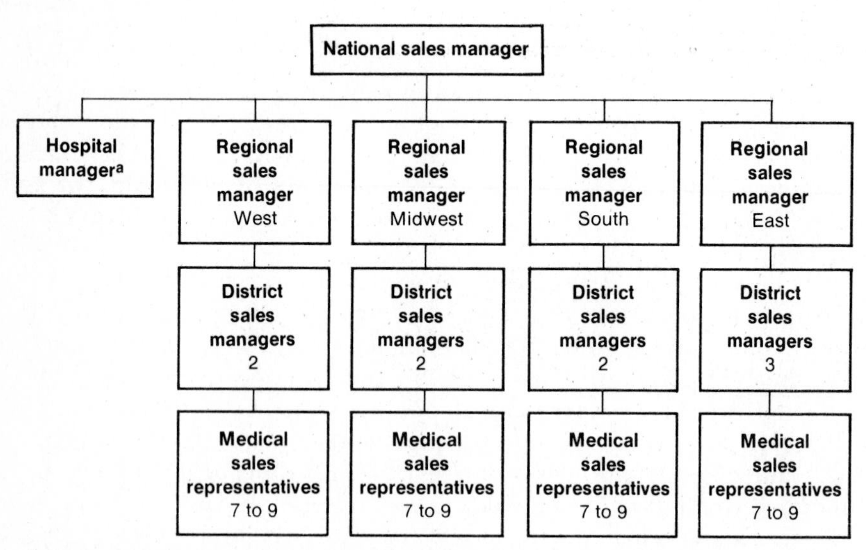


[a]From 1963 to mid-1965 only; dropped in 1965 because of the overlap between calls on doctors when they were at the hospital and when they were at their private office.

**FIGURE 17-1 Sales Group Organization Chart**

### *Regional Sales Managers*

Alcon divided the United States into four large sales regions, each supervised by a regional sales manager. The job description in the company's supervisory manual listed five major functions for the regional sales manager (RSM):

1. Recruitment and selection of candidates for field sales work (medical service representatives) with special emphasis on applicants with management potential.
2. Training and developing the district managers.
3. Supervising, directing, and controlling the activities of the district sales managers.
4. Maintaining communications with the home office through weekly reports and with the sales force through quarterly regional sales meetings.
5. Planning and organizing to help set the objectives for the region and to help the district sales managers set their goals.

The job description stated that RSMs should spend a minimum of 35 percent of their time in personal field visits with their district sales managers. They had no direct customer responsibilities.

Three of the four regional sales managers worked in the home office and spent a good deal of their time working with Leone in planning the national sales effort. They were involved in sales promotion, planning, meetings, and developing company policies and procedures for recruiting, selection, training, and supervision of the sales force. The fourth RSM was in the process of moving from Chicago to the home office.

### *District Sales Managers*

Reporting to each of the four regional sales managers were two to three district sales managers (DSMs). An Alcon district was a subdivision of a region (e.g., the New England states constituted one district of Alcon's eastern region). The district sales manager's job description listed five major duties:

1. Recruiting, selecting, and with approval from RSM, hiring salespeople to become medical sales representatives.
2. Training and developing the field sales force.
3. Supervising, directing, and controlling the activities of the field sales force.
4. Maintaining communications with home office and with RSM, and conducting quarterly district sales meetings.

5. Planning and organizing operation of districts through setting objectives for field salespeople.

The job description further stated that the DSM should allocate his or her time as follows: "a minimum of 75 percent of his time in personal field visits with the medical sales representatives, and the remainder [25 percent] at medical meetings, sales meetings, and visits with regional sales manager." The DSMs, like the RSMs, had no direct customer responsibilities.

### *Sales Force*

Reporting to each of the nine district sales managers were seven to nine medical sales representatives (MSRs). These 70 salespeople were responsible for Alcon's direct customer contacts. Each MSR covered one Alcon territory. The medical sales representatives' job description listed six major duties:

1. Call on each of the following:
   a. All eye physicians within territory
   b. All pharmacies on call list
   c. All hospitals on call list
   d. All wholesalers on call list
2. Follow the sales program including using all sales tools outlined by the program.
3. All MSRs must fulfill their performance standards and objectives each month in the following areas:
   a. Doctor call standards (1a above)
   b. Retail call standards (1b above)
   c. Wholesale call standards (1d above)
   d. Increase sales objective (the DSM and MSR together set a specific objective as to how much sales will increase in the current year over the previous year).
   e. Ration of increased sales to sales cost; for example:

| | 1966 | 1965 |
|---|---|---|
| $\frac{\text{Total territory sales}}{\text{Total territory costs}}$ | $\frac{\$100,000}{12,000} = \frac{8}{1}$ | $\frac{\$120,000}{20,000} = \frac{6}{1}$ |

   f. Featured product (the one being promoted or detailed) objective.
   g. Turnover order objective.[3]

[3]Turnover orders were those that the drug salespeople wrote for the drug retailer and hand-carried or mailed to the drug wholesaler to be filled.

4. Planning and organizing territory coverage by maintaining territory coverage plan and territory records.
5. Maintaining communications with supervisor and the home office by submitting the required daily, weekly, and monthly reports.
6. Meeting standards of self-development by attaining an adequate product knowledge, and knowing and complying with company policies on appearance, conduct, and maintaining company property.

Top management described the sales force's activities as falling into two distinct categories: *creating demand* (when the MSR is in the doctor's office, trying to get the doctor to prescribe Alcon's products), and *distribution* (supporting demand by getting the product to the wholesaler and retailer).

## SELLING IN THE DRUG INDUSTRY

Salespeople in the drug industry as a whole made an average of 48 calls per week. A typical day for a member of Alcon's sales force started by driving 50 miles to a city to make calls, waiting up to 30 minutes to see a doctor, actually seeing only five of the nine doctors called on, and spending only about 5 minutes with each doctor because of busy schedules. In a normal day, the sales representative also called on one drug wholesaler and three drug retailers, spending only about 15 minutes with each.

Alcon salespeople typically saw their DSM only once a month, but maintained weekly contact by telephone. Alcon salespeople generally saw each other only at their bimonthly sales meetings. Although they had infrequent contact with other Alcon salespeople, the typical MSR had the opportunity for more frequent contact with other companies' salespeople detailing the same area.

### *The Doctor Call*

Alcon, as well as other drug companies, considered "detailing" the doctor as one of the best ways to create demand for both new and existing products, thus salespeople called on eye doctors once a month. On a typical visit to an eye specialist, the Alcon MSR was expected to detail one primary product, one secondary product, and one "door-handle" product (one that was just mentioned on the way out). Any one product was usually detailed for three consecutive months, though some were detailed for only one month, while others were detailed for as long as seven consecutive months.

The MSR was supposed to discuss with the doctor whether he now used the product being detailed, or would use it in the near future. Because doctors were so busy, the salespeople had only a brief period to make their presentations. One doctor commented: "The detail men have to see you at your office. I'm very busy there, so it is hard to find time to see them. I can only give them five to ten minutes and that is time away from seeing my patients." Alcon's management hoped that the MSR's brief presentation would make a lasting impression on the doctor. Journal advertising and direct mail promotions from Alcon were timed to support the salespeople's message to the doctor.

### *The Retailer Call*

The Alcon sales force also called on retail druggists. There were 55,000 drugstores in the United States, but according to Alcon management the Alcon sales force called only on the 10 percent that did the most business in ophthalmological drugs. In the course of calls on retail druggists, salespeople would make it known which product(s) were being detailed in the area and thus which drug(s) doctors would probably be prescribing. If Alcon had any promotional deals on over-the-counter items (usually an offer of free goods with each purchase, e.g., 1 free item with each 12 purchased), the MSR would bring these to the druggist's attention. During the call, the MSR checked the druggist's stock of Alcon products and indicated which areas the druggist should replenish. The MSR attempted to persuade the druggist to stock at least one bottle of all Alcon products and several bottles of the fast-moving items. The MSR would write up the order and mail it or take it to the druggist's wholesaler.

### *The Wholesaler Call*

To obtain adequate distribution of a product, it was also important to call on drug wholesalers. The average Alcon territory contained six drug wholesalers who served as intermediaries between drug manufacturers and drug retailers. Wholesalers maintained sales staffs on their own by which they contacted many more retail druggists than Alcon's MSRs were able to see. A wholesaler's sales force would make calls on each retail druggist once a week and would have daily contact with each druggist by telephone. Thus wholesalers, once sold on Alcon products, could shoulder a considerable part of the sales effort.

When a new product was being introduced, or when an existing product was being promoted, the Alcon MSR was expected to call on each wholesaler to gain support for the product(s) in question. The purpose of this effort was to persuade the wholesaler's sales manager to use his or her sales force to give special attention to Alcon's product. The Alcon MSR was supposed to show the sales manager the detail piece on the product, along with any available literature. While at the wholesaler's, the MSR also attempted to see the buyer or purchasing agent to insure that a six to eight weeks' supply of Alcon's products was maintained.

The casewriter observed that few Alcon salespeople were able to execute promotion of new products. The buyer and sales manager of the wholesaler saw about 100 drug salespeople per week and were pressed for time.

### *The Call Mix*

Alcon's management explained that the same MSR called on the doctor, the retailer, and the wholesaler because the calls were highly related and needed careful coordination. For instance, since no order was written in the doctor's office, the MSR would not know if the doctor would actually prescribe the detailed product or not. One of the best ways to find out was to call on the pharmacist a few days after detailing the doctor and inquire whether Dr. X was prescribing the product in question. If the MSR had established a good relationship with the pharmacist, the pharmacist would, in all likelihood, tell the MSR. In fact, the pharmacist often went so far as to let the salesperson check through the pharmacy's prescription file to see what all of the doctors were prescribing. With this type of information, the MSR knew which products were selling well and which products should be discussed with a doctor on the next visit.

In addition, Alcon managers emphasized that distribution and demand creation had to be closely coordinated. By handling all three types of calls, the sales force could assure the doctors that the pharmacists had the drug they prescribed in stock, and they could assure pharmacists that doctors would prescribe the drugs they stocked.

Alcon managers observed that the retailer calls and the wholesaler calls were directly related. First, they were both distribution calls. Secondly, the turnover order took the MSR back to the wholesaler with a definite order from a retailer, thus giving the MSR an opportunity to urge further purchases of Alcon's products.

While Alcon's management had agreed that one MSR should handle both demand creation (doctor calls), and distribution (wholesaler and retailer calls), in the past there had been a difference of opinion in the marketing department as to which of the two areas should receive the greatest emphasis. As a result, emphasis had shifted from time to time.

In the past, when a new product was introduced, Alcon management had emphasized demand creation. Historically, this had resulted in a sales increase that was consistent with top management's commitment to rapid growth. As sales began to level off, however, an easy way to boost sales was to emphasize distribution by loading up the wholesaler and retailer with inventory. The distribution campaigns had included deals, the use of promotion money to the wholesaler's sales force, and sales contests for Alcon's salespeople. In addition, automatic shipments (i.e., shipments of goods which Alcon estimated could be sold, but which had not been ordered by the wholesaler) would often be made to wholesalers during these periods.

There had been a number of distribution campaigns during periods of slow sales growth. One had been held in May 1964, when a six-month distribution campaign was launched and a sales contest was initiated, in which the winner from each of the four regions won a trip to Mexico. When the contest was over, however, some wholesalers shipped goods back to Alcon (all of Alcon's sales were guaranteed; i.e., Alcon agreed to take back products that were unsold after a specific time). In one winner's territory, returns exceeded sales for a month or two. During the nine months following the contest, three of the four winners left Alcon.

Such distribution campaigns caused wide fluctuations in sales, and strained relations with wholesalers and retailers. Management recognized the undesirable consequences of such actions and concluded that enduring sales growth came only from demand creation. With this in mind, in October 1964 George Leone shifted the emphasis of the sales effort to demand creation. He instructed salespeople to spend 75 percent of their time calling on doctors (compared with 40 percent during the distribution campaign). The salespeople told the casewriter they welcomed this shift in their call mix because they preferred doctor calls to distribution calls. Management believed that MSRs who preferred distribution calls, such as the four contest winners, left the company when the shift in emphasis took place. Alcon maintained this emphasis on demand creation, and managers stated that they did not intend to return to the practice of using distribution campaigns to boost sales in periods of slow growth.

## ADMINISTRATION OF SALES FORCE

Alcon, like the rest of the industry, had found that it was difficult to find and keep a person who could perform all of the required functions of the medical sales representative. In the past six years the annual turnover of Alcon's sales force had averaged approximately 33 percent.

*Recruiting and Selection*

District sales managers were responsible for recruiting and selecting salespeople for each of their territories—they had an instruction manual to help them. One page was entitled "The Man You Want"[4] and listed the following characteristics:

> Twenty-five to thirty-five years of age; preferably married—stable domestic life; college degree; scientific and business courses; above-average grades in school; good work history, preferably in sales/marketing; good grooming and physical appearance; good health, past and present; sound financial position; good diction and use of grammar—articulate, able to understand and project emotions and ideas; has self-confidence and poise; self-starter; doesn't object to travel; enjoys working with people; ambitious with maturity, honesty, and integrity; and enthusiasm and capacity for work.

The district managers used several techniques to find people with these qualifications. When a vacancy occurred in an area, the district manager typically first contacted schools if the opening occurred around commencement time.

George Leone said that Alcon recruited at business schools in particular because Alcon liked to hire MBAs. He felt that the training and ambition of MBAs made them compatible with Alcon's objectives and organization. Leone believed that Alcon had hired approximately 20 MBAs within the last 10 years; 4 to 8 had left the company. Leone identified those still with Alcon; he believed that there were two others whom he had not included on the list (see Table 17-4).

A brochure in the Harvard Business School Placement Office contained the following statement: "The company is small by usual standards, but it offers the opportunity for easy recognition of contribution and rapid promotion to greater management responsibilities. Initial assignments are in field sales. MBAs are expected to reach district manager level within 18 to 24 months."

If qualified applicants were unavailable at business schools, the district sales manager next contacted an employment agency, where typically about 40 people were interviewed. After the first round of interviews, the sales manager would narrow the field to 10 to 12 applicants for second interviews. If the sales manager was unable to fill the vacant positions on the sales force using these sources, a district sales manager would then use a classified advertisement to recruit applicants. One district sales manager had used the following ad several times under such circumstances:

This district sales manager reported that the ad brought an aver-

[4]At that time, Alcon's sales force consisted entirely of men.

**TABLE 17-4 Alcon's Sales Force**

| Medical Sales Rep. | MBA Received | Present Position |
|---|---|---|
| A | HBS '57 | Financial vice president |
| B[a] | HBS '58 | Marketing vice president |
| C | HBS '60 | Comptroller's department |
| D | HBS '59 | Product manager |
| E[a] | HBS '62 | Product manager |
| F[a] | HBS '64 | Assistant product manager |
| G | Chicago | International comptroller |
| H[a] | N. Texas | Salesperson |
| I[a] | Northwestern | District manager |
| J | Wharton '65 | NA[a] |

[a]Began by working as a medical sales representative (MSR).
[b]NA = not available.

age of 75 resumes each time it was used in a large East Coast city; 40 to 45 of these resumes could be discarded immediately on the basis of age or educational background. After telephone interviews with the remaining 30 to 35 applicants, the sales manager would discard 10 to 15 more. Personal interviews would be held with the remaining 10 to 15 applicants.

One district manager explained his selection process:

> My selection is generally made during the second interview as to my first, second, and third choices for a man to fill a vacancy. Then I have two or three more interviews with these men and their wives. The average interview time for a man who is hired is a total of approximately 10 hours. By the time he is hired we really know one another and what we expect from one another. In rare instances, where there is competition for manpower from other industries in a given area, I may make a tentative offer on the spot during the first interview. In a case like this, the first interview would run one-and-a-half to two hours.

Selection was based primarily on the characteristics listed previously under "The Man You Want." The extent to which applicants fulfilled these characteristics was determined on the basis of information gathered through interviews, on application forms, and testing.

The district sales manager was required to spend a good deal of time recruiting because of the high turnover rate in the sales force. In 1965–1966 the region with the highest turnover had 6 people out of 19 leave. This region had the equivalent of four sales territories vacant for the year.

### *Training*

Each new MSR entered a four-week training program, which was under the direction of the DSM and took place in the field. In the first week, the DSM worked with the new MSR demonstrating calls on the doctor, the wholesaler, and the retailer. In the evening the new MSR was expected to learn company policies and procedures and to gain an adequate product knowledge, including the following: (1) basic anatomy, physiology, and pathology of the eye; (2) basic ocular therapy and medical concepts; (3) basic pharmacology; (4) Alcon product advantages; and (5) competitive products.

During the second and third weeks, the new MSR went into the territory of a senior salesperson in the district and made as many field calls with the senior salesperson as possible to perfect the first week's training. In addition, the MSR was expected to continue spending evenings on gaining product knowledge.

In the fourth week, new MSRs worked in their own areas under the supervision of the DSM. At this point the MSR was supposed to make most of the calls while the DSM observed. The DSM made sure that the new MSR was prepared to handle the territory.

This concluded the formal training of the new MSR. After this initial training, the DSM worked with the MSR only periodically, giving additional training as necessary. The new salespeople reported to the casewriter that while an effort was made to do this, the DSM was often too busy to carry out the training as planned.

To develop field sales managers, at the end of 1964 Alcon introduced a program for training managers called the advanced development program (ADP). Outstanding salespeople who were interested in advancement were included in this program (there were nine ADPs in the summer of 1966). The program consisted of each ADP doing a number of individual projects that were usually performed by field managers; for example, the ADP would recruit and train new salespeople. George Leone said, "Four of our best field managers today came from this program."

### *Control and Evaluation*

To keep track of what each MSR was doing, Alcon required that two reports be submitted by each salesperson to the DSM and the home office, including the following:

1. A daily report of all calls made by type of call, and the number and amount of turnover orders. This report was cumulative on a monthly basis.

2. An expense voucher to be filled in daily and mailed to Fort Worth on Saturday morning.

In addition, the MSR was required to keep territory records including a doctor call book with information such as the doctor's day off, the best time to call, the doctor's specialty, and so forth.

Once a year the district sales manager conducted a performance appraisal of the MSR. The DSM then made a recommendation for a salary increase based on this performance appraisal and the MSR's commission for the past year. Management maintained that the introduction of regular performance appraisals greatly improved the compensation of the sales force at Alcon, making it more equitable by relating salary increases more closely to performance. In addition, the company made it a practice to terminate salespeople who did not meet the high standards set by the company.

### *Compensation*

Compensation for salespeople was in the form of salary plus commission. Alcon's starting salaries ranged from $400 to $700 per month, depending on the training and experience of the new person. In 1966 Alcon's salespeople's salaries ranged from $500 to $916 per month, and averaged $580 per month. Each MSR was eligible for a yearly salary increase, and the annual increase could be up to one-half of the commission received the preceding year. Table 17-5 presents MSR's salaries from 1962 to 1966.

Management expressed the opinion that although Alcon had been behind the industry in compensation before, significant salary increases had made Alcon quite competitive with the drug industry. Table 17-6 presents data on the drug industry's compensation of salespeople in 1964.

Commissions were handled in the following manner: a new MSR was placed on commission after three months of employment with Alcon, following a performance review and approval by all levels of field

**TABLE 17-5 Salespeople's Salaries at Alcon**

| Year Ending April 30 | Average Annual Salary of all Salespeople[a] |
|---|---|
| 1962 | $5,760 |
| 1963 | 6,168 |
| 1964 | 6,744 |
| 1965 | 6,900 |
| 1966 | 6,960 |

[a]Excludes commissions.

**TABLE 17–6 Salespeople's Total Compensation: Salary and Commission, 1964**

| | |
|---|---|
| 100th percentile | $25,000 |
| 75th percentile | 9,000 |
| 50th percentile | 8,000 |
| 25th percentile | 7,000 |
| 1st percentile | 5,000 |

A group of 28 companies manufacturing drugs, chemicals, and cosmetics reported the following data concerning the compensation (salary and commission) of their salespeople:

| COMPENSATION ($) | MIDPOINT | RANGE |
|---|---|---|
| Highest person | 12,000 | 8,000–25,000 |
| Top half of sales force | 9,000 | 9,000–10,000 |
| Lowest person | 6,000 | 5,000– 7,000 |
| Lower half of sales force | 7,000 | 6,000– 8,000 |

SOURCE: *Sales Management*, January 21, 1966.

supervision. Commissions were paid twice each fiscal year and were based on 10 percent of increased sales after total MSR expenses (including car expenses, motel, telephone, meals) had been deducted. The following is an illustration of the commission plan:

The commission plan had been introduced in 1960 when the company was having trouble controlling salespeople's expenses. Some Alcon managers had expressed the feeling that this plan was not equitable because it penalized those with large territories requiring overnight travel. Total commissions paid to the 70 salespeople in 1965–1966 were $26,000 ranging from $0 to $1,500 individually, but Leone observed that 80 percent of the commission payments went to 20 percent of the sales force.

Thirty-eight salespeople had been hired and retained since 1964. Of these, more than two-thirds were between the ages of 25 to 30 and more than three-fourths were married. Virtually all of them had earned a bachelor's degree in a wide range of fields. Prior to joining Alcon, they had 31 collective years of sales experience and 52 years' experience in a variety of occupations.

### *Attitudes of Managers, Salespeople, and Customers*

In the course of gathering material for the case, the casewriter interviewed individuals at different organizational levels within Alcon. In addition, he interviewed a number of eye doctors, drug retailers, and drug wholesalers concerning their attitudes toward drug salespeople.

The two DSMs interviewed by the casewriter reported that other activities prevented them from spending 75 percent of their time with the MSR as their job description required. With a high turnover in the sales force, it was necessary for them to spend a great deal of time on recruiting and selecting new salespeople. One DSM had three vacancies to fill in a four-month period, and it was necessary for him to spend nearly all his time trying to fill those vacancies during that period. The DSM also reported that "the job has changed a lot in the past two to three years. Before, I just worked with the men, but now I am running an organization. I hire, fire, train, and evaluate men. I also run a good bit of the sales meetings. We have one about every two months."

### *Views of Selected MSRs*

Don Wade, an Alcon salesman for eight years, expressed the following comments, which seemed typical of Alcon's older salespeople:

> The most important thing is to sell the doctor and create demand for your product. If you just get it into the retailer and then the doctor doesn't write it, you have problems because the retailer will send it back. I provide information to the doctor. The doctors ask me about drugs, ours and our competition's; they ask me what they are and what they do, and so on. If I don't know about a product, I don't try to bluff it, so they trust me. If a competitor's product is good, I tell the doctor it is. I've been with Alcon a long time so I know the doctors and they write my products. When I come around with a new drug the doctors trust me so they'll start right in and use it.
>
> The doctor call is indirect selling; you don't write up an order and you don't know if you have sold him. That's what makes it such a challenge. I enjoy trying to match wits with the doctor and I can tell 80 percent of the time whether I have sold him or not. But you have to know what he is saying. A doctor will promise you anything. They want to be nice to you like they are to their patients, so they will say they will use your drug and then they won't follow up and do it.
>
> You have to use finesse with the doctor—it's a soft sell. You have to know where he went to school, his likes and dislikes. The more you can get him to talk, the better you can sell him. The doctor is more professional and more ethical.
>
> A distribution call, on the other hand, is direct selling. The pharmacist is more interested in money, so you have to show how your product will make him a profit. The pharmacist trusts me, so I just check his inventory, decide what he needs, and write up the turnover order. Usually he doesn't even see it. I just send it to the wholesaler. It's the same way with the wholesalers. I have a good relationship with them and they just let me write up the orders.

An interview with John Cook revealed the attitude of the younger, more ambitious salespeople. Cook had been with Alcon just one year and was described by the DSM as a good management prospect. He said:

> It's a hard sell with the doctor. You're in there as a salesman to sell your product. You really have to know your doctors because you can really pin some of them down and get a commitment to write your product, but with others you can't do much. So you have to know which ones to push. You have to get to know the receptionist too because she guards the doctor and can prevent you from seeing him.
>
> I would rather call on the doctor because he treats me like a professional man. It's just a chore to make retail calls. I spend 85 percent of my time calling on doctors because I'd rather call on them. Some of our wholesalers are upset because they say Alcon is high pressure as a result of the distribution campaign two years ago.

Bob Jensen, a salesman with three years' experience at Alcon, commented:

> I studied premed in college but I didn't have good enough grades to get into medical school. However, I still wanted some dealings with the medical profession so after I got some sales experience I came with Alcon. Because the eye doctors know that Alcon only calls on eye doctors, they like to see the Alcon man. So I am accepted more by doctors than the detail men from other companies are.
>
> I enjoy calling on the doctor because he is more professional—ethical. The only problem is that you don't know when you've sold the doctor. You get better feedback from the pharmacist because you write up an order there.
>
> Ninety-nine percent of the doctors accept me very well; about 50 percent of them call me by my first name, but it's taken two years to get on a first-name basis. The doctor would rather discuss products with a friend, so if you have been calling on him a while and he knows you, he'll listen.

### *Comments from Doctors*

Doctor Jones was about 45, had a large practice, and also did some work with a well-respected eye clinic in the large eastern city where he practiced. His views were typical of the busy, successful ophthalmologist:

> The detail man keeps the doctor informed. He makes the information available before it comes out in the journals (the journals are always months behind) and you can ask questions of him directly.
>
> I like a detail man who is pleasant and sincere, and one who has a knowledge of his product or at least is honest enough to let you know

> when he doesn't. I also prefer one that makes no demands. Some of them will say, "I'll be back in 10 days to see how you've gotten along with my product," and it puts you on the spot.

When asked which companies were doing the best job of promoting their products, Dr. Jones replied:

> The question really should be which ones see you most frequently? The answer is Alcon; Smith, Miller & Patch; and Upjohn, I guess. I tend to write more of their products when they call frequently and I have more knowledge of their products. I depend on the detail man to get information on things like products, sizes, availability, etc. They keep me up to date on new developments.

Dr. Barron was about 50 years old. Barron, less busy than some other eye doctors, commented that detail men could be quite helpful:

> I am influenced by the detail man. I have an emotional affinity for him and he leaves a lot of samples. I feel an obligation to him and I'll write his drugs. But I don't like the overpowering salesman. I like a neat, well-dressed, polite man who just gives me information. I think all detail men are frustrated doctors—you wouldn't really want to be a detail man. Generally, the salesmen are very nice people and very cooperative.

### *Pharmacist's View of the Sales Force*

A pharmacist was asked about his feelings toward the sales force and the companies they represented. He expressed his views as follows:

> The ethical drug salesman tells us about new products, price changes, and what's being detailed, because that's what sells. He comes in and writes up the order. Then we check it over and cut back if he's put in too much of any product.
>
> All the major companies do a good job. Upjohn, Merck, and so forth. But the small companies have high turnover. They'll have a new man in here about every month. We sometimes have a problem with them.
>
> The salesman expects us to keep his products in stock; he sells the products to the doctor. He also asks for information on what the doctors are writing. We have a prescription file and he's welcome to look through it.

### *Wholesaler's View of the Sales Force*

The following interview with a buyer at a busy wholesaler gives an indication of his attitude toward the sales force:

> I like salesmen who take care of the details on their products, such as price changes, returns, checking inventory, and giving us information on new items.
>
> Also, I don't like pressure. We are trying to sell merchandise and in or-

> der to sell we have to buy. We don't need anyone to pressure us. It's just the new man or the fly-by-night guy who gets this pitch from the home office and tries to shove it down our throat. But by and large they tend to be quite professional in their approach.

When asked specifically about Alcon, the buyer said: "They're a little pushy, a little bang-bang. But they are less so now than in the past. They tended to put up these deals at the home office and then put them off on us."

### *Sales Force's View of the Marketing Effort*

A number of managers and salespeople pointed out that the quality of the promotion developed by the product managers could greatly influence an MSR's success. With a high-quality program and the support of direct mail and journal advertising, the MSR could significantly increase sales of featured products. The salespeople appeared to agree that the work of the product managers had improved a great deal in the past two to three years, and that they were doing an excellent job. Many of the sales force expressed concern, however, about the infrequency with which Alcon had introduced new products. One MSR said that in the past six years Alcon had introduced only "two big new products," and that it was only in those periods that the company had experienced rapid sales growth. One manager pointed out that Alcon had significantly expanded its R&D effort in the past two years and that "we now have in R&D more Ph.D.'s per sales dollar than anyone else in the industry, and we are currently spending 10 percent of sales for that purpose."

### *Sales Force's Views of the Company, Compensation, and Opportunity for Advancement*

The following is another part of the interview with Don Wade who had been with Alcon over eight years:

> You can't make big money in the drug business, and if you compare Alcon with the others in the industry, their salary is not the best, but they hit a happy medium. I've been offered more money by other drug companies, but Alcon has a great future and they have a good relationship with the doctors.
>
> Alcon has the best opportunity for advancement in the industry, if you're looking for that. I'm not. I just want to be a salesman. The DSM has to travel too much and I don't want to be away from my family any more than I am now.
>
> Our company has been weak in supervision compared with other drug companies. At least we've been weak in the past. But now they're doing a

> better job of training a man before they make him a DSM. Nobody can learn the drug business in two years, so our managers just haven't had enough field experience.

When asked why so many salespeople had left Alcon, Wade replied: "Alcon promises you the sky in terms of advancement and then they just don't come through. So, when the boys have been here a while and they don't get a promotion as soon as they were told they would, they leave."

Nearly all of the Alcon employees interviewed said they believed that there were excellent opportunities for advancement with Alcon. Management indicated, however, that there were no plans to expand the sales force or the number of field managers in the immediate future. When the casewriter presented this apparent contradiction to Dave Colton, a salesman who had been with Alcon for five months, Colton replied that he expected to advance with Alcon. He believed that there would be an opportunity for him to be promoted into a management position in one of the companies that had been acquired or would be acquired by Alcon.

## MANAGEMENT CONCERN

Management was aware that turnover was high among sales personnel throughout the drug industry (12.1 percent in 1964), but Alcon turnover was a great deal higher than at other drug companies. In fact, it had been as high as 42 percent in 1964. (Table 17-7 shows the turnover in Alcon's sales force from 1961 to 1966, and the length of service of those leaving.)

Management was concerned about the high turnover for several reasons. First of all, it was costly. Although Alcon's figures were not available, one survey reported, "The cost of selecting, training, and supervising a new drug salesman averages $7,612 excluding salary." Just as important as cost was the fact that it took one to two years for an MSR to establish a relationship with the doctor, the wholesaler, and the retailer. Most of the men who left had been with Alcon less than two and one-half years; they just barely got to know the customers before leaving.

George Leone was uncertain about why so many people had left Alcon. He indicated that almost all of them said they were leaving because they were not earning enough money, but he was not sure that was the whole reason. Alcon had raised salaries considerably in the past three years, but people were still leaving. Leone felt that part of the problem may have been the shift in emphasis from demand to distribution and then back to demand. Leone noted that Alcon's higher turnover had occurred in the years when they had distribution campaigns.

**TABLE 17–7 Alcon's Sales Force Data**

Turnover of Alcon's Sales Force

| Year Ending April 30 | % Turnover |
|---|---|
| 1961 | 35 |
| 1962 | 27 |
| 1963 | 35 |
| 1964 | 42 |
| 1965 | 34 |
| 1966 | 28 |

Length of Service of Salespeople Terminating

| No. Months Employed | Personnel | | Cumulative Personnel | |
|---|---|---|---|---|
| | *No.* | % | *No.* | % |
| 6 or less | 4 | 14[a] | 4 | 14 |
| 12 or less | 8 | 28 | 12 | 41 |
| 18 | 4 | 14 | 16 | 55 |
| 24 | 2 | 7 | 18 | 62 |
| 30 | 5 | 17 | 23 | 80 |
| 36 | 1 | 4 | 24 | 83 |
| 42 | 1 | 4 | 25 | 87 |
| 48 | 1 | 4 | 26 | 90 |
| 60 | 3 | 10 | 29 | 100 |

[a]Figures do not add to 100 due to rounding.

CASE 18

# MEGALITH, INC.-HAY ASSOCIATES (A)

*John A. Seeger*
*John P. Kotter*
*Anne Harlan*

> Frank, there's no question about it. We're out of line. Way out of line. The situation is real. It's hurting us, and I have two resignations here to prove it.

John C. Boyd, senior vice president of Finance for Megalith, Inc., paced across his office in agitation. Near the door stood Frank C. Nicodemus, Megalith's vice president for Human Resources. The two men, long-time colleagues in the successful multinational firm, were continuing a debate begun much earlier, when Boyd had attempted to raise the salaries of his key managers by 25 percent.

Boyd continued:

> You told me last June that these people were too young and inexperienced to be worth the money. And I told you we'd have to pay based on their competence, not their seniority. Now it's October and two of them have given notice in the past month. You know both of them—Lonny Jackson and George Arnold are two of the best managers in the company. They're half of the team I brought in here to bring the Finance Group out of the Stone Age, and they've been absolutely vital to the development of the group. And now they're both leaving—to get salaries I wanted to pay them months ago.

Boyd turned and shook his head.

> Frank, I know that what's done is done, and we're not going to get Lonny and George back. But what if my other key people take off, too? Where would that leave us? I've got to have more room in the salary schedule to take care of the exceptional people who've made this group click!

Boyd paused, and Frank Nicodemus responded.

> John, you'll remember I showed you that all four of your key people were right at the top of our scale. Megalith's compensation system isn't something we've arbitrarily picked out of the air; every year we check the

schedule against trade associations' published data, and we adjust it to make sure we're above average—that we're competitive with the best in the labor market. To make exceptions to a well-grounded scale would be both hasty and rash. It would raise hell around here, throwing everything out of balance.

So I held the line. But since then I've been checking to see just how sound our schedules are. We found a consulting firm that has a very good reputation in comparative compensation, and for the past month I've been working with one of their partners. His name is Ed Rogers, and the firm is Hay Associates. You know them: they're the people conducting the Climate Study right now, and reviewing all our corporate-level job descriptions. Would you like to talk to Rogers?

Frank, I've got the comparisons I need, right here. [John Boyd waved a file folder at his friend.] Lonny Jackson will start with an extra twelve thousand a year in direct salary, and will make a bonanza if he does well as Executive Vice President of R. G. Miller, and I'm sure he'll succeed. Megalith will have to pay at least twelve thousand to find and break in a replacement vice president for Information Systems. What are we saving by putting our budget into search instead of salary?

And the same thing goes for George Arnold, my treasurer. He's going to take over a new leasing division for Rockwell, and his chance for profit incentive payments there puts anything we can offer to shame.

I just can't compete, Frank. You've got us locked in with a pay schedule that looks competitive on the surface, but when the chips are down, it's a loser. [John Boyd hesitated, then continued slowly.] We've never before failed to reach agreement, Frank, but I'm afraid I'll have to fight you on this one. If we haven't solved the problem by the time Allen Whitfield [Megalith's president] gets back from Europe, I intend to ask him to call the Board's Compensation Committee in, to review the whole damn system.

[A silence of several seconds was finally broken by the Human Resources vice president.] John, what could the Com-Com really *do*? They'd *have* to call in professional help, and they'd probably rely on our CPA's or a firm of specialists, like the ones I've already brought in. Wouldn't it make sense to hear what Rogers has to say, before we admit defeat? Won't you talk to him?

## MEGALITH, INC.

In its 50 years of years of operations, Megalith, Inc. had grown to international prominence as a manufacturer of printing equipment, as a publisher, as a supplier of office equipment and supplies, and more recently as a builder of computer-related printers, plotters, and data recorders. From its beginnings, the firm had led the field in development of lithography and photo-offset printing techniques; basic patents in both printing and plate-making equipment had allowed Megalith to penetrate international markets early in its history. Megalith trademarks were found in virtually every job shop printing house in the world.

Shortly after World War II the company diversified into publishing; by 1975 it operated large-scale printing plants in seven countries. In the late 1950s Megalith attacked the office equipment industry; primarily through acquisitions it had achieved significant shares of markets in copying equipment, dictating systems, and typewriters—although it had failed to threaten the dominance of Xerox or IBM in these fields. Megalith's newest diversification strategy recognized that computers had come of age as sources of the written word; the firm began acquiring technology-based companies making high-speed line printers, plotters, microfilm output printers, and data recorders. By 1975, Megalith was a leading producer of computer peripheral equipment under its own name, as well as a leading supplier to the computer industry itself. Worldwide sales volume reached $1.7 billion in 1974, and profitability remained at traditionally high levels, in spite of generally poor economic conditions. (Exhibit 18–1 shows Megalith's corporate-level organization chart, with annual sales by product group since 1956.)

Megalith executives credited the company's success to well-chosen strategy (dominance in printed communication), to technological leadership and to strength in financial control. They were quick to admit that the company's only failure to reach market dominance—in the office equipment field—was due to the relative unimportance there of financial controls and engineering leadership; marketing genius was required to displace the leaders there. Still, the Megalith Office Products Group contributed significantly to profits and was considered a good investment.

Behind the desk of Megalith President Allen G. Whitfield hung a large, ornately-framed poster, loudly proclaiming, "WE PRINT MONEY." The poster had been commissioned when the company had closed the order to equip the United States Mint; it had become an informal slogan of the firm, and smaller reproductions of the poster were common in executive offices and factory washrooms. Megalith people were proud of their "blue-chip" reputation.

## HAY ASSOCIATES

In its own, much different market, Hay Associates was also proud of its leadership position. Founded in Philadelphia in 1943, the firm originally offered consulting services in the field of management compensation. By 1975 its specialties included comprehensive services in integrated planning systems, performance management, and reward management; it employed 275 professional people, operating from 29 offices in 14 countries. Hay's 1975 billings reached $21 million, and had grown at an annual rate of 30 percent since 1964.

Hay Associates brought an approach to compensation problems that organized known management judgments into a systematic measurement process. It separated the requirements and descriptions of the jobs from the performance of the job-holders, considering each separately in determining appropriate pay levels. Jobs themselves were analyzed according to know-how and problem-solving requirements, and according to the end results for which the position was accountable. The Hay system assigned "content points" for each criterion and gave the firm a basis for measuring the relative importance of different jobs and for ensuring an equitable internal balance of salary scales.

A key part of the process recognized that management positions were based on an organization's need for certain end results, but that each incumbent also had an impact on his job's content. Interviews with job-holders were used to develop descriptions acceptable to both the organization and the incumbent.

A comprehensive data base, collected annually from hundreds of client firms (1,500 participated in 1975) permitted the client to compare his base salary practice and total remuneration including benefits with those of a broad industrial group. Since all contributors to the data base used the same measurement process, comparisons were always made on the basis of uniform content values for any position.

Hay's service allowed a company to compare its own salary practices, benefit programs, or even its "working climate" with others in its own industry or with the economy as a whole. The analysis identified jobs where a client company was overpaying or underpaying its people, compared to the policy or the actual practice reflected in the continually updated data base.

## JOHN BOYD

John Boyd sat comfortably in a leather-upholstered chair beside the window of his Manhattan office. Across a low coffee table, Edmund Law Rogers, partner in the firm of Hay Associates, leaned forward intently, listening.

> So there's my situation, Ed. With this team of four really outstanding managers, we've built the Finance Group from a skeleton crew of budget-assemblers into one of the finest, most professional teams in industry. Now I'm losing the people responsible for breathing life into this outfit,

because our bureaucratic salary system doesn't recognize the difference between talent and mediocrity. Can *your* system tell the difference?

John, that's a judgment no formal system can make. Only the responsible executive—the man in your own shoes—can tell how *well* his people are performing, or how high they can go. But a formal system *can* say something about the jobs themselves. We can compare the jobs in the Finance Group to each other, based on their contents, to give you a measure of internal equity—of how fairly you're paying your people relative to each other. Then we can compare your salaries to those paid for similar-content jobs by a broad spectrum of industry. We can help define what end results each position is accountable for, and those definitions can sharpen your measurements of performance. That can help you decide what ''outstanding'' means, and how much you're willing to pay for it.

I'd like to know more about these key positions. Do you have a group organization chart handy?

## THE MEGALITH FINANCE GROUP

In early 1969, Allen Whitfield had asked John Boyd to move from the group vice presidency for office products to the new position as senior vice president for Finance. The corporation, with advice from a major American consulting firm, had decided to increase the size of its central financial staff, to bring together in the New York headquarters the analytic and control talents which were then scattered rather unevenly between the operating companies. Whitfield wanted a proven leader to build a coherent finance group, and Boyd was his first choice.

The Finance Group, Whitfield and Boyd decided, should be responsible for end results in the areas of strategy, planning, policy, and control. Exhibit 18–2 details the specifics of the Finance Group mandate.

Under Boyd's direction, the Finance Group had grown since 1969 from 110 to 630 employees. (The 1975 organization chart for the department is included as Exhibit 18–3, along with a record of annual employment since 1969.) The expansion had required new personnel, and Boyd had consciously decided to seek out energetic, competent, young people who could respond to the challenge, and to bring his new recruits up through the ranks of the group as fast as possible. This ''fast track'' policy had helped attract the four key people who, Boyd said, had made the concept work. All four of the ''young stars'' had performed beyond all expectations, impressing the entire senior management group with their imagination, forcefulness, and effectiveness. All four had received every possible commendation, promotion, salary increase, and incentive bonus. (Exhibit 18-4 shows annual salaries and brief personal data on the key group personnel.)

John Boyd stated to Ed Rogers:

> It was in June's performance planning meetings with people, I began to feel uneasy. There had been more and more complaints coming from people, about money. Most of them could be handled all right, but with my key people, we were up against the ceilings in both direct salaries and Management Incentive Opportunity. I couldn't offer them enough, and I couldn't get Frank Nicodemus to relax the constraints. You know those personnel people, they always seem to stand in your way. [See Exhibit 18-5 for a summary of the Megalith compensation system.] It's clear now: I should have fought harder. Lonny and George both gave notice in September. Now I'm waiting for the other show to drop; if John Auer and Manuella should also leave, it would be like starting over from scratch, to build a new team.
>
> Was there any connection between the two resignations?
>
> No, Ed. Neither man knew the other was going to quit, and they both feel badly that the Group here will suffer. But the money was too much for them to resist.
>
> Are you sure it's money that made them go?
>
> That's what they both said, and I'm sure they're leveling with me. If we'd been competitive, neither of them would have given the time of day to the recruiters who contacted them. Besides, it all fits in with other comments I've heard—that the pay is inadequate.
>
> But let me get back to the question: would *your* compensation system allow for the exceptional managers? Can we get Frank to give in on those damn ceilings? I need a fast answer, because I'm starting to recruit replacements, and I have to tell them what they can look forward to.

Boyd and Rogers spent the next half-hour discussing the Hay evaluation system, which focuses on the content of the job, rather than the talents of the individual. Rogers briefly described the evaluation process (see Exhibit 18-6). Responding to Boyd's questions, he detailed how a specific job might be evaluated.

Know-how, in the Hay system, is scored according to three different aspects of the job's requirements—technical or practical knowledge, however acquired; managerial knowledge, in terms of degree of integration and coordination with other functions or activities required by the position; and human relations skills needed to perform the job, classified as basic, important, or critical. (A sample section of the guide chart, used by Rogers to demonstrate the rating of three typical jobs, is included in Exhibit 18-7.)

A similar, but more comprehensive guide chart has been developed for Megalith's own job evaluations, Rogers said.

Problem-solving requirements of a job are rated according to two dimensions—the thinking environment, ranging from strictly routine to abstractly defined; and the thinking challenge of the job, ranging from repetitive choice-making to creative concept-formation.

Accountability, the last major area for rating, is measured on three dimensions—the positions's freedom to act, ranging from totally prescribed to unconstrained-except-for-broad-policy; its impact on end results, ranging from indirect-remote to direct-primary; and the dollar magnitude of the area most clearly affected by the job.

> Given a large number of jobs, consistently described and rated, we can compare the salaries and incentives paid for job contents, rather than job titles. [Rogers summed up.] You can't compare on the basis of title, because incumbents, organizations' needs, and/or organizations' styles make the jobs different.
>
> Here in Megalith, we've finished with the updating of job descriptions [see Exhibit 18–8 for a sample description], and I expect to submit our final report to Frank Nicodemus in two weeks. He's said you'll be the first one he sends a copy to.
>
> [John Boyd thought for a moment as he lit a cigarette.] O.K. [he said], You'll tell us how our pay scale stacks up in terms of the jobs we pay for. But you're not going to evaluate the individuals involved, or the problem of identifying exceptional talent and holding it. Is that right?
>
> John, that's got to be your job. We can help, by giving you information, and an analysis of your own system's strengths and weaknesses, and our suggestions for changing the system.
>
> Our numbers data *will* show Megalith's current salary practice, compared with the practice of a broad industrial spectrum. We *will* include an analysis showing what your current salaries would be, if they were fully consistent with the measured content of the jobs. But Frank Nicodemus hasn't asked us to go beyond that in this report.
>
> In addition to the numbers, you'll see the results of the Climate Study we've just finished here. About 50 of your finance people have filled out our survey forms, and we'll digest that information for you, relating it to the answers given by several thousand other respondents.
>
> [Boyd stubbed out his cigarette and stood.] I'll look forward to seeing that report. And I assume we'll meet again to talk about what it means—probably with Frank. [Boyd smiled.] I've tried a couple of times to pin you down on an answer to this, but you've dodged me. Before you go, I'd like to ask you directly . . . do you have any opinion yet on raising these ceilings of ours?
>
> No way, John. [Rogers smiled in return.] But I'll look forward to seeing you again after the report is finished.

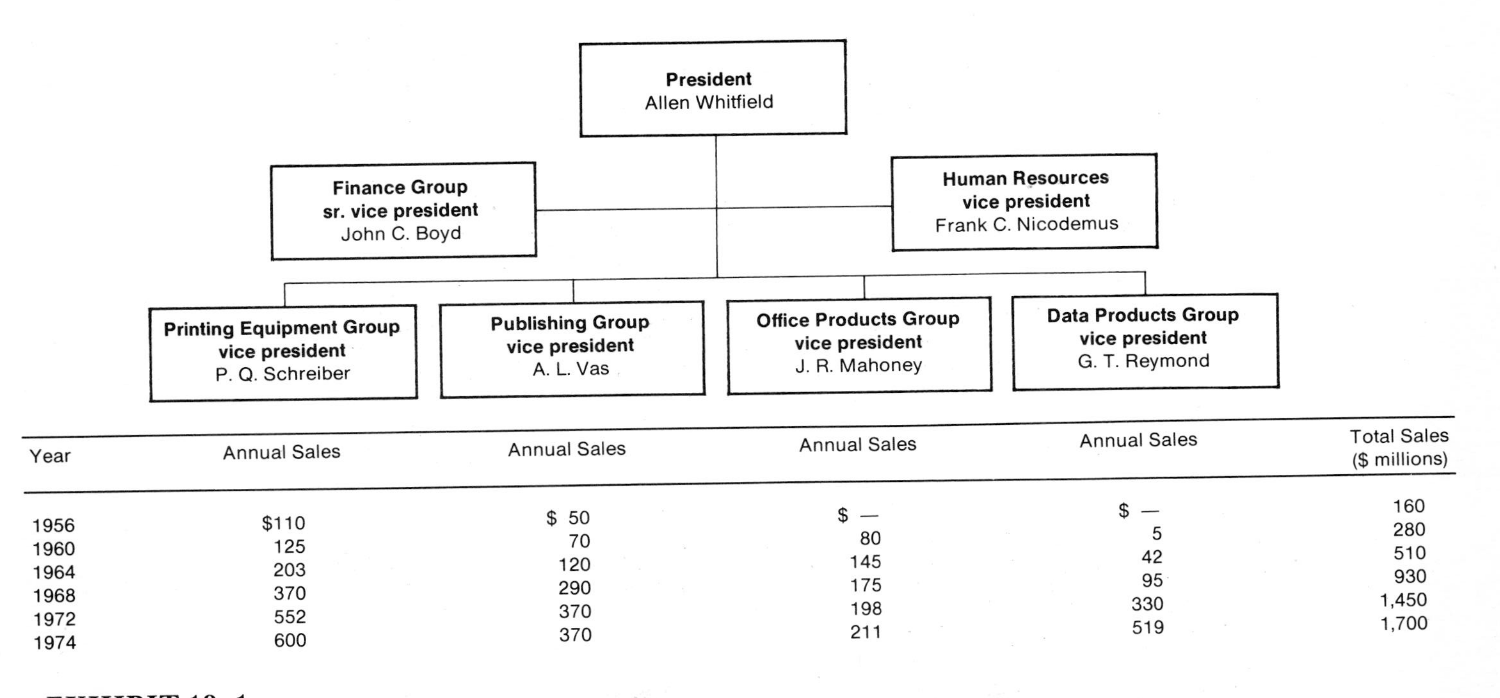


| Year | Annual Sales | Annual Sales | Annual Sales | Annual Sales | Total Sales ($ millions) |
|---|---|---|---|---|---|
| 1956 | $110 | $ 50 | $ — | $ — | 160 |
| 1960 | 125 | 70 | 80 | 5 | 280 |
| 1964 | 203 | 120 | 145 | 42 | 510 |
| 1968 | 370 | 290 | 175 | 95 | 930 |
| 1972 | 552 | 370 | 198 | 330 | 1,450 |
| 1974 | 600 | 370 | 211 | 519 | 1,700 |

**EXHIBIT 18–1**
**Corporate Organization Chart, 1975**

**EXHIBIT 18–2**
**Expected Outcomes for the Finance Group's Activities**

1. Financial strategy which significantly contributes to corporate profit and growth objectives
2. Financial policies, processes, and controls to provide timely and accurate information, comply with accepted practices and regulatory authorities, and protect assets
3. Corporate planning and measurement process which provides an effective means to integrate group operations, evaluate achievement, and assure top management awareness of problems and opportunities
4. Continuity of a corporate financial management team organized and competent to achieve functional objectives and a significant contribution to group financial management continuity and competence
5. Effective asset and liability management which contributes to corporate short-term profit objective and long-term growth and stability
6. Significant contribution to acquisition strategy and effective implementation through development of objectives, evaluations, and analysis
7. Systems and control capability to provide effective management information services
8. An informed top management and board of directors aware of financial results and projections

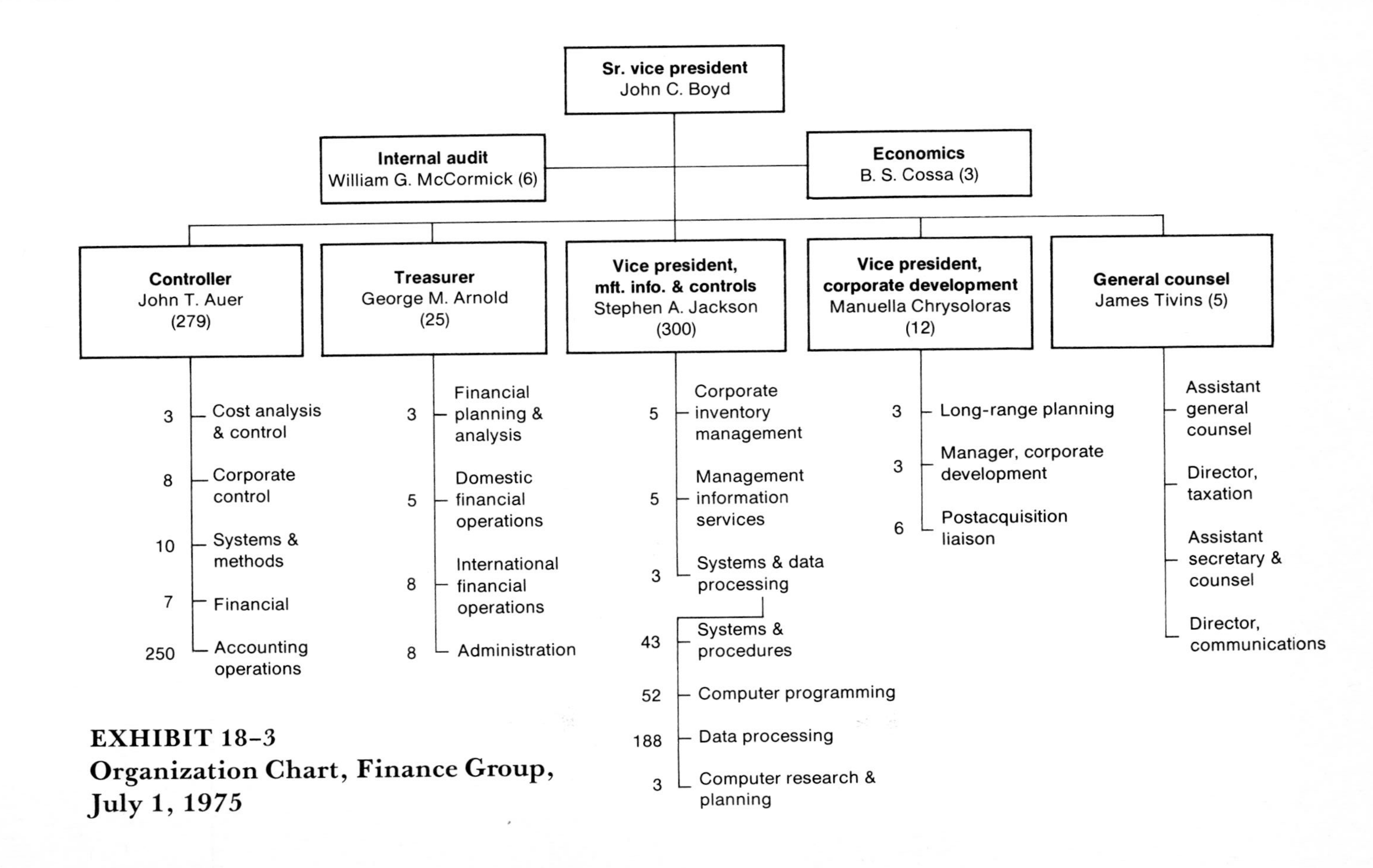


**EXHIBIT 18–3**
**Organization Chart, Finance Group, July 1, 1975**

**EXHIBIT 18-4**
**Excerpts from Personnel Resources Reference, July 1, 1975**

- **Senior Vice President, Finance.** John Covert Boyd, age 47. MBA, Harvard, 1958. Founded Duplicopy, Inc. and served as its president until its acquisition by Megalith in 1963. Became group vice president, Office Products, in 1967, and SVP in 1970.
  1975 salary: $90,000 plus $25,132 incentive[1]
- **Controller.** John T. Auer, age 38. MBA, Wharton, 1960. Financial analyst, then Assistant Controller of Itek International until 1964, when he joined a small consulting firm as an Associate. Recruited by Boyd in 1970 to head the Controller's Systems and Methods group. Promoted to Director of Accounting Operations in 1972, and to Controller in 1974.
  1975 salary: $59,000 plus $21,500 incentive
- **Treasurer.** George Miles Arnold, age 42. MS, London School of Economics, 1959. Lecturer in Finance, University of Bologna, then joined a major international oil company as coordinator of financial planning for Europe and the Middle East. Joined Barclay International in 1965 to form a new consulting services group in international money management. Recruited in 1969 by Boyd, to head Megalith International Financial Operations department; set up the Domestic Financial Operations office in 1970, and reorganized the Accounting Operations department in 1971. Promoted to Treasurer in 1973.
  1975 salary: $54,000 plus $18,160 incentive (plus car)
- **Vice President, Management Information Systems.** Stephen Alonzo Jackson, age 35. BS, MIT, 1962. Partner in a small, Boston-based software consulting firm for three years, then head of systems analysis for McGraw-Hill West Coast operations. MBA, Stanford, 1970. Joined Megalith as Director of Systems and Procedures; became Director of Management Information Services in early 1972; Director of Systems and Data Processing in 1973; and VP for MIS in 1974.
  1975 salary: $55,000 plus $18,700 incentive (plus car)
- **Vice President, Corporate Development.** Manuella Chrysoloras, age 39. MBA, Darden, 1963. Joined an investment banking firm, and three years later set up her own brokerage in mergers and acquisitions. Retained by Megalith to assist in

[1]Incentive plan payments are based on results for fiscal year ended June 30, 1975; they were approved by the Compensation Committee of the board of directors on September 1, and paid the following week.

acquisition of four small computer peripheral manufacturers, and became executive vice president of the largest one. Drafted into Finance Group by Allen Whitfield in early 1971.

1975 salary: $48,000 plus $14,760 incentive

- **General Counsel.** James Tivins, age 61. LLB, University of Virginia, 1940. Joined legal staff of one of Megalith's printing equipment companies in 1949. Extensive work in antitrust, finance, and tax law. Appointed Corporate Secretary in 1960, and General Counsel in 1966.

  1975 salary: $65,000 plus $12,600 incentive

## EXHIBIT 18–5
## Summary: Compensation Policy, Revised July 1, 1971

- **Compensation Objective.** To attract and motivate professional management people, enhancing their positive identification with corporate strategy and goals. Total compensation practice shall be competitive with an appropriate market mix of similar high-growth companies.
- **Compensation Components.** Cash compensation shall consist of base salary (determined by comparison with appropriate markets); and Management Incentive Opportunity (determined by formula and approved in each case by the Compensation Committee of the Board).

  Noncash compensation includes pension plan, deferred savings plan, group life insurance, medical plan, short-term disability, and long-term disability plans. These combined benefits approximate 35 percent of base salary expenditures for the Company; details of all plans are available from the vice president, Human Resources.
- **Compensation Procedures.** All positions shall be described in writing whenever changed or filled following a vacancy; all descriptions shall be audited annually by the Human Resources staff. Changed or added descriptions shall be evaluated by the appropriate Human Resources Review Committee to maintain internal consistency and equity.
- **Management Incentive Opportunity Plan (MIO).** MIO payments apply to all positions specifically determined by the Compensation Committee of the Board to have both a direct impact on corporate earnings and a distinct requirement for individual discretion in their performance.

**EXHIBIT 18-5 (*Continued*)**

- **Corporate Threshold.** Before any MIO awards are paid, Megalith must earn a targeted Earnings Per Share (EPS) as set by the Executive Committee. The EPS goals must equal or exceed the average EPS of the latest three years' operations. The Executive Committee may make an exception to the threshold for a division or group which achieves exceptional results.
- **Performance Planning.** Each MIO participant shall agree with his supervisor, before the beginning of each year, on his own performance goals and implementation plans. Group and Functional heads are responsible for coordination of these goals within the framework of corporate strategy, and shall inform each participant of his own potential MIO earnings for the forthcoming year, at different levels of performance.

- **Performance Growth Plan (PGP).** Participants will be eligible for annual awards, determined by the Compensation Committee and calculated as a percentage of the MOI payments received during the immediately preceding four years.

Participants may accept awards wholly in Megalith stock (with a 20 percent inducement premium for doing so), or half in stock and half in cash. PGP awards may be deferred until after retirement, and taken over a period not to exceed ten years, at the participant's option. Cash-deferred awards will accrue interest at the prime rate; stock-deferred options shall reinvest dividends in additional stock.

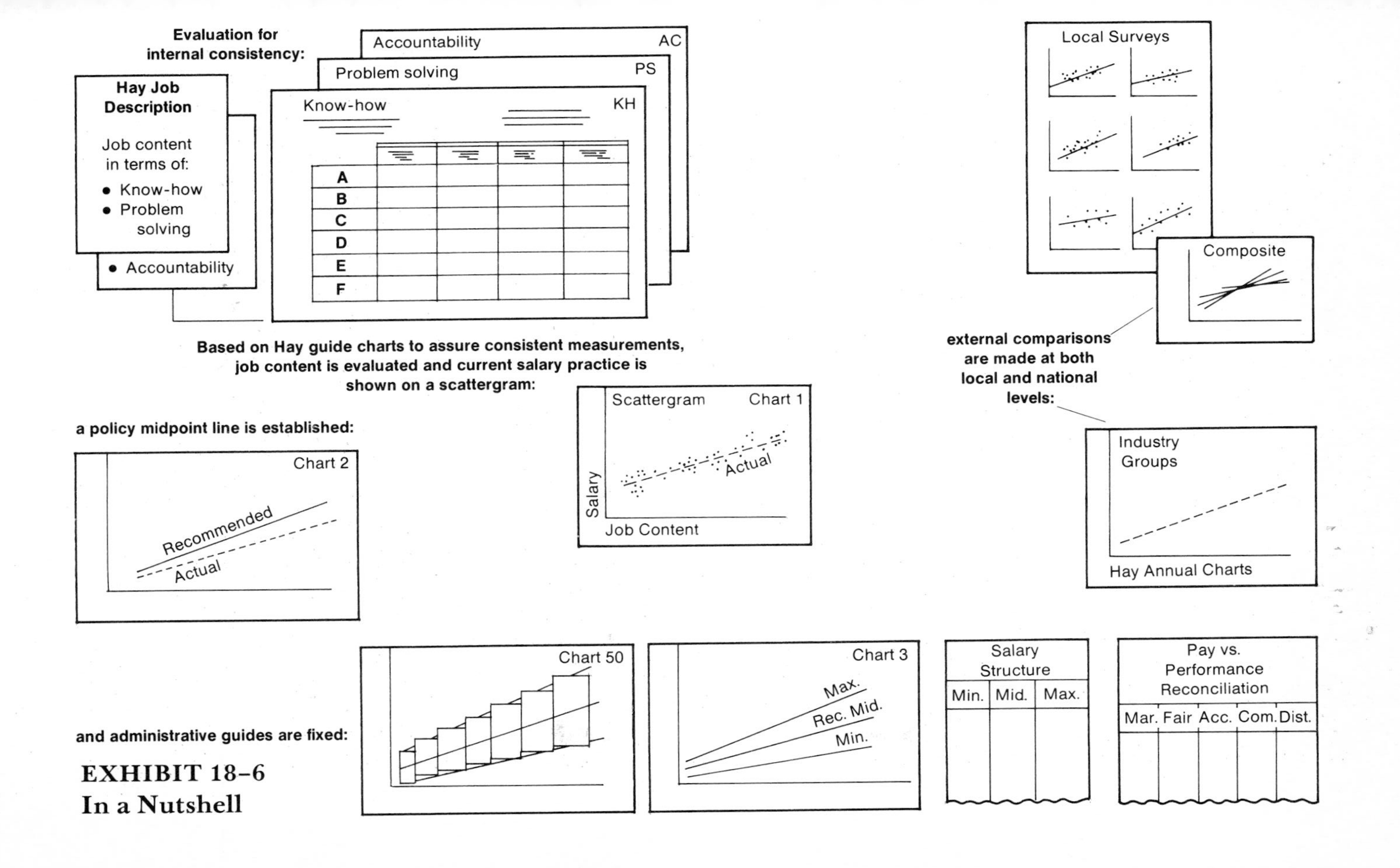


**EXHIBIT 18–6**
**In a Nutshell**

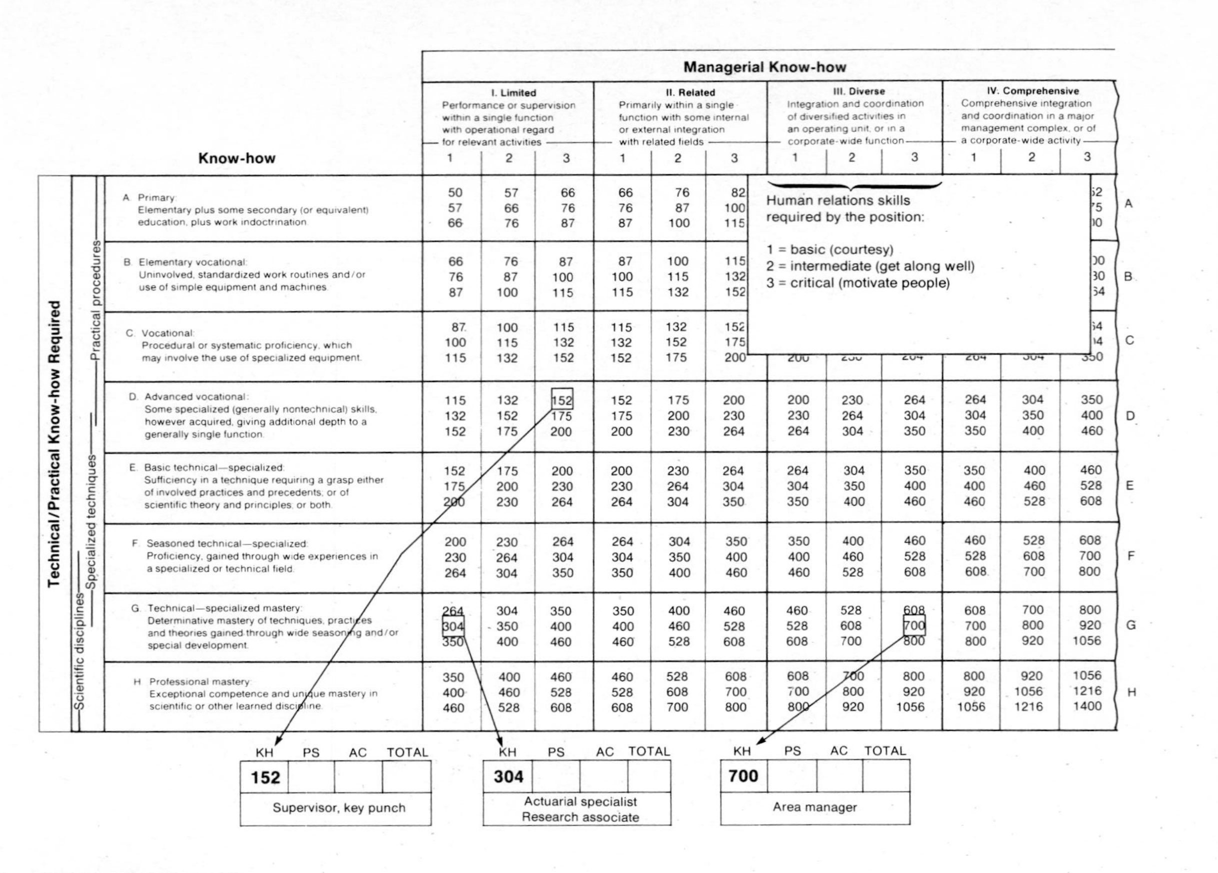

| Know-how | | Managerial Know-how: I. Limited — Performance or supervision within a single function with operational regard for relevant activities | | | II. Related — Primarily within a single function with some internal or external integration with related fields | | | III. Diverse — Integration and coordination of diversified activities in an operating unit, or in a corporate-wide function | | | IV. Comprehensive — Comprehensive integration and coordination in a major management complex, or of a corporate-wide activity | | | |
|---|---|---|---|---|---|---|---|---|---|---|---|---|---|---|
| Technical/Practical Know-how Required | | 1 | 2 | 3 | 1 | 2 | 3 | 1 | 2 | 3 | 1 | 2 | 3 | |
| Practical procedures | A. Primary: Elementary plus some secondary (or equivalent) education, plus work indoctrination. | 50<br>57<br>66 | 57<br>66<br>76 | 66<br>76<br>87 | 66<br>76<br>87 | 76<br>87<br>100 | 82<br>100<br>115 | [illegible] | [illegible] | [illegible] | [illegible] | [illegible] | [illegible] | A |
| Practical procedures | B. Elementary vocational: Uninvolved, standardized work routines and/or use of simple equipment and machines. | 66<br>76<br>87 | 76<br>87<br>100 | 87<br>100<br>115 | 87<br>100<br>115 | 100<br>115<br>132 | 115<br>132<br>152 | [illegible] | [illegible] | [illegible] | [illegible] | [illegible] | [illegible] | B |
| Practical procedures | C. Vocational: Procedural or systematic proficiency, which may involve the use of specialized equipment. | 87<br>100<br>115 | 100<br>115<br>132 | 115<br>132<br>152 | 115<br>132<br>152 | 132<br>152<br>175 | 152<br>175<br>200 | [illegible]<br>[illegible]<br>200 | [illegible] | [illegible] | [illegible] | [illegible] | [illegible]<br>[illegible]<br>350 | C |
| Specialized techniques | D. Advanced vocational: Some specialized (generally nontechnical) skills, however acquired, giving additional depth to a generally single function. | 115<br>132<br>152 | 132<br>152<br>175 | 152<br>175<br>200 | 152<br>175<br>200 | 175<br>200<br>230 | 200<br>230<br>264 | 200<br>230<br>264 | 230<br>264<br>304 | 264<br>304<br>350 | 264<br>304<br>350 | 304<br>350<br>400 | 350<br>400<br>460 | D |
| Specialized techniques | E. Basic technical—specialized: Sufficiency in a technique requiring a grasp either of involved practices and precedents; or of scientific theory and principles; or both. | 152<br>175<br>200 | 175<br>200<br>230 | 200<br>230<br>264 | 200<br>230<br>264 | 230<br>264<br>304 | 264<br>304<br>350 | 264<br>304<br>350 | 304<br>350<br>400 | 350<br>400<br>460 | 350<br>400<br>460 | 400<br>460<br>528 | 460<br>528<br>608 | E |
| Specialized techniques | F. Seasoned technical—specialized: Proficiency, gained through wide experiences in a specialized or technical field. | 200<br>230<br>264 | 230<br>264<br>304 | 264<br>304<br>350 | 264<br>304<br>350 | 304<br>350<br>400 | 350<br>400<br>460 | 350<br>400<br>460 | 400<br>460<br>528 | 460<br>528<br>608 | 460<br>528<br>608 | 528<br>608<br>700 | 608<br>700<br>800 | F |
| Scientific disciplines | G. Technical—specialized mastery: Determinative mastery of techniques, practices and theories gained through wide seasoning and/or special development. | 264<br>304<br>350 | 304<br>350<br>400 | 350<br>400<br>460 | 350<br>400<br>460 | 400<br>460<br>528 | 460<br>528<br>608 | 460<br>528<br>608 | 528<br>608<br>700 | 608<br>700<br>800 | 608<br>700<br>800 | 700<br>800<br>920 | 800<br>920<br>1056 | G |
| Scientific disciplines | H. Professional mastery: Exceptional competence and unique mastery in scientific or other learned discipline. | 350<br>400<br>460 | 400<br>460<br>528 | 460<br>528<br>608 | 460<br>528<br>608 | 528<br>608<br>700 | 608<br>700<br>800 | 608<br>700<br>800 | 700<br>800<br>920 | 800<br>920<br>1056 | 800<br>920<br>1056 | 920<br>1056<br>1216 | 1056<br>1216<br>1400 | H |

Human relations skills required by the position:

1 = basic (courtesy)
2 = intermediate (get along well)
3 = critical (motivate people)

| KH | PS | AC | TOTAL |
|---|---|---|---|
| 152 | | | |
| Supervisor, key punch | | | |

| KH | PS | AC | TOTAL |
|---|---|---|---|
| 304 | | | |
| Actuarial specialist<br>Research associate | | | |

| KH | PS | AC | TOTAL |
|---|---|---|---|
| 700 | | | |
| Area manager | | | |

**EXHIBIT 18–7**
**Sample Evaluation**

**EXHIBIT 18-8**
**Position Description, November 1, 1975**

Position: Treasurer

Organization unit: Financial

Incumbent: George M. Arnold

Location: New York

---

Accountability objective:

This position is accountable for planning of debt/equity financing and the direction and coordination of cash mobilization, short-term investment, insurance, and benefit plan services.

Dimensions:

Department operating expenses: $1.0M

Short-term investment earnings: $2-5MM

Department employees: 24

Nature and scope:

Megalith, Inc. is a major, multinational corporation with financing requirements and cash management operations throughout the world. Major outlays of cash are anticipated to continue an upward trend during the next 8-10 years. Possible changes in accounting for and reporting of off-book financing, the need to generate increased amounts of capital overseas for use in overseas operations, and the uncertainties created by new international monetary arrangements pose formidable challenges to the corporation's financial capability and plans for growth. The Treasurer's function has been recently reorganized to concentrate on these problems.

**EXHIBIT 18–8** (*Continued*)

Reporting to the Treasurer are four Directors. Their areas of concentration are:

Financial Planning and Analysis (three employees)--This unit conducts overall analysis of debt/equity financing and performs similar analyses in developed plans for financing foreign operations from foreign financing sources; develops plans for the management of foreign exchange; makes buy/lease analyses of property from the financial point of view; and generates regularly total forecasts of cash requirements worldwide for short- and mid-term periods of time, and updates forecasts periodically during the year.

Domestic Financial Operations (five employees)--This unit makes short-term investments in the money market including treasury notes, CD's, and banker's acceptances; gathers and deposits cash through the operation and collection of 500 bank accounts throughout the United States; and monitors compensating balances in relation to lines of credit.

International Financial Operations (eight employees)--This unit coordinates overseas project financing; manages more than 40 bank accounts in approximately 12 different foreign countries, including the transfer of funds between accounts; deals with a variety of currencies; borrows money from other than offshore finance companies; and provides advice and counsel to management on the implications of the cash management and financing support for their operations.

Administration (eight employees)--This unit develops working company policies, including those having to do with credit and collection, for the guidance of all operating groups; buys insurance (premiums amounting to $2-3MM per year) for the corporation in the form of blanket policies covering worldwide risks (a $3MM deductible provision is a feature of all covered risks). In addition, this unit performs cost/benefit analyses of group benefit plans and participates in negotiating and placing benefits with carriers.

<u>Principal end results</u>:

1. Financial plans, and forecasts which reliably project the financing needs of the company
2. Optimum cash availability for current needs through effective use of cash mobilization systems and policies, and efficient financial operations
3. Maximum return on short-term investments consistent with the company needs for liquidity
4. A worldwide system of banking relationships which facilitates the management of funds, the availability of cash, short-term investments, and assures required borrowings
5. Risk and benefits plan placement which effectively meets company objectives
6. Knowledgeable advice and counsel to management concerning proposed capital expenditures and investments for domestic expansions, acquisitions, mergers, and other business ventures
7. Continuity and development of a professionally competent staff of financial managers and specialists

CASE 19

# NOTE ON JOB EVALUATIONS

*Bert A. Spector*
*Michael Beer*

In order to reduce actual and perceived internal inequities in the amount of pay received by employees of an organization, a large number of companies rely on some form of *job evaluation system*. By accompanying job evaluations with a wage and salary survey, these companies also hope to increase the perception of external equity.[1]

The essence of any job evaluation system is a ranking of jobs in order of their relative worth to the organization so that an appropriate and equitable rate of pay can be determined for each job. Determining the worth of jobs is, of course, difficult. Such determinations are typically accomplished by some standardized means of describing jobs so that they can be compared on a number of relevant factors and assigned a numerical rating reflecting their relative worth.

By far the most common method of job evaluation utilized in the private sector is some form of a *point system*. The first step of a point system is to draw up a manual which will provide a set of standards against which each job can be compared. Universal *factors* are identified. Two commonly used sets of factors include the following:[2]

| Hourly Rated Jobs | Salaried Jobs (Clerical, Supervisory, and Technical) |
|---|---|
| *Skill* | |
| Education | Education |
| Experience | Experience |
| Initiative and ingenuity | Complexity of duties |

*continued*

[1]For a fuller discussion of the concepts of internal and external equity, see *Note on Reward Systems*, Harvard Business School case 9-482-017, p. 7.

[2]These factors are suggested by the National Electrical Manufacturers Association and reprinted in Wayne F. Cascio and Elias A. Awad, *Human Resources Management: An Information Systems Approach* (Reston, Va.: Reston Publishing, 1981), p. 329, and Paul Pigors and Charles A. Myers, *Personnel Administration: A Point of View and a Method*, ninth edition (New York: McGraw-Hill, 1981), p. 365.

| Hourly Rated Jobs | Salaried Jobs (Clerical, Supervisory, and Technical) |
|---|---|
| *Effort* | |
| Physical effort | Monetary responsibility |
| Mental effort | Contacts |
| *Responsibility* | |
| Responsibility for equipment and process | Type of supervision |
| Responsibility for material and product | Extent of supervision |
| Responsibility for safety of others | Working conditions |
| Responsibility for work of others | |
| *Job Conditions* | |
| Working conditions | |
| Unavoidable hazards | |

Each factor is rated on the degree to which that condition exists in the job. *Anchor points* which describe different degrees of a factor are provided in order to increase the reliability and validity of the rating. Each anchor point is then assigned a numerical rating ranging from 25 to 100. The factor "Responsibility for equipment and process," for instance, could be divided into four anchor points which describe the degree to which it exists, and then assigned points as follows:[3]

| Degree | Points |
|---|---|
| Little possibility for mistakes | 25 |
| Small losses might occur, but mistakes easily caught. Errors might go up to $25 a week | 50 |
| Substantial loss possible before errors are discovered. Losses might be great but normally will not exceed $200 a week. | 75 |
| Responsible for important operation. Errors could cause substantial damage. | 100 |

The second step involves a detailed *description* of all the organization's jobs in which the requirements for each job are described and listed in a standardized fashion. Using those descriptions, each job is rated factor by factor according to the manual. The proper point value is assigned to each factor and the points are added up to give a *point total*

[3]Adapted from Leonard R. Sayles and George Strauss, *Managing Human Resources* (Englewood Cliffs, N.J.: Prentice-Hall, 1981), p. 401.

for each job. Jobs are then bunched together in job classifications or *grades* according to their point total.

The step of assigning wage ranges to each of these grades is usually preceded by some type of *wage survey*. A certain key, or *benchmark*, job is identified within each grade. A wage or salary survey looks at what those benchmark jobs are paid within a certain geographical area or particular industry. The company can then peg its own benchmark job in each grade to the labor market and build a range around that job. If job evaluations are kept up to date, and periodic wage surveys are made to keep the benchmark job rates in line with the prevailing labor market, such a job evaluation system can help to promote both internal and external equity.

Although the point system is the most commonly used method of job evaluation, there are others. *Ranking* involves listing a given set of jobs in order of importance from highest to lowest, taking into account the characteristics of each job as a whole. The *job classification* system, used by many government agencies, first involves establishing a set of classifications or grades (from grade 1 to grade 15, for example). The level of difficulty for each grade is carefully described, and individual jobs are then fitted into what seems like their most appropriate grade. All this is done without the elaborate analysis that is done in the point system. Finally, there is a complex *factor comparison* system which involves a computerized factor profile of each job.[4]

There are some possible limitations to a job evaluation system to consider. The system pays for jobs rather than for the particular individuals performing those jobs. Thus, individuals may be paid below their level of competence, or they may have little incentive to develop more competence unless promotions are possible. Some companies thus feel that a skills-based system would do more to encourage individual growth. A certain amount of inflexibility in personnel transfers or promotions may be caused by a job evaluation system, since the reassignment of employees demanded by organizational needs may involve moving an employee into a new wage range, either so far below his or her current range or so far above that current range that the new range would involve an immediate and dramatic increase or decrease. The reassignment question raises the question of if, when, and how to make exceptions to the job evaluation system. (When an individual employee's wage is made an exception to the prevailing wage ranges, that employee is said to be "red-circled.") And the degree to which employees perceive job evaluations as equitable depends to some extent on the trust they have in the method of rating and scoring jobs. If managers do not trust the system or think it valid, they will find ways

[4]Sayles and Strauss, op. cit., pp. 371–372.

of getting around it and thus increase distrust and escalate even further the desire to circumvent the system.

Whatever the possible limitations might be, most large firms in the United States today employ a job evaluation system for determining the compensation of their employees. But continued problems with all known systems spur the continued search for a means of determining a compensation system that will improve employee perception of equity and enhance pay satisfaction.

CASE 20

# LEP CORPORATION (A)

*E. Mary Lou Balbaky*
*D. Quinn Mills*

The Advanced Technology Division of the LEP Corporation was established in 1957. Its major function was the manufacture of electromechanical relays. In its first year the Division hired 500 employees and occupied 40,000 square feet of space. Production employees comprised 49 percent of the total population of this one-shift operation.

As the electronics industry evolved and expanded over the years, the Corporation kept pace with the changing technology and experienced rapid growth. It historically has maintained substantial profit margins and an annual revenue growth rate of 8 to 10 percent. Today, in 1981, the Advanced Technology Division employs 7,500 people and occupies 3,000,000 square feet of manufacturing and laboratory space, in addition to approximately 300,000 square feet of leased off-site space. A three-shift operation is now required to satisfy demands for the development and manufacture of advanced semiconductor logic and memory components for use in computers and office equipment systems.

In adjusting to the sophistication of semiconductor technology, the skill mix requirements changed. Today a wide variety of scientific and technical employees constitutes 56 percent of the total population and the production population has decreased from 49 percent in 1957 to 23 percent in 1981.

The years of rapid growth have caused the Division to double in population in the last 10 years. It enjoys a stable population with attrition running at approximately 3.0 percent a year; its work force is not unionized; and it has never had to resort to a layoff.

Last year's recruiting effort resulted in the addition of 500 new hires, approximately half of whom were professionals in technical disciplines. This was consistent with past years' recruiting results. However, hiring will be minimal this year because of the economic uncertainties facing all of industry at this time.

One of the major strengths of the company is the integrity of its personnel policies and practices and it is recognized as an industry leader. Considerable time and capital are invested to ensure that employee benefit plans keep pace with industry, that communications channels are open and active, that employee/manager relationships are nurtured, and that the performance planning/evaluation and pay programs are equitably and consistently administered.

At present the Division is faced with the following internal challenges: The current recession in the United States is forcing some internal belt-tightening. The rapid population growth rate of the Division is declining, and is anticipated to result in less internal movement and promotions. Increased demands for product, together with stronger emphasis on quality and reliability, will place even more pressure on production and related operations. New technology development will require heavy investment of capital and resources.

The external environment presents challenges in the areas of high inflation, competition, and the impact of the Division's size on the community. The LEP Corporation is the largest industrial employer in an area which is predominantly rural and obviously has an impact on housing, schools, tax revenues, local employment, local businesses, and environmental protection.

## SITE SITUATION SPECIFICS

### *Evolution of Focus*

Dr. Richard Campbell is the newly hired site manager and president of the Advanced Technology Division of LEP Corporation. Although there has been a strong tradition of filling jobs from within the company, Dr. Campbell was brought in from outside the firm because of his widely recognized expertise in the area of technology which will dominate the Division's efforts for the next few years. Since he assumed his job in August 1981, Dr. Campbell has been having meetings with his staff to become more familiar with all aspects of the business. Although the company with which he was previously associated was a high-technology company, many of the personnel policies were different from those of LEP Corporation, particularly in the area of human relations.

Since next year's salary plan will soon be ready for Dr. Campbell's review, he has asked John Taylor, the division personnel manager and a member of his staff, to prepare and review with him a summary of the Merit Pay and Employee Evaluation programs. (See Exhibit 20-1.) He also requested a review of plans for conducting merit pay training sessions for line management.

After a study of these programs, Dr. Campbell scheduled a review of the upcoming 1982 salary plan. Following are the basics of the plan presented to Dr. Campbell:

### *1982 Salary Plan*

BACKGROUND. Salary programs over the past years had maintained the average salary in the Division at a favorable position to the average salaries paid in other companies. Quality applicants were being attracted for hire and attrition was low. Employee satisfaction with their level of pay had been positive and overall morale remained high.

For the exempt population, the results of the national salary survey indicated that the Division would begin the year in a good relationship to the other companies in the survey. Using wage and economic trends, the average salaries paid in other companies were projected to increase 9.1 percent in 1982. Salary ranges were established based on the projected movement of outside salaries, and an increase guideline was developed that would generate salary increases during the year to maintain the average salary in the Division at a favorable position to the average salaries paid in other companies.

PROPOSED PLAN. The following exempt program, which was similar to the 1981 salary program, resulted from reviewing the salary/performance data of employees against the proposed 1982 salary ranges and increase guidelines:

1. The average increase will be 9.5 percent, with individual increases ranging from a low of 5 percent to a high of 13 percent. This 9.5 percent average increase to the salaries of the current population will yield an 8.0 percent increase in the average salary. This results from the effects of staffing dynamics, through which employees are lost from the Division each year due to terminations, retirements, leaves, transfers, and so forth. To maintain the work force, new employees are hired. Since new hires are generally paid in the lower portion of the ranges and employees leaving the location are paid higher in the ranges, the change in the population mix lowers the average salary.
2. The average time between increases will be 11 months with all employees receiving an increase during the year, the exception being a few employees in an overpay condition.
3. An additional 15 percent of the population will receive a second increase within a 12-month period. The salaries of these employees are in the lower portion of the ranges and their high performance ratings will produce increases in a shorter time span.

The nonexempt program is similar to that for the exempt population as the movement of outside salaries in the local area and the relationship to the salaries paid in those companies will be comparable.

The projected cost of salary increases granted in 1982 is 9.1 million dollars. Since increases are evenly distributed throughout the year, only one-half of their annual cost will be expended in 1982.

To provide the site with flexibility to cover unplanned salary activity during the year, a contingency of approximately 1 percent of the total increase cost (exempt and nonexempt) is built into the final salary plan that is submitted for approval.

## A NEW COMPETITIVE DEMAND

While in the process of reviewing the proposed 1982 salary plan, Dr. Campbell was informed by LEP Corporate Headquarters that his Division's competitive technological position was eroding and that the Division must have a new technology operational two years earlier than was planned. He suspended review of the salary plan, realizing that this new requirement would have an impact on the plan. He then asked each of his staff members, including John Taylor, personnel manager, to redefine his or her needs and identify any anticipated problems in order to meet this new requirement.

John Taylor knew that in order to bring the technology in early, the hiring plan would have to be increased by about 100 engineers and 50 technicians. In addition, approximately 100 employees must be transferred in from another location to support the new technology.

John also knew that the resulting expansion in terms of increased numbers of personnel and the ensuing costs, as well as other personnel issues that have recently surfaced, may have an impact on the 1982 salary plan. After several meetings with his own staff, John Taylor presented the following concerns to Dr. Campbell:

### *Major Concerns*

Engineering Compression in Pay Relationships. The demand for graduates of engineering schools has risen faster than the supply of new graduates. There has been a rapid escalation in the starting rates companies offer to engineers to be competitive in attracting new hires. The college hiring salary rate has increased at a rate of 10 to 11 percent in 1982. Offering competitive starting salaries will be a major determinant in the success of college recruiting.

Salary surveys are conducted annually for engineering positions. Over the last four years the rise in the salaries of engineers in the labor market has been similar to that of all exempts (approximately 9 percent).

As a result of the above factors, a number of engineers hired within the last few years frequently find their salaries equal to or, in some cases, less than the salaries of newly hired engineers. This has been a source of some concern. There is risk of increased attrition of these recent hires because of salary concerns.

The Advanced Technology Division will require a major college hiring program for the coming year to meet the manpower demands imposed by accelerated technology schedules.

### *Employees Questioning Pay Practices*

Constant analysis of the country's economic climate by the various news media has raised the consciousness of employees relative to their personal economic status. The rate of inflation as measured by the Consumer Price Index (CPI) and the continuing recession are indicating to employees that their standard of living is being eroded by forces beyond their control.

In addition, cost-of-living clauses in publicized labor contracts give the impression of offering protection to the unionized worker against inflation which nonunion employees of LEP Corporation feel they do not have. As the CPI increased to a high of 11.2 percent, employees compared this to their average rate of salary increases (9.5 percent) and several questioned the role of the Merit Pay Program in a high inflation environment.

Evidence of employee concern is the increased use of internal communications channels to express salary concerns. Opinion surveys, direct queries to management, employee/manager interviews, and other communication programs all reflect modest increases in employee concerns of salary compression, cost-of-living, and equity. The most common employee suggestion is an across-the-board salary adjustment to compensate for the rising cost-of-living.

### *Transfer in of Nonexempt Technicians*

In order to bring the required new technology on-line early, recruiting efforts have begun to acquire the necessary critical skills. Although engineering requirements will be filled primarily by new hires, many key technician openings must be filled from another LEP location which is phasing out some of its operations. The plan is to transfer in permanently 50 of their nonexempt technicians from the other location within the next six months.

The area of the country from which these transfers-in will be drawn employs a higher-paid labor market. As a consequence, LEP employees' salaries in that area are somewhat higher than those paid to employees with similar skills here. In past mass transfer activity, employees have received prorated merit increases at the time of the move. Proration is based on a proportion of their planned increase earned to the time of transfer.

Managers of the areas involved point out that because some employees in the Division share salary information, such apparent inequities may create doubts among the Advanced Technology Division's existing 500 technicians and could result in employee relations problems.

### *Design Specialists*

A major employer in the area has recently granted an 11 percent increase to the salaries of design specialists. This is the second year in a row that the salaries of this group have been increased locally at a higher rate than the average salaries on the outside. The labor market is extremely competitive for this skill with companies actively seeking new applicants.

There are 30 design specialists in the Advanced Technology Division and they are aware of the increase in outside rates for their skills. Some of the employees have questioned management about their pay rates. The current salary plan provides a yearly increase of 9 percent for this group which will result in their average rate of pay being only slightly ahead of the new rates paid on the outside. Since the skill of these employees is key to the successful implementation of the new technology management is concerned that some may leave to go elsewhere.

After reviewing these issues with John Taylor, Dr. Campbell was now faced with the task of defining a course of action to resolve each one of these concerns.

## EXHIBIT 20-1
## Summary of Merit Pay and Employee Evaluation Programs Presented to Dr. Richard Campbell by John Taylor on September 2, 1981

### Philosophy

LEP Corporation believes that rewarding individuals for their efforts and contributions to the business encourages employees to seek their highest level of productivity, promotes positive employee relations, and provides the company with the best return on its investment. This belief in merit is reflected in the pay program and other practices such as promotion from within and participation in selected developmental programs. The principal factor in this concept is the performance evaluation.

### Employee Evaluation Program

The execution of the merit system is dependent on the yearly evaluation of the employee's job performance, which is essentially a measurement of the employee's net contribution to the business. Because it is the company's practice to reward for performance (both in merit pay and promotions) much effort has gone into the Employee Evaluation Program in terms of attempting to achieve a reliable and fair method of defining and measuring performance. To ensure that employees are given optimum opportunity to achieve the highest level of performance evaluation possible, each phase of the program is given equal emphasis and involves the participation of the employee.

### Planning

Managers determine the key or major responsibilities of the employee's job, using an established job description as a guide. Managers strive to indicate tasks in performance plans which have the quality of being measurable, both in a qualitative and quantitative way. The manager then reviews the document with the employee and (1) explains the purpose of the plan, (2) states the key requirements, (3) states the objectives (departmental, mission, and so forth), (4) seeks the employee's views, and (5) tries to ensure that the employee understands the performance plan and the relative importance of each of its elements.

Performance plans are established annually and revised, if necessary, to reflect any change in job assignment, with the employee's knowledge and understanding.

Counseling

Integral to the sound execution of the Employee Evaluation Program are the counseling sessions held throughout the performance plan period. These sessions between the manager and employee allow each to express any concerns about performance and to assess progress against the performance plan.

Counseling is an ongoing process and can be initiated by either the employee or the manager when necessary. Counseling sessions ensure that the plan is on track and that the employee is not surprised by a less-than-expected appraisal in the final stage of the Employee Evaluation Program.

Evaluation

All employees are evaluated annually by their immediate supervisor, with three exceptions: (1) new hires are evaluated twice during the first year; (2) employees who are promoted or reassigned to significantly different positions are evaluated within six to nine months after assuming the position; (3) when an employee's performance changes and is sustained at the changed level for a minimum of six months.

The rating scale

Four categories of satisfactory performance have been established:

- o One (1)--Outstanding
- o Two (2)--Above average
- o Three (3)--Average
- o Four (4)--Satisfactory

When performance drops below the satisfactory level, the employee is evaluated as "unsatisfactory" and is not eligible for merit increases. Management

**EXHIBIT 20-1 (*Continued*)**

develops an improvement program and counsels the employee in order to help improve his or her performance. If performance is not improved to the satisfactory level, the employee is subject to dismissal.

The completed evaluation form is reviewed by the manager with the employee. The employee has an opportunity to comment on the evaluation form and sign it, signifying only that the contents were reviewed--not necessarily agreed with.

The rating is related to the Merit Pay Plan in that the percentage of the merit increase and the period of time between increases are determined by the rating. For example, an employee performing as a (1) might in a particular salary plan have an increase of 10 to 12 percent and a time period of 10 months between increases. A (4) might have a 7 to 9 percent increase and a timeframe of 12 to 15 months.

Merit pay systems

The company's pay practices are designed to attract and retain superior employees, to reward each individual in accordance with sustained performance on the job, and to motivate each to the highest possible level of performance. These practices have three primary objectives: internal equity, external competitiveness, and individualized pay based on sustained performance.

A. Internal consistency

Internal consistency is achieved through job classification which evaluates and classifies each job according to duties and skill requirements. Jobs of similar value to the company are classified together into the same salary grade for salary administration purposes. Each position is further classified as exempt or nonexempt according to overtime provisions of the Federal Wage and Hour Law.

B. External competitiveness

Salary surveys. External competitiveness is achieved through outside wage comparisons. Regular salary surveys are conducted to assure that LEP's comparisons are based on current outside pay rates. For the most part, national surveys are conducted on exempt positions and local surveys compare nonexempt pay rates.

LEP Corporation intends to maintain an average level of pay that is higher than the average level of pay for similar skills in other companies with which they compete for employees or with which they compete in the marketplace, thus assuring that the company's rates will be competitive.

Below is a graphic example of a typical survey data analysis:

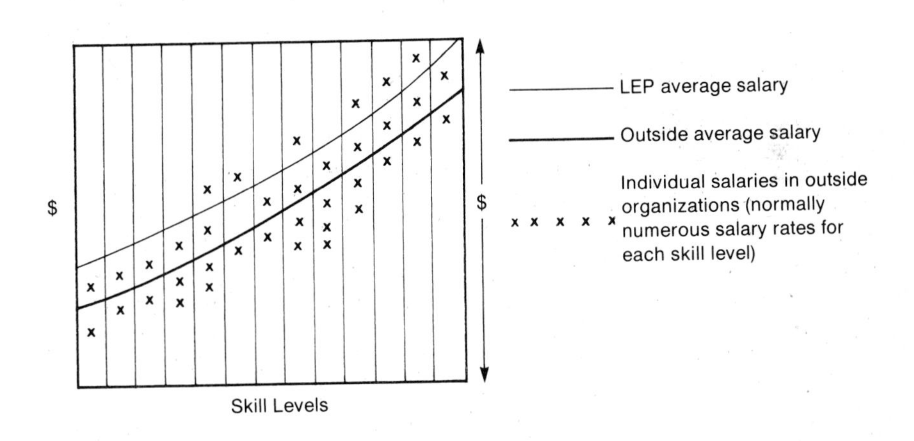


LEP salary ranges. Salary ranges are constructed for each pay grade in the company based on the results of salary surveys. A salary range is the difference between the maximum and minimum salary which is normally paid for a

**EXHIBIT 20-1 (*Continued*)**

job. An example of this structure is shown below:

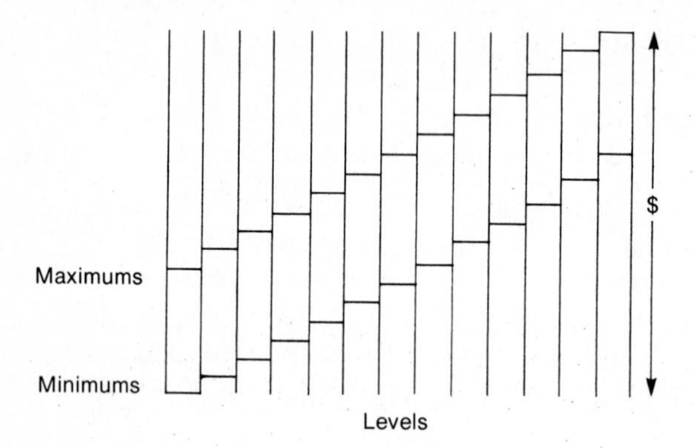


Salary ranges overlap for the following reasons:

1. The degree of skill difference between some skill levels is fairly close.
2. An employee in one level whose performance far exceeds the requirements of the assignment is often worth as much or more than an employee in the next higher level who has a lower performance.

C. Individualized pay

Merit pay allows individuals to directly influence their earnings through performance on the job. Increases are granted as they are earned through sustained or improved performance. The objective is to achieve significant pay differentials based on sustained performance over time.

To reward an employee properly based on a sustained level of performance the salary ranges are divided into areas representing the four categories of satisfactory performance (see figure below).

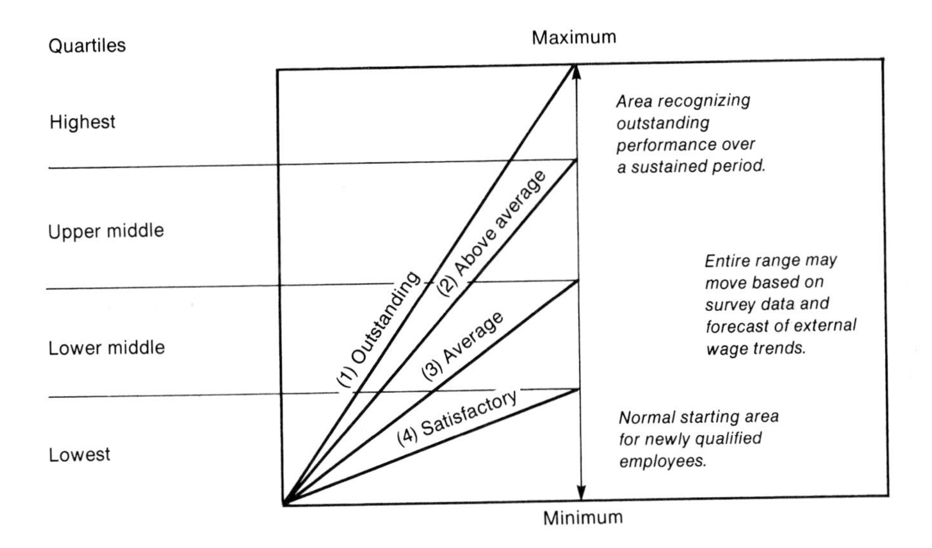


Rate of progress through the range varies and is based on sustained or improved performance. With a range that is 60 percent wide from the minimum to the maximum (not unusual), significant pay differentials can be paid based on performance. Over time a level 3 performer can earn up to 13 percent more than a level 4 performer, a level 2 performer 26 percent more than a 4 performer, and a level 1 performer 39 percent more than a level 4 performer.

A merit guide is provided to each manager for the purpose of achieving appropriate merit pay relationships and ensuring consistency in the criteria used for granting merit increases. To satisfy both objectives stated above, the

**EXHIBIT 20-1 (*Continued*)**

manager has the right to deviate from the guide (see example guide below).

Merit Increase Guide

SAMPLE

| | Minimum | Lowest | | Lower Middle | | Upper Middle | | Highest | Maximum |
|---|---|---|---|---|---|---|---|---|---|
| 1 Outstanding | 13% | 8-10 mos | 11% | 10-12 mos | 9% | 12-14 mos | 7% | 14-17 mos | 5% |
| 2 Above average | 11% | 10-12 mos | 9% | 12-14 mos | 7% | 14-17 mos | 5% | • | |
| 3 Average | 9% | 12-14 mos | 7% | 14-17 mos | 5% | • | | • | |
| 4 Satisfactory | 7% | 14-17 mos | 5% | • | | • | | • | |

The percentage in an employee's salary is based on the current performance rating in conjunction with where the current salary falls in the salary range. The four levels of satisfactory performance are shown in the left hand column while across the top are various positions of pay within the salary range.

The Guide, which is designed to achieve appropriate merit pay relationships within the salary range, indicates the amount by which an employee's salary should change and the approximate time between increases based on performance. For example, as measured against the same guide, an "outstanding" performer whose pay is in the area designated as lower middle would receive a higher increase within a shorter time frame than an "outstanding" performer whose pay is in the area designated as upper middle. The percentage change in salary becomes smaller and the time between increases becomes longer as the employee's salary approaches the maximum rate for the performance level. Once the maximum rate for the performance level has been achieved, future increases will depend upon one or more of the following three factors:

1. Upward movement of the salary ranges
2. Sustained, improved performance in present job
3. Promotion to a higher skill level

Salary program implementation

To grant an increase, the immediate manager recommends an amount which is reviewed by the next level of management. When there is agreement on the increase, it is communicated to the employee and implemented. To assure maximum protection of personal privacy, all salary discussions with an employee should involve only that employee's individual situation and not the salary status of others.

In the third quarter of each year the salary plan is developed for the upcoming year. Development of ranges, increase guidelines, projected costs, program size, and relationship to other companies are prepared by Personnel and reviewed with the Finance Department. The plan is submitted to the division president for approval. Finance may or may not concur.

After Division approval, the plan is forwarded to LEP corporate headquarters where it is reviewed for personnel and cost considerations and ultimately approved by the company president.

In December the approved plan is received from LEP corporate headquarters. It is then printed and distributed to management for implementation.

CASE 21

# FIRST FEDERAL SAVINGS (A)

*Stephen X. Doyle*
*Jay W. Lorsch*

Late in the third quarter of 1974, the board of directors of First Federal Savings requested that their president, Gene Rice, submit a recommendation on whether or not to grant branch managers a cash bonus that year. According to the company's Management by Objectives (MBO) system, the granting of yearly bonuses was contingent upon the attainment of specific corporate profit objectives, in addition to the individual manager's performance against preestablished MBO targets. Earnings in 1974 were targeted for a 15 percent increase over the 1973 profit of $7,800,000. This 15 percent growth objective was established late in 1973 when management fully expected that First Federal could continue compounding its growth at a rate of 15 to 20 percent per annum (see Exhibit 21-1). But the economic slowdown of 1974 hit the savings and loan industry particularly hard, with depositors withdrawing their savings to meet living expenses and taking advantage of the higher interest rates offered on short-term treasury bills. This reduction in savings made it difficult to grant mortgages which, in turn, constrained corporate profits.

Gene Rice clearly knew that the 1974 MBO goals and profit objectives would not be met (see Exhibit 21-2). He commented:

> We did a bad job of picking objectives for 1974. We had been lulled to sleep by a fantastic growth rate and a good economy. In 1974 the market went to hell, and our targeted 15 percent increase in profit before tax was not realistic. You know we base our bonus on the company meeting its profit objectives. In the past years we have been able to give handsome bonuses, and in return I expect a lot of our people. If our managers don't perform, then we are doing them a disservice by keeping them.

Rice considered the MBO system to be the cornerstone of management productivity and morale. He wondered if he should recommend a bonus to reward managers for their exceptional efforts even though the desired results had not been achieved. If he did give the bonus, what impact would it have on the future credibility of the MBO system? (See Exhibit 21-3.)

---

## ABOUT FIRST FEDERAL SAVINGS

First Federal Savings and Loan Association of Phoenix received its charter on November 1, 1934. In 1935 First Federal and the State Building and Loan Association initiated a merger. The merger was completed on February 2, 1938 and the surviving company, First Federal, recorded assets of $1,982,495 at the end of the year.

Management, recognizing the growth potential in the Arizona economy, initiated a program of branch expansion. The criteria established for opening a new branch were the potential economic growth in the area and the marketing advantages of offering convenient services to local residents. By the late 1960s First Federal was serving ten cities located in four counties of Arizona. According to management, the development of these branches gave the company a unique, competitive advantage, since a branch opening, in nearly every instance, was the forerunner of the development of a local shopping center.

This planned expansion continued through the late 1960s and early 1970s. In 1973, First Federal became the twenty-fifth largest savings and loan association in the nation. Combined assets stood at $778,000,000 (see Figure 21-1). By the end of 1974, First Federal planned to operate 27 branches and 5 subsidiaries specializing in management services to the real estate industry and thrift institutions.

## MBO AND THE BONUS PLAN

In the eyes of top management, superior employee performance would be the key to accelerated corporate growth and profits. Both George Leonard, chairman of the board and chief executive officer, and Rice felt that if outstanding performances were to be expected, rewards of a sizable amount must be given at relatively frequent intervals. In 1968 a bonus program was introduced based on the amount of annual profits. The cost of the incentive plan was considered to be self-liquidating, because the bonus pool came from funds that were generated above and beyond the expected profit levels.

In 1968 an MBO system was also introduced. MBO was considered to be a cornerstone of the bonus plan because the MBO structure, with its clear and measurable goals, provided the opportunity to reward managers for results. Rice commented on the MBO and bonus systems:

> In the 1960s we were just an ordinary savings and loan association, but we wanted to be something more. We were in need of an entrepreneurial climate while ours was very much security and image conscious.

**FIGURE 21–1 Recent Financial Trends**

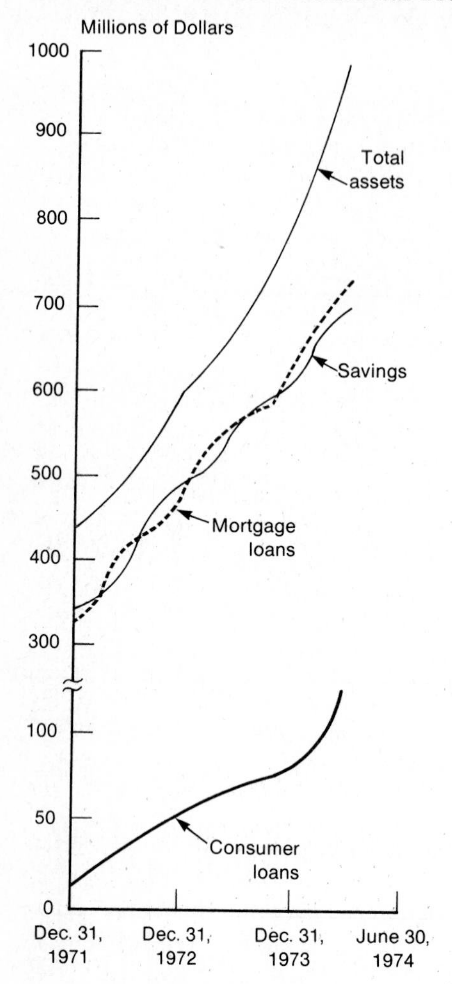


SOURCE: Company records.

> The MBO system was instituted as a planning tool for the future and the changes it would bring. The bonus was added as a sidelight to "help make things happen!" We viewed the bonus program as a vehicle which could be used to recruit the entrepreneurs which the bank's more aggressive stance would require.

The MBO process began late in the third quarter when the branch managers established financial and nonfinancial goals for the coming year. Each branch manager forwarded his or her goals to regional headquarters for approval. The regional manager and the branch manager often renegotiated projections before the final results were forwarded to corporate headquarters in Phoenix; there, all the branch and divisional goals were combined into an annual profit plan. The following MBO targets were typical at the branch-level office:

*Financial Goals*

1. Produce a net savings increase of $x$ dollars
2. Produce a net increase in mortgage loans of $x$ dollars
3. Produce a net increase in consumer loans of $x$ dollars
4. Maintain sales, personnel, and office expenses within budgeted amounts

*Nonfinancial Goals*

1. Give one speech per month to community groups
2. Complete one course at a local college per semester
3. Serve on the board of a community service agency
4. Cross-train two employees per quarter

Rice expected each manager to be an outstanding example of First Federal in his area; he commented:

> The company has a commitment to Arizona and I expect our managers not only to run the best savings and loan in regard to profit, but also to become involved in community service. In fact this commitment is specified in our nonfinancial targets. We don't just want a good looking branch office. I expect every manager to be a statesman in his community, to offer services and leadership just as George Leonard does on a national basis. Sure, it is expecting a lot, but our managers know that they will be rewarded for their performance.

Each month the local manager received individual feedback in the form of a computer report on his or her office's performance against monthly financial objectives. In addition, regional management was expected to interact with local branch managers about performance variances and the local manager's progress on nonfinancial objectives. Participators in the bonus plan were listed as follows (see Figure 21–2):

1. *Upper Management Group*
    - Chairman of the board
    - President
    - Executive vice president
    - President First Service Mortgage Corporation
    - Mortgage Loan Division manager
    - Savings and Branch Operations Division manager

- Consumer Loan Division manager
- Finance Division manager
- Data Processing Division manager
- Vice president personnel
- House counsel
- Association secretary
- Regional managers (3)

2. *Department Heads and Specialist Group*

- Mortgage Loan Administration manager
- P.I. production manager
- Accounting Department manager
- Assistant data processing manager
- Appraisal Department manager
- Loan officers (2)
- Systems and procedures manager
- Mobile home loan manager
- Treasurer

3. *Branch Manager Group*

- All branch managers

As previously stated, the amount of money available to the total bonus pool was based on profit generated above expected levels. The executive salary committee, based on First Federal's yearly forecasted profit plan, determined the profit levels representing expected amounts, as well as the levels that represented superior performance. According to this policy, a bonus would not be paid in 1974 unless 1974 profit exceeded 1973 profits by at least 15 percent.

The amount of the dollar reward to a manager was influenced by the individual's performance against objectives the manager had agreed to at the beginning of the year. The regional managers would review their subordinates and recommend a bonus amount for each of them. The actual determination of the bonus, however, was the prerogative of the executive salary committee. Generally speaking, the committee used the following guidelines to approve individual rewards:

1. The first 50 percent of the bonus pool should be allocated to an eligible employee based on his or her salary's percentage of the total salaries of all eligible employees in the incentive plan.
2. The second 50 percent of the bonus pool should be distributed with discretion by the committee.

FIGURE 21-2 Organization Chart, 1974

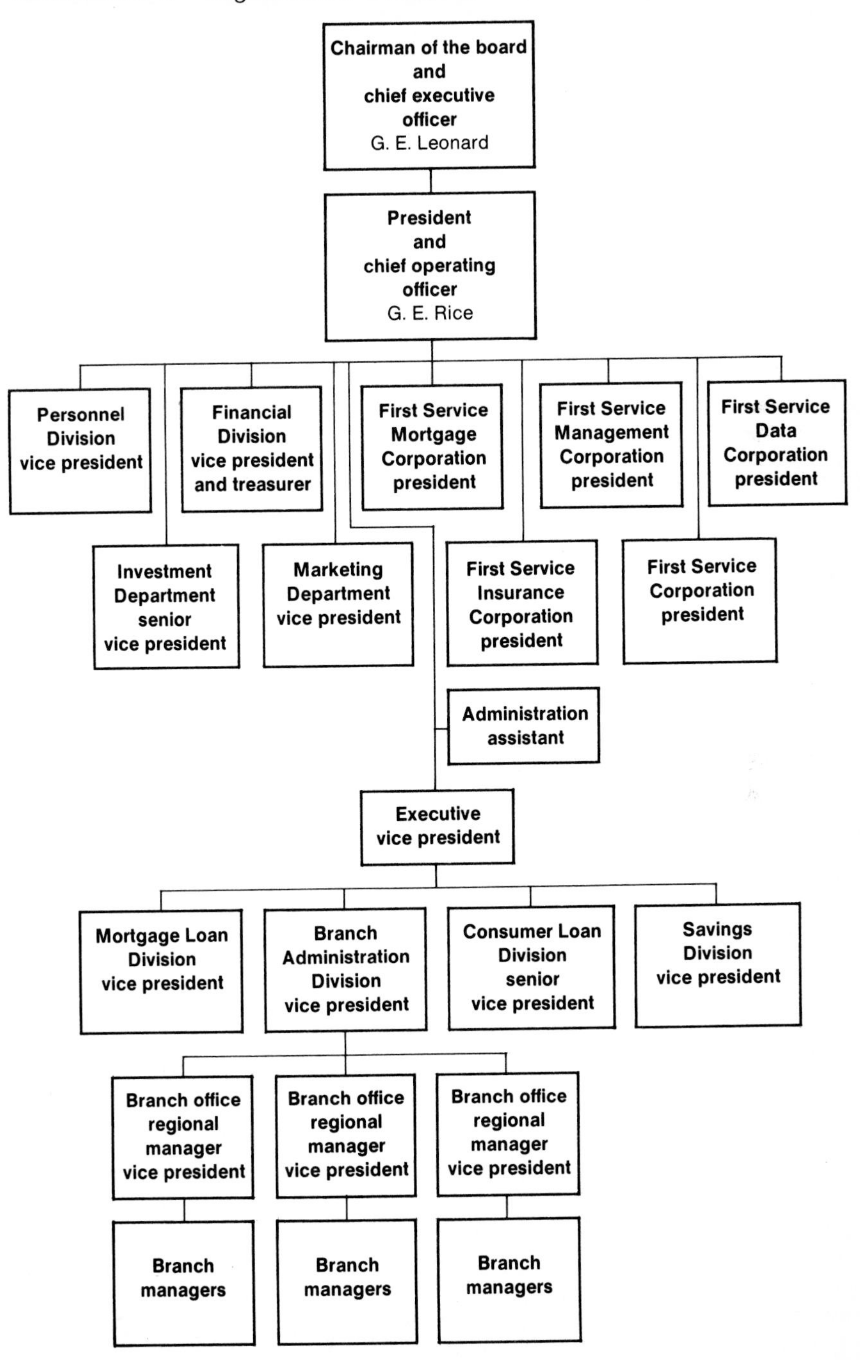

3. No bonus should exceed 40 percent of an individual's base annual salary.

## THE BRANCH MANAGERS

True to Rice's expectations, the branch managers were perceived by the casewriter to be talented, highly motivated "statesmen," who actively sought to increase the influence of First Federal in their respective areas. Typical of the managers under Rice was Harry Turner, who was in charge of the Scottsdale branch. After graduating from Arizona State University (ASU) in 1966, Harry entered the Air Force's flight training school. In 1971, Harry resigned his commission and joined First Federal as a management trainee. Harry commented about his experience at First Federal:

> I was really impressed when I met Gene Rice. He told me that what was important was performance. If I performed, I would get paid for it . . . 1974 has been a hard year. . . . I know that if the company does not hit a certain income level I will not get a bonus. It is hard to admit, but I am programming myself for no bonus. What would bother me is if we hit 75 percent of our corporate profit objective and we get zero reward. The company is still making millions and we should get part of the pie. If the bonus is small or nonexistent, I would wonder what all the heartache, sweat, and struggle are about. This year I think a $4,000 bonus would be fantastic, $2,500 acceptable, and anything under $2,000 very disappointing. Another important part of the bonus is that it has influenced my wife's attitude. . . . Branch managers tend to put in a lot of time. A $4,000 Christmas bonus can have a lot of meaning. From top management's point of view, the bonus could be a real problem because if Gene Rice pays this year, I might not be so concerned about meeting my financial objectives next year.

Another branch manager, Tom Walsh, provided more insight on the implications of Rice's decision. Tom was middle-aged, a vice president, and manager of the successful Tucson branch. Tom was recruited by Rice to open up the new Tucson office. Previously, he had been employed by Prudential Insurance as a district director of mortgage loans. Tom commented about MBO:

> Before MBO, we were all striving and working hard but not in a coordinated manner; MBO has made our goals more precise. We set targets for ourselves and we direct our efforts to meet these goals. The part that I like best about MBO is that it gives me an opportunity to see my own personal contribution to the company. You know, I guess I am a company man. The company has treated me very well and I feel proud about what First Federal is trying to accomplish. When I came on board I had a major hip operation. Both Gene and George Leonard knew about the opera-

> tion and that I would be laid up for a couple of months. They told me not to worry, to go up to Tucson and just talk to customers. . . . In regard to the bonus situation this year, I would love the extra dollars, but if it is not in the cards, I don't think I would feel short-changed. The company and my job reward me in many ways. We have a chance to help others, generate new ideas, and see results from our efforts.

Ray Walker managed a medium-sized branch in the southwest section of Phoenix. Walker's branch was situated at a busy intersection. Each corner of the intersection was occupied by a competing bank or savings and loan company. Walker had two children and was a graduate of Arizona State University with a B.A. in business management. His present assignment was the third management position he had held since graduating from the company's management training program in 1969. Walker had a number of opinions about his work and 1974. He commented:

> I was transferred into this office and I have had to accept someone else's goals. This is a growing problem because of expansion and the promotion from within policy. I am not sure that I agree with all the targets set by my predecessor, but the point is that I still am going to be judged on those targets. Right now I am beginning to think about my targets for next year. As a branch manager I set my own goals in key areas like savings deposit, mortgage loans, consumer loans, and expenses. I submit my forecasts to the regional headquarters; sometimes we disagree and then we negotiate.
>
> This forecasting is a very complex problem. I guess the only way to do it is to thoroughly know your area. But of course no one accurately predicted what happened recently. . . . This year we changed our goals in midyear. We shifted our emphasis from generating new mortgages to developing more savings deposits. In order to meet my new savings objectives, I hired six new tellers and the cost of these six tellers has placed me way above my expense budget. I know it and my boss knows it, but I do not expect to have my bonus penalized for being over budget. . . . The bonus plan is one of the two reasons I am here today. The other reason is the opportunity for personal growth. If there is no bonus this year there will be a tremendous morale problem among managers. . . .
>
> At my last branch assignment in Flagstaff I received a very mediocre bonus, and boy, was I discouraged! It wasn't the dollars that were important, it was my own feeling of self-worth. The bonus tells me how much the company appreciates my work. . . . The severe winter storms hurt the Flagstaff tourist industry. We had over 200 inches of snow. Most businesses, instead of depositing, had to withdraw savings just to survive. . . . I really put out and met four out of five goals, but as I mentioned, my bonus was small. I felt that the company did not appreciate my efforts and that they were inflexible. I was eventually promoted out of the office and I often wonder in my own mind if I did a poor job there. I hope I did OK, but perhaps the company was disappointed in me.

## SENIOR MANAGEMENT

George Leonard, chairman and chief executive officer, was an acknowledged industry leader and spokesman. Leonard had recently returned from Washington, D.C., where he was working with a number of congressmen on legislation that would affect the savings and loan industry. Leonard commented:

> When I joined the Association, it was an autocratic institution. All decision were made by the managing officer. Operationally, we were just not working together and there seemed to be little commitment or cooperation. I also think we tended to be short-sighted and were making decisions that would be beneficial on a short-term basis only.
>
> I soon realized that, if we were to continue our growth and expansion, authority would have to be delegated down. With the delegation of authority and accompanying accountability, I believed that a reward system had to be set up that would motivate young and talented managers to grow with us. While a bonus had previously been paid, I know that there was a lot of discontent because the bonus was being given arbitrarily with people at the top getting most of the dollars. One of the first things I did was to bring in some outside help, a consultant who started to make us think about our own corporate goals and industry position. These sessions led us to the conclusion that we wanted to be Number One in the savings and loan industry. To achieve this goal, we designed and implemented the MBO system and then later on tied the bonus in with achievement of MBO targets. The results have been outstanding. We have clear objectives, there is cooperation, and we have developed a group of talented and dedicated managers. This year we will not hit our target of 15 percent increase in profit before taxes. Our bonus is based on results, but I am concerned that we will ruin the spirit of the organization if we do not give a bonus.

Bill Blodgett was a vice president who had direct line responsibility for the 27 branch offices (Figure 21-2). Blodgett felt that MBO had made significant contributions, but that he had a problem on his hands in 1974. He commented:

> In a bad economy the company may not meet its profit objectives, but I could have a number of branches that are meeting or exceeding their office objectives. How do I tell them that there is no bonus this year? How do I motivate them next year?

Another vice president, Dave Braun, was in charge of the Financial Division. Braun graduated from Arizona State University in 1937 with a B.A. in accounting, and returned to ASU in the late 1950s to earn an MBA. Braun commented on MBO:

> We have the problem of matching numbers with behavior. When McSweeney and Associates, our management consultants, originally sold us on the MBO approach, it was based on a rigid formula of profit attainment; 1973 was a good year with a $7,800,000 profit and we also had a good bonus. This year, the bonus situation has not been decided. We are accruing funds, but I don't know if they will be dispensed. I am not sure what my decision would be if I were Gene Rice. . . .
>
> On one side of the argument is the position that the goals in and of themselves are important. If we don't make our targets as a company, then there just is no dollar bonus that year. Also, how can we establish believable goals if we say one thing and then do another? On the other side of the argument is the fact that everyone has made a tremendous effort this year. We have achieved some of our objectives. If we do not give a bonus, then we are not acknowledging the hard work and flexibility of our staff. We asked our managers to shift gears right in the middle of the year. They shifted from an emphasis on new mortgages to an emphasis on generating new savings accounts. . . .
>
> We came up with a number of innovative marketing ideas, and our branch managers picked up the ball and started generating new accounts. I guess my main worry with the bonus this year is concern for motivation next year. . . . Would suspension of the 1974 bonus have serious negative impact on our managers?

**EXHIBIT 21–1**

**Consolidated Five-Year Growth, First Federal Savings** *($ Thousands Except Growth Statistics)*

| | 1973 | 1972 | 1971 | 1970 | 1969 |
|---|---|---|---|---|---|
| *Deposits* | | | | | |
| Passbooks | $156,270 | $141,450 | $106,066 | $ 89,563 | $ 84,153 |
| Certificates | 461,585 | 344,713 | 235,850 | 160,328 | 127,382 |
| Total | $617,855 | $486,163 | $341,916 | $249,891 | $211,535 |
| *Loans* | | | | | |
| First mortgage | $622,080 | $488,111 | $343,734 | $241,035 | $196,919 |
| Property improvement | 47,868 | 40,464 | 28,966 | 18,348 | 11,512 |
| Mobile home | 35,977 | 11,218 | 6,527 | 2,312 | — |
| Other | 12,614 | 9,029 | 8,687 | 8,395 | 8,310 |
| Total | $718,539 | $548,822 | $387,914 | $270,090 | $216,741 |

| | | | | | |
|---|---|---|---|---|---|
| *Growth Statistics* | | | | | |
| Number savings accounts | 137,703 | 109,415 | 92,867 | 82,610 | 80,019 |
| Number first mortgage loans | 26,072 | 22,540 | 17,998 | 16,099 | 15,409 |
| Number property improvement loans | 15,872 | 13,471 | 10,674 | 8,149 | 6,225 |
| Number mobile home loans | 2,046 | 1,128 | 578 | 177 | — |
| Number full service offices | 27 | 22 | 20 | 19 | 18 |
| *Operating Results* | | | | | |
| Total revenue | $ 57,092 | $ 41,324 | $ 26,979 | $ 19,648 | $ 15,404 |
| Total expenses | 46,414 | 32,810 | 22,493 | 17,548 | 13,885 |
| Income before income taxes & extraordinary items | 10,678 | 8,514 | 4,486 | 2,100 | 1,519 |
| Income taxes | 2,850 | 2,100 | 835 | 370 | 245 |
| Income before extraordinary items | 7,828 | 6,414 | 3,651 | 1,730 | 1,274 |
| Extraordinary items | — | — | 668 | — | — |
| Net income | $ 7,828 | $ 6,414 | $ 4,319 | $ 1,730 | $ 1,274 |

SOURCE: Company annual report.

## EXHIBIT 21-2
## Consolidated Statement of Income, First Federal Savings and Wholly Owned Subsidiaries

| For the Six Months Ended June 30 | 1974 | 1973 |
|---|---|---|
| *Revenues* | | |
| Interest on loans | $29,291,641 | $21,225,843 |
| Loan fees and service charges | 4,462,150 | 3,171,001 |
| Investment income | 2,260,391 | 1,290,610 |
| Real estate operations, net | 624,362 | 368,920 |
| Other | 799,976 | 818,433 |
| | $37,438,520 | $26,874,807 |
| *Expenses* | | |
| Interest on savings deposits | $21,435,918 | $14,673,396 |
| General and administrative expenses | 8,007,838 | 5,083,259 |
| Provision for loan losses | 74,863 | 0 |
| Other interest expense | 3,480,144 | 1,326,407 |
| | 32,998,763 | 21,083,062 |
| Income before income taxes | 4,439,757 | 5,791,745 |
| Provision for income taxes | 1,240,344 | 1,542,180 |
| Net income | $3,199,413 | $4,249,565 |

## EXHIBIT 21-3

# Carrot & Stick

## More Concerns Tie Bonuses to Meeting Goals for Workers

### *Programs Spur Employees To Do More, Firms Say: But Some Problems Seen*

### *A Link to the Crime Rate*

**By ROGER RICKLEFS**

Staff Reporter of The Wall Street Journal

Fourteen years ago, when Gene E. Rice was a branch manager of First Federal Savings & Loan Association of Phoenix, he received an annual bonus of exactly $580, and he didn't like it. "All the branch managers and all the vice presidents got the same thing. I thought I was working harder than the rest and I thought I should be paid more. So it was a negative incentive," he says.

Now Mr. Rice is president of the bank, and he has a bonus plan that he likes a lot better. Today payouts range up to 40% of salary and down to nothing. The amount depends on the individual's performance against pre-established goals, ranging from the number of new savings accounts to the number of speeches delivered to real-estate groups.

The new bonus plan, which grew out of the "management-by-objectives" program the bank started in 1968, has "definitely encouraged people to work harder and has also helped us attract good people," Mr. Rice says.

Like First Federal, hundreds of companies have adopted management-by-objectives or similar plans in recent years, but they operated independently of bonus programs. The more jaded executives have often figured that they were just another management fad. But now companies are giving these programs the bite that counts: They're tying the plans to the size of paychecks.

**"A Growing Practice"**

"Five years ago, setting the bonus on the basis of management by objectives was a rarity, but today it is a growing practice," says George A. Goddu, a principal and compensation specialist at Peat, Marwick, Mitchell & Co., the large accounting firm. Recently, International Business Machines Corp., Bendix Corp., CNA Financial Corp., PepsiCo Inc., and numerous others have all moved in one way or another to relate their bonuses more directly to the recipient's actual performance.

One result is that in companies where almost everybody with comparable rank could count on getting similar bonuses, executives now find their peers getting bonuses much smaller—or much bigger—than their own. Some of them are shocked by the discovery, especially when the difference may amount to thousands of dollars.

At First Texas Financial Corp., a Dallas savings-bank holding company, bonuses used to range up to 10% of salary. Starting last year, they ranged from zero to 30% of pay. Until last year, nobody at Norton Co., the large Worcester, Mass., abrasives maker, received any bonus. But in a new plan for 130 executives, some got a 30% bonus last year, and seven hapless managers again received nothing, the company says.

**Bonuses of 100% of Salary**

One Midwestern conglomerate started a new plan last year with specific performance goals and potential bonuses ranging up to 100% of salary. This replaced a program that left awards completely to management's discretion and paid 10% to 18% of salary, says Frederick A. Teague, vice president and compensation specialist at Booz, Allen & Hamilton Inc., management consultants.

Sometimes the new programs generate enormous sums for executives who rate highly. In a new performance-oriented plan at IBM, Frank T. Cary, chairman, earned a bonus of $246,000 last year, well over his salary of $200,000.

## EXHIBIT 21–3 (*Continued*)

But sometimes, too, subordinates get awards while their bosses get nothing. At CNA Financial, the big insurance, finance and real-estate concern, where corporate earnings declined last year, the top officers didn't receive any bonuses. At subsidiaries, however, bonuses ranged up to $25,000, Frank Metzger, senior vice president, says.

Practically all of the new plans operate by setting fixed goals in advance, usually starting with profits. At First Texas Financial, for instance, the new bonus plan has a profit goal "that has to be met or nothing else happens," John L. Ingle, president, says. But in addition, the Dallas bank-holding company sets profit goals for individual units, then looks at other factors such as penetration of market in a given field, reduction of operating expenses and improvement of facilities.

**What's a "Good Job"?**

Of the nation's largest 100 companies, probably 30 to 40 now set bonuses by some sort of pre-agreed formula for what constitutes "a good job" and vary the awards from one profit center to another, says Graef S. Crystal, vice president of Towers, Perrin, Forster & Crosby Inc., compensation consultants. This figure compares with only five to 10 companies five years ago, he says. In addition, some companies, including PepsiCo, say they are constantly striving to make the goals more specific and detailed.

Companies find that the bonus plans can encourage the pursuit of all kinds of goals, not just increased profit. A plan started last year at Bendix includes routine financial goals but also adds objectives in "management development," minority and female employment and safety and health, says Kenneth I. Otto, vice president for personnel and organization development. Thus, a Bendix executive's bonus now depends in part on how well he conducts college recruiting, provides able executives to other units of the corporation, works with high schools to attract minority employees and meets goals for upward mobility of women and blacks, the official says.

J.C. Penney Co., which has paid cash bonuses based on annual results for many years, started a program in 1971 that awards bonuses in Penney stock based on results over a three-year period. "We wanted to get people interested in longer-range development," Ronald A. Johnson, compensation manager, says.

Outside of business, the incentive-bonus principle is being applied to crime fighting. The Orange, Calif., police department last year started a program that boosts police pay if crime declines in four categories considered responsive to improved police prevention work: burglary, robbery, rape and auto theft. So far this year, crime in these categories has declined 17% from a year ago, and the police have received one raise of 2%, Police Chief Merrill Duncan says. As a check against fiddling with statistics, outsiders audit the program by monitoring reports of police calls he adds.

Many companies say they are pleased with the performance bonus approach. "You see results right away," says Samuel N. Hibbard, Norton Co.'s director of compensation and financial benefits. "An incentive plan focuses effort on what management wants effort to go into."

**Knowing What Is Expected**

By the same token, the new programs also help executives know exactly what management expects and why they are getting the money. Bendix Corp.'s Mr. Otto, who has pushed performance bonuses, says: "When I came here two years ago, I asked people, Do you know how you earned your bonus last year?' Most people didn't really know, and that is what got me on this kick."

In addition, companies say the specific goals and criteria of the new incentive programs force executives to reward the high performers and to squeeze the inept. "Our bonuses previously tended to be more or less the same for everybody," says Roland Beers, PepsiCo's personnel vice president. "Executives are reluctant to differentiate."

Mr. Crystal of Towers Perrin says that "if there isn't some sort of formula, everybody tends to get the same thing because you can't blame the disparity of awards on an inanimate object. If you have an infinite amount of discretion, you don't use any." The consequent similarity of bonuses grates on the strong performers who feel they aren't being recognized, executives say.

**Problems with the Plans**

But performance-bonus plans take time to set up and can create problems of their own. "Nobody has ever designed a plan like this that worked right the first time," says Mr. Ingle of First Texas Financial. "Some of the goals we set had to be shifted around during the year due to things happening over which we had no control," he adds.

Mr. Crystal of Towers Perrin adds: "A lot of companies try basing the awards on meeting budgets. This gives the division manager a motive to set the budgeted profit too low. In some companies, people are always pleading to readjust the formula. It can get to be sort of like the chairman of the board holding night court."

Mr. Crystal says that one New York conglomerate that used to pay executives fairly similar bonuses switched in 1970 to bonuses based on divisional performance, but it went back to the old system last year. "The problem was that half the division heads got nothing, the others got up to $50,000 a year and the chairman wasn't sure that the right people were getting the $50,000. One big problem was a division president who got a huge award. But he had done well mostly because a key competitor was on strike for six months," Mr. Crystal says.

---

CASE 22

# DANA CORPORATION—THE RICHMOND CAMSHAFT PLANT (A)

The following material is provided by Dana Corporation to employees to describe the Scanlon program of the Richmond camshaft plant.

## WHAT IS THE SCANLON PLAN?

The Scanlon plan is a program whereby all Dana people at the camshaft plant have an opportunity to participate in the managing of the local plant. Employees have the opportunity to participate in the managing of the plant by making suggestions through a committee structure as to when, where, why, what, and how their job or other jobs should be performed. The objective of the Scanlon plan is working together as a group (teamwork) in order to be more productive and efficient, to reduce scrap, to reduce costs, and to produce a monthly bonus for all employees who have sixty (60) days or more service.

## WHEN AND HOW DID THE SCANLON PLAN GET STARTED IN CAMSHAFT?

The Scanlon plan is a result of an agreement between the United Auto Workers of America (UAW) and the Dana Corporation. The plan was agreed to by the concerned parties and placed into effect on July 1, 1976. The Scanlon program was placed into effect for a period of twelve (12) months on a trial period basis. At the conclusion of the trial period, the employees will have had the opportunity to vote as to whether or not the Scanlon plan should remain permanently in effect at the camshaft plant.

## WHO STARTED THE SCANLON PLAN?

The Scanlon plan is based on principles developed by the late Joseph N. Scanlon. Mr. Scanlon was a former union official and associated

---

later with the Massachusetts Institute of Technology. Frederick G. Lesieur, former union official, instructor at Massachusetts Institute of Technology and a long-time friend and associate of Mr. Scanlon, is carrying on his work. Mr. Scanlon developed the program with a concept in mind that the employee, employer, and the union had much in common. His thoughts were that every employee has a contribution to make concerning ways to make improvements on the job. He felt that any improvements that could be made on the job would help to solidify the company's business in the market place and, in turn, would provide increased job security.

## WHY DO WE HAVE A BONUS PLAN?

In addition to being a plan whereby all employees work together to better manage our plant and secure our jobs, the plan also pays a bonus in cash when labor-saving improvements are made. This cash bonus is an incentive for everyone to participate in making our plant more efficient. An efficient plant satisfies its customers, earns profits, grows, and provides good wages and secure jobs for its employees. Being an efficient company ensures our competitive position in the work market. This means being able to produce large quantities of camshafts at the highest quality levels for the lowest prices. The greatest productivity gains are made by working smarter, not necessarily by working harder.

The Scanlon concept of participative management provides the framework for all of us to get our productivity-increasing ideas into use; then pays us a higher wage, in the form of a bonus, for the increased productivity.

Our bonus is not a give-away program. It is paid when it is earned by better than normal performance. But if performance is only average or below, it is equally fair that there is no bonus.

## HOW DO YOU PARTICIPATE IN THE SCANLON PLAN?

Each person has the opportunity to make a written or verbal suggestion to any member of his or her elected production committee. The purpose of a suggestion should be to improve:

- Methods:
  - Eliminate any unnecessary operations
  - Simplify your own job
  - Suggest new methods
  - Simplify present methods

- Machinery and equipment:
  - Improve machine output
  - Improve design or construction
  - Reduce machine set-up time
  - Reduce machine downtime
  - Reduce maintenance costs
- Paperwork:
  - Eliminate duplicate work
  - Eliminate unnecessary reports
  - Simplify or combine forms
  - Reduce or simplify filling-in of forms
  - Reduce occasions for errors
  - Reduce phone, postage, or shipping costs

## WHAT IS A PRODUCTION COMMITTEE?

The camshaft plant was divided into eight (8) production committees representing designated areas and shifts within the plant (see Exhibit 22-1). These committees are subject to change and can be structured in any way which would best serve the people whom they represent. Each group has its own production committee made up of a management representative and two (2) elected employee representatives. The production committees solicit monthly suggestions from the employees whom they represent. After gathering the suggestions, they discuss what should be done with each. A suggestion can take one of five dispositions at the production committee level. The five dispositions are:

1. Accept the suggestion and put it into use.
2. Reject the suggestion.
3. Accept the suggestion and put in under investigation (suggestions are normally put under investigation when there are not enough facts to make a decision, and when it is necessary to find out if the savings involved would offset the cost of putting it into effect).
4. Accepted and referred to screening committee (these suggestions normally are those that a production committee feels should be placed into effect but cost over $200 to implement).
5. Rejected—difference of opinion (these are suggestions in which one or more members of any production committee has a difference of opinion with the fellow member of the committee as to whether or not a suggestion should be put into effect). These suggestions are then referred to the screening committee.

A production committee may spend up to two hundred dollars ($200) on any one suggestion.

The production committee may request and will receive whatever assistance is necessary from management, service departments or production departments in order to process and implement suggestions.

## WHAT IS THE SCANLON SCREENING COMMITTEE?

The screening committee consists of five (5) of the elected employee members from the production committees and five (5) management employees, consisting of the plant manager and four (4) other management representatives appointed by him.

The screening committee meets once each month prior to announcing the monthly bonus results.

The screening committee is set up for the sole purpose of assisting the production committees; reviewing the calculations of the monthly Scanlon bonus and for the purpose of discussing what improvements could be made to earn bonus. The committee will also discuss why a bonus was not earned during any month, if we should experience that happening. They review any business that the production committees desire to have them discuss.

## HOW THE BONUS IS CALCULATED

The increases in productivity and the reduction in scrap and other costs resulting from our working smarter, under the Scanlon plan, will generate a monthly bonus expressed as a percentage of each individual's gross monthly income. This bonus is paid monthly, usually around the 22nd of the month for bonus earned the previous month, in a separate check. The basis used to calculate the bonus each month is the ratio of total payroll costs plus vacation and holiday accruals to the sales value of production. The base ratio is established to represent the normal or expected total payroll cost to produce one dollar's worth of sales, expressed as a percent of the sales value of production. In the example, the base ratio is 37 percent. This means that in that period, the normal total labor cost would be 37 percent of the sales value of production or 37 cents for each one dollar of product produced at sales value. Once this base ratio is established, it is changed only to allow for significant changes in the factors which affect its calculation. (See Exhibit 22-2.)

In the example, the total sales value of production is $700,000 and so the allowed or "expected" total labor is 37 percent of this, or $259,000. However, the actual labor cost is only $215,000. The difference of $44,000 then becomes the Scanlon bonus pool.

For each one dollar in the bonus pool, 75 percent will be paid to the people participating in the plan and 25 percent will be retained by the company. The people get 75 percent of this bonus because they have increased productivity by working smarter and the company gets 25 percent of this bonus because it supplied the capital monies needed to implement our labor saving ideas. Prior to making the monthly payment of 75 percent to Dana people and 25 percent to the company, 25 percent of all bonus (both the employees' and the company's share) is set aside in the form of a reserve in case there would be a deficit month. A deficit month is a month when total payroll cost exceeds allowed payroll. (See Exhibit 22-3.)

## THIS IS AN EXAMPLE OF HOW AN INDIVIDUAL PAY RECORD WOULD LOOK WITH BONUS

Bonus pay may vary from one month to another month, based upon the gross earnings for a month, even though the percentage of bonus earned may be the same for both months.

Bonus is calculated on the basis of actual hours worked during a month inclusive of cost of living, shift premium and overtime premium. Since bonus is paid on the basis of work participation, any wage or salary preceived for absence from work, holidays, vacation, bereavement or jury duty will not be considered when computing bonus pay.

At the end of each Scanlon year, which is June 30, all money remaining in the reserve account is distributed 75 percent to the people and 25 percent to the company in what is referred to as a thirteenth monthly Scanlon bonus check. In the event a Scanlon year ends with a

| Name | Total Hours Worked | Overtime Hours | Hourly Rate |
|---|---|---|---|
| John Doe | 190 | 30 | $5.00 |
| **Total Pay** | **Bonus (%)** | **Bonus** | **Total** |
| $1,230.00 | 11.79 | $145.02 | $1,375.02 |

deficit balance in the reserve account, the entire deficit is absorbed by the company and is not charged against any future bonus. The reserve account example illustrates how this works and shows the effect of a deficit month. (See Exhibits 22-3 and 22-4.)

In reading this pamphlet, you have had a brief introduction to the Scanlon plan. With visions of bonus and prosperity in your mind, it can only be said that the Scanlon plan will work only if we want to make it work.

In this program everyone is a partner and it requires people willing to put forth effort as well as ideas. The program offers all employees a great opportunity, so let's do our part as individuals and make it work.

In this example, the actual payroll was greater than the allowed payroll, which results in a deficit bonus pool. This is charged against the bonus reserve account and reduces the amount left in the reserve at the end of the Scanlon year.

The Scanlon booklet is intended to serve only as a general guideline as to the operation of the plan. The plan is flexible in nature and may be changed or altered to best serve the needs of the participants.

The Scanlon program is set forth in a memorandum of understanding between the UAW of America and the Dana Corporation Perfect Circle Division, Camshaft Plant.

## GLOSSARY

- **Accruals, Vacation-Holiday.** The constant amount set aside each month so as to spread the effect of large vacation and holiday pay in any one month over the entire year.
- **Base Ratio.** The expected labor dollar cost of making each dollar's worth of sales value of production.
- **Bonus Percentage.** The monthly bonus pool after deduction of reserve and of the Company's share expressed in relation to the total eligible payroll. This percentage when applied to your month's earnings, gives you your month's bonus payment.
- **Bonus Pool.** The difference between the actual payroll for the month and the allowed payroll using the current ratio times the monthly production.
- **Bonus Year.** The Scanlon year runs from July 1 of one calendar year through June 30 of the next calendar year.
- **Compensation.** Payment for work done; wages and salaries.
- **Costs.** Wages, salaries, employee benefits, materials, heat, light, power, and all other expenses of operations must be kept down if we do not want to lose business to our competitors. Suggestions help to keep them down.

- **Deficit.** Term used to describe the unhappy situation when the actual payroll cost is greater than the allowed payroll cost; means no bonus that month.
- **Incentive.** Something that stimulates or motivates you to do something. When you are walking across the street and you see a truck coming right at you, you have an incentive to move fast.
- **Incentive—Group.** An incentive to motivate the team to better performance.
- **Lesieur, Fred.** Mr. Lesieur is our plan consultant. He was brought up in a shoe town; his parents worked in a shoe factory and he worked in the cutting room. He became associated with Joe Scanlon while a machinist at LaPointe Machine & Tool, where the plan was installed. His immediate grasp of the plan so impressed Joe Scanlon that he was asked to go to M.I.T. as his assistant. Upon Joe's death, Fred was asked by the university to continue his work.
- **Payroll, Actual.** Wages and salaries actually paid for the month.
- **Payroll, Allowed.** Total sales value of production multiplied by the base ratio. This is the target or "bogey" which we must beat, if we are to earn a bonus. If we fail, there is a deficit, no bonus, and a reduction in the reserve.
- **Payroll, Participating.** The payroll on which the bonus percentage is calculated. It differs from the actual payroll by excluding the wages and salaries of employees in the 60-day waiting period, employees taking time off, and so on.
- **Production Committee.** Made up of employee and management representatives, considers cost-saving, efficiency-improving suggestions from its area. Refers all suggestions, reporting all action taken at its meeting to the screening committee.
- **Productivity.** Relation between input (labor, equipment, parts and so forth) and output (finished goods). Productivity improvement means producing more output with the same input or the same output with less input. A rough measure is the ratio of total sales value of production to payroll.
- **Ratio.** The relation of payroll cost and total sales value of production. Total sales value of production multiplied by the current ratio equals allowed payroll.
- **Reserve.** Part of the gross bonus pool (or total savings from increased productivity set aside to compensate for deficit months. Any cash reserve at the end of the year is distributed as a year-end bonus. Any year-end deficit is absorbed by the company.
- **Sales Value of Production.** Actual production for the month valued at sales dollars.

- **Scanlon, Joseph.** The inventor of the Scanlon plan; one-time prize fighter, open hearth tender, steel company cost accountant, union local president, union headquarters staff member, lecturer at Massachusetts Institute of Technology, and leading labor relations advisor to industry. He drew on his vast and varied experiences to devise the Scanlon plan. Mr. Scanlon died in 1956.
- **Screening Committee.** Made up of management and employee representatives; reviews and disposes of suggestions coming up through production committees.

## EXHIBIT 22–1
## Committee Structure

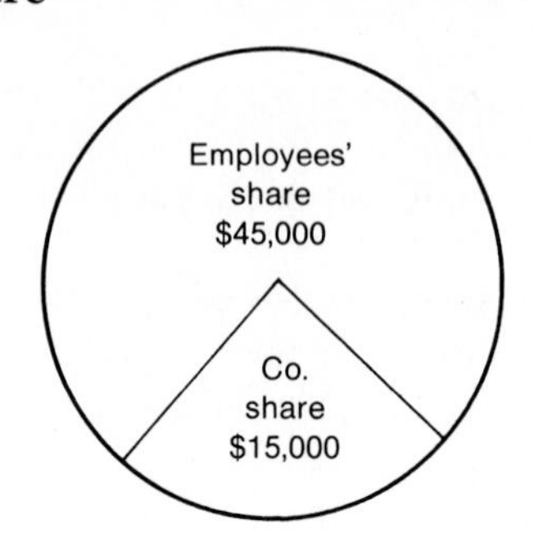


| | |
|---|---|
| **Office 1st**<br>Supervisor (chairman)<br>2 elected/committee[a] | **Turning 1st**<br>Supervisor (chairman)<br>2 elected/committee |
| **Grd. finish line insp. 1st**<br>Supervisor (chairman)<br>2 elected/committee | **Turning 2nd**<br>Supervisor (chairman)<br>2 elected/committee |
| **Grd. finish line insp. 2nd**<br>Supervisor (chairman)<br>2 elected/committee | **Turning 3rd**<br>Supervisor (chairman)<br>2 elected/committee |
| **Grd. finish line insp. 3rd**<br>Supervisor (chairman)<br>2 elected/committee | **Skilled trade G.M.**<br>Supervisor (chairman)<br>2 elected/committee |

[a]Two elected for each production committee

## EXHIBIT 22-2
## Bonus Calculation Example

| | |
|---|---|
| Sales value of production | $700,000 |
| Allowed payroll at 37 percent | 259,000 |
| Actual payroll | 215,000 |
| Bonus pool | $ 44,000 |
| Less reserve for deficit months—25 percent | 11,000 |
| Balance | $ 33,000 |
| Company share—25 percent | 8,250 |
| Employees' share—75 percent | $ 24,750 |
| Participating payroll | $210,000 |
| Bonus percentage ($24,750 : $210,000) | 11.79 percent |

*Note:* The reason that the participating payroll is less than the actual is because no bonus is paid to employees on the job less than 60 days or for nonworking pay for such things as vacation, holidays, jury duty, bereavement, and so forth. In addition to this bonus payment, the employees have a 75 percent stake in the reserve.

## EXHIBIT 22-3
## Reserve Account Example

| Month | Add this Month | Reserve Total |
|---|---|---|
| January | $11,000 | $11,000 |
| February | 17,275 | 28,275 |
| March (deficit month) | (6,000) | 22,275 |
| April | 9,991 | 32,266 |
| May | 14,445 | 46,711 |
| June | 13,289 | 60,000 |
| Company share—25% | | $15,000 |
| Employees' share—75% | | 45,000 |
| Total | | $60,000 |

## EXHIBIT 22-4
## Deficit Month Example

| | |
|---|---|
| Value of productivity | $700,000 |
| Allowed payroll at 37 percent | 259,000 |
| Actual payroll | 265,000 |
| Bonus pool | ( – $6,000) |
| Reserve for deficit months | ( – $6,000) |

CASE 23

# DANA CORPORATION—THE RICHMOND CAMSHAFT PLANT (B) (CONDENSED)

*Richard O. von Werssowetz*
*Michael Beer*

> No Scanlon plan bonus will be payable for November 1980. The actual payroll exceeded the allowed payroll by $40,944 (11.1%)[1] or 3.65 percent of sales. This increases the reserve *deficit* for the five months to date of this Scanlon year to $271,127.

Ronald Cooke, plant manager of the Richmond (Indiana) camshaft plant of Dana Corporation's Perfect Circle Division, looked over the November Scanlon bonus report which had just been compiled. [See Case 22—The Richmond Camshaft Plant (A)—for a description of the plant's Scanlon program covering all plant employees including Ron Cooke.] Last month was another deficit month with no bonus to be paid. The last Scanlon bonus had been paid for April. From the looks of the labor cost to value of production ratio, it appeared unlikely that plant employees would earn bonuses for months to come. This continued to be a demanding year for everyone.

The economic downturn of 1979 and 1980 had resulted in a substantial drop in Richmond Camshaft's volume. Forty-six employees had still not been recalled from layoffs that began last December. Productivity and profits were also down. Ron's first priorities were to help obtain and start up production of new products to restore lost volume in an especially cost-competitive market. At the same time it was critical to maintain the superior quality performance of the plant. But how could a bonus plan which was paying no bonus help him accomplish these goals? Ron wondered whether he should reconsider the Scanlon plan, and look more closely at some other group or individual incentive system.

---

This case was revised by Bert A. Spector, Research Associate, under the direction of Michael Beer, Lecturer.

## RICHMOND CAMSHAFT

Dana had gotten into the camshaft business by acquiring the product line of Muskegon Camshaft in 1971. The operation first was installed in a backroom of the Richmond [piston] ring machining plant. In 1972, this was moved right next door into its own facility as the Richmond camshaft plant. The plant manufactured camshafts for large machinery such as agricultural and construction equipment and locomotives. Production workers in the plant were represented by Local 279 of the United Automobile, Aerospace, and Agricultural Implement Workers of America (UAW). There had been no strikes since the plant began operations. The current contract ran from December 3, 1979 to December 5, 1982.

### *Manufacturing Process*

Camshafts are made to order to customer specifications. Job runs might be as small as 30 camshafts, but most orders were lots of about 150. Physical lots moving from work station to work station were usually 40. Repeat orders were common, but machine set-ups for each job run still were a substantial part of the job cost.

The plant consisted of 80,000 square feet of modern space on one level. Various machine tools were laid out to provide a continuous flow of material through the 24 process steps. (Exhibit 23-1 lists the process steps and gives the number of machines at each work station, the number of machines normally controlled simultaneously by a single operator, the total number of operators for each step, and the number of shifts normally worked for the work station.) In steps one through six, the camshaft is cut and drilled, lathed to remove excess material, hydraulically straightened and spot ground, then cut and fine ground into high tolerance.

Up to this point, all steps have been working on a relatively soft, unhardened forging. Now, to give better wearing characteristics, the camshaft is put into a furnace, and carbon is induced into the material to harden it. There are successive steps of straightening, more grinding and hardening to closer tolerance, on the now-hardened material. Final steps included polishing and final inspection. Each step must follow precisely to insure that the cams are located rotationally on the shaft in such a way that the valves will operate in the proper sequence and at exactly the right moments.

---

[1]All dollar and other numerical amounts in this case have been disguised.

### *Quality Control*

Quality control must be maintained by each operation and the operators check their own work. Constant checks are required to adjust for tool wear and machine slippage. Bad products can be spotted visibly and sent back to the station that caused the problem for reworking. In addition, an in-process inspector randomly checks each station. Three or four days of work might be used as buffer stock held between some steps, so it may be several days before the next station begins work on the same lot. Final inspection checks all qualities of samples from each lot.

### *Sales Drop*

After several years of explosive growth, Richmond Camshaft's sales had dropped to a running rate of around $9 million. Profits, too, had dropped (Exhibit 23–2). The plant currently had 165 employees, down from a maximum of 220 in 1979. Richmond Camshaft was not alone, however, in its market problems. Its parent, Dana Corporation, had a number of problem areas.

## DANA CORPORATION

Dana Corporation had become a leader in the introduction of progressive human relations techniques under the direction of Rene McPherson, chief executive officer of Dana from 1972 until 1979 when he left to become dean of Stanford Business School. Dana extolled a strong commitment to its employees, including belief in "the philosophy of continued employment for all Dana people." This meant a policy of no layoffs for regular employees. It had pursued an aggressive and generous employee stock-participation plan (70 percent of its employees were shareholders), and maintained a good relationship with the UAW, which represented workers at many Dana plants. Dana overwhelmingly promoted from within and had developed an in-house "Dana University" for employee training. Its principles were widely publicized in an employee booklet called "The Dana Story" as well as by focusing the 1979 annual report on "productive people." Under this philosophy, Dana achieved a 10-year compounded sales growth rate of 15 percent and a return on investment of almost 18 percent. (See Exhibits 23–3 through 23–5 for excerpts describing Dana policy and performance.)

Difficult problems arose in fiscal year 1980. In the past, Dana competed in only one market, supplying universal joints, frames, and axles for passenger cars. By 1970 that market had been reduced to about 20 percent of Dana's business by diversifications into light truck components, vehicular replacement parts, and industrial machine and nonhighway vehicular components. Dana's strength in the truck business allowed it to maintain its growth through the 1974–1975 auto slump. However, capacity expansion to meet the explosive demand for vans, recreational vehicles, and pickups pushed this segment to 38 percent of Dana's sales and never allowed the smaller industrial segment to catch up. In late 1979, the light truck market dropped precipitously. Dana found itself with a large amount of idle capacity and the need to close plants and lay off regular employees for the first time. Stanley Gustafson, an executive vice president, commented on this dilemma: "How can a people company close a facility? You close it because there's no business."

Dana laid off or terminated 10,000 of its 29,000 U.S. employees. During this traumatic time, frequent and direct communications to employees continued as before to describe the company's position and actions. Effects of unemployment were buffered for a time by union-negotiated supplemental unemployment benefits and a counterpart, Dana's Management Income Protection Plan. Dana found buyers for some facilities that would employ many of the former Dana employees and in one case chose to rebuild older larger facilities and shut down a new one to keep more people employed. Dana also negotiated changes in contract work rules with the UAW to try to keep some plants going. Around the company, displaced employees received preferential hiring at other Dana plants with Dana paying relocation costs. Various outplacement services were also provided to try to aid those laid off. Gerry Mitchell, McPherson's successor as chief executive officer, responded to scattered bitter comments about these actions:

> We never said we'd employ like a welfare program. Our policy statement says, "The purpose of the Dana Corporation is to earn money for its shareholders." Our people know this because they're our shareholders. . . . Of all the dammed things you have to do, laying people off is the toughest.

During this period, productivity programs remained in effect and Dana continued to contribute to the employee stock purchase plan, which continued to be used by almost the same percentage of employees. Although sales dropped 9 percent and earnings dropped 42 percent in fiscal year 1980, Dana's cash position remained healthy as it went about trying to recover and balance its business to avoid sharp dislocations in the future (Exhibit 23–6).

## THE SCANLON PLAN

In McPherson's quest for productivity, Dana was open to any good ideas. He transformed the company from a highly centralized organization to a decentralized divisional organization in which most decisions are made at the divisional and plant level. Time clocks were discarded and a wide variety of incentive plans were used. One plan that attracted a lot of attention was the Scanlon plan.

Joseph Scanlon had developed the concept of the plan in the late 1930s. A cost accountant by training and a steelworkers' union official of a steel mill facing bankruptcy, Scanlon worked with the owner to enlist the ideas plant workers had to increase productivity. Ultimately, the plant was saved and Scanlon became an exponent of the idea, working for the international union to aid other small, distressed plants. He continued to develop the plan that bears his name at Massachusetts Institute of Technology (MIT) until his death in 1956.

The plan consists of three major elements: a participative management philosophy, joint worker/management committees to stimulate increased productivity, and plantwide productivity financial incentive. The philosophy of openness and participation supports group problem solving. The committee system opens communications and provides support for experimental ideas. The productivity bonus shares the fruits of these efforts between the company and its employees. It is meant as a means of providing a sense of equity and as a supportive device to make the plan acceptable to employees and unions. Collective bargaining and grievance handling are very carefully separated from the Scanlon process to try to buttress the atmosphere of cooperation and minimize role conflicts arising from leaders who must bargain over contract items and cooperate to solve production problems.

The plan has developed diverse support. Estimates of the number of companies using some form of Scanlon range from 150 to 600 firms. Although the plan is generally thought to be more appropriate to smaller, rural companies with less than 500 employees, some larger plants of over 6,000 employees have installed the plan, and at least one distribution company is trying it to cover 35 locations under one plan. Scanlon has been used in both union and nonunion plants. Annual conferences on Scanlon ideas are held at MIT and Michigan State to discuss new experiences and developments in the use of the plan.

In 1969, the Hayes-Dana, St. Thomas, Canada plant (a part of Perfect Circle Division) first adopted a Scanlon plan. This experiment was considered successful and was discussed around the company by participants in several Dana standing committees of operating managers. During negotiations in 1973, the United Auto Workers agreed not to disagree with plants that wanted to vote in a Scanlon plan. (Union attitudes toward Scanlon plans are mixed. As with some managers, some union leaders fear loss of power and control or feel otherwise uncomfortable with the participative aspects of the plan. Joseph Scanlon's union background and that of one of his associates, Fred Lesieur, used by Dana as a consultant, greatly aided union acceptance.) Dana then became the first major U.S. company to embrace the plan at a corporate level for consideration by any of its units. Scanlon was discussed at Dana managers' meetings and training sessions and a set of guidelines of important first steps was circulated (Exhibit 23-7). Dana would provide inside and outside consultants to any plant wishing to consider Scanlon and allow plant representatives to visit Scanlon facilities. By the end of 1975, 10 Dana units had adopted Scanlon plans. (In 1980, 21 Dana plants were using Scanlon plans. Two others using the plan had been closed.)

## INTRODUCTION AT RICHMOND CAMSHAFT

Richmond camshaft plant adopted the Scanlon plan in 1976. Leo Henken, the new plant manager, had arrived recently to find conditions in the plant to be "very poor. They had just come off a big loss and were headed for another financial disaster." The main problem he saw was that the plant was moving from manufacturing soft, relatively low-tolerance camshafts to hardened camshafts that required much closer tolerance. The transition was not a smooth one and production delays were irritating customers. Henken felt the problems had to do with both the previous plant manager, who had no manufacturing experience, and a militant union (the same local represented both the ring and camshaft plants) that had succeeded, over the years, in "taking away management rights through negotiation, primarily by adding job restrictions." Henken continued:

> There was a tremendous amount of distrust of management in both plants, tremendous conflict. Much of it was justified. The union was always out to hurt you financially on grievances and they would actually lay in wait for you to make a mistake.

The results of this distrust and conflict between union and management was poor performance. "We calculated that over 50 percent of the workers," said Henken, "were producing less than 46 percent of what fair standard hour compensations said they should have."

Henken had heard about the Scanlon plan at one of Fred Lesieur's presentations to another plant's bargaining unit, had read his book, and had been exposed to Lesieur through meetings at the corporate office. "In my own mind," he said, "it fitted the way I wanted to manage."

Henken also knew that the Scanlon plan could not be initiated all at once. To lay the proper groundwork, he worked closely with his personnel manager, explaining:

> You have to build credibility and discipline. We worked on those. My personnel manager helped bury them in communications. We wanted them to know where we were at, why they were there, what we needed to do to get out of it. We also worked closely with people who were not producing to find out their problems and excuses, eliminate them, and show them we expected to perform.

When the union proposed individual incentives to supplement Camshaft's day rates, Henken emphatically rejected the notion:

> I was just the bad guy and said we are not going to have an incentive system here. I don't like them. They were bad. They cause problems. As long as I was plant manager, we were not going to have them. I said this publicly a number of times.

Henken was especially strong in his rejection of the Perfect Circle individual incentive plan used at the ring plant:

> I was opposed to individual incentive systems because they are a large burden requiring a lot of manpower. You're always squabbling with the union. In my opinion, any time you set a rate on an operator, he is going to figure out a way to beat that rate, and you won't be allowed to change it because the contract won't allow you to change it.

One problem with individual incentive schemes is that over time, the standard can get out of date. This is usually because individual small changes in tools and methods rarely justify changes in the incentive standards. But the cumulative effect of many such changes can result in the incentive standards having little relation to actual job content. The Perfect Circle incentive system at the ring plant had, Henken felt, "got so far out of whack" that the average operator was earning 160 percent of the day rate.

Similarly, Henken resisted group incentive plans:

> You have exactly the same negotiating problems and other problems. Both systems make it difficult to change. If you are going to change your operation, institute new technology, or a new product, or a new manufacturing line, the process to get that installed and operational is much longer under either an individual or a group incentive system.

The Scanlon plan was, according to Henken, the one incentive system that could overcome these problems:

> In Scanlon, you can institute new methods, new machinery and the people are receptive to it, because they are a part of it. They are part of it from the day you conceive the idea because you have this great communications network up and down the organization.

## GETTING WORK FORCE COMMITTED TO SCANLON PLAN

Although interested in instituting the Scanlon plan, Henken wanted to wait for his own staff, as well as the union, to ask for it:

> As I said, you can't *put in* Scanlon, people have to want it. And how you get them to want it depends on the group of people you're working with. In our situation, I couldn't push Scanlon. In fact, I had to wait until *they* wanted it. I gave my staff the material I had, talked with them about Scanlon, let them talk to people who were in it.
>
> Because we were a member of the Dana-UAW master contract, the union people knew of other Dana-UAW plants that had Scanlon. Gradually we began to have people coming back to us asking about Scanlon. This went on for almost a year to the point that the work force was petitioning the union to come to me to ask me to investigate Scanlon.
>
> I finally said "OK, we'll bring Fred Lesieur in and I'll talk to him, but we really cannot afford his consulting fees."

Use of an outside third-party consultant is considered critical to implementing Scanlon plans. The consultant acts as a neutral party to identify organizational problems and sets an example of effective group interaction. The consultant also helps set and maintain critical ground rules separating bargaining and safety issues from Scanlon discussions and often acts as an "independent accountant" for cost issues. The cost of consulting aid in helping to develop and propose the plan and aid in first-year implementation if adopted was estimated to be $40,000 including expenses. After initial planning discussions, Leo hired Fred Lesieur in May 1976 to work with management, union, and employees separately and together to investigate the plan and to develop a bonus formula suitable for Camshaft.

Lesieur began by holding an informal meeting with a representative plant group to discuss various bonus plans and particularly Scanlon plan principles. Since enough interest was generated, several widely based committees were formed to develop the needed formulas and procedures and to visit a plant currently using the Scanlon plan. Leo described the next steps:

> We let the bargaining committee mingle with the bargaining committee there, we sat in on the Scanlon meeting there, and we kind of stood back and let them get their own feel. We also let the management guys talk to their counterparts. They came back with enough enthusiasm that they wanted to proceed to the next step and get Fred in to talk to the plant.
>
> Fred came down to make his presentation to the work force and a vocal group of union dissidents took over the floor. I felt sorry for poor Fred. They were rude and nasty and had dug up bodies from history that had no bearing on the meeting whatsoever. After the meeting was over, we

> walked back to my office and Fred said, "Leo, are you sure you want to proceed with this?" I said, "I'll have to stop it now and see if they really want it."
>
> I did that. I went out that same afternoon and said I was ashamed of the way the group had performed. If that was the attitude of the work force, forget about it, I was not going to do anything. After my announcement that I was cutting it off, the silent majority came alive and I had them trooping into my office for the next three days speaking up for the plan. Finally I caved in and we proceeded with it.

### *Setting the Ratio*

Setting an equitable target ratio of payroll cost to sales volume of production was one of the more difficult aspects of establishing a plan. The idea is to examine the historical ratio over a representative period of a plant's business cycle, including all ups and downs that are likely to occur.

> Because we had been provided a number of hard to quantify services by the ring plant, our base ratio history was badly distorted. We had to try to reconstruct what our costs would have been if we had existed all along by ourselves.
>
> At the same time, we felt we should look at the fact that the people had been performing at totally unacceptable, very poor levels. We took that into consideration when we developed our ratio.
>
> Fred, however, totally ignored all of that. His position was that if you are operating at 50 percent of efficiency and you want improvements, that is where you measure from.

The best reconstruction of actual performance showed that the ratio had varied between 31.7 and 74.8 percent between September 1974 and August 1975. The average for the 12 months had been 44.6 percent. Other alternative attempts to reconstruct ratios suggested 37.4 percent and 46.2 percent. Lesieur suggested that a target of 45 percent be set. But the plant had not been profitable during that period. The management felt that no plant could be healthy without a profit and no bonuses should be paid until a profit was earned. They suggested that a 33 percent ratio would provide a minimal 5 percent after-tax return on sales.

> After some rather heated arguments, we all agreed to start at 37.0 percent. However, Fred would explain to the employees that the data was poor, that it was a best guess and that it may have to be changed.

### *Adoption of the Scanlon Plan*

By June 1976, a Memorandum of Understanding had been prepared to be presented to all employees for discussion and ultimately a vote to accept or reject the plan. Because a high level of general commitment is required to make Scanlon successful, everyone agreed that a 75 percent favorable vote of all employees would be considered necessary for adoption of the plan. The plan was accepted with 77 percent of the 144 workers voting for the plan.

A Scanlon plan bonus plan agreement was signed by management and union leaders to formalize the agreement. Important provisions included:

- A statement of separation of the plan from the labor agreement
- Technical definitions of eligibility to participate
- Agreement that the plan could be terminated by majority vote of participants
- Agreement to the initial productivity ratio of 37.0 cents in payroll costs to each dollar of sales value of production
- Agreement to a 75 percent to employees/25 percent to company split of labor savings
- Calculation criteria for a reserve for deficit months and year-end bonus distribution of any excess reserve
- The structure and appointment/election method of committees
- Sample bonus calculations

One important aspect of the agreement was a statement on conditions that might necessitate a change in the ratio. Any "substantial" change in variables such as wages, sales volume, pricing, product mix, subcontracting, or technology that lead to increases or decreases in selling prices or standard costs "may be cause" for reviewing and changing the prevailing ratio. "However, not every change in the variables affecting the ratio should require ratio adjustment, since the development of the ratios themselves reflect certain fluctuations which prevailed in the base period."

Production committees and a screening committee were established and the Scanlon plan was put into effect July 1, 1976.

### *Initial Results*

During the first months of the Scanlon program, several reactions in the plant became immediately apparent. One of the most striking was the immediate increase in productivity as measured by the payroll cost-to-sales-value-of-production ratio. Labor productivity jumped in the first month of the plan, before the suggestion system could contribute significant new ideas. It appeared that the possibility of a bonus might be generating increased effort from the plant workers.

In the first month under Scanlon, the actual ratio was 35.41 percent and a bonus of 3.15 percent of pay was paid. Performance slipped badly to 45.95 percent in the second month. Then performance leveled out around 33 percent. The average for the first six months was 35.36 percent. Bonuses paid for months three through six averaged 7.26 percent.

Suggestions also immediately began to be presented through the Scanlon plan committees. Few of the early suggestions had a large direct effect on productivity. Some were purely convenience items. However, as all committee members wanted to encourage use of the system and confirm management's commitment to listen to employee ideas, every suggestion was accepted if at all reasonable and possible. Management even used the committee structure to find acceptance for ideas that might otherwise have been rejected by the union as an attempt to speed up work. Explained Henken:

> One of our engineers might start an idea in an operator's mind and ask "What if we did something like this?" The operator could pick it up and expand on it—it became his suggestion rather than an engineer's.

A development period also was required for the committee system itself to become effective. Henken described this period:

> The elected representatives did not communicate well with their own peers. Their communication from the committee meetings back out to the floor was extremely poor, especially when a suggestion was rejected. It was almost impossible to get a representative to go back and say, "Hey, Joe! Your suggestion was rejected and here's why."
>
> One of my staff or I would go out on the floor after a meeting and talk to a guy who had given a suggestion. We'd ask, "Did Joe come over and tell you the outcome of the meeting?" "No, he didn't." "Wait a minute, and I'll go over and get Joe."

Henken then described monthly communication meetings typical of Scanlon plants:

> We not only covered the results of the prior month in detail, but we would then talk about business conditions as we saw them, what was happening, what new customer we were working with, when we anticipated a new part number coming on-stream, what new equipment was coming in. All kinds of things that we felt would be of interest to them to know about the business. They had never been told this before until we had started it before Scanlon in informal discussions.
>
> Then we'd open up the floor for questions and all questions were fair game. Not many managers will get up and open up for all questions—it's uncontrolled. They understood there were only two restrictions: I would not allow a discussion of somebody's personality and I would not get into a discussion of anyone's pay rate. If there is criticism, OK, "I'll look into it and I'll get back to you." I'd have my staff there and if I couldn't answer a question, I'd ask one of them to answer. I put them on the spot too so that people saw we weren't up to anything and weren't trying to cover anything up.

The achievement of bonuses, use of the suggestion system, and participation in the committees and general meetings reflected a changed atmosphere in the plant. While attitudes and skills weren't completely changed overnight, communication and cooperation had certainly increased among employees of all levels.

## RICHMOND CAMSHAFT PLANT 1976–1980

### *Reactions to Scanlon*

Reactions to the Scanlon plan varied over time. After the initial period of testing, most plant employees seemed to accept the serious intent of the plan. The level of trust and cooperation varied with different managers, union leaders and employees. Those who directly participated in the Scanlon activities developed better relationships. At one point, some union officers demanded that union committeemen attend all Scanlon plan meetings. The company agreed. Other employees expressed indifference. Some claimed not to know the size of their weekly paychecks, much less the amounts of their Scanlon plan bonuses. Over the several years of the plan, most complaints vocalized about the plan fell into two categories: distrust in the bonus calculation and questions of fairness.

DISTRUST OF BONUS CALCULATIONS. Despite open access to the bonus calculations, detailed explanations of the process to all employees, and a review made by Fred Lesieur, some employees continued to feel that the company was manipulating the numbers. There were several bases for this distrust. One important factor was the complexity of the calculation itself. The calculation began with sales results which were then adjusted for returns and increases or decreases in inventory levels. This adjustment began the confusion since the Scanlon computations depended on the *sales value of production* which was different than *shipments*. Furthermore, the "allowed payroll" was calculated and compared to actual payroll costs. This determined the bonus pool. A deduction was then made for a reserve. Next, the amount available for immediate distribution was split between the company and the employees. Finally, the employees' share was divided among eligible employees. In years with deficit months, additional calculations had to be made. There was too much "accounting jargon" in the calculations, according to some employees. They suggested that management might reduce bonuses and sacrifice their incentives to "make their numbers look good and get promoted."

Other factors contributed to this lack of trust. Before introduction of the Scanlon plan, production achievement was measured by total unit production. Each month's units were tracked and widely announced and record months were celebrated. However, the Scanlon bonus measured *productivity*. It was influenced by many factors other than units produced, including the number of days in the month, sales mix, overtime, returns, and inventory shifts. The occasional disappointment felt when a low Scanlon bonus was announced after a record *unit* month led some to be disgruntled.

On one occasion, a mistake in the calculations was not discovered for several months, then led to a lowering of the bonus. This too added to some workers' suspicions about the plan.

Adjustments to the ratio of allowable payroll to sales value of production were another area that weakened the plan's credibility. Changes to the ratio are expected and were discussed in the Scanlon agreement. Such changes are meant only to adjust for changes in products, pricing, technology, equipment and other resources. They are specifically not to be used to create a "moving carrot," absorbing the increased productivity of the employees. A change had been necessary in the ratio as early as January 1977, the sixth month of the plan. In all, four reductions in allowable labor had been made since the inception of the Scanlon plan:

| | |
|---|---|
| July 1977 | 37.0% |
| January 1978 | 35.7% |
| December 1978 | 35.0% |
| August 1979 | 33.2% |
| December 1979 | 32.6% |

In each case of new adjustments management developed the new ratios and explained them during the Scanlon meetings. During the first year, Lesieur also was present to answer questions about the new ratio, but in subsequent years he was not involved.

QUESTION OF FAIRNESS. Even among those who accepted the legitimacy of the bonus and ratio calculations, several questions of basic fairness arose. Some employees always felt that certain others didn't deserve as much of the bonus. Other employees felt that some of the supervisors weren't doing their share:

> People don't have respect for some of the supervisors. Most are people you've worked with. Some had real bad work habits. I think they just promoted some to get them off the floor. Now don't tell me to do what you [the supervisors] didn't.

Partly as a result of some of these feelings, there was little overt peer pressure among operators when someone appeared to be doing less than a fair share. An operator commented:

> Some people do think a guy like that is taking it from my pocket. But that's the supervisor's job. That's their part of the group incentive—why they get part of the bonus. It really burns me up when they don't go after the goof-offs.

Some operators did provide signals:

> They do it in a broad brush sense. They may not go to the foreman and say, "Joe specifically is not doing his job." But they may go to him and say, "The line is not moving and there is a bottleneck here. Now you know, what are you going to do about it, Mr. Foreman?" If you're *listening*, you'll go look, you'll know where to go.
>
> You do have to be careful to consider what you hear. Everything that is wrong tends to be the foreman's fault. They are under a lot of pressure to get production up.

### *Accomplishments*

Nonetheless, during the period from 1976 to 1980, Richmond Camshaft quadrupled its sales while maintaining superior quality. (Richmond Camshaft was designated one of only two "certified suppliers" to a major customer, meaning that customers could so depend on Camshaft's quality that they did not even inspect the vital parts supplied by Camshaft before using them in their equipment.) Camshaft had also become profitable even in 1980 with a severe drop in volume. It had not been profitable before the adoption of Scanlon. At the same time that the plant was achieving growth, profits and quality, the employees had received some good financial rewards. Scanlon plan bonuses had been paid each year in addition to normal wage increases (Exhibit 23-8).

All of the accomplishments weren't apparent in the quantitative measures. Leo had felt that:

> . . . the greatest productivity improvement through the use of Scanlon is not with the production operator but through the nonproduction operator, the indirect labor person, the maintenance guy. Prior to Scanlon, if a man's machine went down, they called the maintenance man. He walked over, he looked at it, said yeah. Then he went back to the crib and got a tool and came back and went back and went back. It just went on and on and on because there was no incentive for him to get the thing up. The operator was not pressuring him. The operator was standing there, making the same money for doing nothing as for working, on a day rate.

So after Scanlon came in, that was the biggest change you saw. When an operator yelled for a maintenance man, he brought his whole tool cart over, all at the same time. The maintenance man knew that until that machine was making chips, he was not going to be making any incentive bonus to share. The operator was helping, handing him wrenches, doing things of that nature, rather than standing back and doing nothing.

In other situations, the operator might be more likely to fix his machine by himself.

### *Recent Developments*

During the 1976–1980 period there were shifts in management, including four different plant managers and two different plant superintendents during this period. The plant superintendents were responsible for the facility during interim periods between appointments of plant managers. There were also shifts in the work force to and from the ring plant next door.

The camshaft plant had maintained several ties with the ring plant even after it had split into a separate operation. The production employees at both plants were represented until 1979 by a single local union of the UAW. Workers had the right of making one move from one plant to the other while retaining seniority rights until that time. After adoption of the Scanlon plan at the camshaft plant, workers had the option of choosing a plant with either that plan or the individual incentive plans which were continued in the ring plant. Most of the production operations were very similar and so employees tended to select work under a compensation plan they preferred. However, that wasn't the only consideration. One worker recalled concern about lay-off protection:

> A lot of people were hesitant to come to Camshaft. This plant had just become profitable and was risky. It could go down just as fast. Camshaft had lost so much money.

Another factor that influenced some workers' decisions was the feeling that incentive work created excessive pressure:

> You can make more money on incentives, but you're always aware of how many units you're turning out. The pressure never lets up. When your machine goes down under incentive, you lose. Here, you stay on straight time. Maintenance wasn't so bad. But it was the *idea* that you could lose.

This feeling of pressure led some workers at the ring plant to shift to the camshaft plant.

Each plant manager introduced new innovations. In January 1979, Thomas Burns tried a program which was a first for Dana. All hourly employees were placed on weekly salary. This meant to employees who had been paid by the hour that "within reason you can expect to receive the equivalent of 40 hours pay even when you have worked less than 40 hours a week." Although made in agreement with the UAW for a 12-month trial, the company could alter or revoke the plan at any time after consulting with the union. Some people thought that the all-salaried plan, operating together with the Scanlon plan, seemed to benefit malingerers who took too much time off or just didn't produce:

> If our section busts our tails to get work out and another doesn't, they get rewarded two ways. First, they get overtime at time and a half, which most people are pretty happy to have. Then, because of the overtime, they get a bigger part of the Scanlon bonus!

In 1980 the salary plan was still in effect.

### *Current Situation*

Most employees Ronald Cooke talked to clearly saw and liked the increased participation and communication among workers of all levels.

> OPERATOR: You find out management's not always going to say no. People listen.
>
> FOREMAN: Although grievance handling is kept separate from Scanlon, it has helped. When you've got that experience of going one on one, you can work things out better.
>
> SUPERINTENDENT: We use the monthly Scanlon meeting to communicate the business climate. We try to relate it to this plant and their future. We talk about scrap and quality, customer requirements and problems, and the steps we're taking. We do this for all employees over one day, all three shifts, in groups of twenty or so. It's a tough grind this way, but we feel we owe it to them.

The communication and trust in the plant had helped Camshaft adjust to the problems of the business decline of 1979–1980. Ron made several observations:

> A layoff is very hard, but at least we could discuss it and everyone knew our reasons. We're all trying hard to get everyone back to work.
>
> One good example is the acceptance of Japanese forgings. We'd all rather use American forgings, but this was the only way we could remain competitive.

> Sometimes changes happen over time and you really don't realize how far you've come. People don't see themselves as a more cooperative work force—it's just a better place to work.

In an effort to help bolster plant morale and reinforce team spirit, Ron had helped sponsor a visit by plant workers to see the use of their product in a customer's plant. Almost 70 of the workers signed up for the five-hour bus ride. When unexpected overtime work was scheduled, almost 30 employees passed up the extra pay to make the visit. Everyone returned with great enthusiasm. Other Scanlon plants had found it useful to develop competition with another facility or create interest with special projects. One plant had had production employees develop a new employee handbook. A Scanlon plan plant manager observed:

> This program is not self-perpetuating. You've got to give it a shot in the arm every so often—however often the work force needs it. You can sense when it is beginning to flatten out.

With business down and some employees on layoff, some aspects of the plan weren't working as well as before. There had been no bonuses paid this Scanlon year. It appeared unlikely that the cumulative deficit could be made up so that any bonus could be paid for the entire year. Another aspect involved the salary plan. When Scanlon bonuses were being paid, the salary plan had been a tradeoff: any additional costs reduced the cost saving split by Scanlon such that 75 percent of the extra cost would have been paid to employees as a higher bonus. On the other hand, the impact of the decline on profits and health of the plant had been buffered by reduction in Scanlon bonus expense. Total compensation was reduced with reduced productivity. Some other Scanlon plants were paying bonuses even when the plant was losing money. That didn't make sense to Ron.

In other areas, with some employees on layoff and those "on the bubble" threatened by any additional reductions, suggestions were reduced and productivity decreased. A good hourly wage with no bonus was better than no wage at all for a worker or for one of his friends. Also, even with the communication built over the past few years, there was some resentment that the white collar work force had not been reduced in an equal proportion to the blue collar workers.

Cooke attempted to explain this resentment:

> It's very hard to get across that we actually don't have enough people—especially in engineering. To fill up the plant we need more machines, more products. These need tender loving care. Rolling up the sleeves and getting with it helps.

## TAKING STOCK OF THE SCANLON PLAN

After taking over as plant manager in July of 1980, Ron Cooke felt he should give the situation some thought. This was his first experience in a plant with a Scanlon plan. He felt many other types of incentive plans had worked well in his plants, including various group bonus arrangements, but never with the whole plant as a group. He also felt that a large part of participative management depended on the manager. He believed he had been able to achieve good communication, trust, and participation without the Scanlon committee system or Scanlon bonus plan. Even within the plant, there was still some active support for individual incentive schemes. One engineer argued:

> We are all different. Each one of us has certain God-given talents that I can do something better than you can. Now if I can be lucky and get you a job that you are especially well adapted to, you can run circles around me. Because I can't do *that* job as well as you can—you just have the knack for doing that.
>
> If you get a station where you have a great talent, you may, say, run 150 pieces a shift when the average is 100. You're putting out 50 more pieces for the plant and you're making more money for yourself. We've gotten better utilization out of the machine which is making the stockholders money. Everybody in your classification is trying to catch you. They say, "If that dirty dog can run 150, I can too somehow."
>
> Now if that's put on a group incentive, you're not going to run that 50 more. Because you're going to say, "What's going on here? We're making 120 pieces average. That's what we're getting paid for, so that's all I'm going to run." You don't get it with Scanlon either.
>
> On an individual incentive, people also move around less. They're very, very careful because they're not sure they can make it at another station. They know what they can make at their old station. In a group, they go on down and let the group carry them if they're not sure.

Ron wondered how a bonus plan that was paying no bonus could provide the necessary incentive to maintain the plant's performance. If there were any changes he might make, this was probably a good time. And as the manager of a Scanlon facility, he might be called upon at any time to give his opinions to other plants considering the Scanlon plan. He wondered what advice he should give.

**EXHIBIT 23–1**
**Manufacturing Process Loading**

| Work Center No. | Description | Total No. Machines at Station | Normal No. Machines Run by One Operator | Total No. Operators All Shifts | No. Shifts Operated |
|---|---|---|---|---|---|
| 1 | Receiving | — | — | 1 | 1 |
| 2 | Mill and center | 7 | 1 | 9 | 3 |
| 3 | First turn | 12 | 3 | 10 | 3 |
| 4 | Straighten/spot grind | 1 | 1 | 3 | 3 |
| 5 | Finish turn bearings | 6 | 2 | 4 | 3 |
| 6 | Cam turn | 5 | 1 | 9 | 3 |
| 7 | Carburize | 1 | 1 | 3 | 3 |
| 8 | Straighten | 6 | 1 | 9 | 3 |
| 9 | Turn ends | 4 | 2 | 3 | 3 |
| 10 | Gun drill | 4 | 2 | 3 | 3 |
| 11 | Cross drill | 2 | 1 | 4 | 3 |
| 12 | Harden/draw | 1 | 1 | 3 | 3 |
| 13 | Anneal | 1 | 1 | 2 | 2 |
| 14 | Straighten | (See 8) | (See 8) | (See 8) | (See 8) |
| 15 | Qualify | 1 | 1 | 3 | 1 |
| 16 | Mill and center (2) | 1 | 1 | 1 | 1 |
| 17 | Plain grind | 2 | 1 | 5 | 3 |
| 18 | Grind ends | 6 | 2 | 8 | 3 |
| 19 | Keyway | 4 | 1 | 8 | 3 |
| 20 | Cam grind | 16 | 4 | 10 | 3 |
| 21 | Miscellaneous finish | 14 | 1/2 | 12 | 3 |
| 22 | Final inspection | 4 | 1 | 4 | 1 |
| 23 | Ship | — | — | 1 | 1 |

## EXHIBIT 23–2
## Sales and Profits *($ Thousands)*

| Fiscal Year Ending August 31 | Sales | Profits | Return on Sales (%) |
|---|---|---|---|
| 1975 | $ 4,720 | ($ 340) | (7.2) |
| 1976 | 4,062 | (1,000) | (24.7) |
| 1977 | 8,397 | 420 | 5.0 |
| 1978 | 10,756 | 742 | 6.9 |
| 1979 | 15,841 | 1,394 | 8.8 |
| 1980 | 11,479 | 861 | 7.5 |

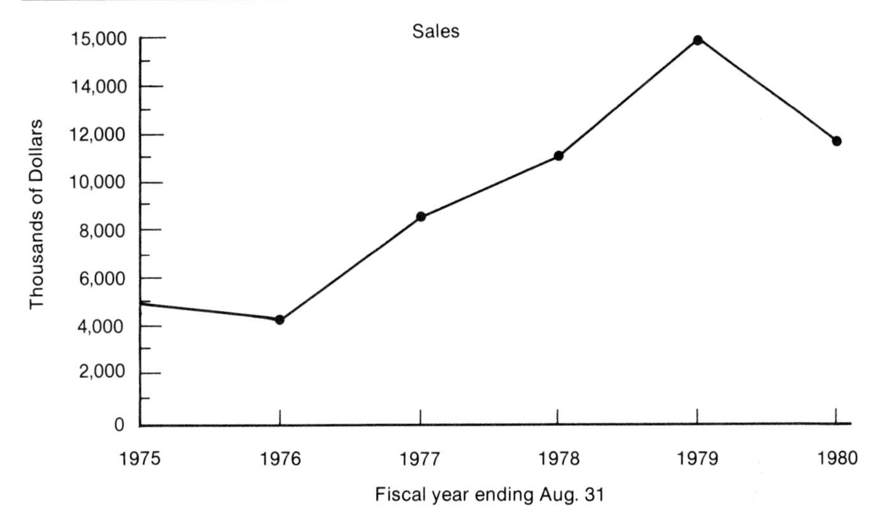


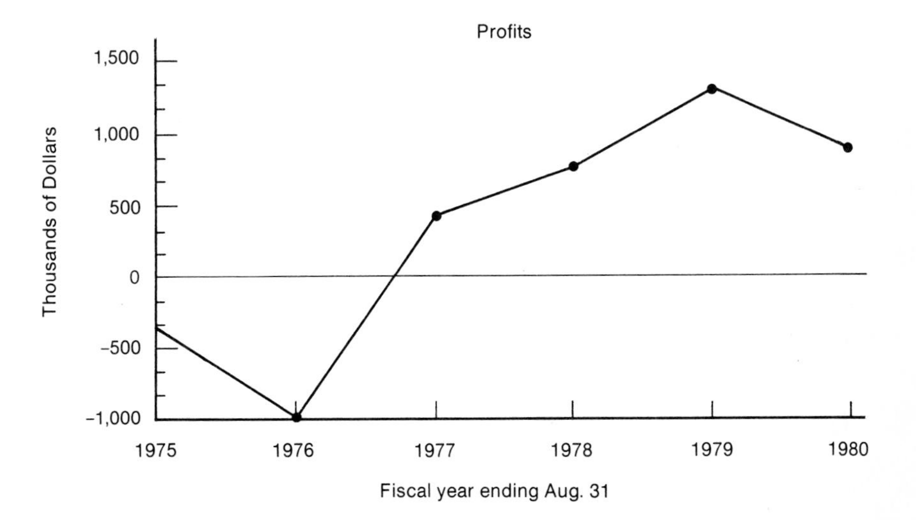

**EXHIBIT 23–3**
**Dana Philosophy**

WE BELIEVE THAT BUSINESS IS 90% PEOPLE AND ONLY 10% MONEY!

Dana is not a unique company, but we feel we are different. More than 16,600 of our people are shareholders in the company under a voluntary Stock Purchase Plan.

We have one of the lowest turnover rates in our industry. We promote from within. We operate our own university. We depend on people and not paper to get things done.

We seek and stress people involvement, and we are responding to the involvement of our people. We listen, discuss, meet, communicate, explain, talk, argue, start task forces—try, and try again, to get involvement from everyone.

The greatest asset in Dana today is the contribution that our people can make in order to keep us growing and to remain competitive. We will continue to seek the involvement of our people and to encourage them to contribute their skills and efforts.

We believe that collectively, we are striving to determine, recognize and achieve acceptable performance levels and to employ our available assets to the best advantage of Dana . . . permitting everyone the maximum possible freedom to develop and utilize their own abilities . . . to fully participate . . . to share in our successes . . . and to accomplish all of this in an air of honesty and sincerity throughout all levels of the company.

**EXHIBIT 23–4**
**Corporate Goals**

TURNING POWER INTO PROGRESS AROUND THE WORLD: Policies

*Earnings*

The purpose of the Dana Corporation is to earn money for its shareholders and to protect and increase the value of their investment. We believe the best measurement of the accomplishment of our purpose is the constant growth in the corporation's earnings per share.

*Growth*

We believe in a steady rate of growth consistent with protecting our assets against the erosions of inflation.

We must enter new diversified markets worldwide that are consistent with our goal and compatible with our management and technical abilities.

The corporation and the divisions share in this growth responsibility.

*People*

We are dedicated to the belief that our people are our most important asset.

We will encourage all of them to contribute and to grow to the limit of their desire and ability.

We believe people respond to recognition, freedom to contribute, opportunity to grow, and to fair compensation. We believe that higher pay follows job performance and endorse the practice of an above average base compensation with a high incentive potential.

We believe in the philosophy of continued employment for all Dana people. We believe that they should identify with the company and that this identity should carry on after they have left active employment.

We believe that wages and related benefits are the concern and responsibility of supervisors. There are some benefits which are a corporate matter and participation in these—the Stock Purchase Plan, the

**EXHIBIT 23-4 (*Continued*)**

Management Resource Program, some form of Income Protection, Matching Gifts, Tuition Refund, Relocation and Foreign Service Benefits—is a privilege of all *career* Dana people.

We believe that on-the-job training is the most effective method of teaching: that everyone must prove proficiency in at least one line of our company's work—*marketing*, engineering, manufacturing, financial control, or personnel; second, these people should then demonstrate ability as supervisors and be able to get work done through other people; third, we recognize the importance of gaining this experience both internationally and domestically.

Periodic changes in duties are desirable but should vary with the individuals and their own capabilities. These changes should not conflict with the operating efficiency of the company.

We believe in utilizing cooperative student programs and summer employment as recruiting devices and for training of people.

In filling vacancies that result in job training and promotion, every effort will be expended to find candidates within the Dana Corporation and its affiliates and subsidiaries. *Career* people interested in other positions in the company are encouraged to discuss the Dana Management Resources programs with their supervisor.

We believe education of all of our *career* people who desire it is very important. Division presidents and general managers and staff vice presidents and directors are responsible for the education of the people in their organizations. The Policy Committee is responsible for the education of officers, division presidents and general managers, and staff vice presidents and directors.

The Dana Board of Regents is responsible for suggesting policies and providing programs to support and encourage the career and personal development of all Dana people.

*Planning*

We believe in planning at all levels of the organization.

Divisions will be responsible for detailed one-year and general five-year plans covering products, growth, profitability, investment, source and use of funds, people, etc. These plans will be reviewed and continually updated.

*Corporate planning will also be done on a one-year detailed and a five-year general basis and will include broad corporate objectives. In developing the corporate plan, consideration will be given to division plans.*

The practice of management by objective is a key part of this planning process. Naturally differences in the various divisions will dictate their own objectives in support of the broad corporate objectives.

### *Organization*

*Dana is a market oriented company supplying the proprietary product and service requirements of our selected markets.*

*We believe in a divisionalized organizational structure with responsibility for performance given to division presidents, general managers, and affiliate presidents. Divisions will be complete with their own marketing, engineering, manufacturing and financial functions.*

These managers must have operating latitude to accomplish their goals within corporate objectives and policies. This environment not only stimulates initiative and innovation, but develops the expertise of management that is the keystone of our success.

In keeping with this philosophy, we do not create corporate procedures. If procedures are mandatory for the operation of a division, it is the responsibility of the division president or general manager to create them.

We believe in a "store manager" concept because it results in management training. We also believe it allows operating situations to be broken down into sizes that are readily manageable.

We believe in a small, highly effective corporate support group to service the needs of the corporate groups and the divisions as requested.

### *Customers*

We believe it is absolutely necessary to anticipate our customers' needs for both product and service, and toward the fulfillment of this policy we must exert every effort. In anticipating our customers' needs for products and services, we must insure our delivery capability based on an internal capacity with an opportunity for outside procurement consistent with sound, economical employment of the corporate assets.

Once a commitment is made to a customer, every effort must be made to fulfill that obligation.

It is highly desirable to maintain a balance between make and buy not only to protect the continuity of employment for our employees through the various swings of business cycles, but also to insure customer supply through these same cycles.

**EXHIBIT 23-4 (*Continued*)**

*Communication*

We will communicate our goals, policies, and objectives to the shareholders, customers, people, plant, city, public, and the financial community.

It is the job of the division presidents and general managers and staff vice presidents and directors to keep people up to date constantly through newsletters, bulletin boards, group meetings, etc. At least once every year they shall make sure that all their people are informed of the results of their particular operation and what is planned for the coming year.

It is the responsibility of supervisors to encourage opinions and ideas from their people. Supervisors shall implement those ideas and suggestions that have merit or explain the reasons why certain things cannot be utilized if they are impractical or improper.

*Citizenship*

The Dana Corporation will be a good citizen at the international , national, state and local levels. We will conduct our business in a professional and ethical manner when dealing with governments, customers, neighbors and the general public worldwide.

Laws and regulations under which we operate worldwide have become increasingly complex. The laws of propriety always govern. The General Counsel and each General Manager can give guidance when in doubt about legal or appropriate conduct. It is assumed that no one would willfully violate the law and subject themselves to disciplinary action.

We encourage active participation on the part of all of our people in community action.

We will contribute to worthwhile community causes consistent with their importance to the good of the community.

The Policy Committee
Dana Corporation

Approved by The Board of Directors
Dana Corporation
10/28/69

| | | | |
|---|---|---|---|
| Rev. 8/1/72 | 7/1/75 | 10/1/77 | 4/1/79 |
| 12/8/72 | 10/15/75 | 2/1/78 | 7/1/80 |
| 7/1/74 | 8/1/76 | 8/1/78 | 12/1/80 |

## EXHIBIT 23-5
## Productivity Comparison

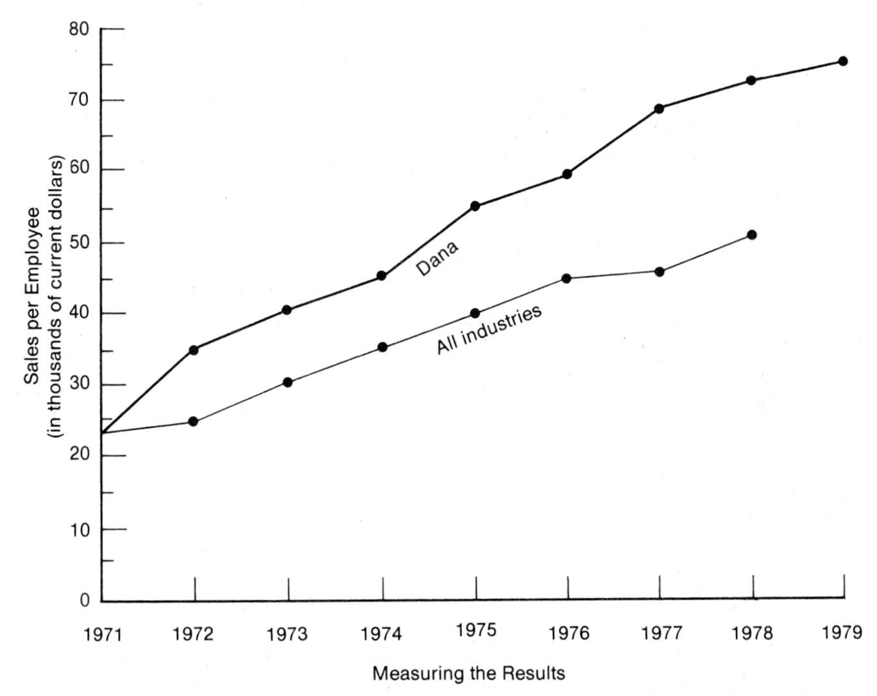


Using sales dollars per person, the accompanying chart compares Dana Corporation productivity with all industries in the Fortune 500 for the years 1971 through 1978, the last year in which industry figures are available. This chart emphasizes, better than words, the outstanding performance of the people of Dana.

This is the story of the productive people of Dana. Through their efforts we have continued to be a growing company. We look forward with great enthusiasm to the challenge of the decade of the eighties.

## EXHIBIT 23–6
## Ten-Year Financial Summary from 1980 Annual Report

| | For Fiscal Years | | | | | | | | | |
|---|---|---|---|---|---|---|---|---|---|---|
| | 1980 | 1979 | 1978 | 1977 | 1976 | 1975 | 1974 | 1973 | 1972 | 1971 |
| Net income per share of common stock[a] | $2.78 | $5.03 | $4.22 | $3.61 | $3.05 | $2.13 | $2.10 | $1.97 | $1.54 | $ .97 |
| Cash dividends declared per share of common stock[a] | 1.57 | 1.42 | 1.26 | .97 | .77 | .68 | .67 | .64 | .61 | .60 |
| Shareholders' equity per share of common stock outstanding at August 31[a] | 27.65 | 26.54 | 22.91 | 19.86 | 17.09 | 14.79 | 13.35 | 11.99 | 10.67 | 10.08 |
| *Summary of Operations (millions of dollars)* | | | | | | | | | | |
| Net sales | $2,524 | $2,761 | $2,253 | $1,794 | $1,444 | $1,136 | $1,078 | $989 | $822 | $686 |
| Cost of sales | 2,106 | 2,263 | 1,843 | 1,456 | 1,183 | 944 | 897 | 830 | 684 | 541 |
| Income before income taxes | 139 | 303 | 263 | 211 | 165 | 116 | 115 | 106 | 88 | 54 |
| Income taxes | 43 | 139 | 129 | 103 | 76 | 54 | 54 | 50 | 43 | 26 |
| Net income | 96 | 164 | 134 | 108 | 89 | 62 | 61 | 56 | 45 | 28 |
| Net income for the year retained for growth | 42 | 117 | 94 | 79 | 67 | 42 | 42 | 38 | 27 | 11 |
| Interest expense | 50 | 30 | 20 | 17 | 17 | 17 | 12 | 9 | 8 | 6 |

*Year-End Financial Position (millions of dollars)*

| | | | | | | | | | | |
|---|---|---|---|---|---|---|---|---|---|---|
| Liquid assets[b] | $421 | $389 | $351 | $271 | $242 | $211 | $145 | $115 | $135 | $113 |
| Working capital | 565 | 584 | 444 | 422 | 362 | 303 | 197 | 193 | 189 | 196 |
| Ratio of current assets to current liabilities | 2.1:1 | 2.4:1 | 2.1:1 | 2.8:1 | 2.7:1 | 3.1:1 | 2.0:1 | 2.3:1 | 2.5:1 | 3.2:1 |
| Total shareholders' equity | 960 | 936 | 733 | 603 | 504 | 431 | 389 | 346 | 302 | 291 |
| Long-term debt | 337 | 292 | 193 | 202 | 201 | 198 | 129 | 111 | 107 | 89 |
| Property, plant, and equipment at cost | 1,059 | 861 | 680 | 593 | 544 | 503 | 480 | 418 | 372 | 343 |
| Property, plant, and equipment, less accumulated depreciation | 636 | 523 | 395 | 323 | 297 | 282 | 276 | 235 | 203 | 183 |
| Total assets | 1,935 | 1,756 | 1,402 | 1,102 | 967 | 822 | 753 | 635 | 561 | 493 |
| Average no. shares outstanding (in thousands)[a] | 34,416 | 32,611 | 31,787 | 29,859 | 29,270 | 29,167 | 29,056 | 28,376 | 29,140 | 28,862 |

[a]Restated to reflect 5% stock dividend declared in October 1973 and one-for-one stock distribution declared in December 1975.
[b]Cash, marketable securities, and accounts receivable.

## EXHIBIT 23-7
## Scanlon Plan—Union Guidelines—March 25, 1976

When considering a Scanlon-type plantwide incentive pay plan, the following principles should be understood and every effort should be made to implement such principles:

1. *Under no circumstances can a Scanlon-type incentive plan be substituted for a collective bargaining agreement with an equitable wage structure.*
2. A Scanlon-type bonus should not be considered a part of wages. In the collective bargaining process a fair and equitable wage rate should be established without consideration to earnings arrived at through a bonus system.
3. When a bargaining unit is approached by management with the proposition of implementing such a plan, the local union officials should immediately contact their international Representative and the UAW department involved.
4. When any type incentive plan is established in a facility, such a plan can affect wages and fringe benefits and is proper subject matter for collective bargaining.
5. A bonus plan should be established on the basis that it will provide an opportunity for employees to achieve additional earnings over and above the negotiated wages established at the plant.
6. In plants where there is an incentive program and the parties agree to implement a Scanlon-type bonus system, it will be necessary that the company and the union establish rates of pay for incentive classifications based upon the average incentive earnings by classification or department. These new rates should fully protect the earnings of incentive workers. Bonuses earned under the Scanlon plan will be based upon these new rates.
7. The agreement should provide that a third-party consultant should be used in the development and installation of a new Scanlon plan and that such third-party consultant be retained in order to insure that the original concept of the plan is being followed.
8. It must be clearly understood that such a plan does not conflict with, supersede, or in any way interfere with the collective bargaining agreement.
9. Union matters should not be discussed during the so-called screening and production committee meetings scheduled for the purpose of Scanlon plan discussions.

10. The plan should include a provision whereby the union may upon request obtain the services of an outside certified public accountant to audit the company's records to determine if the financial data being provided are correct.

**EXHIBIT 23–8**
**Scanlon Plan Suggestions and Bonus Payments**

| Years | Ideas Suggested | Ideas Accepted | Bonus (%) | Average Bonus $ per Person for Year |
|---|---|---|---|---|
| 1976–1977[a] | 358 | 298 | 6.91 | 790 |
| 1977–1978 | 224 | 161 | 4.82 | 766 |
| 1978–1979 | 133 | 94 | 11.17 | 1,995 |
| 1979–1980 | 79 | 65 | 3.70 | 575 |

[a]Scanlon plan year July 1 to June 30.
Source: Plant records.

*Chapter* 6

# Work Systems

When managers are asked what attitudes and behavior they desire to have among the persons they supervise, they ordinarily list the following:

- Initiative, self-starting
- Dependability
- Willingness to take responsibility
- Loyalty to the company and to managers
- Willingness to suggest changes and improvements in the job
- Adaptability, flexibility

To a large degree, this list may be said to envisage a work force strongly committed and involved in the successful performance of work. But when asked if employees exhibit such attributes, managers ordinarily say no, or only to a limited extent.

Instead, employee dissatisfaction, depersonalization, alienation and frustration, physical and psychological stress, low levels of initiative, high turnover and absenteeism, low product quality, and eroding productivity are all too often common at American workplaces.

In the past 20 years we have become increasingly aware of the extent to which negative behavior at work might be tied to the manner in which work is designed and the manner in which people are managed. The relation between work system design and employee productivity and well-being is most obvious at the shop floor level where assembly lines and other applications of so-called rational and efficient production systems have been in evidence since the early days of the Industrial Revolution. However, an examination of work design among office workers, professionals, and managers reveals that many of the same principles of work system design that have been applied to production-level employees may be finding their way to these levels of the organization with some of the same resulting problems. This trend has been heightened by the emergence of increasingly sophisticated office technology and management information systems as well as by the continued adherence to traditional assumptions about people and work.

The productivity crisis now faced by the American economy adds urgency to our needs as managers to understand how work system design affects employee performance and well-being, and how work systems can be designed to achieve desired business and human outcomes. To the necessary concern of businessmen and labor leaders about these issues can be added the concern of government, not only as an interested partner in solving the productivity problem, but as the institution most concerned about the well-being of society as a whole, for there is some evidence to indicate that work system design may have effects on physical health, mental health, and longevity of life itself.

The theme of this chapter is that management choices concerning work system design will have a strong effect on commitment, competence, cost effectiveness, and congruence—the four Cs outlined in Chapter 2. Well-executed changes in work system design can broaden employee responsibilities and result in substantial improvements in all four Cs.

1. *Commitment.* When employees become more psychologically involved in their work, higher levels of motivation, performance, and loyalty will result. There is some evidence that greater involvement in work may increase involvement in the community, thus contributing to the well-being of society.
2. *Competence.* Broader employee involvement increases the attractiveness of the firm to more capable prospective employees. It also develops employee competence and self-esteem.
3. *Cost effectiveness.* Wages and benefits are not lowered by innovation in work system design, and indeed may be increased. However, turnover and absenteeism often decrease; and flexibility, receptivity to change, productivity, and quality often increase.
4. *Congruence.* Management, unions, and employees can achieve a higher perceived coincidence of interest, provided the change itself is achieved by a process all parties regard as legitimate.

Fewer grievances and quicker resolution of local contract negotiations are some specific results that have occurred in unionized settings.

How have our assumptions about work system design been shaped historically? What are the emerging assumptions that are achieving some of the results just described? What are some of the problems and considerations in implementing innovations in work system design? We will turn to these questions after we define what we mean by the term work system.

## WORK SYSTEM DEFINED

The term work system, as we use it here, refers to a particular combination of job tasks, technology, skills, management style, and personnel policies and practices. These are seen as determining how work is organized and managed, how employees will experience work, and how they will perform.

### *Job Content*

As Figure 6–1 shows, at the core of a work system is the design of the work itself; that is to say, the job requirements as determined by the scope and organization of the immediate task. A clerical employee in a sales order-processing department may perform one task such as booking, then pass the order on to another worker who schedules the order then passes it to yet another person who handles special problems with

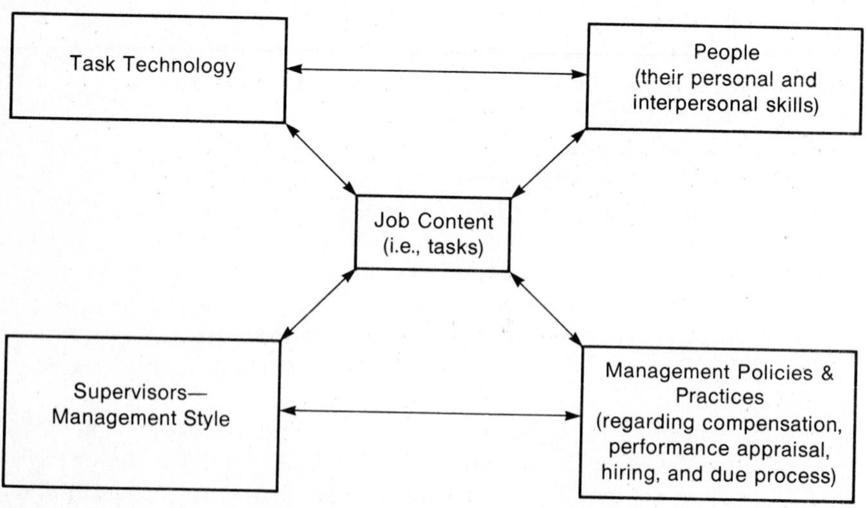


**FIGURE 6–1 Work System**

the customer. Alternatively, these employees can be organized so that each performs all of these order-processing functions for a more limited set of customers. Discretion in their tasks can be very closely circumscribed or it can be broad. Jobs may be highly individualized, or a team may be formally accountable for a whole task. The individual's responsibility may be confined to executing defined tasks or it may include contributing to goal-setting, planning, and problem-solving for the larger organizational unit.

### *Task Technology*

Job design and other components of an overall system discussed below are influenced by features of the job technology. For example, an assembly line in an automobile plant and a continuous process technology in a paper mill present very different opportunities and constraints on job design and supervisory delegation of planning and problem solving. It is possible for a supervisor to delegate to a face-to-face group responsibility for planning and operating a paper machine that embraces the entire process of converting pulp to rolled paper. In contrast, the magnitude and complexity of the automobile assembly task make it virtually impossible for a small group of individuals to be given comparable responsibility for planning and executing the assembly of an entire car.

### *People*

Another component of the work system is the set of skills and attitudes that employees bring to the workplace and those which are developed by the work experience. The selection process can place varying emphasis on mechanical skills, mental skills, and interpersonal skills. It can center on the ability of the employee to perform immedately, or take acount of the employee's potential for development. Management can attempt to select either employees who are predisposed to regard the job in strictly economic terms or those who also bring expectations about challenge and involvement. Apart from the predispositions and entering skill levels represented by new employees, management can choose to work toward some preferred profile of developed skills and attitudes. Obviously, this profile must fit the technology and job design, and must anticipate the type of management style and policy choices discussed below.

### *Supervision—Management Style*

The nature of supervisors, particularly the extent to which a supervisor delegates responsibilities for planning, goal setting, problem solving, and decision making, or allows workers to participate in these activities is a key aspect of a work system. Do supervisors see it as their responsibility to practice their technical skills or to impart them to their subordinates? Do they see their authority simply as delegated authority or do they see it as partly derived from the "consent of the governed?" How much emphasis do they place on developing the capabilities of their subordinates to supervise themselves? These choices about role definitions and management style are critical in conceiving the most appropriate work system.

### *Management Policies and Practices*

One component of work systems includes certain policies already discussed in the chapters on employee influence, flow, and rewards. The performance appraisal system may or may not require a supervisor to sit down and talk to subordinates about current performance and potential. It can emphasize individually oriented or unit-wide contribution. The employment security policy can determine whether employees must be worried about working themselves—or their fellow workers—out of employment. Finally, if the work force is unionized, then management's labor relations policy will influence whether the union resists or supports the other design choices that make up an internally consistent work system.

## WORK SYSTEMS AT DIFFERENT LEVELS

The work organization of a company encompasses many different, albeit interdependent work systems. There are work systems based on the operational tasks to be performed in a plant and in the office. Our illustrations above have emphasized these. There also are work systems related to engineering and research units. Finally, there is a managerial work system.

Before we examine in detail recent trends which have centered on the plant and office work systems, we will briefly note some of the concepts which have reshaped managerial work systems, modifying both the content of managerial work at various levels and the opportunities for manager involvement. Work systems based on divisonalization and/or the creation of profit centers delegate the responsibility and accountability for decision making. Integration of the functions required to compete in the marketplace also occurs at a lower level. Such changes inevitably orient managers to their competitive environment, determine the content of their work, and affect their motivation for performance.

Management work systems employing matrix organizational

forms are designed to provide for dual focus on function and product or product and geographic area. They require some managers and professionals to report to two bosses—one on each axis of the matrix. Matrix work systems require more communication and create higher levels of ambiguity for managers. These and other managerial innovations such as project management systems and "office of the chairmen" are illustrative of the stream of ideas which have affected the shape of managerial work systems—often in an evolutionary way. They are an important part of American industry's efforts to revitalize itself in the face of international competition.

### *Scientific Management*

The dominant pattern for organizing work today in the United States has been strongly influenced by the principles established by Frederick Taylor, coincident with the rise of large-scale manufacturing in the period around World War I.

"Each man must learn to give up his particular way of doing things," Frederick Taylor wrote in *Shop Management* (1919), "adopt his methods to the many new standards and grow accustomed to receiving and obeying instructions covering details, large and small, which in the past have been left to individual judgment."

Taylorism, or Scientific Management as it is sometimes called, came into vogue in the 1920s as an attempt to apply scientific principles to the management of workers, particularly the relationship of workers to newly emerging large-scale manufacturing. Work was to be divided into relatively simple and specialized tasks. In order to gain maximum efficiency at desired costs from technology, managers were urged to define precisely the limited tasks of workers, reduce to the fullest extent possible the need to bring human skills to bear on production, and thus minimize the opportunity for human mistakes and human inefficiencies.

Although Taylor's focus was on the job design, all other elements of the work system supported and reinforced these design choices—close supervision, piece-work incentives, minimal training requirements for single jobs, acceptance of turnover as not too costly, and so on. Taylorism relied on what is now characterized as a pessimistic view of an organization's human resources.

## FOCUSED INITIATIVES TO RESTRUCTURE OPERATING WORK

In the past several decades, a number of ideas have been advanced about how to utilize more effectively employees who work in plants and offices. Especially significant are three focuses for work reform, each of which relates to one element of our definitional model of the work system—supervision, job content, and task technology. Each type of work reform grew partly out of a sense of the incompleteness and insufficiency of prior initiatives.

### *Participative Style*

The idea of employee participation in matters of immediate concern and consequence to them grew steadily through the 1960s. It was a concept of supervision that top management and academics urged individual managers to adopt. Douglas McGregor, in *The Human Side of Enterprise* (1960), argued that, whatever the specific tools that might be employed by managers and theorists, a certain philosophy of management, indeed of human nature itself, underlies those practices. The prevailing theory of human behavior, Theory X, made pessimistic assumptions about human motivation. Taylor's techniques had been based on Theory X. McGregor argued that workers are capable of self-directed effort toward shared managerial goals. He labeled this theory of human nature and motivation Theory Y. The primary challenge of management, as he saw it, was to organize the enterprise in such a way that the potential for self-directed activities, even innovation, could be tapped.

Participative management gained considerably more momentum in the 1970s and early 1980s when the idea became associated with a variety of workplace reforms. In the mid-1970s, U.S. firms began promoting "quality circles," an idea that the Japanese were utilizing to great advantage. Quality circles consist of a number of volunteer employees from a work unit who meet regularly to identify and analyze problems that affect quality, productivity, or cost, and to recommend solutions. These circles frequently do not include a member of supervision. In the United States, the Honeywell Corporation has applied quality circles extensively, particularly in the Defense Group.

Even before quality circles were being discussed in the United States, some managements had begun to experiment with the same idea, referring to the concept then by the more descriptive term, "participative problem-solving groups." In the 1960s Texas Instruments pioneered this idea, reporting significant cost savings and efficiency gains in their manufacturing operations. These experiences led to the publication of *Every Employee A Manager* (1970) by Scott Meyers, who promoted corporate efforts to apply participative management approaches. The book's title reflects the assumption underlying the participative management approach: that employees who are involved in decisions about their immediate work will take responsibility for reducing costs and improving quality in the same way managers are presumed to be able and want to do.

It is not surprising, however, that this idea was found somewhat threatening by unions who saw in these efforts an attempt to reduce employee interest in unions. Indeed many of the firms that applied these ideas in the 1960s and early 1970s were in the electronics industry, which is largely nonunion.

Despite these fears on the part of unions, to which we will return later, it should be noted that participative concepts also were sometimes jointly sponsored by union and management. A prime example is the assembly plant of General Motors in Tarrytown, New York, in which a problem-solving group of workers was successful in finding a remedy for the problem of leaky rear windows. The success of this and similar efforts in the early 1970s led to the spread of such groups throughout the entire plant. The participative problem-solving groups became the main mechanism for improving the quality of work life for workers, a joint objective of plant management and the UAW. It produced benefits for management, union, and workers.[1]

Participative problem-solving groups have also been the primary vehicle for implementing the quality of work life objective of AT&T and the Communications Workers of America. These groups can be initiated without first making other changes in the definition of jobs. Therefore, the barriers to entry appear low. However, the longer-term success of participative problem-solving groups is only possible if management changes other aspects of the work system to encourage the delegation of authority and responsibility, and the improvement of the content of the job themselves. Many programs have foundered because management was not prepared to support fully the spirit of the program and to rethink other aspects of the work system.

### *Job Enrichment*

While the idea of participative supervision was gaining popularity, some observers were emphasizing a different type of reform—what was needed was to change the core task itself.

Frederick Herzberg has argued that there are two sets of factors involved in work tasks.[2] The first set, called "hygiene factors," have to do with the environment of the job and include such things as company policies, supervisory practices, pay plans, and working conditions. The second set of factors, called "motivators," include recognition, achievement, responsibility, advancement, personal growth, and competence. Employees cannot be motivated by improvement in hygiene factors alone, Herzberg argued. But those factors are considered to be of primary importance by employees. Therefore, any attempts to use job design to motivate employees must first minimize dissatisfaction with the hygiene factors. Only when that is done can motivation be enhanced by providing employees with work that allows them to experience the motivators.

In the 1960s Robert Ford and his associates at AT&T pioneered in the application of Herzberg's theories. Production, service, and office jobs were redesigned to allow workers a greater opportunity for motivator need satisfaction. An early experiment involved clerical workers who answered customer complaint letters. Previously required to answer correspondence by selecting from a set of standard letters signed by their supervisors, employees were now given the opportunity to write and sign their own letters. Some individuals were asked to take added responsibility as experts on certain subjects so that they could be resources to the rest of the department in answering difficult inquiries. The results were higher productivity and satisfaction with achievement, responsibility, and growth in competence.[3]

If jobs are to be designed to increase motivation, it would be helpful to know explicitly what job characteristics might be changed to increase involvement. More recently, a conceptual framework has been developed for analyzing many jobs.[4] Five core dimensions in the framework are:

1. *Skill variety.* The degree to which a job requires a variety of different activities in carrying out the work, involving the use of a number of different skills and talents.
2. *Task identity.* The degree to which the job requires completion of a "whole" and identifiable piece of work; that is, doing a job from beginning to end with a visible outcome.
3. *Task significance.* The degree to which a job has a substantial impact on the lives or work of other people, whether in the organization or the external environment.
4. *Autonomy.* The degree to which the job provides substantial freedom, independence, and discretion to the individual in scheduling work and determining the procedures to be used in carrying it out.
5. *Feedback.* The degree to which carrying out work activities required by the job results in the individual obtaining direct and clear information about the effectiveness of his or her performance.

By redesigning jobs to increase variety, identity, significance, autonomy, and feedback the psychological experience of working is changed. As Figure 6-2 illustrates, individuals experience the work as more meaningful, they feel more responsible for results, and they know more about the results of their efforts. These psychological changes lead to many of the improved work outcomes which have been observed following the redesign of work: higher internal motivation, higher quality work performance, higher satisfaction with the work, and lower absenteeism and turnover.

However, according to theory, only employees who have relatively strong needs for achievement, autonomy, and responsibility are likely to be affected by work redesign in the manner specified by the model (depicted in Figure 6–2 as "Employee Growth Need Strength"). This is not surprising, but it raises important strategic questions about the application of work design concepts. If not all individuals want more responsibility and freedom, are special selection efforts needed in organizations that plan to enrich work? What should be done in older plants about existing employees who do not want more responsibility? Are these employees capable of learning to like and want increased responsibility? Indeed, are their relatively low needs for responsibility a function of the traditional work systems in which they have been working? We will return to these implementation questions later in this chapter.

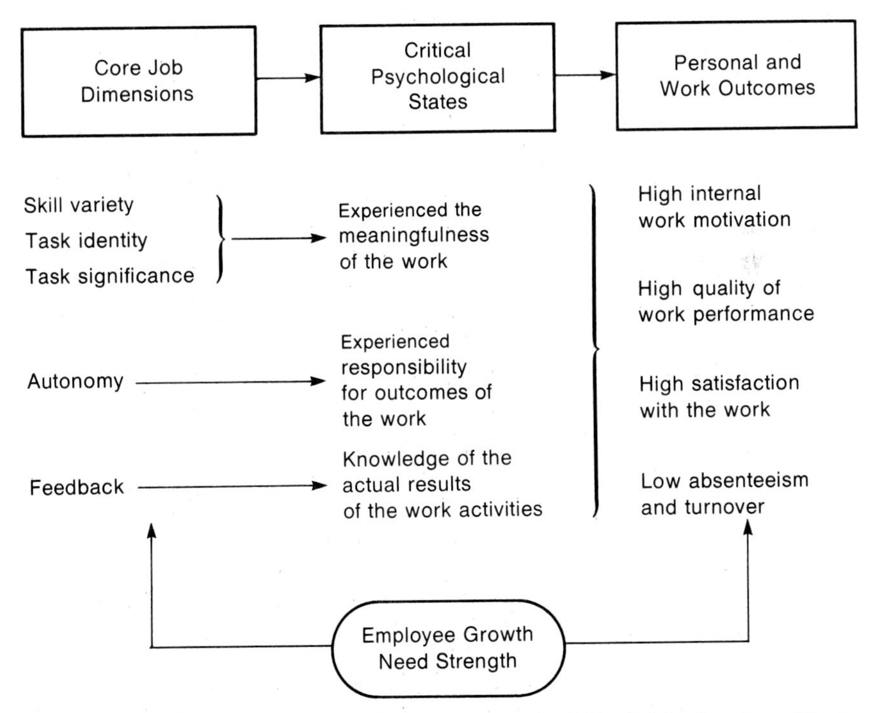


**FIGURE 6–2 The Job Characteristic Model of Work Motivation: Work Design**

SOURCE: From J. Richard Hackman, "Job Design," in J. R. Hackman and J. L. Suttle (eds.), *Improving Life at Work: Behavioral Science Approaches to Organizational Change* (Santa Monica, Calif.: Goodyear Publishing, 1977), p. 129. Reprinted with permission of J. Richard Hackman.

There are five steps a manager can take if he or she wishes to enrich a job by increasing variety, identity, significance, autonomy, and feedback.

1. *Formulating natural work units.* This means grouping tasks so that, as much as possible, they constitute an identifiable and meaningful whole. Units may be formed according to geography, products, or subassemblies, business, or customers.
2. *Combining tasks.* This means combining what may have been separate and distinct jobs into one.
3. *Establishing client relationships.* This means giving the worker contact with a user of his or her product (another production department, a customer, a sales group, and so on) and giving him or her an understanding of the criteria by which the product will be judged.
4. *Vertical loading.* This means giving the worker as much responsibility as possible in planning, doing, and controlling. Thus the control that management may have exercised through other departments is given to the workers. This often means giving workers responsibility for scheduling work, inventory control, budgeting, and quality control.
5. *Opening feedback channels.* This means giving the worker as much information as possible and as directly as possible about results such as cost, yields, setup, customer complaints, production, and quality.

Figure 6-3 illustrates the task dimensions that are most affected by each of the job design steps. It is thus a guide for redesigning jobs once deficiencies in one or more task dimensions have been diagnosed.

### *Technology Policy*

A still more recently articulated idea is that it is not enough for management to try to enrich jobs as an afterthought to the already extant technology of the job. The initial design of the new technology should be responsive to social criteria as well as technical and economic criteria.

This idea is particularly apropos in relation to advanced information technology which is still developing. Increasingly, this technology crosses normal departmental boundaries, is on-line, and involves large numbers of clerical, professional, and managerial personnel who directly utilize terminals as part of their normal work routines. A new procurement system in a large multifacility company, for example, may embrace buyers and their clerical support, receiving personnel, and accounts payable personnel. An electronic mail system may place terminals on the desks of all managers and many support personnel. A

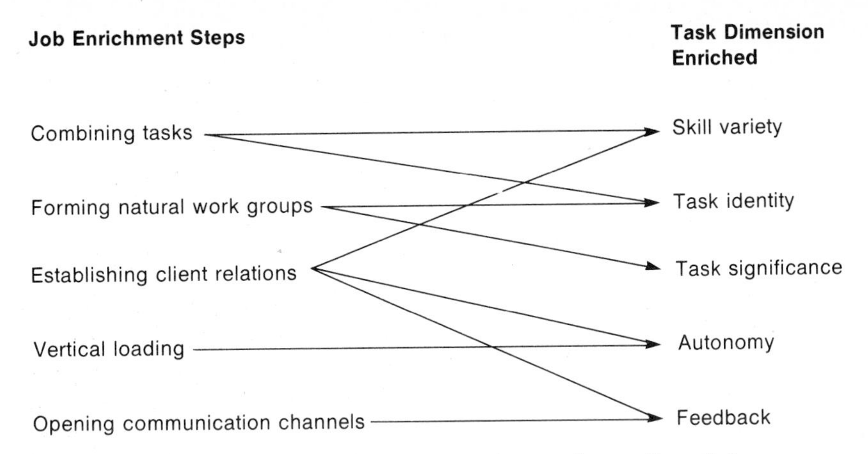


**FIGURE 6–3 Effects of Job Enrichment Strategies on Core Job Dimensions**

SOURCE: From J. Richard Hackman, "Job Design," in J. R. Hackman and J. L. Suttle (eds.), *Improving Life at Work: Behavioral Science Approaches to Organizational Change* (Santa Monica, Calif.: Goodyear Publishing, 1977), p. 136. Reprinted with permission of J. Richard Hackman.

centralized word processing system may link those who generate text and who produce it in a very different way, affecting work content and work relationships. The applications—existing and contemplated—are virtually infinite.

The application of this type of information technology can have a profound impact on other elements of the work system, with second-order consequences for employee commitment and developed competencies. The impact can be either positive or negative.[5] Management can increase the positive impact by considering the following implications of design choices:

1. While work systems based on new technology will usually require less skill and knowledge on the part of *some* employees, they will require *more* skill and knowledge from others. System design can influence whether more jobs are being upgraded or downgraded.
2. Work system design can increase or decrease work schedule flexibility to accommodate human preferences.
3. Work system design can contribute to isolation or bring operators in closer touch with each other and with the end product of the work.
4. New technology may render some individual skills obsolete, but it can open career opportunities for learning new skills.
5. Work system design can change—for better or worse—an employee typist into a subcontractor operating a terminal out of his or her own home.

Computer-based technology is becoming less and less deterministic, allowing planners increasing latitude in making design choices that take into account its human impact. Two factors are responsible for this. First, the rapidly declining cost of computing power makes it possible to consider more technical options, including those that are relatively inefficient in the use of that power. Second, the new technology is less hardware-dependent, more software-intensive. It is, therefore, increasingly flexible, permitting the same basic information-processing task to be accomplished by an ever greater variety of technical configurations, each of which may have a different set of human implications. For example, one system configuration may decentralize decision-making; another may centralize it. Yet both will be able to accomplish the same *task* objectives.

Not many corporations or vendors of the new information technology are incorporating human consideration in the design or installation of new technology. Technical people in the client or vendor organization are simply not attuned to the long-term human implication of the technology. Workers who are affected by the technology and managers who will inherit the long-term human and management problems that will result are generally not given a voice in designing and installation decisions. It has been suggested that organizations develop a social impact statement before introducing any new technology.[6] That statement must account for the human and organizational consequences of the new technology and for how the champions of the technology have chosen to deal with them. Another approach to the problem would require a broadly constituted committee of technical people, managers, and human resource specialists, each with their own perspective on the benefits and costs of the technology, to manage the introduction of any new technology. A consensus of what technology is to be introduced and how it is to be introduced would be required before implementation could proceed. Finally, employees who are to be affected by the technology can be directly involved in the design or choice of equipment and in implementation. Presumably their needs would be taken into account through this process. For example, in a recent introduction of word processing equipment, clerical workers who were affected suggested that the equipment be placed in small centers distributed throughout the office building instead of being consolidated in one large word processing center. They said this would result in closer identity with client managers and greater responsiveness to their needs, a principle of job design we described earlier.

## COMPREHENSIVE REDESIGN OF WORK SYSTEMS

Both in the United States and abroad there have been many years of experimentation with alternative arrangements between employees and employers that embrace all of the above initiatives and others as well. The intellectual and practical pioneering of this comprehensive approach was done by Eric Trist and his colleagues at the Tavistock Institute in London. Their initial project in the British coal mining industry after World War II spawned a theory, a method, and a skilled cadre of advocates of this school of thought. The new paradigm of work they advocated included the following principles:

1. The *work system*, which comprised a set of activities that made up a functioning whole, now became the basic unit rather than the single jobs.
2. Correspondingly, the *work group* became central rather than the individual job holder.
3. *Internal regulation* of the system by the group was thus rendered possible rather than the external regulation of individuals by supervisors.
4. A design principle based on the *redundancy of functions* rather than the redundancy of parts characterized the underlying organizational philosophy. Redundancy of functions means developing multiple skills in the individual and thereby immensely increasing the capability of the group to respond to a variety of task demands.
5. This principle valued the *discretionary* rather than the prescribed part of work roles. Individuals would have more freedom to decide what to do and when to do it.
6. It treated the individual as complementary to the machine rather than as an extension of it.
7. It was *variety-increasing* for both the individual and the organization rather than variety-decreasing in the bureaucratic mode.[7]

Over the two decades after World War II, socio-technical concepts were employed in projects that covered a wide variety of industries in a number of different countries, including a textile company in India, a hospital in Australia, and telecommunications in Holland. An especially important set of projects was initiated under the direction of the Norwegian Industrial Democracy Project in the 1960s. However, in none of these countries, including Norway, did the new paradigm of work become a significant trend before the 1970s.

A few new plants in the United States in the late 1960s and early 1970s were designed according to socio-technical theory, although they did not necessarily follow the design methodology or employ socio-technical language. A Procter & Gamble soap plant in Lima, Ohio and especially a General Foods dog food plant in Topeka, Kansas became visible prototypes that influenced the design of an important fraction of new plants started up in the 1970s. In the United States, the socio-technical approach to work system design was subsumed by and was promoted by the quality of work life (QWL) movement which became a national phenomenon in the 1970s.

The term "quality of work life" was coined in an international conference held at Arden House in 1972 and gained institutional status when the UAW and General Motors used it as the umbrella concept for the work reforms they would sponsor jointly.

When the work system experiments began in American manufacturing in the late 1960s, there were both successes and failures. Most of these early experiments took place in new nonunion facilities. In these situations supervisors and employees could be selected to fit the new work system concept. The restrictive work practices and traditions of union-management conflict often found in older plants did not inhibit implementation. In several instances work system innovations proved to be quite fragile with the passage of time. As new management and/or workers flowed into the experimental plants, regression in innovative practices and their effects took place. In other instances conflict between managers of innovative plants and corporate headquarters began to develop over the number of exceptions from traditional corporate policies these innovative work systems were to be granted. Instead of being seen as pioneers, managers of the innovative facilities felt they were being restricted, perhaps even stymied in their careers. Some innovations began to unravel; a few disappeared completely.

As the years have passed experiments have continued and a great deal has been learned, particularly about implementation. An increasing number of work restructuring projects have been jointly sponsored by management and union in older plants.

What was the nature of these experimental work systems? It is simplest to contrast two alternative work system models. The first model is an attempt to capture the traditional work system, the one that developed with Taylor's principles as its cornerstone. It is the model generally prevailing today. Employees perform jobs which are narrowly defined in content. They stay in jobs and specialize unless they are promoted or transferred. Pay is according to the specific job, and sometimes according to individual performance. The employee works under close supervision, and employee performance is evaluated by direct supervisors. Persons are assigned overtime or are transferred temporarily under elaborate rules, especially in unionized organizations. The employee's career is one of specialization, with little opportunity to grow in competence beyond that specialization. (As a practical matter, ordinarily American business has no concept of a career for any employees other than professional and managerial personnel.)

The experimental model, which we believe signals an emerging pattern, departs in almost every detail from the one just cited. It elaborates upon the socio-technical approach. In the experimental model jobs are broadly defined, teams of employees are assigned to perform a group of jobs, and employees are rotated through the various jobs. In effect, the team is given a business to conduct. The team is responsible for inventory, materials scheduling, personnel scheduling, production goals, cost targets, and product quality. Employees are paid according to the number of tasks which they have mastered. Ordinarily employees are assigned a particular task for six months or more, so that there is a built-in length of service element in the pay system. There is little direct supervision. Employees are supervised and evaluated by the team, and respond to the requests of peers rather than the orders of a supervisor. The assumption is that peer pressure is more compelling than a supervisor's orders. In place of rules about overtime and transfers there are a few general practices (such as six months' job rotation periods) and informal arrangements stressing shared burdens among the team members. An employee may now be said to have more of a career because progression occurs as the employee masters the assorted skills required in the teams. Because the breadth of tasks is large, an employee with an aptitude for technical or administrative advancement is able to demonstrate it. Furthermore, the company considers that it employs a broad-gauge person with various capacities, rather than one with a specialized and limited-usage input to the production process. Thus, the personality, intelligence, flexibility, and general effectiveness of the person become more important in determining effectiveness on the job. Finally, because of broad skills and because of the flexibility that the team approach brings to production (often resulting in better

**TABLE 6–1 Alternate Work Systems**

| Model A—Traditional Work System | Model B—High-Commitment Work System |
|---|---|
| Narrowly defined jobs | Broadly defined jobs |
| Specialization of employees | Rotation of employees through jobs |
| Pay by specific job content | Pay by skills mastered |
| Evaluation by direct supervision | Evaluation by peers |
| Work is under close supervision | Self- or peer-supervision |
| Assignment of overtime or transfer by rule book | Team assigns members to cover vacancies in flexible fashion |
| No career development | Concern for learning and growth |
| Employees as individuals | Employees in a team |
| Employee is ignorant about business | Team runs a business; business data shared widely |
| Status symbols used to reinforce hierarchy | Status differences minimized |
| Employees have input on few matters | Broad employee participation |

productivity), employees' jobs may be somewhat more secure. Recognizing employees as a greater asset, employers will try harder to keep them even in difficult economic periods.

The contrasts between the two models just discussed are summarized in Table 6–1. The theme of the first model (A), which is still the prevailing one used in blue-collar and clerical work, is a direct focus on efficiency and control. In contrast, the theme of the emerging model (B), is to build human commitment by direct attention to the integration of individual needs and organizational requirements, and to achieve control and efficiency as a second-order consequence. Therefore, we will sometimes refer to the emerging models as a "high-commitment work system."[8]

## MANAGEMENT ASSUMPTIONS AND VALUES

As we stated earlier, managerial behavior reflects fundamental assumptions, often implicit, about the motivation and competence of human beings and their capacity to become involved in work. It is not surprising, therefore, that the basic assumptions that underlie the design of "emerging" work systems are considerably more optimistic than those underlying "traditional" work systems. The assumptions most often explicitly articulated by the managers who have designed and started up these high-commitment work systems are:

- People *want* to work hard, perform well, learn new skills, and be involved in decision making that affects their jobs.
- Creative talents are widely distributed at all levels of a work organization.
- Participation can lead to quality decisions and commitment.

It is not uncommon for the founding management team of these new plant work systems to spend up to a week discussing assumptions which should guide the new plant. This is usually done with the help of a consultant, through education on human motivation and management theory, and by examining their own managerial assumptions, beliefs, and behavior. This process finally shapes a philosophy of management that guides all their design decisions.

The design phase itself often takes from several months to a year prior to plant start-up. During this period, team members begin to hire the next level of management and make decisions about job design, compensation systems, mechanism for employee voice, work rules, promotion and employment security policies, and so on. In each of the four policy areas policies are typically articulated and tested for consistency with the basic assumptions and philosophy set forth at the beginning. The design phase and later implementation sometimes cause reexamination of assumptions and values and occasionally changes in them. By and large, however, the three basic assumptions listed above are reflected in all of the high-commitment systems of which we know. And the articulation of a philosophy of management is critical in enabling management to break with the past, examine their own managerial behavior, and design highly internally consistent policies in the employee influence, flow, rewards, and work systems areas. It is the internally consistent nature of these policies that makes it possible for employees to understand management's expectations for performance, involvement, and responsibility.

While the clarification of assumptions may have been useful to management in designing and managing these new work systems, it also contributed to the conflict between management and corporate headquarters to which we referred earlier. The clearer these managers became about the assumptions that guided their innovative plants, the more apparent the differences became between their own assumptions and those of corporate management. When those differences were not managed well by either side, problems arose that ultimately led to the departure of key managers in the innovative plant. These types of problems are associated with many innovations, not only those in human resource management. They will be less in evidence the more the assumptions underlying the new work systems become the assumptions of American management, a transformation that we believe is well underway. The tensions that have arisen from differences in assumption and values underscore that corporate transformations in human resource management cannot occur without a transformation in the assumptions and values of management at all levels.

## SOME CONSISTENT POLICIES AND PRACTICES

It is not surprising, given common assumptions about human motivation and competence, that many new innovative plants have similar human resource policies to support the development of a high-commitment work system.[9]

In the *employee influence* policy area many of the plants have developed mechanisms for giving employees a voice in the governance of the plant. For example, open-door policies, small group meetings of employees at all levels with the plant manager, committees and task forces to study various problems and make recommendations, and permanent boards of employee representatives are not uncommon. Participation of employees is sought in many decisions beyond their immediate work, including layout of machinery, equipment, and the plant itself.

A flat organization structure, with the plant manager only several steps above production workers (sometimes as few as three or four), makes it easier for employees at the bottom to talk to management at the top. Finally, egalitarianism is established by eliminating unnecessary distinctions between employee groups in dress codes, office space, parking, and eating facilities. Egalitarianism is also fostered by an all-salaried work force (see Chapter 5), which eliminates the distinction between hourly and salaried workers (except of course for the legal requirements governing overtime pay for nonexempt employees).

In the *human resource flow* policy area, high-commitment plants depart from the traditional approaches to selection, promotion, and training, often allowing more employee influence in these decisions. For example, the traditional approach to selection (the personnel department carefully screens, tests and selects among applicants) is often replaced with work teams being allowed to select their own members. Extensive front-end training and orientation emphasize not just specific content skills, but interpersonal skills; they help acclimate new employees to the climate of high involvement and high commitment.

In the *reward systems* policy area, new innovative plants incorporate several similar pay policies and again allow more employee influence on these policies. To encourage growth in competence and to allow the flexibility in job assignments required by the team approach, a skill-based pay system (as opposed to the traditional job-based system—see Chapter 5) is typically installed. Employee pay levels are determined by the number of skills they have acquired. Typically, a five- or six-level ladder is established. Teams are expected to evaluate their members and decide when they are eligible for a raise, although not all plants incorporate this feature because it is the most difficult to implement, requiring considerable skill and maturity on the part of the team. Employees help design and administer these pay systems, reevaluating their efficacy from time to time or assessing whether pay levels are equitable compared to other plants in the company or region. Sometimes a profit-sharing or cost-savings bonus is used to encourage cooperative behavior in the plant, reinforcing commitment to the whole rather than the individual or group.

Finally, these high-commitment systems redefine the duties of first-line supervisors. They become facilitators and consultants to work teams and are not supposed to take on the usual directive role of traditional supervisors. Since most teams in a new plant do not have the experience or maturity to work autonomously early in the life of the plant, supervisors must be more directive at first and slowly work themselves out of that role and into one of facilitation. The unique demands of this role make it hard to find people who fit it well or to keep people in it, a special problem of high-commitment job systems that needs continual attention.

As noted earlier, in the United States these experimental systems initially were developed in new production facilities without unions. They are now being introduced into unionized facilities, both newly constructed and old.

It is in the area of attitude changes that the new systems make their greatest demands on management, union, and employees. There is great flexibility in the experimental systems. As a result considerable trust is required between management and labor to make them work successfully. Employees must not be concerned that management will utilize flexibility to exploit workers, and managers must not be concerned that employees will use flexibility to impose inefficient practices on the company. The new systems can build trust between labor and management, but they also depend upon its prior existence.

The life of an employee is different under the new system. Rather than carrying out orders in a repetitive fashion and leaving all problems at the workplace each evening, the employee assumes much more far-reaching obligations. The stress of meeting production targets now falls directly on the team and its members. Employees must learn to accept criticism from other members of the team, and to react in a constructive fashion. Employees must be able to communicate effectively with one another, including the transmission of technical information and production requirements in a clear and understandable fashion. Employees must continue to learn on the job as new skills are mastered and new processes, new technology, and new products are introduced. Employees in effect assume what are now managerial functions, and they experience as well the stress which accompanies administrative jobs. The employee takes the job home at night, and family relationships may be disrupted unless the employee is able to cope with stress successfully. The new systems require a much higher degree of commitment from the employee to the workplace then do the old systems. Their apparent advantage in productivity arises from this higher commitment and the flexibility in production which accompanies high commitment.

## THE CHOICE BETWEEN MODEL A AND MODEL B

Many managers will acknowledge that there are advantages in the Model B approach, including greater employee commitment to their jobs and improved performance. However, managers often are either skeptical that the approach is realistic or fear the apparent loss of control when they relinquish decision-making authority (either formally or in practice) to subordinates. How is a manager to decide when it is appropriate to try to design or develop a Model B type work system?

Some managers and behavioral scientists have suggested that Model A is better fitted to some technologies than Model B and vice versa. Specifically, it has been asserted that in machine-paced processes, such as automobile assembly, there is no room for employee initiative of the type envisioned by Model B. However, some of the most effective experiments with Model B have occurred in the assembly-line environment. By and large it now appears that technology does not dictate the form of work organization, though it is an important influence in detailed work design, as we have mentioned previously.

## UNIONS, MANAGERS, AND QUALITY OF WORK LIFE

Though traditionally not the subject of collective bargaining, the design of work and the involvement of employees in decision making is becoming a matter of joint union-management concern as evidenced by quality of work life (QWL) programs at General Motors and AT&T and the Employee Involvement program at Ford. Such programs are not so much concerned with job design as with ways of seeking, implementing, and institutionalizing participation in and influence over the working lives of employees and the operation of the organization.

Not all union leaders agree on the efficacy of involvement with management on QWL or innovative work system programs. There are two main views. Some union leaders see joint QWL programs as a further step (after collective bargaining) toward industrial democracy. Irving Bluestone of the UAW is the best example of a union leader who had this view when he began the process of building a cooperative relationship with the management of General Motors. But others dismiss the efforts. For example, in 1973 William Winpisinger of the Machinists Union dismissed job enrichment experiments as "a stopwatch in sheep's clothing. . . . The better the wage, the greater the job satisfaction. There is no better cure for the 'blue collar blues'."[10]

The majority of unions have not endorsed QWL, while the AFL-CIO's top leadership has expressed, at best, guarded optimism. Those who do favor QWL programs insist that they should be established only with union presence and involvement. QWL in a nonunion setting becomes, in their view, a paternalistic "gift" that can easily be taken back. Says Glenn Watts of the CWA, without a union "bosses will never give up the idea of being a boss." Still, some union leaders see cooperation as a sellout, "getting in bed with management." Others feel that their role as sole protector of the rights of workers is threatened. Still others find old adversarial patterns and ways of thinking and behaving hard to break. But QWL does raise an important question, even a challenge, to union leaders in the upcoming decade. Traditionally, unions have shied away from questions of participation of job design, concentrating almost exclusively on tangible matters like pay and hours. The shrinking economic pie that seems to be the country's lot in the near future, however, will likely make monetary victories hard to come by. Unions that can no longer promise members ever-increasing wages might find participation and job enrichment promising avenues to consider. An increasingly well-educated work force might, in fact, demand that union leaders break their old habits and move in the QWL direction, or members may seek new leaders. Such innovative union leaders could begin making demands for jointly administered employee surveys or the right to review the performance and effectiveness of supervisors. They might make demands to become involved in decisions about technology as the Communication Workers of America have or to review all job assignments and training plans as Japanese unions regularly do. This approach would require a union leadership educated in human resource innovations, something that—with few exceptions—they are not. It would put management that is lagging in these innovations on the defensive and would be a major force for change in American industry, if not also a source of revitalization for unions.[11]

The National Labor Relations Act raises another set of questions concerning quality of work life activities—those having to do with the legal ramifications of QWL in both union and nonunion settings. The NLRA makes it unfair labor practice for employers to dominate or interfere with *any* labor organization, whether that organization be a union or some sort of employee committee. It is likely that under current labor law and judicial interpretations most QWL programs in nonunion settings are either totally or in part illegal. Does the NLRA allow for *any* formal cooperation? The matter is yet to be decided by the Supreme Court, but scattered circuit court rulings have suggested that a primary consideration should be *intent*. The labor organization must truly represent the wishes of employees, and the employer must not intend to dominate the group in any way. In other words, the more freedom of participation an employer grants under some type of QWL mechanism in a nonunion setting, the more likely is that QWL program to be found legal. The more an employer attempts to restrict, interfere, or control an employee committee, the more likely is that employer to be found in violation of the NLRA. It should be noted, however, that very few legal challenges have been raised to QWL programs in either union or nonunion settings.[12]

## CHALLENGING QUESTIONS ABOUT HIGH-COMMITMENT WORK SYSTEMS

Accepting that there will be individual differences, do most workers want to work under such a high-participation, high-commitment work system? Should prescreening before hiring be used to identify those who do? Can most managers manage effectively under such systems?

Do new measures of success under altered work systems need to be developed? Does managerial competence need to be defined and measured differently? Within an organization, how can different work systems be measured to determine relative success? Should they be compared? Will organizations adopt and continue to support these types of work systems when they don't have hard financial evidence that they are superior?

First-line supervisors are the immediate contact between management and nonmanagement employees, but are often most resistant to changing work systems, to giving up "authority" and control. Do they have the necessary interpersonal skills to manage high-participation systems? What about union stewards, whose role may be similarly affected?

There are many other questions that become salient *after* those high-commitment work systems have enjoyed a period of success.[13]

Will they gravitate toward the conventional patterns they seek to replace? Will the rules and structures developed to solve a particular problem take on a life of their own? Will individuals and groups tire of the flexibility and uncertainty inherent in Model B and instinctively attempt to define and protect their own turf—whether it be differentiated roles or special privileges? Will the initially egalitarian society become stratified to accord more status to those who have accepted more responsibility? If not, why not? How does one repeal or avoid the "iron law of bureaucracy"?

Do these high-commitment work systems, which require careful development and nurturance during their formative periods, remain in a "fragile, handle-with-care" state? Or do they, because they are aligned with both individual and organizational needs, become robust and difficult to destroy?

Will the greater involvement of workers in decision making lead to ever-rising expectations for influence? Does having some voice regarding "managerial agenda" such as machine layout lead to expectation of voice in other areas—subcontracting, plant location, product design, and inventory policy? If so, can these expectations be accommodated? How should expectations be managed, or should they?

These questions are among many that must still be answered in order for the assumptions and concepts underlying innovative high-commitment work systems to become more widely applied, for high commitment work systems to become the norm rather than the exception. We believe, however, that the experience and evidence to date is sufficiently encouraging for effort to be made by American industry to innovate in work system design on a broad front—in traditional and new plants, in union and nonunion settings, at the shop floor and in the office, and at the operating and management levels. Indeed, as we saw earlier, these ideas can be applied to the introduction of new information technology, the area in which rapid change provides potential for innovation but in which traditional thinking can recreate in the office the problems we are now trying to solve in the plant. The experience of innovation is required to grapple with the problems suggested by the questions above. With sufficient commitment to innovation, to the transformation of the relationship between manager and managed: solutions will be found to the new set of problems created by innovation. This after all is the nature of organizational and social change, solutions created to solve old problems are accompanied by a new set of problems which themselves require solution for the innovations to survive. Competitive pressures and changes in work values will demand that management undertake the commitment required to manage major organizational transformations. As we mentioned earlier, several large companies such as General Motors, Ford Motors, Cummins Engine, Goodyear Tire & Rubber, AT&T, and Bethlehem Steel, among others, are making innovations in work systems a major part of their strategy for competing in the 1980s and beyond.

## SUMMARY AND CONCLUSIONS

The productivity crisis and changing values in the work force have stimulated a stream of innovations in work system design that transform traditional relationships between the task, workers, managers, technology, and personnel policies. These innovations have started at the shop-floor level but are applicable to the office and management levels, particularly as new information technology is introduced. Instead of narrowly defined jobs, specialization of employees, pay for specific job content, close supervision, employees assigned to individual tasks, status differentials which reinforce hierarchy and little employee influence (what we have called Model A), innovations in work systems have tended to define jobs broadly, rotate employees through many jobs, pay for skills mastered, emphasize self or peer supervision, assign whole tasks to teams, remove status differentials and emphasize egalitarianism, and allow substantial employee influence and participation. We have called such systems Model B or high-commitment work systems. These systems are based on the assumption that employees want to work hard, that creative talents are widely distributed, and that participation can lead to quality decisions and commitment. High-commitment work systems, therefore, require substantially different managerial values and skills than are found in most organizations, including a willingness to delegate and give employees information and influence. High-commitment work systems have threatened some union leaders and have been embraced by others.

This chapter concludes where it began—with a recitation of the "stakes" associated with work system design. When the Model B-type work systems have been implemented effectively, managements report the following types of benefits of high commitment: higher in-plant quality, lower warranty costs, lower waste, higher machine utilization, fewer operating and support personnel, lower turnover and absenteeism, and faster start-up of new equipment. However, to achieve these gains, managers have had to invest extra effort, develop new skills and relationships, cope with higher levels of ambiguity and uncertainty, and experience the pain and discomfort associated with changing habits and skills.

Union officials who have entered into joint sponsorshop of QWL reforms of traditional work systems report a number of benefits: improved product quality, reduced absenteeism and turnover, reduction in discharge, disciplinary layoffs, and grievance load; re-election of union officials who are proponents of QWL; and enhanced financial rewards.[14] They also expect greater job security to derive from improved competitiveness. Like management, they must make a heavy investment of time, and experience the frustrations associated with change. They also have to be wary of the political risk of becoming too closely associated with management.

The stakes for the worker include the following: higher influence and more autonomy in exchange for accepting more responsibility; more social support from peers in exchange for operating in a more interdependent mode; and more opportunity for development and self-esteem in return for accepting more ambiguity and uncertainty. Apparently for most participants in the emerging work system, but not for all, that is a good bargain.

## NOTES

1. Robert H. Guest, "Quality of Work Life—Learning from Tarrytown," *Harvard Business Review*, July-August 1979, pp. 76-89.
2. Frederick Herzberg, B. Mausner, and B. Snyderman. *The Motivation to Work* (New York: Wiley, 1959).
3. Robert N. Ford, *Motivation Through the Work Itself* (New York: American Management Association, 1969).
4. Ricky W. Griffin, *Task Design: An Integrative Approach* (Glenview, Ill.: Scott, Foresman, 1982), pp. 17-51; J. Richard Hackman, "Work Design" in J. R. Hackman and J. L. Suttle (eds.), *Improving Life at Work: Behavioral Science Approaches to Organizational Change* (Santa Barbara, Calif.: Goodyear Publishing, 1977), pp. 96-162.
5. Richard E. Walton, "Social Choices in the Development of Advanced Information Technology," *Human Relations* 35 (1978), pp. 1973-1983.
6. Walton, "Social Choices."
7. Eric Trist, "The Evolution of Socio-Technical Systems," *Issues in the Quality of Work Life. A series of occasional papers*, No. 2, June 1981, p. 9.
8. Richard E. Walton, "Establishing and Maintaining High Commitment Work Systems," in J. Kimberly and R. Miles (eds.), *Organizational Life Cycle* (San Francisco: Jossey Bass, 1980).
9. Edward E. Lawler, "The New Plant Revolution," *Organizational Dynamics* (Winter 1978), pp. 3-12.
10. William Winpisinger, "Job Satisfaction: A Union Response," *AFL-CIO American Federationist*, February 1973.
11. Michael Beer and James W. Driscoll, "Strategies for Change," in Hackman and Suttle, *Improving Life at Work: Behavioral Science Approaches to Organizational Change* (Santa Monica, Calif.: Goodyear, 1977), pp. 409-11.
12. Thomas J. Schneider, "Quality of Work Life and the Law." A speech given at the Kennedy School of Government and Public Policy, 19 November 1981.
13. Richard E. Walton, "Topeka Work Systems: Optimistic Visions, Pessimistic Hypotheses, and Reality," in R. Zager and M. Rosow (eds.), *The Innovative Organization* (New York: Pergamon Press/Work in America Series, 1982).
14. Irving Bluestone, "Labor's Stake in Improving the Quality of Working Life," in Harvey Kolodny and Hans van Beinum (eds.), *The Quality of Working Life and the 1980s* (New York: Praeger, 1983).

CASE 24

# NEW TECHNOLOGY AND JOB DESIGN IN A PHONE COMPANY (A)

*Richard E. Walton*

In the late 1970s a phone company began to automate a major part of the customer repair system. Previously, customer requests for repair service had been handled as follows:

1. Customer calls were connected with the local repair bureau which serviced the area.
2. The request was received in the repair bureau by a repair clerk who recorded all details on a form, initiated a manual test of the phone service to locate the trouble, and made a tentative time commitment for completing the repairs.
3. The clerk handed the form to a supervisor of the field repairman.
4. If a customer called the bureau again, the clerk could readily check the status of the repair order.

Repair clerks engaged in a number of additional work activities, such as filing and assisting other personnel in the bureau.

The new system utilized on-line computer technology with the objectives of reducing the time taken to process requests and the number of clerks required. The new system operated in the following way:

1. The clerical task of receiving customer repair requests was removed from local bureaus and centralized in one answering center, connected by on-line computer to a large number of repair bureaus over a four-state area. One hundred answering personnel, designated as repair service answerers (RSAs), manned the centralized answering center over three shifts. The floor plan is shown in Exhibit 24–1. Any phone call could be routed to any desk.
2. Customers with repair requests were connected to the answering center where the calls were directed to one of the available RSAs, and the RSA receiving the call elicited precisely the in-

formation required and recorded the details on a visual display console.

3. This information was dispatched automatically via computer to the appropriate repair bureau which received it in printout form. At the same time, the RSA initiated an automatic test of the customer's service.
4. Following prescribed guidelines, the RSA provided the customer with a schedule commitment for the repair.
5. The incoming repair requests and test results were received by operators in the repair bureau and passed on to supervisors, who dispatched field personnel to restore or repair subscriber service.

Organizationally, the answering centers and the repair bureaus reported to company headquarters by different chains of command. Employees in the answering center were represented by the same union which represented all nonsupervisory employees in the repair bureaus.

Technically, the new system promised to reduce both the time taken to process repair requests and the number of answering personnel required, but these objectives were not being achieved. Nor did the quality of service meet performance objectives. The system was plagued by three sets of problems:

1. Problems of task performance and work dissatisfaction among employees of the answering center. Symptoms included conflict, turnover, tension, low morale, and the "worst labor relations in company."
2. Coordination difficulties and conflicts, particularly at the interface between the answering center and the repair bureaus.
3. Some new sources of customer dissatisfaction.

Some of these problems could be associated with the introduction of a new system, but others arose from the effects this particular system was having on the organization and performance of work. These problems were likely to persist.

**EXHIBIT 24–1**
**Floor Plan of Answering Center**

— Clock

Switchboard

Supervisor

Supervisor

Storage room

Conference room

Key: Desk with terminal and phone

x RSA

CASE 25

# KALAMAZOO PLANT PARTS DIVISION—ACME MOTORS

*Frank S. Leonard*
*Wickham Skinner*

Bob Moore, supervisor, Salaried Personnel, returned to his office after a management development discussion with the plant manager, Rich Howards. During the discussion, Bob had informed Howards of the year-end figures for supervisory turnover. Out of a total of approximately 170 supervisory positions at Kalamazoo, the Industrial Relations Department had placed (hired) 78 supervisors during 1978. The plant manager had asked Bob to look into the problem, find out the reasons for the high turnover, and make recommendations. With increasing pressure for cost reductions and improved productivity from Division, the high supervisory turnover was seen by Moore and Howards as a critical problem.

The Kalamazoo plant of the Parts Division of Acme Motors (one of the Big Three auto manufacturers) was one of the largest plastic molding and injection assembly plants in the country. It produced a variety of plastic parts used in an automobile including grilles, instrument panels, instrument clusters and gauges, fender aprons, fan shrouds, turn panels, and so forth. Kalamazoo was one of seven plants in the Parts Division, each of which was a profit center with a fully autonomous organization. Sales at Kalamazoo were about $400M annually. With the trend toward fuel economy and energy conservation, the use of plastics had been increasing, taking on strategic importance. The Kalamazoo plant was the major supplier of plastic parts to the Acme Assembly Division; the operation of the assembly lines was highly dependent on the Kalamazoo production.

The Kalamazoo plant, located in Kalamazoo, Michigan, employed about 3,600 people in early 1979. Of this total, 3,100 were hourly and 500 were salaried employees. The hourly personnel at the plant were unionized [United Auto Workers (UAW)]. The plant operated three shifts on most lines. Six- and seven-day weeks for many of the supervisors and management were commonplace.

The manufacturing supervisors constituted the largest group of salaried employees at Kalamazoo. There were 167 supervisors, 31 general supervisors, and 10 superintendents. Supervisors were employed primarily in four main areas: production, quality control, maintenance (plant engineering), and production control (materials handling). (See Exhibits 25-1 and 25-2.)

Bob Moore had prepared a table (Exhibit 25-3) showing the placement (accessions) of manufacturing supervisors for 1978. Twenty-three of the new supervisors had been attributed to increasing production and line expansion ("volume"). The volume accessions were distributed as follows: Production Control (1), Maintenance (2), Decorating (5), Molding (2), Assembly (5), Regrind and Panel Assembly (2); the remaining supervisors had been temporary hires for the new model changeover and startup ("79 launch").

Approximately 75 percent of the supervisors had been promoted through the ranks from hourly and the remaining 25 percent moved into manufacturing supervision as new hires from several local colleges and from other parts of the plant as part of a development program. Divisional Industrial Relations and Division Management had been pressing Kalamazoo to increase the ratio of college graduates (CG) to those promoted through the hourly ranks (PTR) to 50:50. From Bob Moore's perspective, the rationale for this policy seemed to be:

> that they don't think there are enough people in general supervisory positions with potential to move further into superintendent or production manager slots. There are too many blockers in the general supervisory category . . . I personally feel that, though we might need more college graduates, to go to a 50:50 split is too far. The college grads come in with very high expectations and we just aren't able to offer them movement and development activities, in manufacturing or elsewhere.

At Kalamazoo, the general supervisors had almost always been promoted from the first line supervisory position. Furthermore, the superintendents had almost always been promoted from general supervisor, being "products of the manufacturing system." During 1978 two supervisors had been promoted to general supervisor (one retirement, one death), and no general supervisors had been promoted to superintendent. Bob Moore stated:

> Unless someone is on the fast track, has high potential, and has talent outside manufacturing, they may be best suited to stay in production . . . production people are best there, they just can't compete in other areas; the best opportunities for them are in manufacturing—it uses their skills to the best advantage. . . . however, manufacturing is an excellent area for developing good managers and engineers; a year in there gives them good experience.

The job of manufacturing supervisor at Kalamazoo was considered to be one of extreme difficulty and high pressure. It involved dealing with up to 45 people on a line, absenteeism, tardiness, union officials, grievances, scheduling, checking time sheets, equipment maintenance, obtaining parts, inspecting purchased parts, maintaining quality, keeping down health and safety violations, making performance goals, negotiating work standards, identifying and solving production problems, and disciplining employees, to name a few. Supervisors were caught between the often conflicting demands of management, the union, labor relations, and the workers. Due to increased organizational and technological specialization they were dependent on a series of specialists over whom they had little control, such as maintenance, quality control, industrial engineering, and industrial relations. Every day a printout was sent to the production departments with the previous day's results. On this were the profit (loss) for each supervisor, number of pieces produced, rejects, and number of machine cycles.

The supervisors were evaluated annually with a performance appraisal. As seen by a superintendent, the major criteria for this evaluation (and subsequent salary increases) were "performance" and "how they handle their employees." Performance was measured by the ability to "run black" (high-quality production with standard amount of labor—standards set by Industrial Engineering). The ability to handle people was a more subjective measure, but, in the words of one general supervisor, "It's how they get the job done without lots of grievances and without getting runover." The general supervisors evaluate ("write up") the supervisors under them and the superintendents evaluate the general supervisors.

Bob Moore commented:

> The measures on which supervisors are evaluated in their annual performance appraisal are: budget performance, labor control, housekeeping, absenteeism, and training. It's pretty informal though—the underlying question is how well did they perform.

A management development package, updated twice yearly, was kept on most salaried people, particularly those thought to have "potential." An individual had "potential" at Kalamazoo if he or she was considered to be capable of advancing at least one level of management (general supervisors were in the level above supervisors, middle managers were at the next level). This management development package consisted of a folder with information on an individual's history (including education, Acme experience, and other experience), an evaluation of their potential by the immediate supervisor, specific plans and job assignments for promotions, and specific qualified replacements for their present job. This package was widely used in moving, rotating, promoting, and developing people with potential. In early 1979, a development folder was maintained on very few supervisors or general supervisors.

A Management by Objectives (MBO) system was used for middle and upper plant management. It was fairly well regarded as a development tool at Kalamazoo. Each manager, from superintendent on up, set annual goals and objectives and was evaluated on his or her level of attainment. Although managers did not see the comments which went into the management development package, the content, particularly the evaluation of their potential, was expected to be discussed with them at the MBO appraisal.

One superintendent commented on supervisory promotions:

> Our supervisors are really frustrated—an opening at the general or superintendent level comes up, I make recommendations to the front office (Industrial Relations) on who I want in there—one of my best people—and it always comes back with someone else in the job. IR usually sticks some college grad or developmental in there and my people just don't see any hope of their getting bumped up.

The range of base salary for a new supervisor was $1,465 to $2,008 per month plus $180 a month for a cost-of-living allowance. Afternoon shift carried a 5 percent premium and midnight shift a 10 percent premium. Overtime varied according to the area of the plant but averaged about 4 to 8 hours/week of paid ("compensable") and 4 to 8 hours/week of unpaid ("casual") overtime. Annual merit raises ranged from 0 to 8 percent of base salary. General supervisors' base salary range was $1,640 to $2,500 per month.

In addition to base compensation, new supervisors received special merit raises; a "B" increase at 4 to 6 months of 4 to 6 percent and an "F" increase at 15 to 18 months. These raises were historically based. They were intended to accelerate the supervisors' salary progress since supervisors had traditionally lagged behind their administrative counterparts in increases. The supervisors were pegged, initially, at 15 percent above the average hourly pay. Almost all supervisors, if they stayed in the job, received the "B" and "F" increases.

In recruiting and selecting new supervisors from outside the plant ("walk-ins," local colleges, and referrals), there were four main criteria: (1) desire for a career in manufacturing, (2) appropriate education [equivalent of a Bachelors in Business Administration (B.B.A.)], (3) favorable reactions from interviews with the production manager and two general supervisors, and (4) successful completion of the First Line Supervisory Selection System (FLSSS).

The FLSSS was a company wide, day-long written and oral examination. It included a written portion (½ day) consisting of an in-basket exercise, a production scheduling problem, and an interpersonal skills section. The oral, done by three trained assessors, one for each of the three parts, was designed to probe the decision-making process and judgment of the applicants in regard to the written answers.

Applicants were evaluated on six dimensions. These were with priority weightings, problem solving (1), short-range planning (1), task-structuring (1), interpersonal skills (2), personal work standards (3), and long-range planning (4). The first three, considered the most important, were all given an equal weighting in importance. Two out of five applicants passed the FLSSS.

Hourly people applying for a supervisor's position, also had to take the FLSSS. Their selection process began with a posting of the available positions twice a year. The respondents to this posting, if their employee records were good, were sent to the FLSSS. Those that passed were put into a pool and randomly selected for the available jobs. The system was set up so that anyone applying for a supervisor's job who passed the FLSSS and was placed into the pool of applicants was never passed over more than twice. The third time someone made it to the pool they were selected automatically.

Of the 55 supervisors placed in 1978, Bob Moore estimated that roughly half of them had left voluntarily and half of them "failed" and were asked to step down. Part of the total returned to hourly, part went to other jobs in the plant, and part left the Kalamazoo plant altogether. When asked about the ones that failed, Bob replied:

> They failed because of three main reasons—inability to control the work force, inadequate training, and the self-fulfilling prophesy. In regard to the first, you have to be aggressive to make it on the floor. If the hourlys feel they can get away with something—they'll do it. You have to be able, as a supervisor, to step up to it, set limits, and maintain respect.
>
> Secondly, a lot of our supervisors are put on a line after a few hours training. The general supervisors expect them to just walk in and hit it. They don't have the time to spend three to four months training them. Some supervisors don't know what industrial engineering is, they don't know how to fill out a time sheet, they don't know how to handle a hearing or a grievance, they don't even know their rights from the union contract. Some of the union people, who they have to deal with, have been to school to study their contract rights.
>
> Finally, I think there is a self-fulfilling prophesy operating out there. I think that when general supervisors or superintendents think someone is no good then they end up failing in the end. When they don't think someone has what it takes to make it, then it is hard for them to justify spending limited, precious time training, guiding, assisting, or protecting the new supervisor. Especially when it comes to handling the work force—the general supervisors and superintendents have a tendency to dictate those methods that were successful for them when they were supervisors; they don't want to see the supervisors doing anything different.

In 1978 Bob Moore had instituted a new training program for new supervisors. Under this program, Industrial Relations paid the supervisors' salary and trained them for the first month. This month-long training included rotating through all the main functions in the plant, spending a day with the timekeeper on common time/pay errors, working with the supervisors on their lines, sitting in grievance hearings, and spending a day with Labor Relations on contract, discipline, and hearing procedures. This special program, available only to college graduates, handled two people a month; six supervisors completed the program in 1978. Of those six supervisors, all were still on the job and "getting up to speed." Because of budget cutbacks this program was taken out of the 1979 budget. However, the plant manager was in the process of trying to get it reinstated.

Bob also conducted an exit interview with one of the supervisors who had left voluntarily. The reason he gave for leaving was that he was just not trained for the job. His general supervisor had just said, "do it," and sent him out on the line. In addition, when it came to labor control his general supervisor had imposed his will on how "things were to be done around here." The departing supervisor summed up the exit session by stating that he was effectively left alone, without the required skills and tools, and expected to act toward the hourly employees the way the general supervisor wanted.

In Spring 1978, the Division had taken a salaried opinion survey of all the salaried employees at all locations. This survey confirmed the suspicions of Rich Howards and Bob Moore that there was a "morale problem" among some of the salaried people. In particular, on those questions where the responses of supervisors could be separated from other personnel, there seemed to be dissatisfaction in the area of career development, communication, and supervisory and management practices. Bob Moore said that he thought that a "lack of recognition" was a critical part of that dissatisfaction.

> They are not feeling part of the team, they're alienated; they are the lowest rung on the ladder and no one is paying attention to them—just putting demands on them. Communications is a big key to this. A recent breakfast meeting of all salaried people was very well received, I'm getting good feedback. . . . But you just can't tell a general supervisor to communicate with his people. . . . on top of this they feel that management is selling out to the union, giving the plant away.

This last statement referred to some labor unrest which had been smoldering for the last few months. Although the exact causes of the unrest were vague and complicated to Bob, he said that it seemed to involve several incidents where decisions around the supervisor's authority were reversed in the grievance hearings, a manufacturing superintendent had been threatened, and a particularly troublesome employee reinstated after termination. Most recently, in early February, under the threat of a strike and with the full involvement of Divisional and Corporate Labor Relations people, there had been a settlement around a deluge of industrial safety and health grievances.

In discussions with superintendents and general supervisors about the supervisor's job and the high turnover of supervisors, the following comments were emphatically conveyed:

> Our people are being asked to do more, get more performance, and to be responsible for things that they have no control over (i.e., attendance, parts availability, maintenance, and so forth). The attitude that we get from management if there's a problem is "fix it—make it go away." No matter what happens you're expected to run black or get yelled at. They don't accept any reasons as being realistic or valid . . . they just don't have any authority anymore and yet they still have all the responsibility for production . . . no one responds to them as supervisors, no one reacts . . . you used to be able to pick up a phone and make engineering jump . . . now they do things when they get around to them . . . we just don't get any support anymore from anyone.
>
> The workers out on the line just don't want to work anymore, they just don't give a rip about their job . . . most of the younger workers are happy with three days a week, enough for their car payment and a nickel bag . . . the women are usually the second breadwinner and if one of the kids is sick, if it snows, or something comes up they just take off . . . you always have to keep on your toes or they will stick it to you; it's a jungle out there . . . let's face it, since they all are getting paid the same, if they can come to work and stick it to a supervisor, that's a bonus for the day.
>
> To make it out there you have to know what factory life is about, how the system works, how to beat the local agreement, and how to get revenge . . . you can't be afraid to speak with or confront people . . . you have to be able to deal with people who don't want to work—the 5 percent—you have to be willing to offend someone, to be unpleasant, to be aggressive to get the job done . . . this Maslow stuff and counseling jazz is garbage . . . it takes intestinal fortitude.
>
> And when it comes down to keeping that line going you have to do something—if you come into work and half of your people are absent, if you don't find replacements, matching the right people for the right jobs, get your line started within 15 minutes you have lost it for the day—you're running red . . . management just doesn't understand what we have to deal with.

A labor relations person at the plant offered the following viewpoint on the supervisor turnover problem:

> The younger supervisors are sharp and aggressive but they just aren't given sufficient training—especially in how to deal with the union and how to treat people. It is hard for them to accept that they don't have the power and authority that they used to have . . . let's face it, the union does have power now.

> A lot of labor problems and lost production all focus on the supervisor—the supervisor is the one who interacts with the employee and is responsible for the company-hourly interface. Most of the problems that cross my desk could be prevented if the supervisors knew how to get along with hourly people. They seem incapable of being able to understand the needs and wants of their people, to care about them. The union calls it, "treating us like human beings." Supervisors would be more successful if they could treat their people with respect, courtesy, and recognition and not have such negative attitudes about them.
>
> They also get very frustrated because they think that we [Labor Relations] are down here undermining their authority. They don't understand about compromise and negotiation. They don't see that often I have to give in to the union in one thing if we want to get something else in another part of the plant or in another part of the company. Those are hard things to explain—sometimes you can't explain them. All the supervisors see is one of their disciplines being sent back to the line, laughing at him, waving a check for the lost time in the supervisor's face.
>
> We have to do a better job of communicating with the supervisor, of letting him know, when we make a decision or reverse one, why we did it. Right now they hear it as rumors, second-hand reports, or from the union. We have to do a better job of training our foremen—they often are out there working with little knowledge of the correct way to handle labor situations and they are up against veteran committeemen who have been to long training workshops on the contract, their rights, and their bargaining levers.

Bob Moore knew that he was not faced with a simple problem in trying to solve the supervisory turnover. The ramifications went way beyond the cost of turnover—they infected the morale of half of the salaried work force, productivity, the development of future management, and company-union relations. There seemed to be no simple key to unlock this.

By the end of March he wanted to have recommendations on what could be done about this on the plant manager's desk. He also had to have a specific action plan for implementing them. With this deadline in mind, and the end of February approaching, Bob pondered what could be done.

**EXHIBIT 25-1**
**Organization Chart (abbreviated to highlight manufacturing supervisory positions)**

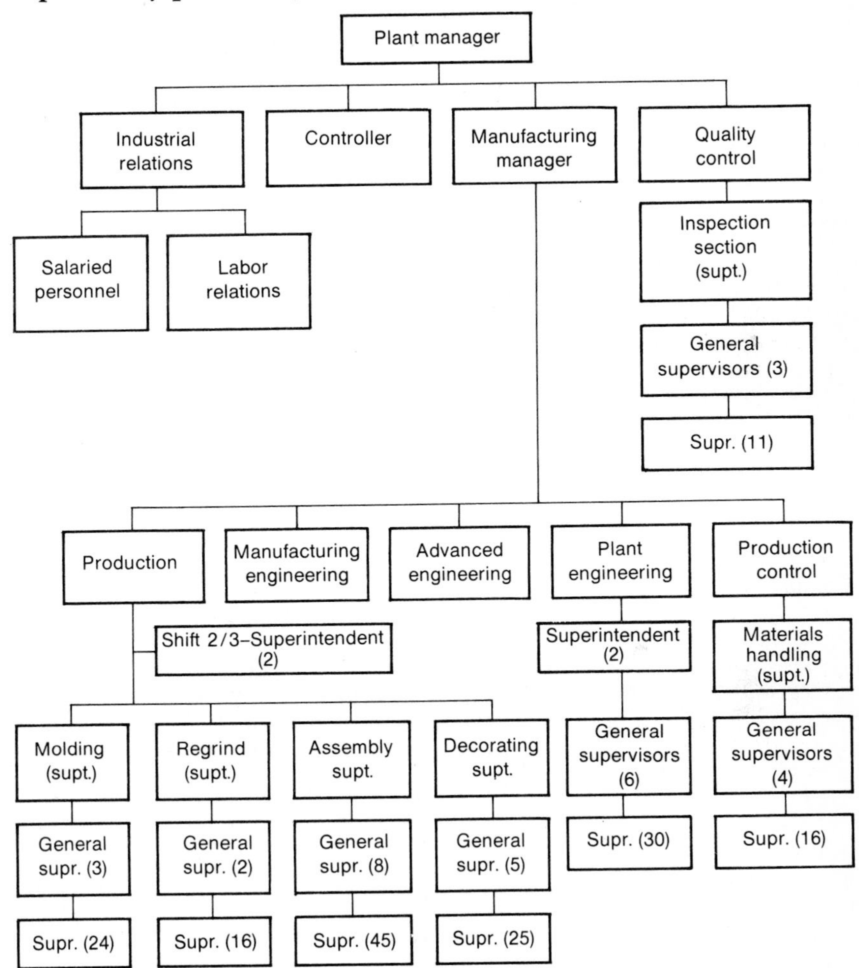

**EXHIBIT 25-2**
**Plant Distribution of Hourly Supervisors**

| PLANT AREA | SUPERVISORS | GENERAL SUPERVISORS | SUPERINTENDENTS |
|---|---|---|---|
| Production | 110 | 18 | 6 |
| Maintenance | 30 | 6 | 2 |
| Quality control | 11 | 3 | 1 |
| Production control | 16 | 4 | 1 |
| Total | 167 | 31 | 10 |

**EXHIBIT 25-3**
**Manufacturing Supervisory Accessions—Kalamazoo, 1978**

| DEPARTMENT | COLLEGE GRADUATES | NONGRADUATES | TOTAL |
|---|---|---|---|
| Production control | 0 | 5 | 5 |
| Quality control | 0 | 2 | 2 |
| Maintenance | 0 | 11 | 11 |
| Production | | | |
| Decorating | 18 | 11 | 29 |
| Molding | 3 | 1 | 4 |
| Assembly | 5 | 10 | 15 |
| Regrind and panels | 5 | 7 | 12 |
| Totals | 31 (39.7%) | 47 (60.3%) | 78 (100%) |

CASE 26

# SEDALIA ENGINE PLANT (A)

*Bert A. Spector*
*Michael Beer*

The transition period for the Sedalia Engine Plant (SEP) would not be easy; of that, SEP's newly appointed plant manager, Danney Goble, was certain. The plant had been manufacturing and assembling diesel engines in Sedalia, Minnesota, since 1974, and SEP's parent company, American Diesel, had allowed the plant to chart an exciting and innovative course. This was a bold venture not only in the redesign of work, but also in the environment in which that work took place—SEP had emphasized a participatory style of management. Since its inception, SEP had been under the firm hand of the original plant manager, Donald St. Clair. Often described by co-workers as charismatic, St. Clair had served as a sort of father figure for the new plant and its employees.

In the fall of 1979, however, St. Clair had been promoted and moved to American Diesel's corporate headquarters in Beacon, Illinois. His successor, Danney Goble, formerly SEP's director of assembly and testing, offered a sharp—and to some, quite disturbing—contrast to St. Clair's managerial style. But the challenges facing SEP went beyond adjustments to a new plant manager. Not only St. Clair, but practically all of SEP's top management team had left, saddling Goble with a massive rebuilding program. That turnover, although a normal step in the career development of those involved, could not have come at a worse time. The declining national economy was forcing SEP to meet its greatest challenges yet. How would these challenges affect the level of commitment that had been from the beginning such a critical feature of life in the plant? Danney Goble could not be sure.

## GUIDING PHILOSOPHY OF SEDALIA ENGINE PLANT

The notion of experimenting with innovative work systems had taken root at American Diesel in the early 1970s. Following a 60-day strike at the Beacon plant in 1972, American Diesel undertook several innovations in its new plants. In 1974 American Diesel decided to move into

Sedalia, Minnesota, and opened the Sedalia Engine Plant. The SEP philosophy, unique within American Diesel, grew out of a series of discussions between Don St. Clair and his operating team. Because of the oil embargo of 1974, American Diesel's business had been reduced sharply. As a result, the company allowed St. Clair and his team considerable slack time in which to work through and carefully develop an operating philosophy.

After visiting a number of innovative plants throughout the country and working with an outside consultant, St. Clair and his operating team selected four words to help identify the type of organization they hoped to create: excellence, trust, growth, and equity (see Exhibit 26–1 for a detailed definition of these goals as provided by the organizing team). Essentially, he hoped to create an organization where the self-interest and creative talents of all employees would be directed to the general well-being of the plant. Allowed a maximum amount of freedom, responsibility, and flexibility, employees would dedicate themselves to a high level of performance. "People want to work hard, perform well, learn new skills, and be involved in the decision-making processes that affect their jobs," said St. Clair in expressing the basic assumptions of his operating team. The work ethic was a powerful force that could be released if the proper atmosphere was created. Thus, the main point of the organizational structure at SEP would be to release that full potential inherent in most workers.

Although American Diesel's main plant at Beacon was unionized, there was to be no union at SEP when it opened. There would be ample protection for the rights of employees, St. Clair's team believed, in an elaborate governance system that would allow all employees to air grievances freely, speak their minds, and seek remedies to perceived inequities. Unions would not be needed to perform such a task, the team hoped. Besides, the operating group felt that at SEP, individuals would represent themselves through their teams and other plant organization. The adversarial relationship which they thought would result from a unionized plant would get in the way of the experimentation in job design. As a result, there would be no union.

The basic unit of organization at SEP would be the team. All employees would be grouped into small teams, and within each team emphasis would be on self-management, learning new skills, and performance. Teams would be trusted to regulate themselves, keep track of their own performance, and encourage growth and the acquisition of new skills on the part of individual members.

Groups of between three and four teams would then be clustered into what were called "businesses." One of the basic assumptions of St. Clair's organizing group was that the maximum number of people any business unit ought to employ should range between 200 and 300 people. That size would allow the business manager to know personally each and every employee. Since it was assumed that SEP would quickly grow to 1,000 employees and eventually to 2,000, the plant was divided into five "businesses," each operating as autonomously as possible under its own business manager. These business managers would oversee and direct the operations of various teams assigned to them.

As a reflection of their belief that, given the goal of creating an open and trusting environment, people would motivate themselves, St. Clair's organizing team replaced the traditional first-line supervisor with a "team adviser." While first-line supervisors usually act as spokesmen for company policy and policemen for the workers assigned to them, SEP's team advisers would work *with,* not above, their teams to facilitate performance and the acquisition of new skills. To fill these positions. St. Clair wanted to find individuals not just technically proficient but also able to work well with people in a nonauthoritarian, nonthreatening manner.

The compensation system at SEP would also reflect the organizing team's belief in growth and responsibility, and a shared commitment to the attainment of plant goals. To reduce the traditional gulf between workers and management, all SEP employees were to be salaried. Machine and assembly workers who traditionally are paid by the hour (as was the case in all other American Diesel plants) would be salaried along with management personnel. Everyone would be expected to work 40 hours a week and to make up any missed time. Furthermore, the compensation system was based not on seniority, but on the acquisition of new skills and the willingness to perform varied tasks. Wages at SEP for machine and assembly workers would be relatively high compared with the prevailing wages of the community—in the seventy-fifth percentile—but, because of the generally depressed condition of the Sedalia area, low in comparison with other American Diesel plants. St. Clair and his team viewed pay not as a motivator, but as a way of achieving equity among plant employees.

Participation at all levels—that was the key. "Participation," St. Clair said, "is a way of doing business effectively through achieving quality decisions or a commitment to carrying them out." St. Clair was adamant on the point that SEP was *not* a social experiment: "We are dealing with ways to develop and utilize the best skills and abilities of our human resources, while at the same time creating a more satisfying work environment."

## INSIDE SEDALIA ENGINE PLANT

SEP's parent company, American Diesel, has been producing, manufacturing, and selling diesel engines, components, and parts since 1919. From corporate headquarters in Beacon, Illinois, American Diesel has constantly held onto a sizable share of the market—usually fluctuating between 40 and 50 percent—despite competition from such corporate giants as John Deere, Caterpillar, and even General Motors. Over the years, American Diesel has built its reputation on high-priced engines of excellent quality and exceptional service follow-up.

The town American Diesel selected in 1974 as the site for its new plant—Sedalia, Minnesota—was home to 55,000 people. The work force was both highly skilled and strongly unionized. SEP set up shop in a 930,000-square-foot plant vacated three years earlier. "Just to give you an idea of how enormous this place is," explained Connie Kelleher, one of SEP's directors, "they tell me you could put nine football fields on the roof. All you have to do is walk back and forth between the front office and the assembly lines once or twice and you'll have no trouble believing that." (See Exhibit 26–2 for a floor design of the plant.)

Once it was operational, the physical layout of SEP reflected its operating philosophy. The south end of the plant was made up of compact, self-contained manufacturing lines for various components of the diesel engine: pistons, piston liners, camshafts, camboxes, flywheels, and so forth. The northern half of the facility housed the elongated assembly lines, added after the plant opened, where between 18 and 22 diesel engines were assembled daily on their way to the small test rooms in the back and, from there, directly to the loading docks.

The 24-foot-high building was open from top to bottom except for a core of offices dividing the plant down the middle. A few of those core offices were built when the plant first opened. Later, in an effort to link staff support personnel more closely to the manufacturing functions, SEP began to enlarge those core offices so that even more of the support people might be placed right in the middle of the plant. When construction was completed on the offices, they stretched from the east end to the west end of the plant, effectively shutting off the ten manufacturing lines from the two assembly lines. Sitting at the front of the plant in a small cluster of offices were the plant manager, his director of organizational development and training, and the finance department.

### *Internal Plant Structure*

There were two separate but overlapping structures set up within SEP: the operating organization and the governance structure.

OPERATING ORGANIZATION. The operating organization was divided into five levels: plant manager, directors, business managers, team advisers, and team members (see Exhibit 26–3). The plant manager, first St. Clair and then Goble, had overall responsibility for the operations at SEP. The seven directors immediately under him served as his operating team and were responsible for manufacturing and/or staff support functions. The combining of these two functions was done in order to create and maintain close ties between support and manufacturing operations, and to develop managerial talent. Thus, three of the directors—purchasing and materials, manufacturing services, and reliability—had both staff support and manufacturing functions under them. The director of purchasing and materials, for instance, had responsibility not only for staff support functions like transportation, shipping, and purchasing, but he also had one of the plant's manufacturing businesses reporting to him. Three directors—finance, personnel, and organizational development and training—had only staff support functions under them; and the director of assembly and test oversaw two manufacturing businesses.

Dropping down another level to business manager, the five managers in the plant reported on a direct line to their assigned director, and they served as heads of the five, semiautonomous businesses in the plant. The assembly-related businesses were named engine business and operations business; the other three were merely assigned letters: *A, B,* and *C* (see Exhibit 26–3). The business manager for operations had responsibility for seven assembly teams as well as a manufacturing support group made up of engineering services, specialized skills trainers, materials, finance, training, and order administration. In fact, every business within SEP had a number of staff support functions as well as a group of manufacturing teams (see Exhibit 26–4).

In point of fact, during St. Clair's tenure as plant manager, the business managers became an important part of the plant's leadership. Tom O'Donnell, business manager, said: "We were a real tight-knit group when Don was here. The business managers spent a lot of time together and a lot of time with Don. I know the organization charts didn't show it, but we really reported on a direct line to St. Clair." St. Clair relied heavily on his business managers for the day-to-day plant operations, while he and two or three of his directors—Danney Goble among them—provided the overall leadership. That close relationship between St. Clair and his business managers tended to blur the precise functions of the director level.

Next, there were team advisers—SEP's first-line supervisors—and, finally, team members. (Their functions will be defined below in the section on teams.)

Governance Structure. St. Clair was convinced that the operating organization of SEP would not be enough to insure a high level of commitment and participation. In addition, he felt the need for some sort of safety-valve mechanism that would allow people to air grievances and work-related problems. There needed to be another structure that would allow people from all five levels to interact, and to work to resolve plantwide issues affecting the work environment. There needed to be some formal forum for workers to air grievances as well as participate in the shaping of management decisions. For that reason, his original team developed a complex and multilevel governance structure to parallel the operating organization.

Atop the entire governance structure sat the plant operating team (POT). Made up of the plant manager and his directors, POT was charged with giving a general sense of direction to the plant. It worked with American Diesel on plant objectives and commitments, and it was responsible for specific strategy, policy decisions, and other matters of plantwide concern.

The second major governance organization was the board of representatives (BOR), made up of 20 elected representatives from all the plant's business and functional areas. BOR acted as a forum or sounding board for SEP employees. New ideas, unique viewpoints, and lingering complaints were aired at regular BOR meetings. Employees used BOR to debate matters ranging from concerns over the compensation system and layoffs to complaints of petty thefts within the plant. BOR could then take suggestions, comments, or complaints to POT to seek some kind of resolution.

St. Clair had hoped that the atmosphere at BOR meetings would be such that all employees would feel free to speak their minds. But when Danney Goble became plant manager, he was somewhat surprised to find a considerable amount of dissatisfaction with the way BOR operated. Staff support personnel in BOR complained that manufacturing representatives often clogged BOR meetings with complaints about petty problems like overflowing toilets and disciplinary matters. Manufacturing team representatives responded by insisting that they had nowhere else to go with such problems. BOR was the only structure in SEP that offered them the opportunity to get together and jointly air their grievances and concerns. Besides, they countered, most BOR discussions were monopolized by staff support people.

Numerous other groups and task forces within the plant focused on specific issues. One informal safety valve mechanism begun by St. Clair and continued by Gobel was the "fireside chat." Once or twice a week, the plant manager invited into his office a small group of employees representing a cross-section of the plant. St. Clair started the chats in order to keep "tuned in" to the plant. By speaking confidentially and keeping those confidences, he also hoped to create a feeling of trust that would allow any plant employee to come to him with their problems and concerns.

### *Plant Leadership*

For five years, the personality of plant manager Don St. Clair galvanized SEP. The plant had been from its founding an intimate and important part of St. Clair's life, and he in turn provided a model of enthusiasm and complete commitment to SEP employees. "He was a father figure to us," explained one of the original business managers. "Whatever 'charisma' means, Don had it," added an adviser.

Everyone, from director to team members, leaned heavily on St. Clair during those startup years, relying on the power of his personality and the force of his commitment to steer SEP through the hurdles of its early development. "This place looked and smelled like Don St. Clair," noted director Doug Pippy. "The whole thing was an extension of his personality."

St. Clair saw himself as a plantwide "agitator." Every day, he spent some time on the lines: talking to people, questioning them, encouraging, prodding them to take responsibility and to live up to the expectations of the plant. "He was one hell of a guy," said a team member who had been with the plant from the beginning. "And we worked harder for him."

St. Clair's managerial style was wide open; Danney Goble observed of his predecessor:

> He was the kind of guy who liked to have his hand in everything. He liked to know everything that was going on. Because everybody in the plant—directors, managers, team members—trusted him, they would come to him with their problems. Anything they couldn't work out on the floor, they brought it right to Don. And he was glad to talk to them and work with them. His door was always open.

### *SEP's Teams*

Manufacturing and staff support personnel at SEP were all organized into small teams, each with its own team adviser. Teams were usually made up of 20 people, although they occasionally grew to 50 people or 80 people over three shifts. If a particular line or machine operated over three shifts, workers on all three shifts would belong to the same team with only one team adviser. At least once a month, team meetings would have to be arranged so that members from all three shifts could gather at the same time. Since all decisions at SEP were meant to be made at the lowest possible level, each team was designed to be as functionally autonomous as possible.

Manufacturing Teams. Each of the 40 manufacturing teams was clustered around a business manager, reporting to that manager through its own team adviser. Team members undertook the usual task of operating on assigned machines or assembly tasks. At SEP, however, a premium was placed on the ability of each team member to perform not just one but a variety of tasks. Thus, each team was expected to handle setup and maintenance as well as operation of the machines or assembly tasks assigned to it. Furthermore, each individual team member was expected, over the course of five years, to learn how to perform these functions on each of the machines. The members of a piston line team, for instance, should eventually be able to perform not just one but each job and support function assigned to the team as a whole. (See Exhibit 26–5 for a description of team responsibilities.) One of the signs of team maturity was the degree to which the team members did, in fact, encourage each other to learn and perform new tasks.

Out of necessity, the assembly teams operated somewhat differently than the machining teams. Teams like the piston team were involved in the manufacturing of a whole product. Each of the seven assembly line teams, however, was assigned just one stage in the assembly of a diesel engine. They completed that stage and then passed the engine along a conveyor to the next team. The line was constructed in such a way that each team could build up a surplus of from eight to ten engines. The plant manager, together with the director of assembly and the business managers from assembly and testing and shipping, set monthly rates of completion based on corporate demand. The entire assembly line was expected to schedule and pace their work in order to meet that monthly goal. Another less formal motivator existed for assembly teams. If one team worked so much more slowly than the next that the faster team depleted its surplus, that second, quicker team would find itself with nothing to do. "If that happens," explained Dave Palmer, director of organizational development and training, "members from the faster team will walk over to the other group and not so politely ask, 'What the hell are you guys doing?' "

The functions of SEP's manufacturing teams went far beyond the operation and maintenance of machines, however. Each team was also expected to do its own administrative housekeeping. Team members kept track of their own team's inventory; ordered and inspected necessary materials; documented their team's production, costs, attendance, and performance; oversaw safety practices; and participated in budgeting and forecasting. In addition, each team was responsible for hiring its own members. Teams were to work with their adviser in setting their own performance appraisal, disciplinary actions, and even determining raises to a higher salary level.

These administrative, housekeeping, and personnel functions were known in SEP as vertical tasks. One or more members of each team was expected to devote some working time to a vertical task such as material ordering, budgeting, inventory control, or keeping cost records. Who does what vertical task? What percentage of the work day should be spent on a vertical task? These were decisions that each team was to make for itself. Such assignments usually lasted a year before being rotated to another team member.

The degree to which individual teams performed up to the ideal established by St. Clair's organizing team varied considerably. Mature teams encouraged individual members to learn new tasks and participate fully in devising ways to reduce costs, evaluating performance of individual members, and helping to correct the behavior of individuals that might be harmful to the team. The most mature teams—about one-quarter of the teams, Dave Palmer estimated in 1979—were virtually self-managing and autonomous. The less mature teams depended almost entirely on the intervention of the team adviser to handle matters relating to training, housekeeping, and evaluation.

Perhaps the most dramatic example of a team handling its own affairs occurred in the cambox team in 1979. Cambox production had begun three years earlier and grown rapidly to 1,500 camboxes a day. The size of the team grew with the production rate: over 80 people spread over three shifts with only one adviser. While the adviser felt his team was operating well, many team members thought otherwise. Said team member Sally Moore: "Everything was chaos. There was absolutely no communication between shifts. You would leave a message for the next shift, telling them what needed to be done. They either didn't get the message, or would ignore it. Nobody really gave a damn."

Signs of poor performance seemed to spread. Low morale led to low energy, high turnovers, and constant overtime. Quality suffered, and there was no way of knowing who or what was at fault. "There were so many people and so little communication," said Moore, "that there was no accountability." Finally, in one month American Diesel had to recall 35,000 camboxes, all made at SEP.

Even then, the team adviser refused to admit that he had a problem. But three months after the recall, Moore and fellow team member Dick Smith decided to take some action. With 80 people crowded into a meeting room for the regular team meeting, and with the adviser not present, the two stood up and expressed their feelings. In the middle of the meeting, Smith phoned St. Clair and asked him to join them. St. Clair did, and he encouraged the team to develop, on their own, some plan for reorganization. Moore and Smith then called for an informal committee to consider the possibilities. Two representatives from each shift met every night after work, sometimes for five hours at a sitting, for five weeks.

Their first conclusion was that the team was too big and should be divided into four smaller teams. Recalled Dick Smith: "Not everyone favored dividing us up like that. They said you'd lose product identification that way. But the committee decided that the number of people on a team is more important than product identity. It's not looking at a cambox and saying 'I made that' that gives me satisfaction. It's team work and cooperation that makes this place special."

In dividing up the tasks among the four teams—casting and drilling (kingsbury), assembly, variable machine timing, and inventory control—the committee made sure that each team still retained some variety of tasks. And to insure better communication between shifts, a coordinator was appointed for the second and third shifts of each team.

The impact of the cambox reorganization was both immediate and dramatic. Averaging 920 camboxes per day for the year prior to reorganization, the reorganized cambox line upped its daily average to between 1,100 and 1,200 camboxes per day. Overtime dropped by 50 percent, scrap was reduced from 17 to 5 percent, turnover from 30 to 4 percent, while machine utilization increased from 42 to 56 percent (a measurement of the total time available over three shifts a machine is in use). Subjective assessments—team morale, communications, and problem solving—were all positive as well. "It seems that whenever we have a chaotic situation, and a team is able to deal with that chaos, then productivity rises," said St. Clair. "I'm not sure why that is, but it always happens."

While nobody at SEP could say for sure what made one team mature and another not, there seemed to be general agreement on the importance of three factors: the size of the team, the length of time the team had been together, and the willingness of the adviser to encourage team growth.

STAFF SUPPORT TEAMS. Like the manufacturing people, staff support personnel in the plant also worked as part of a team. Each team had its own adviser. Staff support teams provided specific services—quality and product engineering; financial analysis; materials planning, purchasing, and handling; performance and/or training of maintenance duties; engineering, procurement, and installation of machine tools—in support of the manufacturing teams. If a manufacturing team member assigned to the vertical task of forecasting and budgeting, for instance, felt the need for expert consultation, he or she could call directly (or indirectly, through the team adviser) on staff support personnel in order to seek their advice.

ORIENTATION. St. Clair felt that in order to acclimate new employees to the drastically different work environment of SEP, all new employees should go through an intensive orientation program. Therefore, once hired, each new team member went through an orientation program consisting of 13 sessions to be attended during the initial six months of employment. They discussed plant history, philosophy, goals, and practices. St. Clair candidly admitted, "As hard as we tried to keep these orientations realistic, we really ended up building unrealistic expectations of the amount of freedom they were going to find, of the excitement and the challenge of working here. When they went back out onto the floor, we hoped they'd turn whatever disappointment they might have felt into a determination to work twice as hard to change their expectations into reality."

The reaction of newly hired SEP personnel to the orientation program was decidedly mixed. Some complained about precisely what St. Clair talked about—building unrealistic expectations. Team member Dick Kirkendall said: "We would be told all about teams, about how independent they are. But then I went to work and found out there were a lot of decisions we just weren't allowed to make as a team." Others found the courses to be over their heads. Said team member Bob Reed: "They kept talking about 'work systems.' I know what that means now. But when I first got here, I was fresh off the streets. I had just barely finished high school, you know? They'd say 'work systems,' and I didn't know what the hell they were talking about."

### *How Did Teams Work?*

Most of the workers at SEP came there after some experience in traditional, often unionized, plants. The idea of maximum flexibility, of responsibilities ranging far beyond the operation of a single machine, and of a commitment to learning new skills often struck them as rather alien when they first arrived at SEP. "I used to work in a plant," said Mike Cassity, whose experience was typical of most SEP workers. "There, I had a job to do and I did the same thing every day." Still, the vast majority of the team members responded enthusiastically to the challenge of increased expectations.

> **Frank McCarthy,** team member: Honest to God, I'm excited to get here every morning. I always hated work, but not now. I like living in Sedalia and raising my family here. But there weren't many good jobs around, and I thought I'd have to move. Then this came along. I'm as happy as can be about it.

> **Ed Purcell,** team member: Before I came here, I was a clothing salesman. I made good money, but I was bored crazy. When I came here I took almost a ten-thousand dollar cut in pay! Can you believe that? And I've never regretted that decision for a minute.

> **Dave Thelen,** team member: This is the best place I've ever worked, no doubt about it. A lot of guys around here say they'd like to move up eventually, maybe become an adviser. But not me. As long as I can make enough money on this assembly line, this is where I'd like to stay.

One of the team problems that attracted Danney Goble's immediate attention had to do with discipline. St. Clair had created a mechanism, called the corrective action process, for correcting ''unacceptable'' behavior—substandard performance, abuse of paid time off and property, disrespect for others. This involved informal counseling with the team's adviser, but some business managers complained that the process was not working. They identified absenteeism as a key concern and heard reports of other disciplinary problems. Some team members on third shifts were sleeping on the job, and there were occasional outbreaks of fighting. In one case, the piston team decided to fire an unruly member—a dismissal upheld by the adviser, business manager, and director. The discharged team member, however, appealed directly to St. Clair who ordered him reinstated. (He lasted another month before being fired again, this time with no appeal.)

''One of the problems,'' said director Connie Kelleher, ''was that we just didn't have any common definitions. What *is* excessive absenteeism? What *is* disrespect for others? Nobody could say for sure, and many teams were asking for better definitions.''

STRESS: A SIDE EFFECT OF HIGH COMMITMENT. ''I'm going to tell you something about this place you probably won't want to hear,'' said a team member. ''There's a lot of stress here, a hell of a lot of stress.''

By pushing down levels of responsibility and increasing expectations of commitment on the part of team members, SEP had introduced a new element into the lives of many line workers. Most team members had previously worked in traditional factory settings. Once they came to SEP, they were told to help set production and cost goals, maintain machines as well as run them, learn budgeting, and make up missed time on weekends. That high level of commitment had its rewards—enriched, interesting work—but also its cost—personal stress. There were no facts or figures on the level of stress among SEP's team members, or the impact that stress had on their families. But most SEP team members recognized the problem after a few years of working there, and they spoke candidly about it.

> **Mike Cassity,** team member: My old job was pretty dull, but at least I knew what I was supposed to do and did it, day in and day out. When I got interviewed for my job here, they told me all the things I would be expected to do: keep books, order materials, go to meetings, things like that. They asked me whether I could do that kind of work, whether I'd enjoy it? I said sure! I wanted the job, right? But when I got here and found out they really meant it. . . . My God!

**Ed Purcell,** team member: Sometimes, to make sure we get everything done, our team will decide to work some extra hours or come in on the weekend. But my wife just can't understand why we do that. She gets really angry.

**Henry Wallace,** team member: We're always being taught and encouraged to talk things out and share our feelings. That was all new to me at first, but eventually it became part of the way I did things. But then I'd go home and want to talk to my wife about things that were happening at the plant. I never did that at my other job. I'd just come home and forget about work. But there's something about this place that makes you want to share everything. And my wife would just look at me like I was nuts.

**Harry Holmes,** team member: We all work so hard together and spend so much time together that we become sort of a family. Maybe that's why there are so many romances and divorces here. People on my team call this "little Peyton Place." I know. That's what happened to me. I got divorced last month.

TEAM ADVISERS. SEP's first-line supervisors, the team advisers, were given responsibility for the training of individual team members and the development of a mature, well-functioning, self-managing team. The SEP adviser was to act as a team builder, communicator, trainer, and occasional fill-in; but not as an autocratic overseer and decision maker. The plant sought advisers with a firm grounding in technical know-how, combined with interpersonal skills.

The team advisers sat in on the daily meetings of their teams, usually held in the first half-hour of the work day, but their function there was to lead discussions rather than issue commands. They held personnel files for their teams, arranged for technical and professional advice from staff support personnel within the plant, and coordinated training for their teams.

When Goble became plant manager, he worried that several of his team advisers did not seem to be effective. The position had always been a difficult one to fill and maintain. While the original advisers came almost exclusively from supervisory positions in traditionally organized plants, their replacements came, for the most part, from within the plant. St. Clair felt tremendous pressure from team members to provide a place within the organization for them to rise to, and that place was the adviser position. But the practice of promotion from within was not entirely satisfactory. Between 25 and 50 percent of all advisers who had been promoted from team members quit their positions within a year or two to return to their team. Why did this happen?

**Bob Kerr,** team adviser: What I'm finding is that the more mature my team gets, the duller my job is. I used to help out on all the machines and teach people how to use them. Now, my team doesn't need my help, and they do their own training. So I spend most of my time settling arguments and talking to people about why they missed a day or two of work. That gets old, fast.

**Jim Gilbert,** team adviser: When I think of all the extra hours I put in, coming around on second and third shift, attending meetings—I often get here at 5:30 in the morning and leave at 5:30 at night—I figure that I'm getting paid less on an hourly basis than when I was a team member.

Goble worried that while team advisers from the inside seemed to be somewhat dissatisfied, he was not getting new people to come in from the outside to fill new openings. Since advisers rarely rose to higher rank at SEP, it seemed like a dead-end job. And the old problem of finding someone with both technical and people skills made it difficult to select the right person. One of the constant complaints Goble heard from team members had to do with the competing pressures placed on the team member by the demands of their adviser for maximum effort on the machine or assembly lines versus the expectation that all team members would participate in vertical tasks. Time spent by a team member budgeting and forecasting, ordering materials, or attending BOR meetings was time away from the line. Some advisers understood, even encouraged, this as a necessary and significant part of the work day; others did not.

**Mike Cassity,** team member: Most advisers here put too much pressure on you. You go off to do a vertical task, and the adviser says to you, "Why the hell are you gone so often?" And then, when you're being evaluated, they say, "Why the hell haven't you done this or that vertical task?"

The pressure from some advisers for members to stay on the line was so great that a few members openly questioned whether the plant was really committed to its professed ideals. "I'll tell you this," said one disillusioned team member, "around here, production is number one. Quality of work life? That's two, three, or even four."

PERFORMANCE MEASUREMENT. The most significant continuing measurement of team performance came from cost-per-piece figures. St. Clair and his organizing team rejected a cost system based on standard costs established by industrial engineers. Instead, SEP had established a cost system based on improvements from previous performance. There would be a base cost for each piece that would be the real cost from the previous year. Each team in the plant would report monthly on its own cost-per-piece, and the figure would be measured against the base cost as well as the previous month's performance. Each manufacturing team would be responsible for computing its own cost-per-piece and for working to reduce that cost.

The monthly reports compiled by each manufacturing team were simple, yet complete. Costs were given for variable manufacturing expenses (broken down to such items as rework, maintenance, scrap, operating supplies, tools, and freight), semivariable expenses (salary, gas, travel, taxes, insurance), and total team costs. (See Exhibit 26-6 for a two-month cost-per-piece report of one SEP team.) Those figures were then compared to the previously supplied base costs. At the same time, the plant manager and his directors set plantwide goals for cost reductions on specific line items (direct materials, team expenses, and so forth). In 1980 the primary goal was to reduce costs by the rate of inflation.

Dave Palmer explained the reasoning behind the continuing stress on this type of measurement: "The cost-per-piece computation is important because it gives each team a feeling of autonomy, a belief that they are key to our productivity." The cost-per-piece figures allowed St. Clair to assess the performance of teams at SEP in terms both of actual costs and cost reductions, and allowed teams access to the information necessary to make good economic decisions.

### *The Compensation System at SEP*

The main distinction made in the plant was not the usual one between hourly and salaried employees, but the legal one between those who must be paid extra for overtime work—nonexempt—and those who are not paid for working more than 40 hours—exempt. (For overtime work—more than 40 hours—SEP's nonexempt workers were paid on an hourly basis.) Team members constituted the nonexempt employees, while advisers, business managers, directors, and the plant manager made up the exempt group.

In keeping with this attempt to minimize distinctions among workers, many of the status symbols typically associated with a plant hierarchy were nowhere in sight at SEP. Dress codes for exempt employees along with special parking spaces and dining facilities were never introduced. St. Clair was convinced that the removal of such artificial distinctions enhanced communications within the plant. At least some team members, however, found this attempt to downplay the gulf between management and workers to be somewhat superficial. "It's as simple as this," commented one team member. "When we have plant athletic teams, they [managers] sign up for the golf team, and we sign up for the bowling team."

EXEMPT COMPENSATION SYSTEM. Initially, SEP placed all exempt employees into three broad pay categories (as opposed to the 13 narrowly defined categories in place at American Diesel's Beacon plant).

This, it was thought, would allow people to progress through a series of pay increases without quickly coming to the top rate for their category. "We hoped this would encourage stability and development," explained Dave Palmer. "People could get their raises without seeking other jobs and moving to different plants."

"That just didn't work," admitted Palmer. "People here were getting the same money as other executives within American Diesel, but they wanted the promotions as well. They complained that their careers were moving more slowly here than they would elsewhere in the American Diesel system." Just before St. Clair left in 1979, SEP moved to seven-level exempt compensation system. Team advisers would be placed on one of the first three levels depending on a combination of education and job experience. Their annual salaries would range from $15,120 to $30,420. Staff support managers were assigned to level four ($21,840 to $34,920); business managers to level five ($26,220 to $41,940); plant directors to level six ($32,280 to $51,600), and the plant manager to level seven ($40,680 to $65,040). A progression matrix was then constructed by POT, clarifying the combination of skills, experience, and performance that would allow individuals to progress from the minimum through the midpoint to the maximum of their salary levels.

NONEXEMPT COMPENSATION SYSTEM. The compensation of nonexempt employees was supposed to be based entirely on the acquisition of skills by individual team members, and the willingness of the individual to perform those skills. "It's a mistake to base pay solely on the acquisition of new skills," explained Palmer. "People will learn something just to get more money, but then never put what they learned to use." There were five skill levels that each team member was expected to reach, one year at a time (there was also a six-month increment for the first year only, contingent on attending the 13 orientation sessions). All nonexempts worked out a yearly performance plan with their adviser, stating in writing what skills they should acquire and tasks they should perform during the year. At the end of each of the first five years, team members would be evaluated—by the team adviser, except in the case of an extremely mature team, in which case the entire team would participate—on how well they had met those expectations. Promotion to a higher level depended on meeting these expectations for performance and growth.

On some teams, members were reluctant to oppose openly the awarding of an increment to a fellow member. "Nobody wants to stand up at a meeting and say so-and-so shouldn't get a raise this year," said one team member. "If you do that, what's going to happen to you when it's time for your raise to be considered?" On those teams, the yearly increments designed to recognize the acquisition of skills became strictly seniority advances. Some team members, advisers, even business managers, insisted that they knew of no instances when a team member was denied a yearly raise. St. Clair acknowledged that while there were several instances when team members were denied a raise, compensation had indeed become a seniority-based system.

Another shortcoming of the five-level plan was the question of what happened after the fifth year. By the time Goble became plant manager, there were a number of five-year employees who wondered about that point. They could still receive general raises along with Beacon; however, they could not receive increments based on the acquisition of new skills.

Each of the five levels was given a flat rate. At first, POT pegged that rate almost entirely to the prevailing wages in the Sedalia area. SEP's wages were competitive in comparison with similar workers in the community, but because it was a depressed area, they tended to be rather low when compared to American Diesel's Beacon employees. In order to achieve greater equity within the corporation, POT sought to upgrade nonexempt wages in 1977. (See Exhibit 26–7 for nonexempt wage scale, prior to and immediately following this upgrading.) According to plant policy, POT reviewed the entire compensation system twice a year. In the summer of 1977 POT decided to tie Sedalia's wages to the union-negotiated wage agreements in Beacon.

A four-year employee at Sedalia was to be given a salary derived loosely from the average hourly rate for all four-year employees at Beacon. Five-year Sedalia employees, in recognition of their broader skills and responsibilities, would receive more than the average five-year Beacon employee. And because of that tie-in, any negotiated increase in the hourly wages at Beacon would result in an increase at Sedalia. Thus, SEP employees received raises in two ways: an annual advance in salary level for their first five years and a negotiated increase in the Beacon contract. Between 1977 and 1979 those increases often reached 5 percent and 6 percent every six months. That shift moved SEP into the ninetieth percentile of wages in the Sedalia community.

St. Clair hastened to add that the tie-in to the Beacon wage was not absolute. He and POT members felt no hesitation about adjusting wage rates up or down. "Compensation is one of those areas that I don't think should be too participatory," said St. Clair. "I tried to keep people informed about what we were doing, but me and my directors made final decisions ourselves. Seeking too much participation on compensation issues can get you in a lot of trouble."

One special category among SEP's nonexempt personnel was created for skilled tradespeople like electricians, machine repairmen, or draftsmen, who were hired to train team members in their skills. Because SEP was having a problem attracting skilled tradespeople, POT created a special wage scale for them in 1976. They were placed on a wage scale considerably higher than the scale used for other nonexempts. POT also tied Sedalia's 90 tradespeople to the hourly wages for the skilled trades at Beacon. Thus, in 1977, the skilled trades entered at $246 a week and topped at $290. From the beginning, the distinction caused resentment within the plant.

### *Concept and Reality at SEP*

A minor but revealing example of tension between concept and reality occurred over the question of precisely how to translate into the question of plant life one of the plant's key philosophical commitments—that of trusting all employees. Team adviser Ed Fremder explained the flap that occurred in the plant over the question of locks:

> We say we trust people around here to act like adults. Because of that, we give people access to whatever tools they need to do their jobs. Somehow, that got translated to mean no locks anywhere in the plant. Doors, equipment, files, everything was kept open. If Don saw a lock anywhere in the plant on *anything,* he'd rip it off. But that's not the real world, is it? People do steal things out there and in here.
>
> Now, at one point, the plant bought three-wheeled bicycles, one for each team, to be used by their members in getting around. Right away, those bikes started disappearing. One team would "borrow" a bike from another without asking, and then "forget" to return it. Teams started hiding their bikes so that others couldn't find them. It got a little ridiculous. Oh, we spent hours debating that one! Meetings all the time. You should have seen it. And we never really decided anything. The bikes just drifted away, and we never bothered replacing them.

That tension between the concept and the realities, and the danger of allowing one to blur the other, had always been a matter of concern at SEP.

### *Performance at Sedalia Engine Plant*

"It may be too early to tell, but there are encouraging signs that our style of management is starting to pay off." That evaluation was offered in the Fall of 1979 by Don St. Clair as he prepared to move on to corporate headquarters in Beacon and pass on managership of SEP to Danney Goble. St. Clair's hopeful appraisal of the plant's performance included the following specific points:

1. Absenteeism, including both excused and nonexcused, was down to about 3 percent, as opposed to about 6 percent at

American Diesel's Beacon plant, and 8 percent in the Sedalia community.

2. SEP's safety record, while poor at first, was improving steadily.
3. Initial warranty data on SEP's engines were extremely favorable.
4. Plantwide machine utilization usually ran between 60 percent and 70 percent and sometimes as high as 75 percent, compared with 50 percent at Beacon.
5. While technological differences existed between the two plants, indirect labor costs were significantly less at Sedalia than the Beacon plant. As the plant reached maturity, that savings could reach 20 percent. Because of the advanced skills of some team members, the need for skilled tradespeople at Sedalia was considerably less than for Beacon. Sedalia also operated with one-half the first-line supervisors at Beacon.
6. Team members were continually performing major machine overhauls and minor maintenance.
7. Except for some startup problems, quality seemed to be running high at Sedalia. For example, the number of engines rejected by testing at Sedalia was 25 percent of the Beacon number.
8. The general climate was positive and focused on plant excellence.
9. The work system and the governance system seemed to be working to the satisfaction of SEP employees. Job satisfaction seemed to be higher than at other American Diesel plants. To support that conclusion, St. Clair pointed to the fact that no serious union drive had been launched at SEP.
10. SEP enjoyed support from American Diesel's CEO, although there was still some skepticism and lack of understanding about SEP from some key people in upper management.

"By far," St. Clair concluded, "this has been the best plant startup American Diesel has ever had."

### *Danney Goble Takes Over*

"He really walked into a mess," said one of the business managers about Danney Goble's first months as plant manager. "You have to feel bad for the guy." Goble himself spoke of the challenge not just to him but to the plant. "We now face our most serious test ever of our strength and moral fiber," he observed.

LEADERSHIP TURNOVER. The contrasts in the personalities and styles of the old and new plant managers were dramatic and obvious to everyone in the plant.

> **Tom O'Donnell,** business manager: I would characterize the difference this way. Don was people-oriented, while Danney is process-oriented. He seems to have less tolerance for ambiguity and more need for structure. Don looked at results, like most manufacturing people. Danney's background is engineering, and he seems more concerned with details than Don was. Don was a visionary; Danney is a tactical leader.

Some worried that Goble could not lead the plant in the same way St. Clair had been able to—among them, Doug Pippy, director, who said: "Danney seems to have problems relating to other people. Like the other new management people he brought in with him, like me in fact, he's a little uncomfortable with other people."

Complicating matters even further was the fact that SEP was undergoing a large turnover among its top management team. Directors, business managers, even some advisers were leaving SEP in large numbers. Out of its top 24 slots, SEP lost 15 people. Only 3 of those left American Diesel; the other 12 went to plants within the American Diesel system. "I can understand that," said Dave Palmer. "People left here because they wanted to get more attention from corporate headquarters. So they went to Beacon, or some of the new plants that American Diesel was opening." Moreover, it was customary for managers to move every several years. Also, American Diesel actively sought experienced SEP managers to help them start up new plants.

"The extent of the turnover and the short time in which it happened was completely unanticipated," said Goble. "I feel like I have to reinvent the wheel all over again, to teach these people from scratch what our operating philosophy is all about. This certainly won't make things any easier."

ECONOMIC DOWNTURN. "Our company business analysts still are projecting a major downturn 'soon.' Our company president stated two weeks ago we can expect it to be the second worst decline in the last 25 years for American Diesel (second only to 1974-1975). All our planning is based on this assumption." (See Exhibit 26-8 for summary of American Diesel's economic picture.) That was Goble's gloomy assessment of economic conditions, communicated to SEP employees just after he became plant manager. Already, the indicators were unmistakable. In the six months prior to Goble's becoming plant manager, engine orders had declined 18 percent and projections indicated only a worsening of conditions.

"What we're faced with," said Goble, "is the possibility of our first layoffs at SEP. The whole corporation is suffering, and we're going to have to shoulder our fair share of that suffering. I'm almost certain that there are layoffs coming, and that those layoffs will be sizable."

In considering the possibility of layoffs, Goble felt that he had an option of two broad policies. SEP could join other American Diesel plants in laying off workers. Although estimates of the extent of that reduction varied from week to week, Goble figured he would have to reduce SEP's work force by about 4 percent, or 20 people. On the other hand, he could commit SEP to attempt at least to maintain current levels of employment. What layoffs would do to the high level of commitment that employees had built up over the years, he could not be sure. What layoffs would do to the fragile team member-management relationship of trust, already severely tested by the turnovers, he was even less sure.

That second course—protecting all jobs—would still require sacrifice on the part of the plant, and a good deal of creativity in deciding how to absorb losses without cutting employment. Goble continued:

> If I go that route, I'm going to ask for even more commitment on the part of our employees. They're going to have to devote their energies to thinking of ways to cut costs. We might ask, for instance, that some people take temporary, voluntary layoffs. Perhaps we could all go on shorter work weeks. We might have to move people around from one team to another, maybe ask them to do work that we've previously contracted out for. We're getting ready to paint the plant, for instance. I wonder if we could get some of our teams to do that rather than hiring outside painters. But what will that do to our team structure?
>
> Another question I've got to decide, and decide right away, is how much to tell people in the plant? Right now, all of this is speculation. I don't know for sure that we're going to have layoffs. Should I tell people now that it's a distinct possibility? I might be getting them upset over nothing. And with all the concern now with me and the other new people, that kind of bad news might be too unsettling. On the other hand, I'd like to get people involved in thinking about the alternatives. How do I do that unless I tell them everything?

NONEXEMPT COMPENSATION. "Danney keeps telling us that we're being paid fairly compared to the people at Beacon," said team member Bob Reed in the fall of 1979. "Now, I'm getting paid well, but not for the kind of work that I do. I do a hell of a lot more than the people at Beacon. Do they have the vertical tasks that we do? No! Most of the guys here don't even look at Beacon for a comparison. Instead, we look at the autoworkers over in Calhoun. They're getting nine and ten dollars an hour, while we get seven or eight.''

With the enriched work and higher expectations of commitment, perhaps it was inevitable that nonexempt workers would begin to reconsider their compensation system. But the economic downturn brought the issue to a head just as Goble became plant manager.

Starting in 1977 nonexempt pay levels at SEP had been pegged loosely to the average wage of all four-year employees at Beacon. The economic downturn of 1979 had a dramatic impact on salaries, both at Beacon and Sedalia. Any large-scale layoff at Beacon could hurt Sedalia wages. If employees at Beacon were laid off in large numbers, quite a few employees there would find themselves bumped down to lower paying assignments; that would significantly reduce the average four-year wage at Beacon. If Goble and POT elected to adhere tightly to that average, it would negatively affect wages at Sedalia. Compounding the problem was the fact that the wages of the skilled trades at Beacon would not be affected by the downturn. Skilled tradespeople at Sedalia were tied independently to those at Beacon, which meant that they were still in line for significant raises.

Goble had an immediate question to consider in the fall of 1979. If he followed the formula of basing four-year Sedalia wages on the precise average of Beacon without making any adjustments, team members would receive only about two-thirds of the increase they had received over the previous several years, while the skilled trades would receive a significantly higher raise. Team members already concerned about the fact that overtime had been virtually eliminated in 1979, might be even more upset by the enhanced inequity between themselves and the skilled tradespeople. Could Goble's leadership withstand the disruption that might be caused by such unhappiness among team members?

Goble was clearly leaning toward the idea of sticking literally to the old formula for 1979 and then rethinking it the following year. He anticipated that such a course would raise some concern among team members, so he needed to devise some sort of a process for bringing them into the discussions. On the issue of equity between team members and the skilled tradespeople, Goble figured it was an old problem that would cause no special concern now.

In fact, he worried more about the costs of suddenly abandoning the formula. Some POT directors were suggesting just that. ''Let's make an exception in this case,'' one director argued, ''and give the same raises to everyone.'' But Goble was skeptical: ''If POT went into a meeting and suddenly changed the formula, we would be setting a horrible precedent for the future. And I think that would really upset people. Sure, they would be happy if they got a little money. But in the long run, they'd be suspicious of us. If we could change this long-held policy behind their backs, so to speak, what else would we change without asking them?''

Besides, as one director told Goble, ''Our people supported the old logic when it led to good raises. They should be willing to support it now that it means some sacrifice. Besides, people know what the economic situation is. They're not expecting much this time.''

The possibility of opening up the process of compensation review to team members immediately after springing on them the news that raises would be reduced promised some disturbing times. Employees might come to view such participation as a kind of formal collective bargaining process over wages. There would be ticklish questions of deciding how employees should be brought in the process. Team members were dissatisfied with their representation in BOR, yet no other in-plant organization included nonexempts.

Then, too, Goble wondered just how high the expectations of Sedalia's nonexempts had risen. They already insisted that five-year Sedalia employees should earn more than their Beacon counterparts because Sedalia expected more of its employees. But just how high had his employee's evaluation of themselves risen, Goble wondered, and how would that affect their salary expectations?

### *A Possible Organizing Campaign*

Goble was aware of one final development. During the same week that he was considering what direction to take with the compensation system, the following article appeared in the *Sedalia Free Press*:

> Production and maintenance personnel of the Sedalia Engine Plant have been invited to attend an informal meeting at 7 P.M. Thursday at the Holiday Inn, being held by the Machine Workers of American union.
>
> Robert Reinhold, a union representative, said his union represents about 6,800 workers in American Diesel's Beacon plant, and that the purpose of Thursday's meeting is not to organize the workers in the nonunion plant here, but simply to provide information on wages and benefits being given union workers in Beacon.
>
> ''Of course, if the workers here wanted to organize a union, we would be interested,'' Reinhold said, ''because we feel everyone would be better off if all the American Diesel workers were represented.''

## EXHIBIT 26–1
## How We Do Business

Our business goals are basically the same as those of any successful business:

- Produce a quality product
- On-time shipment of our product to our customers
- Be efficient in our operations
- Be profitable

Each of us has ideas on how we can best reach these overall goals, and on how we can do business to reach more specific goals which will contribute to reaching these overall general goals.

A way to do business can mean many different things, such as a way to: run a machine, prepare a report, train an employee, solve a problem, evaluate plant performance, communicate an idea, arrange a work area, or practice safety. Each of these and all other ways to do business can be accomplished in many ways. Each different way to do business is assumed to have some advantages and some disadvantages and may be compared to other ways for accomplishing the same thing. The way with the strongest advantages and most acceptable disadvantages will be selected.

A good question to answer at this point is "How do we decide?" because we must do many things in unison as a single plant; we as a plant organization have come up with four basic guidelines to help us decide the *best* way of doing business or the way we think has the best chance of success. These guidelines or key questions which have served as the building blocks of our organization are:

*Excellence*

Does the way we do business allow every employee to perform to the best of his or her ability? Does the way to do business allow the plant to function as effectively as possible? Our assumption is that all people who belong to our organization will want to do their best and will expect the same of others even in the performance of many repetitive, routine tasks which are part of our work. We assume nothing less than such effort will allow us to be an effective competitor in the diesel engine business.

### *Trust*

Does the way to do business reinforce the idea that employees are expected to behave as responsible adults, and therefore, information, equipment, and materials are made accessible to them? If employees are assumed to be responsible adults, then the risks of abuse of information are low and the advantages of accessibility and openness are great. For example, it is assumed that we can solve any problem once it is raised and that all employees will bring us problems, issues, and sensitive information because they are confident that this information will be treated effectively with no harm coming to them simply because they raised an issue. Trust does not mean that information will be handled carelessly or that everything will be available to everyone. However, it is assumed that ownership in and a commitment to accomplishing objectives is strongest when relevant information is available. Therefore, information will be made available as appropriate.

### *Growth*

Does the way to do business encourage both the *learning and performing* of many tasks by said employees? We assume that human resources are too valuable to waste. People have been educated more and are capable of learning and performing more at work. It is assumed that work can be more interesting when people are challenged to perform a series of related tasks that add up to a measurable end product or service, rather than routinely performing only the smallest parts of total jobs. This does not mean that uninteresting or repetitive work is eliminated; for a fact, many such tasks are required to make diesel engine parts, however we organize our work. It is assumed that as employees, we can recognize the need to continue to perform the skills that we have learned, even though without new learning, some tasks may eventually lose some of the initial excitement or interest they held. In our business, we must learn in order to perform. We do not learn for the sake of learning.

It is assumed that we can recognize the value of sharing the skills which we have learned with others even though our instincts and past experience may mislead us to think that protecting some unique skills which we have will make us more valuable employees. A valuable employee is capable of, and willing to train others.

**EXHIBIT 26-1 (*Continued*)**

*Equity*

Does the way to do business treat all employees as adults and as fairly as possible? Our assumption is that we will tend to perform better as an organization to the extent that artificial differences in the way people are treated are eliminated. *Note that Equity does not mean Equality.* There are some differences in such areas as pay, benefits, and work areas, based on levels of responsibility and functional needs. However, equity does mean that *where there is no good business reason* to have differences, such as special parking privileges or less medical insurance, there *are* no differences.

Our business is growing rapidly and our ways of doing business are evolving as we learn from experience. Our experience in orienting new employees has taught us to be careful not to exaggerate the differences between our organization and other business organizations. It is our intention to do business in a few ways which we think will be effective and these ways may be different from what some of us have experienced in the past.

However, we are part of a plant startup situation. This means that many of the intentions that we have are to be found only partially in practice at this time. It is assumed that each of us is committed to devote the extra effort that it will take to make our organization work as it is intended. It is certain that this effort from each of us will succeed.

## EXHIBIT 26–2
## Plant Layout, May 1979

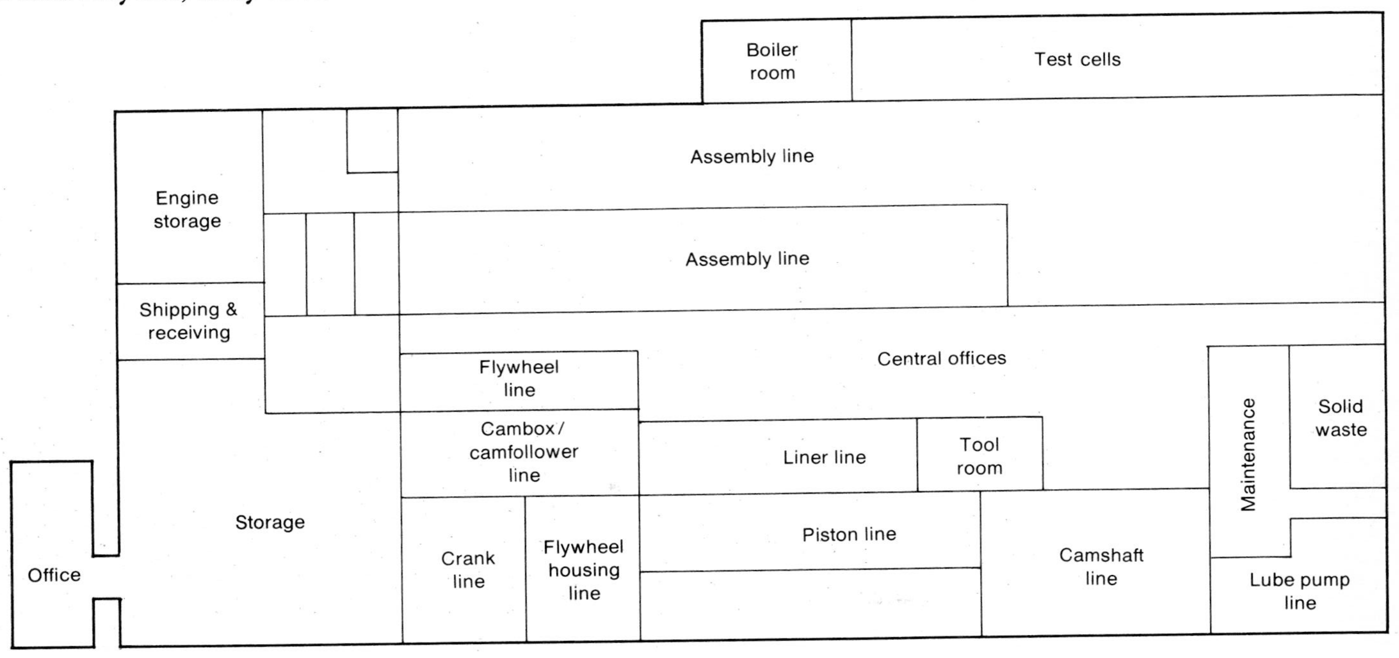

## EXHIBIT 26–3
## Plant Organization Chart

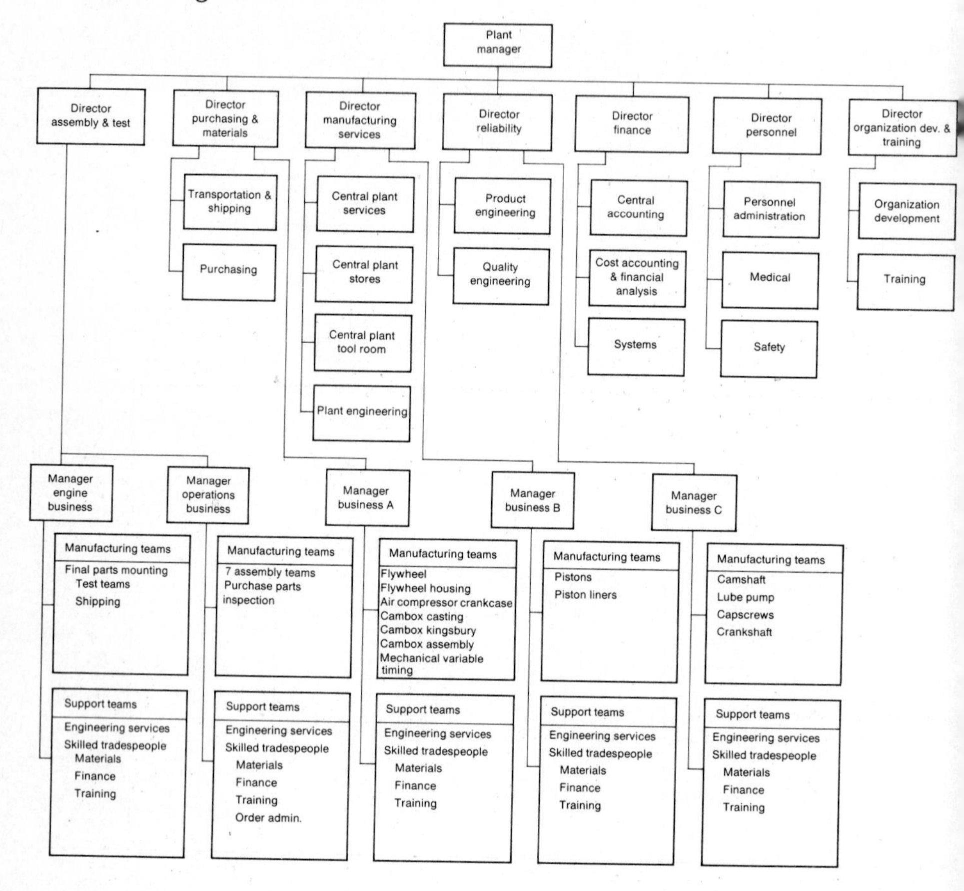

**EXHIBIT 26–4**
**Representative Mature Manufacturing Business**

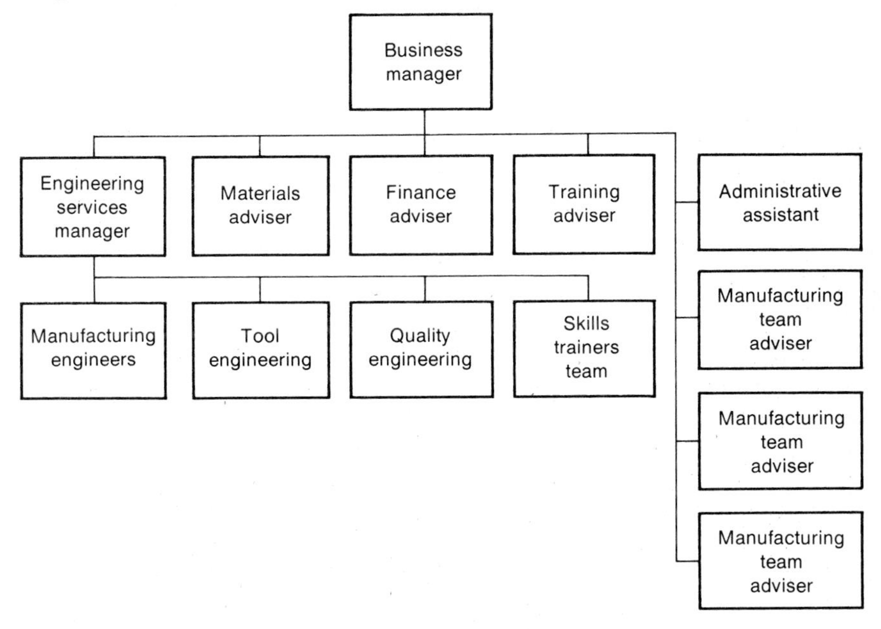


**EXHIBIT 26–5**
**Team Responsibilities**

1. Participation in the selection of team members:
   a. Departing team members
   b. Additional manpower requirements
2. Participation in the setting and administering of rules governing behavior affecting the accomplishment of the team's and organization's objectives:
   a. Attendance
   b. Housekeeping
   c. Safety practices
   d. Quality and quantity
   e. Training and team participation
3. Training of its members:
   a. Evaluation of competency levels of each member
   b. Planning needs of team and individuals
   c. Assume active role in training programs
4. Distribution and assignment of tasks among team members:
   a. To cover for nonparticipation

**EXHIBIT 26-5 (*Continued*)**

b. To provide training opportunities
c. To assign individuals to committees

5. Coping with production problems that occur within or between the teams' areas of responsibilities:
   a. Quality
   b. Delivery
   c. Service
6. Regulations and control of process functions that cross crew boundaries, including planning and scheduling material requirements.
7. Participation in setting of organization's goals and objectives:
   a. Cost reduction
   b. Quality levels
   c. Budget control
   d. Product output
8. Achievement of team's objectives and ensuring that members contribute toward the objectives.
9. Document and communicate the achievements and needs of the team to the necessary organizations in the systems.

*Following Will Be Provided to Team*

1. All relevant resources and information needed to carry out team's responsibility.
2. Rewards according to the individual level of competence attained and contribution to the team's achievement of its goals. These levels of competence will be based on objective measures of the ability to perform more than one combination of tasks.

*Guarantees*

1. No differences in privileges between team members and other members of the organization except as required externally.
2. No barriers to attainment of higher competence levels.

**EXHIBIT 26–6**
**Cost per Piece Cambox/Camfollower**

| | Base Cost | March | | February | | Cost Reduction | Total |
|---|---|---|---|---|---|---|---|
| | | *Total* | *Per Piece* | *Total* | *Per Piece* | | |
| Quantity, production | — | 35,556 | | 26,038 | | — | — |
| Direct material @ base cost | $25.193 | $ 895,762 | $25.193 | $655,975 | $25.193 | — | — |
| Direct labor @ base rate | 4.624 | 130,542 | 3.672 | 103,257 | 3.966 | $ .952 | $33,849 |
| Team manufacturing expense | | | | | | | |
| *Variable* | | | | | | | |
| Rework | .009 | 155 | .004 | 53 | .002 | | |
| Premium | .633 | 23,699 | .667 | 18,313 | .703 | | |
| Maintenance | 1.138 | 45,409 | 1.277 | 39,920 | 1.533 | | |
| Manufacturing, tools, gauges | .086 | 6,430 | .181 | 965 | .037 | | |
| Operating supplies | 1.090 | 41,805 | 1.176 | 29,983 | 1.152 | | |
| Scrap, manufacturing | 1.090 | 27,357 | .769 | 27,465 | 1.055 | | |
| Scrap, supplier | .522 | 42,585 | 1.198 | 173,716 | 6.672 | | |
| Scrap recovery | (.455) | (46,117) | (1.297) | (209,754) | (8.056) | | |
| Others | .047 | 3,519 | .099 | 14,314 | .550 | | |
| Subtotal variable | 4.160 | 144,842 | 4.074 | 94,975 | 3.648 | | |
| Freight | .716 | 28,150 | .791 | 14,608 | .561 | | |
| Total variable | 4.876 | 172,992 | 4.865 | 109,583 | 4.209 | | |

*continued*

**EXHIBIT 26–6** ***(Continued)***

| | Base Cost | March | | February | | Cost Reduction | Total |
|---|---|---|---|---|---|---|---|
| | | *Total* | *Per Piece* | *Total* | *Per Piece* | | |
| *Semivariable* | | | | | | | |
| Salaries, wages, fringes | 1.287 | 42,071 | 1.183 | 38,162 | 1.465 | | |
| Power | .268 | 21,535 | .606 | 6,995 | .269 | | |
| Gas | .011 | 535 | .015 | 233 | .009 | | |
| Travel | .011 | 305 | .008 | — | — | | |
| Depreciation | 1.210 | 29,892 | .841 | 29,643 | 1.138 | | |
| Taxes, insurance | .076 | 2,407 | .068 | 1,980 | .076 | | |
| Total semivariable | 2.863 | 96,745 | 2.721 | 77,013 | 2.957 | | |
| Total team manufacturing expense | 7.739 | 269,737 | 7.586 | 186,596 | 7.166 | .153 | 5,440 |
| Total team cost | $37.556 | $1,296,041 | $36.451 | $945,828 | $36.325 | $1.105 | $39,289 |

*Note*: Figures in parentheses represent increases.

## EXHIBIT 26–7
## Nonexempt Compensation System

| | 1976 | |
|---|---|---|
| *Level* | *Weekly Salary* | *Hourly Equivalent* |
| Entry | $148 | $3.70 |
| 6 months | 154 | 3.85 |
| 1 year | 160 | 4.00 |
| 2 years | 170 | 4.25 |
| 3 years | 180 | 4.50 |
| 4 years | 190 | 4.75 |
| 5 years | 200 | 5.00 |

| | 1977 | |
|---|---|---|
| *Level* | *Weekly Salary* | *Hourly Equivalent* |
| Entry | $186 | $4.65 |
| 6 months | 198 | 4.95 |
| 1 year | 208 | 5.20 |
| 2 years | 224 | 5.60 |
| 3 years | 236 | 5.90 |
| 4 years | 246 | 6.15 |
| 5 years | 256 | 6.40 |

**EXHIBIT 26–8**

**Economic Performance of American Diesel** *($ Thousands Except Earnings per Share)*

| | 1973 | 1974 | 1975 | 1976 | 1977 | 1978 | 1979 |
|---|---|---|---|---|---|---|---|
| Net sales | $637,330 | $801,566 | $761,504 | $$1,030,532 | $1,268,814 | $1,520,742 | $1,770,851 |
| Profit on sales | 48,739 | 63,510 | 36,763 | 127,726 | 136,468 | 130,396 | 106,991 |
| Net earnings | 26,592 | 23,775 | 491 | 58,622 | 67,022 | 64,399 | 57,938 |
| Earnings per share | $3.87 | $3.31 | $0.21 | $7.66 | $8.22 | $7.62 | $6.84 |

CASE 27

# OFFICE TECHNOLOGY, INC. (A)

*Richard O. von Werssowetz*
*Bette L. Witcraft*
*Michael Beer*

The meeting was heading into its fourth hour and there was no indication that things were going to cool down. If anything, the discussion was getting more heated by the minute. Robert Dorr, administrative manager in the Scientific Markets Group was trying to shut out the din and think about how work and workers should be organized in the order administration (OA) function. Some of his managers emphasized the need and desirability of individuals performing multiple functions, becoming involved with problem solving, and becoming familiar with a particular product line and able to identify with the product line people. Others regarded this as a backward step and felt that to meet the goals of standardization and efficiency, a pipeline organization was needed with each individual performing a single function with as little identification or specialization by product lines as possible and with *all* problem solving done by supervisors.

The meeting was held on September 24, 1979. In addition to Robert Dorr and his staff, it was also attended by Jeff Chaney, a representative from the Scientific Products Group personnel staff and Michael Russell, a consultant on the design of work systems. It was the culmination of a process that had started fourteen months earlier when Robert Dorr had been asked to develop a *uniform* order processing system for all five product lines in the group. The objective of this system was to increase the efficiency of OA operations while providing more timely shipments and accurate invoicing.

Robert Dorr had already decided to eventually consolidate all the OA groups. In late August, however, Jeff Chaney urged Dorr to delay such consolidation until some fundamental decisions were made about the design of work flows. There were some differences between product lines in how work was arranged. One OA group had assembly line-like operations with each individual specializing in one OA function while others involved individuals in multiple tasks, known as the team con-

---

This case was revised by Research Associate Bert Spector, under the direction of Professor Michael Beer. Subsequent revisions were made by Professor Richard Walton.

cept. These differences were reflected in the opinions which surfaced in the meeting. Robert Dorr recalled how the decision was made:

> I honestly could not think of a valid reason for *not* going to teams, so I just stood up and said, "Look, what I hear all of you saying is that you can't agree on a decision. Do you want me to make the decision? I'm not averse to it." So I went to the board, announced the decision, and proceeded to lead the discussion around how we would implement the team concept.

## OFFICE TECHNOLOGY, INC.

Office Technology, Inc. (OTI) started as a shoestring operation manufacturing electronic adding machines. OTI research gradually expanded the product line to include special-purpose computing and word processing systems. Prices for OTI products ranged from $30 to over $1,000,000. The quality of OTI products coupled with the company policy of responsiveness to customer needs is the basis of the incredibly strong customer reputation enjoyed by OTI.

OTI employed 35,000 people by 1979. Sales and net income had more than quadrupled in the past five years alone. In 1979, revenues were $1.4 billion and profits were $143.7 million.

### *Organization*

Given its phenomenal rate of growth and its strong customer orientation it is no surprise that after 20 years OTI's structure resembled that of a holding company with 14 different small companies (one for each product group operating pretty much autonomously). Each one was allowed to set its own goals, conduct its own research and development, run its operation any way they wanted to, with the corporation serving more as an evaluator and allocator of resource rather than a coordinator of effort. All of the product groups shared common sales and manufacturing functions resulting in a matrix or product management-type organization.

In 1978, OTI felt the need to reduce repetition of effort and intergroup competition as well as the increasing need to maintain control over the rapidly growing business. The 14 product groups were divided into three major "super" groups organized by market rather than product. However, each product group continued as an individual profit/loss center. One of the market groups is the Scientific Markets Group for which Robert Dorr worked. Now proposals from each product group are filtered through the three group heads before they reach the presidential level.

### *Culture*

The words "people" and "involvement" enter frequently into discussions with OTI management. President James Ingalls is people-oriented and encourages OTI's employees to develop their ideas and set their own goals within an informal work atmosphere. "I believe that the worker always knows more about his job than his boss," he says. "And as the company becomes larger, our challenge is to see that we don't stifle our people."

Ingalls' personnel policies have earned the company a reputation as a nearly ideal place to work. He ordered all workers paid even after heavy rains and a power failure kept them home for a week. An employment policy assures employees that they will be retained even during downturns in business. After one year's employment, they can invest up to 10% of their annual wages in OTI stock at a 15 percent discount.

Despite its growth, OTI's climate continues to reflect Ingalls' determination to encourage initiative. Individuals are rewarded for taking independent action when it is in the interest of the corporation. Thus, individuals or units may not always collaborate and coordinate, a price OTI is willing to pay for individual creativity and initiative.

OTI, like most other firms in the high-technology industries, is not unionized. It maintains an extensive network of employee relations personnel to ensure high levels of communication between management and other employees.

## HISTORY OF ORDER ADMINISTRATION AT OTI

The independent development of the 14 product groups was felt by many to have been a key factor in OTI's successful rapid growth. However, as OTI passed $1 billion in annual sales, it became apparent that the groups were continually reinventing the wheel in administrative systems. Again and again, as a product group went from $25 million to $50 million to $100 million in sales, they went through the stages of systems evolution from being a manual to slightly automated to more completely automated operation except that it was incumbent upon each one of those business managers and his financial and administrative staff to figure out what this system should be and put it together.

Salesmen found there might be fourteen different ways to process an order and began complaining. Manufacturing plants had to deal with fourteen different groups. No one found the separate methods satisfactory.

Jeff Chaney, organization development specialist for the Scientific Group, talked about how the order administration function has traditionally been a convenient corporate "whipping boy."

> In the first place the order administration people, the order administration units, have been the group that has absorbed most of the blame for things that have gone wrong. Giving the customer anything he wants means a lot of individualization around the product, changing things around to suit the individual customer. But the company is too big and the operation too complex to do that anymore.
>
> If you go to manufacturing, they'll tell you that it's order processing's fault if something's late, if you go to the product line they tell you the same thing and if you go to sales, they also blame order processing. But when you go to the order processing people, they're working as hard as they can, they're doing the best job they can but people keep asking them to do unusual things, to make exceptions. And if they don't do it they fail and if they do do it they fail, and so they keep on doing the best they can.

## ORDER ADMINISTRATION IN THE SCIENTIFIC MARKETS GROUP

There were five groups doing order administration work in the Scientific Markets Group, one for each of the product groups. In total these groups employed approximately 40 people, mostly nonexempt white-collar clerical employees.[1] Two of these groups were the focus of the current analysis: the Original Equipment Manufacturers (OEM) Group was the largest of the two and was managed by Tim Everhart. Reporting to him was a supervisor, Jim Hancock, who helped him in the supervision of the group. The Laboratory and Medical Products (LMP) Group was supervised by John Fortier and served the smaller product lines in those two areas. John Haley (who managed Order Administration for three product lines in Menlo Park), Tim Everhart and John Fortier all reported to Robert Dorr, manager of OA in the Scientific Markets Group. He, in turn, reported to the head of Finance and Administration for the group. (See Exhibit 27-1 for organization chart.)

Robert Dorr had plans to put Tim Everhart in charge of both OEM and LMP. Thus, John Fortier would report to Everhart sometime in the future. This was known to Tim Everhart and John Fortier but no formal announcement had been made.

[1]Nonexempt employees are those (usually blue-collar workers, white-collar clerical workers, and technicians) who, according to the wage and hour laws, must receive "overtime pay" for work beyond the normal work day.

## ORDER ADMINISTRATION STANDARDIZATION

The five OA departments under Robert Dorr had not always been part of the Finance and Administration function. In May 1978, concomitant with OTI's reorganization into three product groups, the new vice president of the Scientific Markets Group, decided to take the OA departments away from the product line organizations and consolidate them under the finance and administration manager. However, the OA groups continued to be physically located near the product line groups they served and to be accountable to the product groups for meeting their needs.

According to the finance and administration manager:

> It became very obvious that the systems used to enter orders, really, are sheer administrative functions that could all be the same and that, if you had that, it would all look the same to the field and therefore the salesmen and that it would all look the same to the people in manufacturing. So we decided to relieve the product groups of the function and to standardize the process.

Robert Dorr was hired in May 1978 as the Scientific Markets Order Administration manager. Dorr spent the first three months in his new job examining the problems in OA and developing recommendations for solutions for the OA process within the Scientific Markets Group.

On August 11, 1978, Dorr made a presentation to the Scientific Markets Group vice president, his staff, and the product group managers of what he had uncovered: there were seven computers running three different order processing systems, four computers running four scheduling systems, five different methods of handling OA (one for each of the product groups in the Scientific Group). Dorr detailed his arguments for uniformity of process and everyone agreed. The project was approved.

In April Robert Dorr was asked to report back to the vice president and his staff on the progress made in standardizing the OA process and related the reaction he received:

> They weren't real happy. In eight months of working on the project we had not made the progress we had planned for originally. Part of the problem was the decision made in midstream to change computer systems, but most of it was that while all the product group managers agreed that the process should be uniform, they all assumed that it was going to be done their way and that everyone else would be doing the changing.

In late August 1979, Jeff Chaney, a member of the Scientific Markets Group personnel staff, was asked by the Finance and Administration staff to help Robert Dorr with the standardization project. Chaney and Dorr discussed the project and the types of resistance Dorr had encountered. Dorr indicated that in addition to standardizing the OA process, he wanted to consolidate all OA activities because he thought it would be easier to control. They decided to bring in a consultant with expertise in work innovation and job design to assist them in analyzing the OA process.

## THE ORDER ADMINISTRATION TASK

Order processing is the handling of the customer's order, as transmitted from the field sales organization, from receipt of the master order form through booking and acknowledgement and the invoicing of that order upon notification of shipment. According to Robert Dorr:

> Essentially every order is information which comes from the field that has to be put into a computer system like order processing, backlog administration, scheduling system, and then that information has to be passed on to the same manufacturing world via what we call an SBA—Scheduling, Billing, and Shipping and Billing Authorization. So if you look at it from an overview, you simply see there's information coming in from the field, it comes into a product line system, and then goes on to manufacturing after it's massaged and you add some information to it.

The OA task within the Scientific Markets Group, as documented by Robert Dorr, consists of five functions: (1) distribution, (2) administrative edit, (3) data entry, (4) scheduling, and (5) booking and acknowledgement. The responsibilities of each function are:

- **Distribution.** The job of distribution involved, first of all, going to the computer room every morning and picking up new orders in the form of a master order form (MOF) that have been transmitted by computer from the field sales offices. Each one is put into folders that are color coded according to specific product lines.
- **Administrative edit.** Purchase orders are edited or checked to see that they meet all the requirements of a legal agreement. The person doing the checking must be familiar with "normal" contract language and OTI policies such as pricing and delivery to detect exceptions. The time required to edit a "normal" order with no unusual terms and conditions is approximately 30 minutes.
- **Data entry.** Data entry is performed at an interactive computer terminal. This involves the input of the information gathered and edited changes. Data entry takes from 15 to 30 minutes.

- **Scheduling.** When an order is "loaded" against the material allocation system, the operator is able to verify the availability of materials, the production capability to manufacture the product, and the ability to meet the customer request date in light of materials and production capability. If the order can be met as requested, it is then scheduled and assigned a manufacturing slot number. This normally requires approximately 15 minutes if no problems are encountered. The time lag between scheduling and filling an order, even when materials are available, can stretch anywhere from two to nine months.
- **Booking and acknowledgment.** Once scheduled, the order is considered booked revenue and constitutes a legal and binding contract between the customer and OTI. The field sales office and corporate headquarters are notified via computer of the booked order and followed up by a paper acknowledgement to both the field and the customer.

### *Problem Orders*

Basically there are two kinds of problems encountered in the processing of an order: (1) "system" problems, and (2) problems encountered in the order itself.

System problems or delays might be, for example, due to computer "down" time or a failure on the part of the materials management staff to allocate sufficient materials to be scheduled against. Generally speaking, the supervisor or a lead person will work with the appropriate group (e.g., the plant computer staff or the materials staff) to solve the problem.

Problems encountered in an order itself might include an out-of-date price quoted, an unusual discount allowance or an unrealistic delivery schedule. In this case, the person performing the editing function or the supervisor will work with either the field sales office or the product line staff to resolve the issue.

The impact of erroneous decisions or failure to resolve OA problems could potentially be very significant to the corporations. For example, if a mistake is made on pricing, the customer might refuse to pay; if the incorrect parts are ordered, manufacturing may produce the wrong piece of equipment, and since OA files are the source files for the ordering of materials by the corporation, an incorrect order could result in unavailability of certain materials.

### *End of Quarter Crunch*

The last month of each quarter was described as "absolute mayhem." In spite of the fact that the sales force do not get paid on a commission basis and do not receive a bonus for exceeding their quotas, the salespeople are measured on a quarterly basis and tend to keep all of the orders until the end of the quarter. Sixty percent of all orders for that quarter come in the last weeks. Repeated efforts over the previous decade to break this pattern had failed. There are peak periods where OA has to be working at full speed, night and day and through the weekends to get the orders processed,

### *Measurement of OA Effectiveness*

There were no real measures of the OA process in terms of efficiency, productivity or quality of service. Quality of service is informally assessed by feedback from the field sales organization, but as is usually the case, only when there are problems. No information was kept with regard to the number of complaints or their nature. Part of the problem in measuring such things as turnaround time is that it is influenced by actions in other parts of the company. If, for example, an order is taking an unusually long time to process, it could be due to the field sales organization negotiating with the customer for a different delivery date or it might be a materials allocation problem that prevents it from being scheduled.

The only measure that was routinely used in evaluating the OA process was the "float"—the dollar value of orders in-process, that is, orders that had been entered but not booked. The dollar value, however, did not immediately indicate the number of orders floating at any one time or explain why they had not been processed. Some of the value may be attributed to orders just entered in the system, some may be due to a hold-up in scheduling, some may be due to a materials problem, some may be due to exceptionally large orders or a higher than normal volume of orders, and finally, some of the value may be due to a lack of productivity on the part of the OA personnel. Due to the differences in each of the product groups' businesses, it was impossible to use float as a comparative measure across groups. It was used, however, within a group and a higher than normal float signaled a need to look into the causes. The float was a virtually continuous measure—examined at least once a week.

### *Differences in Work Systems within OA*

A preliminary September 17 meeting between Dorr, Chaney, and Russell had ended with a clear idea of the options available for organizing workers to accomplish these basic OA tasks. It had also surfaced that OEM and LMP, both located at the Los Altos facility, were committed to different work systems concepts.

## LOS ALTOS ORDER ADMINISTRATION

### *The Los Altos Facility*

The Los Altos facility is first and foremost a manufacturing plant. Modifications to support the various administrative activities are minimal. There are no carpets on the floors—only dusty concrete. A plantwide loudspeaker broadcasts rock music primarily for production workers, but it also serves as a distraction (not a cover-up) from production noises heard throughout the plant. There are no electrical outlets, but rather lines dropped from the ceiling to metal conduits on the floor. No one below a supervisory level position has an enclosed (partitioned) working space and enclosed spaces do not have ceilings due to inadequate ventilation capability. The illusion of enclosed space and a sense of privacy is attained by arrangement of desks that are provided with a three-foot modular top attached to the back of each desk which holds a shelf and a desk light.

### *Personnel and Manpower Flow*

The nonsupervisory personnel in OA historically consisted primarily of women with high school educations and in some cases with some secretarial college training. In all cases they had some typing skills. Recently, however, male employees had been hired with primarily a manufacturing/production background who were looking for advancement through administration. Approximately 15 to 20 percent of the female employees were older and working to provide their households with secondary incomes. The remainder were younger, averaging 22 years of age and more career-oriented. No costs of recruiting and training new employees were available.

OEM. Approximately 20 nonsupervisory personnel were employed by OEM. Under Tim Everhart's management, entry level personnel such as data entry operators and schedulers were typically hired from outside of OTI and with the exception of the older female employees who generally stayed put, left the OEM organization within 6 to 12 months to be promoted to other parts of the company. Tim Everhart offered two possible explanations for people leaving his staff:

> Probably half of the people who leave do so just to get away from OEM. They find that there are other comparable jobs in the organization where they can get paid more for doing less—where they have less responsibility and no direct supervision and can do pretty much as they please. The other half, though, are interested in moving up in the organization and leave for other parts of the company that provide better bridges from one wage class to another.

You have to remember that OTI is a very desirable employer. If has rapid growth, excellent benefits, competitive pay, and is known for its people orientation. People are eager to get a job with OTI, so we have many applicants for the most basic jobs. For example, ten applicants for a typist job had associate degrees in administration from junior colleges. These people then often move on to other jobs in OTI that they could only get because of their experience in OA. These are sales service, revenue accounting, and other similar jobs. There is just no career path in OA. I can only make them highly trained and highly regarded by the rest of the company.

LMP. Nine nonsupervisory people were employed by LMP. John Fortier, the supervisor, conducted lengthy recruiting interviews in an attempt to select people who would fit his organization. During discussions that might last three hours, John Fortier looked for several special qualities he felt were important:

- A positive frame of mind—there is so much turbulence in this group you've got to live with.
- The potential for creative thought—these jobs were more involved and had more responsibility.
- The ability to take the ball and run with it.
- A good attitude concerning cooperation—could they fit in a team—not I'm right, you're wrong.

Under John's supervision, two employees left the company in two years—both for personal reasons unrelated to work. Replacements for these employees were from internal hires.

*Performance Evaluation*

All personnel were given semiannual performance appraisals (a corporate requirement). In addition, entry level employees were given a semiannual salary review and higher-level employees (e.g., editors or specialists) were given annual salary reviews provided no promotions had occurred in the meantime. The performance appraisal form used for entry level personnel such as distribution clerks, data-entry operators, schedulers, etc., listed the general criteria for evaluation. Higher-level employees such as administrative editors were evaluated with a more open-ended format. Supervisors were provided with a grid-type guideline for salary increases with permissible percentage increase ranges dependent primarily on performance and to some extent time in grade.

Under Tim Everhart, the OEM performance appraisal process was a joint process. Prior to the performance appraisal interview, employees were given a copy of the evaluation form and asked to rate themselves. At the same time, the supervisor filled out an identical form on each employee. The performance appraisal interview consisted of a comparison of the two evaluations and a discussion of the discrepancies between them.

Performance appraisals in LMP, under John Fortier, were conducted somewhat differently. John conducted once a week informal feedback meetings with all of his employees where he would ask them about any problems they were having and provide them with feedback on their performance. When approaching the formal review process, the dialogues would deal more specifically with problem areas and improvement in performance. The formal performance appraisal interviews, according to John Fortier, contained no surprises.

### *Compensation*

OTI compensation policy is that the midpoint of each salary range is equal to the industry average for that wage class. The wage range for nonsupervisory OA personnel ranged from approximately $3.70 per hour for entry-level positions up to approximately $13,000 per year for salaried exempt positions. The following table provides compensation data for several "core" OA positions:

| Job Title | Function | Wage/Salary[a] |
|---|---|---|
| Distribution clerk[b] | Distribution | $3.70/hour |
| OA coordinator I | Data entry/scheduling/ booking | $4.19/hour |
| OA coordinator II | Administrative edit | $4.50/hour |
| Associate OA specialist | "Problem solver" | $6.50/hour ($13,000 annual salary) |

[a]Minimum.
[b]General job title not specific to OA.

## WORK SYSTEM DESIGN IN OEM

### *Nature of the OEM OA Task*

OEM customers are companies specializing in specific applications of computing and word processing equipment. They buy basic systems from companies like OTI and then either modify or incorporate these systems into their own product for their specialized markets. By nature, OEM customers order computers by the gross and subsequent orders are usually identical. There are a lot of repeat customers.

OEM is the highest volume group within the group, accounting for approximately 40 percent of its overall revenue. They process approximately 2,500 new orders per quarter. Each order received requires the corporate average of approximately 2.5 changes and/or administrative corrections. (Changes may be customer initiated, sales initiated, or corrections of discrepancies uncovered in the administrative edit process.)

Order changes require only a few minutes of data entry once determined. The orders range in size from approximately $10,000 to $200,000 with an average order size of $50,000 and a yearly volume of $200 million.

In 1979, OEM OA had an especially difficult task because of a variety of circumstances. Several product lines had encountered material shortages, so some volume manufacturing plants were not meeting their commitments. At the same time, there were software problems with the order processing computer. At times, no one knew exactly where they were in allocating materials. Some failures required the recreation of several weeks of work. This not only added to a heavy workload but also created confusion since the allocations previously made could not be exactly duplicated. Marketing had to halt OA assignment of scheduled delivery dates and use their best judgment to allocate orders. These stopgap methods were imprecise, which caused OA to have to reprocess revised schedules several times. Tim Everhart commented:

> Under these conditions, I didn't want my OA people making decisions. We had to get out tremendous workloads and minimize errors.

### *Work Organization*

Orders are processed at OEM in a production line manner. A series of slots (open-ended, mailbox-like cubbyholes) that act as "in-process inventory" are used at several different points in the process. Folders are placed in these slots in order of receipt priority and/or by type of order. Employees walk to the slot racks to leave completed work and pick up new orders to process through their step.

To process an order from receipt to booking takes, on the average, about five days in OEM. Problems with an order (pricing errors, customer changes, and so forth) are essentially ignored for as much of the process as possible and resolved either after the order is entered or at that point in time where further processing becomes impossible depending on the nature of the problem. (Problems encountered at any phase of the process are almost always referred to the editor or supervisors handling the particular order.)

The diagram in Figure 27–1 summarizes the OEM processing of a "clean" order (one with no problems):

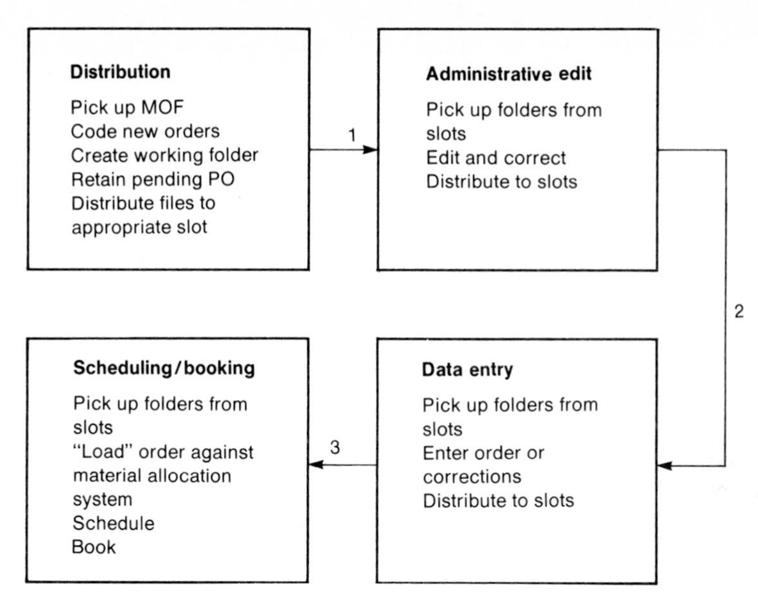


**FIGURE 27–1**

### *Supervision*

Tim Everhart described his present job as manager of the OEM OA group:

> A lot of the things that I have to do day in and day out are what I term babysitting. And that's exactly what it is, you wipe somebody's nose and you wash somebody's booboo and then just send everybody on their way. I haven't had the opportunity to go to school, take a course. I can't afford to be out sick. Because if I'm gone, who makes the decisions? Part of this is because we have a lot of hourly people—people who fill out time cards. People who are not paid to make decisions. That makes up the majority of my group. My faith in human nature isn't exactly what you would call really positive. I subscribe to the school, if you give people an inch, they'll take a mile. And it's just human nature and I probably suppose that I would do the same thing.
>
> The OEM group is perceived to be an extremely strict by-the-book kind of operation and in a way we are but it's also because of the nature of the business we can afford to be . . . there's a certain amount of standardization there so you can sort of set up your business to say that it has to operate by these rules . . . even though you give each order individual attention, it usually turns out to be a standard format so therefore controls can afford to be a little more strict. The fact that we do such a high-volume business and we're responsible for a lot of money increases our chances of liabilities so therefore we want to make sure that the business is managed as closely as we can.

> Most people within OTI who know anything about what it's like to work here won't touch the job because the jobs really are entry level. I ordinarily go to the outside to hire. Within a month or two they're bored out of their tree and the reason for it is it's a very monotonous, dull, boring job. The turnover rate in my group is six months to a year because there are no advancement opportunities. To advance, you're going to have to get out of my group and into another group. And as boring and rotten as the job is, if you do badly at it, you're not going to be able to get out of my group because no one else is going to want to hire you. So, therefore, no matter how poor the job is, you're still going to have to do a terrific job—just to be able to get hired some other place in OTI.

OEM OA personnel characterize Tim Everhart and his supervisory style as follows:

> Tim is strictly business—no fooling around.
>
> He sits in his office most of the time and waits for people to come to him with their problems. He's pretty busy most of the time.
>
> Tim operates strictly by the book.

Other comments included that OEM management keeps to itself and while it's not always clear what they're doing, the operation is a smooth one.

Jim Hancock, the supervisor of the OEM OA group, has been with OTI for nine years, and in supervisory positions eight out of those nine years. Jim talked about his various experiences as an OTI supervisor:

> In my first job, which lasted five years, I was very involved in RHIP—Rank Has Its Privileges. Do as I say, not as I do. I figured that I have worked very hard to get where I am so I should have certain privileges and my subordinates should see those privileges so that they'll be motivated to get to my position.
>
> In my second job in OTI, the plant manager was very people-oriented, and tried to create a democratic plant. I found that it worked much better. I had less problems with my people, less problems motivating.
>
> When I came back to Los Altos into a more structured organization, I had to adjust again. OEM is a tried and true production job where everything moves from one spot to another—a very serialized operation. There were measurements set on how much work you did and the system they use here is old but twigged to maximum efficiency. And now I've adjusted and bought off on the fact that this is about the only way we can do the job given the volume that we've got.

## OBSERVATIONS AND COMMENTS ABOUT OEM

In general, OEM employees perceived their product group to be important to OTI. They are proud of their efficiency in processing a high volume of orders. They feel that the "production line" structure of their job was necessary given the nature of their task. They were satisfied with regard to the work load balancing, yet boredom and fatigue were indicated by most. If there was no work to be done in a particular functional area, people just sat. Overall satisfaction ranged from high for a few older women to low and very low for the majority—especially among those with the talent and motivation to better themselves. Career commitment to OA was the exception with many perceiving OA to be the bottom of the rung. OEM personnel commented that there were no formal training programs, that they were not allowed to go to technical schools (without which they could not advance). What training that was available was "on the job" and usually done by people who didn't really know the job. The OEM group appeared to be highly conscious of status distinctions—aspiring to the administrative edit job (the group considered to be the "policemen" of the unit). They were capable of responding to peak demands but felt that doing so exacted a toll. OEM personnel exhibited skill within their particular functional area but a narrow understanding of the OA work in general. They were told what to do but not why. There appeared to be little respect for higher, classified personnel—they didn't perceive them as coordinated or even very knowledgeable about the jobs.

Representative comments from OEM personnel:

> The way we run things makes a lot of sense—it's logical if we need to find an order, we know right where it is.
>
> As far as I'm concerned, OEM is like a boot camp and as soon as I can, I'm going to get promoted out.
>
> I like it when there isn't any work to do and we just sit around and talk.
>
> We understand a lot more of what's going on than we get credit for and I don't see why we have to go to Tim or Jim for every little problem.

## WORK SYSTEM DESIGN IN LMP

### *Nature of the LMP Task*

LMP customers—research laboratories and medical customers—are end-users of OTI equipment. They, as a rule, order specific and unique combinations of OTI systems and options to meet their own particular needs. By nature, then, LMP customers are usually one-time customers and there are few repeat customers.

LMP processes approximately 2,000 new orders per quarter. Each order received requires approximately four changes and/or administrative corrections. The orders average seven or so items each and average $30,000 in size with a range of anywhere from $1,000 to $1,000,000.

*Work Organization*

LMP's work organization differed from that of OEM. The group had assisted in the development and testing of a new computer program called "Auto-Load." This program makes it possible for orders received from the field to be entered automatically into the OA computer system, thus eliminating the data entry step. As the order is automatically entered into the system, the "Auto-Load" program performs an initial edit and outputs a document called a working SBA (Scheduling, Billing, and Shipping and Billing Authorization). The working SBA is confirmation that the order has been entered in the system and lists line-by-line corrections identified by the computer. (It was planned that all other groups would be using this program within a year.)

The working SBAs, together with the standard MOF (master order form) were picked up by distribution clerks, coded, and placed in a working folder. The folder containing the MOF and the working SBA was then distributed by them to schedulers assigned to either the laboratory or medical product lines. They called up the order onto the computer terminal display and made corrections indicated on the working SBA where possible. They then tested to see if promised delivery dates could be met given the availability of materials and the manufacturing schedule. When manufacturing schedules or material availability indicate a potential missed promise date, schedulers in the LMP negotiate directly with manufacturing or materials personnel without working through their supervisors (in contrast with the OEM process). They then schedule and book the order.

Once scheduled and booked, the folder with the working SBA and MOF was forwarded to the appropriate product lines representative. The product line representative is not a part of LMP's OA group. He or she, upon receiving the PO (original purchase order) completed a final edit, resolved any remaining problems with the field or customers, and sent the working SBA, MOF and PO back to LMP for final corrections to the order.

It takes approximately nine days for LMP to process an order from time of receipt until booking, including the time it takes to send the order out of OA to the product line. If either system or order problems are encountered, the schedulers confer directly with the appropriate people in the organization—e.g., with the materials people if there is a materials allocation problem, or with the product line representative if there is an order problem.

The diagram in Figure 27-2 summarizes the LMP OA process.

John Fortier, supervisor of the LMP order administration group for the past year, commented on their work style:

> Before I came, the product reps outside of OA had all the "knowledge" work and used OA as clerical arms and legs. But these reps were overloaded and began to make mistakes and cut corners. I felt this exposed OTI to unjustified risks and it certainly caused problems for us. My strategy was to get more of the decision making within OA. First I tried to negotiate a change in roles, then just did it unilaterally. We started checking directly with materials, inventory control and scheduling, and so forth. This placed more responsibility on each of our people and led to our approach to work organization. Before, we were always the fall guy, everyone ran roughshod over us. We took more responsibility so people on the outside could influence us less.

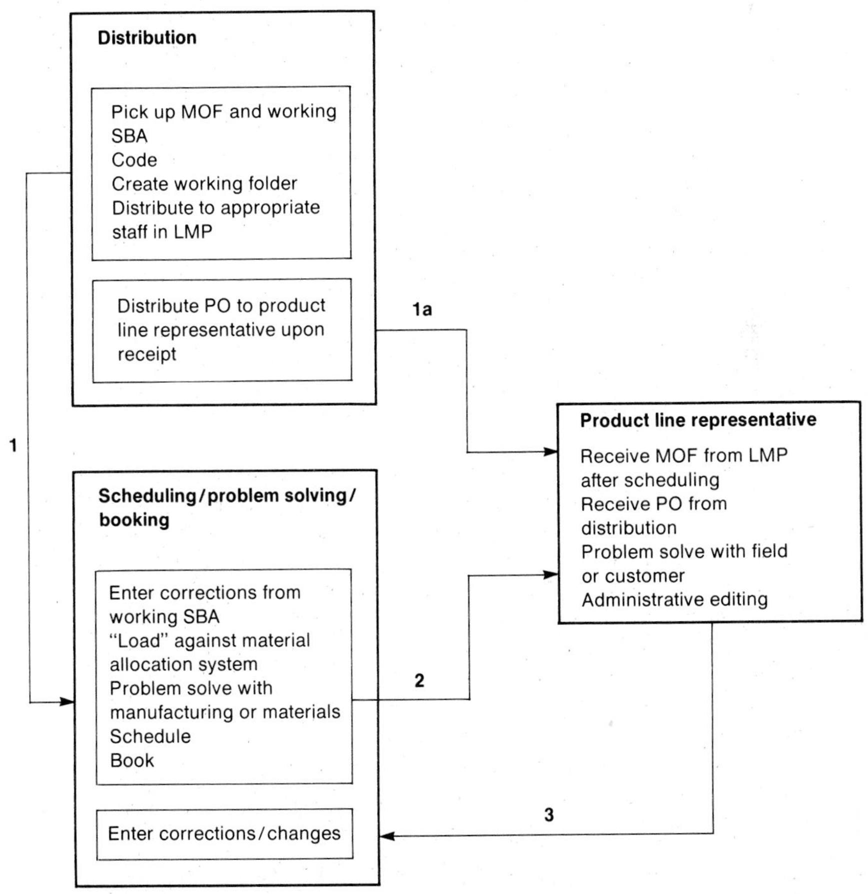


**FIGURE 27-2**

*Supervision*

John Fortier had been with OTI for 13 years, 9 of them in supervisory positions:

> In my career at OTI I've worked for an awful lot of autocrats and I feel fortunate for that because that's helped me as an individual to understand and feel and be able to relate with employees who say that "management" is "on" them for some reason or other. And I decided that my goal in life is to be on the other side and when I have the opportunity, I'll do things different. I wasn't really able to do that with my past supervisory positions but when I came here, I was given the opportunity.
>
> Their prior boss, my counterpart who was here before me, was iron-fisted, didn't understand the order administration world, but understood that people had to be to work on time, and had to do certain things within this environment to survive. And in order to exist, the staff did whatever they were told, right or wrong—they were a bunch of robots. The group was very down, very much told what to do, very ignored, and very misunderstood. So when I came in, I got them all together and asked them what they understood the job to be, what did they know, what could they share with me, what could they teach me? At first, they were very leery and wouldn't share anything. So I kept prodding and kept asking each one, "What type of things do you do? How much work do you have to do?"
>
> In addition, when I came on board, three senior people left so we were understaffed and the end of the quarter was coming. We were in a mess. So I sat down with them, we outlined the problems we were facing, and how we could work them out. Then I rolled up my sleeves and I went out on the floor and said, "I want you to teach me how to process an order," and they did. They first taught me the simplest operation—data entry. Then I told them that since they were all experienced, I'd do the data entry and they could do the other functions—the more intelligent work. So I did just that for three days.
>
> Then I asked them to teach me more—about themselves, the functions of the computer, and what they were expected to do. They started opening up and we built some trust. I began to back off a little and started asking them to come up with, as a group, solutions to problems and suggestions on how to improve the process. I told them that if they would tell me what was wrong or what they didn't like that we would change it piece by piece if we could. On the other hand, I expected them to help me understand the things they did that I didn't like. Eventually, I gradually worked from being "buddy" back into a supervisor and started telling them the way things were supposed to be, helping them to understand the whole OA process within OTI and their opportunities as individuals—how they could grow in Order Administration. So now they hold weekly meetings without me and give me the minutes; they all understand each other and the job, they pitch in and help each other, come in on Sundays if necessary all by their own choice. They're incredible.

John Fortier's people made the following comments regarding him and his supervisory style:

> He let us decide when we want to do what and gives us a lot of freedom. As a matter of fact, he usually makes us answer our own questions.
>
> If someone's absent, we get to decide how to handle the extra work. John left it up to the group.

In addition, it was observed that John Fortier remained physically separated from the group. Yet, people brought their personal problems to him and asked his advice.

### *Observations and Comments About LMP*

In general, LMP staff liked their jobs. They identified highly with the product lines, with their product team, and with their supervisor. In addition, they felt recognized and rewarded for their efforts by product lines, each other, and their supervisor. They had an extraordinary ability to respond to peak demand, and some even claimed to look forward to "all nighters" necessary at the end of the quarter. Given their multiple functions, their flexibility was very high, and if someone was out sick or left the unit, the group decided how to allocate the extra work load. They perceived a great deal of variety in their jobs, they made choices about what they felt like doing (e.g., which part of the process) and there was a great deal of informal and spontaneous learning taking place. There was high internal communication and mutual respect. A very strong "help" norm existed. They felt a commitment to OA and perceived opportunity for growth and development within OA. There was a great deal of respect for their supervisor who they could count on to pitch in and help as well as trust to discuss personal problems with. In summary, the LMP group exhibited high morale, high cohesion, high enthusiasm, and a broad understanding of the OA task.

People in LMP made the following comments:

> We really are a team here. If someone has a problem we all try to help.
>
> We have this thing that we do every quarter, at the end, where we all come in and work 36 to 48 hours straight and you wouldn't believe how much fun we have. I really look forward to it.

## THE SEPTEMBER 24 MEETING

After the September 17 meeting that took place between Jeff Chaney, Robert Dorr, and the consultant Michael Russell, it was decided that it was time to meet with all the managers involved to discuss alternative work systems. That meeting was held on September 24 and included in addition to the above, Tim Everhart, John Fortier, Jim Hancock, and John Haley. The initial question addressed by the group was what criteria should be used in evaluating different work system alternatives. The meeting revealed sharply contrasting preferences between Tim Everhart and Jim Hancock and all of the others. The following list was generated: (names in parentheses indicate who provided the item.)

- Simplicity of organization, clear-cut areas of responsibilities within OA and between OA and customer support people (Tim Everhart)
- Standardization of methods (Tim Everhart)
- Permits measurement of performance at individual level for control purposes and permits measurement of capacity for planning purposes (Tim Everhart)
- Flexibility for filling in at peak loads and for balancing lines and creating variety (John Fortier)
- Attractiveness to individual by variety and enriched work and by advancement opportunities (John Fortier)
- Meets real needs of customers in coordinating with customer service. Responsive to specialized requests even as volume grows. (John Haley)
- Reassuring to product lines, e.g., by enabling them to identify part of OA they are dealing with
- Utilizes existing personnel
- Can be implemented in a way that will maintain/improve quality and progressively improve efficiency
- Will be able to absorb technological change and growth in volume

The OA managers and supervisors were asked to suggest the work system design they would like to see. Tim Everhart and Jim Hancock (OEM) stressed a pipeline organization with as little specialization by products as feasible and with *all* problem solving done by supervisory hierarchy. They regarded any other organization as a backward step. John Fortier (LMP) and John Haley (Menlo Park) emphasized the need and desirability of individuals performing multiple functions, becoming familiar with a particular product line, and being able to be identified by the product line people.

The team concept was introduced last. Tim Everhart and Jim Hancock were strongly opposed and John Haley and John Fortier were sympathetic.

Tim Everhart expressed several other concerns regarding the team concept or any other product line-oriented structure:

- It would be inefficient internally by limiting options in balancing work load.
- It would be unable to enforce standardized procedures.
- It would be marked by many more interpersonal problems requiring management time and skills (which may not exist).

It was generally felt by Tim and Jim that the team concept ran counter to OTI's emphasis on individual achievement.

Robert Dorr described some of the interaction that took place in the meeting between Tim Everhart and John Fortier:

> There's Tim saying, "I want it this way." Jim wasn't going to accept anything else—John wasn't going to accept anything else and they kept going back and forth at one another and understand that here's John realizing that it is in the plans that he's going to be working for Tim and he's trying to be as delicate as possible.

Tim Everhart commented on his stand:

> I was especially opposed to all of the radical changes being proposed to be made in concert, reorganization, standardization, and consolidation. To soften the magnitude of these changes, I tried to incorporate some of the values of what we were accomplishing in OEM. I also had doubts arising from pure human nature. I believed that the OA people would take the freedoms, authority, and higher wages but might very well shirk their duties. They just had no experience in decision making and I didn't see how we could do this all at once.

John Fortier expressed his position:

> I felt that from the point of view of the task itself, I had no disagreement with Tim about the production line approach. Especially for his area which was much more routine. However, I felt the team approach made much more sense from the point of view of the people. I think the different turnover rates are a good indication of this.

John Hancock related his perspective on the meeting:

> Tim and I presented a formidable opposition; for probably the first four or five go-rounds, we were very very anti-team concept and tried to . . . it was politically obvious that we were going to get it [the team concept].

## EXHIBIT 27-1
## Scientific Markets Group Order Administration

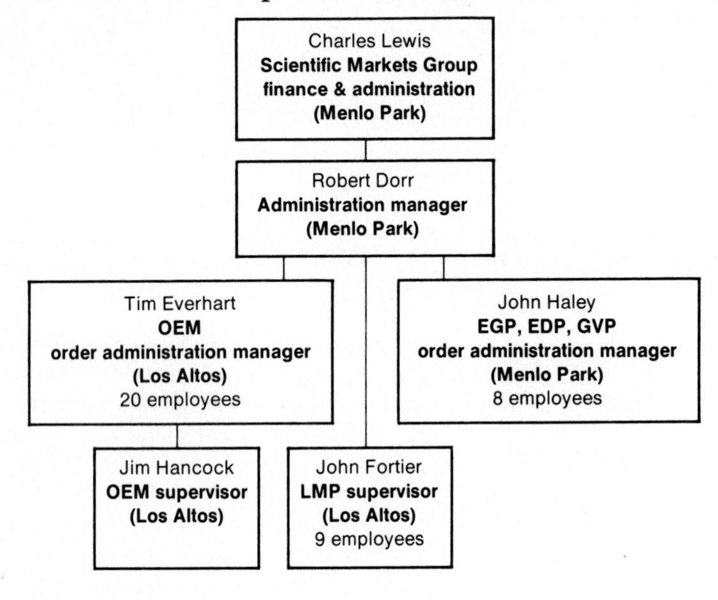


Key:

OEM = Original Equipment Manufacturers
EGP = Engineering Products Group
EDP = Educational Products Group
GVP = Government Products Group
LMP = Laboratory and Medical Products Group

*Chapter* 7

# The Integration of Human Resource Management Policies

THIS FINAL CHAPTER concerns the difficult task all managers face in integrating their organization's many human resource policies and practices into a coherent whole that meshes with the other aspects of the firm's operations. In all too many firms today HRM policies and practices are not well coordinated, the right hand actively blocking the work of the left hand. For example, a firm can be redesigning its plants to increase the challenge of the work at the same time it is introducing new office technology in a way that diminishes the work challenge. The reasons why the coordination of HRM efforts ought to be a central concern of senior line managers as well as human resource managers are not hard to find. When, as is so frequently the case, HRM policies and practices are treated as a long list of isolated tasks, they get farmed out to specialists whose concerns are limited to avoiding obvious problems and assuring technical consistency and accuracy within their particular practice areas. For instance, the expert in pension benefits generally consults only with other pension specialists and is consequently focused on the logic of devising what he sees as the ideal pension system for the company. All too often the impact of such planning on other HRM practices and especially on the firm's overall business strategy is a neglected issue.

In considering the integration of HRM policies, it is important first of all to review the conceptual overview we presented in Chapter 2. The map of the HRM territory (Figure 2-1) has obvious utility in working out an integrated set of HRM policies in any given firm. It helps to clarify the multiple factors that must be considered in shaping HRM policy. It also highlights the relevant constraints, the multiple stakeholders, and the types of outcomes that are directly relevant to management's choices in the four policy areas. In this chapter we propose to supplement this basic analytical tool with the consideration of four additional topics: integrating approaches, the choice of one or two cultures, management values, and the HRM change process.

## INTEGRATING HRM POLICIES: BUREAUCRATIC, MARKET, AND CLAN APPROACHES[1]

In the interest of integrating HRM policies, the first question we must answer is to what end or purpose integration is sought? Clearly, from the *organizational* standpoint, any HRM system should be integrated so as to attract and hold the right mix of people and to establish the type of working relationship between these people that will carry out the organization's strategic plan, once that plan has taken into account any relevant human resource constraints and opportunities. In other words, HRM policies need to *fit* the business strategy. Later in this chapter we will elaborate and expand on this definition of the purpose of an integrated HRM system, but for now it serves as a useful starting place for our discussion by immediately suggesting a second question: How should one define a good fit between a given strategic plan and the design of an HRM system? Toward this end earlier chapters in this book have sorted all HRM practices into the four major policy areas: employee influence, flow, rewards, and work systems. Further toward this purpose, we will now propose three generalized approaches to integrating across the four policy areas of any HRM system: the bureaucratic approach, the market approach, and the clan approach. To see how these methods of analysis can help managers integrate their human resource policies and practice, we will first discuss the distinction between the three approaches.

The *bureaucratic way* of unifying HRM policies is based on the assumption that employees are subordinate and responsive to traditional authority. Its use in industry has grown with the expansion of large industrial organizations in this century, this industrial application having been anticipated by its earlier development in church and military organizations. Over the years it has been successful in coordinating the work efforts of a great many people, but in recent years it has faltered as the primary way to achieve employee involvement and adaptation to changing environments.

The strength of the bureaucratic way of unifying an HRM system lies in its contribution to achieving control and efficiency. Not surprisingly, the chief symbols of this approach are the chain of command (traditional lines and boxes of the organizational chart) and the rule book (standard operating policies). From the employee's standpoint the approach appeals to a desire for order, building as it does upon legitimated authority and property rights, and on a desire for equity in terms of due process. From the organizational standpoint, this approach is based on the necessity for an organization's being able to coordinate its methods of collecting relevant information, making commitments based on such information, and, in turn, giving directions for actions necessary to fulfilling the commitments. Implicit in any such information/decision/command network is the necessity of clearly establishing a division of labor for both operational acts and coordinating acts.

A number of specific HRM practices have evolved which support and implement the consistent use of the bureaucratic way of establishing employment relationships. For convenience these bureaucratic practices can be grouped into the four policy areas of flows, rewards, work systems, and employee influence. In terms of flows, the usual career track begins with lower-level positions that can lead to promotion within each specialized chain of command. Superiors evaluate the employee with criteria for advancement focused on technical qualifications, compliance with the direction of superiors, willingness to pass all relevant information upward, and willingness to supervise in detail the work of all subordinates. In terms of rewards, the bureaucratic method relies on the development of detailed job descriptions that are then rated for their relative economic value to the firm (the job evaluation system described in Chapter 5). This approach generates a pay-for-the-job system of wages and salaries.

In terms of work systems, the bureaucratic way of handling HRM relies on making jobs as simple and unskilled as possible at the bottom of the organization with the supervisory structure entirely responsible for coordinating these jobs (in keeping with the principles of Frederick Taylor). The chain of command is thought of as the way for workers to express their opinions and influence their work life. In this familiar "open-door" policy, management expects that all workers will take problems to the boss for resolution within an accepted procedural framework. In sum, when a consistent set of bureaucratic HRM policies and practices, including competitive pay rate, are carefully and fairly executed, they work to provide a competent, compliant, predictable work force—as long as the technology remains stable and the level of employment does not decline. If either changes dramatically, however, and employees are considered expendable as a way of cutting costs or are required to adjust to new technologies, this method is almost certain to run into serious trouble.

The *market approach* to integrating an HRM system is based on the principle of explicit and immediate exchanges between the organization and its members. Because exchange, in its broadest sense, is probably the most basic principle governing human relations, it is also relevant to bureaucratic and clan approaches. Although in prosperous times the underlying dynamics of market exchanges can become somewhat obscured, they come back into focus in times of adverse economic conditions. The market approach to HRM draws upon the universal norm that there should be reciprocity in exchanges between people and also draws upon the tendency of individuals to repeat behavior that is given positive reinforcement. Market mechanisms appeal to the calculative self-interests of employees and are designed to achieve a congruence between these self-interests and the interests of the organization. The symbol of market HRM practices, the paycheck, represents the exchange of work for money. The rewards policy area, discussed in Chapter 5, is the means by which the organization defines this exchange. As we shall see, however, the paycheck is only the first step in an elaboration of HRM practices that are market-like in character.

The market approach to designing and selecting HRM systems can be described in still other ways: in the language of contributions and inducements and the language of the psychological contract.[2] Employment relationships in organizations where the market approach is dominant are characterized by the high turnover and the bidding for talent associated, for example, with the high-fashion merchandiser, the advertising account executive, the newsbroadcaster, the professional baseball player, the actor or actress, and the stockbroker.

HRM practices that have market-like qualities can best be understood by examining the market flows system that can be summarized as "in-and-out." At its extreme, the employee is virtually a subcontractor in a deal struck with the employer to perform a specified amount of work for an agreed-upon price. When this transaction is completed the relationship is ended until another contract is made. There is no single entry point; employees come into the system at any level, depending upon the needs of the organization and the availability of required talent. Neither is there an established promotion ladder. The market for jobs is not only external but also internal, witness the practice of job posting. In a market-oriented HRM system, employee evaluation is clearly a two-way process; employees as well as employers are constantly evaluating the quality of exchanges, with each party prepared to seek a better deal elsewhere. In terms of rewards, the epitome of the market HRM system is piece-rate payment. There are other variations on this theme of paying for individual performance: executive performance bonuses, sales commissions, merit increases. Other reward practices built upon the exchange principle are cash awards for suggestions, prizes for sales performance, special recognition for technical achievements, and the like.

The way employees influence a market-oriented firm is through negotiation and bargaining. This can take the form of individual bargaining for a formal, or more frequently an informal, employment contract, or the form of collective bargaining carried out by unions on behalf of employees. The work system that is consistent with the market approach involves breaking work into discrete, individualized tasks that are filled by a bidding process. The market-oriented HRM system is particularly effective when flexibility in the employment relationship and responsiveness to sudden environmental changes are important. The price tag for the employer is uncertainty when needed talent is scarce, and uncertainty for the employee when jobs are scarce. Contracts are used to help reduce the uncertainties. A logical, consistent, and integrated set of HRM practices built around the market approach can work in those special instances when it truly fits the nature of the business.

The *clan approach* to integrating HRM policies and practices has not been clearly identified as one aspect of customary practice but is still important. As the name suggests, this ancient form of employment relationship derives from early kinship systems. The clan approach also has thoroughly modern relevance, however, as industry realizes its potential for increasing employees' involvement more than is possible with only bureaucratic and market mechanisms. Based on shared values, shared risks, and shared rewards, and oriented to a joint or collective achievement, the clan approach appeals to employees' desire to identify with and contribute to a social entity and to goals beyond immediate self-interest. For the clan approach to work there must be a gradual evolution within an organization of a shared set of beliefs that are regularly backed by supporting policy and action. An emphasis on this approach is associated with such consistently well-managed firms as IBM, Texas Instruments, and Kodak, as well as some of the outstanding Japanese firms.

HRM practices can be gathered into a unified clan system beginning with a flow policy of assuming long-term employment of all employees. People are chosen not for their immediately available specialized skills but for their anticipated long-term adaptability to the organization. Once employed, they go through an extensive learning and indoctrination process, both to acquire basic skills and knowledge of the industry and to learn how to be effective to the organizational culture. As in the bureaucratic approach, the point of entry is usually at the lower job level, but mobility is as often lateral as upward as employees broaden and deepen their skills. The employee evaluation process relies on the judgments of peers as well as superiors. With the clan approach rewards are linked to group and total organizational performance. This linkage most often takes the form of profit sharing or other means of gain sharing. As we indicated in Chapter 5, interest in organization-wide incentives is growing as companies seek to develop the clan approach. People who are promoted have demonstrated not only their competence but their fit with the company culture; misfits are either discharged or given more peripheral roles. Thus, using terminology we introduced in Chapter 4, these firms tend to define effectiveness in terms of behavior as much as results.

The work systems in a clan-oriented firm make extensive use of teams—of semiautonomous work groups at the operating level, and of special task forces at the managerial level. The hallmark of these teams is cross-training and task-sharing with the goal of creating a climate of interchangeability, enrichment, and group independence. Symbols of status are understandably minimized. In Chapter 6 we described a high-commitment work system—Model B—that highlights these features of clan-oriented firms. With this approach, worker input affecting procedure and policy is voiced through discussion and consensus. Involving all employees in relevant aspects of the decision process not only takes advantage of their experience and ideas but reinforces their commitment to the decisions that are finally put into effect. A significant part of HRM in a clan-oriented company is the time and attention given to wide circulation of facts concerning the business environment: trends in products, sales, competition, regulations, and technology. This provides all organizational members with a broad understanding of the problems to whose solution everyone is expected to contribute. The clan approach to integrating an HRM system aims at building the high level of mutual commitment between an organization and its employees that is necessary if the organization's success depends on quality and especially on innovation.

Table 7-1 is a diagrammatic summary of HRM policies that we have discussed as characteristic of the bureaucratic, market, and clan approaches. Now that we have described in general the differences between these three approaches to integrating human resource management, a host of practical questions present themselves. Are the three systems either/or options, or are combinations of these approaches viable? How does one match a firm's product/market strategy with the appropriate HRM approach or combination of approaches? Must a single approach be taken for all categories of employees or can different approaches be used with different groups within the same organization? This last question can be further sharpened by asking if compa-

**TABLE 7–1 Matrix of HRM Policies**

| HRM Policy Areas | Nature of Employment Relationship: *Bureaucratic (employee involved as subordinate)* | *Market (employee involved as contractor)* | *Clan (employee involved as member)* |
|---|---|---|---|
| Employee influence | Up through chain of command | Negotiated contracts | Consultation and consensus (e.g., quality circles) |
| Flow | Bottom entry—rise to level of competence within functions | In-and-out employment (i.e., job posting) | Long-term employment with lateral as well as vertical movement |
| Rewards | Pay based on job evaluation | Pay based on performance (i.e., piece rates or executive bonuses) | Pay based on seniority, skills, and gains-sharing |
| Work systems | Fine division of labor coordinated by chain of command | Group or individual contracting | Whole task with internal coordination; peer pressure as motivator |

nies are to have one set of HRM practices for exempt managers and professionals and a different set of HRM practices for nonexempt employees. Is there to be one overall corporate work culture or are there to be two, one for managers and one for the managed, as has been typical in American industry?

On reflection, it should be clear that every organization of any appreciable size makes at least some use of all three approaches regardless of which is emphasized. The U.S. Postal Service, for instance, is known for its heavy use of bureaucratic HRM methods but still makes a limited use of such market mechanisms as merit raises and such clan mechanisms as sponsored athletic teams. The question, then, is not whether some mix is possible, but which approach can most suitably be emphasized under given conditions. The choice must take into consideration the importance of establishing a dynamic three-way fit between situational constraints, the firm's strategy regarding products, markets, and financial requirements, and the chosen HRM approach (see Figure 7-1).

Calculating the merits of the various possible fits between strategy, situational factors, and combinations of bureaucratic, market, and clan HRM systems is clearly a complex procedure. It helps to simplify the choice when we realize that certain paired combinations of approach have special merit. The combination of bureaucratic and market approaches is particularly relevant to situations where economies of scale are possible, where markets and technology are stable, and where prices are highly competitive. In such circumstances emphasis needs to be placed on efficiency, and the bureaucratic/market combination does just that. If a firm is competing in a highly complex and uncertain environment, and innovation and flexibility are the key success factors, the combination of clan and market approaches would be most likely to fit the need. Under business circumstances in which the essential resource is a steady and reliable work force, the combination of clan and bureaucratic methods would be most likely to create the needed quality of work life. Finally, if the firm's strategy and environment call for the simultaneous achievement of high efficiency, innovation, and quality of work life, some creative blend and overlap of all three approaches would be indicated.

The suggestion that all three approaches be given equal emphasis may seem like an impossibility, but analysis of the way rewards are sometimes determined will show how practical the simultaneous use of the three approaches can be. The construction of a reward system can begin with the customary base of job descriptions that are evaluated relative to one another to determine basic pay levels (a bureaucratic method). These basic pay levels can then be supplemented by merit increases determined in terms of sustained levels of individual perform-

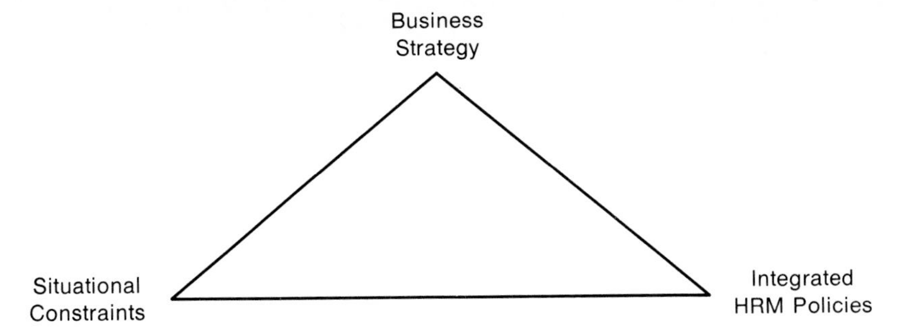


**FIGURE 7-1 An Integrated Approach to HRM**

ance (a market method). Finally, an overall profit sharing or another type of gain-sharing bonus based on total organizational performance can be added (a clan method). Combining all three approaches is not always so easy, of course; in fact, in some instances the respective methods are clearly incompatible so that a choice must be made. For example, a firm cannot possibly reconcile the long-term employment practices of a clan system with the in-and-out employment practices of a fully developed market system for the same employees. Making a choice is inevitable. One useful way to analyze the upcoming Hewlett-Packard case is to sort its HRM practices into the matrix shown in Figure 7-1 to discover which of the three approaches the company emphasized and to what extent it was able to use all three.

The interest in seeking ways to emphasize all three HRM approaches is no accident. In today's competitive world more and more firms are finding it essential to be leaders in efficiency, innovation, and quality of work life. Being leaders in one or two areas is often not quite enough. For instance, if United States Steel wants to compete with its Japanese counterparts, can they neglect any of these three areas of performance? A company is also motivated to find ways to combine all three approaches by the different attractions these approaches have to employees. If the HRM strategy calls for getting employees as involved as possible in the affairs of the business, why not use all the ways of doing it? From the employee's standpoint the biggest appeal of the bureaucratic approach is the promise of equitable treatment. For the clan approach it is the appeal of membership and personal caring. For the market approach it is the appeal of being rewarded in a realistic, supply-and-demand manner for one's own contributions. This combination of organizational and individual payoffs is shown in Figure 7-2.

It must also be acknowledged that each of the three approaches is prone to certain abuses. In fact, the possible abuses inherent to each approach and the capacity of the other approaches to counteract them add a final reason for the attractiveness of the threefold combination.

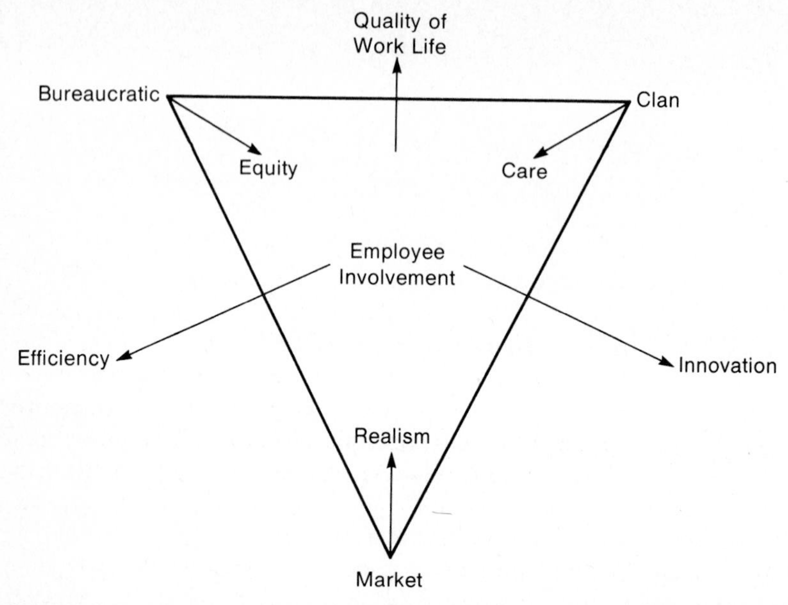


**FIGURE 7–2 Organizational and Individual Payoffs of HRM Strategies**

The clan approach, for instance, carries the hazard of becoming paternalistic; market realism can help correct this tendency. It is almost certainly a mistake for any company to promise explicitly or even infer that it can deliver lifetime job security. Since business uncertainties will almost certainly force some degree of employment fluctuation, HRM policies should provide for these contingencies. Companies cannot and should not try to shield people entirely from economic realities. Clan practices also carry the hazard of breeding favoritism; the due process provided by bureaucratic procedures can counteract this tendency. Market mechanisms, while they promise needed realism, can by themselves be harsh and also unfair to employees. The addition of the caring associated with the clan method can take into account hardship cases—for instance, during a layoff period—even as the due process associated with bureaucratic procedures can assure fair use of rules such as seniority. An exclusive use of bureaucratic methods is prone to the simultaneous hazards of being totally impersonal and being overly expensive. The former problem can be softened by the caring spirit of the clan, while the excessive red tape characterizing the latter problem can be disciplined by the pressure of market mechanisms. Getting the best from all three approaches is by no means automatic, however; it will always take skillful management to achieve these multiple outcomes.

## ONE CULTURE OR TWO CULTURES

An important question which is becoming increasingly critical in U.S. industry remains: can one set of HRM practices serve all types of employees or should different systems be used for different groups, especially for the exempt and nonexempt? Ever since the industrial revolution became well established, the split between the organizational worlds of the managers and the managed has been pointed out by political commentators, social scientists, novelists, and even the writers of folk songs. The distinction has been expressed in many ways: thinkers and doers, capitalists and proletarian workers, skilled and unskilled employees, master and servant. In many large organizations this division of labor has evolved into two ways of life, two different work cultures, which are typically adversarial. We submit that it is no exaggeration to refer to both sides of this split as being work cultures. Local culture has often evolved in the sense of embodying beliefs and rituals that reinforce complex friendship networks. A richness of association has grown out of shared adversities and pleasures that are reinforced by language and custom. The terms and symbols of the crafts or trades of those who work with their hands are rich in meaning; as are also the terms of the professional manager. But in many organizations these cultures have been polarized. Although many say that this split is unavoidable in large organizations of any kind and in any known political system, firms like Hewlett-Packard come close to being a one-culture work system characterized by a mutuality of interests and association throughout the work force. Many of these one-culture firms are not only economically viable but outstandingly successful and—whether American, Japanese, or whatever—are making life very difficult for their competitors. This new well-documented phenomenon of the successful competitive pressure generated by one-culture organizations is receiving more and more attention throughout the business world.

While the competitive pressure from one-culture, high-commitment firms is the primary stimulus to questioning traditional adversarial systems, several other important developments push in the same direction. Low-cost, high-performance microprocessors are now making the long-awaited automated factory at least a partial reality; in fact, industry's entire tool box is rapidly changing as this technology plays out its present potential. The impact on jobs is usually to minimize the importance of motor dexterity and to increase cognitive requirements, so that operators' jobs can frequently be redesigned to include certain managerial responsibilities. These increased mental requirements may combine with the generally higher educational achievements of the new work force to break down the sharp distinction between manager and managed. Meanwhile, as has been widely noted in the press, the traditional distinction between owner and wage earners is eroding as the latter group, through their pension funds, own an ever-larger share of the total industrial equity. The reduced birth rate in the United States also signals that before too long we will need to run industry with a relatively smaller work force or else delay retirement significantly. Finally, the evidence compiled by those who analyze our value systems indicates that Americans at all levels increasingly expect to influence their workplace in some meaningful way. Although all of these factors are converging to break down the time-honored distinction between manager and worker, counterforces to such basic change are equally in evidence.

Federal legislation is a pervasive, although unintentional, reinforcement to the adversarial, two-culture system. For instance, federal wage and hour legislation, which was passed to protect working people from being pressured into working long unpaid hours, establishes the distinction between exempt and nonexempt employees (note the puzzling, double-negative term). Although this law had no part in the original rise of the adversarial work system, it has inadvertently become an unnecessary and stubborn force perpetuating the two-culture system. Business firms are virtually required to keep two sets of records on their employees and to have two sets of ground rules governing employment; often they wind up having two separate personnel departments. The law started a causal chain that has, in a multitude of subtle and not-so-subtle ways, strengthened the wall that divides the two cultures. The federal labor laws legitimating collective bargaining have had a similar unintended consequence. Although the intent was to outlaw phony "company" unions, the laws have sometimes been interpreted to preclude management's being able to encourage workers to participate in the organizational decision process. We suggest that such unintentional side effects might suitably be addressed by fresh legislation.

Many historical reasons have also contributed to the prevalence of the adversarial or two-culture system. Americans, while priding themselves on a relatively classless society, have, in fact, perpetuated a diminished version of the class system they inherited from their European ancestors. To the extent that this class system persists, it is likely to be reflected in industrial hierarchies. Although the beginning of the industrial revolution has aptly been described as a replacement of muscle energy with hydrocarbon energy, human hand and motor skills were still essential for manipulating physical objects. Such work first appeared in quantity in the early textile mills and is seen today in all forms of assembly work. Until these jobs can be automated, industry needs employees who are virtually willing to check their brains at the door; clearly technologies based on this need both create and perpetuate two-culture systems. Industry's response to the growth of higher education also perpetuates and strengthens the two-culture system. When college education was for the few, industries invented special points of entry and special promotion ladders for their college-trained recruits. As the number of college graduates going into industrial organizations grew, the gap between the two cultures grew correspondingly. Educational differences have tended severely to limit the chances of promotion for the noncollege worker, giving college-trained middle managers a vested interest in maintaining the status quo. Middle managers, in fact, not only defended but even invented distinctions and perquisites to separate them further from the nonexempts. Support for the growth of unions was built on the backlog of workers' repressed anger and resentment. Collective bargaining with its periodic and often bitter strikes has institutionalized the adversarial relationship between management and labor. Although the collective contract started out as a market-like mechanism, as it accumulated more and more work-rule clauses it evolved into a strongly bureaucratic mechanism and a frequent bulwark of the two-culture work system. Finally, the rather recent growth of large investment institutions backed by high-speed information systems has pushed industrial managers toward a focus on short-term profits and the related view of seeing employees as variable costs. The consequent tendency for managers to turn quickly to the layoff of nonexempt workers in response to a dip in the economy is also a compelling reinforcement of the two-culture system.

In its extreme form, the two-culture work system consists of a management group governed by HRM practices that emphasize clan methods, facing off against a separate population of nonexempts governed by a heavily bureaucratic set of HRM policies. Because many firms that have followed this course are now in serious competitive trouble, some have begun searching for ways to move toward a one-culture work system and a mutality of interests in order to involve all employees with the company's competitive problems.

By way of contrast, Hewlett-Packard represents a company that was founded upon an explicit set of HRM beliefs, which have successfully guided corporate strategy and policies toward the goal of creating a one-culture company. It is hard to say whether the founders' desire to live by certain HRM beliefs, including the expectation of long-term employment, dictated their choice of product/market/financial strategy or whether the chosen strategy dictated their choice of HRM policies; probably influence flowed both ways. In any case, the two elements clearly dovetail advantageously. Certainly the founders knew what kind of employment relationship they wanted, visualizing their employees as involved, enthusiastic, and creative. Their HRM practices accordingly emphasized clan methods fully supported by an extensive use of compatible market and bureaucratic methods. As a result, Hewlett-Packard has a strong record of continually reconciling the seeming opposites of innovation and efficiency and providing a quality of work life that is highly valued by most of its employees. It is not surprising that we should have chosen this firm as the leading example of an integrated HRM system: Hewlett-Packard subsequently tied with IBM in the *Fortune* poll for being the best-managed company in the United States, a fact that serves to confirm our choice. Our analysis of Hewlett-Packard also suggests that HRM practices must be initiated and nurtured by open expression of appropriate beliefs and values by top management. The Hewlett-Packard story simply does not make sense without acknowledging the importance of the two founders' values regarding their employees.

## TOP MANAGEMENT VALUES AND HRM

The values held by top-level management must, in fact, be considered a key factor in determining whether or not HRM policies and practices can and will be unified. No discussion of integrating an HRM system can be complete without considering these values and the way they are transmitted. The values of senior management, as expressed in words and deeds, either do or do not give employees a sense of confidence about the many different HRM practices. The degree to which management's respect for individual employees infuses HRM practices is especially crucial. Employees will not continue to be emotionally involved in the affairs of the business if their contributions are not respected by their managers. Similarly, employees cannot be expected to be actively committed to the organization if the organization does not show its commitment to them. The institutional commitment must be rooted in the sincerity and durability of the values of top management; managers who adopt expedient solutions at the expense of employees cannot expect employee commitment in return. Various contractual and institutional guarantees of due process are helpful, but they are by no means a substitute for senior management's belief in the importance of equity.

The values managers hold are revealed in many ways besides direct verbal expression. In fact, the old adage that actions speak louder than words applies incontrovertibly to the transmission of values. Earlier in this book we enumerated the three levels of analysis we proposed to use in examining our cases: organizational, individual, and societal; the predicted impact of proposed action was to be tested at all three levels. Managers who regularly analyze their options at all three levels are manifesting their concern and respect for every level even though trade-offs among all three levels will have to be made. Management values also come through in the style of day-to-day action. An example of this was apparent in the Office Technology case when the managerial style of Tim Everhart, for instance, raised questions in employees' minds about his commitment and respect in contrast to their reaction to the style of John Fortier. Certainly the established style of some of the more traditional plant managers in the General Motors case made it almost impossible for them to provide QWL leadership. We are not suggesting that only one style will work, however, for, as we have already seen, a variety of managerial styles have been compatible with building mutuality: in spite of highly contrasting styles, both St. Clair and Gobel successfully encouraged the growth of mutuality at Sedalia because the underlying similarity of their values came through in spite of their different styles.

We have discussed the major variables that influence the development of a consistent and integrated HRM system; we have considered the need for fitting HRM policies to both business strategy and situational constraints, we have indicated how a knowledge of the distinctions between bureaucratic, market, and clan approaches can help make HRM practice coherent in all four policy areas, and, finally, we have examined the critical role of management values. We would like now to consider how this all bears on the pressing issue many companies face in today's competitive environment of finding ways to work out of a traditional adversarial relationship between managers and the managed.

HRM policies are central to the question of whether adversarial two-culture relations are to be superseded by mutuality and a one-culture system. In Figure 7-2, which diagrams these elements, employee involvement is shown to be the critical linkage between HRM policies and the successful achievement of efficiency, innovation, and quality of work life. Although evidence supporting this hypothesis concerning the role of employee involvement is not yet conclusive, management in many companies is still sufficiently impressed by rapidly accumulating evidence to undertake serious and multifaceted steps to move from an adversarial relationship with the work force to a relationship of mutuality. Companies where this change is being effected find that the transition is difficult, but see it as essential all the same.

## CHANGING HRM POLICIES AND PRACTICES

A brief consideration of how companies change HRM practices in general and of how, in particular, they can bring about a change toward a one-culture system concludes our discussion of the integration of HRM policies. Most corporations change HRM policies and practices in response to crisis. When turnover among senior professionals in a professional service firm is high, for instance, it is easy enough to respond quickly by raising salaries and increasing bonuses. But such a move may increase cost without solving the problem, or may create problems of equity with another group of employees. It is still rare for a corporation to examine its human resource management policies and practices as a whole and to chart a course consistent with its long-term situational factors and business strategy, yet this is exactly what we are proposing.

Charting a new course is never easy, but the conceptual framework based on the four policy areas and the bureaucratic/market/clan approaches should make it possible for managers to think systematically about human resource management. The framework is a guide for the necessary analysis, conceptualization, and planning. There are two approaches to the problem of deliberately changing HRM practices: one we call the situational approach, the other the normative approach. Both should be used in parallel.

The *situational approach* (sometimes called environmental scanning) charts future trends. Companies such as Exxon and General Electric typically start their HRM planning by asking a number of questions: What is our long-range strategy and what are its implications for our human resource needs? When we recruit, what skills and what values will we find among prospective employees? How will demographic and educational trends affect labor markets? What changes in ideology, culture, and society's expectations can we anticipate and how might they affect government legislation and the expectations of individual employees as well as of the community? What changes in the role and attitudes of the unions can we expect?

Having grappled, however imperfectly, with these general questions, these firms next address questions centering on HRM policies: How might these possible environmental trends affect us in each of the four major policy areas? If we were to retain our current policies, what would happen to HRM outcomes as perceived by management, employees, and society? If we are dissatisfied with these predicted outcomes, what policies do we need to reformulate? Should we put more emphasis on one or another of the bureaucratic, market, and clan approaches?

The situational approach to HRM planning goes from the outside in; it analyzes given and projected situational factors and fits HRM policies and practices to them. The *normative approach* asks different questions; it works from the inside out. What are our values and beliefs about people at work? What needs and expectations do they share in common? What do we know about the conditions under which people become committed, develop competence, and show a coincidence of interest with the organization? What do our answers to these questions imply for our choice of particular HRM practices in each of the four policy areas?

The importance of top management values in shaping a one-culture company, in communicating to all employees the principles that should shape day-to-day decisions and interventions, has led a number of companies who have not had one-culture values or have not articulated them clearly to do so. Such a process, sometimes aided by outside consultants, typically begins with the chief executive officer examining his or her own values. He or she might then involve other top executives in this process by asking them to define their own management values and inviting them to attend a series of meetings where similarities and differences in these values are discussed. When a consensus emerges, a statement of values is communicated widely throughout the organization by means of the company newspaper, speeches, and perhaps videotaped statements. Moreover, examples of plants and managers that are developing organizations which reflect these values can also be widely publicized and held up as examples of the values management wishes others to adopt.

Such a formal process of value definition and communications will have to be undertaken by companies that do not have one culture and whose top management has not previously articulated these values. Of course, the process itself informs the top managers of the company about their own values and how well they will fit with one-culture values, a necessary step for adapting or exiting from the firm to take place over time. Such a value definition process requires a CEO who believes in the one-culture idea and is willing to lead. As Chester Barnard has said, the task of leadership is essentially one of shaping values.

The situational and normative approaches to HRM policy formulation each have advantages and disadvantages. The normative approach has the advantage of assuring greater internal consistency between HRM policies over a long period (20 to 30 years). As the situation changes, efforts to adapt HRM policies to new realities are usually made in a way that is consistent with the existing philosophy. The disadvantages of the normative approach, as with any general belief, are that it may not fit all employee groups or all situations. A normative approach can be too rigid, generating policies which are outdated by changes in the environment. Depending on its philosophical foundation, the normative approach can be either overly optimistic and naive or overly pessimistic and cynical. If the philosophy is optimistic, it tends to raise employee expectations beyond the organization's capacity to fulfill them. If it is overly pessimistic, it tends to dampen employee motivation and capacity to develop.

The disadvantages of the normative approach are the advantages of the situational approach: reality-based, pragmatic policies can be fit to each group and to any situation. However, the very flexibility of the situational approach makes it more difficult for employees to develop a stable, long-lasting identification with the organization. Likewise, the approach is significantly dependent on an accurate reading by managers of just what the situational reality is. A reading that fails to correspond in some important way to the reading of various stakeholders can seriously undermine the trust of managers, erode the commitment to organizational goals, and replace congruence with costly conflict.

Clearly, it is wise for managers to apply both situational and normative thinking to HRM policy formulation if the interests of both pragmatism and idealism are to be served. The tensions that often exist between the two are actually likely to strengthen the resulting HRM policies and practices. The situational approach to planning is, of course, keyed to the environmental constraints discussed above even as the normative approach is tied to top management values. Both approaches are needed for the creation of a model for future integrated HRM policies, and such a model is one of three requisites for effective implementation of HRM change.

The second factor in successful change is a negative one—discontent with the status quo. Without dissatisfaction with things as they are, it is unlikely that members of an organization will rally the energy needed to effect significant change. Important change always requires time and resources, and it will not happen if people are content with the current situation. Only serious problems triggered the drive for change at General Motors and at Bethoney. Even at Sedalia, St. Clair's normative perspective on change was reinforced by competitive pressures and the negative results of a long strike at the Beacon plant. At MEED the discontent stemmed from its inability to expand as fast as its market growth potential. Dissatisfaction seems always to be a necessary element in any meaningful change in HRM policies.

To be successful, any change must, moreover, move through a sequence of events and employ a variety of change mechanisms; these are the process factors of change. Different organizations select different policy areas as the initial locus of change. At Dana, for example, the Scanlon reward system was the first step toward a more complete change in the employment relationship. At General Motors the leading edge was their QWL employee influence mechanisms; at Sedalia it was the work system design; at Nippon it was their lifetime flow policy.

Each of these very different starting places was part of a more comprehensive process of change.

Skillful leaders are usually well aware of the potential power of models and symbols of change.

GM's Tarrytown and Livonia operations were used as tangible symbols of new possibilities for other GM plants. Sometimes a key individual, such as St. Clair, can symbolize the change. At Sedalia it was he who articulated the desirable future and gave people faith in its realization. Belief in the future always involves a subtle attention to the level of expectations. Expectations that are too high bring disillusionment; expectations that are set too low fail to inspire the necessary energy. In other words, for leaders to be successful in effecting change, they must paint a realistic picture of the considerable time, resources, and commitment involved but they must also describe an exciting picture of the possible future.

The process of change also requires the right mix of skills and competencies. In the examples in this book of successful cases of change, education often plays a crucial role in the acquisition of necessary skills. At times people must also be replaced to get the right skills into key organizational positions; this question arose as regards the plant manager in Highland Products and some of the plant managers in General Motors. In addition to having appropriate skills, key leaders need both the consistent values and the courage that must underlie every significant change.

In conclusion we would like to say that as we review the current scene in human resource management, we are struck by the many opportunities for significantly improving existing conditions. Existing HRM practice is all too frequently a hodge-podge of policies based on little more than outmoded habits, current fads, patched-up responses to former crises, and pet ideas of specialists. HRM practice urgently needs to be reformed from the perspective of general management. HRM issues are much too important to be left largely to specialists. A company's policies and practices in this area (whether, for example, they are pursuing the traditional adversarial employment relationship or attempting to move toward greater mutuality), can make the difference between success and bankruptcy.

We believe that fundamental forces are moving organizations toward the increasing involvement of all employees in the important affairs of the enterprise. We cannot be sure about the immediate future of this trend: near-term changes in the economy, in popular ideas, and in the political climate could speed up or even reverse it. In the long run, however, we believe this movement is the best hope for achieving a better reconciliation of the needs of the organization with the needs of the individual and of the broader society.

## NOTES

1. This approach is based on a framework suggested by William G. Ouchi, "Markets, Bureaucracies, and Clans," *Administrative Science Quarterly* 25 (March 1980), pp. 129–141.
2. C. I. Barnard, *The Functions of the Executive* (Cambridge, Mass.: Harvard University Press, 1938); H. A. Simon, *Administrative Behavior*, 2d ed. (New York: Free Press, 1957); Harry Levinson et al., *Men, Management, and Mental Health* (Cambridge, Mass.: Harvard University Press, 1966).

CASE 28

# GENERAL MOTORS AND THE UNITED AUTO WORKERS (CONDENSED)

*Bert Spector*
*Paul Lawrence*

> Before explaining what our Quality of Work Life (QWL) program at General Motors is, let me explain what it *isn't*. It is not a job enrichment program, because that usually means something that is engineered or imposed unilaterally upon job holders. It is *not* a productivity gimmick. We are not talking about working more or harder for the same pay, eliminating jobs, weakening the union's role in representing the interests of the worker, or, for that matter, giving either party to the collective bargaining process another "bargaining chip" to use in its adversarial relationship. At the same time, it is *not* a loss in management prerogatives. Experience shows us that QWL allows both management and those who are managed to achieve new influence.
>
> —*Howard C. Carlson, Director QWL Research and Administration Organizational R&D Department, General Motors*

QWL was defined by GM as a process for improving the utilization of human resources, developing in all members of the organization an awareness and understanding of the concerns and needs of others together with a willingness to be more responsive to those concerns and needs, and improving the long-term effectiveness and success of the corporation. But one of the most important and unique aspects of QWL at GM was the joint union-management commitment to the program. Although GM began experimenting with job improvement programs in the late 1960s, it was not until a 1973 letter of understanding between GM and the United Automobile Workers (UAW) that the program ceased to be one unilaterally imposed by management and became—from the national level down to the local plants—a truly cooperative effort.

The sagging fortunes of the auto industry, in the face of the continuing energy crises of the 1970s, added fuel to the commitment by GM and UAW officials to use the QWL banner as a way of turning the corporation into both a better place to work and a more efficient competitor in the world auto market.

---

UAW suspicions that some executives within GM saw QWL as a means of enticing workers in newly built plants away from the union presented a major obstacle to continued cooperation. That potentially divisive issue had to be faced and overcome before GM management and the UAW could again combine their talents and energies to help the company and its employees face the major challenge of the 1980s: the need for a dramatic and, from the point of view of the work force, disruptive increase in the use of automation as a means of meeting new competition.

## JOB IMPROVEMENT: GM'S UNILATERAL INITIATIVES

By the early 1970s, GM management could not fail to recognize signs of growing dissatisfaction within its work force. Despite a record level of profits in 1971, income as a percentage of sales was off considerably. From the 10 percent level achieved by GM during the 1960s, income had slumped to 6.8 percent of sales by 1971. (For an overview of GM's financial performance for the years 1965 to 1979, see Exhibit 28-1.) Many in the corporation felt that the problem was essentially one of job performance, and one of the most dramatic causes of that decline in performance, they insisted, was a tremendous increase in absenteeism. Between 1965 and 1969 unexcused absences had risen 50 percent, with the sharpest incline coming in 1969. On Mondays and Fridays, employees absent without excuse often reached 20 percent.

Sharp increases in turnover rates—up 72 percent between 1965 and 1969—provided further evidence of the deep dissatisfaction with which auto workers viewed their jobs. A local union president in 1970 explained: "Every single unskilled man in my plant wants out. They just don't like it. This whole generation has been taught by their fathers to avoid the production line, to go to college to escape, and now some of them are trapped. They can't face it. They hate to go in there."

Absenteeism and turnover were not the only indicators of trouble. The number of grievances rose 38 percent between 1965 and 1969, while disciplinary layoffs shot up 44 percent. Both in and out of the auto industry, the perception of increased dissatisfaction among assembly-line workers became known as the "blue-collar blues." At GM, the phenomenon attracted a more specific label: "the Lordstown syndrome."

### *The Lordstown Syndrome*

In late 1970, the General Motors Assembly Division (GMAD) redesigned a plant in Lordstown, Ohio, for the purpose of assembling

GM's entry into the compact car market: the Chevrolet Vega. Equipped with the most modern automation yet to be developed by the American auto industry, the Lordstown plant would operate at a line speed nearly twice that of conventional GMAD plants—100 cars per hour as opposed to between 55 and 60 at other plants. The average age of the 6,400 assemblyline workers was 23. After some initial months of smooth sailing, the plant began to develop major problems. Absenteeism climbed to 7 percent. Workers complained bitterly of harsh discipline and company speedups. Quickly, Lordstown became a battleground between the young workers and GMAD, with walkouts and strikes seriously undermining the corporation's high hopes for maximum production.

Dissatisfaction over working conditions, called the Lordstown syndrome in the press, soon became apparent in GMAD plants like Norwood, Ohio, and St. Louis, Missouri. GM executives insisted that the press was seriously misreading the distress. There were other plants with work forces younger than Lordstown that did not suffer the same turmoil. Management also insisted that the disputes, when they did occur, were really traditional union-management fights over working conditions. In any event, the phenomenon forced corporate executives to look at their assembly-line workers, particularly the younger ones.[1] They were better educated than their older companions on the line and often sported long hair, sandals, and beads as a symbolic display of their affiliation with the antiauthoritarian counterculture of the 1960s.

To some extent, at least, these new workers were seriously questioning the American work ethic. The notion of working hard and performing well out of a sense of duty, as well as a desire for maximum material gain, no longer seemed to motivate younger workers.

The phenomenon of blue-collar blues was by no means isolated in a few midwestern plants—it was recognized as being widespread. Neither was it the exclusive domain of young, white workers. Older workers felt alienated, frustrated, and bored by their repetitious and fragmented tasks. The civil rights movement of the 1960s served to sensitize black factory workers to the racism inherent in many supervisory practices; and black workers joined young white workers in rebelling against the strict authority of plant life.

### *GM's Response*

Some top GM executives reacted to the Lordstown syndrome not with sympathy for the plight of the blue-collar workers, but with ex-

[1]GM conducted its own job-satisfaction survey at the time and found that younger workers (under age 35) did express lower job satisfaction. The more critical finding was that job satisfaction was significantly shaped by the match between job expectations and job realities, irrespective of age.

pressions of disappointment that their workers were so ungrateful. "Management and the public have lately been shortchanged," complained GM chairman James Roche in 1970. "We have a right to more than we are receiving." With an investment by GM of $24,000 per hourly worker in 1969 (as compared with $5,000 in 1950) and an average weekly wage of $134.60, Earl Bramblett, vice president for personnel, insisted that absenteeism resulted from affluence and abundance rather than boredom and frustration. It was time for young workers to show more appreciation for what they had.

Upon taking over as chairman in 1972, Richard C. Gerstenberg summarized GM's defensive posture in a speech to the Tax Foundation:

> So the current wave of concern for the automobile worker may not be fully warranted when we consider that the builders of our cars earn more than the teachers of our children. The American automobile worker is paid for 14 percent more hours than he works and for up to a year when laid off; he is paid more for not working than most people when they are. As I said, by way of any standard, his work place is a good place to work. And he can, if he chooses, draw from his labor the personal satisfaction of being part of an industry which contributes to the well-being of almost every American.

Absenteeism and other performance problems were symptoms of deeper trouble, insisted Delmar "Dutch" Landen, Ph.D. in psychology and director of GM's Organizational Research and Development (OR&D) Department. "For too long," he said in 1970, "the auto industry has assumed economic man was served if the pay was OK." But other satisfactions were required, and not prizes like the monogrammed glasses one GM plant gave away for good attendance. "One thing is for sure," observed Landen of that particular gimmick. "If they won't come in for $32.40 a day, they won't come in for monogrammed glasses."

Landen's call for greater participation by employees at all levels of the organization received important corporate support from Joe Godfrey, vice president at GMAD; Richard Terrell, executive vice president; and even Gerstenberg himself. And that support provided the basis for GM's early ventures into the area of what would eventually be called quality of work life.

The first step had actually been taken in 1968. GM President Edward Cole, who met regularly in a discussion group that included Ren Likert, founder of the University of Michigan's Institute of Social Research (ISR), raised the question of what GM might do to reduce the possibility of a strike in 1970. Likert suggested that the ISR would be willing to work with Landen and his OR&D staff to develop some sort of a pilot project designed to increase job satisfaction. The result was a survey of 5,000 workers—both hourly and salaried—in four pilot plants to determine their attitudes toward their jobs and the corporation.

The GM—ISR project suggested that employees at all levels felt they had something to contribute to the management of their plants and believed they should be given more of an opportunity to participate. It also indicated a clear relationship between plant performance and how employees felt about organizational climate, quality of management, and employee-management relations.

A major step toward implementing the lessons learned from the ISR survey came in 1971 when GM split its personnel staff into separate labor relations and personnel staffs. That move was designed to free the director of personnel from the traditional, often adversarial role of chief labor negotiator, and allow him to concentrate his efforts on achieving improved working conditions through cooperative rather than combative methods. As vice president for newly designed personnel administrative and development functions, GM went outside the corporation and hired Harvard Business School Professor Stephen H. Fuller. Shortly after his appointment Fuller said: "What we are doing is signaling as obviously and as frequently as we can the commitment of top management that it is interested in improving job satisfaction. We are trying to open the doors and give people an opportunity to share in improving the quality of what they do."

The stage was now set for GM to act on the findings of the GM—ISR survey and the calls of Landen and Fuller for improvement, openness, and participation in the realities of divisional and plant life. In one innovation, Frank Schotters (manager of GMAD's Lakewood, Georgia, plant) set up an extensive orientation program for new employees in 1970. First-line supervisors went through special leadership courses that encouraged a more open attitude in dealing with subordinates. The results were promising—grievances dropped by nearly 50 percent in two years. When the model change was made, workers were asked to help in rearranging the plant's work areas.

In 1971 the manager of GMAD's Tarrytown, New York, plant approached the officers of the UAW Local and proposed involving workers in helping in a major plant rearrangement. A 1972 experiment introduced the idea of team stall building into the GMAD Detroit Truck Plant. GMAD halted the experiment when an upturn in market demand led to a sharp increase in production. It was believed that the organizational design of the plant could not sustain such production demands.

Other improvement projects involved limited grants of minor power to workers. The Oldsmobile Division's engine plant used worker task forces to seek ways to reduce absenteeism. Another project involved bringing together employees from different functions to examine ways of improving quality and increasing the number of engine blocks produced per hour. In both instances, the task forces produced significant improvements. What had not been learned was that in order for the improvements to be sustained, an employee-involvement process had to be maintained. Shortly after the task forces were suspended, the performance returned to previous levels.

## JOINT UNION-MANAGEMENT EFFORTS

As of 1973, GM's project to improve job satisfaction and performance lacked two important elements: the name *Quality of Work Life*, and, more critically, the support and cooperation of the UAW. Without a joint commitment from union and management, the improvements would be a set of principles and policies imposed from above. Warned UAW Vice President Irving Bluestone, "Unless the union is involved as an equal partner, these programs amount to paternalism. Whatever management gives, management can take away."

### *Enter Irv Bluestone*

"I got wind of what GM was doing in what was then being called *Organizational Development* in 1968," said Irving Bluestone who, in 1970, became the UAW's director of the General Motors department, "so I started reading about job improvement myself."

"In 1970 we sat down with Irv Bluestone and his staff and began filling them in on what we were thinking," said Howard Carlson, director at QWL research and administration at GM. "We found out Irv was reading some of the same books we were."

The ascendancy of Bluestone to the head of the UAW's GM department marked another major watershed in the emergence of a joint commitment. Bluestone asserted that the UAW had been concerned with the quality of its members' work life since the 1930s. Unlike his counterparts at GM, Bluestone placed the matter of job satisfaction within the broader context of a push for industrial democracy. He meant not only the right to bargain collectively, but also the extent of influence and responsibilities workers have in the management of their work and the decisions of the enterprise. Collective bargaining, which resulted in material advantages and a level of job security, was the first necessary step toward the goal of industrial democracy. Challenging management's sole responsibility for prerogatives, Bluestone believed, was the second.

In his 1970 discussions with Howard Carlson, Bluestone suggested the phrase *Quality of Work Life* to replace *Organizational Development*. That change was symbolically significant, felt Carlson:

> When GM used the phrase *Organizational Development*, we scared people. Workers perceived OD as something "done" to them from above. "I've been OD'ed," they would joke. But when you're talking about QWL, you're talking about transferring skills and values to people. We spent a year and a half deciding whether or not to use the term QWL. But we eventually decided to use it because it aroused less suspicion among union people.

In the 1970 UAW-GM negotiations, which broke down and led to a 67-day strike, Bluestone first suggested the possibility of a joint union-management QWL committee. GM declined to participate. The whole notion of job improvement was still quite new within GM, and it was viewed with suspicion by traditional manufacturing and labor relations people. It was considered to be an unorthodox, even slightly dangerous program of the OD people, and Bluestone's suggestion was given little consideration.

### *The 1973 Joint Agreement and Its Aftermath*

The breakthrough agreement on QWL came in 1973 when Bluestone again asked for a joint commitment. GM's tradition-minded chief labor negotiator, George B. Morris, vice president for labor relations, saw QWL as a surrender of management powers. But job improvement programs were, by then, showing some real gains at places like Lakewood and Tarrytown. As a concession to both Bluestone and Stephen Fuller, Morris agreed to a letter of understanding with the UAW. In it, he recognized the "desirability of mutual effort to improve the quality of work life," and he agreed to a joint Committee to Improve the Quality of Work Life with responsibility for reviewing and evaluating all QWL programs. (See Exhibit 28-2 for the complete text of the letter.)

The committee was made up of four men—Morris and Fuller from GM, Bluestone and Don Ephlin from the UAW— and met only occasionally in the first years of its existence. The failure of the committee to pursue actively any QWL programs was due to the suspicion with which Morris viewed the notion of QWL. Fuller still represented a small minority within GM committed to QWL as a joint undertaking. Most other GM executives saw QWL either as a meaningless passing fad, or worse, as a surrender of power and authority to unions.

"I knew what was going on with George," said Bluestone, "but it didn't really bother me." He was determined to continue his work with Fuller, Landen, and local management and union officials to implement QWL programs wherever he could. In August 1975 the GM—UAW committee sponsored a one-day joint QWL seminar. The UAW was represented by 12 of its top executives, as was GM. The major focus of the meeting was on getting to know one another a little better and sharing some experiences about what QWL was all about, how it worked, and what it might help accomplish.

Because of the joint accord, as well as the GM–ISR survey and the early indications of success at several plants, there was growing interest within GM. Local initiative came from both local unions and management. At Tarrytown, for instance, the plant manager had approached union leaders, while at plants like New Departure–Hyatt Bearing (Bristol) and Fisher Body (Fleetwood), local union officials urged plant management to consider QWL programs. Together, plant managers and local officials would then invite in representatives from corporate headquarters and the UAW. Landen would assign someone from his staff to work as a team with either Bluestone or Bill Horner, Bluestone's administrative assistant, and with the local plant.

Both GM and the UAW carefully avoided imposing any set QWL package or program on the local plants. One of the first local joint efforts, in fact, would be to draft a definition of QWL for the individual plant (see Exhibit 28–3 for sample definitions of QWL from six GM plants). QWL was to be a broad, loosely defined goal that local management and unions would work toward based on their own understanding, ideas, needs, and mutually acceptable programs.

Even so, the efforts of GM and the UAW did follow a similar pattern. The representatives from GM and the UAW met first with top plant and union leadership in order to explain the aims of QWL, and, more importantly, to begin a process of building trust and respect. Horner explained:

> We tell them that they will have to start doing little things like being nice to each other on the plant floor. They should start talking to each other and try to settle their differences informally instead of through a grievance procedure. We also warn them that there will still be problems. After all, management is there to manage the plant, and we're there to represent the workers. So there'll be differences of opinion, maybe even strikes. But that doesn't mean you can't have trust and respect for each other. Now, this might be a slow process. Sometimes it takes a couple of months, sometimes a couple of years. But unless it's done, there's a good chance that QWL will fail.

Even though they agreed to meet with Bluestone and Horner, Local union leaders were often still suspicious of the QWL notion, particularly with its implication of cooperation with management. To overcome that typical reaction, Bluestone and Horner developed several techniques. They told committee members that QWL meant less hassles for the workers and fewer problems for them. If it succeeded, they would get the credit and enhance their chances of reelection. Often, the UAW would fly skeptical Local officials into Tarrytown, New York, to see what had been accomplished there.

One of the most frequently voiced concerns on the part of union leaders was that QWL would be used by management as a way of speeding up the assembly line or somehow getting more work for less costs. On that point, Bluestone was adamant. Whether talking to representatives from union or management, Bluestone forcefully rejected this view of QWL: "Let me repeat, if the first emphasis by any manager in the introduction and acceptance of a QWL program is, 'How do I reduce labor costs? How do I get more out of the workers?' there will be no QWL program. You can't count at that point on the workers' cooperation or the union's cooperation."

As for the fear that QWL would somehow sap the union of its strength and militancy, and be used by management to promote speedups and other violations of hard-fought collective bargaining agreements, Bluestone developed six guidelines that would govern all joint undertakings:

1. Management could not use QWL to support a speedup. Line speed was a matter to be decided in collective bargaining.
2. QWL could not be used to reduce manpower. That was not to say, however, that management could not cut manpower because of cyclical changes in the economy of the industry.
3. Management could not coerce workers to participate in QWL; it was strictly voluntary.
4. QWL could not be used to waive any agreements contained in the national or local contracts.
5. The elected union representatives had the right to be in on *any* discussion or meeting involving QWL.
6. If either party felt disadvantaged, it could get out at any time.

Bluestone and Horner preferred to keep those rules unwritten as a sign of trust; however, if a Local should insist that they be written—4 of the 84 participating Locals did insist—then GM supplied a written agreement. Now, Bluestone could ask the Local leaders, "If we adhere to those rules, what have we got to lose?"

Some Local union leaders supported QWL because working conditions at their plant were, in their view, so bad that any change would be an improvement. Others saw it as a chance to put the union in the vanguard of a movement to treat workers with new dignity and respect.

Said Ray Calore, president of Tarrytown's Local 664: "We, as a union, knew that our primary job was to protect the worker and improve his economic life. But times had changed and we began to realize we had a broader obligation, which was to help the workers become more involved in decisions affecting their own jobs, to get their ideas, and to help them improve the whole quality of life at work beyond the paycheck." In other instances, such as GMAD's final assembly plant in Framingham, Massachusetts, the adversarial relationship between union and management was so set that Local union leaders would not participate.

More typically, local union membership was divided on the notion of a joint QWL program. At Tarrytown, for instance, a group of workers described by Horner as "militant blacks from Harlem who had been disciplined many times and felt that no one cared about them," actually sought to sabotage the joint efforts. They volunteered for the joint planning committee with the intent of undercutting QWL. But six months of participation in the planning converted them, according to Horner, into true believers. At other times, Bluestone would address a letter to each and every Local member explaining the purpose of QWL.

Once both sides agreed to participate, they would establish a joint union–management QWL committee and appoint one individual from each side to act as a QWL facilitator. The facilitators, often with the help of national GM or UAW people or outside consultants, would set up and run QWL workshops and seminars that would emphasize the aims of QWL and the skills of communication, team building, and cooperation (see Exhibit 28–4 for a complete program of a three-day QWL workshop). Management mandated attendance for its personnel; the participation of hourly workers was left voluntary, but in most cases, participation ran between 90 and 99 percent. The workshops were kept small and divided into separate levels: top staff, first-line supervisors, assistant supervisors, and hourly workers each had their own workshops. The costs of pulling hundreds of workers off the line for 16 hours or 24 hours of workshops was absorbed in the local plant budget.

In most cases, management found their first-line supervisors to be the group most threatened by and antagonistic toward QWL. A one-day, off-site QWL session for assistant supervisors at a New Departures—Hyatt Bearing plant in Connecticut raised a fear found in many supervisors throughout GM: QWL meant capitulation to the union. New Departures's management QWL facilitator, Elizabeth Lynch, explained: "I wish I could tell you this was a complete success, but it wasn't. They came looking to see what management could gain up front from QWL in terms of increased productivity. For why else, they thought, would we be interested in participating? And they were concerned that the end result of all this would be a loss of their prerogatives."

In some cases, the workshops themselves seemed to encourage a new relationship between union and management. At Tarrytown, a plant with high absenteeism—usually around 7 percent—and unsettled grievances often numbering 3,000, the cooperative spirit generated by QWL seminars led to a markedly improved working environment. Tarrytown's production manager said: "From a strictly production point of view—efficiency and costs—this entire experience has been absolutely positive, and we can't begin to measure the savings that have taken place because of the hundreds of small problems that were solved on the shop floor before they accumulated into big problems."

Fisher Body's Fleetwood plant, a serious trouble spot, was turned around by QWL workshops coupled with a commitment to changing the overall managerial style. Encouraged by Al Warren, Fisher Body's head of personnel and a strong QWL supporter, and a new plant manager brought in by Warren, the plant put virtually all employees—management and hourly workers—through a two-day program. Jim Peltier, personnel director, said in late 1980:

> Absenteeism is down from 18 to 8 percent. We've hired an absenteeism counselor, and we hope to reduce the figure to 2 percent. Our costs used to run 134 percent of sales price; now we're in the black. Where we used to run 5,000 grievances on the docket, we now have 69, and not a single work-load grievance. Our quality audit was the worst in all of Fisher Body, and now we're number three. [In early 1981 the plant was rated number one.] And the union is really behind the effort. Jim Adams, who used to be Local 15's committeeman and a militant opponent of QWL, is now the union's QWL facilitator.

A more specific outcome of QWL workshops was increased participation by workers in decisions that had previously been the exclusive domain of management. At Chevrolet-Bay City, a plant with an exceptionally good reputation, worker participation encouraged by a commitment to QWL led to even better performance. In 1979 the plant prepared to begin manufacturing diesel-engine push rods. Jim Fowler, Bay City's general superintendent of manufacturing and engineering, drew up a cost estimate: a variable cost-per-piece of 29 cents, and an investment of $349,000 in new machinery and equipment changeover. Before the investment was made, however, the plant's joint QWL committee urged Fowler to meet with the employees who would actually be involved in the changeover. Fowler reported:

> Let me tell you what happened. One operator suggested that he could handle six cutoff machines instead of four by modifying our material handling system which simplified his job. Another operator stated that he

> could run *two* welders instead of one with a minor rearrangement. The jobsetter said that with the rebuilt equipment he could service this job along with his current assignment. Another operator noted that he could use a current welder for both service and the diesel rod, thus saving the purchase of new equipment. In addition, there were several other proposals to improve the efficiency of the operation. The final result of this effort is the elimination of any M&E investment and a piece-cost reduction of five cents. This cost reduction will result in a savings to the corporation of 16 cents per engine.

The variety of QWL experiments went well beyond those described here. By late 1980, GM reported that at least 84 of its 155 bargaining plants were involved in some sort of a joint QWL project. A few of those plants introduced the concept of quality circles used in Japan. A Grand Rapids plant convinced 100% of its employees to undergo training in transactional analysis ("I'm OK—You're OK"), while another plant encouraged transcendental meditation.

One of the overall positive outcomes of QWL, to which both management and union pointed with pride, was the increase in the number of plants that reached agreement on local contracts *prior* to a national settlement by GM and the UAW. In 1970, for instance, only two Locals and plants within the entire GM system came to an agreement prior to the termination of the national contract. But with QWL working to improve local union-management relations considerably, that number started to rise: 5 in 1973, 8 in 1976, and 54 in 1979. "I can't say that QWL by itself has led to those improved relationships," admitted Howard Carlson, "but it sure has helped. In fact, out of those 54 that settled early in 1979, 42 had joint QWL committees in place."

Another outcome that seemed to flow from QWL programs was a dramatic reduction in grievances and absenteeism. "When I started promoting QWL, I hoped, but didn't really know, that the number of unexcused absences would drop," admitted Bluestone. "What I did not expect was the dramatic drop in grievances." Buick's Plant 81 offered a prime example of that effect. After converting to a team operation in 1980, absenteeism fell from 9 to 0.7 percent and grievances virtually disappeared. "We haven't had a grievance there in two months," said an amazed union representative.

There have been occasional failures, especially when union and management would not agree to work together, and at least one dramatic case of backsliding. After Frank Schotters—Lakewood's plant manager and a strong QWL supporter—left Georgia for corporate headquarters, the efforts that had begun in 1970 disintegrated. The new plant manager was not supportive of QWL, and the pro-QWL union officers were defeated by an openly anti-QWL slate. As of early

1981, Lakewood had become one of the worst-performing plants within GMAD.

### *Managing a Cooperative Effort*

In 1973 both Fuller and Bluestone represented a small group within their organizations committed to joint QWL programs. Each set out to overcome the deep mistrust and suspicions with which one side viewed the other. Fuller sought to build QWL support within corporate headquarters; Bluestone worked on the executive board of the UAW.

For their part, Fuller and his OR&D Department developed three major undertakings to spread the commitment to QWL throughout GM. Landen organized a national GM-QWL conference, first in 1975 and every year thereafter, to provide a platform for sharing information about QWL experiments. Representatives from divisions and plants would stand in front of their colleagues and report on their progress in improving the quality of working life. Howard Carlson said: "Meetings of this kind are very powerful prods to action. There's nothing like some old salt who's been with the company for years standing up in front of his peers and telling them that he's seen the light, that QWL works, and that they'd better get on the bandwagon. That does a lot more to boost QWL than anything our department could ever do."

Then, in 1976 Landen's department developed a QWL survey. Seeking UAW approval when it involved union members, GM instituted a policy of annual QWL surveys for the entire company. The new survey would provide a continual update of the attitudes of GM employees—salaried and hourly—to their work, supervisors, and employer.

Bluestone also found it necessary to build a base of support for union-management cooperation within the UAW's national headquarters at Solidarity House. When he first proposed the joint committee in 1970, he was virtually alone on the executive committee in believing that such an idea would be worth trying. To help build a base, Bluestone encouraged individual union officials to visit Tarrytown and see for themselves all that could be accomplished. Visitors to Tarrytown—like Jim Adams of Fisher Body's Fleetwood plant—often became converted after spending time there; but the process of converting large numbers was painstakingly slow. To overcome that, Bluestone arranged for a major conference to be held at Tarrytown in 1978. Dozens of union officials heard representatives from union locals and GMAD plant management testify to the effectiveness of QWL. Doubters could see the results firsthand by visiting the Tarrytown plant. "That meeting turned things around," said Bluestone. Whereas in 1970 he had been the only one of the 26-member committee to support QWL, by 1980 supporters made up a large majority of the board.

Each side, labor and management, credited the other for making the concept easier to sell. For his part, Bluestone went to some length to assure GM executives that the UAW would always recognize certain business principles: "I tell them, as I tell our members, that there are certain concepts of business that we recognize. Technical progress is inevitable and desirable; a better standard of living for all depends on increased productivity and expanded GNP; and the purpose of business is to make profits."

Fuller and Landen, for their part, took pains to assure the union that QWL was not just another gimmick to speed up the line or get people to work harder. Fuller said:

> I tell my people not to talk about improving efficiency, productivity, or profits when they are talking about QWL. Those may be interesting by-products, but they are not the main point. The union wouldn't accept QWL if we said they were. Besides, I sincerely believe that QWL is not a means to an end; it's an end in itself. It is morally right to involve people in the decision-making process, and it would be right even if it didn't lead to improved productivity, profits, and cost.

Bluestone agreed that Fuller's emphasis on the rightness rather than the utility of QWL made the notion easier to sell to union leaders and members.

### *1979 Negotiations: Threat to Cooperative Efforts*

Between 1972 and 1978 GM opened ten new plants in southern states. Although these plants represented a tiny fraction of GM's overall operation, they attracted a great deal of attention from union and management and threatened the fragile cooperative relationship that had built up between GM and the UAW. GM moved South, management insisted, because of the relatively less expensive costs of fuel and labor and the desire to gain added political clout in a region where GM's influence had been weak. The fact that most of these states were right-to-work states, and that GM fought against union representation, led UAW officials to fear another possible reason for moving South—the hope of running nonunion plants. In addition, the fact that all of these new plants had some type of QWL project raised the possibility that QWL might be used as an antiunion device. Said Bluestone: "I believed that GM was seeking a 'union-free' environment, not just in the South, but also in their new plants in the North. And I thought that GM was using QWL as part of that approach."

In a 1976 letter from management to the union, GM pledged to neither discourage nor encourage future UAW organizing efforts. Still, a major battle over representation erupted in 1979 at a new Oklahoma City plant designed for 2,000 employees to make GM's new X cars. Although GM officially stood clear of the representation campaign, the UAW organizer, Carlton Horner, felt that the fact that the plant was paying $2 to $3 an hour more than the best-paid production workers in the area, and that the work force would be divided into teams, was part of a strategy on the part of management to attract workers away from the union. Oklahoma City teams would, according to management, discuss and vote on job assignments, allot overtime, and report to a team adviser. Horner was unimpressed: "Team concept, team advisers. You can call it anything you like—it still smells. All they can really vote on is where to put their lunches and how many sheets of toilet paper they can get in one pull."

Although the Oklahoma City election resulted in a UAW victory, the UAW had succeeded in organizing only five of the ten new southern plants. If QWL programs were to be introduced into new plants, Bluestone felt the union needed some assurance from GM that such improvements would not be used to attract workers away from union representation. He decided to make his demand: "It was at the 1979 bargaining session that I decided to settle this thing once and for all. QWL was not going to be used to keep us out of new plants. I simply said to GM that I wasn't going to sign an agreement unless the company guaranteed us automatic recognition."

Facing the possibility of a companywide strike just prior to the new model changeover, GM agreed to allow a preferential transfer policy for unionized northern workers who wished to move into the new Southern plants, thus virtually assuring the UAW's victory in all ensuing representational elections.

## THE FUTURE OF QWL

Having settled potential battles over future representational fights, GM and the UAW looked forward to carrying their cooperative efforts into the 1980s. A major turning point in GM's commitment to QWL came in late 1979 when F. James McDonald, executive vice president for North American Automotive Operations, strongly encouraged every GM plant to undertake a QWL program based on five minimum standards:

1. Each GM plant must have a designated group within the plant to oversee the QWL process.
2. Each plant must have a statement of long-range objectives incorporating QWL along with other desirable business targets.
3. Each plant must carry out a regular QWL survey process.
4. Each plant must hold seminars and other activities to make their people more knowledgeable about QWL concepts and techniques.
5. Internal resources must be available to assist in implementing QWL projects.

"In all cases, specific approaches to QWL are optional," explained Fuller. "But as of 1979, quality of work life improvement is mandatory."

Reinforcement of GM's strong commitment came in 1980. GM's Executive Conference on QWL, involving over 350 GM executives from all over the world, included Bluestone of the UAW as one of its main speakers. To have a union officer sharing the dais with GM's newly installed officers—among them, new president James McDonald—sent the QWL message throughout the organization.

That same year, GM gave further signs of corporate commitment to QWL. Al Warren, former personnel director at Fisher Body and a man described by Bluestone as "a QWL supporter from the beginning," took over the labor relations department from George Morris. "That was a signal up and down the system," said Fuller of Warren's appointment, "QWL is here to stay."

Yet another example of that commitment was the expansion of GM efforts to support QWL concepts through supervisory and managerial training. Starting in 1975, an annual corporatewide training program was established and promulgated to improve the skills, knowledge, and attitudes of the supervisors and managers of hourly and salaried employees. In addition, in 1980, all newly appointed supervisors at the first three levels of management were required to attend a five-day, regional training program within six months of their appointment. Therefore, each program had representation from a variety of divisions and plants and the participants were taught GM corporate policies, systems, and values which were now officially QWL values.

### *Livonia: A Bold Step*

The most ambitious QWL program proposals came with GM's decision in 1980 to open a new Cadillac plant in Livonia, just outside of

Detroit. Scheduled to begin operations in June 1981, Livonia had the capacity for 2,000 workers to produce 200 bodies an hour. In 1980 Bluestone met with the leadership of Local 22 (from Cadillac's main Detroit plant) to encourage them to participate with management in some type of QWL program. The assigned Cadillac management team created a 12-person planning committee including four representatives of the Local.

The committee suggested for Livonia the increasingly familiar signs of a QWL plant—no executive cafeteria or parking spaces, management in open-collar shirts rather than coats and ties—but much more was planned. "This could be the most innovative social system going," said the plant's designated superintendent of manufacturing. "If the committee's plan is approved, all hourly workers will be part of a 15-person business team organized around a product line (like a block line) or a function (like an assembly line). Each team will be involved not only in production but also quality control and material handling, and will be responsible for daily job placement and rotation, housekeeping, safety, and the coordination of the 'pay-for-knowledge' compensation system."

The proposed compensation system proved to be the most controversial and troubling aspect to the union representatives on the committee. The plan finally suggested by the committee called for the abandonment of the traditional multilevel job classification system in favor of a single classification for each team. Team members would be brought in at the bottom of the classification, placed in the middle after demonstrating mastery of half the various tasks assigned to the team, and advanced to the top when all the tasks were mastered. Since all Livonia workers were to be transferred in from other Cadillac plants, this could mean a cut in wages for some highly classified workers until they mastered the assigned tasks. The planning committee felt a single classification for a team was necessary if a cooperative team spirit was to be built. The safety-valve feature of the pay-for-knowledge system would be that either side—union or management—could, with 30 days' notice, veto the system in favor of the traditional classifications.

The planning committee at Livonia also attempted to redefine the role of the traditional first-line supervisor. That individual, they agreed, was the key to a successful team. Now called a team coordinator, he or she would sit in on all team meetings (one hour a week during work), share information with the team, and work with an assistant coordinator—an hourly worker from the team elected by the team—to solve any team problems. In order to give that team coordinator maximum flexibility, the traditional level of general foreman would be abolished in all but a few functional areas of the plant.

Livonia was in the unique position of being a new plant starting

QWL from the beginning. Because virtually all employees—salaried and hourly—would be transferred from other plants, the planning committee proposed an unusually rigorous screening process. Foremen or general foremen from any Cadillac plant interested in working at Livonia would participate in a two-day training program prior to making an application. If they were still interested, they would go through an assessment center to determine their suitability for the newly defined foreman's role. Hourly workers interested in transferring would go through two days of orientation before applying. Selections would then be made from the pool of interested workers on the basis of seniority.

Once hiring decisions were made, all Livonia employees would go through another orientation program, for two hours, and then participate in a one-week, off-site, problem-solving seminar. At Livonia, employees would have the option *up front* of deciding whether or not to work in a team system; once there, they would all participate.

Both GM and the UAW had committed themselves to allowing local plants and unions to decide for themselves on the type and scope of their QWL program. But there were certain aspects of the Livonia plan that needed approval by top management in GM's Cadillac Division and by the GM department of the UAW. The most difficult decision that faced Cadillac was whether it could afford the expensive front-end orientation program suggested by Livonia's planning committee. The cost of the orientation program for hourly workers alone would run up to half a million dollars. Were the benefits gained from the extensive front-end screening process worth such costs? For the UAW, union officials had to decide whether or not to allow what amounted to a change in the national contract agreement on compensation, since Livonia was proposing the abandonment of the traditional multiclassification compensation system. Thus, both GM and the UAW needed to determine whether or not to allow their local plant and union officials to undertake what Livonia's plant manager called GM's "most innovative social program" to date.

### *Potential Problem Areas*

In early 1981 the future of QWL at GM was still not absolutely assured. There were still several potential problem areas that could lead to a breakdown in cooperative efforts.

GM COMMITMENT. The majority of executives in GM, from the president down to plant managers, saw QWL as a means of increasing the competitive strength of the corporation. Top management people knew not to present their support of QWL to unions with an emphasis on increased productivity, but the message had not filtered down to all plant managers. There were still managers who saw QWL entirely as a productivity program, and if they presented it as such to the union, the program in all likelihood would never get started.

ECONOMIC AND COMPETITIVE PRESSURES. GM's worst year in almost five decades proved to be 1980, with the company reporting a loss for the first time since 1921. Would the economic downturn force GM executives to reevaluate their commitment to QWL, particularly the costs involved in training programs? Spokesmen for union and management insisted it would not. "If anything, the demand for QWL is up," said Howard Carlson. "People want better performance so the industry can survive, and QWL is a way of achieving that." Bill Horner agreed:

> Overall, the commitment to QWL at GM is stronger rather than weaker. It's true that they've cut back from three-day training programs to two-day programs. Also, more QWL seminars are now being held in factories rather than offsite. But I think that's a better idea, anyway.

There was little question that the sluggish auto market had some impact on future wage settlements. In February 1981 UAW's Chrysler workers ratified a $622 million cut in wages and benefits. Union officials quickly warned GM that this concession would not set a precedent for future negotiations.

In early 1981, most GM executives agreed, the American automobile industry was in a "shake-up situation."[2] GM was no longer the cost leader among the world's automobile manufacturers. Japanese companies, for instance, enjoyed a net cost advantage of anywhere from $1,000 to $1,700 per car brought into the United States over U.S. manufacturers. A report by the Department of Transportation suggested three reasons for that advantage:

1. **Lower Wage Rates.** As of mid-1980 the average hourly compensation for U.S. automobile workers was $15, as compared to about $7 for Japanese workers. (When considering the dollar's decline against the yen, the comparable Japanese wage rate would be even greater ($8.27 in 1982).[3]

[2]Special thanks to Mark Fuller, senior research associate, Harvard Business School, for providing information for this section.

[3]In late 1980, New England's UAW director Ted Barrett visited Japan to study its auto industry. Upon his return, he cautioned that a strict hourly wage comparison between the auto makers of the two countries could be misleading, "Their hourly rate is far below ours, but they enjoy many benefits American workers do not." Among those benefits he mentioned were company-purchased work clothes, subsidized groceries from company-owned stores, medical benefits, generous bonuses often amounting to one-third of yearly wages, retirement bonus at age 55, interest-free loans from companies to purchase homes, and company-owned apartments or dorms with low rents.

2. **Fewer Man-hours per Vehicle.** The Japanese automobile industry seems to have the advantage over U.S. companies in such efficiency-improving areas as quality control, lower unscheduled absenteeism, and the use of robotics.
3. **Quality.** Whether accurate or not, surveys indicate that American consumers perceive foreign-made cars as being of higher quality than domestically manufactured ones, and they express a higher level of satisfaction with those foreign-made cars.

"What we're talking about," said one executive, "is survival." That competitive pressure was echoed on the plant level where plant managers were under intense pressures to produce, and produce right away. An executive in the OR&D Department said:

> We say we absolutely need managers now who have a broad background, who know not just manufacturing but how to work with and get along with people. Steve Fuller has said over and over that there is no room in GM for plant managers not committed fully to QWL. But under the pressure of competition, you have to ask when you open a new plant: do you bring in a manager who has been successful elsewhere, but who maintains the old values and beliefs? That would run contrary to our philosophy, of course, but it does happen. That's what happened when we opened a plant in Oklahoma City. There is a lot of pressure to start producing right away.

AUTOMATION AND ROBOTICS. A large part of the competitive edge enjoyed by non-American manufacturers that were able to hold down unit costs came directly from the use of automation, specifically robotics.[4] Explained one GM executive: "There's a plant in Japan where 65 people, together with robots, build a new car body. Fiat-Strada is built entirely by robots. We've got to compete with that. We're going to have to change Buick, Pontiac, Oldsmobile. Build whole new plants. This is all going to be done by 1984."

In 1980 Japan averaged 45 cars per employee per year, compared with a GM average of 12 to 20 cars per employee per year. Even more startling a contrast, however, was provided by Nissan's Zama plant where 96 percent of the approximately 3,000 welds on a car were done by robots. At that plant 6,500 workers averaged 67 cars per employee per year. Across Zama's five assembly lines, 74 of the 86 welding stations were automated, using only 24 employees. The automated body shop turned out 450 bodies per shift, or one every 64 seconds.

[4]The data in this section are largely taken from Keith Joseph Krach, "Utilization of Robotics in the Japanese and U.S. Auto Industry" (unpublished), 1980.

Through the 1970s the UAW took the position that robotics represented no real threat to their jobs. ''They replaced the lousiest jobs,'' said an international service representative from the UAW, ''that nobody wants anyway.''

But GM hoped to vastly expand its use of robots, projecting the use of over 5,000 by 1985. ''The quality of our product will depend on technology and a few highly skilled technicians who back up that technology,'' said one executive. ''The quality of work life for semiskilled workers may become less important. They may also lose their jobs.'' ''We're talking about displacing maybe a quarter of our work force,'' said another executive. ''How long will our friends in the UAW cooperate with us over QWL after we tell them that?''

Union representatives were still taking a philosophical view of the invasion of the robots. ''As always, automation and displacement of workers will be a matter for collective bargaining and not affect QWL,'' said Bluestone. ''Even if it does lead to layoffs, that's better than laying off the entire industry,'' said another union representative.

Not all GM executives were convinced that union–management relations would remain so harmonious in the years to come. Can QWL continue to exist as the use of more and more robots leads to more laid-off workers? ''We're still scratching our heads on that one,'' said a GM executive.

**EXHIBIT 28–1**

**General Motors Corporation Performance, 1965–1979** *($ in Thousands)*

| Year | Net Sales | Net Income | Net Income (% of Sales) | Employees | Total Payroll | Payroll (% of Sales) |
|---|---|---|---|---|---|---|
| 1965 | $20,733,982 | $2,125,606 | 10.3 | 734,594 | $ 5,488,342 | 26.5 |
| 1966 | 20,028,505 | 1,993,392 | 10.0 | 745,425 | 5,559,742 | 27.8 |
| 1967 | 20,026,252 | 1,627,276 | 8.1 | 728,198 | 5,634,192 | 28.1 |
| 1968 | 22,755,403 | 1,721,915 | 7.6 | 757,231 | 6,540,143 | 28.7 |
| 1969 | 24,294,141 | 1,710,695 | 7.0 | 793,924 | 6,928,279 | 28.5 |
| 1970 | 18,752,354 | 609,087 | 3.2 | 659,796 | 6,259,841 | 33.4 |
| 1971 | 28,263,918 | 1,935,709 | 6.8 | 773,352 | 8,015,072 | 28.4 |
| 1972 | 30,435,231 | 2,162,807 | 7.1 | 760,000 | 8,668,224 | 28.5 |
| 1973 | 35,798,289 | 2,398,103 | 6.7 | 810,920 | 10,308,510 | 28.8 |
| 1974 | 31,549,546 | 950,069 | 3.0 | 733,860 | 9,771,416 | 31.0 |
| 1975 | 35,724,911 | 1,253,092 | 3.5 | 681,000 | 10,028,441 | 28.1 |
| 1976 | 47,181,000 | 2,902,800 | 6.2 | 748,000 | 12,908,500 | 27.4 |
| 1977 | 54,961,000 | 3,337,500 | 6.1 | 797,000 | 15,270,800 | 27.8 |
| 1978 | 63,221,100 | 3,508,000 | 5.5 | 839,000 | 17,195,500 | 27.2 |
| 1979 | 66,311,200 | 2,892,700 | 4.4 | 853,000 | 18,851,000 | 28.4 |

*Note:* In 1980, GM reported net sales of $57.7 billion, down 13% from 1979, and posted a loss of $763 million.

## EXHIBIT 28-2
## 1973 Letter of Understanding

Mr. Irving Bluestone
Vice President and Director
General Motors Department of UAW
Detroit, Michigan

Dear Mr. Bluestone:

In discussions prior to the opening of the current negotiations for a new collective bargaining agreement, General Motors Corporation and the UAW gave recognition to the desirability of mutual effort to improve the quality of work life for the employees. In consultation with Union representatives, certain projects have been undertaken by management in the field of organizational development, involving the participation of represented employees. These and other projects and experiments which may be undertaken in the future are designed to improve the quality of work life, thereby advantaging the worker by making work a more satisfying experience, advantaging the Corporation by leading to a reduction in employee absenteeism and turnover, and advantaging the consumer through improvement in the quality of the products manufactured.

As a result of these earlier discussions and further discussions during the course of the current negotiations for a new collective bargaining agreement, the parties have decided that a Commmittee to Improve the Quality of Work Life composed of representatives of the International Union and General Motors will be established at the national level.

This Committee will meet periodically and have responsibility for:

1. Reviewing and evaluating programs of the Corporation which involve improving the work environment of employees represented by the UAW
2. Developing experiments and projects in that area

**EXHIBIT 28-2** (*Continued*)

3. Maintaining records of its meetings, deliberations, and all experiments and evaluations it conducts
4. Making reports to the Corporation and Union on the results of its activities
5. Arranging for any outside counseling which it feels is necessary or desirable with the expenses thereof to be shared equally by the Corporation and the Union

The Corporation agrees to request and encourage its plant managements to cooperate in the conduct of such experiments and projects, and recognizes that cooperation by its plant floor supervision is essential to success of this program.

The Union agrees to request and encourage its members and their local union representatives to cooperate in such experiments and projects, and recognizes that the benefits which can flow to employees as a result of successful experimentation are dependent on the cooperation and participation of those employees and the local union representatives.

Very truly yours,

George B. Morris, Jr.
Vice President for Labor Relations
General Motors Corp.

**EXHIBIT 28-3**
**Definitions of QWL from Six GM Plants**

- **GMAD—Linden.** Joint commitment to achieve greater personal satisfaction in everyday work life. This is done by establishing an atmosphere of mutual trust and respect and by recognizing the values and needs of the individual.
- **GMAD—Wilmington.** The process by which union and management will develop an attitude within the organization that

provides an environment which will ultimately result in meeting goals mutually beneficial to both employees and management.

- **GMAD—Framingham.** Union and management working together with the people to meet their needs and accomplish plant objectives in a positive atmosphere which encourages involvement from everybody.
- **GMAD—Lordstown.** Creating an environment of understanding and responsibility toward the needs of an organization, its people, and the union through involvement, recognition, respect, and participation of all parties.
- **GMAD—Baltimore.** The involvement of all members of the organization in matters that relate to their relationship within the organization and the fulfillment of its goals.
- **Fisher Body—Fleetwood.** To create a positive and lasting change for the benefit of all, which provides a greater sense of value toward one's self, fellow employees, company, union, and the product we make, thereby allowing for an atmosphere of mutual trust, understanding, and honesty.

## EXHIBIT 28-4
## Review of Three-Day Sessions, by Al Romney, UAW QWL Coordinator, Tarrytown, New York

### *First Day*

*Introductions*

- Trainers to group
- Group members to each other

*Walking Through the Gate* (life as seen by a former hourly worker at Cadillac Motor Division)

- Use of words and slides
- Participants watch slides and then engage in informal discussions
- This part of the three days lets them get involved for the first time.
- Trainer's role is to limit discussion to things the entire group can deal with.

*Transparencies Reviewed and Discussed*

- What is quality of work life?
- What is employee involvement?

**EXHIBIT 28–4 (*continued*)**

- Union's position
- Management's position
- Benefits for all: employees, union, management
- What is the decision-making process at Tarrytown? (top management to the hourly worker)
- How are decisions made? (input from hourly workers, supervision, general supervision—with the final decisions made at an appropriate level)
- The structure of General Motors Assembly Division is reviewed
- Tarrytown is one of 19 plants
- What people are located in Central Office in Warren, Michigan?
- Where does Tarrytown fall into the big picture?
- What is the Tarrytown structure? Who are the people at the top
- What is the union structure? ? Who are the people who are involved in key positions?

*Win as Much as You Can*

- An experience-based exercise designed to discuss competition and cooperation
- When is competition healthy and when is it destructive?
- How does it involve the hourly worker?

*Plant Tour—Slides*

- A 4- to 6-hour tour of the plant through the means of slides and discussions
- Hourly employees are encouraged to participate
- The slides are presented in a way so that the hourly employees understand where they fit into the organization and the importance of their role

*Second Day*

*One-Way vs. Two-Way Communications*

- An experience-based exercise designed to discuss ways to communicate
- Hourly workers discuss ways of communicating in the plant
- When is one-way communication necessary? When could we use two-way communication?

*Available Information*

- Quality, costs, efficiency, safety
- Quality of audit—what does 145 mean? How is it computed? What is the role of the hourly worker in the quality audit?

*Ways to Organize Information*
- A look at the use of charts—ways to display information effectively

*9-Dots Puzzle*
- An experience-based exercise designed to look at constraints
- What are the constraints that hourly employees have? (time clocks, hours, plant rules, and so forth)
- Are we sometimes putting false constraints on ourselves—how does this relate to employee involvement?

*Brainstorming—Generation of Many Ideas*
- An experience-based exercise designed to look at the idea of generating many ideas
- Many employees can generate many ideas when given the freedom to do so
- How can we use this approach when generating ideas that affect your job?

*Involvement*
- It should be easy, important, and something we can do something about
- Get involved in things that affect you or your work place

## *Third Day*

*Disappearing Squares* (four squares into three squares with sticks)
- An experience-based exercise designed to look at how we use information
- Did we use all of the information we had?
- Is one solution the best or are there other solutions available?

*Constraints That Exist in the Organization* (discussion)
- Before we can input or develop solutions we must know what our limits are
- By realizing these limits we can develop solutions or input realistically and have a chance for our solutions to be implemented

*Ten-sticks Puzzle*
- An experience-based exercise designed to look at the steps we come up with to find a solution
- A look at working backward from the end product

*Process Control and Goal Orientation*
- Trainers talk through these steps
- A look at patterns that develop and steps in arriving at solutions to achieve a goal

**EXHIBIT 28–4 (*Continued*)**

*Pony Exercise*

- An experience-based exercise designed to look at what happens when groups get together to solve problems
- What kind of behavior goes on in a group when there seem to be different answers to a problem?
- What methods are used to convince others of our answer—Were they listening?
- Group discussion after exercise

*Final Assignment*

(Last half of the third day)

Involve all participants in an assignment that tries to use much of the information that was discussed during the first 2½ days.

Participants are asked to come up with ideas about what changes would they like to see in this plant

Some considerations

- Who is responsible for making the change? (management—union—employees)
- Consider all factors before developing solutions
- Develop solutions that you feel make sense

Discussions after assignment include

- Is it easy to develop solutions to make a change?
- Do changes involve more than one person or department?
- What is the role of the hourly worker in helping with these changes?
- Is it a two-way street?

*Wrap-up of Session*

- Trainers take a substantial amount of time in wrapping up the three days
- What happens when you go back to the floor?
- Stress the importance of remembering that things don't change overnight
- Hourly workers have to work together with the union and management
- This is just the beginning . . . not the end.

CASE 29

# HUMAN RESOURCES AT HEWLETT-PACKARD

*Richard O. von Werssowetz*
*Michael Beer*

> Our company . . . has developed over the years with a very specific and carefully defined management philosophy. . . . It is important for us to recognize that . . . our own management philosophy is not consistent in every aspect with what other people do, nor consistent with every aspect necessarily with what some of the best scholars of management might say is necessary (of course, not everybody agrees on what the best policies of management are).
>
> We do not believe that the thinking of other people should necessarily be accepted without the most careful consideration and without some actual testing in practice.
>
> We have developed over the years a rather unique, and I think, effective way of working with our people.
>
> I think we've done a really remarkably good job to maintain this so called "HP Spirit" as the company has grown larger. . . . Let's work on that because it is just one of the real strengths. It's the key to productivity and to leadership and continuing progress and success in our company.
>
> —*From an address by Dave Packard to a training class for company managers*

## "THE HP WAY"

In 1939 Bill Hewlett and Dave Packard set up shop in a one-car garage. Their first product was a new type of audio oscillator—an electronic instrument used to test sound equipment. By 1980, sales of the Hewlett-Packard Company were $3.1 billion from a line of more than 4,000 products—precision electronic equipment for measurement, analysis, and computation.

During the early years of the company, the founders developed a number of management concepts that evolved into a directing set of corporate objectives and a business style known as "the HP Way." These objectives and style are credited within the company as the basis for its successful growth and for the strong loyalty and satisfaction expressed by HP employees.

---

> From their responses to [survey] questions about personal identification with the company, it's clear that HP people like working for HP. Some 93 percent said they would recommend HP as a place to work, and 83 percent actually said they feel personally responsible for contributing their share to HP's success. Overall, their identification with the company is 25 percent above the national norm—a figure the survey specialists saw as extraordinarily rare and even "mind boggling."
> —*From HP company magazine discussion of results of a survey of U.S. employees*

> You said you don't think making printed circuit (PC) boards is much different here from other places; I think probably it is. People making PC boards here don't punch time clocks and they haven't for over the 15 years I've been here. They do have flexible work hours. They got them as soon as I did. They've got considerable freedom to input about how they are doing their job. They make suggestions for changes. They have every bit as much access to John Young [HP president] as I do. They don't see him as frequently, because they don't have as many reasons to talk to him. But the door is as open to them as it is to me. I think there are significant benefits at that level of the organization.—*An HP group vice president*

The HP Way is difficult to define, both within the company and to those outside. It includes a participative management style that supports, even demands, individual freedom and initiative while emphasizing commonness of purpose and teamwork. According to this style, the company provides employees direction in the form of well-defined negotiated goals, shared data, and the support of necessary resources. Yet employees are expected to create their own ways of contributing to the company's success. As the company has grown, a conscious intent has been made to retain the sense of purpose, closeness, and informality that HP had as a small company. The set of policies, and attitudes that foster this style are all collectively part of the HP Way.

> The HP Way is a subtle way, and that is why we have so much trouble describing it. It is basically a faith in people to use their discretion and to be sure along the way to make some mistakes as well as to make some contributions. In a way that, over time, generally will continue to take the company in the direction it wants to go—consistent with its basic underlying set of objectives. These objectives continue to drive us, they really do.—*An HP manager*

> There's just sort of a feeling, I guess, that we have of how people are to be treated.—*An HP manager*

> There is something useful in not being too precise—a value to fuzziness. No one can really define the HP Way. If it weren't fuzzy, it would be a rule! This way leaves room for judgment. Without that, there wouldn't be room for the constant microreconciliations needed in a changing world. This is designed as an adaptive company.—*An HP vice president*

One reason for the difficulty in defining the HP Way is that perhaps heavier attention than in other companies is paid to the *way* things are done as well as to *what* is accomplished. The *process* within HP provides the strength and structure to help assure the desired *products* of their efforts.

> You can't mess with the process. There's not a lot of flexibility in the way you use the process. The process has got a very good track record and people don't like you to mess with it. Also, if individuals start to mess with the process, then I think the company breaks down pretty quickly.
> —*An HP group vice president*

Consequently, understanding the HP Way is considered a necessity for being effective within HP:

> There is a widespread belief or conviction that consultants just don't have much to offer HP. Many have the feeling that you just can't trust consultants, that they only want to use HP. Some feel they only want to wiggle their way in here to see what they can get away with.
>
> In addition, there might be some elements of style that are incompatible with the HP Way. They are thought of as being all form—very good at going in and motivating people and getting them enthusiastic about a project, enough to buy it. But the real value is in getting things done. —*An HP employee*

Trying to engender a common, supportive process while retaining individuality requires exceptionally subtlety in approach and trust and openness in relationships. These too are part of the HP Way. New employees often find this different from their prior experiences and must adapt to this style.

> The clan is very nice in terms of being a much broader network and giving you a much better support base. But it can also feel intrusive. It can feel presumptuous and it's much, much, more demanding than any other company that I've ever been affiliated with. . . . You just have to do the right thing.—*An MBA hired by HP two years ago*

> We hear about the "HPWay" almost ad nauseam. It's sort of "truth, justice, and the HP Way." I went through a real struggle with the concept. When I was initially exposed to it, I thought: Boy! There's an awful lot that makes sense. But I guess I came to the point where I said this is overindoctrination . . . some of it must be baloney. I've come not quite full circle, but part way back to the realization that, gee, there is an awful lot that is distinctive, an awful lot that is good in the "HP Way," an awful lot that as an employee I feel grateful for.—*An HP employee of one year*

> [Trying to describe HP] I gave them copies of the corporate objectives. I said one of the things to keep in mind is that the seven objectives guide operational decisions on an hourly-by-hourly basis. Sometimes that is the

only guide you have to knowing if something is the right thing to do. By this time they were absolutely beside themselves. They couldn't believe that it was really this ambiguous. They thought I must have been embellishing the truth quite a bit. So all these things violate completely the expectations that other MBAs have. . . . —*An HP employee*

I thought: These people are putting me on. Why, there's not a shop in the world where someone isn't bad-mouthing the management. So it bothered me that no one was saying anything really bad about HP. I still can't say I really understand why it works, but it does. Peer pressure has something to do with it. New people with bad attitudes quickly learn that it's not acceptable to be that way at HP. And another factor is that you're given work assignments days in advance instead of one at a time every couple of hours. They aren't looking over your shoulder. No matter how much they give you, you seem to get it done.—*An HP model maker*

## BACKGROUND

HP's products for the first 20 years were primarily electronic test and measuring instruments for engineers and scientists. Since then, HP has added computers, calculators, medical electronic equipment, instrumentation for chemical analysis, and solid-state components. In 1980, sales had grown at a compounded rate of 23 percent over the last ten years while net profits had compounded at 27 percent. HP had 57,000 employees worldwide. There were 20 manufacturing locations spread across the United States and 8 others around the world. In addition, there were more than 60 U.S. sales and service locations with over 100 more in 64 other countries. About half of the sales were to the United States with the rest to other parts of the world. (See Exhibits 29-1 through 29-4 for ten-year earnings summary, balance sheets, and sales given by business segments and geographic areas.)

### *Objectives*

Early in the history of the company, while thinking about how a company like this should be managed, I kept getting back to one concept: If we could simply get everybody to agree on what our objectives were and to understand what we were trying to do, then we could turn everybody loose and they would move along in a common direction.—*Dave Packard*

Hewlett's and Packard's strong beliefs in several areas shaped the company from the beginning. These were first put into writing in 1957 as the objectives of the Hewlett-Packard Company. With minor modifications, they remain the most fundamental, active guiding forces at

HP. Exhibit 29-6 gives excerpts from HP's description of these objectives, which must be absorbed to understand HP.

### *Product Strategy*

HP's product strategy embodies several aspects of the corporate objectives. By far the dominant emphasis is on research and development to create products which will compete by new technical contributions rather than through marketing or other competitive devices (see Exhibit 29-5). This product strategy reflects the technically oriented no-nonsense approach of the people who started the company. Furthermore, product strategy and the company's approach to human resource management complement each other. For example, the commitment to HP employees results in avoidance of contract business and design of general-purpose devices suitable for a broad range of customers. (All commercial customers buy from a catalog which lists almost all products HP makes. Only external modification such as special colors or extra protection for environmental extremes are made. The basic designs or purposes of the instruments are not modified. These rules are the same for government purchases.) The focus on technical contribution and profit rather than volume has led HP to conclude that, for HP, it is not appropriate to try to gain market share with a low introductory price:

> It is just as easy to make a profit today as it will be tomorrow. There are, of course, occasions when actions should be taken which will jeopardize the short-term profit and have the hope of improving your long-term profit. These need to be considered very, very carefully because, more often than not, they tend to be rationalizations which simply put off what you should be doing today. . . . They are often the result of wishful thinking and they almost always fail to achieve their overall optimum performance.
>
> If a new product is really as good as we think it is going to be, we'll be able to sell more than we can make in the initial period anyway, and so you are jeopardizing the whole situation with really nothing to gain. . . . You can reduce the price later on, if, in fact, you are able to achieve your lower production costs and keep your costs down.—*Dave Packard*

In addition, there is the belief that it is easier to maintain great individual freedom of action in smaller work units. This, together with the seeking of the most profitable opportunities, leads to an emphasis on many modestly sized market segments where HP can achieve a strong position. The HP organizational structure is designed to maintain flexibility and responsiveness by decentralizing responsibility and authority to divisions responsible for each market segment.

### *Organization*

The fundamental business unit at HP is the product division:

> The division . . . is an integrated self-sustaining organization with a great deal of independence. The aim is to create a working atmosphere that encourages solving problems as close as possible to the level where the problems occur. To that end, HP has striven to keep [product divisions] relatively small and well defined.
> —"*The Hewlett-Packard Organization*"

No product area is a division until it contains the six basic functions of R&D, manufacturing, marketing, quality assurance, finance, and personnel. (Advanced fundamental research is performed by the corporate R&D group, HP Labs.) New divisions are created by a process similar to cellular division:

> New divisions tend to emerge when a particular product line becomes large enough to support its continued growth out of the profit it generates. Also, new divisions tend to emerge when a single division gets so large that the people involved start to lose their identification with the product line.—*An HP general manager*

At the end of 1980, there are 40 HP divisions. Coordination of division activities is the responsibility of ten product groups. Each group is responsible for the overall operations and financial performance of its members. All sales organizations report at the group level as do some nondivisional manufacturing operations (although there is still cross-group selling of products from other areas of the company). A complete company organization chart with other corporate support functions is given in Exhibit 29-7.

### *Financial Elements*

Important financial elements of HP also reflect the company objectives. The emphasis on self-financing results in minimal long-term debt (primarily foreign borrowings for the company's international operations).

> Now in some industries, particularly those which require large capital investments, the pay-as-you-go approach is not feasible. There is also a school of thought in management that capital needs should be attained by leveraging your profits with equity financing and large amounts of debt financing. This school of thought says you can make your profits go further if you do this. Now whatever the arguments, it is not Hewlett-Packard Company policy to lever our profits with long-term debt. We want

> every manager to know this and to act accordingly. . . . I see no possible circumstance that would justify a change. You can argue if you want to, but it isn't going to get you very far!—*Dave Packard*

> Our feeling is there is enough risk in the technology—we have all we can handle there. This philosophy provides great discipline all the way down. If you want to innovate, you must bootstrap. It is one of the most powerful, least understood influences that pervades the company.
> —*An HP vice president*

To help support growth under those conditions, there is a strong emphasis on the management of assets, particularly receivables and inventory. This includes establishing close working relationships with vendors and the use of computer information systems to help pinpoint problem areas. There is a constant evaluation of the relative merits of increasing capacity by adding new fixed assets versus introducing new production equipment in existing facilities. The financial reporting system also provides special statements to view each division's success in worldwide management of its product lines.

Each division is measured along two dimensions: the financial results of the actual manufacturing of products in the division and the total worldwide activity in the divisions's product lines, wherever they are manufactured. (Divisions may produce other divisions' products to improve service and reduce transportation costs around the world.)

Reporting of worldwide results is accomplished by adjustments to the divisional profit and loss statement. Intracompany sales discounts structured to minimize customs and tariffs are reversed so the selling division will consider domestic and international customers evenly. Because there are many "incestuous" products with divisions buying from each other, incorporating those purchases into more complex assemblies, and then selling the combined products, each division is allowed credit only for its own value-added (which is negotiated between the divisions). In addition, a "license fee" is paid by divisions entirely manufacturing products designed by other divisions. A division may be both receiving these fees for products it has designed that are made by other divisions and also paying fees to other divisions for products of others it is making. (These fees are percentages of sales revenues negotiated between the divisions.)

The adjusted worldwide profit and loss statement is the basis for allocation of each division's research and development funds (usually 9 percent of sales). This rewards the innovative divisions with additional funds for further innovation and acts as an indirect form of asset allocation. Plants started purely as desirable manufacturing locations can only attain full divisional status by somehow creating a new product. Only then will it be allocated R&D funds that are the key to its growth.

Balance sheets are produced only at the group level. Below that level, HP feels that the large allocations necessary for such items as corporate overhead, the sales force, and marketing assets create too much distortion to the statements to make them useful.

Capital allocations are negotiated during the yearly budgeting process, although divisions are expected to be self-financing over any period of time. However, for startups or major expansions in any one year, a division may be allowed more capital spending than it can provide for itself. Most capital rationing negotiations are resolved within each group.

## HUMAN RESOURCE ELEMENTS

### *Hiring and Training*

HP feels it is very selective in considering job candidates. There is great emphasis on adaptability and cultural fit. (This selectivity is widely discussed to help instill a sense of pride in the work force at all levels.) This is acomplished by normal interviewing processes. Testing is rare and then limited to specialized skills tests particularly pertinent to a position.

> It starts with the hiring decision. Everybody we hire, we hire forever—at least that's the basic premise. We are not hiring anybody for a program. We don't hire somebody for specific short-term skills. Given our fundamental objectives that we will promote from within and grow our own management people, grow our own supervisors, grow our own technical people, we look for people who have a lot of growth potential.

(Contrary to the expectations that many people have about HP, the casewriter found that the mix of skills and competencies of newly hired HP production workers was very similar to those he had observed at other, non-HP manufacturing operations he had visited. When joining HP, these workers seemed to include typical samples of the mixes of production workers available to other companies in the same areas. However, because many workers have heard good things about HP from friends, they come to the job excited about the opportunity of working for HP.)

Because of the feeling that working at HP *is* different, it is very unusual for someone to be hired into a manager's position:

> Now there are some who say that a person is a good manager who has mastered managerial techniques; he can manage anything. Well, maybe he can. But I hold very strongly that he can manage it a hell of a lot better if he really knows the territory.—*Dave Packard*

> It would be quite rare that you could come right into a management position new to the company and handle it. You're really not trusted or known for at least the first year. It takes you that long to kind of go through the receiving line if you will, or just to become part of the group. Because it is so subtle and there's so much that needs to be handed down like a tradition. So you know what you are doing. So that you know how to make a decision.—*An HP employee*

> There are a lot of different types of people who have been successful in the company. There is no prescription for background. There probably *is* a prescription for style. If you look at the makeup of the Executive Committee or the Operations Council, there are very definitely some different personalities and different styles. But the similarities are probably greater than the differences when it comes to style. Each one of those people has strong belief in individual freedom. We can accept widely different backgrounds, but don't accept divergent style.—*An HP division manager*

New employees at all levels tend to go through a period of adaptation that often includes considerable frustration within the HP style:

> There's a conditioning period for people who have worked other places. Maybe it's the informality they see or the nondirectiveness at HP. Where suddenly instead of being told point by point what you're supposed to do, your boss is relying upon you to be able to use your head. I think maybe that's sort of frightening to some people.

> As with any culture, you begin to talk about it. People understand: discretion, O.K.; a lot of latitude, fine; ability to make mistakes, learn from my mistakes, not high punishment, nor high reward, all trying to pull together and make it happen. But after you finish saying all that, someone who comes from a different kind of a culture, different kind of an environment will say, ''Tell me what to do.''—*Comments by HP employees*

One of the most important tools for conveying the HP ''personality'' is the telling of company stories. These are used not only during employee orientation (and recruiting) periods, but are repeated in many different circumstances on a continuing basis. These stories describe important historical moments in the company history or exemplify role models in the HP Way. Some of the most common stories known by most HP employees concern the following:

- How Bill and Dave [as Hewlett and Packard are commonly addressed] started the company with $538 in the garage behind the Packard's rented house. Bill rented a spare room there.
- How they called their first instrument the ''200A'' so that people would not know they were just starting out and would not be afraid of doing business with such a small, new company.

- How Dave Packard physically smashed up an instrument in a laboratory one day because he thought it was poorly designed, unreliable, and generally a "hunk of junk."
- How Bill Hewlett challenged HP Labs to build a scientific calculator he could put in his shirt pocket (whick led to the introduction of the world's first small scientific calculator and one of HP's most important business segments).
- How during the 1970 business downturn when electronic companies across the United States were laying off employees, every employee at HP took a 10 percent pay cut and worked nine of ten days—taking every other Friday off. There were no HP layoffs.
- How the need for a contemplated issue of $100 million in long-term debt was avoided in 1973 by a tough, corporatewide concentration on asset management. The executives of the company were shaken by the realization that they had almost violated one of their most fundamental objectives when their problem wasn't money, but management. There was a rededication to the company objectives.

Stories such as these are used in classes, recalled during management meetings and retirement parties, are subjects of articles in the in-house magazines, and are incorporated into remniscences in speeches and letters from Bill, Dave, and other company leaders. There is a similar store of equally popular anecdotes concerning the individual divisions and other operations of the company.

The confrontation with the problems of growth in 1973 also led to the expansion of training in the values and methods of HP. It was becoming more difficult to pass the culture on simply by example and word-of-mouth. There were increased executive seminars and a new series of courses for supervisors on managing at HP. This led to the reorganization of the same materials to be presented to all HP employees as a course called "Working at HP":

> The course actually got started in a couple of divisions which is often the way things work here. Their rate of growth was so high and they were having such a hard time assimilating people.
>
> We said, "Gee, if this is what we're telling managers and supervisors, then let's hold a mirror up to it and tell them the same thing, that that's what they should expect."—*An HP manager*

"Working at HP" is normally presented in four half-day modules to groups of less than 30 employees. It is felt to be most effective when attended after about six months of employment. However, during the first several years of the course, a large percentage of *all* employees had attended the classes. Depending on the location and needs of each area, the class may have homogenous mixes of only nonexempt, professional, or other employees or may include employees of all types mixed together.

The course is taught by a member of the local personnel staff and by at least one line manager. The instructors attempt to let employees discover HP by establishing a continuous dialogue with the employees, both by teaching style and by a large number of participative exercises. For example, each group of six or eight employees sitting around a table may develop independent lists of questions about the company and about their area for the division general manager who visits each class for a no-holds-barred discussion.

The first module concentrates on the history of HP and the development of the HP Way. It presents stories about the people of HP which tend to humanize the company and instill pride in the company's past accomplishments. This module also includes exercises that help the employee better picture HP. Examples include the division of pie charts into HP's geographic and product market segments and into how it spends each dollar of revenues. There are also exercises to help illustrate that well-meaning people can have valid different points of view about the same subjects.

The remaining modules provide comprehensive coverage of personnel policies, performance evaluations, salary administration, and personal development. This is also very open, including candid discussions of how HP develops competitive salary information and how its salary philosophy rewards outstanding performance. Each employee fills out a management by objectives (MBO) form for his or her own job. (A later section deals with the pay system in more detail.)

A typical example of the independence of the divisions is that the only way the corporate training group can estimate the number of employees who have attended the class is to count the number of course binders which have been ordered.

### *Structural Devices and Work Systems*

The day-to-day activities of HP employees are primarily directed by a comprehensive system of MBO. This is seen as an iterative process, beginning with the establishment of short- and long-range objectives (called tactical and strategic plans) which are derived from the corporate and group objectives. At each company level, the overall objectives are communicated and subunit objectives are negotiated.

Objectives are to be goals, not tasks, to provide a large measure of freedom in how the goals will be accomplished. At the same time, the goals must be made to mesh horizontally and vertically throughout the organization. Therefore, the entire MBO process is a part of the annual tactical and strategic planning processes. This flows through to individual employee "position planning," which is HP's term for describing the objective of a job along with its major responsibilities and performance measures.

Although the MBO process is initiated from the top, the iterative nature of the MBO/planning cycle is meant to provide ample opportunity for individual initiative and influence in setting of overall objectives. The employee is expected to suggest the ways she or he can contribute to the attainment of the unit's goals. This process is intended to be used for all employees at every level, although employee surveys indicate the MBO may be weak in some areas. One objective of the "Working at HP" program is to make both managers and employees more skilled at this process.

> MBO says that a manager, a supervisor, a foreman, given the proper support and guidance (that is, the objectives), is probably better able to make decisions about the problems he or she is directly concerned with than some executive way up the line—no matter how smart or able that executive may be.
>
> This system places great responsibility on the individuals concerned, but it also makes their work more interesting and more challenging. It makes them feel that they are really a part of the company, and that they can have a direct effect on its performance.—*Bill Hewlett*

Through the managers, the MBO system is also the main control system over the product divisions. Strong and semiautonomous, some even describe these as "feudal baronies." At the same time, interdivisional cooperation is seen as a strength:

> We could allow each division or group to operate as a completely separate business. Under this arrangement life would be much simpler—each would have its own profit center, and you would simply observe how each was doing.
>
> No doubt we could be very successful at that—but I think we would then be just another company.
>
> On the other hand, our strength lies in the fact that our divisions have real freedom of choice in their operations, yet we have learned to talk across these divisional and group boundaries. This has enabled us to share our problems and strengths, thereby building a much stronger company.—*Bill Hewlett*

The common thread seems to be in overall agreement (through the planning process) about what is to be accomplished by each division with great freedom of each division to decide how it is to be accomplished.

A corollary to strong, relatively autonomous divisions is the moderate size and influence of the corporate staff. The special "cross-boundary'' types of projects that are often undertaken by corporate staffs in other companies are instead given to ad hoc task forces drawn from many parts and levels of the company.

This desire to minimize corporate direction and to encourage individual inventiveness and initiative can be seen clearly in the minimization of formal corporate policies. For example, the entire book of HP personnel policies is contained in a 1.5-inch binder.

> When the company was much smaller, quite small, I didn't think we should *have* a personnel department. The reason was that I thought that personnel should be everybody's responsibility and I didn't want to have someone around that they could pass the buck to.—*Dave Packard*

In fact, the corporate personnel function was only initiated in 1957 when HP had 1,200 employees.

Maintaining effective common purpose within this framework that offers freedom of method and divisional autonomy depends heavily on the openness, trust and cooperation so fundamental to the HP Way. These are manifested in a commitment to teamwork and participative decision making.

> One of the things that we have tried to achieve and I think we have achieved is this concept of teamwork. That's one of the reasons we don't have special awards for a division or something that does particularly well. The only way this company is going to run successfully is if we can insure that there is the maximum flow of information and cooperation between all the elements of it and this is a very tricky situation.
> . . . I've often expressed this in terms that everybody in the company is equally important. It's just as important that the fellow that is responsible for sweeping the floor does a good job as it is if Bill and I do a good job. We shouldn't separate this out. . . . In the type of work we are doing, it's the little details that will make the difference between a good quality product and one that isn't very good. So what we've tried to engender is this attitude that it is everybody's business to do a good job. And hopefully we'll all benefit if we do so.—*Dave Packard*

The need for teamwork is easily seen in the sales force. Each of six major product groups has developed a selling strategy that is highly individualized to the needs of its particular market. Yet there are many customers and potential customers who may buy products from several different product areas:

> Many of our customers, especially the major accounts, need products and service from two, three or more product lines. So there has to be a lot of interaction between the salespeople in servicing these customers. They have to work together as a team, using common sense as to who should lead the team.—*HP's marketing vice president*

This multiple product line approach with many divisions trying to meet the needs of what are often the same customers, demands the same cooperation and teamwork in all of the other aspects of the company, from R&D to manufacturing to accounting. This teamwork applies not only across business units, but also includes the ability of all members of a unit to influence the way the unit's task is accomplished. In addition to the MBO process, this occurs through use of a wide variety of communication devices and a philosophy of participative decision making.

### *Communications*

HP uses a variety of techniques to encourage an ongoing dialogue with its employees. One way it tries to do this is by an open door policy. (In most places in HP there literally are no doors to individual offices. Top executives, including President John Young, have offices within large administrative areas that are divided only by freestanding low partitions.)

> A supervisor is expected to promote an atmosphere wherein an employee feels comfortable and free to seek advice and counsel regarding problems of either a personal or job-related nature. The employee may seek counsel from a supervisor, member of the personnel staff, or any level of management with the assurance that no adverse consequences will result from that action.—*HP personnel policy manual*

This formal policy is more of a last resort "insurance policy" to guarantee the right of any employee access to any other. Of more importance is the day-to-day continual mixing of employees of all levels. The clean nature of electronics research and manufacture mean that administrative and manufacturing operations can be and are located in the same areas, often within a single large open floor space. Common coffee breaks have become practically a ritual at HP with the company providing coffee and snacks to all employees every morning and afternoon. In this way, managers and nonmanagers get to know each other and discuss projects and problems more informally. There are periodic "beer busts" and picnics for the whole plant, often at excellent recreational facilities owned by the company. In addition, employees at any level of the organization can stay without charge at company-owned cabins located at these facilities. There are frequent plant meetings to discuss the latest company and plant news. There is also a loudspeaker system that allows company executives to announce company operating results and to discuss topics of wide concern. All of these practices are meant to reinforce the sense of common purpose and belonging and to widen each employee's sources of information.

In addition to the *ability* to seek the advice of anyone in the company, there is the *expectation* that those who can contribute will be sought out:

> I guess one of my first reactions was seeing how many people I had to check things with before I went ahead and did something. And it wasn't the tone of saying, "Look, you have to get their approval." It was in the tone of saying, "Here are some people that probably really have something to say about what you're doing, you really ought to talk to them." It was that kind of subtle difference, but it really ended up in getting approval.
>
> It comes across as, "There are some people that you really ought to check bases with and if you've got a reasonable proposal, they'll support it." I thought several times that if somebody said you *have* to do this before you can do something, I would have said forget it! But it's more of selling the idea. And you do that on a very personal basis. Not very many times does anybody ever come along and say you can't do something. It's a subtle influence process.—*An HP engineer*

An important outgrowth of the open door policy is what HP calls "Management by Wandering Around" (MBWA). Development of the concept is attributed to John Doyle, an HP vice president who had had division manufacturing and general management, corporate personnel, and corporate R&D responsibilites:

> It seemed to John that there had to be a way of describing the extra step that HP managers needed to take in order to make the HP open door policy truly effective. It was not enough to sit and wait for people to come through the door with their problems and ideas—they probably wouldn't in many cases. The managers had better get off their chairs and go out and get in touch with people. In that way people would know the managers were accessible whenever they had something important to communicate.
>
> Straightforward as it sounds, there are quite a few subtleties and requirements that go with MBWA. For one thing, it is not always easy for managers to do—so some of them do it reluctantly or infrequently. And its purpose is not always apparent to people—especially new HP people—at the receiving end of visits, so they may view it suspiciously and respond uneasily.—*Excerpt from* Measure, *the HP magazine*

HP has tried to spread and institutionalize this concept by wide exposure in company publications, meetings, and training sessions and by the example of upper management. Managers at all levels are encouraged to spend a part of each day wandering through the organization, often without specific purpose other than to see what is going on and to build new channels of communication with other employees.

MBWA by high executives is also coupled with another communication device in the form of division reviews:

> Divison reviews didn't really start at some specific time, but are the natural outgrowth of the personal interest and hands-on style so characteristic of HP. As a small company, a group of managers might collect at an engineering bench to evaluate a new product ready for production. As divisions were formed, and particularly those remote from Palo Alto [HP's home location], we found more and more business matters besides R&D programs were of interest.
>
> Today's division or sales region reviews cover a full range of business matters: financial performance for the past year, outlook for orders, shipments and facilities for the next three years, detailed presentations on product development strategy and key programs, and very importantly, a look at people management including training, recruiting, and affirmative action goals and results. A very broad cross-section of division personnel are involved in organizing for and presenting reviews. This is an excellent forum to become acquainted with the growing numbers of people that are key to the success of all these programs.
>
> The visiting group of reviewers shifts a bit depending on location and schedules, but generally includes several members of the executive committee, heads of corporate staff departments such as personnel and controller, appropriate group managers, and usually [other] division managers with a special interest in the programs. [also outside directors on occasion].
>
> Often the technical portion of the review is repeated a second day for a broad representation of engineering management. This proves to be a very effective means of stimulating the flow of technical information across the company.
>
> With all the top policy originators and implementors in one place at one time, the usual communication paths are short-circuited, and we can focus on results.—*HP President John Young*

Outside managers usually spend part of their time during such visits practicing MBWA—investigating techniques that might be of interest to their areas, passing along ideas from their units, and just getting to know more of the people.

Corporate openness is also communicated by example. Management meetings, retirement parties, and division parties often include skits written by employees and acted out by those managers and others they select without warning. These attempt to affectionately caricature management foibles and mannerisms. They help demonstrate the humanity of important managers and hopefully increase the feeling of approachability (besides being a lot of fun). The same idea is used for comic pictures and posters. Managers also normally cook and help serve other employees at division picnics.

*All* employees have the same profit sharing (initiated in 1940) and eligibility for stock options. There are no executive performance bonuses. (No one contends that the *amounts* of the stock options are or should be the same—that's a function of contribution.) In the same way, flexible hours were introduced simultaneously (in 1973) for managers and nonmanagers alike. In addition, everyone at HP is salaried—no one punches a time clock. Other examples are the offices, which are all modest in comparison with many other companies. Helping people remember the 1970 10 percent across-the-board pay cut also demonstrates equal treatment in a tangible way.

Tolerance for the differing needs of individuals is another form of openness. HP employees cite case after case of the great latitude and aid given to them during periods of personal crisis. This same tolerance is demonstrated in HP's remarkable willingness to rehire employees who have left HP to try other fields or to attempt their own company startups. (This does not extend so readily to those who leave to join a large direct competitor.) One employee's struggle with this phenomenon illustrates some common HP traits:

> It's a win-win situation for an individual. They go to work for some small company and if the company is a success, so are they. If the company dies, they can almost always come back to HP. Particularly if they're good people: we like to get them back, sorry to see them go.
>
> [What are the strategies to try to minimize it? For example, what about not being quite so nice about coming back?]
>
> That might be a possibility. This has been raised as a major concern by a lot of people. But I don't think it's gotten beyond the concern stage. It wouldn't be the HP Way to hold that against someone. When you suggest that, it doesn't sit right with me. It's something I don't agree with. I think the approach would be to try to encourage them not to leave. In other words, to make conditions better or to figure out what need is going unsatisfied at HP and try to figure out a way of satisfying that.

In a relatively recent example, HP demonstrated its interest in two-way communication by conducting a survey on employee attitudes and concerns. Dubbed "Open Line," the results, management interpretations, and planned responses were published in the company magazine (Exhibit 29-8). Other internal magazine and newsletter articles discuss company people, problems and progress.

### *Promotion and Reward Systems*

The HP culture and value system play a role in the system of promotions and rewards:

> The sense of doing the job at HP is one of communications—dealing with a lot of people working in a team environment. Not taking your particu-

> lar project and doing an outstanding job on that particular project by yourself in a corner. If you're doing an excellent job within the HP context, that means you're affecting and involved with a lot of other people in a lot of functional areas. And as openings come up, there are going to be people aware of your skills, of your ability to deal with groups and other people, of your potential.
>
> People find out about individuals here by direct contact. There is a lot of that here, and people recognize those that are sharp, that they feel comfortable with, that have the skills. There is a lot of informality at HP and you get to talk to many people for lunch or something to discuss ideas you have or areas you would like to work.—*An HP employee*

Career paths may be as random as the contacts discussed above may seem. At HP, this is called the "career maze." This phrase acknowledges the normalcy of cross-functional, cross-divisional, and lateral moves that often occur over the course of a career at HP.

> There is no prescribed career development or progression pattern. In a lot of companies, you can sit down and literally do a flow chart. If you want to get to point F, you do A, then B, then C, then D and E and you're ready for F. You can describe each job. It's not at all true in this company. When it comes time to promote, we try to look for the best people. There are many examples of unusual progressions at HP. There are many paths you can follow to any particular end.
>
> For example, in my first eight years, I guess I had about seven or eight different jobs and four different functions. A couple of them were lateral moves, some of them were promotions. It's not necessary to get a bigger title or to jump a level in the pay system to be given a new responsibility. I feel very positive about that.—*An HP manager*

Not only does HP feel this is the best use of people, but the constant cross-fertilization across functions aids the coordination of the design, manufacturing, and distribution process. However, this attitude towards promotion requires different kinds of mechanisms for identifying candidates since the candidates often are not within the same area of the company, nor along some common "preparation path," nor even within the same specialty area.

> There is a lot of very purposeful mixing of people. One way is through the division review process. In additon, we spend a fair amount of time talking to people, having communications luncheons, things like that. There are a fair number of social and quasisocial gatherings like the beer busts and picnics.
>
> We use a lot of task forces—it's an important vehicle we use for getting things done in the company. It's a way we get along with a relatively small staff. We sometimes call this real people involved solving real problems. First of all it gets work done. As a matter of fact, it is a very, very

important part of the way we do busines. But it also gives a lot of visibility to people.—*An HP group manager*

The performance appraisal and salary administration processes also expose individual employees to many managers around the company. In this system, "wage curves" for various levels are set to be competitive with relevant labor markets. (All employees are salaried, although nonexempt employees must, by law, be paid for overtime hours which are submitted by the employee.) Individual pay is set by a combination of relevant experience and "sustained performance."

The performance component strongly predominates in line with the HP philosophy. Within each wage curve, normal laws of distribution are expected to result in a 10, 40, 40, 10 split of employee performance. That is, 10 percent will be exceptional performers, 40 percent will be very good, 40 percent will be good, and 10 percent will be acceptable or new in the range. (Unacceptable performance should quickly result in job counseling and quickly improved performance or a repositioning or involuntary termination of the employee.)

The pay positions of the employees should correspond closely within the related performance bands of the wage curve (see Exhibit 29-9). Employees who improve their relative performance positions are given raises over several quarters to bring their pay in line with their higher performance. Because this measurement is based on *sustained contribution,* sudden dramatic changes in performance position are rare. Those whose performances have declined are given small or no increases until the yearly shifts of the pay curves to adjust for inflation result in proper pay alignment. Adjustments to salaries for performance are not expected to be governed by artificial budget limits.

To help determine this distribution of performance, it is common for managers to rank employees within their groups. Where similar groups exist, there is a great deal of effort to correlate these rankings. Managers at the functional level in divisions and higher and senior technical and sales personnel are ranked within each category on a quarterly basis by the Operations Council. This council consists of the top management of the company: group general managers, corporate vice presidents and executive vice presidents, and the HP president. Managers at lower levels also often use the ranking technique. Those who do trade opinions with other managers to help them calibrate their evaluations.

This continuing review of performance every quarter not only helps maintain equity within employee pay, but also spreads extensive knowledge of employee accomplishments throughout the company. The performance band of each employee is discussed during the annual individual performance appraisal and when salary changes are made. This reinforces the HP commitment to using contribution as the standard of value for the company.

Open discussion of hiring needs also helps to identify candidates for job openings:

> We just recruited a national sales manager who reports to our group marketing manager. I solicited far and wide. We had several serious internal [within the group] candidates and I looked at them. But I also contacted the Operations Council, told them about the opening, the kind of person we were looking for, the kind of experience we wanted. I got eight or ten inputs back from that.
>
> I already had a half-dozen people in mind outside the group that I had heard about during the quarterly review process. You don't always get to meet the person, but you hear a little about the individual from the person's boss or boss's boss. That doesn't sound like a big deal, but you do it every quarter and the repetition sinks in. In addition, every year the Operations Council spends three days together scoping [for curve level] and ranking all company executives as a single group.
>
> I also let it generally be known that we were looking for a national sales manager. It was the world's worst kept secret by design. Two people picked up the phone and called to say they'd be interested, could we talk about it. We depend on giving people a lot of visibility.
>
> —*A group vice president*

There is a posting system for nonexempt and lower-level exempt jobs, but that level does not include upper middle-managment positions and above.

All aspects of the salary administration are very open. Each employee sees his or her wage curve and the one on the next level up. Both employees and managers receive extensive training in position planning and the MBO process. HP is candid about the sources of the competitive wage information it uses in setting its salaries and about the fact that the curves are structured with a skew to rewarding the outstanding contributors. To HP, all of these are demanded by respect for the individual and by the essence of a merit-based system.

## THE FUTURE

The growth, financial results, and employee attitudes observed by many and indicated by the Open Line survey have given HP a wide reputation as a well-managed company. Several developments HP faces will further test the adaptability and durability of its methods and its managers. Among other challenges, these executives must deal with the compounding pressures of growth, the requirements of newer markets and intensified competition for its people.

The compounded sales growth rate of 23 percent over the last ten years also resulted in a rapidly growing work force. This growth dilutes the average experience as seen by the fact that more than half of HP workers have been with the company three years or less (Exhibit 29–10). This dilution of experience is especially telling on supervision. Although some experienced supervisors are hired, the HP desire to "grow its own" management and supervision means that there is little time to prepare new employees for leadership roles before those responsibilities must be assumed. New managers are still assimilating the HP culture and style while they are trying to use it effectively and pass it on to even less senior employees.

Because HP is such a young company, there has been a balance to this growth of new employees by the lack of substantial retirements. Now, the normal cycle of experienced people leaving due to retirement increases the need to replace them with new employees at the same time that the experience base in skills and culture is being lessened.

> It is still important to be able to sit at somebody's feet and listen to them talk about how they do their job. Why they don't issue memos that say, "Here's our objective and here's how we're going to achieve it" versus "here's our objective we agreed to, let's get on with it."—*An HP manager*

The challenge to continue to provide leadership is seen to be especially critical for the company's executives:

> Our leaders, Bill and Dave and others, have been fairly unique fellows who have been able to have a personal impact on this company. That amount of leadership is rarer than average—they're on the high part of the curve. As you create more and more little small companies which is what our divisions are, the direct leadership on the average would probably be lower. We've got to insure that we have people who can nurture others.
>
> As we've become larger, we really spread the people who have the ability to pass along the HP Way in subtle kinds of ways: by the way they carry out their jobs; by the way they get around and talk with people; by the way they deal with problems; how they set and get ownership for objectives for the coming year; by the way they deal with the difficult situations where there is conflict. We, as a company, still depend on those leaders who have these characteristics to continue to pass them on to the current management structure which is very diverse, very matrix-oriented, with a lot of dotted lines.—*An HP manager*

The problems of assimilating the numbers of new employees and new supervisors are compounded by the increasing geographical spread of operations throughout the United States and around the world. While HP uses the same management style in non-U.S. locations and feels it has been effective, the HP Way must be made to work in more and more different cultures.

HP's move in the computer systems markets also created changes which are still being felt. Prior to that time, almost all HP divisions made low production-volume products that were hardware-performance oriented. Computer systems and peripheral devices tend to require high-volume production and have much larger components of software development and service. These both require a different set of skills than HP's traditional mix. The new skills must be added and assimilated by those with little experience in these areas.

In another area, HP faces growing challenges to retain key employees. As a company that tries to attract exceptional people, it should be no surprise that some will leave to start their own companies. Former HP employees have been principals in quite a few of the new startups in "Silicon Valley." The examples of past successes by such new ventures and the recent increased availability of startup capital make it increasingly difficult to retain exception employees. This is also seen in the increasing desirability of HP employees as recruits for other ongoing enterprises. Recognition of a difference in the way HP manages has made HP people more attractive to those that would use similar techniques themselves.

**EXHIBIT 29–1**

**Ten-Year Consolidated Summary for the Years Ended October 31**

*(in Millions of Dollars Except for Employee and Per Share Amounts)*

| | 1980 | 1979 | 1978 | 1977 | 1976 | 1975 | 1974 | 1973 | 1972 | 1971 |
|---|---|---|---|---|---|---|---|---|---|---|
| Domestic orders | $1,517 | $1,280 | $ 977 | $ 769 | $ 592 | $ 501 | $ 468 | $ 424 | $ 307 | $ 233 |
| International orders | 1,623 | 1,247 | 898 | 664 | 558 | 501 | 425 | 311 | 200 | 164 |
| Total orders | $3,140 | $2,527 | $1,875 | $1,433 | $1,150 | $1,002 | $ 893 | $ 735 | $ 507 | $ 397 |
| Net sales | $3,099 | $2,361 | $1,737 | $1,368 | $1,121 | $ 985 | $ 893 | $ 669 | $ 483 | $ 378 |
| Costs and expenses: | | | | | | | | | | |
| Cost of goods sold | 1,475 | 1,106 | 808 | 625 | 538 | 467 | 425 | 316 | 224 | 186 |
| Research and development | 272 | 204 | 154 | 125 | 108 | 90 | 71 | 58 | 44 | 39 |
| Marketing | 459 | 362 | 264 | 208 | 177 | 162 | 142 | 124 | 81 | 65 |
| Administrative and general | 370 | 291 | 215 | 181 | 137 | 117 | 111 | 76 | 59 | 42 |
| | 2,576 | 1,963 | 1,441 | 1,139 | 960 | 836 | 749 | 574 | 408 | 332 |
| Earnings before taxes | 523 | 398 | 296 | 229 | 161 | 149 | 144 | 95 | 75 | 46 |
| Provision for taxes | 254 | 195 | 143 | 108 | 70 | 65 | 60 | 44 | 37 | 22 |
| Net earnings | $ 269 | $ 203 | $ 153 | $ 121 | $ 91 | $ 84 | $ 84 | $ 51 | $ 38 | $ 24 |
| Per share[a] | | | | | | | | | | |
| Net earnings | $ 4.47 | $3.43 | $2.63 | $2.13 | $1.62 | $1.51 | $1.54 | $.95 | $.73 | $.46 |
| Cash dividends | $ .40 | $ .35 | $ .25 | $ .20 | $ .15 | $ .12 | $ .10 | $.10 | $.10 | $.10 |
| Common shares outstanding at year-end[a] | 60 | 59 | 58 | 57 | 56 | 55 | 55 | 54 | 53 | 52 |
| No. employees at year-end (in thousands) | 57 | 52 | 42 | 35 | 32 | 30 | 29 | 28 | 21 | 17 |

[a]Based on shares of common stock outstanding at the end of each year, giving retroactive effect to the two-for-one stock split in June 1979.

**EXHIBIT 29–2**

**Consolidated Balance Sheet, October 31, 1980 and 1979** *(Millions of Dollars)*[1]

| | 1980 | 1979 |
|---|---|---|
| *Assets* | | |
| Current assets | | |
| Cash | $ 7 | $ 30 |
| Temporary cash investments, at cost which approximates market | 240 | 218 |
| Accounts and notes receivable | 622 | 491 |
| Inventories: | | |
| Finished goods | 148 | 120 |
| Purchased parts and fabricated assemblies | 397 | 358 |
| Other current assets | 77 | 52 |
| Total current assets | 1,491 | 1,269 |
| Property, plant, and equipment: | | |
| Land | 69 | 53 |
| Buildings and leasehold improvements | 645 | 491 |
| Machinery and equipment | 447 | 348 |
| | 1,161 | 892 |
| Accumulated depreciation and amortization | 372 | 301 |
| | 789 | 591 |
| Other assets | 57 | 40 |
| | $2,337 | $1,900 |

*Liabilities and Shareholders' Equity*

| | | |
|---|---|---|
| Current liabilities | | |
| Notes payable and commercial paper | $ 143 | $ 147 |
| Accounts payable | 104 | 109 |
| Employee compensation and benefits | 156 | 140 |
| Other accrued liabilities | 141 | 97 |
| Accrued taxes on earnings | 147 | 106 |
| Total current liabilities | 691 | 599 |
| Long-term debt, less current portion included in notes payable (1980—$7;1979—$9) | 29 | 15 |
| Deferred taxes on earnings | 70 | 51 |
| Commitments and contingencies | | |
| Shareholders' equity: | | |
| Common stock, par value $1 a share, 80 million shares authorized | 60 | 59 |
| Capital in excess of par value | 333 | 267 |
| Retained earnings | 1,154 | 909 |
| Total shareholders' equity | 1,547 | 1,235 |
| | $2,337 | $1,900 |

[1]The accompanying notes are an integral part of these financial statements.

**EXHIBIT 29–3**

**Business Segments** *(1977, 1976, and All Order Amounts Are Unaudited; Millions of Dollars)*

| | 1980 | 1979 | 1978 | 1977 | 1976 |
|---|---|---|---|---|---|
| *Orders* | | | | | |
| Electronic data products | $1,502 | $1,154 | $ 809 | $ 601 | $ 471 |
| Electronic test and measurement | 1,230 | 1,049 | 787 | 617 | 501 |
| Medical electronic equipment | 250 | 196 | 171 | 135 | 118 |
| Analytical instrumentation | 158 | 128 | 108 | 80 | 60 |
| Total orders | $3,140 | $2,527 | $1,875 | $1,433 | $1,150 |
| *Segment Sales* | | | | | |
| Electronic data products | $1,546 | $1,092 | $ 769 | $ 588 | $ 461 |
| Electronic test and measurement | 1,215 | 998 | 741 | 593 | 501 |
| Medical electronic equipment | 230 | 193 | 163 | 135 | 120 |
| Analytical instrumentation | 159 | 122 | 98 | 76 | 58 |
| Intersegment sales | (51) | (44) | (34) | (24) | (19) |
| Segment sales | $3,099 | $2,361 | $1,737 | $1,368 | $1,121 |

*Earnings Before Taxes*

| | | | | | |
|---|---|---|---|---|---|
| Electronic data products | $ 285 | $ 183 | $ 124 | $ 106 | $ 69 |
| Electronic test and measurement | 271 | 242 | 180 | 134 | 103 |
| Medical electronic equipment | 37 | 27 | 26 | 22 | 21 |
| Analytical instrumentation | 24 | 16 | 16 | 12 | 7 |
| Eliminations and corporate | (94) | (70) | (50) | (45) | (39) |
| Earnings before taxes | $ 523 | $ 398 | $ 296 | $ 229 | $ 161 |

*Electronic data products* are the responsibility of our computer groups and the personal computing products division. Their products include small- to medium-scale computer systems for business, scientific and industrial applications, desktop computers, personal computers, personal scientific and business programmable calculators, data terminals, printers, and disc and tape memories. Also included are a wide variety of software and support service for these products.

*Electronic test and measurement products* are the responsibility of our instrument and components groups. Their products include microwave semiconductors, light emitting diodes, logic analyzers, voltmeters, frequency analyzers, power supplies, board testers, plotters, recorders, counters, frequency sources, network and signal analyzers, signal generators, and automated test equipment.

*Medical electronic equipment* is the responsibility of our medical group. Their products include continuous monitoring systems for critical care patients, medical data management systems, fetal monitors, electrocardiographs and related interpretive and stress systems, pulmonary function analyzers, cardiac catheterization laboratory systems, blood gas measuring instruments, ultrasonic imaging systems, portable x-ray devices, cardiac defibrillators, and hospital supplies.

*Analytical instrumentation* is the responsibility of our analytical group. Their products include gas chromatographs, liquid chromatographs, mass spectrometers combined with chromatographs, spectrophotometers, laboratory automation systems, and integrators.

**EXHIBIT 29–4**
**Geographic Areas** *(All Order Amounts Are Unaudited; Millions of Dollars)*

| | United States | Europe | Rest of World | Elimina-tions and Corporate | Total |
|---|---|---|---|---|---|
| *1980* | | | | | |
| Orders | $1,517 | $1,160 | $ 463 | — | $3,140 |
| Net sales | $1,525 | $1,136 | $ 438 | — | $3,099 |
| Exports | $ 831 | $ 40 | $ 145 | $(1,016) | — |
| Earnings before taxes | $ 432 | $ 154 | $ 55 | $ (118) | $ 523 |
| Identifiable assets | $1,557 | $ 565 | $ 153 | $ 62 | $2,337 |
| *1979* | | | | | |
| Orders | $1,280 | $ 859 | $ 388 | — | $2,527 |
| Net sales | $1,201 | $ 805 | $ 355 | — | $2,361 |
| Exports | $ 624 | $ 25 | $ 98 | $ (747) | — |
| Earnings before taxes | $ 344 | $ 102 | $ 32 | $ (80) | $ 398 |
| Identifiable assets | $1,313 | $ 400 | $ 132 | $ 55 | $1,900 |

| *1978* | | | | | |
|---|---|---|---|---|---|
| Orders | $ 977 | $ 616 | $ 282 | — | $1,875 |
| Net sales | $ 911 | $ 581 | $ 245 | — | $1,737 |
| Exports | $ 427 | $ 19 | $ 66 | $ (512) | — |
| Earnings before taxes | $ 246 | $ 85 | $ 17 | $ (52) | $ 296 |
| Identifiable assets | $ 997 | $ 302 | $ 106 | $ 57 | $1,462 |

The data presented above reflect the worldwide aspect of the Company's manufacturing and marketing activities.

Exports are primarily intercompany transfers to affiliates outside the region. In addition, direct shipments from the United States to trade customers in the "rest of world" are included as exports from the United States and as net sales in the "rest of world." These direct shipments amounted to $192 million in 1980, $180 million in 1979, and $111 million in 1978.

The Company's policy is to transfer products between affiliates at the prevailing market price, less an allowance to compensate the receiving entity for subsequent production and/or marketing services.

Corporate items included in earnings before taxes are corporate research and development, marketing, administration, company-wide interest income and interest expense, and the minority interest in our 49%-owned unconsolidated Japanese affiliate.

Corporate assets included in total assets amounted to $409 million in 1980, $352 million in 1979, and $259 million in 1978. These represent temporary cash investments, leasing receivables, and headquarters facilities.

**EXHIBIT 29–5**
**HP Orders by Year Introduced**
*(Excludes Service, Components, and Parts)*

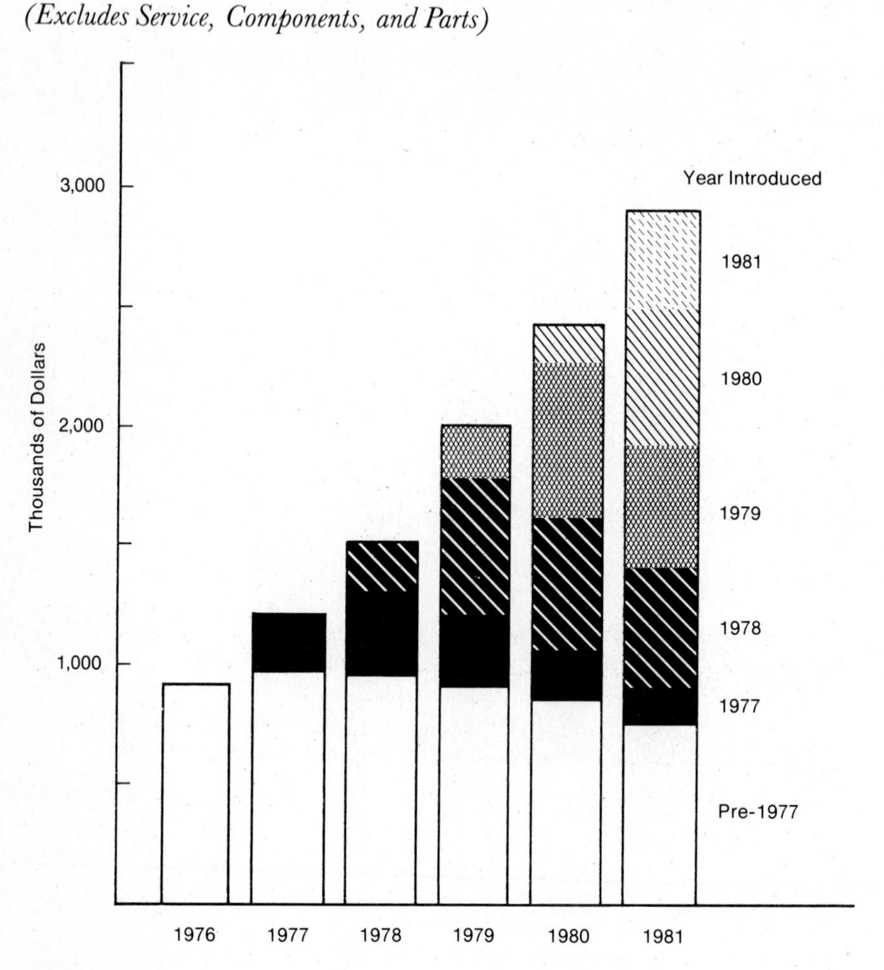


**EXHIBIT 29–6**
**Excerpts from HP's Statement of Corporate Objectives**

The achievements of an organization are the result of the combined efforts of each individual in the organization working toward common objectives. These objectives should be clearly understood by everyone in the organization, and should reflect the organization's basic character and personality.

If the organization is to fulfill its objectives, it should strive to meet certain other fundamental requirements:

- Highly capable, innovative people at all levels of the organization
- Objectives and leadership which generate enthusiasm at all levels: there can be no place, especially among . . . management, for halfhearted interest or halfhearted effort
- Uncompromising honesty and integrity
- All levels work in unison . . . through effective, cooperative effort

## *Objectives*

### 1. PROFIT

To achieve sufficient profit to finance our company growth and to provide the resources we need to achieve our other corporate objectives.

> It is the one absolutely essential measure of our corporate performance over the long term.
>
> Our long-standing policy has been to reinvest most of our profits and to depend on this . . . to finance our growth. This can be achieved if our return on net worth is roughly equal to our sales growth rate.
>
> Profits vary from year to year . . . our needs for capital also vary, and we depend on short-term bank loans to meet those needs. . . . However, loans are costly and must be repaid; thus, our objective is to rely on reinvested profits as our main source of capital.
>
> Meeting our profit objective requires that . . . every product . . . is considered a good value . . ., yet is priced to include an adequate profit.

### 2. CUSTOMERS

To provide products and services of the greatest possible value to our customers, thereby gaining and holding their respect and loyalty.

> Products that fill real needs and provide lasting value.

### 3. FIELDS OF INTEREST

To enter new fields only when the ideas we have, together with our technical, manufacturing, and marketing skills, assure that we can make a needed and profitable contribution to the field.

**EXHIBIT 29-6 (continued)**

The key to HP's prospective involvement in new fields is *contribution*. This means providing customers with something new and needed, not just another brand of something they can already buy.

4. GROWTH

To let our growth be limited only by our profits and our ability to develop and produce technical products that satisfy real customer needs.

5. OUR PEOPLE

To help HP people share in the company's success, which they make possible; to provide job security based on their performance; to recognize their individual achievements; and to help them gain a sense of satisfaction and accomplishment from their work.

Relationships within the company depend upon a spirit of cooperation among individuals and groups, and an attitude of trust and understanding on the part of managers toward their people. These relationships will be good only if employees have faith in the motives and integrity of their peers, supervisors and the company itself.

Job security is an important HP objective . . . the company has achieved a steady growth in employment by consistently developing good new products, and by avoiding the type of contract business that requires hiring many people, then terminating them when the contract expires. . . .

6. MANAGEMENT

To foster initiative and creativity by allowing the individual great freedom of action in attaining well-defined objectives.

Insofar as possible, each individual at each level in the organization should make his or her own plans to achieve company objectives and goals. After receiving supervisory approval, each individual should be given a wide degree of freedom to work within the limitations imposed by these plans, and by our general corporate policies.

7. CITIZENSHIP

To honor our obligations to society by being an economic, intellectual, and social asset to each nation and each community in which we operate.

To make sure that each of these communities is better for our presence.

EXHIBIT 29–7

Hewlett-Packard Corporate Organization November 1980

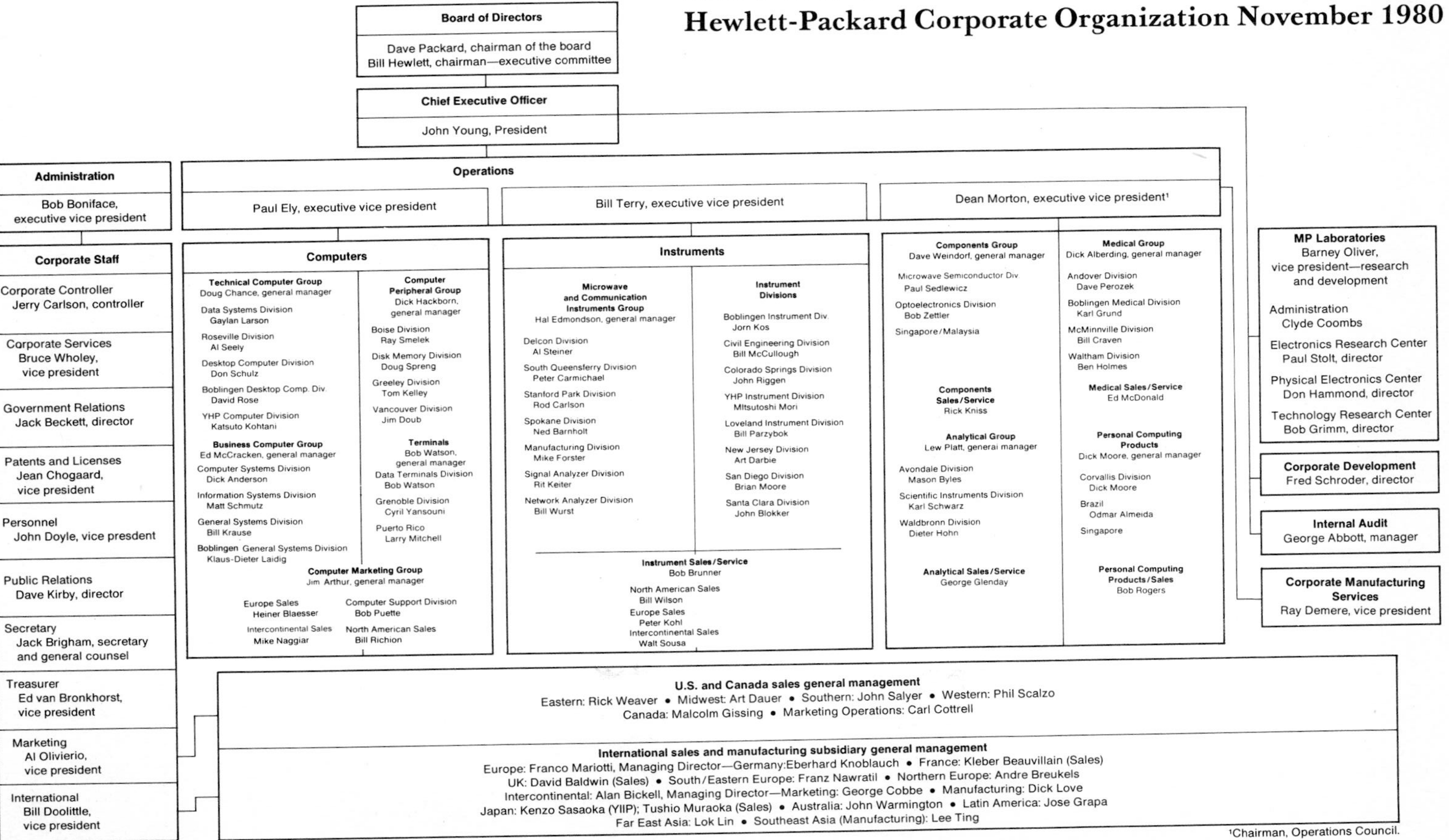

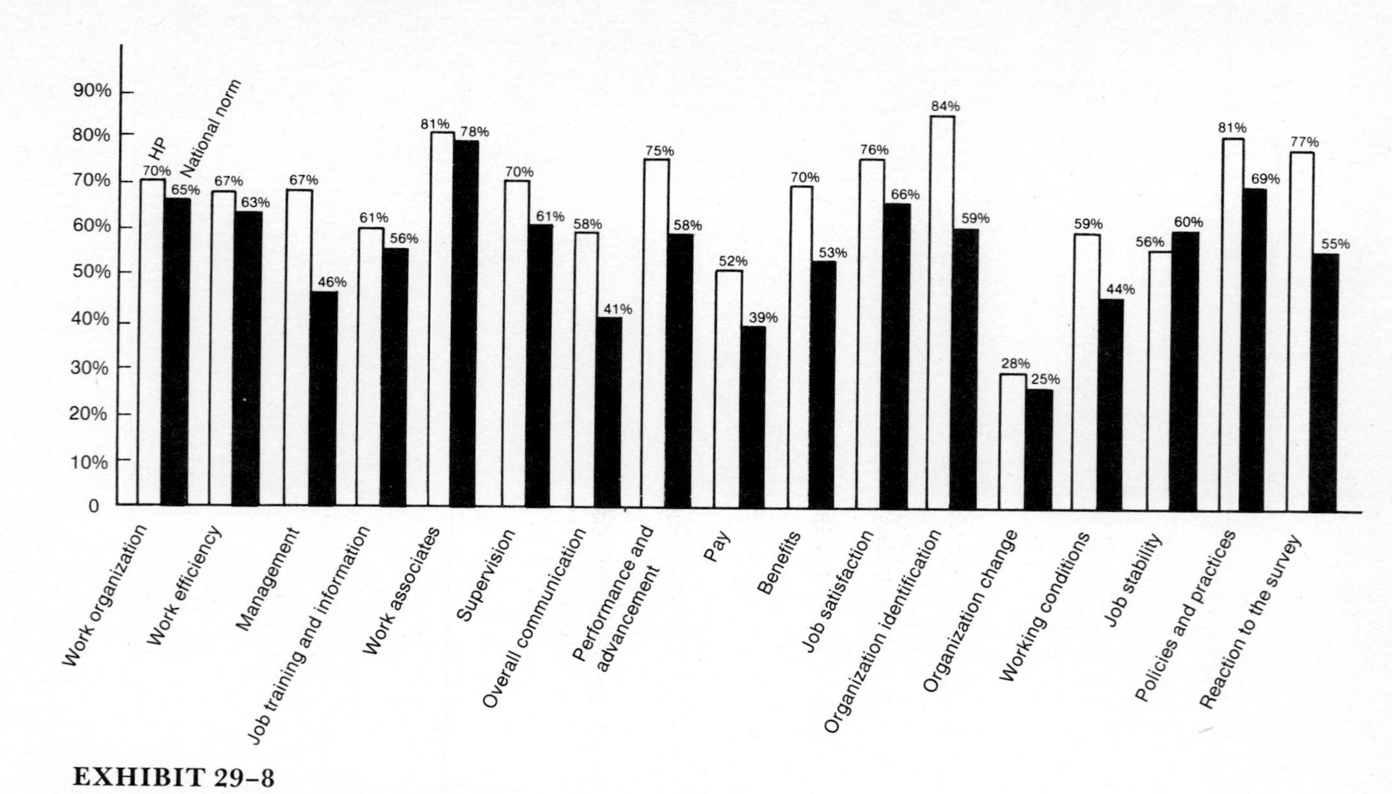


**EXHIBIT 29–8**
**Responses to Open Line Attitude Survey: Percentage of favorable responses of HP employees to a national sample of employees in 200 top U.S. companies, by category**

## EXHIBIT 29–8 (*continued*) Percentage of Responses Above or Below National Norms

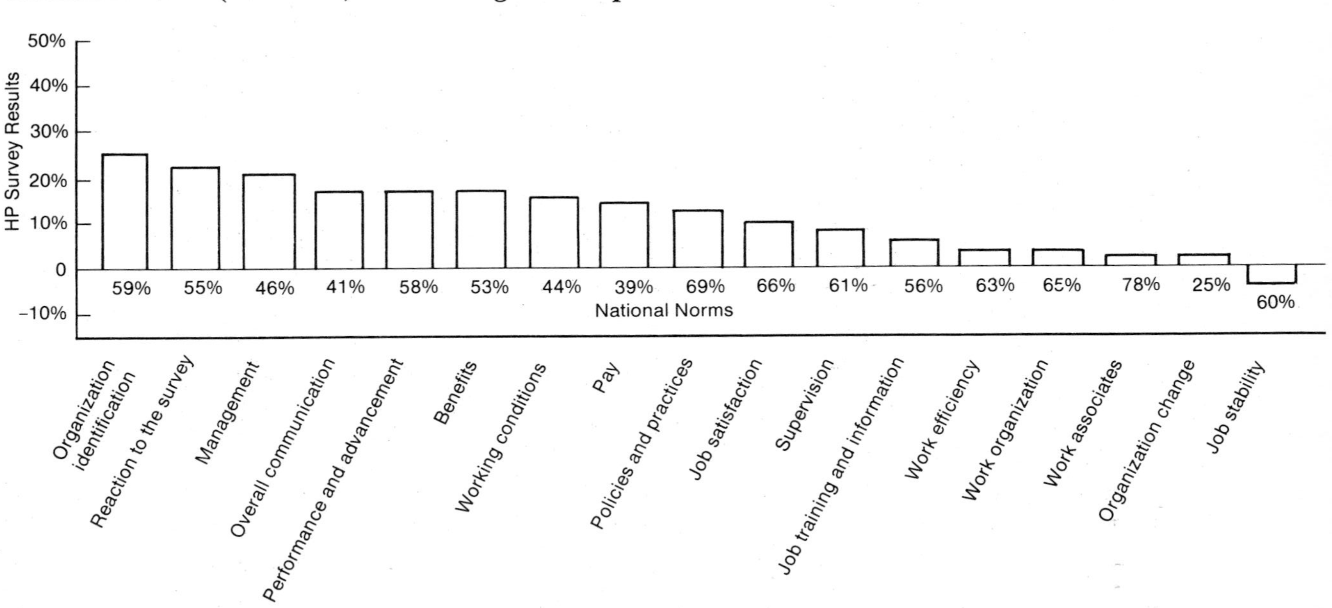


The 17 general categories of HP's Open Line results are shown in their order of ranking in percentage points above or below the national norms. In this Delta profile, the first eight categories (from Organization identification through Pay) show HP margins that are significantly above relatively low norms. In this series, HP averages 18.5% above a 49.4% norm average. In the next seven categories (Policies through Associates), HP's margins are only moderately above rather high norms. Here, HP averages 7.1% above an average norm of 65.4%. Actually, in total favorable responses, the HP averages in both of these two series were at a very similar high level—68.9% average for the first, and 72.5% for the second. The last two categories show a different picture: In Organization change we are only 3% above a very low norm of 25%, and in Job stability we fell some 4% below a 60% norm.

**EXHIBIT 29-9**
**Performance Bands Within One Pay Curve**

| QUADRANT DISTRIBUTION | PERFORMANCE DESCRIPTION | |
|---|---|---|
| Top 10% range: | Exceptional | Performance consistently *far exceeds* expectation and is superior to the vast majority of employees. |
| Upper 40% range: | Very good | Performance *consistently exceeds* expectations and job requirements. |
| Lower 40% range: | Good | Performance *consistently meets* expectations and job requirements. |
| Lower 10% range: | Acceptable or new on curve | Performance *usually* meets expectations and minimum requirements for the job. |

We can anticipate, then, that approximately 10% of employees at HP are Exceptional performers, while 10% are Acceptable. Similarly, 40% of HP employees make Very Good contributions while another 40% are Good contributors.

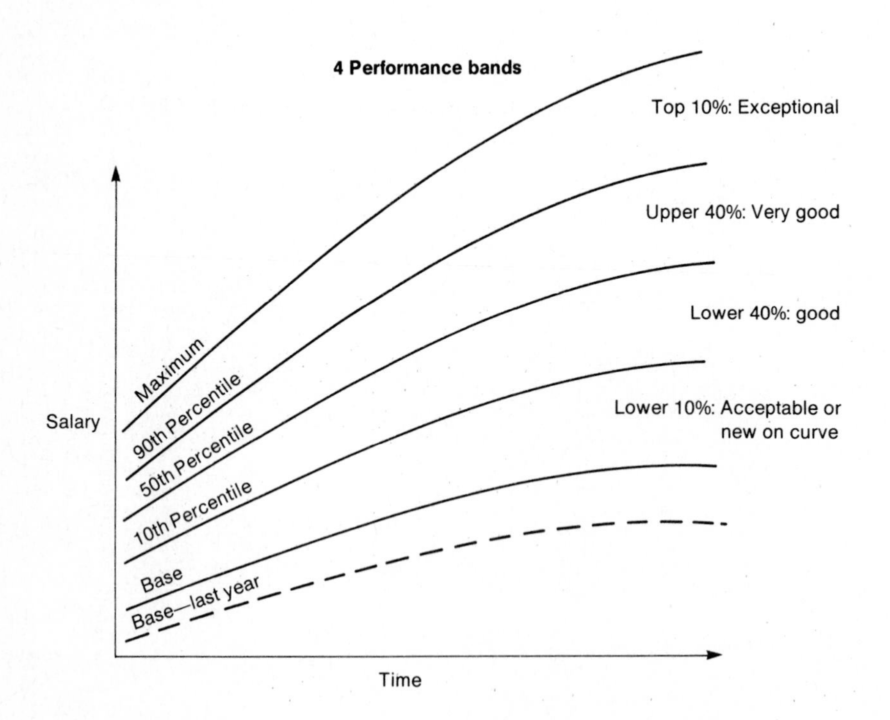

# EXHIBIT 29–10
# Distribution of Work Force by Time with HP

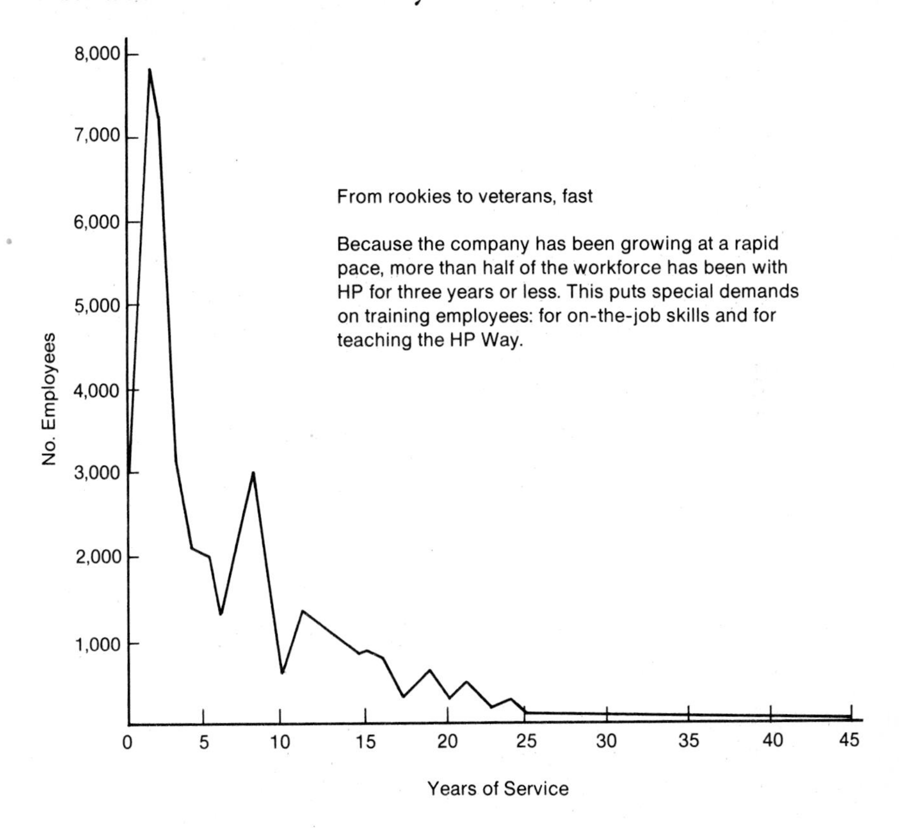

CASE 30

# PEOPLE EXPRESS

*Debra Whitestone*
*Leonard A. Schlesinger*

> We're now the biggest air carrier in terms of departures at any New York airport. We've flown almost three million passengers and saved the flying public over one quarter of a billion dollars (not including the savings from fares reduced by other airlines trying to compete with us). We expect to see a $3 million profit this year. . . . We have a concept that works and is unique.
>
> But with no growth horizon, people have been disempowered. We've started slowing down, getting sleepy. So, we've decided to set a new growth objective. Instead of adding 4 to 6 aircraft as we planned for this year, we are now thinking in terms of 12 or more new aircraft a year for the next few years.

With this announcement, Don Burr, founder, president, and chief executive officer (CEO) of People Express (PE) airline, concluded the business portion of the company's third quarterly financial meetng of 1982, graciously received rousing applause from several hundred of his stockholder/managers there to hear about and celebrate the success of their young company, and signaled for the music to begin.

## ORIGINS AND BRIEF HISTORY

People Express had been incorporated on April 7, 1980. In July of that year it had applied to the Civil Aeronautics Board (CAB) for permission to form a new airline to be based in the New York/Newark metropolitan area and dedicated to providing low-cost service in the eastern United States. Organized specifically to take advantage of provisions of the 1978 Airline Deregulation Act, PE was the first airline to apply for certification since its passage. (The act, which was designed to stimulate competition, allowed greater flexibility in scheduling and pricing and lowered the barriers to new entrants.)

In applying to the CAB for a "determination of fitness and certification of public convenience and necessity," PE committed itself to:

1. Provide "a broad new choice of flights" with high-frequency service

2. Keep costs low by "extremely producive use of assets"
3. Offer "unrestricted deep discount price savings" through productivity gains
4. Focus on several high-density eastern U.S. markets which had yet to reap the pricing benefits of deregulation
5. Center operations in the densely populated New York/Newark metropolitan area with service at the underutilized, uncongested, highly accessible Newark International Airport

The CAB was sufficiently impressed with this stated intent that it approved the application in three months (compared to the usual year or more). On October 24, 1980 People Express had its certificate to offer air passenger service between the New York/New Jersey area and 27 major cities in the eastern United States.

## STARTUP

People Express's managing officers proceeded to work round the clock for the next six months to turn their plans and ideas into a certificated operating airline. They raised money, leased a terminal, bought planes, recruited, trained, established routes and schedules, and prepared manuals to meet the FAA's fitness and safety standards. "We were here every night . . . from November until April when they [the Federal Aviation Administration (FAA)] gave us our certificate. . . . It was hell" [Burr]. People's operating certificate was granted April 24, 1981.

### *Operations Begin*

Flight service began on April 30, with three planes flying between Newark and Buffalo, New York; Columbus, Ohio; and Norfolk, Virginia. By the following year, the company employed a work force of over 1,200, owned 17 airplanes, and had flown nearly 2 million passengers between the 13 cities it was servicing. People Express had grown faster than any other airline and most businesses. It had managed to survive a startup year filled with environmental obstacles, a severe national economic recession, a strike of air traffic controllers, and bad winter weather—all of which had serious negative effects on air travel. By June 1982, though the airline industry in general was losing money, and though competition resulting from deregulation was intense, PE had begun showing a profit. Exhibit 30–1 lists milestones in the growth of People Express.

In the spring and summer of 1982 People underwent an extensive review of its infrastructure, added resources to the recruitment function so as to fill a 200-person staffing shortfall, and modified and attempted to implement more systematically a governance and communication system for which there had been little time during startup. By the fall of 1982 three more planes were about to arrive and three more cities were scheduled to be opened for service.

## BACKGROUND AND PRECURSORS

Donald Burr had been president of Texas International Airlines (TI) before he left it to found People Express with a group of his colleagues. The airline business was a ''hobby business'' for Burr; his love of airplanes went back to his childhood and he began flying in college, where as president of the Stanford Flying Club he could get his flight instruction paid for. After receiving an MBA from Harvard Business School in 1965 he went to work for National Aviation, a company specializing in airline investments, thus combining his affinity for aviation with his interest in finance. In 1971 he was elected president of National Aviation. While at National Aviation, Burr began a venture capital operation which involved him in the startup of several companies, including one which aimed at taking advantage of the recently deregulated telecommunications industry.

Eighteen months later he decided he wanted to get into the ''dirty fingernails'' side of the airline business. He left Wall Street and joined TI as a director and chairman of the executive committee. In June 1973 he became executive vice president and in 1976 assumed the responsibilities of chief operations officer. Between 1973 and 1977, Texas International moved from a position close to bankruptcy to become a profitable business. Burr was largely credited in the media for managing the turnaround. In June 1979 he was made president of Texas International. Six months later, he resigned.

Looking for a new challenge, one option he considered at that time was starting a new airline. The day after Burr left T.I., Gerald Gitner, his VP of planning and marketing, and Melrose Dawsey, his own and the CEO's executive secretary at TI, both submitted their resignations and joined Burr to incorporate People Express.

By the fall of 1980, 15 of TI's top managers and several more experienced staff from the ranks followed Burr to become part of the People Express management team and startup crew. Some gave up their positions even before they knew where the new company would be based, how it would be financed, whether they would be able to acquire planes, or what their exact jobs would be. In spite of the personal and financial risks, the opportunity to start an airline from scratch, with people they liked and respected, was too good to pass up. It was an adventure, a chance to test themselves. Burr at 39 was the oldest of the officers. Even if People Express failed, they assumed that they could pick themselves up and start again.

According to Hap Paretti, former legal counsel and head of government relations at TI, who became the fifth managing officer at People Express,

> We weren't talking about my job description or what kind of a budget I would have. It was more, we're friends, we're starting a new airline, you're one of the people we'd like to have join us in starting the company . . . what you do will be determined by what your interests are. The idea of getting involved and letting my personality and talents come through to determine my job appealed to me. I'm not happy doing just one thing.

Bob McAdoo, People's managing officer in charge of finance, had been corporate comptroller at Texas International. For McAdoo, joining People Express "was an easy decision, though I was having a good time at Texas International . . . I happen to be a guy driven by things related to efficiency. This was a chance to build an airline that was the most efficient in the business."

Lorie Dubose had become director of human resources at TI—the first woman director there—within a year after being hired.

> When Burr called to offer me the "People" job he explained that we would all be working in different capacities. I'd get to learn operations, get stock—I didn't know anything about stock, never owned any. At 28 how could I pass it up?

She came even though she was married and her husband decided not to move with her to Newark.

## FINANCING AND AIRPLANE ACQUISITION

To finance this adventure, Burr put up $355,000, Gitner put in $175,000, and the other managing officer came up with from $20,000 to $50,000 each. Burr secured an additional $200,000 from FNCB Capital Corp., a subsidiary of CitiCorp. The papers for the CitiCorp money, People Express's first outside funds, were signed on May 8, 1980, Burr's 40th birthday. Subsequently, the investment firm of Hambrecht & Quist agreed to help raise additional startup funds. Impressed with Burr's record and the quality of his management team, and aware of the opportunities created by airline deregulation, William Hambrecht agreed to Burr's suggestion of taking People Express public. (No other airline had ever gone public to raise startup money.)

As soon as the CAB application was approved in October 1980 all eight managing officers went on the road explaining their business plan and concepts to potential investors throughout the country. They were able to sell over $24 million worth of stock—3 million shares at $8.50 per share.

The official plan stated in the CAB application had called for raising $4 to $5 million, buying or leasing one to three planes, and hiring 200 or so people the first year. According to Hap Paretti, "We thought we'd start by leasing three little DC-9s, and flying them for a few years until we made enough money to buy a plane of our own." According to Burr, however, that plan reflected Gitner's more cautious approach and what most investors would tolerate at the beginning. Even with the additional money raised, Gitner thought they should buy at most 11 planes, but Burr's ideas were more expansive. From the beginning he wanted to start with a large number of planes so as to establish a presence in the industry quickly and support the company's overhead.

With cash in hand they were able to make a very attractive purchase from Lufthansa of an entire fleet of 17 Boeing 737s, all of which would be delivered totally remodeled and redecorated to People's specifications. While other managing officers recalled being a bit stunned, Burr viewed the transaction as being "right on plan."

## BURR'S PERSONAL MOTIVATION AND PEOPLE EXPRESS'S PHILOSOPHY

Government deregulation appeared to provide a "unique moment in history," and was one of several factors which motivated Burr to risk his personal earnings on starting a new airline. At least as important was his strong conviction that people were basically good and trustworthy, that they could be effectively organized, and if properly trained, were likely to be creative and productive.

> I guess the single predominant reason that I cared about starting a new company was to try and develop a better way for people to work together . . . that's where the name People Express came from (as well as) the whole people focus and thrust. . . . It drives everything else that we do.
>
> Most organizations believe that humans are generally bad and you have to control them and watch them and make sure they work. At People Express, people are trusted to do a good job until they prove they definitely won't.

From its inception, therefore, People Express was seen as a chance for Burr and his management team to experiment with and demonstrate a "better" way of managing not just an airline but any business.

While Burr recognized that his stance was contrary to the majority of organized structures in the United States, he rejected any insinuation that he was optimistic or soft.

> I'm not a goody two-shoes person, I don't view myself as a social scientist, as a minister, as a do-gooder. I perceive myself as a hard-nosed businessman, whose ambitions and aspirations have to do with providing goods and services to other people for a return.

In addition, however, he wanted PE to serve as a role model for other organizations, a concept which carried with it the desire to have an external impact and to contribute to the world's debate about "how the hell to do things well, with good purpose, good intent, and good results for everybody. To me, that's good business, a good way to live. It makes sense, it's logical, it's hopeful, so why not do it?"

Prior to starting service, Burr and the other managing officers spent a lot of time discussing their ideas about the "right" way to run an airline. Early on, they retained an outside management consultant to help them work together effectively as a management team and begin to articulate the principles to which they could commit themselves and their company. Over time, the principles evolved into a list of six "precepts," which were written down in December of 1981 and referred to continually from then on in devising and explaining company policies, hiring and training new recruits, structuring and assigning tasks. These precepts were: (1) service, commitment to growth of people, (2) best provider of air transportation, (3) highest quality of management, (4) role model for other airlines and other businesses, (5) simplicity, and (6) maximization of profits.

From Burr's philosophy as well as these precepts and a myriad of how-to-do-it-right ideas, a set of strategies began to evolve. According to People's management consultant, the "path" theory was the modus operandi—management would see what route people took to get somewhere, then pave the paths that had been worn naturally to make them more visible.

Thus, by 1982, one could articulate fairly clearly a set of strategies that had become "the concept," the way things were done at People Express.

## THE PEOPLE EXPRESS CONCEPT: THE PHILOSOPHY OPERATIONALIZED

The People Express business concept was broken down and operationalized into three sets of strategies: marketing, cost, and people. (Over Burr's objections, the presentation prepared by investment company Morgan Stanley for PE investors began with the marketing and cost strategies rather than the people strategies.)

*Marketing Strategy*

Fundamental to People's initial marketing strategy was its view of air travel as a commodity product for which consumers had little or no brand loyalty. People Express defined its own version of that product as a basic, cut-rate, no-nonsense air trip. A People Express ticket entitled a passenger to an airplane seat on a safe trip between two airports, period. The marketing strategy was to build and maintain passenger volume by offering extremely low fares and frequent, dependable service on previously overpriced, underserviced routes. In keeping with this strategy, the following tactics were adopted:

1. VERY LOW FARES. On any given route, People's fares were substantially below the standard fares prevailing prior to PE's announcement of service on that route. For instance, People entered the Newark-to-Pittsburgh market with a $19 fare in April 1982, when U.S. Air was charging $123 on that route, Typically, peak fares ran from 40 to 55 percent below the competition's standard fares and 65 to 75 percent below, during off-peak hours (after 6 P.M. and weekends).

2. CONVENIENT FLIGHT SCHEDULES. For any route that its planes flew, People tried to offer the most frequent flight schedule. With low fares and frequent flights, People could broaden its market segment beyond those of established airlines to include passengers who would ordinarily have used other forms of transportation. In an effort to expand the size of the air travel market, People's ads announcing service in new cities were pitched to automobile drivers, bus riders, and even those who tended not to travel at all. People hoped to capture most of the increase as well as some share of the preexisting market for each route.

3. REGIONWIDE IDENTITY. People set out to establish a formidable image in its first year as a major airline servicing the entire eastern United States. Large established airlines could easily wage price wars and successfully compete with a new airline in any one city, but they would probably have to absorb some losses and would be hard pressed to mount such a campaign on several fronts at once.

4. PITCH TO "SMART" AIR TRAVELERS. In keeping with its product definition, People's ads sought to identify People Express not as exotic or delicious or entertaining, but as the smart travel choice for smart, thrifty, busy travelers. The ads were filled with consumer information, as well as information about PE's smart people and policies.

Unlike most airlines, for instance, every People Express plane had roomy overhead compartments for passengers' baggage thereby saving them money, time, and the potential inconvenience of loss.

5. MEMORABLE POSITIVE ATMOSPHERE. Burr's long-term marketing strategy, once the airline was off the ground financially, was to make flying with People Express the most pleasant and memorable travel experience possible. The goal was for passengers to arrive at their destination feeling very well served. Thus, People Express's ultimate marketing strategy was to staff every position with competent, sensitive, respectful, up-beat, high-energy people who would create a contagious positive atmosphere. The message to staff and customers alike was: "At People Express, attitude is as important as altitude."

*Cost Structure*

People's cost structure was not based on a clear-cut formula so much as on an attitude that encouraged the constant, critical examination of every aspect of the business. According to Bob McAdoo, the management team "literally looked for every possible way to do things more simply and efficiently." McAdoo could point to at least 15 or 20 factors he felt were important in keeping costs down while preserving safety and quality. "If you look for one or two key factors, you miss the point." Cost savings measures affecting every aspect of the business included the following:

1. AIRCRAFT. Since fuel was the biggest single cost for an airline, People chose, redesigned, and deployed its aircraft with fuel efficiency in mind. Its twin engine Boeing 737-100 planes were thought to be the most fuel-efficient planes for their mission in the industry. By eliminating first-class and galley sections, interior redesign increased the number of all coach-class seats from 90 to 118 per plane. Overhead racks were expanded to accommodate more carry-on baggage. The planes were redecorated to convey a modern image and reassure potential passengers that low fares did not mean sacrificing quality or safety.

PE scheduled these planes to squeeze the most possible flying time out of them, 10.36 hours per plane per day, compared with the industry average of 7.08 hours. Finally, plane maintenance work was done by other airlines on a contract basis, a practice seen as less expensive than hiring a maintenance staff.

2. LOW LABOR COSTS. Labor is an airline's second biggest expense. Though salaries were generally competitive, and in some cases above industry norms, People's labor costs were relatively small. The

belief was that if every employee was intelligent, well-trained, flexible, and motivated to work hard, fewer people (as much as one-third fewer) would be needed than most airlines employed.

People kept its work force deliberately lean, and expected it to work hard. Each employee, carefully selected after an extensive screening process, received training in multiple functions (ticketing, reservations, ground operations and so on) and was extensively cross-utilized, depending on where the company's needs were at any given time. If a bag needed to be carried to a plane, whoever was heading towards the plane would carry the bag. Thus, peaks and valleys could be handled efficiently. This was in sharp contrast with other airlines which hired people into one of a variety of distinct ''classes in craft'' (such as flight attendants, reservations, baggage), each of which had a fairly rigid job description, was represented by a different union, and therefore was precluded from being cross-utilized.

3. IN-HOUSE EXPERTISE AND PROBLEM SOLVING. In addition to keeping the work force small and challenged, cross-utilization and rotation were expected to add the benefits of a de facto ongoing quality and efficiency review. Problems could be identified and solutions and new efficiency measures could be continually invented if people were familiar with all aspects of the business and motivated to take management-like responsibility for improving their company.

The Paxtrac ticketing computer was commonly cited as a successful example of how PE tapped its reservoir of internal brain power rather than calling in outside consultants to solve a company problem. Many of PE's longer routes were combinations of short-haul flights into and out of Newark. The existing ticketing system required a separate ticket for each leg of the trip, resulting in higher fares than PE wanted. Burr spotted the problem when he was flying one day (he tried to spend some time each month on board the planes or in the ground operations area). An ad hoc team of managers was sent off to a hotel in Florida for a week to solve the problem. They came up with a specially designed microprocessor ticketing machine with the flexibility to accommodate the company's marketing plans and fast enough (7 seconds per ticket versus 20 seconds) to enable on-board ticketing of larger passenger loads.

4. FACILITIES. Like its aircraft, PE's work space was low-cost and strictly functional. The main Newark terminal was located in the old North Terminal building, significantly cheaper to rent than space at the West and South terminals a mile away. People had no ticket counters. All ticketing was done either by travel agents in advance, or by customer service managers on board the planes once they were air-

bound. Corporate headquarters, located upstairs over the main terminal had none of the luxurious trappings associated with a major airline. Offices were shared, few had carpeting, and decoration consisted primarily of People Express ads, sometimes blown up poster size, and an occasional framed print of an airplane.

5. RESERVATIONS. The reservations system was kept extremely simple, fast, and therefore inexpensive. There were no interline arrangements with other airlines for ticketing or baggage transfer; no assistance was offered with hotel or auto reservations in spite of the potential revenue leverage to be derived from such customer service. Thus, calls could be handled quickly by hundreds of easily trained temporary workers in several of the cities People served, using local lines (a WATS line would cost $8,000 per month) and simple equipment ($900 versus the standard $3,000 computer terminals).

6. NO "FREEBIES." Costs of convenience services were unbundled from basic transportation costs. People offered none of the usual airline "freebies." Neither snacks nor baggage handling, for example, were included in the price of a ticket, though such extras were available and could be purchased for an additional fee.

### *People*

Burr told his managers repeatedly that it was People's people and its people policies that made the company unique and successful. "The people dimension is the value added to the commodity. Many investors still don't fully appreciate this point, but high commitment and participation, and maximum flexibility and massive creative productivity are the most important strategies in People Express."

## STRUCTURE AND POLICIES

As PE moved from a set of ideas to an operating business, People's managers took pains to design structures and develop policies consistent with the company's stated precepts and strategies. This resulted in an organization characterized by minimal hierarchy, rotation and cross-utilization, work teams, ownership, self-management, participation, compensation, selective hiring and recruitment, multipurpose training, and team building.

1. MINIMAL HIERARCHY. People's initial organizational structure consisted of only three formal levels of authority. At the top of the

organization was the president/CEO and six managing officers, each of whom provided line as well as staff leadership for more than one of the 13 functional areas (see Exhibit 30-2 for a listing of functions).

Reporting to and working closely with the managing officers were eight general managers, each of whom provided day-to-day implementation and leadership in at least one functional area, as well as planning for and coordinating with other areas. People's managing officers and general managers worked hard at exemplifying the company's philosophy. They worked in teams, rotated out of their specialties as much as possible to take on line work, filling in at a gate or on a flight. Several had gone through the full "in-flight" training required of customer service managers. They shared office furniture and phones. Burr's office doubled as the all-purpose executive meeting room; if others were using it when he had an appointment, he would move down the hall and borrow someone else's empty space.

There were no executive assistants, secretaries, or support staff of any kind. The managers themselves assumed the activities that such staff would ordinarily perform. Individuals, teams, and committees did their own typing, which kept written communications to a minimum. Everyone answered his or her own phone. (Both practices were seen as promoting direct communication as well as saving money.)

Beyond the top 15 officers, all remaining full-time employees were either flight managers, maintenace managers, or customer service managers. The titles indicated distinctions in qualifications and functional emphasis rather than organizational authority. *Flight managers* were pilots. Their primary responsibility was flying, but they also performed various other tasks, such as dispatching, scheduling, and safety checks, on a rotating basis or as needed. *Maintenance managers* were technicians who oversaw and facilitated maintenance of PE's airplanes, equipment, and facilities by contract with other airlines' maintenance crews. In addition to monitoring and assuring the quality of the contracted work, maintenance managers were utilized to perform various staff jobs.

The vast majority of People's managers were *customer service managers,* generalists trained to perform all passenger-related tasks, such as security clearance, boarding, flight attending, ticketing, and food service, as well as some staff function activities (see Exhibit 30-2).

By and large, what few authority distinctions did exist were obscure and informal. Managing officers, general managers, and others with seniority (over one year) had more responsibility for giving direction, motivating, teaching, and perhaps coordinating, but *not* for supervising or managing in the traditional sense.

2. OWNERSHIP, LIFELONG JOB SECURITY. Everyone in a permanent position at PE was a shareholder, required as a condition of em-

ployment to buy, at a greatly discounted price, a number of shares of common stock, determined on the basis of his or her salary level. It was expected that each employee in keeping with being a manager/owner, would demonstrate a positive attitude toward work, and participate in the governance of the company. As Managing Officer Lori Dubose pointed out, "We'll fire someone only if it is (absolutely) necessary. . . . For instance, we won't tolerate dishonesty or willful disregard for the company's policies, but we don't punish people for making mistakes." In exchange, People Express promised the security of lifetime employment and opportunities for personal and professional growth through continuing education, cross-utilization, promotion from within the company, and compensation higher than other companies paid for similar skills and experience.

3. Cross-Utilization and Rotation. No one, regardless of work history, qualifications, or responsibility, was assigned to do the same job all the time. Everyone, including managing officers, was expected to be "cross-utilized" as needed and to rotate monthly between in-flight and ground operations and/or between line and staff functions. (The terms "line" and "staff" in PE parlance differentiated tasks which were directly flight-related from those related to the business of operating the company.)

Seen by some as unnecessarily complicated and troublesome, cross-utilization and rotation were justified by PE in several ways. According to Burr, they were conceived primarily as methods of continuing education, aimed at keeping everyone interested, challenged, and growing. Bob McAdoo appreciated the flexible staff utilization capability which eventually would result from everyone having broad exposure to the company's functions. Rotation did create some difficulties:

> It takes people a while to master each job. It might seem better to have an expert doing a given job. Cross-utilization also means you need high-quality people who are capable of doing several jobs. This in turn limits how fast you can recruit and how fast you can grow.

These were seen, even by McAdoo, the efficiency expert, as short-term inconveniences well worth the long-term payoff.

> When you rotate people often they don't develop procedures that are too complicated for newcomers to learn and master fast. This forces the work to be broken down into short simple packets, easily taught and easily learned.

4. Self-Management. People were expected to manage themselves and their own work in collaboration with their teams and coworkers. According to Jim Miller, coordinator of training, "We don't

want to teach behaviors—we want to teach what the end result should look like and allow each individual to arrive at those results his or her own way. . . . When desired results aren't achieved, we try to guide people and assist them in improving the outcome of their efforts."

The written, though never formalized, guidelines regarding "self-management" read as follows:

> Within the context of our precepts and corporate objectives, and with leadership direction but no supervision, individuals and/or teams have the opportunity (and the obligation) to self-manage, which encompasses the following:
>
> - Setting specific, challenging, but realistic objectives within the organizational context.
> - Monitoring and assessing the quantity/quality/timeliness of one's own performance ("how am I doing?") by gathering data and seeking input from other people.
> - Inventing and executing activities to remedy performance problems that appear and exploiting opportunities for improved performance.
> - Actively seeking the information, resources, and/or assistance needed to achieve the performance objectives.

When it came time for performance reviews, each individual distributed forms to those six coworkers from whom feedback would be useful. Again, growth rather than policing was the objective.

5. WORK TEAMS. Dubose observed that "even with smart, self-managed people, one person can't have all the components to be the answer to every situation." People therefore had decided to organize its work force into small (3- to 4-person) work groups as an alternative to larger groups with supervisors. "If you don't want a hierarchical structure with 40 levels you have to have some way to manage the numbers of people we were anticipating." Teams were seen as promoting better problem solving and decision making as well as personal growth and learning.

Every customer service manager belonged to a self-chosen ongoing team with which he or she was assigned work by a lottery system on a monthly basis. Though monthly staff assignments were made individually according to interests, skills, and needs, staff work was expected to be performed in teams. This applied to flight managers and maintenance managers as well as customer service managers. Each team was to elect a liaison to communicate with other teams. Each staff function was managed by a team of coordinators, most of whom were members of the startup team recruited from Texas International. Managing officers also worked in teams and rotated certain responsibilities to share the burden and the growth benefits of primary leadership.

6. GOVERNANCE, BROAD-BASED PARTICIPATION. People's governance structure was designed with several objectives: policy development, problem solving, participation, and communication.

While Burr was the ultimate decision maker, top management decisions, including plans and policies, were to be made by management teams with the assistance of advisory councils. Each of the eight managing officers and eight general managers was responsible for at least one of the 13 functional areas (see Exhibit 30–2) and served on a management team for at least one other function. The 13 function-specific management teams were grouped into four umbrella staff committees: operations, people, marketing, and finance and administration. For each staff committee, composed of managing officers and general managers from the relevant functional areas, there was an advisory council made up of selected customer service managers, flight managers, and maintenance managers serving on relevant line and staff teams. The councils were intended to generate and review policy recommendations, but until August 1982 they followed no written guidelines. A study done by Yale University students under the direction of Professor Richard Hackman showed considerable confusion as to their purposes (influencing, learning, solving, communicating issues) and role (advising versus making decisions).

To minimize duplication and maximize communication, each advisory council elected a member to sit on an overarching "coordinating council" which was to meet regularly with Don Burr (to transmit information to and from him and among the councils). These ongoing teams and councils were supplemented periodically by ad hoc committees and task forces which could be created at anyone's suggestion to solve a particular problem, conduct a study, and/or develop proposals.

In addition to maximizing productivity, all of the above practices, teams, and committees were seen essential to promote personal growth and keep people interested in and challenged by their work.

7. COMPENSATION—HIGH REWARD FOR EXPECTED HIGH PERFORMANCE. People's four-part compensation package was aimed at reinforcing its human resource strategy. Base salaries were determined strictly by job category on a relatively flat scale, ranging in 1981 from $17,000 for customer service managers to $48,000 for the managing officers and CEO. (Competitor airlines averaged only $17,600 for flight attendants after several years of service, but paid nearly double for managing officers and more than four times as much for their chief executives.)

Whereas most companies shared medical expenses with employees, People paid 100 percent of all medical and dental expenses. Life insurance, rather than being pegged to salary level, was $50,000 for everyone.

After one year with PE all managers' base salary and benefits were augmented by three forms of potential earnings tied to the company's fortunes. There were two profit-sharing plans: (1) a dollar-for-dollar plan, based on quarterly profits and paid quarterly to full-time employees who had been with PE over one year, and (2) a plan based on annual profitability. The former was allocated proportionally, according to salary level and distributed incrementally. If profits were large, those at higher salary levels stood to receive larger bonuses, but only after all eligible managers had received some reward. The sustained profits were distributed annually and in equal amounts to people in all categories. Together, earnings from these plans could total up to 50 percent or more of base salary. The aggregate amount of PE's profit-sharing contributions after the second quarter of 1982 was $311,000.

Finally, PE awarded several stock option bonuses, one nearly every quarter, making it possible for managers who had worked at least half a year to purchase limited quantities of common stock at discounts ranging from 25 to 40 percent of market value. The company offered five-year interest-free promissory notes for the full amount of the stock purchase required of new employees, and for two-thirds the amount of any optional purchase. As of July 1982, 651 employees, including the managing officers, held an aggregate 513,000 shares of common stock under a restricted stock purchase plan. Approximately 85 percent were held by employees other than managing officers and general managers. The total number of shares reserved under this plan was, at that time, 900,000.

8. SELECTIVE HIRING OF THE PEOPLE EXPRESS "TYPE." Given the extent and diversity of responsibilities People required of its people, Lori Dubose, managing officer in charge of the company's "people" as well as in-flight functions, believed firmly that it took a certain type of person to do well at People Express. Her recruiters, experienced CSMs themselves, looked for people who were bright, educated, well groomed, mature, articulate, assertive, creative, energetic, conscientious, and hard working. While they had to be capable of functioning independently and taking initiative, and it was desirable for them to be ambitious in terms of personal development, achievements, and wealth, it was also essential that they be flexible, collaborative rather than competitive with co-workers, excellent team players, and comfortable with PE's horizontal structure. "If someone needed to be a vice president in order to be happy, we'd be concerned and might not hire them" [Miller].

Recruiting efforts for customer service managers were pitched deliberately to service professionals—nurses, social workers, teachers—with an interest in innovative management. No attempt was made to attract those with airline experience or interest per se (see Exhibit

30-3). Applicants who came from traditional airlines where "everyone memorized the union contract and knew you were only supposed to work x number of minutes and hours" were often ill-suited to People's style. They were not comfortable with its loose structure and broadly defined, constantly changing job assignments. They were not as flexible as People Express types.

The flight manager positions were somewhat easier to fill. Many pilots had been laid off by other airlines due to economic problems, and People Express had an abundant pool of applicants. All licensed pilots had already met certain intelligence and technical skill criteria, but not every qualified pilot was suited or even willing to be a People Express flight manager. Though flying time was strictly limited to the FAA's standard 30 hours per week (100 hours per month, 1000 hours per year), and rules regarding pilot rest before flying were carefully followed, additional staff and management responsibilities could bring a flight manager's work week to anywhere from 50 to 70 hours.

Furthermore, FMs were expected to collaborate and share status with others, even nonpilots. In return for being flexible and egalitarian—traits which were typically somewhat in conflict with their previous training, and job demands—pilots at PE were offered the opportunity to learn the business, diversify their skills and interests, and benefit from profit sharing and stock ownership, if and when the company succeeded.

9. Recruitment Process. As many as 1,600 would-be CSMs had shown up in response to a recruitment ad. To cull out "good PE types" from such masses, Dubose and her startup team, eight CSMs whom she recruited directly from TI, designed a multistep screening process.

Applicants who qualified after two levels of tests and interviews with recruiters were granted a "board interview" with at least one general manager and two other senior people who reviewed psychological profiles and character data. In a final review after a day-long orientation, selected candidates were invited to become trainees. One out of 100 CSM applicants was hired (see Exhibit 30-4 for a CSM profile).

In screening pilots, "the interview process was very stringent. Many people who were highly qualified were eliminated." Only one of three flight manager applicants was hired.

10. Training and Team Building. The training program for CSMs lasted for five weeks, six days a week, without pay. At the end, candidates went through an in-flight emergency evacuation role-play and took exams for oral competency as well as written procedures. Those who tested at 90 or above were offered a position.

The training was designed to enable CSMs, many without airline experience, to perform multiple tasks and to be knowledgeable about all aspects of an airline. Three full days were devoted to team building, aimed at developing trainees' self-awareness, communication skills, and sense of community. "We try to teach people to respect differences, to work effectively with others, to build synergy" [Miller].

On the last team-building day everybody chose two or three others to start work with. These groups became work teams, People's basic organizational unit. Initially, according to Miller, these decisions tended to be based on personalities and many trainees were reluctant to choose their own work teams. They were afraid of hurting people's feelings or being hurt. Trainers would remind them that People Express gave them more freedom than they would get in most companies, more than they were used to, and that "freedom has its price . . . it means you've got to be direct and you've got to take responsibility" [Kramer].

Over time, trainers learned to emphasize skills over personalities as the basis of team composition and to distinguish work teams from friendship groups. Choosing a work team was a business decision.

## BOTTOM LINES: BUSINESS INDICATORS

As of the second quarter of 1982 People was showing a $3 million net profit, one of only five airlines in the industry to show any profit at that time. In addition to short-term profitability, Burr and his people enjoyed pointing out that by several other concrete indicators typically used to judge the health and competitive strength of an airline, their strategies were paying off and their innovative company was succeeding.

MARKETING PAYOFF. Over three million passengers had chosen to fly with PE. The size of air passenger markets in cities serviced by People had increased since People's entrance. In some instances the increase had been immediate and dramatic, over 100 percent. Annual revenue rates were approaching $200 million.

COST CONTAINMENT. Total costs per available seat-mile were the lowest of any major airline (5.2¢ compared to a 9.4¢ industry average). Fuel costs were ½ to ¾¢ per-seat-mile lower than other airlines.

PRODUCTIVITY. Aircraft productivity surpassed the industry average by 50 percent (10.36 hours/day/plane compared to 7.06). Employee productivity was 145% above the 1981 industry average (1.52

compared to .62 revenue passenger miles per employee) for a 600-mile average trip. Return on revenue was 15.3 percent, second only to, and a mere .9 percent below, Southwest—the country's most successful airline. (Exhibit 30–5 shows operating statements through June 1982, and Exhibit 30–6 presents industry comparative data on costs and productivity.)

## EXPLANATIONS OF SUCCESS

How could a new little airline with a funny name like People Express become such a formidable force so fast in such difficult times? Burr was fond of posing this question with a semipuzzled expression on his face and answering with a twinkle in his eye! The precepts and policies represented by that "funny" name—People—had made the difference. To back up this assertion, Burr and the other managing officers gave examples of how the people factor was impacting directly on the company's bottom line.

Consumer research showed that, notwithstanding heavy investments in award-winning advertisements, the biggest source of People's success was word of mouth; average customer ratings of passenger courtesy and personal treatment on ground and on board were 4.7 of 5.

Several journalists had passed on to readers their favorable impressions of People's service: "I have never flown on an airline whose help is so cheerful and interested in their work. This is an airline with verve and an upbeat spirit which rubs off on passengers." Others credited the commitment, creativity, and flexibility of People's people with the company's very survival through its several startup hurdles and first-year crises.

Perhaps the biggest crisis was the PATCO strike which occurred just months after PE began flying. While the air traffic controllers were on strike, the number of landing slots at major airports, including Newark, were drastically reduced. This made People's original hub-and-spoke short-haul route design unworkable. To overfly Newark and have planes land less frequently without reducing aircraft utilization, People Express took a chance on establishing some new previously unserviced, longer routes between smaller, uncontrolled airports, such as Buffalo, New York to Jacksonville, Florida. This solution was tantamount to starting a new airline, with several new Florida stations, new advertising, and new route scheduling arrangements. The costs were enormous. According to Hap Paretti:

> We could have run out of $25 million very quickly and there wouldn't be any People Express. The effort people made was astronomical, and it was certainly in their best interest to make that effort. Everybody recognized

> truly and sincerely that the air traffic controllers strike was a threat to their very existence. They rearranged their own schedules, worked extra days, really put the extra flying hours in, came in on their off days to do the staff functions, all things of that nature, people just really chipped in and did it and did a damned good job. So when we went into these markets from Buffalo to Florida, we could go in at $69. If we went in at $199 like everybody else we wouldn't have attracted one person. We could go in very low like that because we had a cost structure that allowed us to do that. That's where the people strategy, from a cost standpoint, resulted in our survival. If it wasn't there we'd be in the same situation many other carriers are today, hanging on by a toenail.

By way of comparison, New York Air, a nonunion airline started by others from Texas International around the same time as People Express with plenty of financial backing, economical planes, and a similar concept of low-cost, high-frequency service, but different people policies, was losing money.

## THE HUMAN DIMENSIONS: POSITIVE CLIMATE AND PERSONAL GROWTH

In addition to becoming a financially viable business, People Express had shown positive results in the sphere of personal growth, the number one objective of its "people strategy." High levels of employee satisfaction showed up in first-year surveys done by the University of Michigan. Less tangible but nevertheless striking were the nonverbal and anecdotal data. A cheerful, friendly, energetic atmosphere permeated the planes and passenger terminals as well as the private crew lounge and hallways of corporate headquarters. Questions about the company were almost invariably answered articulately, confidently, and enthusiastically. Stories of personal change, profit and learning were common:

Ted E., CSM:

> I was a special education teacher making $12,000 a year, receiving little recognition, getting tired, looking for something else. I started here at $17,000, already have received $600 in profit sharing, and will soon own about 800 shares of stock worth $12 on the open market, all bought at very reduced rates. (Two months after this statement the stock was worth $26 a share.)

Glenn G., CSM:

> I was running a hotline and crisis program, then was assistant manager of a health food store before seeing the People Express recruitment ad in the newspaper and coming to check it out. I'm about to sell my car in order to take advantage of the current stock offer to employees.

Both Glenn and Ted had worked primarily in training but had also done "in-flight" and "ground-ops." jobs. They wanted more responsibilities, hoped to get them but even if they didn't get promoted soon they expected to continue learning from and enjoying their work.

Michael F., flight captain:

> I'm making $36,000. With my profit-sharing checks so far I've got $43,000 and on top of that I'll get sustained profit-sharing deals . . . I'm doing O.K. . . . Granted, at [another company] a captain might be making $110,000 working 10 days a month [but] they're not really worth it. [In other companies] the top people might make over $100,000 but they throw on 200 guys at the bottom so they can continue to make their salary. Is that fair? [Also, the seniority system would have kept Michael from being a captain at most other airlines.] We're radically different and I believe radically better.
>
> Most pilots know very little about what's going on in their company. In a People flight manager position, the knowledge people gain in this ratty old building is incredible. It's phenomenal opportunity. It's very stimulating and exciting. I never thought I would have this much fun.

The stories of People's startup team members and officers were even more dramatic. Each had profited and diversified substantially in their two years with People.

Melrose Dawsey, Burr's secretary at Texas International, was a managing officer at People with primary responsibility for administration. She owned 40,000 shares of stock, purchased at $.50 a share and worth, as of November 1982, over $20/share. For her own career development, she had also begun to assume some line management responsibilities in the in-flight area. In her spare time, she had earned her in-flight certification and run the New York marathon (as had Burr).

Lori Dubose, the youngest officer, had come to People to head the personnel function. In addition, she had taken on primary responsibility for the "in-flight" function as well as assuming the de facto role of key translator and guide vis-a-vis the company's precepts. As others came to see the value and purpose of People's precepts and human resource policies, Dubose's status among the officers had also risen.

Jim Miller had been a flight attendant for a year and base manager of in-flight services for four years at Texas International. As part of Dubose's startup team, he had been coordinator of training, played a key role in recruitment, and then took on added responsibility for management and organizational development as well.

Hap Paretti, who began as legal counsel and head of government relations, quickly became involved in all aspects of the marketing function, and then went on to head flight operations, a move he acknowledged was "a little out of the ordinary" since he didn't have a technical background as a pilot. He spoke for all of the officers in saying, "As a managing officer you're expected to think about virtually every major decision that comes up for review."

Many spoke of the more subtle aspects of their personal development. Hap Paretti enjoyed the challenge of motivating other people and "managing by example" so as to enhance the growth of others.

Geoff Crowley, a general manager in charge of ground operations and manpower scheduling, talked of becoming "less competitive" and "less uptight about winning alone" and more interested in working together with others to accomplish group and company goals.

## THE DOWNSIDE OF PEOPLE'S GROWTH AND STRATEGIES

People Express's growth rate and strategies were not without significant organizational, financial, and human costs. By Burr's own observation,

> I would say, at best, we're operating at 50 percent of what we'd like to be operating at in terms of the environment for people to do the best in. So we're nowhere near accomplishing what we would really like to accomplish in that regard. [But] I think we're better off today than we ever have been. And I think we're gaining on the problem.

## CHRONIC UNDERSTAFFING

Lori Dubose saw the hiring rate as the most difficult aspect of the company's growth process, causing many other problems:

> If we could get enough people to staff adequately in all three areas of the company so that people got some staff and some line responsibility and would have some time for management development . . . I think things would be a lot different. [There's been] constant pressure to hire, hire, hire, and we just haven't gotten enough.

She was adamant, however, about not relaxing People's requirements.

When Dubose came to PE she expected to have to staff a company flying three planes which would have required rapid hiring of perhaps 200 to 300 people. The purchase of the Lufthansa fleet meant five to six times as many staff were needed. Given the time consumed by the selective recruiting process, and the low percentage of hires, the staffing demands for supporting and launching 17 planes stretched people to the limit. The result was chronic understaffing even by People's own lean staffing standards.

As of November 1982 the 800 permanent "managers" were supplemented with over 400 temporaries, hired to handle telephone reservations, a function trained CSMs were originally expected to cover. Some of these "res" workers had been there a year or more, but still were not considered full-fledged People people, though many would have liked to be. They received little training, did not work in teams, own stock, receive profit-sharing bonuses, or participate in advisory councils. They were just starting to be invited to social activities. For a while those wishing to be considered for permanent CSM positions were required to leave their temporary jobs first on the theory that any bad feelings from being rejected could be contagious and have a bad effect on morale. That policy was eventually seen as unfair, and dropped. Indeed, some managers saw the reservation area as a training ground for CSM applicants.

In August 1982 several managing officers estimated that aside from reservation workers, they were short by about 200 people, though the recruiting staff was working 10 to 12 hours daily, often 6 days a week, as they had since January 1981. This understaffing in turn created other difficulties, limiting profits, policy implementation, and development of the organization's infrastructure.

> If we had another 100 to 150 CSMs without adding an additional airplane we could just go out and add probably another half a million to a million dollars a month to the bottom line of the company. . . . There is additional flying out there that we could do with these airplanes . . . we could generate a lot more money . . . almost double the profits of the company.—*McAdoo*

The policy of job rotation, critical to keeping everyone challenged and motivated, had been only partially implemented. Initial plans called for universal monthly rotations, with 50 percent of almost everyone's time spent flying, 25 percent on ground line work, and another 25 percent in "staff functions." Due to staffing shortages, however, many people had been frozen in either line jobs without staff functions or vice versa. Some had become almost full-time coordinators or staff to a given function like recruiting and training, while others had done mostly line work and had little or no opportunity to do what they expected when they were hired as "managers." Since neither performance appraisal nor governance plans had been fully carried out, many felt inadequately recognized, guided, or involved.

There were also certain inherent human costs of People's people strategies. Rotating generalists were less knowledgeable and sometimes performed less efficiently than specialists on specific tasks. High commitment to the company plus expectations of flexibility in work hours could be costly in terms of individuals' personal and family lives. For many who were single and had moved to Newark to join People Express, there "was no outside life." As one customer service manager described it, "People Express is it . . . you kind of become socially retarded . . . and when you do find yourself in another social atmosphere it's kind of awkward."

For those who were married, the intense involvement and closeness with co-workers and with the company was sometimes threatening to family members who felt left out. Of the initial 15 officers, three had been divorced within a year and a half. The very fact of People's difference, in spite of the benefits, was seen by some as a source of stress; keeping the hierarchy to a minimum meant few titles and few promotions in the conventional sense.

> You might know personally that you're growing more than you would ever have an opportunity to grow anywhere else but your title doesn't change, (which) doesn't mean that much to you but how does your family react?"—*Magel*
>
> Even People's biggest strengths, the upbeat culture, the high-caliber performance, and positive attitude of the work force, could be stressful. "It's not a competitive environment, it's highly challenging. Everybody's a star . . . but, you know," said one CSM, "maintaining high positive attitude is enough to give you a heart attack."

High commitment and high ambition, together with rapid growth and understaffing, meant that most of People's managers were working long, hard hours and were under considerable stress. Said one CSM, "Nobody is ever scheduled for over 40 hours (a week), but I don't know anybody who works just 40 hours."

Dubose recognized that the situation had taken a toll on everybody's health. "I was never sick a day in my life until I worked for People Express and in the last two years I've been sick constantly." Other managing officers, including Burr, had also been sick a lot, as had general managers. "And startup team members—oh my God, they've got ulcers, high blood pressure, allergies, a divorce . . . it's one thing after another . . . we've all been physically run down." She added, however, "It's not required that we kill ourselves," asserting that personality traits and an emotionally rewarding work place accounted for the long hours many worked.

Burr's stance on this issue was that there were no emotional or human costs of hard work, "Work is a very misunderstood, underrated idea. In fact human beings are prepared and can operate at levels far in excess of what they think they can do. If you let them think they're tired and ought to go on vacation for two years or so, they will."

By the Fall of 1982, though people were still generally satisfied with their jobs and motivated by their stock ownership to make the company work, many of People's managers below the top level were not as satisfied or optimistic as they once were. A University of Michigan 18-month climate survey taken in September 1982 showed signs of declining morale since December 1981. "People are feeling frustrated in their work (and feel they can't raise questions), cross-utilization is not being well-received, management is viewed as less supportive and consultative, the total compensation package (including pay) is viewed less favorably. Clearly there is work to be done in several areas." (Exhibit 30–7 contains excerpts from the 1982 survey.) The report found significant differences in the perceptions of FMs and CSMs: flight managers were more skeptical of cross-utilization and more uncertain of what self-management meant; they felt most strongly that management was nonconsultative.

When questioned about such problems, those in leadership positions were adamant that both business and personal difficulties were short-term, and the costs were well worth the long-term benefits. They felt that virtually every problem was soluble over time with better self-management skills—including time management and stress management, which everyone was being helped to develop—and with evolving improvements in organizational structure. Even those responsible for recruitment insisted, "The challenge is that it seems impossible and there's a way to do it" [Robinson].

> I don't think the long-term effects on the individual are going to be disastrous because we are learning how to cope with it. And I think the short-term effects on the organization will not be real bad because I think we're trying to put in place all the structure modifications at the same time that we're continuing the growth. That makes it take longer to get the structure modifications on the road. Which isn't real good. But they'll get there. Long term I think they will have a positive effect. I think. I wish I knew, for sure.—*Dubose*

Within two months of the climate survey report, Dubose and others from the People advisory council made a video presentation to address many of the items raised in the report. For almost every major item a solution had been formulated.

In spite of all the new initiatives, each of which would entail considerable time and energy to implement, People's officers did not believe they should slow down the company's rate of growth while attending to internal problems. Their standard explanations were as follows:

> If you don't keep growing then the individual growth won't happen. People here have a very high level of expectation anyway, I mean unrealistic, I mean there's no way it's going to happen. They're not going to be general managers tomorrow, they're not going to learn each area of the airline by next month. But they all want to. And even a reasonable rate of

> growth isn't going to be attainable for the individual if we don't continue to grow as a company. And the momentum is with us now we're on a roll. If we lose the momentum now we might never be able to pick it up again.—*Dubose*

Burr put it even more strongly:

> Now there are a lot of people who argue that you ought to slow down and take stock and that everything would be a whole lot nicer and easier and all that; I don't believe that. People get more fatigued and stressed when they don't have a lot to do. I really believe that, and I think I have tested it. I think it's obvious as hell and I feel pretty strongly about it.

He was convinced that the decrease in energy and decline in morale evident even among the officers were not reasons to slow down but to speed up. For himself, he had taken a lot of time to think about things in his early years and had only really begun to know what was important to him between his 35th and 40th years. Then he had entered what he hoped would be an enormous growth period, accelerating "between now and when I get senile. It's sensational what direction does. The beauty of the human condition is the magic people are capable of when there's direction. When there's no direction, you're not capable of much."

As 1983 approached, the big issue ahead for PE, as Burr saw it, was not the speed or costs of growth. Rather, it was how he and People's other leaders would "keep in touch with what's important" and "not lose sight of their humanity."

## EXHIBIT 30-1
## People Express—Major Events

| | |
|---|---|
| April 1980 | Date of incorporation |
| May 1980 | 1st external financing—Citicorp Venture |
| October 1980 | CAB certificate awarded |
| November 1980 | Initial public offering—$25.5 MM common stock |
| March 1981 | 1st aircraft delivered |
| April 1981 | 1st scheduled flight |
| August 1981 | PATCO strike |
| October 1981 | Florida service emphasized |
| January 1982 | One millionth passenger carried |
| March 1982 | 17th aircraft delivered |
| April 1982 | Reported first quarterly operating profit |
| July 1982 | Filed 1,500,000 shares of common stock |

## EXHIBIT 30–2
## Organizational Structure, November 1982—Author's Rendition

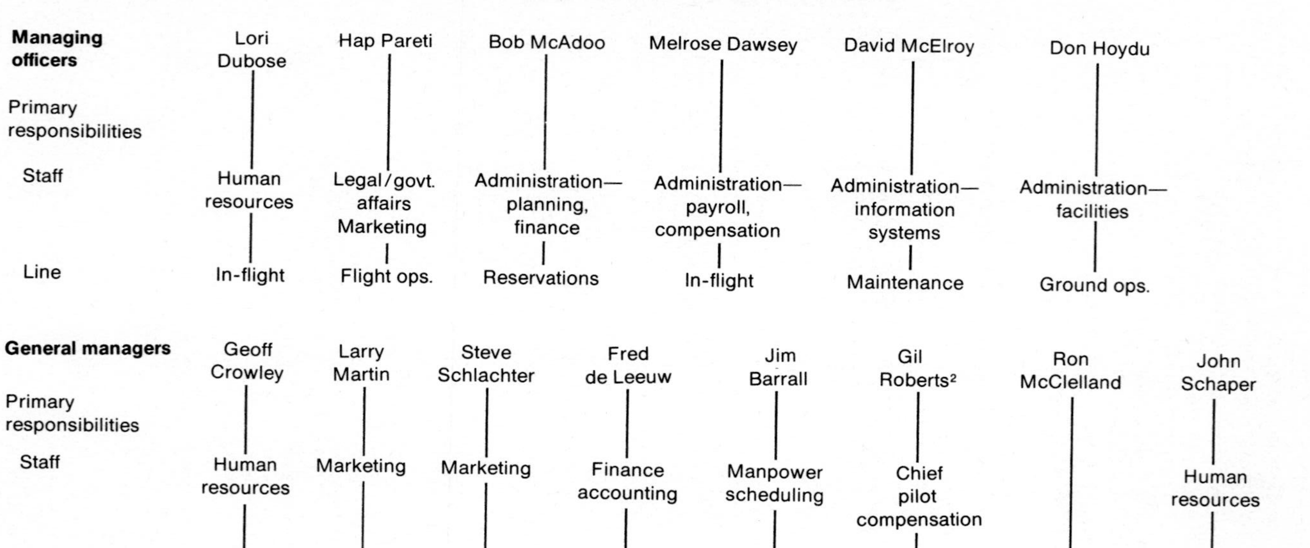


[1]Original president, Gerald Gitner, resigned March 1982 and Burr assumed presidency.
[2]Gil Roberts appointed Chief Pilot November 1982.

**EXHIBIT 30–3**

# TEAMWORK TAKES ON A WHOLE NEW MEANING AT PEOPLExpress!

# TOTAL PROFESSIONALISM

## *Customer Service Managers*

PEOPLExpress has a whole new approach to running an airline! As a Customer Service Manager, you'll be a vital part of our management team, working in all areas from In-Flight Service, Ground Operations, and Reservations to staff support functions such as Marketing, Scheduling, Training, Recruiting, Accounting, and more.

This cross-utilization takes a lot of hard creative work–but it's the best way we know to achieve greater professionalism and productivity! Instead of doing just one limited job, you'll be involved in both line and staff activities–so you can learn the airline business fully. Faced with our variety of challenge, you'll develop and *use* all your decision-making skills. That's how bright people grow at PEOPLExpress... by finding simple creative solutions to complex problems... solutions that contribute to our productivity and growth... and *yours*.

Even better, your productivity can show a direct return. As a Customer Service Manager, you'll have the opportunity to participate in our unique STOCK PURCHASE PROGRAM (subject to legal requirements) and our profit-sharing plan.

If challenge stimulates you, if you really want to pursue management and growth... and are willing to invest the time it takes to achieve TOTAL PROFESSIONALISM, joining PEOPLExpress could be the turning-point in your career (we're already one of the phenomenal success stories in the history of American business).

Our basic requirements are that, preferably, you've had previous business management experience–and that you be poised, personable, have some college education–and be between 5'2" and 6'4" with weight proportional.

If you would like to learn more about the opportunities available to you...

COME MEET PEOPLExpress

at: Baltimore Hilton 101 West Fayette St. Baltimore M.D.

on: Tues., Oct. 26, 1982 12 noon Til 7 P.M.

(NO PHONE CALLS ACCEPTED) (ALL POSITIONS REQUIRE RELOCATION)

OR send your resume to:
PEOPLExpress, Newark International Airport,
North Terminal, Building #55, Newark, N.J. 07114
Attn: Customer Service Manager Recruiting Office.

**PEOPLExpress**

**EXHIBIT 30–4**
**Profile of a Customer Service Manager**

Look for candidates who:

1. Appear to pay special attention to personal grooming.
2. Are composed and free of tension.
3. Show self-confidence and self-assurance.
4. Express logically developed thoughts.
5. Ask intelligent questions; show good judgment.
6. Have goals; want to succeed and grow.
7. Have strong educational backgrounds, have substantial work experience, preferably in public contact.
8. Are very mature, self-starters with outgoing personality.
9. Appear to have self-discipline, good planners.
10. Are warm but assertive personalities, enthusiastic, good listeners.

*Appearance Guidelines*[1].

- Well-groomed, attractive appearance
- Clean, tastefully worn, appropriate clothing
- Manicured, clean nails
- Reasonably clear complexion
- Hair neatly styled and clean
- Weight strictly in proportion to height
- No offensive body odor
- Good posture
- For women, makeup applied attractively and neatly
- Good teeth

[1]Above-listed guidelines apply to everyone regardless of ethnic background, race, religion, sex, or age.

**EXHIBIT 30–5**
**Statement of Operations**

| | From April 7, 1980 to March 31, 1981 | Nine Months Ended December 31, 1981 | Six Months Ended June 30, 1982 (Unaudited) |
|---|---|---|---|
| | (In thousands, except per share data) | | |
| Operating revenues: | | | |
| Passenger | $ — | $37,046 | $59,998 |
| Baggage and other revenue, net | — | 1,337 | 2,302 |
| Total operating revenues | — | 38,383 | 62,300 |
| Operating expenses: | | | |
| Flying operations | — | 3,464 | 4,240 |
| Fuel and oil | — | 16,410 | 22,238 |
| Maintenance | 21 | 2,131 | 3,693 |
| Passenger service | — | 1,785 | 2,676 |
| Aircraft and traffic servicing | — | 7,833 | 10,097 |
| Promotion and sales | 146 | 8,076 | 7,569 |
| General and administrative | 1,685 | 3,508 | 2,498 |
| Depreciation and amortization of property and equipment | 6 | 1,898 | 3,087 |
| Amortization—restricted stock purchase plan | — | 479 | 434 |
| Total operating expenses | 1,858 | 45,584 | 56,532 |
| Income (loss) from operations | (1,858) | (7,201) | 5,768 |

**EXHIBIT 30–5 (*Continued*)**

| | From April 7, 1980 to March 31, 1981 | Nine Months Ended December 31, 1981 | Six Months Ended June 30, 1982 (Unaudited) |
|---|---|---|---|
| | *(In thousands, except per share data)* | | |
| Interest: | | | |
| Interest income | 1,420 | 1,909 | 763 |
| Interest expense | 14 | 3,913 | 5,510 |
| Interest expense (income), net | (1,406) | 2,004 | 4,747 |
| Income (loss) before income taxes and extraordinary item | (452) | (9,205) | 1,021 |
| Provision for income taxes (note 4) | — | — | (470) |
| Income (loss) before extraordinary item | (452) | (9,205) | 551 |
| Extraordinary item—utilization of net operating loss carryforward (note 4) | — | — | 470 |
| Net income (loss) | $ (452) | $(9,205) | $ 1,021 |
| Net income (loss) per common share: | | | |
| Income (loss) before extraordinary item | $ (.20) | $ (1.92) | $ .11 |
| Extraordinary item | — | — | $ .09 |
| Net income (loss) per common share | $ (.20) | $ (1.92) | $ .20 |
| Weighted average number of common shares outstanding | 2,299 | $ 4,805 | 5,046 |

# EXHIBIT 30-6
# Comparative Industry Data on Costs and Productivity

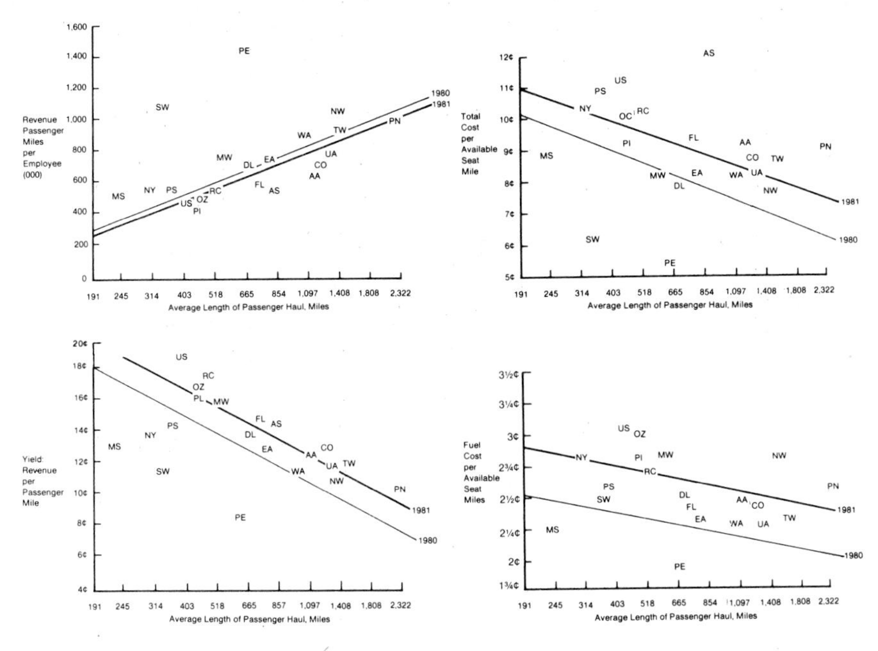


Key to Charts

| Symbol | Airline | Symbol | Airline |
|---|---|---|---|
| AA | American | PN | Pan American |
| AS | Alaska | PS | Pacific Southwest |
| CO | Continental | PE | People Express |
| DL | Delta | PI | Piedmont |
| EA | Eastern | RC | Republic |
| FL | Frontier | SW | Southwest |
| MW | Midway | TW | Trans World |
| MS | Muse | WA | Western |
| NY | New York Air | UA | United |
| NW | Northwest Orient | US | US Air |
| OZ | Ozark | | |

All data have been drawn from calendar 1981 results, except People Express and Muse, for which the first quarter of 1982 is used in order to offer comparisons not influenced by the startup of operations.

Notes:

Total cost is operating cost plus interest expense net of capitalized interest and interest income.

Yield represents passenger revenues divided by revenue passenger miles (RPM).

Average length of passenger haul is plotted on a logarithmic scale.

The average line in each graph is a least-squared linear regression curve, based on 16 carriers which evolved in the regulated environment. Southwest, People Express, New York Air, Muse, and Alaska were not used in the calculations to determine the average. The 16 carriers were assigned equal weightings in the average.

**EXHIBIT 30–7**
**Excerpts from the 1982 Survey**

*Changes Since the December 1981 Climate Survey*

In comparing the responses from the December 1981 and September 1982 surveys, the following significant changes have apparently taken place[1]:

- Getting help or advice about a work-related problem is not as easy.
- What is expected of people is not as clear.
- People are not being kept as well informed about the performance and plans of the airline.
- Satisfaction with work schedules has decreased.
- The number of perceived opportunities to exercise self-management is lower.
- The process used to create initial work teams is viewed less favorably.
- The work is generally perceived to be less challenging and involving.
- The overall quality of upper management is being questioned more.
- Fewer opportunities for personal growth and career development are apparent.
- People are not very comfortable about using the "open door" policy at People Express.
- People feel that their efforts have less of an influence on the price of People Express stock.
- The buying of discounted company stock is being perceived as less of a part of the pay program.
- The compensation package is thought to be less equitable considering the work people do.
- People feel they have to work too hard to accomplish what is expected of them.
- The team concept at People Express is being questioned more.
- Officers and General Managers are thought to be nonconsultative on important decisions.
- People Express is thought to be growing and expanding too fast.

SOURCE: Numbrecht and Quist, June 1982.

[1]Responses on many of these items were still quite positive in an absolute sense, though showing statistically significant decline from earlier studies.

- There is a stronger perception that asking questions about how the airline is managed may lead to trouble.

All of these changes are in a negative direction. Clearly, people are frustrated with the "climate" at People Express: morale and satisfaction are on the decline.

On the positive side, people's expectations of profiting financially were somewhat greater.

HIGHLAND PRODUCTS, INC. (A)

**EXHIBIT 14-6**

**North Haven Plant Affirmative Action Goals**

| | | Females | | | | Minorities | | | |
|---|---|---|---|---|---|---|---|---|---|
| | *12/31/79 Plant Population* | *12/31/79 Plant Female Population* | | *Ultimate Goals Based on 12/31/79 Population (Parity)* | | *12/31/79 Plant Minority Population* | | *Ultimate Goals Based on 12/31/79 Population (Parity)* | |
| | (No.) | (No.) | (%) | (No.) | (%) | (No.) | (%) | (No.) | (%) |
| Officials and managers | 21 | 0 | 0 | 3 | 16.4 | 1 | 4.8 | 2 | 8.3 |
| Foremen | 17 | 0 | 0 | 5 | 30.5 | 1 | 5.9 | 3 | 16.8 |
| Professionals | 19 | 3 | 15.8 | 5 | 25.1 | 1 | 5.3 | 2 | 8.1 |
| Technical | 5 | 1 | 20.0 | 2 | 33.4 | 0 | 0 | 1 | 13.2 |
| Sales | 7 | 1 | 14.3 | 1 | 15.0 | 0 | 0 | 1 | 8.0 |

# Index